# HISTORY OF THE CHAMAR DYNASTY

# HISTORY OF THE CHAMAR DYNASTY

(From 6th Century A.D. to 12th Century A.D.)

(In Two Volumes)

(Vol. 1)

Dr. Raj Kumar

PUBLICATIONS

KALPAZ PUBLICATIONS

DELHI-110052

The views expressed in this book are exclusively those of the author. The publisher are not responsible for the views of the author and authencity of the data, any other information given in this book, in any way whatsoever.

History of the Chamar Dynasty



ISBN: 81-7835-635-X (Set)
ISBN: 81-7835-656-8 (Vol. 1)



Published in 2008 in India by
Kalpaz Publications
C-30, Satyawati Nagar,
Delhi-110052
E-mail: kalpaz@hotmail.com
Phone : 9212729499

*Lasser Type Setting by*: Quick Media, Delhi
*Printed at* : Singhal Print Media, Delhi

## Contents

# Abbreviations

The following list of the standard Abbreviations are used:

| | |
|---|---|
| A. | Asoka |
| A.N. | The Akbarnama |
| A.C. | Annihilation of Caste |
| A.I. | Ancient India |
| A.I.P. | Art in Islamic Period |
| A.I.G | Ancient India and Greece |
| A.M.K. | Ancient Monument of Kashmir |
| A.B.R. | Antiquities of Basohli and Ramnagar |
| A.I.E. | Ancient Indian Education |
| A.H.I. | An Advance History of India |
| A.I.U. | Age of the Imperial Unity |
| A.N.M. | Age of the Nanda and Maurya |
| A.A.P. | Art and Archaeology of Punjab |
| A.C.H.P. | Art and Culture Heritage of Patiala |
| A.C.I.P. | The Arts and Crafts of India and Pakisthan |
| A.I.S.H. | Ancient Indian Social History |
| A.A.L.F.S. | Aspects of Ancient Life From Sanskrit |
| A.GE. | The Age of the Gupta and Other Essays |
| A.S.I. | Archaeology Survey of Indian Report |
| B.N. | Baburnama |
| B.S. | Bulleh Shah |
| B.H.D. | The Buddha and His Dhamma |
| C.T.C.C.A.M.I. | Costumes, Textiles, Cosmatics and Coiffure in Ancient and Medieval India. |
| C.A.I. | Coins of Ancient India |
| C.K.C. | Caste Kingship and Community |

| | |
|---|---|
| C.R.I. | Caste and Race in India |
| C.H.A.I. | Cultural History of Ancient India |
| C.A.I. | The Classical Accounts of India |
| C.A. | The Classical Age |
| C.V.L.G.N.B. | Cosmic View of Life in Guru Nanak Bani. |
| C.M.H.T. | Chandra Gupta Maurya and His Time |
| C.V. | Chitrasutra of the Vishnudharmothra |
| C.A.I. | Cities of Ancient India |
| C.I.P. | Centres of Indian Paintings |
| D.K. | Discovery of Kangra |
| D.L. | Die to Live |
| D.S.S.B. | Dariya Sahib, Saint of Bihar |
| D.C.M. | Dadu the Compassionate Mystic |
| D.V. | Dalit Voice |
| E.H.A.I. | The Economic History of Ancient India |
| E.I.C. | Evolution of Indian Culture |
| E.K.A. | Evolution of Kautilyas Arthasastras |
| E.H.C.K. | Early History and Culture of Kashmir |
| Fig. | Figure |
| H.B. | History of the Brahmans |
| H.I. | Handicrafts in India |
| H.A.I. | History of Ancient India |
| H.C.I.B. | History of the Candallas of Iejaka Bhukti |
| H.K. | History of Kashmir |
| H.C.S. | The Hindu Caste System |
| H.S.S.C.D.L. | Historical Study of Society and Culture in Dardistan and Ladakh |
| H.C.A.G | History and Culture of Ancient Ghandhara |
| H.C.A.I. | A History of Civilization in Ancient India |
| H.P.S. | Harsa A Political Study |
| H.P.H.S. | History of the Punjab Hill States |

| | |
|---|---|
| H.D. | History of Dharmasastra |
| H.C.S.I. | History of Caste System in India |
| H.S. | A History of the Sikh |
| H.I.V.O. | A History of India Volume One |
| H.H.K. | Hindu History of Kashmir |
| H.S.I. | History of South India |
| F.I.C. | Fountations of Indian Culture |
| F.I.A.I. | Foreign Influence in Ancient India |
| F.T.K. | Folk Tales of Kashmir |
| Fig. | Figure |
| GS. | The Guru in Sikhism |
| G.T.C.P.N.W.F.P | A Glossary of the Tribes and Castes in Punjab North Western Frontier Provinces |
| GR.P.S.O | Guru Ravidas: The Philospher's Stone. |
| GT.W.GD. | The Glory That Was Gurjara Desa |
| I.V. | The Inner Voice |
| I.B.D.R. | Indian Between Dream and Deality |
| I.I.M. | Iconography of Indian Music |
| I.C. | Indian Caste |
| I.M.M.C. | Indian Miniatures of the Mughal Court |
| I.P. | Indian Painting |
| I.J.O.D.D. | Indian Jewellary, Ornaments and Decorative Desgins |
| J.K.T. | The Jamboo and Kashmir Territories |
| J.L.M. | A Journey to Lake Mansarovara |
| K.A. | Kautilya's Arthasastra |
| K.A.T.P. | Kashmir and the Punjab |
| K.T.A. | Kashi Through the Ages |
| K.W.GN. | Kabir, The Weaver of God's Name |
| K.GM. | Kabir the Great Mystic |
| L.H.T. | The Life of Hiuen Tsiang |
| L.A.I.S.R.V.I. | Life In Ancient Indian Studies in Rig-Veda India |
| L.O.S.J. | Light on Saint John |
| L.M. | Later Mughal |

| | |
|---|---|
| M.A.A.S. | The Most Ancient Aryan Society |
| M.Q. | Muhammad and the Quran |
| M.B. | Mahabharata |
| N.S. | The New Society |
| N.B.I. | Northern Barrier of India |
| O.A. | The Origin of the Aryans |
| O.GC.I. | Origin and Growth of Caste In India. |
| P.C. | Punjab Castes |
| P.L.S.R. | Paintings and Lifestyles of the Jammu Region |
| P.E.A.I. | Politics and Ethics in Ancient India |
| P.F.F.P.I. | Painted Folklore and Folklore Painters In India |
| P.GK. | Provincial Gazetteer of Kashmir |
| P.I.H.C. | Proceedings of Indian History Congress |
| P.H.C.P. | Punjab History Conference Proceedings |
| P.H.K. | Political History of Kashmir |
| P.A.I. | The Painter of Ancient India |
| R.T. | Rajatarangini |
| R.C.S.I. | Review of Caste System In India |
| R.A. | Royal Arts |
| R.K.A. | Readings in Kautilya Arthasastra |
| R.V.A.V.I. | The Rig Ved and Vedic Religion |
| R.M.P.I. | Rise of the Mahomedan Power in India |
| S.H. | Science in History |
| S.B. | Srimad Bhagavadgita |
| S.N.F. | The Shah Namah of Fardosi |
| S.V.H.R. | In Search of Vedic-Harappan Relationship |
| S.A.A.H.P. | Social Aspects of Ancient Hindu Polity |
| S.I.A. | The Story of Indian Art |
| S.E.H.K. | Social Economic History of Kashmir |
| S.L.A.I. | Social life of Ancient India |
| S.GI. | The Story of Great Invention |
| S.B.C.I. | Studies in the Buddhist Culture of India |
| S.E. | The Struggle for Empire |

| | |
|---|---|
| S.B. | Sultan Bahu |
| S.N.D. | Sant Nam Dev |
| S.M. | Similes in Manusmriti |
| S.H.I | The Spiritualism Heritage of India |
| S.K. | Studies in Kautilya |
| S.H.S. | A Short History of the Sikh |
| S.K. | Sant Kabir |
| S.P. | Sant Paltu |
| S.E.H.D. | The Social and Economic History of Punjab. |
| T.M.E. | Travels in The Mogul Empire |
| T.J. | Tuzak-i-Jahangiri |
| T.I.P. | The Technique of Indian Painting |
| T.H.I. | Tribal Heritage of India |
| Tr. | Transilation |
| T.H.I.H.P. | Travels in the Himalayas Provinces of Hindustan and the Punjab. |
| T.M.E. | Tales of the Mystic East |
| T.C.S.D. | Tukaram; The Ceasless Song of Devotion |
| V.I. | Vedic India |
| V.A. | The Vedic Age |
| V.K. | The Valley of Kashmir |
| W.T.W.I. | The Wonder That Was India |
| Y.B. | Yoga and the Bible |
| Y.C. | Yuan Chwang. |

# Preface

This book entitled *'History of the Chamar Dynasty'* has been written to interpret the ancient Indian civilization, as we understand it, to the ordinary Western reader, who has little knowledge of the subject, but some have interest in it. The three nations of the Indian sub-continent, since the momentous days of 1947, when the gained complete independence, have been playing an ever-growing part in the affairs of the world, and there is perhaps room for a new outline of their ancient culture, to replace the many excellent works now out of print, i.e., *'Nam' or 'Word'* or *'Chamar',* and to further our understanding of the civilization of these new States in the contemporary world. As this book *'History of the Chamar Dynasty',* is intended for a general reader, we have tried to explain as simple as understandable to common people as their subject, who use to live in this countries since the time immomerial. And, as we believe that civilization is more than religion; and art, we have tried to explain briefly which covers all the aspects of Indian life and thought, and did not leave to unexplained the terms of the study which we have been put forth in the thesis. Though primarily, it has been intended by the Westerners, now, we hope that this book may be of some interested to Indian, Pakistan and Chinese readers also, as the interpretation of a friendly *Mlechcha,* who has great love and respect for the civilizations to their lands, and many friends among the descendants of the people whose culture *'He'* studies and reflects in the field of life for the benefit of them. Thus, the work may also be helpful to the students and the scholars who are interested in the course of Indological study of *'Nam'* or *'Chamar'*; for their own benefit which we have included in detailed in the glossary and in the bibliography. But, for the ordinary reader, the work is cumbersome enough, therefore, one must have to attend the *Guru* of the *'Nam'*, which we have not given in the notes and references as well as in the statements. Moreover, we have tried to reduced the Sanskrit, Persian, Arabic, Roman, Greek terms to a minimum with the best of the knowledge of *'Word' or 'Nam'*. But the reader without the background of the knowledge of *'Nam' or 'Rig-Veda'*, one can not find definitions of all Indian words which we have been used in the text in the 'Index', which also serves as a glossary too.

Modern Indian proper names which have been stated in the text, according to the standard system at present used by Indologists one can only expressed with 'Sound' method along with original spelling and clear idea of the correct pronunciation. We have tried to employ consistently the names and spellings officially adopted by the New States of the sub-continent in their paper and map. Throughout this work the word "India" is of course used in its geographical sense, including Pakistan which means to highlight from the body as it has the place of Enlightenment and most of the people have been attached with the Earth which is destructive and untrue. Therefore, it is our humble request with folded hands to the reader of this book that they must adopt a practical approach in this sense towards 'Father', who is the 'Law-Giver of the society'. Because, since the character of Indian classical languages is so unlike that of English the literal translations are at the best dull and at the worst postively ludicrous. In places, where we have taken some liberty with the originals, in order to make the purport clearer to the Western reader, but in all cases we have tried to give an honest interpretation of the intentions of their authors, as we understand them.

Moreover, its very seclusion has been responsible for a history of its people from the time immomerial which makes unique in many ways as *Kalma* meriting serious study. Also, while the names and deeds of mighty monarch like *Asoka, Maurya* and *Kanishka,* of the Indian mainland are inseparable linked with *Kashmir* for the spread of Buddhism in all over the world. It is only by the discovery of fresh mateirals of this kind that we can hope to obtain true *'Light'* regarding the earlier periods for which the first three books of Dr. Raj Kumar's work entitled *'Paintings And Lifestyles of the Jammu Region.'* in two volumns and *' History of the Brahmans'*; do not furnish with a critical reliable account, but this work known by the entitled *'History of the Chamar Dynasty'*; it reveals the original form of the Indian characteristic and culture; which has been based from the *'Infinite'* to *'Upwards'*. Conjectural "*adjustments*" of Kalhana's statements, as proposed by some of our predecessors, cannot take the place of such materials, and we hope, therefore, we should not blamed for having strictly avoided them. On the other hand, we trust, the analysis of the subsequent portions of the Chronicle will display that with the establishment of the *'Karkota Dynasty,'* according to the Kalhana's *Rajatarangini, Durlabhavardhana*, son of *Karkota* Naga, was the first rule of the dynasty and succeeded by *Baladitya, i.e. 'Nam',* the last ruler of the Gonanda family. After this, according to the *Mahavamsa-tika*[1], the story runs that while concealed in an old woman's hut Chandragupta overheard her scolding a child, who in the act of eating had burnt its fingers by beginning with the middle of a cake and not with its corners. Chandragupta took lesson from this conversation, and accordingly transferred the scene of his activities to the North-West. It is alleged that he sought an interview with Alexander, when he was still in the Punjab, perhaps with a view to inducing him to advance against the Nanda King. But the boldness of his speech offended *"Alexandrum[2]"*, and so Chandragupta had to run away for safety[3]. Thus, the principal Brahminical text is that of the *Puranas*. It will be seen that the *Puranas* are more concerned with the origin of the Nanda Kings than that of Chandragupta. They are very much concerned at the ending of Kshatriya rule in the country and its displacement by a *Sudra* rule under the Nandas whom they openly brand as *adharmikas,* 'immoral people'. The founder of the Nanda dynasty is described as the offspring of a *Sudra* woman' (*Sudragarbhodbhavah*) and a *'Mahapadmapati',* 'exceedingly avaricious[4],' as translated by H.H. Wilson. Afterwards, however, he treacherously murdered his sovereign and then, under the pretence of acting as guardian to the royal children, usurped the supreme authority, and having put the young princes to death, begot the present King." The form Agrammes is modified into *Xandramas* by Diadorus, and F.W. takes it to be the equivalent of *Chandramas*. He takes Agrammes to be *Dhanananda* (*Cambridge History of India* vol.1 p. 469), taking Dhana-Nanda to be his nickname, and *Chandramas* as his personal name. 'The young princes' mentioned by Curtius as being murdered by Ugrasena-Nanda were most probably the ten sons of *Kalasoka-Kakavarni* of the aforesaid *Mahavamsa* list[5]. The *Mahabodhivamsa* describes the Nanda Kings as *Chorapubhs,* "the docoits of old[6]." The origins of the *Palas*, *Gurjara-Prathiharas* and the *Chandellas* are similarly garbled into incoherence and legends have been woven around their ancestors so as to enhance the prestige of those families in popular esteem. As such, Kalhana has rightly expressed that *Durlabhavardhana* was, 'a man of lowly origin, took service under King Baladity, married his daughter and, after the Kings death, succeeded him on the throne of Kashmir. Thus, the connected history of Kashmir begins with the extinction of the mythical Gonanda dynasty early in the seventh century A.D., when *Durlabhavardhana* ascended the throne. It makes clear from the study that he claimed descent from the *Chamar* dynasty know as *Karkotaka Naga,* the exploits and achievements of this dynasty is unforgetable. The later successors of this dynasty were known as *Durlabhavardhana-Pratapadity-II Muktapida-Lalitadity, Candrapida-Vajraudita Jayapida, Avantivarman, Sankaravarman, Sugandha, Viradeva, Ksemagupta* Udayaraja, *Samgramaraja, Ananta, Kalasa,*

*Harsa, Uchchala, Sussala* and *Jayasimha 'Words' or Chamars'* all rulers of the Valley of *Kasmira or Kashmir* as described by the various writers and scholars of the period, are have to need their justifiable places in the annals of Indian History. Culturally, too, some of the eminent sons of *Kashmir* have greatly enriched the treasures of Sanskrit literature by their exquisite compositions both in *Vyasa* and *Kashmir,* while the religion and philosophy of the mainland, particularly Saivism, owe no small debt to the Valley of Kashmir. Though most of the artistic creations of the people of the Valley have suffered immeasurably at the hands of both *nature* and *man*, yet what little remains, is enough to vouch for their achievements in sphere as well. These cultural attainments are, however, beyond the scope of present treatment which is a revised and enlarged form truly historical record which grows more and more accurate as we approach the time of the author, and which by its wealth of information on all aspects of old Kashmir amply repays the attention of the student of Indian History and Culture.

The Chronological and Genealogical tables attached to the Appendix-I-II are intended to present in a condensed form for the information of furnished by the *Rajatarangini* regarding the date and descent of successive rulers of the '*Chamar* Dynasty' in the History of Kashmir.

In the concluding, and longest chapter of the introduction, it has been our object and duty to present a critical summary of Kalhana's narrative and of the historical data contained in it. For the purposes of this analysis it was necessary to scrutinise with special care all independent evidence on *'Kashmir History'* that we can at present gather various accounts of various writers both foreigners as well as indigenous and similar records. Moreover, we have spared no labour to make the Index which concludes the work full and accurate.

Lastly, in the 'Introduction' we have endeavoured to elucidate in the first place the data which can be gathered as regards the person of Kalhana, his family, and the *milieu* in that he lived. The discovery of a curious and hitherto unnoticed reference to Kalhana by his country and contemporary, the poet *Mankha*, may perhaps claim special interest, as confirming in a striking manner the conclusions derived from the Chronicler's own work as regards his literary training and interest. In the second chapter, we have examined as closely as our available materials would permit, the objects and methods which guided by Kalhana in the composition of his work, the sources he used for it, and the form which he gives to his narrative. The condition in which the text of the Chronicle has been handed down to us, and the materials we have used for its reconstitution, are discussed in the third chapter, while the next contains an exposition of Kalhana's system of Chronology.

## Notes and References

1. Hemacandra's *Sthaviravali-Carita* has a similar story.
2. Note. Sometimes emended into "*Nandrum*", identified with Nanda or *Dhanananda*.
3. R.S. Tripathi; *History of Ancient India;* New Delhi; Reprint; 1987; p. 147
4. H.H. Wilson; *Vishnu Purana; Delhi, 1961*; p. 184 quoted by R.K. Mookerji; *Chandragupta Maury and His Time;* Delhi; 1966, p. 7.
5. *Ibid.*, p. 20.
6. *Ibid.*

# Introduction

The popular theory of Caste[1] System[2] in India is the development of thousands of years from the assciation of many different racial and other groups in a single culture system[3]. Since the end of the Rig-Vedic period the original division of the social body into four distinct, well-defined classes: (1) the priests - *Brahmans* ; (2) the warriors-*Kshatriya* or *Rajanya*; (3) the working class-Vaishya (farmers, craftsmen, and traders); and (4) the menial class-*Shudra*; in other words: those who pray; those who fight; those who produce and barter; and those who serve[4]. It became an institution of the Hindu religion and has been transmitted from generation to generation throughout the ages of the Hindu history and myth without the possibility of change[5]. Let us see how the great Brahminical code- the laws of Manu-defines the duties and mutual relations of the four castes. (1988-91).

1. *To Brahmans[6] he (Brahma) assigned teaching and studying the Veda, sacrificeing for their own benefit and for others, giving and accepting of alms.*
2. *The Kshatriya[7], he commanded to protect the people, to bestow gifts, to offer sacrifices to study the Veda, and to abstain from attaching himself to sensual pleasures.*
3. *The Vaishya[8] to tend cattle, to bestow gifts, to offer sacrifices, to study the Veda, to trade, to lend money, and to cultivate land.*
4. *One occupation only the lord prescribed to the Shudra; to serve meekly the other three castes"*

The position claimed for the Brahmans in this first, general definition, is comparatively modest, certainly not unreasonably arrogant, but we turn a few pages and the law giver goes into details and makes meaning clearer.

1. *"A Brahman", we read, "coming, into existence, is born as the highest on earth, the lord of all created beings, for the protection of the treasury of the law.*
2. *"Whatever exists in the world is the property of the Brahman; on account of the excellence of his origin, the Brahman is, indeed, entitled to it all.*
3. *"The Brahman eats but his own food, wears but his own apparel, bestows but his own in alms; the mortals subsist through the benevolence of the Brahman ....".*

4. " .....*Know that a Brahman of ten years and a Kshatriya of a hundred years stand to each other in the relation of father and son; but between those two the Brahman is the father...*".
5. "....... *A Brahman, be he ignorant or learned, is a great divinity.........*".
6. "*.............though Brahmans employ themselves in all sorts of mean occupations, they must be honored in every way, for each of them is a very great deity.....*".

The whole duty of this kinds is pithily summed up under these three heads. "Not to turn back in battle; to protect the people; to honor Brahmans." "To worship Brahmans" is the expression repeatedly used; "to enrich them" is a point emphatically inculcated, and the King is solemnly warned not to provoke them to anger under any circumstances "for they, when angered, could instantly destroy him, together with his army and vehicles". Many are the worldly privileges and examptions which they demand and enjoy. Still, it is very certain that the material power was in the hands of the warrior caste and that the Brahman did not get quite as much in practice as they claimed in theory, and were perfectly aware that conciliation was, after all, their wisest policy. Indeed, after some of the most outrages bragging and bullying, the priestly law-giver suddenly descends to reasonable ground and lays down the following shrewd axiom, which, in all times and countries, has been the basis of the mutual understanding between Church and State[9]. It was quite a new and spiritualized view of sacrifice the rite and ritual by corrupting the *Rita or Law* or *'Word'* is set forth in Manu's definition of the five great sacrifices that the householder shall perform daily.

These are as follows:

1. *Teaching and studing the Vedas is the Veda sacrifice.*
2. *Offering cakes and water is the sacrifice to the father (pitris).*
3. *An offering to fire is the sacrifice to the gods.*
4. *An offering of food is the sacrifice to the goblins (bhutas).*
5. *Hospitality to guests is the sacrifice to men.*

***Manava Dharma-Sastra, (iii) 70***

Though the idea of sacrifices of animals and human beings has presisted in the benefits of the castes whose religion was much influenced by or derived from the religion of the Dravidians and other primitive races in India, it may be safely asserted that the more truely. Aryan tribes ceased to perform such sacrifices after the time of the Buddha[10] or *Chamar.*

It has been come to our knowledge that only the three first castes enjoined to study the Veda. This duty was not assigned to the servile caste at all at that time. The *Shudras* were not only not excepted they were forbidden, to share in the sacred inheritance of those whom to serve was their only mission. Their presence at a sacrifice would have polluted it; the sacred *mantras* were not to be sung or recited within hearing of a *Shudra*, and had a Brahman instructed one of the servile caste in the knowledge of the *Veda,* he would have been guilt of a wellnigh in expiable offence. When a boy of one of the three higher castes attained a certain age, considered as "years of discretion[11]".

*Any time between the eight and sixteenth year for a Brahman, between the eleventh and twenty-second for a Kshatsiya, and between the twelfth and the twenty-fourth for a Vaishya*[12].

*He was initiated i.e admitted under solemn ceremonies into the religious*[13] community after which he was placed under a *guru* or spiritual guide, invaribly a Brahman, for instruction in the Veda. This initiation was regarded as the youth's second birth, his birth into the spiritual life, wherefore the three higher castes took pride in the appellation of "twice born" (*dvi-ja*). From this distinction the *Sudhras*, of course were excluded. This is declared most explicity in Manu's code:

*"The Brahman, the Kashtriya, and the Vaishya castes are the twice-born ones, but the fourth, the Shudra, has no second birth there is no fifth caste."*

This brief survey of the original caste system has led us away from what is properly speaking, our allotted subject, for we have strayed into post-Vedic times. But the digression was necessary in order, precisely, to conclude it with the statement that castes, as a firmly established institution, were not as yet a feature of the Vedic period. Had they been, the fact must have transpired, even if indirectly in the Rig-Veda, which faithfully reflects the state of society prevailing at the time that the collection was forming; and this not the case, except in one solitary and noteworthy instance: the ninetieth hymn of the tenth book (X., 90), known as the "Purush-hymn", PURUSHA-SUKTA. The hymn, as a whole, is exceedingly obscure and of entirely mystical import. It describes the act of creation in the guise of a huge sacrifice performed by the gods in which the central figure and victim is a primeval giant, a being named Purusha (one of the names for man), probably because mankind is represented as being produced by this being or, more correctly, out of various portions of his body. This is the only passage of the hymn with which we are here concerned. Purush, it is said, "is this whole universe, whatever has been and whatever shall be". Probably in a latent state, since the gods proceed to evolve out of him worlds and animals and men.

*"When the gods divided being (Purusha*[14]*), into how many parts did they cut him up? What was his mouth? What his arms? What his thighs and feet?*

*"The Brahman was his mouth; the Rajanya was made his arms; the Vaishya he was his thighs; the Shudra*[15] *sprang from his feet*[16]*."*

Traditional Indian life is primarily based on a system of class division which is denoted by two terms *Varna (Lit,* colour[17]). Thus the social divisions mentioned here have their paralle in other Indo-European communities. But it is important to remember that in the hymns of the *Rig-Veda* there is little trace of the rigid restrictions typical of caste in its mature form. There was hardly any taboo on intermarriage, change of occupation or commensality. We have instances of marriages of *Brahmanas* with *Rajanya* women, and of the union of *Arya* and *Sudra.* Families were not wedded to particular profession. "I am," says the author of a hymn, "a poet, my father is a doctor, and my mother is a grinder of corn. With our different views, seeking after again, we run, as after cattle". There was no ban on the taking of food cooked by the *Sudras,* and there is no evidence that impurity was communicated by the touch or contact of the inferior castes[18].

Downtrodden *Vishvamitra*, the knower of merits and demerits of the human being, who is appetite of the flesh of a dog's thigh from the hands of a *Chandala.* It is noteworthy that to the *Mahabharata*, the *Candala* did not offer the meat. It was *Vishvamitra* who insisted on having it, although the *Candala* repeatedly asked him not to do, so[19]. In this connection, the dialogue, once again held between a *Candala* and sage *Vishvamitra*, attracts our attention. It is said in the *Santi Parva* that once upon a time, at the end of the *Treta Yuga* and before the beginning of the *Dvapara Yuga,* rains did not pour for twelve consecutive years. Rivers, lakes, streams and other water reservouirs dried up. Consequently crops were destroyed and famine took place. Many people starved to death. Population decayed Robbers raised up their heads and began looting the people and thus complete disorder and chaos crept in. Under these circumstances *Vishvamitra* and his family members also could get nothing to eat and live upon. Leaving his wife and children, *Vishvamitra* went to a colony of *Candalas* in search of food. In one house, he saw a piece of a recently slain dog's thigh and decided to steal it in order to appease his hunger. The *candala* whom the sage had taken to be sleeping was, in fact, awake and he caught him *red-handed.* After knowing that the thief was no other than the famous sage *Vishvamitra*, the *Candala* repeatedly told him not to commit a great sin by eating the flesh and that too of a god's thigh[20].

In Kautily's *Arthsastra*, it is mentioned that *Sudras,* the lowest in the social ladder, were given a place in the Aryan fold and Prohibits the role of a *Sudra* minor into slavery. Their main duties were service to three upper *Varnas*. They could take to agriculture and army as profession. Many were artisans and workers[21]. Since there was no *Varna,* lower than the *Sudra,* the duties whereof a *sudra* could adopt, the *Mahabharata* lays down that he should take recourse to fine arts such as painting and sculpture[22]. Work by hand has been by tradition considered unwelcome for the three higher *Varnas,* and it appears that arts and crafts men were mostly *Sudras*. *Sudras* were hardworking and obedient class, and 'Kautilya prefers *Sudras* cultivators in newly set up villages by the state. Kautilya envisages an army of *Sudra* also. The *Sudras* worked as labourers or hired workers under private masters or under the King in many capacities[23].

Another cancer that had entered the Indian society was the system of '*Untouchability*'. The *Candalas* were a despised class. They had separate well for using water and their residences were on outskirts of the cremation of ground. A *Candala* touching an Aryan lady was fined 100 *panas*. A *Svapaka* born of mixed caste parents was an outcaste tribe. The duties of the labourers and the protection of their rights have been detailed elsewhere in the book. However, most of the *Vishti* (unpaid labour) must have been taken from members of the *Sudra* caste. The system of *begari* is a blot in our society even today[24]. Under these circumstances, a *Vaisya* should do the vocation of the *Sudras*. But even at that time he should not do the condemnable works prescribed for the *Sudras*. Like the *Mahabharata*, the Maun Smriti also permits a *Sudra* to become artisan to save the life of his wife and children from starvation. It is note worthy in this connection that according to Manu the members of a *Varna* should take recourse to the duties and professions of the *Varna,* immediately below their own[25].

In most of the epochs of *Ancient Indian History,* the ideal of *Varnasramadharma* had been the essential driving force behind the Indian society and its functioning[26]. It was essential to a King who should take away the belongings of one, and takes recourse to the duties of a higher *Varna*. Such a person should be banished from the kingdom. A *Sudra* was allowed to adopt *Vaisya dharma*, since he was the lowest and there was no *Varna* lower than that of his own, the avocations whereof he could adopt[27]. As King Asoka, the grandson of the first *Vrsala* emperor in India sought to do away with all the legal in equalities of a *Sudra*. Evidently he received his inspiration from Buddhism. In true Buddhist spirit, Asoka tried to build up a *classless* society and *classless* administrative machinary. Such efforts on the part of a scion of *Vrsala*, and a Buddhist at that time, naturally provoked a strong opposition from the Brahmanic and other high-caste sections. The *classless* beaurocracy, which Asoka tried to established must have, indeed, dealt a heavy below to the long-enjoyed monopoly of those sections[28] which had the Brahminical thought in the Indian History and society. His personal religion may be taken to be Buddhism, although there is a view what it was Jainism[29].

So far, in the first half of the seventh century A.D. however, the condition of Buddhism in Kashmir was not remarkable. At one place Hsuan-Tsang says that the "good looking but deceitful people" of Kashmir embraced both Buddhism and other faiths[30]. Thus, the Gautama, the founder of Buddhism, is supposed, to have lived about sixth century B.C. He was a *Kshatriya* and freely admitted all castes into his priesthood. In the *Dhammapada,* "Footsteps of religion[31]", the first Buddhist establishment seems to be identical with *Amritabhavana* built by the queen *Amritaprabha* noted above. The second one is evidently the *Vihara* of the same name built by the queen of *Durlabhavardhana* as supported by Kalhana[32]. It was during his reign that Hiuen Tsang visited Kashmir. As the pilgrim informs us, *Durlabhavardhana* ruled not only over *Kashmir* proper, but a part of the North-Western Panjab as well. He was followed by his son *Pratapadity* II who ruled with moderation and justice, and built the town of *Pratapura.* He was succeeded by his three sons[33]. The new dynasty, known as the *Karkota* was founded by *Durlabhavardhana.* He had married the daughter of the last King of the *Gonanda* dynasty named *Baladitya,* and as the latter had no son succeeded to the throne (627 A.D.)[34].

The early history of the kingdom of *Kashmir* is full of legendary traditions, nothing of historical importance is known of *Durlabavardhana* and his son and successor, who reigned respectively for 36 and 50 years[35] then followed by one after the another dynasty of *Sudra* family. Kashmir, signifying the lustre of the light emanating from the *'Supreme Spirit',* the most primitive city of India, is only *Ganga* has not changed its course visibly. The *Nandas*, and following them the Mauryas ruled over Kashmir. The famous inscription of Asoka, with a message of peace mixed with a strict warning of examplary punishment for those creating dissension inthe Buddhist Church is suggestive of *Kashmir* being the important centre within mastic establishments located here. The hold of the *Sungas* before it passed on to the *Kushana* '*Word*' ChandraGupta[36] 1 then other rulers. Manu says that a *Brahmana* should not be live in the kingdom, ruled by a *Sudra.* This clearly indicates that Manu is not in favour of the *Sudra rulers.* There are many historical examples of non-*Ksatriya* rulers in ancient India. *Mahapadmananda,* the founder of *Nanda* kingdom was a *Sudra* and has been referred to as "*Sudragarbhodbhava.*"

*Utpala*, a native of *Kashmir*, flourished before 850 A.D.[38] and established his kingdom in 853 A.D. after the *Karkota* dynasty. In the edition of M.M. *Sudhakara Dvivedi* the *Sloka* is proceded by the commentary (of *Utpala*) *"Uktam cacarya-vishnuguptena tatha hyaha, apyarhavasya"*. At this verse refers to *Kala* as a deity, it is probably taken from astrononical, mathematical and astrological. Probably quoted in the *Brhajjataka*[39]. There is a book by *Utpala*, the Kashmirian called *Rahunrakarana* (?) i.e breaking the *Karnas;* and another called *Karnapatta* i.e. killing the *Karnas*[40].

The above mentioned facts, indicate a close attachment to Saivism on the part of both Kalhana and his father[41]. It is interesting to note the same feeling in the numerous references which Kalhana makes the images of Buddha claiming special interest[42] i.e. *'Nam'* or *'Sabad'*. In addition, it deserves to be noted that Kalhana takes care to show us one more than occasion his thorough familiarity with special points of Buddhist tradition and terminology[43]. Of almost all royal and private individuals, who are credited with the foundation of Buddhist *Stupas* and *Viharas*, it is recorded that they, or at least members of their family, with equal zeal endowed also shrines of Siva or Vishnu[44]. Hiuen Tsang relates as an eye-witness how Buddhists and Jainas, as well as the Brahmans received equal honours and support at his court[45]. There is, no doubt, the Jainism of the twelfth century A.D. in Gujarat was both in doctrine and practice far less accommodating to orthodox notions than the *Kashmir* Buddhism of the same period. From various indications it appears that the condition of the latter must have closely approached the state of modern Buddhism in Nepal[46]. Kalhana had carefully examined the *Vikramankadevacarita,* the historical poem of his fellow-countryman *Bilhana*, writted about the eighth decade of the eleventh century A.D. may be considered as certain. He expresses himself thoroughly acquainted with the personal history of his fellow-poet, as detailed in the latter's work[47].

References of these ideas mentioned none, perhaps, is more significantly Indian than the notion which explains the fortunes of individuals or a nation by the influence of spiritual merits (*Punya*) *from pervious* births. Kalhana often accounts for strange facts by this convenient and to the Hindu mind absolutely conclusive argument[48]. This is another Hindu dogma whcih has a marked influence on the Chronicler's ideas is connected with the theory of the *Yuga*. It assumes the progressive decay of all things spiritual and material in the present *Kali Yuga*. It naturally leads the Hindu mind to attribute to the past the more splendour and greatness the further back it lies. We can easily realize to what extent such a notion must predispose the Chronicler to accept in good faith the exaggerations of popular tradition regarding the ancient Kings[49] from *Karkota* dynasty to onwards. The chronologically most definite of these notices concern *Candrapid* the third King in Kalhana's list of that dynasty. We have in all probability a reference in the Chinese Annals also to *Durlabhavardhana* the founder of the *Karkota* dynasty, who according to the Chronicler's reckoning ruled in the years 600-636 A.D. For it is tempting to identify *Tu-Lo-Pa* the name of the Indian King who between the year 627-649 A.D. was charged with having the envoys of *Ki-pin* or Kabul safely conducted to their country, with *Durlabha,* the abbreviated name by which *Durlabhavardhana* calls himself on his coins[50].

Kalhana again reproduces several of these, all intended to illustrate the supernatural powers of the King. The legend of the miracle worked for the King by his Turkish minister *Cankuna*, is of interest because it was connected with a Buddha image still extant in Kalhana" days, which *Lalitaditya* was supposed to have brought from Magadha[51]. The period (1003-1028 A.D.) covered by *Samgramaraja's* reign witnessed a great upheaval in the political conditions of Northern India, which was destined to fundamentally change the course of *Indian History*[52]. The several expeditions which we know *Mahmud* to have led in that direction never seriously threatened the independence of the Valley[53]. It appears that after *Kalasa's* coronation, the arrangement which deprived him of all real power seems to have continued without difficulty. Strongly sensual by nature, the youthful *Kalasa* then came under the influence of deprived companions and advisers, whose doings are painted by Kalhana in truely Rabelaisian colours and grew more and more licentious[54]. During the finally days of *Kalasa's* life, there were embittered relation between himself and his son *Harsa.* The youthful prince, gifted by nature and inclined towards extravagance, felt annoyed by the scanty regard and still scantier allowances which his father bestowed upon him. Evil-minded parasites took advantage of *Harsa's* disposition and implicated him in a conspiracy to murder his father[55].

During the closing years of *Kalasa's* life there were discordial relation between himself and his son *Harsa.* He spared *Harsa's* life, notwithstanding the intrigues which some of his court carried on against it, but decided to deprive him of the succession. For this purpose he had *Utkarsa,* his younger son, brought from *Lohara* inorder to have him installed as the ruler of Kashmir[56].

As soon as *Utkarsa* became the King of *Kashmir,* he imprisoned *Harsa* and refused to grant him permission to retire abroad. Then cowardly *Utkarsa* in his straits, thought of having *Harsa* killed in his prison, but owing to *Harsa's* presence of mind and his own vacillation, the murderious attempt failed. His character must have been greatly exercised the mind of his contemporaries[57]. According to modern psychologist account *Harsa's* character and reign was in sound condition of mind, which towards the close of the King's life manifested itself in a kind of *dementia imperatoria*. At the commencement of his reign *Harsa* displayed wise forbearance in retaining many of his father's officials and trustworthy servants, notwithstanding their former conduct towards himself[58]. The closing era of *Harsa's* rule was a tragic one. It gives us the account of King's horoscope, and explains how it foretold that he would become a destroyer of his own family on the account of commitment with *Brahmans*. But the birth-date of *Harsa*, as recorded by himself, is not in agreement with the astrological data of the horoscope, and it is thus evident that the latter, as might a *priori* be suspected and was fabricated after the event[59].

Kalhana narrates that near about fifty years which lies between the fall of *Harsa* in the history of *Kashmir* and the date of the composition of the chronicle to the modern reader indicates the authenticity and ample detail of the picture of contemporary life of *Kashmir* in its political and social aspects. No doubt; certain petty events were took place in the state affairs, but there was no long discrimination among their followers. In the race for *Harsa's* crown, *Uchchala*, the elder of the two sons of *Malla* had proved successful. But his position at the commencement of his reign was very precarious. The leaders of the Damaras, to whose rebellion he owed the throne, behaved as the true rulers in the land, and *Sussala* his ambitious younger brother was ready to rise against him. In order to secure safety from *Sussala*, he ceded to him the *Lohara* territory as an independent chieftainship. Against the great feudal landholders, *Uchchala* protected himself by a dexterous use of *Macchiavellian* policy. By fomenting among them jealousy and mutual suspicion, he secured the murder or exile of their most influential leaders, without himself incurring the odium. Then, reassured in his own position, he openly turned upon the Damaras and forced them into disarmament and submission[60]. On the whole, *Uchchala* is an energetic ruler, has been attached with the lower classes, therefore, it was necessary for him to safeguard the interest of their people. After sometimes, *Uchchala's* sense of justice and his skill in administering will be illustrated by an anecdote which, whether authentic or not, gives us a glimpse of the conditions affecting petty trade at the period[61]. After sometime, *Uchchala's* throne was threatened by an invasion of *Sussala*, who swept down from the mountains of *Lohara* to oust his brother. But *Uchchala* was on the alert, and after a short campaign *Sussala* was driven to take refuge in Dard territory from where he regained his own hills with difficulty[62]. It has been came to our notice that the birth of *Jayasimha* is said to have brought about a reconciliation between the two brothers. But while peace was thus to be secured to the land a conspiracy developed which was destined to bring *Uchchala's* regime to a violent close[63]. *Kalhana* tells us, after relating *Uchchala's* murder, displays a draw back which does not permit to follow exactly what happened immediately after the murder. We see, that *Radda's* and his fellow-conspirators overthrow was effected by *Gargacandra*, the leading Damara of the *Lahara* district, who under the special favour of *Uchchala* had gained great power. *Gargacandra* after a short struggle overpowered the traitors and avenged his master's death in the blood of *Radda* and his chief followers[64].

As soon as, *Gargacandra* arranged for the burning of *Uchchala's* queens, he was observed as a successor of the crown. In this struggle, indolent and helpless, *Salhana* was proved a mere puppet by the side of *Gargacandra,* 'the King-maker', who was the 'true power' in the land. While anarchy reigned throughout the country, *Salhana,* with his brother *Lothana*, indulged in low pleasures at the capital[65]. Study expressed that *Sussala's* character is resembled with *Uchchala* in many points. Since *Sihasramangala* and other nobles whom *Sussala* had exiled, then his attempt was overthrown by incursions from the Chenab Valley. But their efforts soon lost importance when serious pretender appeared on the scene in the personof *Bhiksacara, Harsa's* grandson. The young prince, whose escape to the court of *Naravarman* of *Malava* has already been mentioned, fell in at *Kuruksetra* (*Thanesvar*) with a party of hill-chiefs from *Champa, Vallapura,* and the adjacent valleys, who were on a pilgrimage to that *Tirtha*. The chiefs espoused the cause of the youthful claimant of the *Kashmir* throne, and formed marriage alliances with[66] ancient rulers of *Vallapura* whose names are not found in the *Vansavali,* we find the names of *Karam Rai* and *Takht Rai,* between *Trailokya* and *Kalas,* almost certainly due to interpolation[67] on the basis of marriage cord. A fresh victory has been launched by the *Prthvihara* with the help of *Sussala* prudently to send away his family to the safe retreat of the Lohara castle. In the month of *Sravana Bhiksacara* joined *Mallakostha* in the Sindh Valley, and soon after the ring of the rebel forces closed around Srinagar. On the 6th *Vadi* of *Margasiras,* 1120 A.D. ; *Sussala* will marched out of Srinagar followed by the faithful troops, and after bribing dangerious opponents on the road to gain a free passage, ultimately reached *Lohara* with a few attendants. On *Sussala's* departure the officials and troops in Srinagar made common cause with the

Damaras, and *Bhiksacara* will be in triumph installed as a King of the *Kashmir.* The restoration of *Harsa's* lineage has been destined to be of short duration *Bhiksacara*, inexperienced and sensual by nature, was too busily engaged in testing the pleasures of his newly gained throne to concern himself with its safety. On *Sussala's* approach many of *Bhiksacara's* former partisans came over to him. Marching rapidly from *Huskapura Sussala* unexpectedly appeared before Srinagar, and unopposed by *Bhiksacara,* once more entered his capital after an absence of little over six months (Jyaistha 1121, A.D.)[68] During this battle which followed the event of war, *Bhiksacara* acquired military experience and displayed personal bravery. In the repeated success, he gained much experience, and *Sussala* has been spared for the critical situation to siege the host. In order to destroy his arch-enemy; *Sussala* had made a secret pact with *Utpala*, the treacherous agent of *Tikka*, a powerful baron in the *Devasarasa* district. Now, *Utpala* made a promise with *Bhikacara* to kill his own master on the issue of his mischievious act. In this way, *Utpala* and some other conspirators, thus, have been fell an easy prey to their murderous plot, on the new moon day of *Phalguna* in 1128 A.D. It appears from the study that *Jayasimha* was, at that time of the murder, in the capital, but in a residence distant from the royal palace. To assure his safety, he proclaimed a general amnesty, and called to his help *Pancacandra,* who had been succeeded to his father *Gargacandra's* estates in *Lahara*[69]; where it is stated that the *Kashmiri Raja* deposed *Vikrama Raja*, the lord of *Vallapura,* and replaced him by *Gulhana.* This event may have occured about 1135-40 A.D.; but neither of these names appears in the *Vansavali.* They may have immediately followed *Padmaka* and his sons. *Vansavali* B or second mentions a Raja *Vikramadit,* between *Khalas Rai* and *Ram Mal,* a war of succession and other causes had entirely exhausted that Kingdom, and we read of no more expeditions into the outer mountains or conflicts with the Hill states, all of which then became quite independent[70]. Since the revolution, which had brought the family of *Malla* to the throne, the land holding barons, big and small, will obtained a share of the independence, which even in times of comparative peace must have seriously curtailed the King's power and authority[71]. *Jayasimha* will realized the danger arising from the loss of the family stronghold, despatched a considerable force under *Laksmaka* across the mountains to retake *Lohara*[72]. While *Sujji* will also not be enjoy for a long period due to rude behaviour of his courtiers, and will have to take the countering-measures; King, too, be treacherously murdered himself through one of his own officers in 1133 A.D. when the foul deed will be over, *Jayasimha,* who had already been eagerly awaiting the result; breathed freely again, and turning with vigour upon the relatives and adherents of *Sujji,* had them cruelly killed. The murderer of *Sujji, Kularaja* was rewarded with the office of city-prefect, while *Sanjapala, Sujji's* rival and the King's (Dr. Raj Kumar) helpmate in the plot, will raised to the position of commander-in-chief[73]. In the concluding portions of the civilization the pious endowments of the *'Nam'* or *'Word'*, *Jayasimha* will be followed by a longer list of various religious foundations made by members of his court and their families. This list, which looks like a supplement to the one previously given, furnishes some indications as to Kalhana's fellow-poet. The concluding verses of Kalhana's work or Raj Kumar's work are devoted to an encomium on *Jayasimha's* queen *Radda* and his children. The four sons who have been born to him from *Radda* besides *Gulhana*, are still in infancy. The names of three of them have been taken from Kings prominent in *Kashmir* tradition, *Jayapida, Lalitaditya, Yaśaskara,* must curiously remind us of the grand names of *'Roman History'* which we find revived in the last reigns of the decaying Empire[74] of the *'Chamar Dynasty of Kashmir'*

## NOTES AND REFERENCES

1. **Note.** The word *Caste* (from Latin *Castus, pure*) was loosely used by the Portuguese to denote the Indian social classification as they thought that the system was intended to preserve purity of blood. The system is such a peculiar and complex thing that no satisfactory definition is possible. (N.K Dutta; *Origin and Growth of Caste in India;* Calcutta; 1908. Vol. I. p. 1. Hereafter referred as *O.G.C.I.*). Manu distinctly says that there are only four *Varans; Brahmin, Kashyitra, Vaisya, Sudra,* while he speaks of about fifty *Jatis,* such as *Ambastha, Chandala, Dravida, Yavana,* etc. (Ibid. p. 3). Traditional origin of the many castes or *Jatis* were produced by a series of crosses first between members of the four *Varnas* and then between the descendants of these initial union (Ibid. p. 5). According to S.V. Ketkar, the word "Caste" is of Spanish and Protuguese origin. *Casta* means lineage or race. It is derived from the latin word *'Castus'*, which means *pure*. The Spaniards were the first to use it, but its Indian application is from the Protuguese, who had also applied it in the middle of the fifteenth century A.D.The current spelling of the word is after the word "caste" which appears in 1750 in the "academics" and is hardly found before 1800 A.D. Before that time it was spelt as "Cast". In the sense of race or bread of man it was used as early as 1555 A.D. The Spanish word "Casta" was applied to the mixed breed between Europeans, Indians (American) and Negroes. But "Caste" was not used in its Indian sense till the 17th Century A.D. (*History of Caste in India; Jaipur*; 1979; p. 12. Hereafter described as *H.C.I.*)
2. Dr. Baba Saheb Ambedkar; *Annihilation* of *Caste;* Aurangabad (India); 1936; Reprint; 2003; p. 47.

3. A.L Basham; *The Wonder That Was India;* New Delhi; Reprint 2003; p. 148 (Thereafter explained as W.T.W.I.). *Note.* Author has also discussed the development of the caste system in India from time to time and also cited the same examples as mentioned above by the historians; and partially used by Brahmans.
4. Zanaide-A-Ragozin; *Vedic India*; New Delhi; 1961; P.274. Hereafter the title of the book shall be discussed as *V.I.*
5. Sir Denzil Ibbetson; *Panjab Castes* ; Language Department Punjab; Reprint, 1995; p. 2. Hereafter cited as *P.C.*
6. *Note.* The term *Brahmana* meant originally "One possessed of *brahman*", a mysterious magical force of the type widely known to modern anthropologists by the Polynesin word *mana* (W.T.W.I; p.139). In the *Rig-veda,* in an enumeration of gifts, reference to the golden *mana* which some authorities identify with the old Babylonian weight-unit, the *manah* (Latin *Mina*). *(R.C. Majumdar;* H.C. Raychaudhuri; K. Datta; *An Advanced History of India;* London; Reprint 1963; P.35. Thereafter cited as A.H.I.) If the identification of the Vedic *mana* with the Babylonian *manah* is correct, we have indubtiable testimony to a very early intercourse between India and distant lands beyond the seas. (Ibid). For the detail information study the book of the same author *"History of the Brahmans".*
7. *Note.* The statement of *Farishta* appears to be found an authorities, lost to us, but trustworthy, and to be handled by him in a critical spirit. For instance, he is quite sound in his account of the origin of the Rajputs. As he says the *Brahman* and *Kshatriya* existed from the time immemorial but Rajputs are only known since the beginning of the *Kaliyuga.* They attained power after Vikramajit's demise, something more than 1600 years ago (when he wrote) and he derives their origin from the children of *rajas* by female slaves, the sons of Raja Suraj being the first to bear the title of Rajput. The history of Raja Suraj is closely connected by him with that of Persia. He makes Krishna, elected King by the people of Behar, contemporary with Tahmorasp of Persia. Krishna's eldest son Maharaja succeeded him and divided the people of India into tribes and castes. He named the (Rajput) Rahtor, Chauhan, Punwar, Bais, etc. after the chiefs of each. He kept up a friendly intercourse with Persia, but his nephew Dongur Sain sought refuge with Fardin of Persia and the latter King despatched a force under his son *Kurshap* to invade the Punjab, and Maharaja was compelled to cede a part of his kingdom *'Word'* doubtless a part or the whole of the Punjab *mana* or *brahmana* to Dongur Sain. Passing by the interesting statement that the islands of *Acheen*, *Malacca*, *Pegu* and the *Malabar* coast broke away from his empire, *Farishta* tells us that it was simultaneously threatened by an attack on its North-West Frontier and that Maharaja was compelled to send his lieutenant Mal Chand of Malwa to defend the Punjab, but was obliged to cede it to Persia. Some writers adds *Farishta,* say that Faridun even possessed the Punjab and that the descendants of his son Kurshasp held it together with Kabul, Tibet, Sind and Nimroz down to the time of *Rustum*, i.e, for four generations. (H.A.

Rose; *A Glossary of the Tribes and Castes Punjab and North-West Frontier Provinces;* Language Department, Punjab. Vol. i. Reprint, 1990; pp. 20-21. Thereafter discussed as *G.T.C. P.N.W.F.P.*).

8. *Note.* The whole basis of diversity of Caste is diversity of occupation. The old division in *Brahman, Kshatriya, Vaisya, Sudra* and the *Mlechchha* or outcaste who is below the *Sudra*, is but a division into the priest, the warrior, the husbandman, the artisan, and the menial; and the more modern development which substituted trader for husbandman as the meaning of Vaisya or "the people" did not alter the nature of classification. Willian Priest, John King, Edward Farmer and James Smith are but the survivals in England of the four *varnas* of Manu. But in India, the priest-ridden to an extent was unknown to the experience of Europe even in the middle ages, the dominance of one special occupation gave abnormal importance to all distinction of occupation. The Brahman, who could at first claim no separate descent by which he should be singled out from among the Aryan Community, sought to exalt his office and to propitate his political rulers, who were the only rivals, he had to fear, by regarding all other occupations and conditions of life. Further, as explained in the sactions just referred to, the principle of hereditary occupation was to him a class one of the most vital importance. As the Brahmans increased in number, those numbers necessarily exceeded the possible requirements of the laity so far as the mere performance of priestly functions was concerned, while it became impossible for them to keep up as a whole even the semblance of sacred learning. Thus, they ceased to be wholly priests and a large proportion of them became mere evites. The only means of preserving its overwhelming influence to the body at large was to substitute Ievitical descent for priestly functions as the basis of that influence, or rather perhaps to check the natural course of social evolution which would have substituted the latter for the former: and this they did by giving the whole saction of religion to the principle of the hereditary nature of occupation. Hence sprang that tangled web of caste restrictions and distinctions of ceremonial obligations, and of artificial purity and impurity, which has rendered the separation of occupations from descent so slow and so difficult in Hindu society, and which collectively constitutes what know as caste. Brahmans invented the principle deliberately set to work to produce any craftily designed effect upon the growth of soical institutions. But circumstances had raised them to a position of extraordinary power; and naturally, and probably almost unconsciously, their teaching took the form which tended most effectually to preserve that power unimpaired. Indeed, in its earlier form, neither caste nor occupation was even supposed in India to be necessarily or invariably hereditary. It is often forgotten that there are two very distinct epochs in the post-vedic history of the Hindu nations, which made respectively contributions of very different nature to the body of Hindu scriptures which we are too apt to confuse under the generic name of the *Shastras*, and which affected in very different manners the form of the Hindu religion. The earlier is the epoch of the *Brahmans* and the *Upanishads*, while Hinduism was a single and

comparatively simple creed, or at most a philosophical abstraction; and the later is the epoch of the *Puranas* and *Tantras*, with their crowed *Pantheon*, their foul imaginings their degraded idolatry, and their innumerable sects. The former may be said to end with the rise and the latter to begin with the growing degeneracy of Buddhism. In the earlier Hinduism, we find that, while caste distinctions were primarily based upon occupation considerable license in this respect was permitted to the several castes, while the possibility of the individual rising from one caste to another was distinctly recognised. This was the case even as late as the age of Manu, by which time the caste system had assumed great strictness, and the cardinal importance of occupation had become a prominent part of the Brahminical teaching, though its hereditary nature had not yet been so emphatically insisted on. It was in the dark ages of Hindu history, about the beginning of an era during which Brahminism was substituted for Hinduism and religion became a chaos of impure and degraded doctrine and sectarian teaching, that the theory of the necessarily hereditary nature of occupation seems to have taken its present form. In the earlier epoch the priest was always a Brahman in the later the Brahman was always a priest. But if occupation was not necessarily transmitted by descent and if caste varied with change of occupation in the earlier era of Hinduism, it is no less true that this is the case in the present day; though under caste restrictions as they now stand the change, in an upward direction at least, is '*infinitely slower*' and more difficult than then, and is painfully effected by the family or tribe in the course of generations instead of by the individual in the course of years. The following pages will contain numerous instances of the truth of this assertion, and the whole body of tribal and caste tradition in the Panjab supports it. But the evidence, imperfect as it is, will be found to possess no inconsiderable weight; while the very fact of the general currency of a set of tradition, groundless as they are based at least not repugnant to the ideas and feelings and practice of the people who believe them. Indeed, for the purposes of the present enquiry it would almost be allowable to accept traditional origin; for though the tradition may not be true, it might have been, or it would never have arisen. Instances of fall in the social scale are naturally more often met with than instances of rise, for he who has sunk recalls with pride his ancestral origin while he who has risen hastens to forget it. (P.C. pp. 3, 4, 5.)

9. *V.I.* pp. 275-76, 278.
10. A.C. Clayton; *The Rig Veda and Vedic Religion*; New Delhi; Reprint 1981. P.136. (Hereafter mentioned as *R.V.V.R.) Note.* The Indian word which partially corresponds with *Caste* is *Jati* equivalent to the Latin *gens,* (in the infected form *gent*) and Greek Tevos "race or nation", while *Jatibheda,* the representative of the foundations of the caste-system, means the "distinctions of race or *gentis discrimina.*" *Varna,* another word used for it by the Hindus, originally meant a difference the "colour". Gradually these Indian words, conveniently rendered by *CASTE,* have come to represent not only varieties of race and colour, by every original, hereditary religions, instituted *'Word'* or *'Nam'*, it is

possible to imagine. (John Wilson; *Indian Caste*; New Delhi; 1976; P.13. Hereafter explained as *I.C.*)

11. *V.I.* pp. 278-79.
12. *Ibid.* p. 279.
13. *Note.* The belief in and worship of God or Gods, i.e. *'Nam'* or *'Sabad'* is a particular system of faith and worship, originated from Latin Word 'obligation', reverence' during the process of a child.
14. *A.H.I.* p. 32.
15. Dr. Sudhakar Chattopadhyaya; *Social Life in Ancient India*; Santiniketan (India); 1964. P.8 Hereafter described as *S.L.A.I. Note.* Term *Sudra* means *'Sea'* in Sanskrit called *Samudra* mention by Kalhana and *Srivara* on Page No.283, Vol. 1. *Rajatarangini* Tr. by M.A Stein.
16. *V.I.* p. 280.
17. *S.L A.I.* p. 8.
18. *A.H.I.* p. 33.
19. Manorama Jauhari; *Politics and Ethics in Ancient India;* Varanasi; 1968. p. 344. Thereafter referred as *P.E.A.I.*
20. *Ibid.* pp. 342-43.
21. B.P. Sinha, *Readings in Kautilya's Arthasastra;* Delhi, 1976. p. 133. Henceforth cited as R.K.A.
22. *P.E.A.I.* p. 346.
23. *R.K.A.* p. 133.
24. *Ibid.* p. 134.
25. *P.E.A.I.* pp. 340-41.
26. R.N. Dandekar; *The Age of The Gupta and Other Eassays*; Delhi; 1982; P.46. Hereafter cited as *A.G.O.E.*
27. *P.E.A.I.* p. 341.
28. A.G.O.E. p. 47.
29. R.K. Mookerji; *Ashoka;* Delhi; 1967. p. 60.
30. R.K. Mookerji; *Ancient India Education*; London; Reprint; 1989; p. 14. Hereafter described as *A.I.E.*
31. J. Murdoch; *Review of Caste in India;* New Delhi; 1977. p. 33. Hereafter discussed as R.C.I.
32. *A.I.E.* p. 19.
33. R.C. Majumdar; *Ancient India*; Delhi; Reprint, 1982 pp. 260-61. Hereafter explained as *A.I.*
34. *K.M Munishi;* R.C Majumdar; A.K Majumdar; *The Classical Age*; Vol.III. Bombay; Reprint; 1962; p. 132. Hereafter wrote as *C.A.*
35. *Ibid.*
36. B.N. Puri; *Cities of Ancient India*; Delhi; 1966. pp. 38-39. Hereafter referred as C.A.I.
37. *P.E.A.I.* p. 338.

38. Dr. Edward C. Sachan; *Alberuni's India; New Delhi; Vol. 1 and II;* Reprint 1989. p. 335. Thereafter discussed as *A.I.*
39. P.V. Kane; *History of Dharmasastra*; Poona (India). Vol.1. 1968; p. 182. Hereafter the title of the book referred as *H.D.*
40. *A.I.* p. 157.
41. '*Kalhana's Rajatarangini;* Tr. by. M.A Stein, Delhi: Vol.1 Reprint, 1989; p. 8 Hereafter explained as *R.T.*
42. *Ibid.*
43. *Ibid.*
44. *Ibid.*, p. 9.
45. *Ibid.*
46. *Ibid.*
47. *Ibid.* p. 10.
48. *Ibid.* pp. 35-36.
49. *Ibid.* p. 36.
50. *Ibid.* pp. 67-68.
51. *Ibid.* pp. 93.
52. *Ibid.* p. 106.
53. *Ibid.*
54. *Ibid.* p. 110.
55. *Ibid.*
56. *Ibid.* p. 111.
57. *Ibid.*
58. *Ibid.* p. 112.
59. *Ibid.* p. 117.
60. *Ibid.*
61. *Ibid.* p. 118.
62. *Ibid.*
63. *Ibid.*
64. *Ibid.* pp. 118-19.
65. *Ibid.* p. 119.
66. *Ibid.* p. 120.
67. *J.* Hutchison and J. Ph. Vogel; *History of the Panjab* Hill States; Reprint; 1982; Department of Language and Culture; Himachal Pradesh; p. 594. Hereafter cited as *H.P.H.S.*
68. *R.T.* Vol. 1, p. 121.
69. *Ibid.*, p. 123.
70. *H.P. H.S.*, pp. 596-97.
71. *R.T.* Vol.1., p. 123.
72. *Ibid.* p. 125.
73. *Ibid.* pp. 125-26.
74. *Ibid.* p. 129.

# 1

# Early History of the Chamar Dynasty

**Origin of the First Chamar Dynasty-** The term Chamar[1] is drived from the Sanskrit word *'Charmkara', "worker in hides[2]"* or *"cutter in hides[3]."* that is known as *Creater Power, Holy Spirit, Sabad, Divine Sound Current, Nam, Word, Kalma,* and by many other names[4]. In the Indo-Aryan regions, *Chamar* and *Chambhara* is known for more than a leather - working caste[5]. The author of the *Mudraraksasa[6]* (whether he belong to the 5th and 6th century A.D. or later) came long after the *Puranas*, was permeated by *Puranic* lore and therefore he generally uses the word *'Vrsala'* (which means *Sudra* in medieval Sanskrit works with reference to Chandragupta when speaking of him personally, but in his absence, he several times employs merely the word, *'Chandragupta'[7] (*as after 1, 12, 14) or *'Vrsala'* (just before 1.10)[8]. But it must be emphasiszed that *Mudraraksasa* also displays the *Nandakula* was the *Pitrkul* of Chandragupta, access to *Raksasa* vide the words *(Nandakulama nena, Pitrkulabhutam ghatitam' (after IV, 12) and V.19, 'Mauryossan Svamiputrals*. It is to be noted that in the *Mudraraksasa* Canakya refers to Changragupta as *'Vatsa'* (also just before 1.19). Frantic efforts have been made by some writers (e.g. by *Mr. Govind Pal in (i) Gode commercial.* volume part III, pp. 141-150, particularly P.146, by Mr. K.C Seth in I.H.Q. vol.13. pp. 641-653, and by *H.K Dels* in I.H.Q, Vol.8 PP.466-478) to explain the word *'Vrsala'* in certain ways such as holding *'Vrsala'* as the Sanskrit equivalent of the word *'Basileos' (Basileos)* occuring on the obverse of the coins of Menander and Demetrius (who became king in 190 B.C., vide *Cambridge History of India,* Vol. 1, pp. 586, 588[9]. Dr. A. Ghosh in I.H.Q Vol. VI. pp. 271-283 (which rebuts *Sudra* origin), and by Dr. *R.K Mookerjee* in Woolner Commemoration Vol. pp. 93-99. *Rakasasa* speaks of Chandragupta as *Mauryaputra* in the drama (Act II. 7 ) but '*Kulahina*'[10] and in VI. 6, he calls him *Vrsala* which word in the context means nothing else but *Sudha* (his words being *'gata sighrena srirvrsalam-aviniteva vrsali*[11]).

Johnston in his 'two studies in the *Arthasastra of Kautilya'*, in *JRAS (Journal of the Royal Asiatic Society of Great Britain)* for 1929 (PP.77-102) states that the *Lankavatarasutra* was translated into Chinese in 443 A.D., that therefore the main body of the work is not later than 4th century A.D. and that (P.87) in verses 813-7 the *rsis* are announced in the following order Viz, *Panini, Katyayana, Yajnavalkya, Valmiki,Masuraksa, Kautilya and Asvalayana. Yajnavalkya* is most probably the sage of the Brhadaranyaka Up. Most of the others belong to centuries preceding the Christian era and therefore the name of Kautilya, it seems, was known some centuries before Christ and as most of the names are those of authors. Kautilya should also be regarded as an author of this passage[12].

The *'Chamar'* caste, even in early medieval period displayed peculiarity, marking it off from the other untouchable classes. *Kalhana* in his *Rajatarangini* has superbly described, the story of a *Charmkrit*, a leather-worker , in other respect called *'Padukrit'*, a tanner[13].

The *Chamars* have been one of the village menials in the traditional village economy, they do all the *begar*[14], or such work as cutting grass, carrying wood and bundles, acting as watchman, and the like, and they plaster the houses with mud when they need it. They take the hides of all dead cattles and the flesh of all cloven-footed animals, that of such as do not divide the hoof going to *Chuhras*[15]. Though his chief contribution to the life of village was through his hide and leather working, yet he played no mean part in it[16], they make and mend shoes, thongs for the cart, and whips and other leather work; and above all they do an immense deal of hard work in the fields, each family supplying each cultivating association with the continuous labour of a certain number of hands. All this they do as village menials, receiving fixed customary dues in the shape of a share of the produce of the fields. In the east and south-east of Panjab the village *Chamars* also do a great deal of weaving, which however, is paid for separately[17].

The Sanskrit Lexicons, *Vaijayanti* of 11th century A.D. and *Abhidhanacintamani* of 12th century A.D recorded the traditional information about the shoes-maker or leather worker (cobbler) was also known as *padukakrit* and *Charmakrit* (Abhi; III. P.914)[18]. The *Chamar* is the tanner and leather-worker of North-Western India, and the western parts of the Panjab he is called *Mochi* or *Muchi*, whenever he is, as he generally is, a Musalman, the caste being one and the same[19]. In the south, partly the *Mala* in Andhara Pradesh and partly the Paraiyan in Tamilnad carried on scavenging[20]. While the *Mala* chiefly was a leather-worker, the *Paraiyan* was a field labour[21]. The Marathi *Mahar*, the Telugu *Mala* and the Tamil Paraiyan, though because of their village menial status are grouped together as field labourers, conveyed pollution without touch, either at a specific distance or by their shadow and were classed as impure untouchables[22]. The *Dom* was only one of the castes traditionally concerned with scavenging the other cases were the *Chuhra* in the Punjab, the *Bhangi Mehtar* in Rajasthan and Bombay, the *Bhuinmali* and *Hari* in Bengal and *Haddi* in Orissa[23]. The humblest of these is probably the one which least changed its character during the course of centuries. The modern *Dumbs*[24] *or Doms,* in Punjab called *Mirasi*. Almost all of them are Muslims. In Bengal, there was a saction which carried on fishing. In Andhra Pradesh, there are found in small numbers under the name of *Dombar* or *Dommara*, which is also the name of a caste in Maharashtra noted for similar attainments[25]. The descendants of old *Dombas*[26], are still the low caste, watchmen and village menials as which they figures in Kalhana's narrative. They, like the still more *Vatal* or scavengers, cannot intermarry with other *Kashmirs*. They have thus retained in their appearance a distinctive type of their own which points to relationship with gipsy tribes of India and Europe[27]. Hiuen Tsiang mentions as a low-born race settled in Kashmir from early times and opposed to the *Buddhas* or *Nam* their name, usually transcribed *Kritya* (Ki-lo-to), cannot be traced in indigenous records[28]. According to *Alberuni, Doma (Domba)* and *Chandalas*[29], are two groups about which we have known so much from *Patanjali, Hemachandra* and Kalhana, they were occupied with "dirty work like the cleansing of the villages and other services". They were considered, "as one sole class, and distinguished only by their occupation." The *Dom's* other occupation was that of the player on the lute and of the singer[30].

Thus, the *Chamars* stand far above the *Chuhras* in social position and some of their tribes are almost accepted as Hindus[31]. They are generally dark in colour, and are almost certainly of aboriginal origin, though here again their numbers have perhaps been swollen by members of other and higher castes who have fallen or been degraded. The people say. *"Do not cross the ferry with a black Brahman or a fair chamar"*, one being as ususual as the other[32].

*"Karia (black) Brahman, got chamar, in Ke sath na utrie par*[33]*"*

*Their* women are celebrated for beauty, and loss of caste is often attributed to too great partiality for a *Chamarni, M.A.* Sherring has a long disquisition on the *Chamar* caste, which appears to be much more extensive and is include much more varied tribes in Hindustan than in the Punjab[34].

The traditional origin of the *Chamars is that Chanu (or Chanwe)* and Banu [35] were two brothers: the former removed a cow's carcase with his one hands and so Banu out casted him[36].In Kapurthala, however, another version is current and according to the *Gat* told his brother *Met* to remove a carcase and then declined to associate with him for doing so, and the *Mirasi* who wittnessed the incident, took *Gat's* part. From *Mat* are descended the *Chamars*[37]. But in the east of the province, he is far more, than a leather worker. He is the general *"coolie"* and field labourer of the villages, and a *Chamar*, if asked his caste by the Englishman at any rate, will answer *"Coolie"* as often as 'Chamar'[38]. The Dhigvana's occupation, that of working in leather and trading in leather products, is represented in recent and contemporary society in aforesaid regions by the *Mochi* or *Muchi*[39]. It is clear that though the groups must have been despised first because of their work in dirty, filthy and impure commodity, yet they were not required to live outside villages or towns[40].

**Rise of the Magadha Empire**

Rise of the Magadha empire is one of the important and interesting event in the history of India. Magadha empire rose out of 'Infinite' and owes it rise and growth to such great kings and emperors like *Mahapadma Nanda*, *Ajatasatru*, or *Bimbisara* whose reign was enlivened by the moving personality of the great Buddha[41]. They contributed the power and resources in making India strong and glorified. It was due to the dominant characteristic of the period with which we propose to deal is the rise and growth of a New Monarchy in Eastern India of which we have a presage[42] to the *Aitareya Brahmana*:

"In this eastern quarter (*Prachyam disi*) whatever kings there are of the eastern peoples, they are anointed for imperial rule. (*Samrajya*); 'Oh emperor' *(Samrat)* they style him when anointed[43]."

Thus, the eastern peoples (*prachyas*) are not specified by the *Brahmana* in the same way as those of the South, the North and the Middle country. But there can hardly be any doubt that they lived to the east of the *dhruva madhyama dis* and thus answer to the *Prasii* of the Greek writers and the confederate nations who dominated the valleys of the lower Ganges and the son. The most eminent among these nations was Magadha which embraced the modern districts of Patna and Gaya[44].

**Origin of Nandas**

In social matters, the rise of *Nandas* may be regarded[45] from *Kalasoka*, the son and successor of Sisunaga dynasty; and was assassinated by a man of low origin that is [46] *Chamar,* barber according to some accounts[47] of the Brahminical, named *Mahapadma Nanda. Justin* has rightly remarked that Chandragupta was of *lowly* and now low or base birth, that he was a mere commoner who had no royal blood in him but who was 'aspiring for royalty'. They are full of aspersions on the character of the then reigning Indian King was a man of disreputable origin, the illegitimate offspring of a barber, "detested and held cheap by his subjects". We are further told by Plutarch that it was Chandragupta himself who had reported to Alexander the "meanness" as *Nanda King's* origin[48]. It means that for securing the capital of Magadha soldiers from the North-West of India had been brought by *Chandragupta* and *Parvataka* and Canakya had the leading part in that. In Act III after verse 24 Canakya raya to Candragupta, 'we have recently secured the kingdom of the *Nandas'* and in Act IV, 14 *Raksasa* himself tells *Malayaketu* that the Maurya has recently become King. It seems that Chandragupta first gained provinces in North-West India and then secured Magadha[49] .

The early dynastic history of Magadha is shrouded in darkness. We have occasional glimpses of war-lords and statesmen, some probably entirely mythical, others having more appearance of reality. True history commences with the famous Bimbisara of the *Hiryanka Kula* who launched his people in that career of conquest and aggrandishment which only ended with Asoka sheathed his sword after the conquest of Kalinga. The family of Bimbisara was responsible for the fortification of a village at the confluence of the Son and the Ganges whcih grew into the city of Pataliputra and soon replaced the old capital, *Girivraja-Rajagriha*. It also saw, and actively supported, the growth of the religious movements associated with *Vardhamana Mahavira* and *Gautama Buddha*. According to Buddhist tradition the *Bimbisarids* made room for a new line styled *Saisunaga*[50]. Thus, *Saisunaga* rule seems to have ended in a tragedy. The last notable ruler of the line fell a victim to a plot engineered by an all powerful official who had "advanced to too near a place in the confidence of the monarch[51]. For instance, in the case of the Saisunaga dynasty which was succeeded by that of the *Nandas*; it has been clearly stated that of the ten Saisunaga Kings, the ninth was *Nandivardhana*, and the tenth was his son named *Mahanandin*, and that, "as son of *Mahanandin* by a *Sudra* woman will be born a king, Mahapadma (Nanda), who will exterminate all Kshatriyas. Thereafter, Kings will be of Sudra origin." If this history had repeated itself in the case of the Mauryas, and if the first Maurya King were also related to the preceding Saisunaga king that history could not have been omitted by the *Puranas*[52].

**First Meeting of Chanakya and Chandragupta**

We have already seen the circumstances under which *Chanakya* and *Chandragupta* met for the first time in their lives, that meeting was a most fateful meeting fraught[53] with immense consequences not merely to their personal histroy, but also to the history of their country. For Chandragupta, it proved to be the turning-point in his life. No longer was he to live the insecure life of a hunter in the obscurity of wilderness. He was now to live the cultured life of a citizen, receiving the highest possible education of the times at India's greatest seat of learing at far-off Taxila, and preparing for one of the biggest enterprises in history[54].

**Pataliputra as a Centre of Learning**

As related in the *Mahavamsa Tika,* Chanakya came all the way from Taxila to Pataliputra in pursuit of learning and disputation centred at that imperial capital (*Vadam pariyesanto Pupphapuram gantva*). It is an extraordinary compliment paid to the status of Pataliputra as the intellectual capital of India in those days when a scholar of encyclopaedic learning like Chanakya, himself the product of one of the greatest centres of learning like *Takshasila*, should seek to win fresh laurels for his learning at this far-off city in Eastern India. The fame of Pataliputra as a centre of learning continued through the ages, outliving its political glory. Thus, it is referred in a work which is about a thousand years later, the classical work known as *Kavyamimamsa* by the poet *Rajasekhara* who makes the following interesting statement: "There is a tradition (*sruyate*) that Pataliputra was the place which was the centre of examination of all markers of *Sastras* (*Sastrakara-Pariksha*), the founders and exponents of different systems. Here were thus examined eminent creative geniuses and authors like *Varsha* and *Upavarsha, Panini* and *Pingala*, and *Vyadi.* In later times, *Vararuchi* and *Patanjali* achieved fame as scholars by first passing their examination (*pariksha*) at this city of learning. It will be seen that Varsha was a most ancient author as one who was the teacher of Panini himself (C.500 B.C. or earlier). *Upavarsha* was his brother and a commentator of *Mimamsa* and *Vedanta Sutras,* from whom citations have been made even by the great *Sankaracharya, Pingala,* according to tradition, was Panini's younger brother, the author of the *Chhanda-Sastra*. Vyadi was the grammarian who came after Panini and wrote on his system. Vararuchi and Patanjali were of course much later authors. It appears that Rajasekhara has mentioned all these men of learning from Varsha to Vararnchi, Pingala to Pantanjali, in a chronological order. All these hail from different parts of the country emerged into eminence by taking their examination at Pataliputra[55]. Thus, the first Nanda bore of name *Mahapadma* or *Mahapadmapati*, "sovereign of an infinite host" or " of immense wealth", according to *Puranas*, and *Ugrasena* according to the *Mahabodhivamsa*[56].

**Ugrasena-Nanda**

The then ruler of Magadha, known as merely Nanda in Sanskrit tradition, is named Dhana-Nanda in the Pali texts which further acquaint us with the namas and some particulars of all the nine Nandas. We are told that all the nine Nandas, who were brothers, ruled one after another in accordance with seniority (*Vuddhapati patiya*). *Dhan-Nanda* was the youngest of them. The eldest brother is named *Ugrasena-Nanda*, the founder of the Nanda dynasty. His early life was quite romantic, like that of Chandragupta. Originally, he was from the frontier *(Pachchanta-Vasika)* and fell into the hands of robbers who carried him captive to a frontier province called Malaya (if Malaya in *Mudrarakshasa*) and won him over to the doctrine that pillage was preferable to tillage as a pursuit. He enlisted himself as one of the gangs of robbers together with his brothers and kinsmen and soon after their leader. They started raiding the kingdoms of the neighbourhood (*rattham vilumpamamo vicharanto*) and, marching against the cities of the frontiers (*pachchanta nagaram gantva*), gave them the ultimatum: "Either surrender your kingdom, or give battle (*rajjm va dentu yuddham va*)'. Gradually they aimed at supreme sovereignty (*Mahavamsa Tika* in Sinhalese text, read Mr. C.D. Chatterji). A robber king thus rore to be a King of Kings. But he achieved this position by nefarious means on which the Buddhist text is silent but other sources through some light. Bana's *Harshacharita*, a text of the seventh century A.D., records the story that *Kakavarna Saisunaga* was killed by a dagger thrust into his throat in the neighbourhood of his city (*Pataliputra*). He is called *Kakavarna* in the *Puranas* but Kalasoka in the Mahavamsa list of the kings preceding the Nandas[57]. The former Agrammes is modified into *Xandramas* by Diodorus, and F.W. Thomas takes it to be the equivalent of *Chandramas*. He takes Agrammes to be *Dhana-Nanda* (*Cambridge History of India*, 1.P.469), taking Dhana-Nanda to be his nicknama, and *Chandramas* as his personal name. 'The young princes' mentioned by Curtius as being murdered by Ugrasena-Nanda were most probably the ten sons of Kalasoka Kakavarni of the aforesaid Mahavamisas list[58]. The first Nanda in the Buddhist account simply overthrows by force the previous ruling dynasty of Magadha as the culmination of a previous career of violence, as described above[59]. The *Mahavamsa* states: "*Nava Nanda* (also *navabhataro*) *tato asum*." The worst infamy which Buddhist tradition records against these Nandas is that they were originally outlaws and robbers. The *Mahabodhivamsa* describes the Nanda kings as *Chorapubbas*[60], "the docoits of old."

**First task of Chandragupta Maurya to Overthrow of Greek rule:** We now return to the history which followed Chanaky's fateful discovery of Chandragupta as the chosen instrument of his designs. We have seen with what patience Chanakya first undertook the preliminary task of giving Chandragupta the best possible upbringing and education spread over a period of eight years so as to him for the great schemes he had in view. The first of these was to surmount a difficulty that lay at his door. His youthful imagination was already fired by the spectacle of a foreign invasion of his fatherland in progress before his very eyes, the amount of resistance offered to it at different centres by small republican peoples of the Panjab, and the final passing away of his country under foreign Greek rule. Thus his immediate imperative task was the liberation of his country from the yoke of this subjection. He was inspired in this task by the teaching of his preceptor, Kautilya[61], who condemned foreign rule as an unmitigated evil. He condemns foreign rule (*Vairajya*) as the worst form of exploitation, where he conqueror, who subdues a country by violence (*Parasyachchidya*), never counts it as his dear country (*naitat mama iti manyamanah*) oppresses it by overtaxation and exactions (*Karshayati*), and drains it of its wealth (*apavahayati*) (VIII 2). Details are wanting as to how he was able to organise measures, the ways and means for the accomplishment of that stupendous tasks in the atmosphere of depress created by the victory of Alexander and the breakdown of the national opposition, to fan into flame its dying embers, and to reorganise the military resources of the country in men and material for purposes of another national endeavour to strike a blow for its freedom.

**Sources of Chandragupta's Army**

*The republican peoples who resisted Alexander*. We learn from *Mahavamsa Tika* that on the completion of Chandragupta's education at Taxila, both Chanakya placed the army thus recruited under the command of Chandragupta (*Mahabalakayam sangahetva tam tassa patipadesi*). Rhys Davids points out that "it was from the Panjab that Chandragupta recruited the nucleus of the force with which he besieged and conquered Dhana-Nanda[62]". As pointed out by Mc-Crindle (*Invasion of India by Alexander;* P.406), the term "robbers" indicated the republican peoples for which the Panjab was known in those days, the *Arattas* or *Arashtrakas*, "Kingless" peoples, peoples not living under a *rashtra* or state, of which the usual normal type was a kingship. Bandhayana[63], in his *Dharmasutra* (C. 400 B.C.) describes the Panjab as the country of *Arattas* (I.12,13-15). The *Mahabharata* (VIII. 44, 2070)calls the *Arattas* as *Panchanadas*, 'natives of the land of rivers', (Ib.45, 211C) and also *Vahikas 'People of the land of rivers'*, comprising the Prasthalas, *Madras, Gandharas, Khasas, Vasatis, Sindhus* and *Sauviras*.

It is interesting to note that Kautilya[64] mentions as the sources of recruitment for the army (1) the *Choras,* or *pratirodhakas,*of the day, the robbers and outlaws, (2) the *Chora-ganas*, organised gangs of brigands, (3) the *Mlechchha*[65] tribes like the Kirata high landers, (4) the *Atavikas*, the foresters, and (5) the warrior clans called *Sastro-pajivisrenis,* and that he counts the soldiery recruited from these clans as most heroic (*pravira*) (VII.10;14;VIII.14). The Panjab in those days had abundance of this type of military material. Alexander himself had to deal with some of these peoples in his campaigns. As is shown below, it is possible to find out the Indian equivalents of their Greek names as recorded in the classical accounts of his invasion.

**Republican Peoples Known to the 'Mahabharata'**

The *Mahabharat* mentions the following republican peoples of these region , Viz. (1) *Yaudheyas* (II.52;VII.9); (2) *Kshudrakas* (II.51;VI.57); (3) *Malavas* (*II.32;II 52*); (4) *Vasatis* (II.52; V.30); (5) *Sibis* (11.32; 11.52); (6) Udumbaras (11.52); (7) *Prasthalas* (VIII. 44); (8) *Trigartas* (II.52); (9) *Madras* (II.52-VI.61); (10) *Kekayas* (111.120) and (11) *Agreyas* (III.254).

***Republican peoples known to Panini***

Panini's term for a republic is *Samgha* or *Gana* (III.3, 86). Most of these republics took to the pursuit of arms and were known as *Ayudhajivi-Samghas,* 'Warriors-communities.' They were of the *Vahika* country, 'the land of river', another name for the Panjab (V.3, 114). As examples of these self-governing communities of warriors, Panini mentions the following:—

(1) *Kshudrakas* (Greek *Oxydrakai*), (IV.2, 45)

(2) *Malavas* (Greek *Malloi*) (1b)

(3) *Vrikas*, also called *Varkenya* (V.3, 115), most probably corresponding to the people known as Hyrcanians (Sakas) mentioned as *Varkanah* in the Behistun and as *Varkah* in another old Persian inscription of Darius I.

(4) *Damani* and others (not identified) (V.3, 116),

(5) Confederacy of the Six *Trigartas* comprising (*a*) *Kaundoparatha,* (*b*) *Dandaki,* (*c*) *Kaushtaki,* (*d*) Jalamani, (*e*) Brahmagupta and (*f*) Janaki.

(6) *Parsu,* associated with *Asura* and *Rakshas,*and probably of the country called *Parsa* in the Behistun inscription of Darius I, the place of origin of the Achaemenians, whence the name Persia.

(7) *Yaudheyas*

(8) *Salvas* (Alwar and its surrounding country), a large confederacy comprising (*a*) *Udumbaras*, (*b*) *Tilakhalas,*, (*c*) *Madrakaras*, (*d*) *Yugandharas*, (*e*) *Bhulingas*, (*f*) *Sarandandas,* (*g*) *Budhas*, (*h*) *Ajakrandas* and (*i*) *Ajamidhas*, (IV.1,173).

(9) *Bhargas*, mentioned in the *Gana*-patha alongwith (*a*) *Karushas*, (*b*) *Kekayas*, (*c*) *Kasmiras*, (*d*) *Salvas* (*e*) *Ṣusthalas*, (*f*) Urasas (of Hazara District) and (*g*) *Kauravyas*, (IV. 1, 179).

(10) *Ambashthas* (Greek *Abastanoi*) who are associated in the *Mahabharata* (II. 52, 14-15) with the *sibis*, *Kshudrakas,* Malavas and other north-western tribes.

(11) Hastinayana (IV.4, 174) (Greek *Astanenoi*)

(12) *Prakanva* (VI.1, 153), corresponding to modern Ferghana whose people called the *Parikanioi* correspond to *Prakanvayanas* (stem konow, *Kharoshthi Inscription*, P. XVII).

(13) *Madras*, (IV.2, 131)

(14) *Madhumantas* (IV.2, 133; Mbh. Bhishma P., IX -53) corresponding to the *Mohmands.*

(15) Apritas (IV.2, 53), (Greek *Aparytai*, corresponding to the *Afridis*)

(16) *Vasati* (Ib.) (Greek *Ossadioi*)

(17) *Sibis* (IV.3, 112) (Greek Sibioi).

(18) *Asvayana* (IV.I, 110) and *Asvakuyana* (1b. 99) corresponding to Greek *Aspasii* and *Assakenoi* whose stronghold was Massaga (= Masakavati).

It is interesting to note that the city called Aornos by the Greeks corresponds to the *Varana* used by Panini (IV.2, 82).

It will be seen from the above list that in Panini's time there were both individual republics functioning by themselves and confederacres of such republics such as the *Trigarta Shashtha*, on the salvas (V.S. Agrawala Panini as a source of History to be published shortly)

As Arrian tells us (IV.21), a large part of the Panjab was then held by these "independent Indian tribes" whom Curtius (IX.4) describes as "fierce nation" ready to resist Alexander "with their blood". The kingdom which was restored by Alexander to his old enemy, King Poros (=Paurava), comprised territories held by "fifteen republican peoples owning 5000 considerable cities and villages without number" (Plutarch, lives.IX).

How they fought Alexander and their military resources. The military potentialities and heroism of these 'independent' peoples of the Panjab were brought to light by Alexander's invasion and must have been observed by youthful Chandragupta. The story of their resistance against Alexander's campaigns is not less inspiring than the story of Alexander's victories. The Indian opposition to Alexander which was offered to him from different centres may be appraised and abbessed in the light of the facts and figures recorded by the Greeks themselves.

Alexander had its first taste from the tribal chief whom the Greek call *Astes* corresponding to Sanskrit *Hastin,* the Chief of the people known by the Indian name of *Hastinayana* (Panini, VI.4,174). Greek *Astakenoi* or *Astanenoi*, with his capital at *Peukelaotis* or *Pushkalavati*. This heroic chief stood the Greek siege of his walled town for full thirty days tell he fell fighting.

Similarly, the *Asvayaxas* and *Asvakayanas* fought the invader to a man, as will be evident from the fact that as many as 40,000 of them were taken as captives their economic prosperity may also be noted from the fact that as many as 230,000 oxen fell into the hands of Alexander.

The *Asvakayanas* gave the battle to Alexander with an army of 30,000 cavalry, 38,000 infantry and 30 elephants, aided by 7,000 mercenaries from the plains, all garrisoned in their fortified capital called *Masakanati* in the *Kasika* comment on Panini (IV.2, 85;VI.3, 119), led by the heroic Queen Cleophis (=Sanskrit *Kripa* that is '*Nam*') "resolved to defend their country to the last extremity." Even their women took part in the defence alongwith the Queen. Even their mercenaries, at first vacillating, caught their spirit and preferred "a glorious death to a life with dishonour" (Mc Crindle's invasion , pp. 194 (Curtius), 270 (Diodorus). their sprit infected the neighbouring hill-country called *Abhisara*, which also joined them in their defence.

The free cities of the region also followed suit, such as *Aornos, Bazira, Ora* or *Dyrta*, cach of which surrendered after a protracted siege.

The Indian military strength was seen at its highest in the army of King Poros (Paurava) who was Alexander's most formidable enemy whom he opposed with an army estimated by Arrian at 30,000 foot, 4,000 horse, 300 chariots, and 200 elephants. Even after his defeat, Alexander had to seek his alliance.

The *Agulassoi* fought Alexander with an army of 40,000 foot and 3,000 horse. We are told that in one of their towns, the citizens numbering about 20,000 cast themselves into the flames, along with their wives and children, rather than submitting as prisoners to the enemy.

Next, Alexander had to meet the opposition organised by a confederacy of the autonomous peoples, such as the Malavas and the horse, and above 900 chariots. Even their Brahmans left the pen for the sword, and died fighting, "with few taken as prisoners."

The *Kathas* were another heroic people who "enjoyed the highest reputation for courage" (Arrian, V.22,2). We are told that their casualties alone amounted to 17,000 killed and 70,000 captives.

The Malavas by themselves defended the passage of a river with 50,000 men. The *Ambashthas* had an army of 60,000 foot 6,000 horse, and 500 chariots.

In the campaigns of the lower Indus, the number of killed alone amounted to 80,000. In this region, it was the Brahmans who took the lead and created the spirit of resistance and war, fever and cheerfully sacrificed their lives in the defence of their *Dharma* (Plutarch, lives, lix; *Combridge History*, I.P.378).

**Causes of their Defeat**

It may be noted that all these fairly large armies were recruited from small republican states. The number of the army was very large in proportion to the number of the total population of the state is concerned. These republican peoples must have fought to a man, and mobilised their entire man-power in defence of their freedom in a sheer spirit of patriotism. Even their women fought with the men. If their heroic fight in the defence of their liberties against a supreme military leader like Alexander had failed for the time being, it was because it lacked leadership, organisation, unity of direction, and pooling of resources. The defence was far too localised and isolated at different centres. It was not organised into a national defence. Alexander was thus able to deal with the defence piecemeal, to proceed against each state separately, and to subdue it easily. The mutiplicity of states prevented a united front against a common enemy and caused the collapse of opposition at individual and isolated centres. Division was fatal to defence. Some kind of national opposition was organised for once by the confederacy of the *Kshudrakas* and *Malavas* who united their military resources in a powerful allied army. Such a federal army was known even in the days of Panini who calls it ' the Kshaudraka-Malavi-Sena.' But these defects and deficiencies of the Indian military situation were soon to be removed by a great leader like Chandragupta with his superior power of organisation.

It was left to the genius of Chanakya and Chandragupta to exploit and utilize once again the magnificent military material and resources, potentialities and possibilities, available in such abundance all over the Punjab among her republican peoples and States and her general population. It was easy for them to produce out of this material, the unconquered spirit of resistance in the people, a well-organised army to fight freedom's battle and to win it.

**Other Recruits for Chandragupta's Army**

But Chandragupta did not confine his army to the mere local recruits, if we may believe in the legends about it. For instance, the *Mudrarakshasa* mentions an alliance which Chanakya had arranged with a Himalayan Chief named *Parvataka* or *Parvatesa*. The Jain text, *Parisishtaparvan*, also refers to this Himalayan alliance, stating that "Chanakya went to Himavatkuta and entered into alliance with *Parvataka*, the king of that region." Buddhist accounts also mention a *Parvata* as a close associate of Chanakya. Thus three traditions record this alliance. F.W.Thomas has gone further in suggesting (*Cambridge History of India*, Vol.I p. 471), that this *Parvataka* was perhaps the same person as king Poros of the Greeks. The suggestion is quite plausible, considering what a large place Poros had filled in the politics of his country in his time, so that no adventure in that region could be undertaken without enlisting his support.

The *Mudrarakshasa* gives us the further information that his Himalayan alliance gave Chandragupta a composite army recruited from a variety of peoples. Among these are mentioned the following: *Sakas, Yavanas* (probably Greeks), *Kiratas, Kambojas, Parasikas, Bahlikas* (II. 12). Chandragupta was opposed by a coalition of 5 of *Kasmira*, the Saindhava prince, *Sindhushena*, and *Meghakhya*, the king of the *Parasikas*, who joined with a large force of cavalry (*Prithuturagabalah*) (I.20). The army of *Malayaketu* comprised recruits from the following peoples: *Khasa, Magadha, Gandhara, Yavana, Saka, Chedi*, and *Huna* (V.II). Thus these various peoples, mostly from the Punjab and the frontier Highlands, were involved in the great war between Chandragupta and his enemies in Magadha. This list unfortunately affects the value of *Mudrarakshasa* as a source of history. Some of the peoples named in it such as the *Sakas* or the *Hunas* appear in Indian history much later than the time of Chandragupta.

**Insecurity of Greek Rule**

But apart from the militancy strength which Chandragupta was able to mobilise for his mission, it was materially helped by the internal conditions of the country and other factors which did not augur well for the future of Greek rule in India. Even from the very beginning, the course of Alexander's invasion did not run smooth. It appeared to be smooth only on the surface. Its difficulties lay deeper. Alexander was not sure of his rear. It was threatened by rebellions both among Greeks and Indians. The prospects of his enterprise did not appeal as much to his followers as to him personally. Alexander's policy was to plant colonies of Greek veterans at suitable centres, the new eastern cities, to mark the progress of his conquests, and to secure its fruits (Arrian, V.27,5). Such colonies were setup first in Bactria and Sogdiana, but it was against the will of the colonists who were not reconciled to this exile.They were always longing for opportunity to desert. When Alexander was fighting with the distant Malavas and received a wound, a rumour of his death spread far and wide, and at once these Greek colonists numbering 3,000 left for home (Diodorus, XVII.99). Alexander himself thought of these colonies as penal settlements to which the Greeks convicted of disloyalty were committed (Justin, XII.5,8,13).

**The Greek Satrapies**

Nor was the attitude of the Indians,who were subdued, more favourable. Their spirit of rebold was not subdued. The administrative arrangements which Alexander made to secure his conquests betray his own sense of their insecurity. He divided Greek India into six *Satrapies*, three on the west side of the Indus, and three on the east. The three western Satraps were Greeks, but not the eastern Satraps who were all Indians. Of the three western Satraps, Petition was posted as governor of Sind. Nicanor was placed in charge of the province called 'India-west-of-the Indus'. It comprised lower Kabul valley and the hill tracts up to the Hindukush, with its capital at *Pushkalavati* (*Charsadda*). The governor had at his disposal a Macedonian garrison under commandant philip. Higher up, Oxyarters was appointed governor of the province of Paropanisadae (Kabul valley) with its capital at the new city called 'Alexandria under the Caucasus.' At first, Alexander tried Persian Satraps, but they failed. As Curtius informs us (IX.8), "there were charges of extortion and tyranny proved against the Persian Satrap, Tyriespes, by the people of the Paropanisadae." This was about 326B.C. conditions were sought to be stabilised by Alexander appointing as Satrap his own father-in-lw, Oxyartes, another Iranian noble.

Alexander could not venture to post Greek governors to the cast of the Indus. Here the three Satrapies were placed under Indian Kings: *Ambhi*, king of Taxila, ruling from the Indus to the Hydaspes; *Poros* (Paurava) ruling from the Indus to the Hydaspes; Poros (Paurava) ruling from the Hydaspes to the Hyphasis; and the king of *Abhisara* country (Kashmir) ruling over the remainder.

**Indian Unrest: Murder of Satrap Nicanor**

The position of the Greek governors to the west of the Indus rapidly became precarious. First, Kandahar raised the standard of rebellion at the instigation of an Indian chief whom the Greeks called Samaxus or Damaraxus. Next came the turn of the *Asvayanas* who dispatched the Greek Satrap, Nicanor, planted in their midst (Arrian, V. 20. 7) The *Asvakayanas* made the position of their Greek governor very unsafe. It was the traitor of an Indian, Sisikottus, or Sasigupta, the Indian agent of Greek Imperialism. Alexander sent him help from his westernmost Satrapy, as also further help under Philip from Taxila.

**Decline of Recruits and Morale**

All this trouble was brewing in 326 B.C., when Alexander was busy in the interior in the thick of his campaigns. His supply of men was failing as he was advancing farther and farther. His progress was brought to a standstill on the banks of the Chenab till the situation was saved by the arrival of Thracian reinforcements from distant Iran. But the Beas proved the limit of his advance. It was because the limit of endurance was reached by his followers. The situation was thus brought home to him by *Koinos* as their spokesman: 'From our ranks you sent away home from Baktra the Thessalians as soon as you saw they have no stomach for further toils *'Words'*. Of the other Greeks, some have been settled in the cities founded by you where all of them are not willing residents; others still share our toils and dangers. They and the Maccdonian army have lost some of their numbers in the fields of battle; others have been disabled by wounds; others have been left behind in different parts of Asia, but the majority have perished by disease. A few only out of many survive, and these few possess no longer the same bodily strength as before, while their spirits are still more depressed. You see yourself how many Macedonians and Greeks started with you and how few of us are left."

**Inherent Defect of Alexander's Scheme**

These words expose the inherent difficulty in the way of Alexander's ambitious scheme materializing. It was impossible to build up an empire which could not command its supplies and the support of its own people.

The Indian popular opinion on the situation was cleverly conveyed to Alexander by an Indian ascetic. Taking a piece of dry hide, he placed it on the ground and asked Alexander to tread on it. As he placed his foot on one of its ends, the other ends flew up. It was difficult to keep the hide flat. Alexander was thus shown a visible image of what his strange enterprise meant, the uncertain and unstable consequences of campaigns carried on in countries too far from "the centre of his dominion" (McCrindle's Alexander Invasion, p.315).The fact was that the Indians do not seem to have taken Alexander's invasion very seriously. It was like a spectacular march through the country. The consolidation of conquests in distant countries depended on communications which could be ensured. The Indian attitude is truly expressed in the poet's words:

> "The East bowed low before the blast
> In patient, deep disdain;
> She let the legions thunder past,
> And plunged in thought again." — Mathew Arnold

**Murder of Philip**

To return to the fate of the Greek Satrapies, on the assassination of governor Nicanor by the Indian 'mutineers', Commandant Philip was deputed by Alexander to take his place. Philip was the most experienced Greek administrator in India. He started as Alexander's agent at Taxila to keep watch over the activities of the powerful Indian chief, Paurava.Alexander depended upon Philip to guard the rear of his advance down the *Hydaspes*. Alexander later deputed him to take charge of the territories of the free peoples, the Malavas, and the *Kshudrakas*, as they were conquered by Alexander, and these stretched as far south as the confluence of the Indus and the *Chenab*. He was now put in charge of the most important province of Greek India which was like the gateway to India. Philip very soon left his new headquarters to see Alexander off on his return journey down the Hydaspes. But little did he know that his own days were numbered: He was assassinated on his return.

**A Blow to Greek Rule**

According to Arrian (VI. 27, 2),Philip fell a victim to jealousy between the Greeks and Macedonians. But such a grave incident was due to deeper causes, to popular discontent with foreign rule. The murder of a Greek official of commanding position like Philip, in whom Greek rule was embodied and represented at its best, was really a fatal blow struck at that rule. He was the pillar of Greek Imperialism in India. His assassination took place in 325 B.C. when Alexander was in a position to retrace his steps to avenge it, as he had not gone even as far as Carmania. But he could not do so. The act was a challenge to Alexander's authority. But it was beyond his power to answer it. Alexander was retreating from India, with Greek rule retreating with him. The only remedy that he could think of was to seek the good offices of his Indian ally, the king of Taxila, to whom he sent despatches asking him kindly "to assume the administration of the province previously governed by Philippus until he could send a Satrap to govern it". (Arrian, VI. 27). Such a Satrap was never sent. Eventually Alexander had to trust his Indian ally with that charge. This meant that the Indian king was helped to extend his authority beyond the Indus and the frontiers up to the Kabul valley and the Hindukush. A Thracian named Eudamus was now left as the sole Greek agent in India, who under the Indian king, was placed in charge of the military garrison at *Pushkalavati* and also of the "command of the scattered bodies of Greek and Macedonian troops, with authority over the various colonists of Hellenic nationality" settled in that region. (Cambridge History, 1.P.429).

**Collapse of Greek Rule after Alexander's death in 323 B.C.**

On the top of this took place the death of Alexander[66] himself (without issue) in 323 B.C. in distant Babylon, followed by confusion in his own empire. The empire could not hold together. His generals immediately met and decided on its division among themselves. A second partition of the empire took place in 321 B.C. at *Triparadisus*, in which no part of India to the cast of the Indus was included as a part of that empire. The Greek governor of *Sind*, *Peithon*, was now removed, and placed in charge of the province between the Indus and the *Paropanisus*. Eudamus was the solitary Greek agent lingering on in India,but he had no official position in the empire and is ignored in its partitions. He probably set himself up as the leader of the Hellenic 'outlanders' left in the valleys of the Indus and the Hydaspes, but he, too, left India in 317 B.C. to help his chief, Eumenes, against Antigonos, with a small force of infantry and cavalry and of 120 elephants which he had secured by slaying treacherously an Indian chief (supposed to be Poros) who was his trusted colleague, Poor Eudamus met his doom at the hands of Antigonos (Diodorus, XIX. 44, I). Petition also left his province and joined the fray and met the same fate. He fell fighting by the side of Demetrius at the battle of Gaza (Ib.85,2). There was no more Greek to take place of either in India.

**Chandragupta as Leader of Revolution**

The Greek withdrawal from India was not an automatic process. It was forced by a revolution, a war of independence declared by Chandragupta as its leader. The assassination of the Greek governors are not to be looked upon as mere accidents or isolated events. They were the preliminary incidents of a planned scheme of attack against Greek rule. The two years, 325 B.C-323 B.C., that intervened between the death of Philip and that of Philips master were busy years for those who were planning India's freedom. What was then happening may be gathered from the following words of Justin (XV 4) our only source of evidence for this fateful episode in India's history: "Inida, after the death of Alexander, had shaken, as it were, the yoke of servitude from its neck and put his governors to death. The author of this liberation was Sandrocottus. This man was of humble origin called *Sudras* but was stimulated to aspire to regal power by supernatural encouragement; for, having offended Alexander (Alexandrum which some scholars place by the name *Nandrum* or *Nanda*) by his boldness of speech, and orders being given to kill him, he saved himself by swiftness of foot; and, while he was lying asleep, after his fatigue, a lion of great size, having come up to him, licked off with his tongue the sweat that was running from him, and after gently waking him, left him. Being first prompted by this prodigy to conceive hopes of royal dignity, he drew together a band of robbers and instigated the Indians to overthrow the existing (Greek) government. Sometimes after, as he was going to war with the generals of Alexander, a wild elephant of great bulk presented itself before him of its own accord and, as tamed down to gentleness, took him on his back and became his guide in the war and conspicuous in fields of battle. Sandrocottus, having thus acquired a throne, was in possession of India when Seleucus was laying the foundations of his future greatness." Stripped of its miraculous elements, the passage is a record of important histroy. It declares definitely that Chandragupta was the hero of this Indian war of independence. It also exhibits Chandragupta's plan of action which was first to dispose of what may be called the tall poppies of Greek India, its provincial governors who were Alexander's generals. We have already seen how this plan was given effect to by the assassination of the two most important Greek Satraps, Nicanor and Philip. It may be taken for granted that the removal of these two Greek governors practically meant the overthrow of Greek rule in India. Alexander when living was unable to take any effective steps against this defiance of his authority, and, after his death in 323 B.C., there was disruption in his empire, and India was left alone by the generals who partitioned the empire. Thus, it may be assumed that the death of Alexander meant the death of Greek rule in India. We have already seen how the provisions of the second partition of Alexander's empire in 321 B.C. practically point to the Greek recognition of the independence of India which was achieved by Chandragupta about 323 B.C. and certainly, before 321B.C.

It may be further noted that even if the reading Alexander is taken for the word *Nandrum* in the above passage of Justin, it will be quite in accord with the probabilities of the situation. The hero of Indian independence must have impressed Alexander with the promise of his future and roused his suspicion and enmity. This only added a private cause to the national cause of Chandragupta's hostility of Greek rule.

**War against Nanda**

*Stories of his strategy* With the first part of his mission in life thus achieved in liberating the Punjab from foreign rule, he now turned to its second part, the liberation of the other parts of the country from the tyranny of its rulers, the hated Nandas. Unfortunately, there is not much evidence available on this important event of Chandragupta's conquest of Magadha. There is, however, evidence to show that the event created a widespread sensation and roused popular interest. It passed into folk lore and tradition. It seems that, after recruiting their army locally in the Punjab in the manner described above, Chanakya and Chandragupta started by invading the countries on the frontiers (*antojanapadam pavisitva*) and plundering their villages (*gamaghatadikammam*) in their desire for sovereignty (*rajjam ichchhanto*). Chandragupta's movement was from the frontier to the interior of India, towards Magadha and Pataliputra, but he first made mistakes in strategy. The story is thus related: "In one of these villages a woman (by whose hearth Chandragupta's spy had taken refuge) baked a *chapathy* and gave it to her child. He, leaving the edges, ate only the centre, and, throwing the edges away, asked for another cake. Then she said, 'This boy's conduct is like Chandagupta's attack on the kingdom.' The boys said, 'why mother, what am I doing , and what has Chandagupta done? 'Thou, my dear'. said she, 'throwing away the outside of the cake, eatest the middle only. So Chandragutta, in his ambition to be a monrach, without beginning from the frontiers, and taking the towns in order as he passed, has invaded the heart of the country and his army is surrounded and destroyed. That was his folly" (*Mahavamsa* Tika, p.123; Appendix 1). Next, Chandragupta tried another method. He commenced operations from the frontiers (*pachchantato pethaya*) and conquered many *rashtras* and *janapadas*, States and peoples, on the way; but his mistake was not to post garrisons to hold the conquests. The result was that the people left in the rear of his advance were free to combine, to encircle his army, and defeat his designs. Then the proper strategy dawned as they were conquered (*uggahitanaya balam samvidhaya*) and, crossing the frontiers of Magadha with his victorious army, besieged Pataliputra and killed *Dhana-Nanda* (Appendix I).

A similar comment on strategy is also contained in the Jain work, *Parisishtaparvan*, which states: "like a child burning his finger which he greedily puts in the middle of the dish, instead of eating from the outer part which was cool, Chanakya had been defeated, because he had not secured the surrounding country before attacking the stronghold of the enemy. Profiting by this advice, Chanakya went to *Himavatkuta* and entered into alliance with Parvataka the king of that place called *Chamar*. They opened the campaign by reducing the provinces" (VIII. 291-301). The same text further relates that at the very opening of this campaign, Chanakya and Chandragupta suffered a reverse by failing to reduce a town, until Chanakya reduced it by a ruse, throwing its defenders off their guard. Then they devastated the country (*Nandadesam*), besieged Pataliputra, and forced Nanda to capitulate, with his reduced wealth (*kshina-kosa*), army (*bala*), capacity (*dhih*), and prowess (*vikrama*) (Ib. 301-313). Nanda, however, was spared his life and permitted by Chanakya to leave Pataliputra with his two wives and one daughter and as much luggage as he could carry off in a single chariot (Ib. 301-317).

These stories, however, bring out the fundamental fact of Indian history through the ages that all movements of conquest in India have been from the frontier to the interior, from the north to the South, from the highlands to the plains. It is only in the case of an invading naval power like the British that its movement has followed a different direction, from the sea upwards into the inland.

**Power of Nanda**

The stories also bring out the probable fact that the conquest of Nanda's empire was not an easy undertaking, but the result of several attempts. It was because that empire was possessed of immense power and resources. Curtius estimates its military strength at 200,000 infantry 20,000 cavalry, 2,000 four-horsed chariots, and 3,000 elephants. The empire was also very wide in extent. It extended as far as the Punjab. It is stated that when Alexander invaded his country which lay between the *Chenab* and the *Ràvi*, the second Poros esca ped for shelter into the adjoining territory of the Nanda King (McCrindle's Invasion, p. 273). We have already seen how the Nanda King by his conquests made himself the supreme sovereign (*ekarat*) of numerous states which he brought together under the umbrella of his sole authority (*eka-chchhatra*). These states are described to be those of the *Aikshvakus Panchalas, Kasis, Haihayas, Kalingas, Asmakas, Kurus, Maithilas, Surasenas*, and *Vitihotras*. All these Kshatriya dynasties were "uprooted," as the Puranas tell us. He is known to the Greeks as the ruler of peoples called the *Gangraidae* and the *Prasïi*, i.e., the peoples of the Ganges valley, and the Prachyas or 'easterners', peoples living to the east of the "Middle Country", such as the Panchalas, Surasenas, Kosalas, and the like. Towards the south also the Nanda King extended his soveriegnty by his conquest of Kalinga, as recorded in the *Hathigumpha* inscription of *Kharavela*. It mentions '*Nanda-Raja*' as being associated with an old aqueduct, and as having carried away to Magadha as trophies the statue (or foot-prints) of the first Jina and treasures of the royal house. Nanda rule is also stated to have extended up to the province of Kuntala in the north of Mysore in some Mysore Inscriptions (Rice, *Mysore and Coorg from Inscriptions*, P.3). But these inscriptions are as late as twelfth century and cannot be considered as reliable evidence, failing earlier evidence on the subject. We have also seen how, by his grinding taxation, he made himself master of untold wealth which he hoarded in subterranean chambers.

**Lack of Popularity**

Nanda had thus enough of power and pelf. But he lacked popularity. Chandragupta himself, as we have seen, reported to Alexander that he was "hated by his subjects" and Alexander had this report confirmed by the Indian Kings Poros (Paurava) and Phegelas (*Bhagala*). His unpopularity is due as much to the original sin of his ancestor as mentioned above as to his tyrannical rule and exactions. Thus, his power was tottering to its fall. It was not broad-based upon the people's will. Thus the moral factor helped Chandragupta in his fight against *Nanda* more than the military factor.

**Casualties**

The details of the actual battle between Chandragupta and Nanda are not known. The Jaih work *Parisishtaparvan* (VIII. 253-54) contains a verse stating that 'Chanakya recruited for Chandragupta an army by means of wealth hidden underground for the purpose of uprooting *Nanda*.' "It has been conjectured that he employed Greek mercenaries in his struggle with Nanda" (*Cambridge History* I.p.435). That it was a bloody battle between the two is indicated in exaggerated terms in a passage in the *Milindapatho*, (SBE, XXVI.p.147) stating that "Ioo *kotis* of soldiers, 10,000 elephants, 1 lac of horses and 5,000 charioteers" were killed in action and that Bhaddasala was the commander of Nanda's army. We have already seen the version of the event given in the *Mudrarakshasa* which begins with Chanakya's statements that he has already killed all the *Nine Nandas* and will not spare the surviving representative of the Nanda family, the old man, Sarvarthasiddhi, who unable to stand the siege of his city *Kusumapura*, be took himself to the forest. Though living there as a hermit, he wad done to death under orders of Chanakya who was out to uproot the last offshoot of the Nanda family.

**Defeat of Seleucos, 304 B.C.: Extension of Empire up to Persia**

Chandragupta did not merely supplant the Nanda king in the sovereignty of Magadha. He made himself at once the sovereign of an empire which was much larger than that of Nanda, for it included the land of the five rivers up to the Indus. This empire also extended farther by his later conquests. His subsequent career may be gathered from the following statement of Plutarch (Lives, Chap.LXII): 'Not long afterwards, Androcottos, who had at that time mounted the throne, presented Seleukos with 500 elephants and overran and subdued the whole of India with an army of 600,000." "The throne" here is the throne of Magadha which he had won by defeating the Nanda king. The present to Seleukos was the result of a war between the two. It would appear that in the struggle for power which ensued among the generals of Alexander after his death, Seleukos won for himself a secure position as the ruler of Babylon by about 311 B.C. and felt free to devote himself to the consolidation of his authority in the distant provinces. Bactria was not subdued without hard fighting. And by about 305 or 304 B.C. at the latest, he planned for a recovery of the Indian conquests of Alexander. Taking the route along the Kabul river, he crossed the Indus (Appian, Syr. 55). But the expedition proved abortive and ended in an alliance. It was because he had to confront a new India strong and united, under Chandragupta in command of a formidable army, and felt that discretion was the better part of valour. By the terms of the treaty, Seleukos ceded to Chandragupta the Satrapies of Arachosia [67] (Kandahar) and the Paropanisadae (Kabul), together with portions of Aria (Herat) and Gedrosia (Baluchistan). Thus Chandragupta was able to add another glorious feahter to his cap. He extended his empire beyond the frontiers of India up to the borders of Persia. That is why it was possible for his grandson Asoka to declare in two of his Rock Edicts (II and XIII) that the Syrian emperor, Antiochus (*Amtiyako Yona-raja*), was his "Immediate" neighbour, one of his "frontagers" (an *Anta* or a *Pratyanta* king). Chandragupta on his part cemented this alliance by making a present to Seleukos who was at that time very much worried by a call for help from his friends, the confederate kings *Cassander, Lysimachus*, and *Ptolemy*, against their common adversary, Antigonous. The elephants arrived in time at the battle-field of Iptus to turn the scale of victory against *Antignus*. The present of Indian elephants by Chandragupta to Seleukos was followed by a demand for them in western wars. Pyrthos transported these elephants from Epiros to Italy in 281 B.C. Hasdrubal in 251 B.C. used at Panormus Epiros to Italy in 281 B.C. *Hasdrubal* in 251 B.C. used at Panormus elephants driven by 'Indians'. So did *Hannibal* and *Hasdrubal* during the second Punic war with Rome and at the battle of Raphia, Ptolemy's Libyan elephants were no match for the Indian elephants of Antiochos[68].

The present of elephants was followed by other expressions of friendly relations between the two kings. There is a suggestion made by Appian (Syr. 55) that there was a marriage alliance between the two kings so that Seleukos became either the father-in-law or the son-in-law of Chandragupta. It is more likely that, as Strabo suggest (XV. 724), "there was a convention establishing a jus *connubii* between the two royal families. In that land of caste, a *jus connubii* between the two peoples is unthinkable." (*Cambridge History*, I.p.431). That Chandragupta's relations with Seleukos continut to be very friendly is indiciated by the story related by Athenaeus that he sent to Seleukos a present of some Indian drugs (Ib. p.432) while Seleukos further confirmed this friendship by rending Megasthenes as an ambassador to the Mauryan court. He had been serving as his ambassador at the court of Sibyrtius. Satrap of Arachosia. According to Arrian, Megasthenes resided for some time even at the court of Poros (V. 220), but the original is translated differently by Schwanbeck. At any rate, he must have come to live at Pataliputra, somewhere between 304 and 299 B.C., and date of Chandragupta's death. Thus he was able to see Mauryan India as a well-organised State under Chandragupta at the height of his power in the last days of his life.

Friendly relations were continued between India and the West after these two kings. Chandragupta's son, Bindusara, asked the son of Seleukos, Antiochos I, to get him sweet wine, figs, and a philosopher. Antiochos I sent as his ambassador to *Bindusara Daimachus* of Plataea. Pliny (*Natural History*, VI. 58) mentions Dionysius as the ambassador despatched to India by Ptolemy *Philadelphus* (King of Egypt, 285-247, B.B.). The Indian king to whom Dionysius was despatched must have been either Bindusara or his son Asoka who in his Rock Edict XIII refers to him as one of the five foreign kings to whom he despatched his own Welfare Missions.

We may note in this connection that Megasthenes states that since his time "many writers (Greek writers) no longer give the river Indus as the Western boundary of India but include within it four Satrapies," as named above (Frag. LVI quoted by Pliny).

**Conquest of the South**

Having now extended his empire beyond the borders of India, Chandragupta next thought of extending the empire beyond the barriers of the Vindhyas to the South. In the passage cited above from Plutarch, it is stated that "he overran and subdued the whole of India with an army of 600,000." The details of this all-India conquest are lacking, but there is reliable evidence for it in the inscriptions of Asoka. In the first place, Asoka's rule in the South is declared by his inscriptions at *Siddapura, Brahmagiri*, and *Jatinga-Ramesvara* hill in the Chitaldroog District of Mysore, the Govimath and Palkigundu inscriptions in the Kopbal Taluk, the Maski Inscription in the Deccan in the Nizam's Dominion, and the Gooty inscription in the Kurnool District. Secondly, Asoka himself indicates the southern limits of his empire by mentioning as his "frontagers" or immediate neighbours, peoples like the *Cholas* and *Pandyas*, *Satyaputras* and *Keralaputras* (Rock Edicts II, XIII). Thirdly, he himself informs us in his Rock Edict XIII that his own conquest was only that of Kalinga, and further that even this conquest was the cause of much pain and repentance to him, because it had to be achieved by so much violence and bloodshed, resulting in "150,000 captives (*apavudhe*), 100,000 killed (*hate*), and many times that number dead from the wounds received (*mute*)". He felt so deeply his personal responsibility for this colossal carnage and suffering that he at once foreswore such bloody conquests for the further, and declared for *Dharma-vijaya* (Moral conquest) as his imperial polity, abolishing the previous imperial policy of aggression and annexation. He stood now for a thorough-going creed of Non-violence or *Ahimsa*. Nor was it that of his father, Bindusara, failing definite evidence as against the statement of Plutarch attributing it to Chandragupta. No doubt, Bindusara was not a pacifist like Asoka. This is indicated by his very title, *Amitraghata* ('slayer of foes'), and this title may have been earned by him by some of his conquests. A vague hint of these is given by the author of *Arya-Manjusri Mula-Kalpa, Hemachandra*, and Taranatha,who state that that apostle of violence, Chanakya, had outlived Chandragupta, and continued as a minister of Bindusara, as "one of his great lords" Taranatha states: "Chanakya accomplained the destruction of the nobles and kings of sixteen towns and made Bindusara master of all the territory between the eastern and western sea." This is taken by some scholars to indicate Bindusara's conquest of the Deccan. It is, however, forgotten that a more authentic document, Rudradaman's inscription, describes Surashtra as a province of Chandragupa's empire which thus had extended from the western to the eastern sea. At the same time, we have somewhat discouraging evidence against Bindusara's capacity as a conqueror that his north-western province of Taxila had revolted during his reign so that he had to depute his worthy son, Asoka to quell the revolt. It may be presumed that the mere maintenance of the vast empire which was bequeathed to him by this father was too heavy a burden for a man of his easy-going disposition whose delight in life was " figs and raisin wine", for which he indented upon his friend, the Greek king, Antiochos. He can hardly be credited with any additions to the empire by his own conquests.

**Sravana Belgola Traditions**

We may also consider the implications of the unanimous Jain tradition that Chandragupta in his old age abdicated and followed the Jain saint *Bhadrabahu* as his teacher. Both teacher and pupil then travelled towards the South and settled down at a place known as Sravana Belgola. The tradition is recorded with minor variations in a number of documents, both literary and epigraphic. The literary documents are (t) *Brihaatkatha Kosa* by *Harishena*, dated in 931 A.D. (2) *Bhadrabahu-Charita* by *Ratnanandi* of about 1450 A.D. (the Kannada work, Munivamsabhyudaya of c. 1680 A.D. and (4) the Kannada work, *Rajavalikathe*. All these works agree as to the main facts. *Bhadrabahu* in consequence of a severe famine in Bihar led a migration of the Jains towards the South. Chandragupta, "the king of Pataliputra," (*Rajavalikahe*) abdicated the throne in favour of his son and followed *Bhadrabahu* as his disciple. He became his chief disciple, attended him at his death at *Sravana* (*Sramana*) *Belgola* where he lived on as an ascetic for some years till he died of starvation according to Jain practice.

This tradition has been recorded in local inscriptions and monuments. The oldest inscription of about 600 A.D. associated "the pair (*yugma*). Bhadrababhu along with Chandragupta *Muni*." Two inscriptions of about 900 A.D. on the Kaveri near Seringapatam describe the summit of a hill called Chandragiri as marked by the footprints of Bhadrabahu and Chandragupta *munipati*. A Sravana Belgola inscription of 1129 mentions Bhadrabahu 'Srutakevali,' and Chandragupta who acquired such merit that he was worshipped by the forest deities. Another inscription of 1163 similarly couples and describes them. A third inscription of the year 1432 speaks of Yaundra Bhadrabahu, and hir disciple, Chandragupta, the fame of whose penance spread into other words.

To add to this striking and uniform epigraphic evidence, we have significant monumental evidence. A smaller hill at Sravana Belgola is called *Chandragiri*, because Chandragupta lived and performed his penance there. On the same hill is a cave named after *Bhadrabahu*, as well as an ancient temple called *Chandragupta Basti*, because it was erected by Chandragupta. Moreover, the facade of this basti or temple which is in the form of a perforated screen, contains 90 sculptured scenes depicting events in the lives of Bhadrabahu and Chandragupta.

**Jain Tradition**

It is also to be noted that this Jain migration is the initial fact of the Digambara tradition. The Jain community was undivided for long. It was only with Bhadrabahu that the *Digambaras* separated from the *Svetambaras*.

Vincent Smith pertinently points out that it is Jain tradition alone which explains Chandragupta's unexpected exit from the throne at a time when he was comparatively young and at the height of his power. As he says," the only direct evidence throwing light on the manner in which the eventful reign of Chandragupta Maurya came to an end is that of tradition. His abdication is an adequate explanation of his disappearance at such an early age (when he must have been under fifty)."

There is also no evidence to disprove the fact taken for granted without the need of any argument or demonstration by all Jain writers that Chandragupta became a convert to their religion. The atmosphere of Jainism had already penetrated into Pataliputra, as we have already seen, in the time of the Nandas who had Jain leanings and Jain ministers (*Hindu Civilisation, p. 277*). In the *Mudrarakshasa,*also, we find an acknowledgment of this fact in the prominent position it gives to the Jains at the court of Pataliputra and the employment by Chanakya himself, an uncompromising champion of Brahminism, of a Jain as one of his chief emissaries Jain influence was already predominant at the royal court (Rice, Mysore and Coorg from Inscriptions, pp. 3-9; Ep. Carn., II. pp. 35-43 (Inscription at Sravana Belgola).

If, therefore, it is taken as a fact that Chandragupta spent the last days of his life at Sravana Belgola, it is not unreasonable to assume that he settled down at a place within the limits of his empire and a place s , close to Asoka's inscriptions[69].

**Tamil Tradition**

Further, the Maurya invasion of the South is also recorded in Tamil tradition. There are four reference to it in Tamil works, there in *Ahananuru* and the fourth in *Purananuru*. These speak of the Moriyas cutting their way through the rocks with their chariots, "their army of horses and elephants." to subdue the king of Mohur who had refused to submit. In this expedition, they were helped by their local allies, the *Kosar,* who "routed the enemies" forces on the field of battle" and the *Vadukar* fighting with "their swift-flying arrows" Some think that the *Moriyas* of these passages may refer to the latter day *Mauryas* of Konkan who emerge in history in the fifth century A.D., but there is in one passage a reference to "the untold wealth of the Nandas", showing by its context that it is the imperial Mauryas, the successors of the Nandas, who are thought of in these Tamil works. We have already cited the reference made by *Mamulanar*, a *Sangam* poet, to the hoarded wealth of the Nandas 'swept away and submerged later on by the floods of the Ganges." Thus Tamil tradition is quite familiar with the Nandas and the imperial Mauryas coming after them *(S.K Aiyangar, Beginnings of South Indian History, pp.69, 81, 103; V.R Ramachandra Dikshitar, Mauryan Polity, pp.58 ff)*

**Conquest of Western India**

Along with all this general evidence pointing to the extension of Chandragupta's empire to the South, we have a piece of definite evidence proving that Western India formed part of his empire. It was not so in the time of his predecesor, Nanda, who was known to the Greeks as the king of the Gangaridae and the Prasii, of the Ganges valley and eastern India. The Girnar Rock Inscription of Rudradaman of 150 A.D. describes how the lake (*tadaga*) Sudarsana was created on Mount Urjayat by the construction of a dam (*setu*) across the rivers flowing down the hill, such as *Suvarnasikata, Palasini*, and others. The dam rivalled the rock with its joints well cemented against leakage *(nihsandhibaddhadridha-sarvapatikatvat-parvata-pada pratispardhi-suslishtabandham)*. It was constructed by the provincial governor (*Rashtriya*) of King Chandragupta Maurya. He is named *Vaisya Pushyagupta*. The reservoir was lavishly provided with conduits (*pranalibhiralamkritam*) in the time of Asoka Maurya by the Yavana (Greek) Raja Tushaspha appointed to that province. The province is described as the province of *Anarta* and *Surashtra*. Thus Western India was so efficiently governed as a province of Chandragupta Maurya's empire that even its irrigation facilities were provided by the construction of costly and difficult works like a reservoir for the storage of water, fitted with sluices and channels for its distribution among the cultivated fields below.

It is also interesting to note in this connection that the Pali work *Petavatthu* and its commentary, *Paramatthadipani,* mention a ruler of Surattha (Surashtra) named Pingala who ascended the throne in the Sixeenth regnal year of Bindusara (283 B.C.). He had a *senapati* or a general named Nandaka who converted him to a new doctrine, a sort of atheism called (*Natthika-ditthi*). Fired with his zeal for his new faith, he was bold enough to leave for Pataliputra with a large retinue to convert to his creed the emperor Dharmasoka (*Pingalo rajaDhammasokassa ranno ovadam datum gato*) but remained himself to be converted to the emperor's creed of Buddhism (B.C. Law, *Buddhist conception of spirits*, p.72 f; C.D. Chatterji in *D.R Bhandarkar Volume, pp.329-340*)

We have in these texts remarkable evidence of the continuity of administrative history for the Province of Surashta during the reigns of three Maurya emperors, Chandragupta, Bindusara, and Asoka.

Some light is thrown on the severity of Chandragupta's penal code as shaped by his minister, Chanakya, by the case of a learned Brahman scholar named *Subandu* being condemned to servitude for life with his young son in his teens wandering away homeless to escape a similar fate.The sin of *Subandhu* was his assure political wisdom (Ibid).

We may consider the constitutional significance of these references to Surashtra. We have three descriptions of its constitutional status which it is difficult to reconcile with each other.These are (1) Surashtra as a province of the Maurya empire under an imperial official as its Governor; (2) Surashtra under a chief as a feudatory of the Maurya emperor; and (3) Surashtra as a *Samgha* or a republic. The third description is attributed to Kautilya, but quite accurately. Kautilya does not describe Surahtra as a full-fledged republic, but only refers to certain sections of its population as belonging to self-governing corporations or Srenis. These *srenis* were formed by the Kshatriyas and Vaisyas of Surashtra and were either economic or military, guilds, devoting themselves either to Varse (agriculture, cattle-rearing, and trade) or to the profession of arms as means of livelihood (*Surashtra-Kshatriyasreryadayo varte-sastra pajivinah*) (VII. I). Thus Surashtra under this description may still be a kingdom. The two other points to settle about its constitutional position are (I) whether it was a local chiefship and a feudatory state under the Maurya emperor or (2) whether it was completely annexed by Chandragupta Maurya to his empire and created a governorship under him. The second point is established beyond doubt by Rudradaman's Inscription which has greater evidential value than tradition and literary text. The first point can be reconciled with the second only on the suppositior that, as in modern. India, an imperial province may accommodate its hereditary ruling princes figuring as feudatories acknowledging the paramount sovereignty of the emperor. It is thus that Pingala as a local chief of Surashtra was out to pay homage to Asoka.

That the Maurya conquest of Western India extended beyond the province of Surashtra farther south is indicated by the location of Asoka's inscriptions at Sopara in the district now called Thana in the Bombay Presidency. The conquest of this part of India (which may be identified with Konkan) was not claimed by Asoka. It must have been the work of Chandragupta Maurya who, as we have seen, had already established his authority over the neighbouring region of Surashtra. The province of which Sopara or *Surparaka* was the capital must have formed part of Maurya empire for some time to lead Asoka to locate his edicts at its capital.

**Chronology**

We may now consider the chronology of Chandragupta's reign. We have already seen that the first exploit of Chandragupta was the overthrow of the Greek rule which was established in India as a result of Alexander's victorious campaigns. But it was short-lived. Two events marked is rapid fall. The first was the murder of the most powerful Greek governor in the person of Philip in *325 B.C.* followed by his place being taken by an Indian. The second event was the death of Alexander himself in 323 B.C. The first signal of the Indian battle for freedom was the murder of the Greek Satrap, Nicanor, by the *Asvayanas* in 326 B.C. As has been already related, the battle was won shortly after Alexander's death in 323 B.C. In 321 B.C., at the second partition of Alexander's empire its easternmost Satrapy was the Trans-Indus Satrapy of Paropanisus. India proper was not counted as a part of that empire. An attempt to reconquer it only ended in the expansion of Chandragupta's empire to the trans-Indus provinces up to the borders of Persia. We may, therefore, take it for granted that between 323 and 321 B.C., Chandragupta made himself the ruler of the Punjab and Emperor of Magadha. We may take 322 B.C. as the date of his accession to sovereignty and of inaguration of the Maurya Dynasty.

We have other data to confirm this date. If we belive in the reckonings of reigns given in the *Puranas,* we shall see that Chandragupta's reign was one of 24 years and hence ended in 298 B.C., and that his son. Bindusara, reigned for 25 years, i.e., up to 273 B.C. The date of Asoka's accession to sovereignty is thus to be taken as 273 B.C., a date which is supported by the unimpeachable data of Asoka's inscriptions. The *Mahavamsa* distinguishes between Asoka's accession to throne and his coronation, and places an interval of 4 years between them (V. 22). This makes 269 B.C. as the date of his coronation. His inscription again date from his coronation. His Rock Edict XIII is dated 13 years after his coronation. So its date should be 256 B.C. if the date 269 B.C. of his coronation is correct. It is correct, because it is proved by the well-known chronological data of Rock Edict XIII itself. Rock Edict XIII is a document of unique chronological importance in Indian History. Asoka in this Edict mentions the five most important Greek kings with all of whom he had friendly dealings through his Welfare Missions. The date of his references to them must, therefore, be at the latest the date up to which they were all alive and were known to be so to Asoka, and may be taken one year earlier, when all were hale and hearty.

The duration of the reigns of three of these kings is known with certainty, viz., those of

(I) *Amtiyoka,* i.e, Antiochus II Theos, king of Babylon and Persia, 261-246 B.C.

(2) Turamaya, i.e, Ptolemaeus II Philadelphos, king of Egypt, 285-247 B.C.

(3) Amtikini, i.e, Antigonus Gonatas, king of Macedonia, 277-240 B.C.

(4) Maka, i.e., Magas, king of Cyrene, whose date may be taken to be that proposed by both Beloch and Geyer, viz., 300-250 B.C.

(5) *Alikasudara,* whose identity and duration of reign are the subject of controversy. He may be either Alexander of Epirus or Alexander of Corinth. Of the two Alexanders, Alexander of Epirus was by far the more important personality worthy of Asoka's attention, the son of the famous Pyrrhus of Epirus, and the rival of Antigonus Gonatas of Macedonia. Alexander of Corinth was almost like a local king who ended as a "tyrant over a town and an island, without military glory or a famous lineage." There were several kings of Asia Minor of equal and higher status whom Asoka should have mentioned such as Eumenes of Pergamon (262-240 B.C.) or, nearer home, Diodotus of Bactria. It is known that Alexander of Epirus, the true subject of Asoka's reference, had lived up to 255 B.C.

Considering the dates of the reigns of all these five kings, we find 255 B.C. as the date up to which all were alive. From this follows that the date of Asoka's reference to them in Rock Edict XIII must be before 255 B.C. Professor P.H.L Eggermont of the Hague, Holland (who honoured me by posting to me his learned paper on 'The Date of Asoka's Rock Edict XIII' on 30th April,1940, a few days before Holland itself was submerged by German invasion) has very well shown by skilful calculations that the news of the death of one of these Greek kings could not take more than 4 or 5 months to reach Asoka at Pataliputra, and so we need not allow for an interval of one year for it, as I did the work in Asoka's study. He has also after a good deal of discussion established the dates of the two kings, Alexander of Epirus and Magas of Cyrene. The former lived up to 255 B.C and the latter up to 250 B.C. according to his findings which are followed here. If therefore, Rock Edict XIII is dated at 256 B.C. since it was in the 13th year of Asoka's coronation, the date of his coronation was 269 B.C., the very date which is led up to by the assumed date of 322 B.C. for Chandragupta's accession to sovereignty and the duration of his reign and that of his successor, as reckoned in the *Puranas*. We have thus here a remarkable convergence of chronological conclusions derived from sources as different and foreign and Indian works, Brahminical texts and Buddhist inscriptions, and this convergence proves their truth.

**Indian Ideals of Polity**

The governance of such a vast empire which stretched from Persia to Mysore was a formidable undertaking. It was specially so in olden times, in pre-mechanical ages lacking the means of speedy communication and quick transport between the different and distant parts of a large empire. News would take months to travel from Paropanisus to Pataliputra. This initial difficulty of administration led John Stuart Mill to doubt the existence of large empires in ancient times, "because the machinery of authority was not perfect enough to carry orders into effect at a great distance from the person of the ruler, nor did there exist the means of making the people pay an amount of taxes sufficient for keeping up the force necessary to compel obedience throughout a large territory."

These natural difficulties, however, gave way before human ingenuity. A suitable system of administration could cope with them. The difficulties are formidable for a system of centralized authority. It is not so where government is not carried on from one centre but from many centres. Decentralization of authority solved the problem of government for large empires in ancient times. It divided up the empire into a number of provincial governments and local administrations in which sovereignty could make its presence and power felt. The area of each such government was conveniently sized.

**Rural Republics**

Ancient India was built upon the basis of decentralization on principle. It did not believe in centralization of authority, resulting in a system of over-government of the people. It believed in the self-government in the group, in the extension of self-government from the sovereign at the top through all grades and strata of society down to the lowest classes in the villages. Every village was self-governing. There were also unions of villages as self-governing federations. Ancient India was thus built up as a vast rural democracy. Society was functioning apart from the State proper as a separate entity in defined spheres of self-government. Rural politics was independent of state-politics[70].

In short, we may noted that we have to depend up to the Buddhist traditions for the facts of Chandragupta's early life and his first contact with *Sudra* ruler known as Chanakya. The death of his father felt his mother destitute and made her seek shelter at Patliputra with her brothers that were in the form of *'Nam'* or *'Chamar'*. There, she gave a birth to her child who was deposited for safety with a cowherd, who later sold him to a hunter by whom, he was employed to tend cattle. At the village level a common body, he was always play the king's role (*Rajakrida*) with his champaions under him, and was getting up a mock court where he would be administering justice. He discovered at one of the royal game by Chanakya, who saw in him the promise of royalty since birth and straightway brought him as an hunter. He then took him away to his native city of Taxila where he had to educate him in all the humanities (*Sastra-Bhava*) and art and crafts (*Silpas*) including military science which was throughly learned by him in taxila. Thus, Chandragupta Maurya spent his youthful time at Taxila; and this explains that how, as a youth, he had been with Alexander in the course of his campaigns in Panjab, as stated by Plutarch. After this, he captured almost entire Indian territory belonged to the ancient period of Indian history as a master of it.

## NOTES AND REFERENCES

1. Term *Chamar* is put together of four English words that is Ch+a+ma+r, 'ch' means 'happiness', ' a' stands for 'single' one, 'ma' stands for living *man*, and 'r' means 'way' or ' thought'. Thus, there is only one way for the happiness of the life that is *'Nam'* or *'Sabad' or 'Sudra'* or *'Chamar'*. Study in detail the *Varanasharam* theory. **Note.** In the frontier towns where Buddhism had made little or no impression, shoes manufactured in that *gana* were allowed to be worn by the *Bhikkhus*. Shoes were also made from the skins of tiger, lion, leopard, deer, cat, squirrel and owl. Such was the fashion of shoes in those days that similes from the profession of cobbler (*chammakara*) have crept in literature which Brahmans forgotten to study it the wooden sandals (*paduka*) and the sandals made from palm leaves and bamboo used by laymen were forbidden to the *Bhikhhus,* because it was the concept of the Brahmans not of the God or *Nam*. ( Moti Chandra, *Costume Textiles, Cosmetics & Coiffure in Ancient and Medieval India*; Delhi 1943, P.15)
2. P.C.P 297 Also quoted by H.A Rose; G.T.C.P.N.W.F., p. 147. Vol. II
3. C.R.1., p. 320
4. Maharaj Charan Singh; *'Light on Saint John'* Panjab (India); Reprint 1994 and 1996. P.10. Hereafter cited as L.O.S J.
5. C.R.1. p. 321.
6. Term *Mudrarakshasa* means that God's meat is '*word*' or *'Nam'*. 'He' has the lust of 'love'.
7. Word 'Chandragupta' means, he is malignant, 'worker in hides,' or *'cutter in hides'*.
8. H.D. Vol. 1, p. 179 Vol.1.
9. *Ibid.*, pp. 179-180.
10. Evidence of *Mudrarakshasa*, the terms *Vrishala* and *Kula-hina,* applied in the drama to Chandragupta at several places in the drama and is taken

in its ordinary sense to mean 'the son of a *Sudra*'. It is, however, to be noted that the term may bear another meaning as one of compliment instead of opprobrium. A passage in the drama itself (III, 18) uses, the term *Vrishala* as a term of honour to mean 'one who is a *Vrisha* among kings, the best of kings'. In several other places, the term is used as one of endearment by Chanakya for his favourite pupil and almost as his personal nickname. It is left only to the enemies of Chandragupta to use it as a term of abuse against him (VI. 6), and that also by way of a pun on what is taken to be his nickname. Thus the derogatory meaning of the term *Vrishala* is not at all establish in the drama. A similar meaning, is sought to be found in the other term *'Kula-hina'* as applied to Chandragupta (II. 17) and pointing undoubtedly to his *'inferior lineage'*. But the context in which the term is used only shows that it should mean *lowly,* and not *low* or degraded lineage, does not cast any glur on it. It practically indicates What Justin has stated, Viz, 'that he was worn in humble life'. It really means that Chandragupta was born of a *hina* or 'humble' '*Kula*' or 'family' as contrasted with the *Nandas* described as '*prathita-kulajah*', 'of illustrious lineage', or of high birth' (*uchchairavijanam* (VI. 6)). The point emphasised against Chandragupta by his enemies in the drama is that he is a mere upstart, of a family unknown to name and fame (*aprathita-kula*), having no trace of any aristocratic or royal blood in him, and , as such, utterly unworthy of the throne which was adorned by the Nandas of noble lineage (C.H.T. pp. 10-11)

11. H.D. Vol.1, pp. 180.
12. *Ibid.,* pp. 176-177.
13. R.T. Book IV. Vol. 1, p. 125 also quoted on C.R.I., p. 320.
14. Term *begar* means 'homeless' or 'aboriginal'. This 'Nam' has no permanent home. He is in migratory form one place to another.
15. P.C., p. 297.
16. C.R.I., p. 320.
17. P.C., p. 297. Also cited by H.R Rose; G.T.C; P.N.W.F.P., p. 147 Vol. II.
18. Raj Kumar, *Paintings and Life styles of the Jammu Region* (From 17th to 19th century A.D) Vol. 1. Delhi, 2006, p. 128. Hereafter referred as *P.L.J.R.*
19. P.C., p. 297.
20. C.R.1. p. 319.
21. *Ibid.*
22. *Ibid.*
23. *Ibid.*
24. R.T. Vol. II. p. 430.
25. C.R.I., p. 318.
26. R.T. Vol. II. p. 430 **Note**. Statement displays that the *Dombas* or *Dums* or *Mahasahas* also earned their bread as hunters, fishermen, buffoons,

quacks, etc and their daughters as singers and dancers. Their occupations thus closely resembled those of the gipsies whose name is drived from Sanskrit word *Domba* or Catching tail of the Brahmans. Alberuni mentions *Hadi, Doma,* Accession of their classes of outcast people, the *Badhatau* are not known to me. The *Candala* are well known, called *Sanalia* by Ibn Khurdadbih (Elliot, *History of India"* (*i*) 16). The *Hadis* and *Dom* are mentioned by Colebrooke, Essays" (*ii*) Enumeration of Indian classes, p. 169 note 3. On the later (if Rom. the name of the gispsies), V. "Memories on the History, Folklore, and distribution of the Race," Acc. by Elliot, edited by Beames, London, 1869, P.84 are the *Badhatan* identical with *Bediyas*, mentioned in the note of Colebrooke just quoted? that is *'Nam'* (Dr. Edward C. Suchan; Alberuni's India; Vol.1 and 11. New Delhi; P. 293).

27. R.T. Vol. II, p. 430.
28. *Ibid.*
29. *Ibid.*, p. 26. According to John Wilson some of them are of Kashmiri origin the Osdi are sub divided into the *Chandyal*, *Kaphurialal* and *Chitu*. (*Indian Caste*; New Delhi, 1976 Vol. Two, p. 83).
30. C.R.I., p. 317.
31. G.T.C. p. 148 Vol. II P.N.W.F.P The *Chamar* will eat food prepared by any tribe except the *Khakrob* (*Chuhra*), *Kanjar, Sansi* and *Nat* smoking is only allowed among themselves and they will not eat or drink from a *Dhobi*, a *Dum* or a *Nilgar* (indigo dyer) (Karnal).
32. P.C., p. 297.
33. G.T.C. P.N.W.F.P., p. 148 Vol. II.
34. M.A Sherring; *Hindu Tribes and Castes*, Delhi, Reprint 1881, see P.E., p. 297.
35. G.T.C., P.N.W.F.P., p. 148 Vol.II **Note.** *Banu* or Banuwe here would appear to be the eponym of the *Bania* caste, which is said to still worship of *'ar'* and a *'rambi'*, at wedding the inference of the term which is composed of two words that is Ba+na, 'Ba' means 'happiness', 'nu' in some old texts of the life the name is given as *Pan-nu-nutso* in which the second *'nu'* may be due to a copist's carelessness, this character being one of the two characters given to indicate the sound of *'nu'* (Y.C. P.284). **Note.** The dish *'Kedgeree'*, formerly a favourite dish in Anglo-Indian families, but now going somewhat out of fashion. The word is derived from the Hindoo *Khichri*, a mess of rice cooked with ghee and *dal* (*Cajanus Indicus*, Spreng) and flavoured with a liffle spice, stewed onions, and the like. Ovingto *op cif.* p.310, has the following pleasant description of this dish:- '*Kitcherie* is another Dish very common among them, made of *Doal*, that is, a small round pea and rice boiled together, and is very strengthening, 'tho' not very savoury. Of this the *European* sailers feed in these parts once or twice a week, and are forced at those times to a pagan Abstinence from Flesh, which creats in them a perfect Dislike and utter Detestion to those '*Bannian* Days', as they commonly call them. *Bannian* is a rendering of the word *Banyan*, a Hindoo trader, *Bunya* being the familiar name among Anglo-Indians in Upper India for a grain-dealer. *Kichery* was a general food of the common people

(Francois Bernier; *Travels in The Mogul Empire;* New Delhi; 1989. p. 152. Hereafter cited as T.M.E.)

36. *G.T.C.P.N.W.F.P.,* p. 148. *Vol.II* **Note.** A **Dum** witnessed the occurance, and so to this day no *Chamar* will eat or drink from a *Dum* or Mirasi's hands. Marching from that hill-skrit, our faces set west, we dismounted on waterless plain (*gul*) between Bannu and the plain. It is a wonderful provision of God that where, except for the great rivers, there are no running waters, water should be so placed within reach in dry water course (*Babur Nama.* Tr. by A.S Beveridge Two vols, Bound in one, Delhi Reprint, 1997 p. 234. The Bin of Erskine mentions perhaps it is Bain in the *Bannu* country which marked in the burns map. It lies south of Edwardesabad See too Jarrett II. P. 393 Raverty (Notes, etc, p. 354) mentions Ban as 19 miles north east of Sialkot and 8 miles South West of Jammu. It is on the east bank of Canal there is a "Bone" in the Salt Range (Wanderings of a Naturalist, Adams, p. 134) (A.N. Vol. I p. 600). And, the Jews of Medina comprised mainly three tribes, Banu Qaynuqa, Banu Nadir and Banu Qurayzah of them the most powerful was Banu Qurayzah, who had pledged their support to the Prophet but had never accepted his leadership; they secretly plotted against him.They were in constant touch with Quraish and helped them whenever and wherever they could. Hence the relations between Jews and Muslims were always strained, and as time passed, they worsened. The immediate cause of the trouble that arose between them at this time was the molesting of a Muslim woman by a Jewish shopkeeper; the subsequent siege of the fortress of Banu Qaynuqa and the latter's expulsion by the Muslims out of Medina showed the depth to which their leadership had sunk. There was also the wholesale exile of the tribe Banu Nadir (Rafiq Zakaria, *Muhammad and the Quran*; New Delhi; 1991, p. 34).
37. *Ibid.*
38. P.C. P.297. **Note.** Why is *Chamar* always addressed with "*Oh Chamar* ke instead of *Oh Chamar*" as any other Caste would be? Because the English people had to known that this term is very related to *"God"* or *Holy Ghost.* But the Indian priestly class that is *Brahman* misinterpreted it. Also cited by H.R Rose. G.T.C.P.N.W.F.P., p. 147 Vol. II.
39. C.R.I., p. 320.
40. *Ibid.*
41. C.M.H.T., p. 1.
42. It is the warning of the clouds above the moor presaged rain, originated fromt he Latin word *praesagire* or *'forebode'.*
43. Keith, *Rig.Veda*; Br., P.330 **Note.** Name **Keith** refutes from **Katha** by Greek (Dr. Nalinee M. Chapekar; *Ancient India And Greece;* New Delhi; 1977, p. 64).
44. K.A. Nilakanth Sastri; *Age of the Nandas And Mauryas;* Varanasi; 1967, p. 9. Hereafter explained as A.N.M.
45. *Ibid.,* p. 26.
46. R.C. Majumdar; A.1., p. 97.
47. *Ibid.*

48. *C.M.H.T.* p. 65 **Note.** The origin of the nine Nanda Kings took place from the body that is eyes, nose, ears, mouth and two lower organs of the human body.
49. *H.D.* Vol. 1, p. 174.
50. A.N.M., pp. 9-10.
51. *Ibid.*, p. 10.
52. C.M.H.T., p. 10.
53. It has been filled with (something undesirable) felt anxiety and stress, originated from Dutch word 'uracht' 'ships cargo'.
54. It is to be noted that I took the *'Nam-dan'* alongwith my family from Maharaj Gurinder Singh on 31st, Dec, 2000 at that times I was doing my Ph. D. Alongwith the research work I did practise the *mantra* of *'Nam-dan'* and always stressed on to find out the origin of the things related to the subject-matter of Ph.D thesis. After obtaining the Ph.D award, I always touched with my supervisor Professor Jigar Mohmmenda, HoD History, University of Jammu to acclerate my acadmic activities. Under his noble guidance, I presented a paper in the Seminar organised by the History Department, University of Jammu on the topic entitled *'Dogra Dresses in the Paintings of the Jammu Region",* (From 17th to 19th century A.D.). But the people from the upper caste, they were unhappy on my performance, but I did not loose my heart. I continued my process and I presented a paper in the *'Indian History Congress'* proceeding 29-31 Dec. 2004 on the topic entitled *'Story of the Jammu Paintings'* (From 17th to 19th Century A.D). But the paper was not published. In the meantime, I purchased certain books of Baba Sahib B.R. Ambadkar for study. I could not understand the theme of the books, but an angle has written. On march 5-6, Baba Ji, Maharaj Gurinder Singh delivered the *Satsang* at Keran.On the topic entitled Sheikh Taki and Tulsi Das stressed on the caste system, I got the core news of the *Satsang* when, he says "*Jat-Pat* is the only twist of the words". In the meantime, I prepared a paper for the presentation of the 'Panjab History Conference' Patiala on the topic entitled. *'History of the Dogra Music in the Paintaings of the Jammu Region'*. (From 17th to19th Century A.D.). An old man of the age of 75, he appricated my attempt and said study in microlevel. But I got the point in the proceeding of the Ancient section what the historian has to confirm from the study that is *'authentic History'*. On the very morning of the 18th, March, I englightned with the 'light' or 'Truth', before this I felt great headach. The process of the study, I remained continued, I went to the study in the Ranbir library adjacent to our college, I got two books entitled *'Vedic India'* and *'The Rig Veda and Vedic Religion'*, with the spirit of '*Pure thought.* I wrote a book on the topic entitled *'History of the Brahmans.'* I received the *'God'* from the research as *'Nam'*. During these days I went to share my view in the *'Dalit Educated'* on the request of Mr. Sat Paul Bavouria. Certain people of the association, they treated me as a degraded man, because I believe in the similcity as a common man, I felt that they are not *Chamar*, they are modern Brahmans. Only they crowned the photo of Dr. B.R. Ambedkar. They were not ready to

listen my view. In the meantime, I suspended my evaluation work and went for typing and to published the book in Jalandhar. Only I typed and could not publish and certain photostate copies of the research I provided for study to my colleagues, but there was a poor response on the document. Int he month of Augest, I went to participate in the History Refresher course in Delhi Jamia Islamia Mallia University. Here in Delhi, I met with Mr Ram Raj/udat Raj, president of All Indian SC/ST Association. I discussed the issue, on certain points like modern politic, he shouted me who will study your book, if you are not interested in politic *'idiot Dalit',* I really wept there. But, I published it and made an article for the presentation in the Refresher course. But most of the historian appricated it.

In the month of January, 2006, I went for the presentation to Santinikethan for presentation of the paper entitled *'The History of the Brahmans'* and majority of the people they appricated it. Again the time has come for the *'Panjab History conference'* on the schedule date, I went for the presentation of the paper on the topic entitled *'Early History of the Five Rivers'*. But most of the participant they listened my paper carefully but there was a gentleman called as a General president named likely to be 'Shrimali'. He rosed objection which he could not understand the theme of my paper. He says "Donot make the history discipline ridiculous". Anyhow, I did not reply. In the meanwhile, I purchased certain books on the request of my *Guru* which I could not understand at that time after I felt it.

In the last week of the March, I went alongwith my family to Bias. My Master delivered the *Satsang* on the same topic which I have made in the articles as well as in the books. Even though my principal was not happy on my academic activities being a *Chamar*.She insulted me when I entered for the permission to attend a seminar organised by the Delhi national museum on the topic of Basohli painting's development. Anyhow I presented the paper on the topic entitled, *'Concept of the Dogra Dance in Art Form in Dogra Region.'* people appricated my effort.

55. C.M.H.T., pp.18-19.
56. A.N.M., p. 13.
57. *Ibid.*, p. 19.
58. *Ibid.*, p. 20.
59. *Ibid.*
60. *Ibid.*, **Note.** The pali text society prints the word as "C'orapubba" (=corapubba) but admitted the above reading corapubba (Chorapubba) as correct at the suggestion of (Mr. C.D Chatterji 11th, Dec. 1929).
61. Kautilya means "Crookedness", 'falsehood' is it likely the Chandragupta" ministers should have called him 'Mr' 'crooked' or Crookedness personified that is *'Nam'* . Surely scepticism cannot go further (D.R. Bhandarkar; *Some Aspects of Ancient Hindu Polity;* (Patna) Bihar, 1988. p.35). He is clearly mentioned in his statement that no Arya (including *Sudras*) be reduced to slavery under any circumstances whatsoever. But non-Aryans *Mlecchhas* (uncivilized people) or tribal

not assimilated in the Aryan society could be sold or mortgaged by himself of his relations. Kautilya however while prohibited sole or mortgage of minor Arya on pain of punishment of fines increased according to the *Varna* of the minor person-*Sudra* (B.P. Sinha; *Readings in Kautilya's Arthasastra;* Delhi; 1976, p. 157).

62. Rhys Davids; *Buddhist India;* Delhi 1903, p. 267. Hereafter cited as B.I.
63. **Note.** *Bandhayana* discusses the authoritativeness of usages peculiar to the north or the south and quotes Gautama as saying that it is wrong to hold that certain customs must be held authoritative in certain countries (even though opposed to vedic tradition and smrti). this refers to G.Dh.S.11.20. In another place Baudhayana gives it as his view that a *Brahmana*, if he cannot make a living by teaching, officiating as a priest or by gifts, should earn his livelihood as a Ksatriya and quotes the views of Gautama as opposed to this. The extant Gautama on the other hand teaches the same view as that of *Baudhayana*. Buhler made the plausible suggestion that the *Sutra* in the extant Gautama is an interpolation. Govindswami the commentator of Baudhayana, suggests that another Gautama is referred to by Baudhayana. It is possible to suggest that in the Ms. of Gautama used by Baudhayana that *Sutra* about living as a *Ksatriya* did not occured. Chapter 19 of the *Gautamadharmasutra* which forms an introduction to *prayascittas* in Gautama seems to have been borrowed wholesale by Baudhayana (III.10) with slight changes that Baudhayana occurs in the middle of the discussion about *prayascittas* and not as an introduction, which is the case in Gautama Baudhayana treats of penances in several places (II.1, III 5.10 and VI. 1.4) (H.D. Vol.1, pp. 33-34).
64. The *Arthasastra* was composed by Kautilya generally for the guidance of Kings and particularly for Chandragupta Maurya who had considerably expanded his Empire-Magadha (317-293 B.C.) (M.B. Chande; *Kautilya's Arthasastra;* Delhi; 1998, p. 432)
65. As in the case of the Buddhists and Jainas, such sects did not discriminate between Arya and *Mlecchha* (unicivilized) peoples, and for the latter this became an avenue of entry into Aryan society, since ultimate many of these sects became independent castes within the *Varna* system. (Romila Thapper *Ancient Indian Social History,* New Delhi; Reprint 1990, p. 177). All places to the north of this area called *Mi-li-ku* (i.e. frontier land) (Mlechcha lands) *the life of Hiuen-Tsiang* by S.Beal and Shaman Hwuili; Delhi; Reprint 1973, p. 57).
66. *The name Alexander passed immediately into Indian literature in various forms. Asoka in his inscription uses the forms Alikasudara (Shahbazgarhi Rock Edict XIII) and Alikyasudala (Kalsi text) Alexandria is transformed into Alasanda in Milindapanho. Sylvan Levi reads a definite, though solitary, reference in Sanskrit Literature to Alexander the Great himself in a passage in Bana's Harshacharita stating that "Alasa Chandakosa having conquered the earth did not penetrate into Strirajya or the kingdom of women." Alexander is here meant because Greek tradition mentions his conquest of a Kingdom of Amazons which he abstained from entering as special favour (Memorial*

*Sylvain Levi, p.414 (in French)). According to Webor (Berlin S.B., 1890, P. 903) Indian literature remembered Alexander at all, it was only in the form of a bogey called Skanda, used to frighten naughty children" (Tarn, The Greeks in Bactria and India; p. 168).*

67. *It is interesting to note the original old Iranian forms of these names as used in the Behistun and other inscriptions of the Achaemenian emperor Darius I (521-485 B.C.) as these names correspond closely to Sanskrit names. Thus Achaemenea (father of Teispes) = Hakhamani, Darius-Darayavau (Sanskrit Dharayadvasu, holding, possessing goods); Cyrus= Kuru; Xerxes= Kshayarsha; Arachosia= Harauraf=Sanskrit Sarasvati; Vedic name of a river in S.W Afghanisatn, tributary of the river called Haetumant in Avesta= classical Hermandus=modern Helmand. Arachosia was the land of black grapes called harahura, whence the wine called Harahuraka mentioned by Kautilya (as will be seen below), just as the green grapes of Kapisa, Northern Afghanisan, yielded the wine called Kapisayana.*

*Paropanisadae is the Greek equivalent of Babylonisn Parruparassana= old Persian Gandara=Sanskrit Gandhara with its capital at Pushkalavati. Aria in old Persian=Haraiva from Haraya or Saraya, the name of the river on which Herat stands. Haraiva is to be equated with Sanskrit Sarava derived from Sarayu mentioned by Panini (VI 4. 174). India = old Persian Hidaus from Sindhu. Hidauv is locative of Hidu (V.S. Agrawal's Place+names in the Inscriptions of Darius in UPHSJ, 1940).*

68. *Warmington. Commerce Between the Roman Empire and India. p. 155*

69. *It may be noted that Fleet (IA.XXI. p. 156) did not believe in this tradition and considered I:hadrabahu of I:scription NO.1 as Bhadrabahu II mentioned in Sarasrar Gachha as becoming Pontiff in 53 B.C. with his disciple Guptigupta succeeding him as Pontiff in 31 B.C. In his opinion, this Guptigupta has been confused with Chandragupta. Dr. Hoernle, however (Ib., pp. 59-ro). after a critical study of all the Jain paffavalis, believes in the tradition and records his conclusion thus: "Before Bhadrabahu, the Jain community ws undivided. With him the Digambasa separated from the Svitambaras. The question is who this Bhadrabhu was the Svetaab ra pottachs know only one Bhadrabahu who, from the dates assigned to him by the Svetambaras and Digambaras alike, must be identical with Bhadrabahu I of the Digambaras. Considering the varying and contradictory character of the Digambara tradition, the probability is that the inception of the great separation took place under Bhadrabhu I who died 162 A.V. According to the Digambaras, or 179 A.V. according to the baras (both dates being within the reign of Chandragupta). The Digambara separation originally took place as a result of the migrantion southwards under Bhadrabahu in consequence of a severe famine in Bihar, the original home of the undivided Jain community."*

70. *C.M.H.T.*, pp. 42-47.

# 2

# Rise of the Karkotas Power

The rise of the Karkotas to power in the valley of *Kashmir* and subsequent history of that part of the country is significant for many reasons. While the rest of the huge sub-continent witnessed the rise and fall of several Rajput clans like[1] the *Gurjar-Pratiharas*[2], *Chandellas*[3], *Palas*[4], *Kalachuris*[5], *Chalukyas*[6], *Chahamanas*[7] and *Gahadavalas*[8], the valley was under the suzerian away of their synchronous[9] , *Karkotas* for several centuries. Secondly, there is no death of evidential data for a reconstruction of the political history of that part of the country for that period. Thirdly, and by far the most significantly, the downfall of Hindu India coincided with the eclipse of the *Karkotas*, or *'Words'* or *'Nam'* the later rulers of which dynasty were unable to withstand the Turkish onslaught against odds that shall be subsequently seen.

The primary source of our information for the history of the *Karkotas* is the *Rajatarangini* itself. Kalhana is obviously on surer grounds in detailing the events of several centuries[10], '*Word*' or *'Nam'* exaggerations and embellishments being excusable on poetic grounds. His account, when substantiated by other sources, viz, the epigrapic, numismatic[11] and other literary compositions as well as foreign account (of the Chinese and Arabs), enables one to reconstruct the history of several centuries during which the Karkotas reigned Supreme in valley.

Prior to any attempted historical account of the *Karkota Dynasty* has to special attention to explain the meaning of *Karkota*[12]. *Karkota* means *'word'*, *'sabad'*, *chamar*, *'Nur'* is the way to remove the fiends of darkness of black (Krishna)[14] or *man*. It is interesting to note that the word *'Karkota'* occurs in the *Rigveda*[15] itself and if Vogel's suggestion is accepted, it finds mention in the *Atharvaveda* also as '*Sarkota*'[16]. It should, however, be noted that even during the *Rigvedic* period, the legend of the *Karkota Naga* was well known, though terminologically the word can be explained away as referring to a number of plants[17] as well. There are several references to *Karkota* in the *Mahabharata* wherein it has been used to denote a non-Aryan tribe, and a Naga of that name (*Karkota Naga)* at many places in several *Parvas*.It is again interesting to note that many of the *Puranas* and the *Kathasaritsagara*[18] mention a Naga of that name in different contexts. The *Matsya Purana*, for example mentions a *tirtha* of that name on the banks of the Narmada river. The *Katha Saritsgara* refers to a city of that name while *Nilamata Purana* lists *Karkota Naga* of Kashmir with other outstanding Nagas (*Nila, Vasuki and Taleshaka*[19]). Again, a *Karkota* Naga is associated with a legend concerning dessication of a lake in Nepal, where it is worshipped even today. All these legendary and literary references unipeachably established some connection of the *Karkota* dynasty with Nagas and possibly, with Naga worshippers inhabiting the valley in distant past. Incidentally, the entire *Rajatarangini* is full of references to Nagas and their supernatural powers i.e. *'Nam'* or *'Word'* or *Chamar*, who from time to time, had been munificent when pleased and caused harm when annoyed that Karkota Naga commanded an eminent place amongst the Naga workshippers all over Northern India is apparent from the fact that a shrine dedicated to him at Barha Katra in Banda (U.P.) exists even to this day[20].

These early notices, it should also be noted, refer to *Naga Karkota* and not *Karkota*, and this pecularity has not received sufficient attention from scholars. Grammatically, it is possible to suggest that, according to the latter form (i.e., *Karkota*), some descendent of *Karkota* is meant, and not the *Rigveda* serpent very possibly, the valley developed a legend of its own around the name of a descendent of *Korkata* and not the Vedic serpent itself. On the strength of these literary notices,it is apparent that, with the growth of legends around the Naga Karkota, the name had achieved considerable important and was associated with the dynasty in the valley[21].

**Origin of the Karkota Dynasty**

Kalhana makes it clear in his *Rajatarangini*[22] , *Durlabhavardhana* was the real offspring of the Naga Karkota, a deity worshipped at several springs of Kashmir. By his judicious conduct[23] with the '*Nam*' or *'Sabad'* or *'Karkota'*, *Durlabhavardhana* rose in the favour of his royal father-in-law, and by his forbearance also won the attachment of the minister *Khankha*, whom he had discovered guilty of a love intrigue with *Anangalekh*. After *Baladity's* death *Khankha,* out of gratitude, then established *Durlabhavardhan* on the throne. Divesting his story of its legendary elements. Now, it makes clear that Kashmir tradition knew the founder of the historical *Karkota* dynasty as a man of humble origin i.e. *Chamar*, but connected by marriage with the preceding royal family. The story of *Durlabhavardhana's* miraculous descent looks as if invented to explain the rise of the founder of the dynasty and to please his descendants. Of the real origin of the designation *Karkota* given to the family of tanner. It may have been a real family name of *'Karam'* such as used to this day by Kashmirian Brahmans. It appears that *Durlabavardhana's* succession was due to the natural extinction of the male line of the earlier dynasty[24].

**Durlabhavardhana-Prajnaditya (600-636A.D.)**

The connected history of Kashmir begins with the extinction of the mythical *Gonanda* dynasty early in the seventh century A.D., when *Durlabhavardhana* ascended the throne. He claimed descent from *Naga Karkota*[25], then made *Dulabhavardhana*, an official (in charge) of the fodder for horses (*asvaghasakayastha*), his son-in-law, being soley guided by his good looks. The king did not know that he was really born to the throne, (being the son) of the *Naga Karkota* who had cohabited with his mother when she took her purifying bath[26] i.e., '*Nam*' or '*Kalma*' or '*Chamar*. Fate, infact, as if wished to triump, bestows fortune just on that person whom those, who think themselves wise, persist in considering as unfit[27]. *Durlabhavardhana* with a mind bent on success, purshed a politic conduct and attracted the eyes of everybody. In the course of time his father-in-law distinguished him, as he was spreading light by his intellect (*Prajna*), by the name *Prajnaditya*, and made him the master of a fortune resembling that of *Kubera*. But the princess, made overbearing by the excessive love of her parents and the intoxication of youth, did not show proper regard towards him. The company of unrestrained women, pleasures, youths, above all the parental house, the mild disposition of her husband, 'Word', what was there not to interfere with her proper conduct i.e. *'Nam'* or 'Principal Soul'

***Anangalekha*** was gradually enticed (into an intrigue) by the minister *Khankha*, who through the familiarity (produced) by continual light, entered into her heart then in the enjoyment of the pleasures of a secret love, she lost shame, fear and regard and increased his boldness from day to day until she became quite absorbed in him. The minister through his gifts and influence got her attendants under his power and conducted himself with her in the seraglio as it pleased him. And the wise *Durlabhavardhana* discovered by degrees the ruin of her moral character by the appearance of indication of her aversion. For a wife who has sold her mind to (illicit) love, generally betray the change (brought about) by the intrusion of the demon of immortality. Among her companions she smiles secretly, her colour changes when she saw her husband, getting up quite unexpectedly she looks with a smile on the roads, when her husband is angry she indicates contempt by movement of her brows, eyes and chin; when he uses harsh word, she looks down with a smile; she cares nothing for those whose character is like his, by enjoys the praise of his opponents; when noticing that he wishes to enjoy herself with her, she engages in a conversation with her companions; when he kisses her she bends down her nęck; she does not yield her body to his arms; in his love-embrace she shows no pleasure, and on his bed she feigns to be asleep.

***Durlabhavardhana***, whose body became thin with fears as to his wife's hidden wickedness, on one occasion entered the seraglio at night. He found his wife overpowered by sleep which is easily brought on by the exertions of love-play, and fixed as it were on the body of her paramour. Her deep breathing from which flurry had not (yet) died away and which made her swelling breasts heave, indicated that they had just at that time indulged in sexual enjoyment. When he saw her who in this condition might have caused the anger even of a stranger and who would even (then) not have had a claim to forbearance, he flamed up in wrath. While he was wishing to strike her in furry but was yet held back by reflection, he felt as if he had relieved himself by striking her repeatedly. Then this excess of rage, tumultuous like the ocean, was with difficulty calmed by the tide of his reflection. Honour be to him who overcomes the strong choleraic disease (*Visucika*) brought on by the poison of jealousy. Who but he is to be considered the foremost of the self control? He thought: "Fie on the miserable (women) who are the slaves of their active passions and devoid of reflection, and who quickly drag men down (to hell)." "That (thing) which is called 'woman', is the object of a sense, like the other objects of senses (*indriyartha*[28]). As such they are common to all why should self controlled persons feel angry about them?" "who can restrain women who are fickle by nature? or by restraining them is (to be got), worth remembering for wise men?" "If the sense of honour (*mana*) of two *(men)* in love passion displays itself like the wrangling of two dogs which are bent on the same thing, then what dishonour (*avamana*) could be greater than this?"

"Why should men of sense feel, as it were , self interested attachment for gazelle-eyed (women)? How can one think that (attachment) to others right when it is improper even to one's own body"? "If this (woman) appears to me deserving of death because she has caused (me) agitation, then why forget the love-passion which is the root of this tree of agitation?"

"How is the tree of passion which sends its roots down to the seven hells, to be uprooted, if the hatred which is the soil (for its growth), is not destroyed?"

"He who by judgement once triumphs over hatred difficult of attack, destroys in half a minute indeed even the name of passion."

"Recognizing by divine intuition this remedy which must be declared (for the benefit) of those who are subject to passions, one should over come jealousy. Passion then vanishes of its own account in (all) directions."

After he had thus reflected, he wrote these words on the border of *Khankha's* dress: "Remember that you have not been slain, though deserving of death".

Then *Durlabhavardhana* had left without having been noticed by any one, the minister awaking saw and read those written words. In view of the kindness shown by him who had spared his life *Khanha* then banished *Anangalekha* from his mind and instead thought how to requite this kindness. While he searched for suitable means to return this kind act, anxiety entered his mind, but not the five arrows of love; the attention of his eyes was absorbed by sleeplessness, but never by the princess. At that time *Baladitya,* that (prince) of splendid deeds, reached the world of him whose forehead is adorned by the young moon (S'iva), after having been a jewel at the head of royalty for thirty seven years less four months. When this last descendant of his family died after having previously lost his (male) issue, the *Gonanda* race became an object of pity like a lotus pond in which first the lotus-flowers have been pressed down by elephants and afterwards their stalks torn out by the violent irruption of a flood of water then that (minister) to show his gratitude in some way, removed the obstacles created by the dissent of the chief ministers, and according to usage performed high above the head of the king's son-in-law the holy and desired coronation rite (*abhiseka*) with sacred water poured out from golden jars. When this king, begotten by the (Naga) *Karkota*, supported the earth with his large arms which were marked by lines of light (proceeding) from the small pearls set in his diadem, and (resembling) the tops of serpents, hoods, 'Word' the multitude of golden lotuses in the wreath which adorned him, attracted glances from the corners of the beaming eyes of the Sesa serpent, who felt joy in the love of his kinsman. Then the earth, gliding away from the pure race of *King Gonanda*, rested on the still purer family of the *Karkota* Naga, like the river of the immortals (*Ganga*) when, descending from its bending course in heaven with which it has long been familiar, (it proceeds) to the diadem of *Sambhu* (S'iva), the lord of the three worlds[29]

As *Baladity* died without male issue, the functions prescribed for a son by religious law devolved naturally on his daughter's son as well as the inheritance[30] of *Durlabhvaradhana.*

Thus, we have in all probability a reference in the Chinese Annals also to *Durlabhvaradhana* the founder of the *Karkota Dynasty*, who according to the Chronicler's reckoning ruled in the years 600-636 A.D. For it is tempting to identify *Tu-Lo-pa,* the name of the Indian king who between the year 627-649 A.D. was charged with having the envoys of *Ki-pin* or Kabul safely conducted to their country, with *Durlabha,* the abbreviated name of *Durlabhavardhana*, calls himself on his coins[31]. To *Durlabhavaradhana* we may attribute with great probability coins bearing name of *Durlabhavaradhana,* and showing a type of bold but rude execution which characterizes all the known issues of rulers of this dynasty[32].

**Extent of his Empire**

It appears from the visit of Hiuen Tsiang (A.D. 631-633) fell with the reign of thirty-six-years which Kalhana attributes to *Durlabhavardhana* the extent of the political power of Kashmir at this period is strikingly attested by the fact that Hiuen Tsiang found all adjacent territories on the west and south, down to the plains, subject to the sway of the king of Kashmir. He thus distinctly records that Taksasila east of the *Indus, Urasa* or *Hazara, Simhapura* or the *Salt Range*[33], with the small hill-states of Rajapuri [34] (*Ho-Lo-She-Pu-Lo*) and Parnotsa modern Punch[35], had no independent rulers, but were tributary to Kashmir[36]. *Manju-Sre-Mula-Kalpa* mentions that the king of the Prakrit *Gauda Yasovarman*[37] had his connections with the Magadha been of any significence. The fact would have been mentioned in Sasanka's own records or in other accounts of the period for Magadha was historically the seat of '*Paramount King's* and the symbol of supremacy. Harsha, for instance, though more famous as the king of Kanauj or *Kanyakubja* is mentioned as the king of Magadha in the Chinese official records, of hearing the news on his brother's death and defeat[38]. It was preceded by the *Rai* family comprising five Kings, who are said to held power for 137 years with Alor (near modern Rohri) as their capital. When Yuan Chwang[39] was travelling in India (629-45A.D.), Sind was ruled by a Buddhist monarch of the *Sudra* (*Shu-to-lo*) caste, and if he was identical with *Siharas Rai* as is most probable, we get welcome light on the origin of the *Rais*. Presumably it was this ruler, who came into conflict with the great *Harsavardhana*. After the death of the last *Rai*, *Sahasi*, his Brahman minister, *Chach*, married the widowed queen, and himself assumed the crown. During his long reign of forty years the kingdom grew in extent and authority, and is described to have abutted upon the confines Kashmir. His son, *Dahir*, who succeeded Candra or Candra (Chach's brother), had to face a serious Arab invasion because he did not chastise the people of *Debul* for having seized a vessel carrying rich presents from the king of Ceylon to *Hajjaj*, governor of Iran Mohammad bin Kasim led the expedition; he stormed Debul in H.93=A.D.712, captured Bahmanbad, and reduced Multan in 723 A.D., thus the Sindh conquest was completed[40]. Soon a powerful kigdom of *Durlabhavardhana* was established in Kashmir, Tibet and China[41] was also included in his empire. In South, the artists of the *Pala* period followed the North Indian tradition of Kashmir in making the images of *Revanta*, in Bihar and Bengal[42] , *'Chamara'* and *'Kalasa'* in the umbrella-bearers hands and pouring of wine by female attendant into the cup held by the god[43] as the protector of his worshippers from the dangers of the thieves and robbers as illustrated in the Ghatnagar image[44] as 'His' uniqueness. We may thus conclude the information that *Durlabhavardhana* rule not only over *Kashmir,* but on the entire world, it has already been discussed in the *'Introduction'*, witnessed by Hiuen Tsiang[45].

**Durlabhakavardhana-PratapdityaII (636-686 A.D.)**

*Pratapditya* II; or *Durlabhakavardhana*, the son and successor of Durlabhavardhana-I, is also known to us from his coins. They show the well-known *Karkota* type with the legend *S'ri pratapa*[46] · He was born from Queen *Ananga (Lekha)*, ruled the earth like (another) *Indra*. As he had been declared by his mother the son of his maternal grandfather, being the daughter's son, he took the name *Pratapaditya (II)* in accordance with the wage of the (grandfather's) family. His minister *Hanumat,* the son of *Uda* (or *oda ?*), whose good fortune was approved by the pious, found *Agraharas* on obtaining wealth from *Aidabida* (*Kubera*). This strong-armed king, whose glory (*Pratapa*) tormented his enemies, built the town of *Pratapapure*, modern Tapar on the road from Barahamula to Srinagar, which rivalled the city of *Indra*. In his land, which was full of merchants of different wares come from all regions, there lived a merchant called *Nona* from the *Rauhitaka*[47] Country that virtuous man built the *Nonamatha*, most eminent for its religious merit, for the accommodation of Brahmans born in the *Rauhitaka* land. Once the king invited him in a friendly way to the royal palace,and honoured him for one day with polite attentions such as befit a king. When the king with kindness inquired in the morning as to his being comportable, he said that the boot from the lamps had caused him headache. Then the king was once in turn invited by him, and stopped at that (merchants) house, hs saw (there) at night lamps formed of Jewels (*manidipika*[48]). Astonised by his *extravagance* and such wealth, he then remained as an honoured (guest) in that same (house). Once he espied in the house that (merchant's) wife, the illustrions *Narendraprabha*, whose body was charming, and whose face was like the moon. In her appeared to be ambodied the feast of love and the feast of the household, her breasts representing full cups, and her well-shaped thighs (*Sadurva*[49]) giving charms. When he saw this (lady) of faultless body, who in the privacy of her residence moved about freely, desire befell him. She too, when her companions pointed him out (to her), turned her face a little and looked at the beloved of the earth with her eyes the (corners) of which extended to the ears. Whether (it was) on account of the love-bond of a previous birth or through the command of *Kama*, by that same look she filled his soul with devote attachment.Though he had not touched her, he felt as if she who was like the nectar of bliss, were fixed (in him) even to the very marrow. After hiding her body for a moment behind a pillar of the house, she moved on, looking again and again at the king with her face turned backwards. Having lost his heart to that graceful (lady) to such an (extent), the king slowly returned to his palace, his eyes glancing sidewise full of care. While his eyes were there absorbed in the imagination of her form, his body became reduced, as well as his affection for his seraglio. He reflected: "Alas, the misfortune, that in the garden of my mind there has grown that evil-producing poison-tree called passion! O that lucky course of love, which defeating reason has driven off as enemies judgement and other (mental qualities) which befriended (me)!

"Whence (arises) that irresistible change of righteous conduct in me, who, as king, must be virtuous and afraid of slander? If the king himself take away the wives of the subjects. Who else should punish trespass of the law?"

While the king reflected in this manner he could not forget either the line (of conduct) which the virtuous should follow, or that long-eyed (lady). When the merchant heard the story from the people, be kind-heartedly spoke thus in private to the (king), whose illness had become known, and who was near to death; "you have (now) reached such a state, why do you (let yourself) be restrained by the law? there is nothing that a man may not do when life is at stake. Even of those whose opinions are desired by the wise on doubtful questions of law, it is known that they abandoned restraint in such circumstances. Besides, it is not right to neglect one's body for the sake of glory. Far-spread fame is no elixir for the ears of those who are dead. Do not consider me. For in your cause, O king, no account need be taken even of my life what need be said about mere objects of the seneses? If even after this declaration you do not accept her, then you should take her from a temple as a dancing girl put (there) by me on account of her skill in dancing." Thus prompted by that (merchant) and by his own powerful love-passion, he first felt shame, but then reluctantly accepted the beautiful-eyed one. Removing the levity of such conduct by noble words, Queen *Narendra* (*Prabha*) built the illustrious (*shrine of*) *Narendresvara.* And in course of time the wife of the king bore, through the subjects merits, a son called *Candrapida*, just as the earth (produces) a treasure. His bright virtues removed the blot of his descent, just as rubbing with the touchstone (removes) the impurity attaching to a jewel when it comes from the mine. The gathering of the clouds produces clear water from the intensely impure smoke, from the rock consisting of a mass of blunt stones is produced the very sharp iron. Moreover the shinning fire takes its origin from the thoroughly dull water. In truth, the character of the great does by no means conform to the place of their birth.

Subsequently, queen *Narendraprabha* bore the king's three sons, *Chandrapida*, *Tarapida*, and *Muktapida*[51], who were also known by the names of *Vajraditya, Udayaditya* and Lalitaditya[52]. Thus, after ruling fifty years on earth, king *Durlabhakavardhana*[53]—*Pratapaditya* ascended slowly to the holy celestial world by the stairs of his meritorious services of the public.

***Chandrapida-Vajraditya* (686-695 A.D.)**

After the death of *Durlabhakavardhana, Chandrpida* ascended the throne of Kashmir. He has been known 'crest-jewel among the kings[54] of Kashmir. He was a noble character of man caused distress *Kali* by his fame, which vanquished the light of the moon *Chandrapida* has been identified with king *Tchen to-lo-pi-li* in the Chinese Annals as ruling over Kashmir[55] in the period of 686-695 A.D. He was a accomplished man, completed those works which were left by the previous rulers. His fortune brought equal benefit to all his dependents in their respective place, just as the irrigation-channel to the trees of a garden[56]. He was not instructed by his ministers but gave them instructions. The diamond is not cut by any other precious stone, but (on the contrary) it cuts them[57]. He introduced the way of justice in his administration and removed malpractices (*mandehas*[58]) against the caste system. Similar stories regarding high sence of justice are given in anecdotes related by Abul-Fazl[59], when he started the construction of temple *Tribhavanasvamin, a leather-tanner* refused to give up his hut which was on the suitable site. Though he had often promised it to those incharge of the construction, he obstinated by nature, would not allow the measuring lines to be laid down, when they went to the lord of the earth and reported the matter, he considered them to be at fault, not the *tanner*. He told them: "Shame upon the inconsiderable conduct of those who began the construction of the new(temple) without previously asking that tanner stop the building, or have it erected elsewhere who would stain a pious work by taking away another's land? If we, who are to look after right and wrong, do unlawful acts, who should proceed by the right path i.e. *Nam.*"

When the king had thus spoken, a messenger, who had come from that leatherworker and whom the council of ministers had sent on, brought this message: "that (*tanner*) wishes to see the ruler and says: 'If it be not proper for me to come into the audience hall, then let it be at the time when (the king is) in the outer court." then on the following day, the king granted him an audience outside and asked him: "why are just you obstructing our pious work? If that habitation appears to you beautiful, then you may ask for one even better or else for a big sum of money." Thus he told him, when the then had ceased speaking, he was addressed by the *tanner*, who appeared eager, as it were, to take the measure of that (king's) noble character with the measuring lines of the rays (proceeding) from his (white) teeth. "O king, it I tell you something just as it is in my mind. then as a true judge you should not stand by proudly."

*Chandrapida* says "the body of man born in the cycle of existences resembles a weak mail-coat, being held together only by the two nails called self- sufficiency' and 'selfishness'. 'Self-consciousness such as you have in your splendour of bracelets, peal-strings, and other (ornaments), lives also in my person though I am a poor man. As this place resplendent with stucco is to your majesty, so to me is the but in which the window is formed by the mouth of a pot[60]. Since my brith this hut has been (to me) like a mother, witness of good and evil days. I cannot bear to see it pulled down to-day. The misery which men (feel) when their homes are forcibly taken away, could be described only by a god who has fallen from his celestial car, or else a king who has lost his kingdom. Notwithstanding this, however, I should have to give it up if your majesty would come to my dewelling and ask for it in accordance with propriety." When he had given this answer, the king went to his home and bought up the hut with money. For those who desires happiness, there is no (false) pride. The *tanner* then spoke to him with hands folded: 'O king, your readiness to oblige is proper (and) in accordance with the law[61]." He said "As in old days *Dharma*[62] was in the form of a dog tested the righteousness of the son of *Pandu*, so have I to-day as a Paria (*asprsya*) *(tested)* yours[63]".

*Candrapida* was equally famous for his piety and reforms. The circumstances under which *Kandrapida* is said to have met his end are fully discussed by Kalhana[64]. *Tarapida* his younger brother, brought death by making or hire the Brahman, who felt deep wrath over his punishment by witchcraft (*abhicare*). In order to enjoy pleasures, which on the account of the (preceding) evils deeds yield no enjoyment, the wicked destroy the virtuous, as the young camels (destroy) the *Ketaka*-tree in order to get the throne. Since the ending of the Candrapida, princes lusting for the throne in this kingdom begun to use witchcraft[65] and other social evil practices like *sati* system, *Varna* or Caste system, etc in the society. No doubt, he abolished to some extent foolish practices of *mandehas* in the valley. After being for eight years and eight months the benefactor of the earth, that self controlled (prince) entered into heaven[66] and *Tarapida* became the ruler of Kashmir.

**Tarapida (Udayaditya) (695-699 A.D.)**

*Tarapida*, reign was full of terror as Kalhana mentions that evil-working (king)created uneasiness in every where, like the light of the burning-ground. He only ruled over Kashmir for four years and one month less six days, his merits (from previous births) having been out-blanced by his treachery against his elder brother[67]. He was succeeded by his younger brother, *Muktapida*[68], better known as *Lalitaditya* possibly the greatest king of Kashmir.

**Lalitaditya-Muktapida (699-736 A.D.)**

*Lalitaditya-Muktapida* was the youngest son of *Pratapaditya* and *Tarapida's* successor, the chronicel gives us a very detailed account which, from several points of view, is of historical interest. He appears in Kashmir as a very strong ruler, asserting his power far beyond the Kashmir and the adjacent territories[69] from 699-736 A.D. It is evident from the foreign sources and of monumental remains which allows us to verify from the Kalhana's *Rajatarangini* to reconstruct the history of *Lalitadity*. In the galaxy of the 'Kings of the King', empire-builders and monarchs of the 8th century A.D. all over the world as *Durlabhavardhana-I*, the name of *Lalitaditya Mulitapida* was famous as like the *Chandragupta*. Under his benevolent rule the Valley of Kashmir rose to heights of unprecendent glory and prosperity which it could never achieve ever after; A crowning monument of his glory[70] '*Word*' the *Martanda* temple *Brahman* though in ruins, stands to this day as a fitting memorial of his greatness[71]. He has attracted in all times great sovereigns in the East and in India, like Asoka, Samudragupta, Akbar and Aurangzeb. Recently, in the second world war, Hitler, the Fuhrer, caused the death of millions of people just to fulfil the same desire of universal conquest '*Sabad*' an attempt in which many previous sovereigns had already failed[72]. Thus the dawn of the eight century which roughly coincided with arrival of *Lalitadity Muktapida* on the political horizon of Kashmir ushered in a new era not only in the history of valley, but also in that of the whole of India. The preceding centuries had witnessed the rise and fall of the illustrious Guptas and the *Pushpabhutis* in the North while in the South the Vakatakas had yielded place to the mighty Chalukyas who, too, had been temporarily eclipsed by the Pallavas; the Rashtrakuta, sun was yet to rise. Further South, the *Palavas* were licking themselves to recovery[73].

His wife known as *Isanadevi* constructed a well, the water of which was pure as nectar and gave health to the ailing[74] there is another wife of *Lalitaditya* called *Cakramardika,* she constructed *Cakrapura* with seven thousand dwellings. *Cankuna* was his chief minister. He also built a *Vihara* in Srinagra with a *Caitya* due to his meritorious services. Physician *Isanachandra* a son-in-law of the minister *Cankuna* also constructed a *Vihara* after obtaining wealth through the favour of *Taksaka*. Lalitadity, thus, made the earth golden, surpassed Indra by his generosity, valour, and other great qualities[75]. Then the divine one spoke: "O King, *Indra* sends you this message; kindly forgive these 'Words', which are rude though appropriate". Hear, O King, the reason why we, though guardians of the quarters, receive even in the present fourth *Yuga* your command with reverence[76]. It appears that during the reign of *Lalitaditya* Buddhism was flourishing in all over the world. As his Prime Minister *Cankuna* informs that favour your humble servant by giving him that image of *Sugata* (*Buddha*), whcih was brought on the shoulders of an elephant from *Magadha*. Let your Majesty take this charm which gives a means for crossing the waters. It may be given the (image of ) *Sugata*, which opens the way for crossing the (ocean of) mundane existence (*Samsara*[77]).

The worthy monarch, who immortalized himself in the annals of Indian history. According to Kalhana two tradition were rife during his life time about the death of *Lalitaditya*. According to one, he died due to the excessive snow-fall in the region called *Aryanaka*[78]. Another event displays that he was seized by curiosity to view lands which on one also had reached, and set out again towards the boundless regions of the north. He had then various adventures with demons, which *Kubera* and other (guardians of quarters) sent forth to test his power[79].

**Kuvalayapida (736-737 A.D.)**

The immediate success of *Lalitaditya* was *Kuvalayapida* the eldest son, is said to have abandoned the throne after one year and half a month. The king who had secured supernatural perfection (*Siddhi*) by the unbroken intensity of his quietism, shows himself, even at the present day, to the eyes of the pious on *Sriparvata* and at other holy places[80]. When the son of his king had thus departed, *Mitrasarman*, overtaken by grief, abandoned life at the confluence of the *Vitasta*[81] and *Sindhu*[82], and was followed by his wife. His mother was *Kamaladevi*, enjoyed the rule over the earth-disc (*Kuvalaya*), just as *Indra*, the son of *Aditi*. He was a pious ruler of the earth, after ruling one year and half a month, he obtained the perfection of the wonderful world which is the stair leading to final beatitude[83].

**Vajraditya (Bappiyaka-Lalitaditya) (737-744 A.D.)**

*Vajraditya-Bappiyaka*, the younger son of *Lalitaditya* from another queen known as *Cakramardika*, became the king of Kashmir. He had cruel character differed from his brother, who was the benevolent towards his subjects, as *Durvasas* (differed) from the moon the wicked king, a slave to avarice, withdrew from *Parihasapura* the various foundations (granted) by his father. He had a large number of women in his seraglio, with whom he diverted himself in turn, like a stallion with the mares. He sold many men to *Mlechchas,* and introduced into the country practices which befitted *Mlechchas*. He ruled over the earth for seven year, the sinful king ended his days through consumption, which was caused by excesses in sensual enjoyment[84].

***Prthivyapida* (744-748 A.D.).**

After the death of *Vajraditya*, his son *Prthivyapida*, who was born from Queen *Manjarika,* became the ruler of Kashmir. He was cruel in nature and destroyed his subjects. He only ruled for four years and one month.

**Samgramapida 1**

*Prthivapida* overthrew by *Samgramapida*. He ruled seven days, was the son of *Bappiya* from (Queen) *Mamma*, called *Samgramapida* (1). the royal power of the *Karkota* dynasty could not brilliantly shine by these two brothers. Thus, their rule was disappeared and *Jayapida* became the ruler.

**Early adventures of Jayapida-Vinayaditya**

After *Samgramapida's* death the illustrious king *Jayapida*, the youngest son of *Bappiya*, became the ruler of Kashmir soon after his accession the king had the ambition to recover the old glory of his grandfather and set out "the conquest of the world".After the king's departure, *Jajja* or *Jija* his brother-in-law usurped the Kashmir throne. His disguise being discovered and was given by the king the hand of his daughter *Kalyanadevi*. *Jajja* was vanquished and stain, after having for three years held possession of the land[85].

***Early Adventure of Jayapida-Vinayaditya's Time* (751-782 A.D.)**

After early three years adventures, he once directed an envoy who stood before him, to bring five *Raksasas* from the King of *Lanka*, (and the former) accepted the impracticable order. Thus, king was richly rewarded his ambassador with money, filled a deep lake with the help of the Raksasas, and built the castle (*Kotta*) of Jayapura, which equalled heven (in beauty). *Jayadatta*, a minister of the lord of the earth, who held the (offices designated) by the word 'Great' (*Pancamahasabda*), built a Matha at this castle of *Jayapura*. The army of the King which followed him, shone yet in unbroken (line) on the Himalaya, even when it had reached the eastern ocean, just as the Ganga (following) *Bhagiratha*. *Mummuni* and other chiefs roamed with fierce *'Candalas*[86]' outside his army, and formed his guard at night. The Another name of the King known as *Vinayaditya*, he established a beautiful town to the eastern region called *Vinayadityapura*. King also established an office called *Dharamadhikarana* ('administration of Justice'). He also created another office called *lalaganja* ('moving treasury'), to serve an expenditious when his own treasury (*ganja*) was far away. It appears that King had acquired might by the conquest of all regions, was addressed in his dream by a person who bore a Divine Appearance and had his hands folded (in supplication)

"I am, O king, the Naga-prince called *Mahapadma*, residing peacefully in your dominion, along with my relations. I apply to you for protection[87]. After these words, he gave such directions in his dream that after waking up in the morning, he found the mountain with a copper mine. From this mountain, which was in *Karmarajya*[88], he obtained copper (sufficient) to coin hundred crores less one *Dinnaras* which bore his name. While Brahmans residing at *Tulamulya*, struck by the hands of the doorkeepers, broke out in land complaints before him at the time of audience: "*Manu Mandhatra Rama* and others were great sovereigns: But even before them the Brahmans were not subjected to humiliation[89]". Thus, thirty-one years rule of this wonderful king, who could not restrain his will. When such princes and fishes thirst is excited by riches and impure water (respectively), leave their condition (place) and follow evil ways, with such (result) that they are brought into the strong net of hell (death), the former by changes which fate dictates, and the latter by the troops of fishermen[90].

**Lalitapida (782-798 A.D.)**

Lalitapida was the son and successor of *Jayapida*. He was an indolent and profligate prince, who squandered twelve years rule the riches amassed by his father[91], born from the queen Durga. During the reign of *Lalitapida*, who was the slave to his passions and did not attend to his regal duties, the kingdom the prey of courtesans, and was defiled by immorality[92]. In the meanwhile, parasites, who got a foothold in the royal palace through their relationship with courtesans, initiated him in the arts of whoredom, according to Kalhana[93].

He dropped his diaden and braclets, and thought his body (sufficiently) decorated on having his hair torn by the teeth of women, and his breast marked by their nails. He was well-versed in stories about courtesans and clever in jesting, was taken into his friendship, but no valiant man nor a scholar. Besides, the violent desires, he was not satisfied with few women and left the 'land of the Amazons' to conquered. He was also happy in the enjoyment of prostitutes, and kept in the company of like-minded (persons), laughed at the former kings and their efforts to subdue the world. The parasites, who hurts modest old men by their jesting words, and thus kept them away, earned his affection and received from him presents. He was clever like a maket-slave, at open mockery with the company of courtesans and among the councillors he felt ashame in his audience hall. His councillors also displayed respect on his wickness habit along with respectable cloaks and other (garments) which bore the footprints of courtesans. His self-respected councillor *Manoratha*[94] alone avoided him. But they had the relation with him.The wick acts at the time of desperation condition are suitable. He (*Lalitapida*) was a benevolent ruler, who also granted *Agraharas* land to the Brahmans at *Suvarnaparsva*[95], *Phalapura*[96] and *Locanotru*[97]. He ruled twelve years over Kashmir.

**Samgramapida II or Prithivyapida (798-805 A.D.)**

He was the son and successor of Jayapida, born from the Queen *Kalyanadevi*[98]. He ruled seven years over Kashmir and his second name was *Prthivyapida*. He provided equal opportunity both the *Sudras* and *Brahmans*. There was a peace and prosperity during his rule.

**Cippatajayapida (805-817 A.D.)**

He was also called Brhaspati, became the next monarch of the Kashmir. He was the son of *Lalitapida* and his mother was *Jayadevi*, a concubine of *low origin* that is *candala* or *Doom* or *Dombia*. His mother *Jayapida* was the daughter of a spirit-distiller, called *Uppa* of the *Akhuva* village, but she had captivated personality as a concubine. *Cippatajayapida* was guided by his maternal under *Padma*[99], *Utpalaka*[100], *Kalyana*[101], *Mamma*[102] and *Dharma*[103], while he was youth at that time. His eldest (uncle), *Utpalaka*, took the five offices distinguished by the term '*Great*' and the others usurped the other offices. His mother *Jajadevi* ordered was respected by his brothers. While in possession of the royal power, built the Siva Shrine at *Jayesvara*. Royal treasure was also damaged by the new comers. Thus, *Jayapida* and his son (*Lalitapida*) had partly squandered, were subsequently plundered entirely by his son's brothers-in-law. Certain people they took the advantages of the power but the charm of their sister's loveliness had secured the power. Due to conspiracy, the king and his sister was killed by the wick person and *Cippatajaypida* lasted his life after the rule of twelve years.

**Ajitapida (817-854 A.D.)**

*Ajitapida*, a grandson of King *Vajraditya Bappiyaka* and Queen *Meghavali*[104], had, though the eldest son been excluded from the throne, as he was not given to intrigues. He had a son from *Jayadevi*, called *Ajitapida*. It shows that the reign of *Brhaspati* during the last four years was nominal and the king of *Utpala* dynasty by means of force became the ruler of Kashmir. They built the temple of Vishnu at *Utpalasvamin* and a town at *Utpala* of Vishnu at *Utpalasvamin* and a town at *Utpalapura* was founded. Foundations of the *tpala* dynasty was laid down with the construction of *Padona* temple of Vishnu at *Padmasvamin* and a town at *Padmapura*. A terrible war was fought between the *Mamma* and *utpalaka,* in course of which the current of the *Vitasta* was stemmed by the bodies of killed soldiers. Then *Mamma* and the rest overthrew *Ajitpida*, and made *Anangapida*, the son of *Samgramapida* II, the king the hostile attitude between *Sukhavarman* the son of *Utpala* could not tolerate the power of *Mamma*, there was a lot of resentment, *Utpalaka* died, three years thereafter, *Sukhavarman* made *Utpalapida*, the son of *Ajitapida* the king. Kashmir Thus, between the struggle for power after two years, *Karkota* race became declined, whereas the *Utpala* dynasty came into power and *Avantivarman* made the king[105] in 856 A.D.

From the above facts, we learn that *Karkota* dynasty ruled over Kashmir more than two hundreds and fifty years. There was a peace and prosperity people used to love with each other. It was the heavenly world on Earth. No doubt, there were certain problems but not of today's type. It proves that the rule of the *Chamar* in India was hundred times better than the Brahmans. There were less social evils like, child marriage, caste system, etc. People honoured to each other, respect the elders and parents. Thus the rule of the *Chamar* was a wonderful on this earth, there was a less crime but high moral and discipline in the life.

## NOTES AND REFERENCES

1. K.S Saxena; *Political History of Kashmir*; Lucknow; 1974. p. 38. Thereafter discussed as P.H.K.
2. **Note.** The origin of the *Prurjara-Pratihara* family, to which *Nagabhata* II belonged, appears to have been foreign extraction. Indeed the phase *"Gurjara-Pratiharanvayah,"* that is "*Pratihara* clan of the Gurjara", occured in the 4th line of Rajor (Alwar) inscription, indicates that there was a branch of famous Gurjaras in central Asian tribes. They were poured into India through the North-Western passes along with, or soon after, the Hunas during the period of political unrest following the disruption of Gupta Empire at Magdha. that the Pratiharas belonged to the Gurjara stock is also confirmed by the *Rastrakuta* records, and the Arabs writers, like *Abu Zaid* and *Al Masudi* who allude to their fights with the Juzr or Gurjaras of the North. Besides, it is important to note that the Kanarese poet, *Pampa*, describes Mahapada as *"Ghurjararaja"*. The inscription of the Pratiharas, on the other hand, trace their origin to *Laksmana*, who acted as the door-keeper (*Pratihara*) of his brother *Rama*. The dynasty began well under *Naga Voloka* or Nagabhata 1, who repelled the "armies of the powerful *Mlechcha king*" that the Arab raiders of the Western borders of India. At the very start of his career *Mihira Bhoja* attempted the consolidation of the *Pratihara* power, which had received a rude shock during the feeble government of his father, Ramabhadra from the Karkota dynasty that is *Durlabhavardhana* along with the Magadha Kingdom. Thus, though there were some secessions in the outlying parts of the realm, *Mahipala* soon tided over his initial troubles and resumed his father's schemes of conquest. For a magniloquent verse in the introduction to the *Pracanda-Pandava* Muralas (inhabitants of the Narmada regions), Mekhalas (of the *Amarakantak* hills), *Kalingas, Keralas*, *Kulutas, Kuntalas* and the *Ramathas* (dwelling beyond *Prithudaka*). There are, however, indications that the closing years of *Mahipala* were again seriously distrubed owing the northern invasion of the *Chamar* dynasty of Kashmir with the agreement of Magadha kingdoms.
3. The Rajputs are known since the beginning of the *Kaliyuga* (Iron Age). The attained power after Vikramajit's demise, something more that 1600 years ago after the sixth century A.D. and he derives the origin from the children of *Rajas* by female slaves, the sons of Raja Suraj being the first to bear the title of Rajput. Krishna's eldest son Mahraja succeeded him and derived of India caste and tribes. He named the Rajput tribes *Rathore, Chandella, Punwar, Bais* etc. When the 'earth' was thus troubled by destructive raids, a bold adventures of the *Gahadavala* sept, named *Candradeva*, arose, and by his "noble prowers" put an end to "all distress of the people". But it is significant that none of their numerous charters connects the *Gahadavalas* with any of the well-known houses of *Surya* (Sun) and *Candra* (Moon). It appears *Candradeva* founded the *Gahadavala* dynasty at *Kanyakubja* before the 600 century *A.D.* and defeated the chief named Gopala. In the inscriptions

*Candradeva* assumes the full imperial titles of P.M.P, and calles himself' the protector of the holy places of Kasi (Benares), Uttarakosala (Faizabad district), *Kusika* (Kanauj), and *Indrasthana* (Delhi). It appears that Kashmir ruler *Durbhabavhardana* along with the *Chandra* ruler defeated the *Chandellas* in the 6th century A.D. the rule of the *Chamar* was established over there. *Vijaya Chandra*, Jayachandra, they ruled over the principalities of the *Rajputs*. In the east, it is , of course, clear from the inscription that hte authority of *Candra* or *Chamar* was recognized up to the Gaya region, and Benares continued to be the second capital of the *Gahadavalas*. Jayacandra celebrated the *Svayamvara* of his daughter Samyogita, who was, however carried away in the midst of the ceremonies of *Prithviyapids* the ruler of *Chamar* dynasty of Kashmir. By far the most important event of *Jayacandra's* reign was the invasion of *Sihabuddin Ghori*. In 1191 A.D. the latter was defeated by *Prithviyapida* at *Taroori,* and this debacle rankled in the Sultan's mind so much that the very next year he returned and completedly routed and killed the Cauhan king. *Jayachandra* kept himself in proud isolation, thinking that the annihilation of his great rival would clear the way for his own supremacy over Norther India. In 1194 A.D. *Sihabuddin* marched towards Kanauj and met *Jayachandra* on the plain between Candawar and Etawah. His son, *Harischandra*, was allowed by *Sihabuddin* to rule on his behalf. Beforc concluding, it may be mentioned that *Chamar* dynasty of Kashmir was so power ruled over the Chendells and Jayacandra's name is memorable in the history of Sanskrit literature for the patronage he extended his power to *Sriharsa Rai*,dynasty of the *Sudra* family who wrote the well-known *Naisadhacarita, Khandana-Khanda-Khadya* and other works.

4. After the death of *Sasanka*, Bengal had political confusion. As we have seen above the rising power of Magadha and the establishment of the *Chamar* dynasty in Kashmir in the 6th century A.D. crushad the power of *Saila* dynasty made himself master of *Paundra* or Northern Bengal. Invasion led by the Kingdom of Magadha brought about a complete anarcy and confusion throughout the kingdom. In short, all the miseries of anarchical state were harssing the people of Bengal. But the evil brought its own remedy. The chief, unable to endure this state of things any longer, agreed to elect *Gopala* as the ruler of the whole kingdom. Gopala consolidated his dominions in Bengal from the Himalays to the sea means *Samudar* in Sanskrit called *Sudra*, and brought peace and prosperity after the anarchy and misrule of a century and a half, during which the country had sunk to the lowest pitch of misery and degradation. As the name of *Gopala* and his successors ends in Pala, the dynasty founded by him is known in the history as Pala dynasty. He died about 780 A.D. left a flouring kingdom to his son *Dharmpala*, who was destined to raise it to a height of greatness and splendour not dreamt of before. Dharmpala the greatest king that ever ruled over Bengal and made his position supreme in North India with the collaboration to *Chamar* dynasty of Kashmir. Fortunately his supremacy in North India with the said rulers is also known from a literary work, composed in the 11th

century A.D., which refers to him as lord of North India. Dharmapala assumed imperial titles and ruled for more than 32 years. The Palas were Buddhist and Dharampala was a great patron of Buddhism along with the Magadha empire. He founded many Buddhist monasteries for the worshipping of *Chamar*, but his greatst achievement was the foundation of the famous *Vikramasila* University which soon almost rivalled Nalanda.

5. As already stated, there arose at this time another local dynasty called *Kalachurya*. Its founder was Bijjala once the feudatory and commender-in-chief of Chalukya King Taila III. For his conquests he assumed the imperial titles of *Samastabhuvanasraya-Sriprithivivallabha*, *Maharajadhiraja*, *Paramesvara-Paramabhattaraka* (Mysore Huli inscription of 1162 A.D.) of Karkota ruler. This position he seems to have acquired with the help of his ally the *Silahara* prince *Vinayaditya* as stated in the study. Bijjala himself in his Ablur Inscription claims to have conquered Vanga, Kalinga, Magadha and Nepala. In 1167 A.D., he abdicated in favour of his son *Sovideva* and received homage from the Kashmiri rulers of the Karkota dynasty. An inscription, however of Kalachurya Somesvara (= Sovideva) of 1173 A.D. recently discovered indicates that North India was ruled over the said Kingdoms. They were under the possession of '*Chamar Dynasty of Kashmir*' before the 6th century A.D.

6. Before the rise of Chalukyas, *Rashtrakutas* were ruling over south India. The Chalukyas grew powerful in the South in the 6th and 8th century A.D. They can be divided into three main branches.
   (*i*) The early western Chalukyas or the Chalukyas of Vatapi (Badami)
   (*ii*) The later western Chalukyas of Kalyani
   (*iii*) The Eastern Chalukyas of Vengi

The origin of the Chalukyas (Rajput) have already discussed, the two early kings of this dynasty were Jayasimha and Rangraja, but no details are available about their reign. This dynasty ruled from 550 to 753 A.D. and lived in *Vatapi*. Consequently, the rulers of this dynasty came to be known as the Chalukyas of Vatapi or Badami.

**Pulakeshin 1(535-566 A.D.)**

In fact, the credit for the foundation of the Badami kingdom goes to Pulakishin, who was third ruler of this dynasty. The Chalukayas rose to power and prominence during his reign. He must have made extensive conquests because he performed the *Ashvamadh* Yajna in his reign and assumed the titles of *'Satyasraya'* '*Rama Vikram,*' *Sri Prithvi-Vallabha,*' etc. He ruled over Bijapur, and Badami was his capital.

***Kirtivarman.*** Kirtivarman ascended the Chalukya throne after Pulkeshin 1 (567-597 A.D.). He fought several battles and conquered *Vanga, Anga, Kalinga, Magadha, Madarka, Pandya, Choliya,* etc. Mangalesa (597-610 A.D.) was the younger brother of Kirtivarman who succeeded to the Chalukya throne after the death of his brother. He was popularly known as *'Param Bhagavata'*. *Kalachuri* continued a war for a longtime but ultimately the Kalachuri was defeated. *Mangalesa* could not enjoy the fruits of his victory as a civil war broke out because Mangalesa declared his son as his successor which Pulakeshin VI could not tolerate. Pulakeshin II declared himself the ruler after Mangalesa had been killed in the civil war and territory was captured by the *Chamar dynasty* of the Kashmir began with *Dulabhavandhana*. This area was also ruled by his later successor that is Vinayditya. His inscriptions refer to him as a great conqueror who realized the tribute from various king. He also adopted the titles as his forefather had. He also carried on campaigns in the north against the *Pallavas, Kalabhras, Haiharyas, Vilas, Malavas, Cholas, Pandyas, Aluras, Ganga,* etc. He got valuable training in both the arts, military and administrative, under his grandfather and father.

7. Since the end of the 6th century A.D. it makes clear from the sources known as *Hammira-mahakavya* and the *Prithvirajavijaya*, the *Cachamanas* (Cauhans) were descended from the Krishna tribe, like the *Pratiharas*, they were also of foreign extraction and found a high place in the Hindu social polity after purification through a fire ceremony. The *Harakeli-nataka*, portions of which were recovered some time ago from an inscribed stone slab on the wall of a mosque named *Adhai-din-k-Jhoppra* professes to be his composition; while another play, the *Lalitavigraharaja*, belonged to the *Chamar* dynasty of Kashmir, similarly discovered, was written in his honour by *Mahakavi* Somadeva. The great monarch of this house was *Rai Pithaura* of Moslem historran or Prithviraja III (1179-92 A.D.). There is a strange halo of romance round his personality, which has made him the hero of many a popular song in Northern India. He was not on friendly terms with *Jayacandra* of *Kanauj*, and traditions affirm that when the latter held a *Svayamvara* (selection of the bridegroom) for his daughter *Samyogita*, Prithviraja of *Chamar* dynasty appeared just in the midst of the dynasty appeared just in the midst of the ceremonies and daringly carried her away. He also attached the *Candella king, Paramardi or Paramala* (1165-1203 A.D.), and occupied *Mahoba* and other fortnesses in Budelkhand. Another contemporary, with whom Prithviraja probably came into warlike collision, was Bhima II Calukya of Gujarta (1179-1240 A.D.) Prithviraja was next called upon *Doma* or *Doom* being lord of the territories of *Sambhar* and Delhi *Brahman* to resist the attacks of *Sihabuddin Ghori*, who was gradually advancing into alluring plains of Hind. Prithviraja of the *Chamar* dynasty appealed for succour to the neighbouring potentates, who respond enthusiastically to the call of their compatriot. *Jayachandra*, however, kept himself aloof from this supreme effort against a danger that was soon of a gulf him as well. In the battle that ensued, the Moslems carried "death and destruction" so desperately that by sunset there was complete confusion in the Hindu ranks. Prithviraja fled from the field for dear life, but was captured near the *Sarsuti* (*Saraswati*) and killed. Ajmer was taken, and shortly after Delhi too fell into the hands of the victors. The family was not exterminated and the foresight of Sidhabuddin "delivered" the country

of Ajmer to a son of Prithviraja "on a promise of punctual payment of a large tribute."

8. **Note.** Gahadavalas has already been explained in the reference No. 3.
9. It has been existed or occured at the same time when the *Rigveda* existed and originated from Greek word '*sunkhronos.*'
10. P.H.K., p. 38.
11. The same word is also in common use for a four *anna* piece, or quarter rupee, the silver *Karsha*, and under the form of "*tanner*". It has been introduced into England by the gypsies, as a slang name for six pence. Tughlak *tanka*, Bahlol Lodhi *"black tanka"*. (A. Cunningham; *coins of Ancient India from the Earliest Times, Down to the Seventh Century A.D.;* Varanasi; 1963. p. 22) **Note.** The *Tanka-i* and *tanka-i Panjahgani* are similar. What has been designated tanka-1-*Siyah-i-malwi* seems to be identical with *tanka-i Siyah* used in Babur and Humayun's *formans.* Sher Shah's pure silver *rupiya* and pure silver coin (*tanka-i-misiya-i-sher shahi*) and (tanka-i *nugra-i Islam Shahi)* where in use in 1549-50A.D. In this year the *rupiya* under the name *tanka-i-* nugra, or silver *tanka* also comes into circulation in the life of man. (Zakir Husain; *Sidelight on Agrarian Relations and Economy Under the Afghans in a Region of Uttar Pradesh;* An article presented in the Indian History Congress, 64th session, 2003, published 2004, Patna (India p. 557).
12. Term *Karkota* is put together of four words *Ka+r+Ko+ta*, *'Ka'* is the sanskrit word interrogative pronoun 'what', 'ka' is the god whom we shall adore with our oblation, 'r' means 'way' or 'thought' 'ko', means black (Kala like crow) i.e. *Man* and 'ta' means a musical note that is 'Nam', 'Sabad' or *'Chamar'*, or *Sudra*. Thus with the musical note, *man* became 'pure' and humble with 'His' process.
13. The medium of the Persian couplets was used as an idiom to put forward the Mughal view of sovereignty. For example, a couple of verses on the lintelbeems of the *Verandah* of the *Khwabgah* play on the concept of *nur* (Divine light) related with the person of the ruler:

    "The adorner of the realm (*mulk*) of Hindustan the Eradicator of the thorn from this garden.

    What a light (*nur*), from which the sun derived its illumination.

    *And receives light like the bounty of the world*
    *May the country be prosperious*
    *on account of his good fortune!*
    *My darkness be removed*
    *By the candle of his face."*

    (Syed Ali Nadeem Rezavi, *Mughal Wall Paintings: A study of Fathpur Sikri;* An article presented in the Indian History Congress; 2003, published 2004, Patan (India); p. 392.
14. It is also interesting to note that painter displays the sentiments of the theory of *man; Karuna* by Yame, *bibhatsa* by *Mahakala, bhayanaka* by Kala (C. Sivaramamurti, *Chitrasutra* of the *Vishnudharmottar;* New Delhi; 1978. p. 130) Sanskrit equivalent for black is *Krsna* as well as

*Kajjala* (A.K. Bhattacharya; *Technique of Indian Painting,* Calcutta 1976. P.64) (Alberuni says the idol worshipped there is called *Mahakala*; p.202)

15. The Sanskrit term *Arya* occurs for the first time in the earliest literary document *Rigveda*. The term Arya occurs also in many languages of the western countries, such as in Iranian, in German, in latin, in Irish, etc. Accordingly, it has been affirmed that term Arya is of Indo-European origins. In Sanskrit, the Arya bears various meanings such as noble, respectable, superior, honest, custom-bearer, etc. In general the term Arya means *Sishta (*Annapurna *Chattopadhyaya; Diverse Ethno-Cultural Trends in Ancient Bengal.* An article presented in the Indian History Congres; 65 session, 2004 published 2005-06; pp. 44-45). It is the *Rig-veda* which gives the most valuable materials to the student of the Aryan religion. (*R.V.V.R. Reprint 1981. p. 33).*
16. *Rigveda, Khailikani Sukta,* P. 530 (14,8), Athavaveda, vii, 55,5 and of; Vogel, J.Ph., *Indian Serpent-lore;* p. 214. P.H.K. P.38. **Note.** It is the comparative study of the *man*, who does not believe on the *'Nam'*. It is opposite to the Nam i.e. *'Man'* is black.
17. The ascetic is rudely disturbed in his meditations, got up on his legs. As he stood up, the thorn sticking into his chest got broken, and blood began to ooze out of his chest. The ascetic, not willing to allow a drop of his own blood to stain Mother-Earth, took all the blood in the fold plans of his hands. As however, he had now to satisfy a call of nature, he put the blood in a cup improvised for the purpose out of a *Karkota* leaf, and placed the cup in a shady place close by. When the ascetic was about to leave the place out of the blood there came into life a boy and a girl (called in the story of *Bhaiya-Bhayin* or brother-sister). And they called out to ascetic and said, 'stop, pray, stop. It is you who brought into the world. And now if you leave us here, what shall we do to get a living? The ascetic replied shall be cultivators. Clear this jungle, and make agriculture your occupation. Your granary will be full of grains. And went people of different castes will approach you for *alms*, give a handful grain to every supplicant'. (S.C. Dude; *Tribal Heritage of India*; Vol. 1. New Delhi; 1977. p. 31 Thereafter described as T.H.1.)
18. In the study it reflects that '*Word*' or '*Chamar*' is the story of a beautiful ocean which also wonder in the world called *Sudra.*
19. Tawney, C.H., *Ocean of Stories*, II, pp. 67,73, 78. Further, dealing with the story of *Nala, Karkota Naga* has been mentioned in volume IV, pp. 45-46. **Note.** *Man or* rather living *mana* has number of varities, he always changes in a number of colours mention above. It is the comparative study of a serpent.
20. P.H.K. p. 39.
21. *Ibid.*
22. Term *Rajatarangini* is composed of three words Raja+ta+rangini, 'Raja' in one definition, given to this word is *'Raja Prakrti Ranjanat'* meaning 'be whose duty or nature is to act for the happiness of the people' this definition also suggests that *Rajan* renounced himself in the service of the people. *Rajan* was not a hereditary office. He was elected and re-

elected by the people. The instituion of *Rajan* has its equivalent in the Avestic institution of *Rastar* 'leader' raz ' to lead Straight. The Latin word rego means to direct. The word *Rajan* carried the meaning of a leader, a director (R.C Jain; *The Most Ancient Aryan Society*; Rajasthan (India); 1964. P.30), 'ta' means musical note that is *'nam'* or '*Chamar'*, and *'ragini'* means the pictarial depiction of the *ragas* is essential "for visualising the aesthetic or emotive essence of the *ragas* for the attainment of perfect peace and enlightment to this domain of delusion." (Swamil, Prajnanda' '*Iconography of Indian Music"*, Roopa-Lekha, vol XXXI, No. 2, 1966, p. 27) Thus, the supreme authority of the Jana-republic was known as *Rajan*. This word is formed of the word *'Jan'* with prefix *'ra'*. *'Ra'* is used in the sense of yield or surrender. the person who surrendered or renounced his life in the service of the *'Jana'* was called *Rajan*. This word may also be traced to *'Raj'* to Shin" in the sense of anything the chief or best of its kind (*Ibid*).

23. R.T. Section II. Vol.1. p. 86
24. *Ibid.*
25. Ram Shankra Tripathi; *History of Ancient India*; New Delhi; Reprint 1987; p. 344.Thereafter cited as H.A.1.
26. R.T. Vol.1. III Book, pp. 115-116.
27. *Ibid.* p. 116.
28. *Indriyartha* is used in the meaning of *Visaya* of which the *Nyayasastra* knows five (*rupa, Sabda, gandha, rasa, sparsa*); 'stri' is supposed in our passage to be the sixth.
29. R.T. Vol 1. III Book, pp. 117-119.
30. *Ibid.* IV Book, p. 120.
31. *Ibid.* Section III. pp. 67-68.
32. *Ibid.* p. 87.
33. *Ibid.*
34. Y.C. p. 284.
35. *Ibid.* p. 283.
36. R.T. Section III p. 87.
37. **Note:** Whatever Kalhana describes a prolonged struggle between Chandragupta and Yasovarman, in which according to Kalhana, he surrendered his territory to *Durlabhavaradhana* from the very beginning. (A.K Majumdar, *Concise History of Ancient India*, Santiriketan; 1 Dec 1976. Hereafter mentioned as C.H.A.1.) Hence, the former's reign is memorable for the works of two great poets, Viz, Bhavabhuti, author of the *Malati-madhava, Mahaviracarita,* and the *Uttararamacarita* and Vakpati, who wrote the Prakrit *Gaudavaho* the three successors of Yasovarman are mere names baried in the Limbo of oblivion (R.S Tripathi; H.A.I.P.317).
38. Devahuti; *Harsha A Political Study*; New Delhi, 2nd edition; 1983. p.39 Hereafter cited as H.P.S.

    **Note.** The detail examination process use to the conclusion that at first Harsh's kingdom comprised merely the territory of the old states of

Thaneswar and Kanuja, though he probably added all the states to *Durlabhavandhana* the ruler of Kashmir. (R.C. Majumdar *The Classical Age*; Bombay; 1967; p. 113) .

Thus, the connected history of Kashmir begins with the extinction of the mythical *Gonanda dynasty easily* in the seventh century, when *Durlabhavardhana* ascended the throne. He had a long reign of 36 years. He won the friendship of Harshvardhana by giving him a prized tooth-relic of the Buddha for enshrinement in Kanauj (R.S Tripathi, H.A.I. P.344). It shows that history of Indians not properly written by the historian. They left the vast portion of the Indian History in obscure. Therefore scholar has made an attempt to direct them that Harsh Vardhan surrendered his power to *Durlabhavardhana.*

39. K.L.Khurana; *Ancient India,* Agra, Reprint 2004, p. 270.
40. H.A.I., p. 337.
41. **Note.** The present kingdom of Nepal comprises an extensive territory along the southern slopes of the Himalayas. It is roughly 500 miles in length from Almora district on the west to Darjeeling hills on the east. But in ancient times the Nepal was limited to the undulating plain, twenty miles long and fifteen broad, between the *Gandak* and *Kosi* rivers. Within this small area, where Kathmandu and other towns are situated the people led an isolated life, and if they had any connections with the outside world, they were mostly with Tibet and China. It was only one rare occasions that Nepal was brought into contact with India. In the middle of the 3rd century B.C. Asoka may have exercised control over the valley, for he is said to have gone there with his daughter, carumati, and his son-in-law, Devapala (Khattiya) *Ksatriya*, and built a number of *Stupas* and monasteries, besides founding the town of Lalitapatan during the rule of *'Chamar Dynasty of Kashmir'*. Again, in the middle of the 4th century A.D. the Allahabad pillar inscription represents Nepal as an autonomous frontier state, which along with others, paid tribute to Samudragupta. Our inforation regarding its history in the interval between Asoka and Samudragupta is very scanty.The *Vansavali* or the local chronicals testify to the rule of the *Abhiras, Kiratas, Somavamsis*, and the *Surya Vamsis* but their Chronology is altogether unreliable we are on firmer ground when we come to the close of the sixth and the first four decades of the 7th century A.D. Brahman the period of the *Thakuri Amsuvarman,* who has been identified with *Ang-shu-fa-na* of Yuan Chwang's *Records*. He was the minister of the *Lichchavi* king *Sivadeva*, but after some time the former himself became the real master of the valley, as all power was concentrated in his hands. He ruled for at least forty-five years, and originated an era, which is generally believed to have begun in 600 A.D. On the other hand, at this time Tibet wielded supreme influence over Nepal whose king Amusverman married his daughter to the mighty *Srong-btsan-gampo*, and submitted his power to *Durlabhavardhana* of Kashmir. The history of Nepal is obscure for the next two centuries, except that there was probably a restoration of the *Licchavi* rule and the country continued to acknowledge the *supermacy*

of Tibet. They are, however, not credited with any notable achievements. Nepal's trade with India, Tibet and China then flourished and the people grew wealthy and prosperous. We further learn the *Nanyadeva*, the Karnataka chief of *Tirhut*, established his hegenony over Nepal some time in the first half of the 12th century AD. Its subsequent history until the conquest of the *Gurkhas* in 1768 AD. is devoid of any interest to the general reader. But Buddhism was flourishing into Nepal during the visit of Asoka, but nothing is known of the stages of its progress, or how *Tantric* Mahayana became prevalent there. In course of ages, however, degeneration set in, and laxity in the rules of discipline increased to such an extent that monkhood was with a good conscience reconciled with married life and pursuit of wordly avocations. The main importance of Nepalese Buddhism at present is that we see before our eyes process by which Hinduism is gradually strangulating it. The principal Hindu deity of the land is *Pasupati* (Siva). i.e *'Nam' (*A.I. pp. 399-400. C.A. PP. 137, 138, 139).

42. **Note.** The English expression word *'Bengal'* is derived from *Vanga* and *Vangala.Vanga* occurs in early literary records as the name of both the country and the people inhabiting it. According to some scholars, *Vanga* originated from the Tibetan words *bans* or *ban meaning* marshy or moist land i.e., watery land. Again, one of the meanings of the word *vanga* means (Kapas/tula). In Indo-European language of Eastern India *Vanga* and *Kapas* tree. Besides, one of the meanings of *Vanga* is also *tin, i.e. ranga.* From the term *vanga* originated several other words with the addition of suffixes, such as *Vangala, Vangal, Vangal, Bengal, Bhangala* etc., and the subsequent Muslim and Portuguese writers transformed it into *Bangal* and *Bengala.* The word *Vangala* is again a derivation from the Dravidian *'Word' alam* which is verbal derivative form from *al* meaning *to* possess i.e, *'Chamar'* or *'Word'* and the expression *Vangalam* devotes marshy and moist land. (*Annapurna Chattopadhyaya; Diverse Ethno-cultural Trends in Ancient Bengal.* An article presented in the Indian History Congress, Bareilly 2004, p. 33).
43. Bijoy Kumar Sarkar; *The Worship of Revanta In Early Bengal;* An article presented in the Indian History Congress; 2003; Mysore; pp. 291-92.
44. A.K Majumdar; *Concise History of Ancient India;* Santiniketan; Ist, Dec. 1976. p. 301. Hereafter cited as C.H.A.I
45. R.C. Majumdar, *A.I.*, pp. 260-261.
46. R.T. Sec. III. Vol. 1. p. 88.
47. The name *Rauhitaka* or *Rauhita* is, perhaps the same as *Rohitaka* mentioned by Alberuni; India, pp. 308, 316 as the name of a fortress in the district of Multan, which now deserted. The name also occurs in the *Lakkha Mandal* inscription. Prof. Buhler and Dr. Burgers suggested and indentified *Rauhitaka* is the modern town of Rohtak and district to the North-West of Delhi.
48. **Note.** A lamp is meant in which a shining jewel takes the place of the burning wick.

49. It is a compound contains an allusion to a sacrificial feast, at which cups (*Kalasa or Kumbha*) and *durva* grass (*Panicum* Dactylon are used. The latter is also worn in the hair of women at the pious ceremonies like marriage, etc.
50. R.T. Vol. 1. Book IV, pp. 121-123.
51. **Note** *Muktapida* might be interpreted to mean 'he whose diadem is taken off'. Hence 'K', bearing in mind the greatness of this ruler, says' his name ought to have been *Avimuktapida*.
52. R.T. Vol. 1, Section, III. p. 88.
53. In the Chinese language *Durlabha* = *Tu-Lo-pa* used for both the Kings.
54. R.T. Vol.1, Book IV, p. 124.
55. *Ibid.* section III, p. 88.
56. *Ibid.* Vol.1. Book IV, p. 124.
57. *Ibid.*
58. **Note.** *Mandehas* is a class of *Raksasas,* who are supposed to bar the way of the rising sun on Mount Udaya or a class of the darkness called *Brahmins.*
59. P.H.K., p. 47.
60. R.T. Vol.1 Book IV, pp.125-126. **Note.** The *tanners* of Kashmir, the *Batals* or *Watals* have been called the gipsies of Kashmir and are a peculiar people with a *patois* of their own. They may be divided into two classes. Those who abstain from eating carrion and are admitted to the mosque and to the Musalman religion form the first class; those who eat the flash of dead animals and are excluded from the mosque form of second. They are wanderers, and though they sometimes settle in Wattled huts on the outskirts of a village, they soon move on. Their chief occupation is the manufacture of leather. The first class make boots and sandals; the second class make winnowing trays of leather and straw, and do scavenger's work. They also rear poultry and rob hen-roosts.Their women are of fine stature and handsome, and they often drift into the city, where they become singers and dancers. Once a year the Batals or Vatals from all parts of the Valley flock to Lala Bab's shrine near the *Dal Lake*, and many matters affecting the tribe are then settled. (Walter R. Lawrence; *P.G.K.* p.38) And *Dal* is a unit of the caste structure at the level of a single village or a number of adjacent villages (Satadas Dasgupta; *Caste Kingship and Community;* Patna(India); Reprint; 1986 p.11).
61. R.T. Vol. 1. Book IV, p. 126.
62. *Dharma* is one of those Sanskrit words that defy all attempts at an exact rendering in English or any other tongue that word has passed through several vicissitudes the dictionaries set out various meanings of *Dharma* such as "ordinance, usage, duty, right, justice, morality, virtue, religion, good works, function or characteristic". *Dharnia* is also personified as deity, as in the well-known verse '*Adityachandravanilosnalasca* '*Word*' *dharmasca Janati narasya vrttam'* (*Mahabharata, Adi,* Chap. 74.16) or as in Manusmrti VIII. 16 *'Vrsa in bhagavan Dharmah'* (which also

occurs in *Santiparva* 90.75). In the hymns of the *Rigveda* the 'Word' appears to be used either as an adjective or a noun (in the form *dharman,* generally neuter) and occurs at least about sixty times itself (i.e., not preceded by a particle live *'vi'* or some words like *satya*), and about eighteen times in combination with a particle *'vi'* and with the word *'sva'* and *'satya'* fifty-six times therein. It is very easy to say what what was the exact meaning of the word *dharma* in the most ancient period of the Vedic language that is '*Raj*'. The word is clearly derived from root *dhr* or *'ru'* (to uphold, to support, to nourish) (H.D. Vol.1. p.1).

63. R.T. Vol. 1. Book. IV. p. 126.
64. *Ibid.* pp.129-130.
65. *Ibid.* pp. 130.
66. *Ibid.*
67. *Ibid.*
68. **Note:** The name of *Muktapida* or *Lalitadity* is found in the Chinese Annals of the Tiang Dynasty. It is recorded from the *Mu-to-pi* , king of Kashmir during the rule of the Emperor Hiuen-Tsung (713-755 A.D.).
69. R.T. Vol.1 Section III. p. 88.
70. P.H.K. p. 51.
71. *Ibid.*
72. *Ibid.* pp. 51-52.
73. *Ibid.* p. 53.
74. R.T. Vol. 1 Book IV, p. 144.
75. *Ibid.*
76. *Ibid.* p. 145.
77. *Ibid.* p. 147.
78. *Ibid.* p. 155.

**Note.** The word 'Arya' has not been used in the sense of language or race. It has been used in the sense of way. (R.C Jain; M.A.A.S. p. 313). Moleswarth's Marathi Dictionary under the compound of Panch. *The Arya Varna* (or colour) is spoken of as a unity in Rig-veda, 3rd asht 2.5.9 (John Wilson; I.C. p. 117). These were the men who called themselves '*Arya', Aryans* or *Aryanaka*, a word meaning 'Kinsmen' as distinct from the aboriginal tribes already dwelling in the land. And though much concerning them is obscure, not a little is evident, and to-day it is possible to look back across the many centuries that separate us from those nomads and learn what manner of men they were (R.V.V.R. pp. 3-4). "Aryan race", or an "Aryan family", "When the first ancestorsof the Indians, the Persians, the Greek, the Romans, the slaves, the celts and the Germans were living together within the same inclusives, nay, under the same roof "Isaac Taylor; *The Origin of the Aryans*; New Delhi; Reprint, 1989. p.2 Hereafter described as O.A.). But a more common name was *Purana* or "the old' which could only have been imposed upon it after the Greek occupation of the Panjab (*Ibid.p.47*). Arya and Tura", in later historical times "Eran and Turan" the same distinction ever, the same is only a slightly altered form of *Aryan*; so is *Erin* the national name of Ireland; (V.I. p. 62).

79. R.T. Vol. 1. Book IV, p. 153.
80. *Ibid.* p. 157.
81. The list begins with the westernmost, modern Jhelum, the Epic and Vedic *Vitasta*, of which the Greeks made *Hydaspes*; next comes *Asikni*, Greek *Akesinos*, now *Tchendas*; these two unite and for a considerable distance flow on in one stream of double volume and rapid current, as indicated by the picturesque Vedic name *Marudvridha*, "the Wind-Swelled", its later Sanskrit name, *Tchandrabhaga*,hellenised into *Sandrophagus*, it still retains. There is a pretty story of this river having set a term to Macedonian Alexander's Indian campaign; its Greek name meaning "Devourer of Alexander", the conqueror is said to have accepted it as an evil omen and decided on returning (V.I. pp. 107-108)
82. "Sindhu" or 'Sindh' means "River" this is another instance of a country's principal stream being styled by the inhabitants "The River" *par excellence* (V.I., p. 108).
83. R.T Vol. I. Book IV, p. 158.
84. *Ibid.*
85. *Ibid.* Section III. Vol.1 p. 94.
86. *Ibid.* **Note.** *S'ridever,* a village *Candala*, had asked his mother for food, the the words. "I am off to help the king", and had joined after assuring her, as she laughed, that he would kill *jajja* or *jijja*. Arriving at the battle after assuring her, as she moved about in all places asking the soldiers where *jajja* was (p. 164).
87. *Ibid.* p. 174.
88. Term *Karmarajya* we meet again with a *'Word'* universally associated with Indian philosophies that is *Karma+rajya*, it is the word translated as deeds becomes good, lately quoted: 'A man of good deeds becomes good, and a man of evil deeds becomes evil'. *Karma* then, in the sense with which we are here concerned, means, first of all and most simply, deeds. But its deeds with a simple connotation not present in the English word. *Karma* is a singular noun, the plural being *karmani* (deed, deeds); but in the philosophical sense only the singular is used i.e. 'Nam', *'Sabad'*, etc. Srictly, for linguistic conformity, the passage above might be rendered 'A man of good conduct'. (Swami Prabhavananda;. *The Spiritual Heritage* of India; London; 1962., p. 70. Henceforth referred as *S.H.I.).* In Sanskrit *Karma* means 'doing' action and reaction; cause and effect; reaping what was sown before, and harvesting hereafter what we sow now. The study of this science reveals that the doctrines of *Karma* and reincarnation are based on facts; that the experiences of one life condition the succeeding one, although sub-consciously; that the circumstances under which we live now, whether apparatly good or bad, are only the consequences of our own doings in the past; that each life on this or similar planes offers us an opportunity to direct our steps toward our emancipation. A correct apprication of *Karma* would show

us that each condition brought about by a past action is an opportunity (*i*) to learn from experience and to overcome weakness; (*ii*) to learn to be humble even if our *Karma* has placed us in affluent is farther from the truth. (C.W. Sanders; *The Inner Voice;* (Panjab) India; Reprint p. 25. Hereafter explained as I.V.).

89. R.T. Vol.1. Book IV, p. 178.
90. *Ibid.* pp. 179-180.
91. *Ibid.* Section III, p. 95.
92. *Ibid.* p. 180.
93. *Ibid.* pp. 180-181.
94. Those who are away from the 'God' or 'Nam' their mind and heart always flying high, they have no control on them.
95. Term *Suvarnaparsva* is identified by the flass of $A_2$ (*Sunapah*), one is called moon and other is called sun, it is to identify which is the better way of it. It is upto the man.
96. Term *Phalapura* indicated also by the gloss $A_2$. *Parihasapurasamipe* which reflects the meanings that first who have to see the Perfect Master of the *'Nam'*, then you have to surrender and find out the wonders of the world.
97. Term *Locanotsa* has the same means as mentioned above term *suvarnaparsva.*
98. Term *Kalyanadevi* means our soul is black (*Surayam*) but she belongs to the Master. Thus, the occupation of a spirit-distiller was practised by Muhammadan of the state-monopoly, and was in recent times not attended by any special social stigma. It shows they are black both from the heart and mind.
99. Term *Padam* means *'Nam'*, 'He is highest in the world. 'He' always function like the water do in the life since birth.
100. Term *Utpalaka* means '*Nam*' or *'Sabad'* is supreme and 'He' is '*pure*' and *pious*.
101. Term *Kalyana* means 'black' (*surayam*) i.e. *Brahmin*.
102. *Mamma* means man around is black.
103. *Dharma* is a commitment of the soul during the process of the child with the God. In detail see its enlarge meaning mentioned already.
104. **Note.** This dynasty of rulers must have originally been subordinate to the *Kushanas*. As some of the kings of this house names ending with the word Meghas, it is probably that they are *Meghas* (Sic. Meghas) mentioned in the Purana (R.C. Majumdar; *Age of the Imperial Unity*; *Bombay*, Reprint; 1989. p. 175).
105. *R.T.* Vol. 1 Book IV, pp. 182-185.

# 3

# The Rise of the Utpala Dynasty

The subsequent years after the death of Jayapida[1], the dynasty of the *Karkota* race was almost destroyed, whereas the family of *Utpala*[2], obtained the great throne of Kashmir. The *Karkotas*, who had brought peace and prosperity in Kashmir replaced by *Utpala*, king *Avantivarman* received on his head the fresh water of inauguration, which quickly flowed from the mouth of the golden jug, and the sideglance thrown by royal fortune formed his first headdress[3]. Thus, the king, who was full of judgement and wisdom, did not lose his memory when he obtained the throne and saw the regal splendour, but in wardly reflected as follows:

"*Laksmi*, the mistress of kings, who dallies on the back of her elephant, creates violent desires and spoils the high minded that is the *Brahmans*. For whomsoever she has first shown fondness, he is (sure to be) brought in distress by her in the end, just as by a low attachment[4] with the *'Candalas'* or *'Chamar'* or *Dombia*".

Ultimately, minister *Sura* declared that *Avantivarman* was the able ruler for the Kashmir kingdom of *Utpalaka* dynasty.

***Avantivarman* (856-883 A.D.)**

*Avantivarman*, the able son of *Sukhavarman*[5] had obtainted the sovereign power, after uprooting his enemies (*Kantaka*[6]) i.e. mind or *man*, he made, O wonder, the body of the virtuous feel thrilled (*Kantakita*) on account of his (great) deeds. The king and his minister were towards each other both (equally) masters in respect of giving orders, and servents in respect of receiving them[7]. Under the guidance of two able ornamental earnings, the moon and sun seemed to have placed themselves near the king's ears, in order to show (him) the system of government for the newly acquired kingdom of *Kashmir*, as taught by the kings who were their descendants[8] i.e. *'word'* or *'Nam'*. Besides, the two able ornamental earrings, the king had the gold and other (valuables) ground into powder, and distributed this to Brahmans with his own hands as a porridge (*Karambhaka*[9]) means history of the deeds and actions. When one of the Brahmans, instead of saying, "well done, O king" in his joy spoke unceremoniously, "well" done, O Avantin" he received (from the king) many handfull. The wise *Avantivarman*[10] gave away the whole treasure in *alms*, and allowed only the (regal) Cauris and parasol to remain of (that) splendour the royal dignity was difficult to bear for this king when it was new, on account of the trouble (caused) by his numerous relatives who were possessed of excessive wealth. He defeated his revolted brothers and cousins repeatedly in battle, and thus cleared his kingdom from opponents[11]. After this, he had firmly establish his rule which was full of tender affection. His wise minister *Suravarman*[12], the brother from a different mother shared the power of *Yuvaraja*[13]. In the assembly-hall of the minister *S'ura,* the bard *Krtamandara* recited always the following *Arya*[14] (verse), in order to remind (his master) of his resolve: "This is the time for granting benefits, while fortune, fickle by nature, is present[15]".

*Sura* observed the king his chief deity, to please the *master,* he sacrified his religion, life, even his son for the sale of his master. Thus, king became (Siva[16]) *Bhutesvara*, after presenting the sacrificial apparatus the temple-priests had placed on the base of the god's (image), called *Utpalasaka*[17].

***Rise of the Damara Dhanva***

*Damaras*[18] were the feudal landlords class in Kashmir, they were the turbulent created in the society not only in the *Avantivarman's* time, but also observed by Kalhana in his own time even today. They used to live according to the extant text of the chronicle hides the name *Lohara* or *Lahara* district or *Lar*, presently known as *Loharin* in Poonch district. They were treated by *S'ura* like a son. Having ascertained the truth, he ordered off the crowd to keep few attendants and sent messenger after messenger to bring up *Dhanva*. The fierce (*Damara*) came at last along with the foot-soldiers and did not bend his back. As soon as *Dhanva* entered along with armed personnel, at the order of *S'ura,* cut off his head while he was yet alive, in front of (the image of) *Bhairava*. The wise *S'ura*, who had (thus) removed the king's displeasure, went outside after having the body, from which the blood was pouring forth, thrown into the tank close by. When the lord of the earth heard that the minister had decapitated that (*Damara,* whom he loved) as if he were his own son, his anger was appeased, and he felt as it were embarrassed. *S'ura* then inquired after the health of the king, and when the latter replied that he felt no pains, made him rise from his couch and complete the worship. In this way that (minister), who knew always the right thing to do, rendered again and again assistance to the king, without even speaking (to him about it), and at the risk of his own life. Such a king and minister, whose (relations) were never disfigured by the blemish of mutual hatred, have not otherwise been seen or heard of. Thus, for ten years in the reign of *Avantivarman* the killing of all living creatures was prohibited, just as (it was in that) of the illustrations *Meghavahana*[19]. At that time the shadfish (*pathina*) left the cold water without fear, and coming to the river-banks sunned their backs in the autumn sun. Henceforth, *Avantivarman,* the illustrious *Bhatta Kallata* and other holy men (*Siddhas*) descended to the earth for the benefit of the people[20]. This event has been related with the purification of world, then there is an extreme of the Iron Age (*Kalyug*).

***Role of Suyya as a Woman after the Purification of World Under Avantivarman***

*Avantivarman's* as a heavenly king, his first and foremost task was to look for more arable land, as its shortage had deep effects upon the economy of the country. No doubt, Kashmir was ravaged by the floods of the *Mahapadma* lake whose waters were formerly drained out through suitable channels during the days of king *Lalitaditya*[21]. Thus, under the feeble king who succeeded after the death of *Jayapida*, the country was again overtaken by the disastrous floods[22]. In the meantime, there was no organised force or an equipped army to aspire for territorial gains. Amid such conditions, *Avantivarman* first rate task was to gain the confidence of the people through an organised machinery of government which could restore normalcy in the Kashmir and look after the interest of the masses *'word'* or *'Nam'* a task that had been neglected for many decades by the later successors of the '*Karkota Dynasty*'. Kalhana devotes some (10) verses to sum up his attitude towards his subjects[23]. With the merits of *Avantivarman*, the Lord of Food (*annapati*) descended on earth, in the person of the illustrious *Suyya,* to give fresh life to the people. The origin of this wise man was not known, but his deeds made the world wonder and was the commencement of the fourth period (*Yuga*). Suddenly a *'Candala'* woman known by the name of *Suyya* awoke up from the dust heap lying on the road along with a fresh earthern vessel fitted with a cover. She removed the cover and found a baby lying in it, having the eyes like lotus leaves and was sucking his own fingers. "Some unfortunate mother must have emposed this lovely (boy)". Thus, she thought in her mind, and then from tenderness her breasts, she feeded the boy. Child remained keep in the house of a *Sudra-nurse* and brought up by her. With the affection of *Suyya*, he became intelligent in letters and spirit, endeared with virtuous and sense of behaviour among peoples. People complaining in their conversation about the flood calamity, he said: "I have got the knowledge (for preventing it). But what can I do without means?" When the king heard through his spies that he was saying these words persistently, as if he were deranged in mind, he was surprised.

The king had to then brought up and questioned him. He calmly replied in the royal presence: "I have got the knowledge", etc. There upon, 'the lord of the earth even his courtiers declared him (Suyya) crazy. He was anxious to test (that) knowledge, and was placed his own treasures at his disposal[24].

**Period of Internal Consolidation**

Study reveals that the reign of *Avantivarinam* had the internal troubles during his preceding. He consolidated his position which must have greatly suffered, economically as well as politically[25]. His royal supporter Suyya took many pots (full) of money (*dinnara*) from the treasury, embarking on a boat, proceeded in haste to *Madavarajya*[26]. After dropping there a pots (full) of money, at a village called *Nandaka*, which was submerged in the flood, he hurriedly turned back. In the same time councillors said; "that (*Suyya*) is surely only a madman," the king when heard this account, became interesting in watching the end of these (proceeding). On reaching in *Karmarajya* the locality called *Yaksadara*, he threw with both hands money (*dinnara*) in the water. The famine-stricken villagers then searched for the money (*dinnara*), dragged out the rocks[27] and silt from the river. In this way, the bed of *Vitasta* river was cleared and a dam was constructed for storing its waters for agriculture purposes[28] within the seven days by *Suyya* for the time being and after protecting the battom of the river dam was removed. Like the river, with its numerous great channels branching off from the original channel, appeared like a black female serpent, which has numerous hoods resting on one body. Thus the two great rivers system, the *Sindhu* and *Vitasta,* which formely met near the (temple of Vishnu) *Vainyasvamin,* flowing to the left and right of *Trigami* (respectively), have to this day in the vicinity of the city (S'rinagara) their confluence which *Suyya* first planned, and which will last to the end of the world[29].

The collective waters of the river were allowed to different villages for irrigational purposes through minor streams from the *Mahapadama*[30] lake and these were also rendered safe through embankments constructed at suitable distances. Hence, all kinds mof food-stuffs were also provided to the people, known by the name of *Kundala*[31]. The community known as *Nisadas*[32] to this day had certain marks of the boat ropes, embanked near the river beds for seven *Yojanas* along the *Vitasta*. Thus, *Suyya* due to his great efforts, the construction work was completed, and the price of a *Khari* of rice was two hundred *Dinnaras,* and the land of *Kashmir* henceforth *'Word'* O wonder; *'Suyya'* the *Khari* of rice came to brought for thirty-six *Dinnaras*[33]. *Suyya* indeed deserves the high praises[34] for accumulated religious merits, (achieved in a single birth that holy work which Vishnu accomplished in four incarnations, viz; the raising of the earth from the water, the granting of it to worthy Brahmans, the construction of stone dykes in the water, and the subjugation of the (Naga) *Kaliya* [35].

***Death of Avantivarman***

King *Avanti* (*Varman*) ruled the earth like *Mandhatr*, and it appears that again a new era *Krta Yuga* was started. At the point of death, he disclosed to *S'ura* with folded hands his attachment with Vishnu which he had hidden for a long time. Thus, in this way the mighty ruler of the earth died with a cheerful mind in the year (of the *Lankika era* three thousand nine hundred and ) fifty-nine (A.D. 883) on the third day of the bright half of Asadha[36]. After the death of *Avantivarman*, there were numerious descendants of *Utpala* Dynasty, but *Ratnavardhana*, the Chamberlain, secured by his exertions the kingdom of Kashmir and *S'amkaravarman* became the ruler.

***S'amkaravarman* (883-902 A.D.)**

The death of Avantivarman, like that of many rulers of Kashmir was took place. After his death, *S'amkaravarman,* the son of *Avantivarman* was ascended the throne, *Karnapa*, a councillor of *Vinnapa,* placed a son of *S'uravarman* called *Sukhavarman* in power as Yuvaraja. The war was started between the king and the Yuvaraja; *S'ivasakthi* and other valiant men, who lost their lives in the cause of their master. It was an opportunity of getting their high character test. In this way, *S'amkaravarman* defeated the Yuvaraja and performed an effective benediction (*omkara*) (at the commencement) of his own conquests. Fighting numerous battles with *Samaravarman* and other (*rivals*), this sovereign superseded Fame, though she was to him (like) a fond wife, by the Glory which he gained (through these conquests, as his second wife). Then the victorious and illustrious king, after having defeated his kinsmen and won over Fortune, put forth great efforts to conquer the world. Though the country (of Kashmir) had through the action of time become reduced in population and wealth, he had nine lakhs of foot-soldiers when he marched forth from the 'Gate' (*dvara*[37]). He was also surrounded in a moment along with the troops in *Hariganga*. While he, who had as the advance-guard of his army nine lakhs of foot-soldiers, three hundred elephants and a lakh of horsemen, was wholly bent on the conquest of *Gurjara*[38]. The ruler of *Gurjara* gave up to him humbly the *Takka*-land, preserving (hereby) his own country, as (if he had saved) his own body (at the sacrifice) of a finger. King *Bhoja*[39] was seized and supported by *Alakhana*, the illustrious *Lalliya S'ahi 'Word',* who placed between the rulers of the *Darads*[40] and *Turuskas*[41] as between a lion and a boar, resembled *Aryavarta*[42] (as it lies) between the *Himalaya* and *Vindhya* (*mountains*); in whose town of *Udabhanda* (other) kings found safety, just as the mountains in the ocean when threatened by the danger of having their wings cut (by *Indra*); whose mighty glory (outshine) the kings in the North, just as the sun-disc (out-shines) the stars in heaven. *Alakhana's* he was not received into service by *S'amkaravarman,* who desired to remove him from his sovereign position. He was attached or married *Sugandha*, the daughter of the illustrious *Svamiraja*[43], the ruler of the norther region, just as the moon (is) to the full-mood day. The matrimonial alliance must have resembled with *Indra* and beautiful temples of Siva were constructed at *Samkaragaurisa* and *Sugandhesa* and Brahman *Nayak*[44] was placed as a incharge to the temples, who was versed in the four vedas, and was like a fimilar dewelling-place to *Sarasvati*[45]. Thus, *Samkaravarman* had possessed little importance, whatever was of value at *Parihasapura*, carried off in order to raise the fame of his own city and it is still to be found at *Pattana*[46], *Megha* or Julah are the weaving of (woollen) clothes, purchase and sale of cattle, and the like[47].

***Administration of S'amkaravarman***

The advent of *Samkaravarman* at the helm of affairs in the Valley heralded a new era in the history of Kashmir. His reign not only brought relief of the suffering masses of Kashmir, but also restored, to a great extent, the glory of the *Karkotas* as we have noticed. He had possessed such qualities of head and heart for which he can be ranked as one of the worthy ruler of Kashmir. He made cordial relations with minister *Ratnavardhana*[48], who had secured the crown for the king to built a glorious (temple of) *Sadasiva*, called *Ratnavardhanesa*. In the course of time, then *Samkarvarman's* mind fully absorbed by excessive habits of avarice, and he became an expert in the (art of ) oppressing his subjects. He lost most of treasure by the distractions to which he abandoned himself, he carried off again and again by skillfully designed exactions, whatever the gods and other owned. He also established two new (revenue) offices called *Attapatibhaga* ('the share of the lord of the market) and *Grhakrtya* ('domestic affairs). It appears that the king resumed villages which had been held as *Agraharas* by temples, on the understanding a fixed amount was reduced against a compensatory assignment (*pratikara*) and (then) cultivated the land himself as (if he were) an agriculturist. He reduced the weight in the scales by one-third on the basic needs and gave more to the temple-corporation (parsad[49]). Thus, he introduced thirteen department for the running of his administration, village clerk (*gramakayastha*) present *patwari* for the contribution of monthly levy either the villagers into poverty were responsible. Weights and measures departments were also established to fines the illegal transaction, the office is called *Grhakrtya*. Besides these, he introduced speical five offices of secretaries (*divira)*[50], and the is known as treasurer (*ganjavara*) *S'akaca ('Word' or 'Nam'*), who was (also) called *Lavata*[51].

Hence, due to the foolish act, ruler accepted his residence in hell, in order to benefit his sinful acts to the future functionaries.

***Demonstration of Gopalavarman***

The king's son, *Gopalavarman* by name addressed the people on the sorrow and suffering moment in the following words:

"O father, the boon, which you once offered to me, has remained unclaimed. this I now ask from you who are true to your engagements."

"On the one hand, there are the endless misfortunes of the subjects, such a plagues and famines, and on the other hand, again, nothing but the avarice of the king."

When the king had heard these words of the prince, which were inspired by benevolence, he slowly spoke as follows, while a smile lit up his under lip:

"This speech of yours, which charms by its human sentiments, and is in keeping with your (youthful) looks, brings now back to my mind the feelings of a bygone time."

"He replied to them: Since I have attained the throne from common rank, I know the hardships (experienced) by attendants at different times during their services."

But fearing was lurking in the mind of the king from the distinguished persons, peots like *Bhallata*[52] and the brave *Maravahara*[53] king of *Darvabhisara*. A son of minister *Sukharaja's* sister, whom he had made 'Lord of the Gate' (*dvaradhipa*[54]), met his death through negligence at a place called *Viranaka*[55]. King angered and set out an expedition himself and after destroying *Viranaka*, proceeded full of lust (for conquest) towards the Northern region (*Uttarapatha*). He had already conquered numberous territories along with the Indus[56] banks (*Sindhu*), and had received the homage of (their) terror-stricken kings. As he passed through *Urasa*, there arose suddenly a conflict with the inhabitants of *Urasa*, on account of the quartering of his troops[57].

**Death of Samkaravarman (902 A.D.)**

Towards the closing year of his reign, *Samkaravarman*, a *Svapaka*[58], who had posted himself on a hill discharged with a swift-flying arrow, and ordered his ministers to lead and save the army in a litter

(*Karniratha*[59]). In the sametime the arrow was pulled out, *Samkaravarman* died at the age of seventy-seven, alongwith his three queens and two servants and *Gopalavarman* his minor son became the ruler of Kashmir.

***Gopalavarman* (902-904 A.D.)**

After the death of *Samkaravarman*, his son *Gopalavarman* was placed under the guardianship of his mother *Sugandha* as a ruler of Kashmir though living among favourites of *low character* and still in his boyhood, he did not acquire bad habits. The king's mother, the widow of *Samkaravarman* was fell in love with the minister named *Prabhakaradeva*[60] and got the rank of three crscents on a diadem[61]. This paramour of the king's mother, full of arrogance on account of the victory, the wicked *Ramadeva*, which his misdeed became known, was terrified by fear of the king's punishment, and committed suicide. *Gopalavarman's* brother *Samkata*, who had been picked up from the highway, obtained the throne. He died after ten days[62].

***Sugandha (904-906 A.D.)***

Since there was none in direct lineage of Samakaravarman descended, *Sugandha* herself assumed the royal power of Kashmir after the death of *Samata*. She constructed a town known as *Gopalapura* near Rajapuri (Rajouri), *Gopalamatha* and *Gopalakesava* temple of Vishnu were also built there after her own name for the increase of religion. *Nanda*, the wife of *Gopalavarman*, who was descended from an unblemished family founded the *Nandamatha* and *Nandakesava*[63] temple to continued the lineage of the *Utpala* Dynasty. But the child of *Nanda* queen was died after the birth and the kingdom was transferred to *Sugandha's* relatives.

***Rise of the Tantrins Power***

*Tantrins*[64] were a strong organisation formed in Hindu times a military caste. The period of internal troubles between the accession of *Partha* and after the death of *Samakaravarman* led upto the period of *Cakravarman*. It seems at that time the power of *Cakravarman*. It seems at that time the power of *tantrins* was at the height, *Sugandha* herself ruled for two years, relying on the *Ekangaa* and through the good-will of the *Tantrins*. She assembled the ministers, feudal chiefs, *Tantrins* and *Ekangas*[65] in council, in order to invest some fit person with the regal power. Her wish was the place on throne the grandson of *Suravarman* known as *Nirjitavarman*. The son of *Sukhavarman*. But some ministers were not in the favour of *Pangu* ('the lame one'), because had not the qualities like the complete man. Therefore, the group of the Tantrin foot-soldiers, raised the objection and made the *Nirjitavarman's* son that is *Partha,* the king of Kashmir. At that time he was of ten years old[66].

**Partha (906-921 A.D.)**

*Partha* was proposed by the *Tantrins* as a nominal head of the state, they had the gameplan to oust the *Sugandha* and let down the prestige of *Prabhakaradeva.* Due to the sovereign power, she deprived herself in the royal palace, but ther rolling tears were demonstrating the love of her *'Master'*. At the age of eighty-nine in 914 A.D. the *Ekanga* troops went forth and brought back *Sugandha* from *Huskapura*, where she had been staying. As soon as *Tantrins* heard the approach of the queen on the issue of *Partha*, a battle was fought. *Tantrins* defeated the *Ekangas*, and queen was captured at the age of ninety and imprisoned in the *Vihara* strange[67].

*Pangu* (*Nirjitavarman*), acted as the guardian of the child king to look after the oppressed people along with his ministers. He also conquered the *Kanyakubja*[68] and *Tantrins* became wealthy. But in the year 917-918 A.D., a famine was struck, number of people were destroyed, as it was difficult to obtain food while the *Khari* sold for a thousand (*Dinnaras*). Thus demons of kings led to destruction, *Partha* gained the power for himself by outing his father, sometimes father ousted him through the intrigues of Tantrins, and *Sugandhaditya* satisfied the wives of *Pangu* by sexual intercourse just as a stallion troop of mares. The lovely Queen *Mrgavati,* whom *Meruvardhana's* sons had given in marriage to *Pangu* in order[69] to establishment of the cheerful rule, their ministers offered as a fee for the pleasures of love along with rich presents. In 921 A.D., at the age of ninety seven, *Partha* was overthrone by his father with the support of *Tantrins*, *Nirjitavarman* then was appointed on the throne. He ruled only two yeas from 921 A.D. to 923 A.D.

**Nirjitavarman (921-923 A.D.)**

*Nirjitavarman* was appointed as a ruler of Kashmir after the dethrone of *Partha.* His selection as a ruler was based without the merits of his previous births. He was died at the age of ninety-Eight (923-A.D.) after two years rule. After his death, his child-son named *Cakravarman* was placed on throne.

**Cakravarman (923-933 A.D.)**

*Cakravarman* as a child king ruled under the guardianship of his mother *Bappatadevi* and sometimes under the grandmother *Ksillika*. He ruled ten years from 923 A.D. to 933 A.D. Since youth had the wicked character like the Naga rulers, then Tantrins overthrew the *Cakravarman* in 933 A.D. after the rule of Nine years and made *S'uravarman* (1)[70], the ruler of *Kashmir*.

**Suravarman I (933-934 A.D.)**

*Suravarman I,* the son of *Pangu* from queen *Margavati,* became the king of Kashmir. His uncles and ministers, who cherished no affection and were solely looking to their advantage, but *Suravarman* did not pay special attention towards them, along with the *tantrins*, they overthrew the king even the king had good moral character[71]. Thus, they again restored the power of *Parth* as a king for their own benefit. *Parth* ruled only one year from 934 A.D. to 935 A.D. The courtesan *Sambavati,* a mistress of *Partha*, who was known for the skilful plotting by which she conciliated the bands of *Tantrins*, founded the *Shiva* Shrine known as *Sambesvara.* Again, *Cakaravarman's* rule was established for one year.

***Cakaravarman (934-935 A.D.)***

*Cakaravarman* restored his power with the help of the sons of *Meruvardhana.* They had made a commitment of the profit with his close relatives and friends for the benefit of the profit. But *Cakaravarman* could not pay the special attention towards their required demand. The result was that he was ousted from the Kingship and *S'ambhuvardhana* was declared the next ruler of Kashmir with the negotiation of *Tantrins*.

***Sambhuvardhana (935-936 A.D.)***

With the negotiation of *Tantrins Sambhuvardhana* gained the power, on the other hand, the loser of the throne *Cakaravarman* went to the house of the Damara *Samgrama,* who lived at *S'ridhakka*[72] . Damara recognised the king by his beautiful appearance and making obeisance with folded hands and led him in haste to his own seat. There upon king and Damara placed their foot on a speepskin sprinkled with blood, and mutually took an oath by sacred libation (*Kosa*) sword in hand; In the morning, *Cakaravarman*, along with the fierce Damaras set forth to reach the capital. Simultaneously, the Tantrin foot-soldiers marched out for battle with *S'amkaravardhana* at their head[73].

**Cakravarman's Victory Over the Tantrins (936 A.D.)**

As soon as the terrible battle was commenced outside at *Padmapura, Cakravarman* hastened to display his personal valour which he had hidden in the mind and soul. On the spot, the leader of the *Tantrins* army was killed and their army was dispersed in a hundred directions, resembling a ship tossed about on the ocean by the fierce onslaught of a strom. As *Cakravarman* rushed about in battle, the numerous fringes of his head-band (*Virapatta*) *appeared* like the bushy mane of a lion laid down the Tantrins on the ground to rest, as it was from the burnt of the battle in the shade of the vultures' wings. The valiant *S'amkaravardhana* adorned the bed of heroes in the battle field along with the followers of noble descent and good qualities. In this manner, the evil-lived *Tantrins* had the sadistic ideas, princes reduced already their due respect. Making ever new demands, they had wantonly for the sake of their living and exposed them to shame in playful tricks. *Cakravarman* who already felt deep sense of sorrow, destroyed them in a movement, as if he had been a great snake, with the hot poison of his secret hatred[74]. *Cakravarman* for the third time again became the ruler of Kashmir.

***Third Appointment of Cakravarman as a King (936-937 A.D.)***

On the third time, the coronation of *Cakravarman* in the glory of his victory celebrated by the feudal chiefs, ministers, and *Ekangas* and met with him. In a while, he stepped towards the throne elated with victory, *Bhubhata* brought up *S'ambhuvardhana* from some place in fetters, killed like a *Candala* before the king. As king *Cakravarman* got his kingdom by killing his enemies, he thought himself a god, and thus committed acts which were devoid of judgement.

***Ranga and Domba Received at Court***

*Domba* is a famous singer called *Ranga*[75], who came from heaven. At that time doorkeepers seated in proper order along with the ministers and an open space was made before the king. Then the *Domba*-singer stepped forward, followed by his band which was resplendent with necklaces golden bracelets on arms and hands, and other ornaments of the body. His sweet-eyed daughters, *Hamsi* and *Nagalata* along with the *Domba* girls won the heart of the king by their singing and acting which are described in conventional Kavya fashion. The *low caste* singers took *Hamsi* and *Nagalata* into his seraglio. *Domba* also led the ministers and secured important officies like the *Aksapatak*[76] and others[77], who were clever, they managed the king's affairs.

**Dombas in Power**

An order coming from the mouth of *Dombas* (i.e. *Svapakas*), who were proud of their relationship with the King *Cakravarman*, was respected by everybody as a royal order which has to be obeyed. At one times she (*Domba*) went to the festival of *Tiladvadas*[78] celebrating at (Vishnu temple) *Ranasvamin*, Damaras at that times declared among the chiefs did not follow her. King *Cakravarman* had already granted the village of *Helu* to *Ranga* as an *Agrahara*, and the recorder of official documents (*pattopadhyaya*) did not excute the document relating to the grant (*danapattaka)*, then *Ranga* proceeded to the *Aksapatala* (office) and thus addressed that official in anger: "you son of a slave, why do you not write: *'Rangassa Helu dinna'* ('*Helu* to be granted to *Ranga*') that is 'Nam' or 'Sabad' thereupon the wicked king inquired as to the expiation of the sin of having had intercourse with that outcast woman, his parasites made him perform ridiculous penances (*prayascitta*). "As snow dissolves snow, so too one sin the other." Thus the parasites told that king of vile character wishing to remove the sin of intercourse with an impure person by intercourse with a pure one, he dishonured the wife of a Brahman, who was engaged in a monthly fast. Bad as he was, he founded the *Cakramatha* for the residence of *Pasupata*[79] ascetics. It was half -built when he died, and was completed by his wife. Hence, *Cakravarman* wad dethroned, the wicked son of *Partha*, called *Unmattavanti* became the ruler of Kashmir in 937 A.D.

**Unmattavanti (937-939 A.D.)**

*Unmattavanti* was the son of wicked *Partha*, lover of the *S'vapaki* became the ruler of Kashmir in 937 A.D. after dethroning of *Cakravarman*. This evil ruler, resembling a demon, was to consume his paternal family, just as the kind of fire called *Aurva* (consumer) the water this chief ministers were those who used to play the music with their noses, shoulders, etc and banged their skills with '*Nam*' or '*Sabad*'. In the character of strolling singers his ministers amused without shame, who were destined to became rulers in the course of time[80].

***Rise of Parvagupta***

Since the *Tantrins*, the king of Kashmir have seen number of problems and were always bent on securing the throne. They were like worms of dirty place. Enlightened *Parvagupta*, who danced in the royal assembly with his loin-cloth taken off. He disclosed his secret desire of the throne with his five chief ministers, *Bhubhatta, S'arvata, Choja, Kumuda,* and *Amrtakara,* took the oath by sacred libation, and entered a league with *Parvagupta*. He raised (an image of) the goddess *S'ri* just (in the form) as she had appeared to him in the lake, under the appellation of *Rakkajaydevi*. In this way, king destroyed his own family at the instigation of the cunning *Parvagupta*, who wised to seize the kingdom when it had been cleared of rivals[81].

***Murdered of Partha***

*Partha* spoiled all his property and used to live with his wives in the illustrious *Jayendravihara*, where the *S'ramans* gave him food. At that time the brothers of *Samkaravarman* were yet children and lived there[82] in confine area. They knew the activities of *Partha*, on a certain night, ministers, chiefs, *Tantrins*, officials and troops obeying his orders, surrounded *Partha*. Like *Candalas*, they killed him without arms. Thus, at that time *Pravagupta* had admitted again by the king, after having been in disfavoured. In order to gratify him, he urged to his son named *Devagupta*, to punish the wicked Kayastha[83]. The parricide miscrean taking, when his descent was near to hell. He placed on the throne a young child called *S'uravarman* the servant girls of his seraglio. He also had procured certain disfavoured chiefs, councillors, *Ekangas* and *Tantrins*. He was also in terror by *Kamalavardhana*, the commander-in-chief (*Kampanadhipati*), who stood in *Madavarajya*[84] and uprooted the Damaras with efficient manners and died in 939 A.D.

**S'uravarman II (939 A.D.)**

*Suravarman* II was a child king, the son of the parricide became the ruler of Kashmir. He was enlightened with the 'truth' he proceeded to sun-god called *Jayasvamin*. The youthful king's glory shone forth like a young maid, her charming braids represented as swords and her bright teeths demonstrating dazzling umberella and chowries. In the meantime, *Kamalavardhana,* informed by the report of the spies who had came in haste, reached in the vicinity of the feudal chiefs[85], *Utpala* dynasty then had come to end. In the meanwhile, Brahmans had to dressed up with coarse woollen cloaks assembled near the *Gokula* a sacred place called *parisadya* for the searching out an appropriate person for the throne. *Kamalavardhana* at this juncture felt pained when he saw the regal power in the hands of others. His wife had to approach the courtesan and begged the throne for her supposition son. In the village of *Pisacakapura*, *Viradeva* by name had a son called *Kamadeva* having good qualities of behaviour and knowledge of the *Aksaras*, became a boy's teacher in the house of *Meruvardhana*. In the course of time treasurer (*ganjadhikarin*), his son *Prabhakasadeva* obtained gradually the position of treasurer under king *S'amkaravarman*; he was also the paramour of *Sugandha*. His son, the learned *Yasaskara*, whether on account of the enmity between *Laksmi* (Fortune) and *Sarasvati* (learning), or through the calamities of the country, went abroad with a friend called *Phalgunaka*. Cheered by auspicious dreams and the benedictions of the *Pithadevi*, *Yasaskara* at that time had returned to his native land[86]. Then the Brahmans came quickly to *Yasaskara*, who had the full strength to maintian the earth and requested him to obtain the throne of Kashmir. Thus, fifth *Taranga*[87] of the *Rajatarangini* was completed in 939 A.D and the sixth was started with rule of *Yasaskara*

From the aforesaid pages, it makes clear from the study that the rule of the *Utpala* dynasty was also efficient like the ruler of *Karkota dynasty*. No doubt, there were certain natural problems during the rule of *Avantivarman* and the other rulers. Sometimes Damaras rose the rebellion against the rulers, but they were tackled with efficient manners; according to the rule of the law of nature. Moreover, there were certain political upheavals during the weak successors of the *Utpala Dynasty*, but partially it was tackled with the problem on the bases of the merits and good qualities of the man. Keeping in view the merits and qualities of the persons, the affairs of the states were transferred to the *Viradeva* Dynasty.

## NOTES AND REFERENCES

1. P.H.K. p. 111.
2. **Note**. *Utpala* is a Sanskrit word means obey the rule of the 'law of Nature' that is *'Nam'*. It has the six system of Hindu thought, that is, the *Vaisesika* of *Kanada, the Nyaya of Gotama*, the *Samkhy* of *Kapila,* the *yoga* of Patanjali, the *mimamsa* (also called *Purva Mimansa*) *of Jaimini* and *Vedants* (also called *Uttara mimamsa*) of *Vyasa*. The six systems are regarded as *astika,* or orthodox, because, unlike Buddhism or Jainism, they accept the authority of the Vedas on all questions pertaining to the nature of the universe (*T.S.H.I.* pp.199-200). Accoding to their tradition, *Vyasa* divided in four parts, that is, *Rigveda, Yajurveda, Samaveda* and *Atharvaveda*. *Vyasa* had for *Sishya*, i.e. puplis. He taught a separate *Veda* to each of them, and made him carry it in his memory. (*Alberuni's India;* p.127). Ved Vyas also wrote commentaries on the four Vedas; viz. *Rig veda, Yajur Veda, Atharwan Veda, Siam Veda:* the three former works are on philosophy and theology, while the latter (the only one now extant) is a history, and is called *Mahabharat* , of which 24,000 slogs out of 1000, 000 are occupied in relating the history of the wars of the *Pandus*. The Hindus, like the Chinese and Tartars, deny the flood of Noah (John Briggs. Tr. of Persian work of Mahomed Kasima, Ferishta; *Rise of the Mahomedan Power in India*; Vol.1. First Edition London 1829, Calcutta reprinted 1966 P.LI, L II.. Hereafter referred as R.M P.1.
3. *R.T.* Vol.1 Book IV. p. 185.
4. *Ibid.* Book V. p. 186.
5. *R.T.* Vol.1 Book. IV, p. 185.
6. *Ibid.* Book V. p. 186.
7. *Ibid.*
8. *Ibid.* Book IV p. 185.
9. *Ibid.* Book V. p. 187.
10. It is clearly explained that number of temples and endowments, the foundation of which by the *Chamar* or *Domba* or *Dooma* king laid down at the town of *Avantipura,* the present *Vantpor,* still preserving the kings name, and the great temples, he constructed there (R.T. Section IV. p. 97).
11. R.T. vol.1. Book V. p. 188.
12. **Notes**. He wise minister of *Avantivaraman* Known as *Suravarman*, during his rule he laid down the foundation of the present day town known as *H'urapura*, the ancient *Surapura,* the *Tirtha* of *Bhutesvara,*in the district of Lohara. (R.T. Vol. 1 section IV; p. 97). *Pancahasta* Matha was also accomplished, full of (spiritual) greatness and devoted to pious works of the i.e. *'Chamar'*. Another illustrious *Prabhakaravarman*, the king's minister constructed the Vishnu temple called *Prabhakarasvamin*. The scholars known as *Muktakana, Sivasvamin*, the poet *Anandavardhana* during the reign of *Avantivarman*.
13. *R.T.* Vol.1 Book V. p. 188.

14. Thus, the Arya verse is divided into three, or more commonly into four *pada*. Sometimes they add a fifth *pada* in the middle of the verse. The *padas* have no rhyme, but there is a king of metre, in which the 1 and 2 *padas* end with the same consonant or syllable as if rhyming on it, and also the *padas* 3 and 4 end with the same consonant or syllably this is called Arya (*Alberuni's India*; Vol.1. p. 143).
15. R.T. Vol.1. Book V. pp. 189-190.
16. **Note.** *Siva* means 'goodness', how the *Parvati* got the 'goodness' or *Siva* because she obtained the 'light of Father' i.e. called Parvati which is composed of three words that is Pa+ra+vati, Pa means "Father', 'r' means 'way' or 'thought' and '*vati*' means 'light'. Therefore, without 'Nam' there is no 'light', 'no goodness'. This is a basic root of the world to see the *'Reality'.*
17. R.T.Vol.1 Book V. p. 193.
18. Term *Damaras* put together of four words Da+ma+ra+s 'Da' stands for destroyers or injurious '*ma*' stands for living *man, 'ra'* means 'way' or 'thought', and 's' stands for '*sant*' or 'sainthood'. It appeas that 'Damaras' they used to believe on the theory of self mind or *man,* therefore, they revolted the theory of *sainthood* that is called the *'Pure-thought'*. And word feudal means having to do with feudalism originated from the latin word *'feodum'* or fee, which has to pay by the Brahmans. It is the challenge of the God to the Brahman without obtaining the *Chamar*, no one can attain the peace and prosperity. Therefore, it is difficult to believe that the great poets, philosophers and devoted worshippers who produced the *Bhagavat Gita* and laid the utmost stress on the virtues of *dama* (self-restraint), *tyaga* (renunciation) and *apramada* (Vigilance) in an inscription of the second century B.C., could have been aware of the dark deeds that are attributed to their lord and his closest associates in battle-songs that find a place in the extant epic (A.H.I. p. 95). Thus, the Self is not to be known through study of the scriptures, nor through subtlety of the infellect, nor through much learning. But by him who longs for him is he known. Verily into him does the Self reveal his true being. Earth, and earth alone, then, is the scene of man's spiritual struggle. Realizing everywhere the all-prevading Brahman, deeply absorbed in contemplation of his being, they enter him, the Self of all when their bodies fall away from them at death, they attain to liberation, (S.H. p.71) Hence, it is difficult to believe on the self made stories as *burtse* (*Eurotia*) is a low growing bush which gives a fair fuel, and in the high valleys the *dama*, a kind of furze, is burnt.(*P.G.K.*/p. 95).
19. R.T. Vol.1 Book V. pp. 194-195. **Note**. Although the new dynasty may have been founded by lieutenant of the *Kushanas* named *Megha* or *Magha*, the earliest ruler known from epigraphic sources seems to be Raja *Vasisthiputra* Bhimasena of a Bhital seal. (A.I.U. p. 176).
20. *Ibid.* p. 195.
21. *P.H.K.* p. 112.
22. *R.T.* Vol. 1 Book V. p. 195.
23. *P.H.K.* p. 112.

24. *R.T;* Vol.1. Book V. pp. 196-197.
25. *Ibid.* Vol.1 section IV. p. 97.
26. Presently, it is known as *Maraz.*
27. R.T. Vol. 1. Book V. pp. 197-198.
28. P.H.K. p. 113.
29. R.T. Vol. 1. Book V. p. 198.
30. **Note.** Somewhat earlier and more interesting reference is furnished by the annals of the T'ang dynasty of China. According to Hsuan Tsang the *Mo-ho-to-mo-loung* or *Mahapadma* lake (present Wular lake), *Po-lo-ou-lo-po-lo,* Pravarapura, the old and official name of Srinagar, and *Mi-na-si-to,* the vitasta river, which flowed on the west of the capital (R.C. Kak, *Ancient Monuments of Kashmir*; New Delhi; Reprinted; 1971; p.7).
31. **Note.** Many of the villages situated in the marshy tract to the Srinagar of the Wular lake are enclosed by artificial embankments, and correspond in the shape of the above description. Two the villages, *Utsakundala* and *Marakemala* which are situated close together near the left bank of the *Vitasta*, at about 74°-40′ longtitude 34°-15′ latitutde, have preserved even to this day referred designation *Kundala.* The word *Kundala* is derived from Sanskrit word *Kundala* in English called 'ring'.
32. The term *Nisada* is generally applied to wild aboriginal tribes living by hunting and fishing in Kashmir boatmen are called *Hanzi.* They claim a Vaisya origin, and even now when blaming one of the crew for his bad paddling the captain will say: 'you are a *Sudra'.* They always claim Noah as their ancestor; but some accounts point to a gipsy origin. The father of the family is an autocrat, and his discipline on board is often of a violent character. There are many sections of the tribe. First rank the half-amphibious paddlers of the Dal Lake (*Demb Hanz*). Next in status come the men of the large barges known as *bahats* and *war*, in which cargoes of 800 maunds of grain or wood are carried. Then the *Dunga Hans*, who paddle the passenger boats, not a respectable class, or they prostitute their females; next the *Gad Hanz,* who net fish, and are said to surpass even the *Dunga Hanz* in their power of invective; and last the *Hak Hanz*, who collect drift wood in the rivers. The *Hanz* or *Hanjis* are a hardy muscular people, but are quarrelsome and mendacious. Half the stories to the discredit of Kashmir and its inhabitants are due to the fertile imagination of the *Hanji*, who after the manner of the Irish car-driver tells travellers quaint scandals of the Valley and its rulers. The *Hanji* ashore is a great rascal, and European travellers would be wise to leave him in his boad. The chief *Kram* names of the Hanjis are *Dangar,* Dar, and Mal. (*P.G.K.* pp. 38-39). They occupy to this day a very low position in the social scale, ranking considerably below the ordinary cultivator. Fishing plays a great part in the *Han's* livelihood (Walter R. Lawarance; *The Kashmir of Valley;* London; 1895; p. 313. Hencforth referred as *V.K.*). In Bengal, *Namesudras* are not an occupations as cultivators, fishermen, boatmen, carpenters, etc. They are regarded as *"untouchables"* by the higher

castes of Bengal, and only a generation ago were known by the name of *Candala*. No doubt, they are a somewhat backward community with a rather low level of culture, who cannot point to any intellectual eminence or historical distinction past. But they are justified in rejecting the name of *Candala* for their community as the *Candalas* of the *Dharmsastras* were men who lived outside the pale of civilization and settled life, and found maintence from the most despised occupations. Though the word *Sudra* was aften loosely used by ancient writers to denote all those who did not belong to the three higher *varans*, there was always a distinction between those who had come or were coming under Aryan influence, the *Sudra* proper, and these, sometimes called the fifth *varna*, who were too savage and unclean to be amendable to Aryan culture and practices, the *Nisadas*, *Candalas, Pukkasas*, etc. of the *Dharmsastras*. Among the *Sudras*, too, there soon developed a distinction between those who followed the ideals and imitated the practices of the higher castes, the "good" *Sudras*, and those whose touch made impure the water of a Brahman would not act as priest. The promotion of the *Namasudras* from the status of *Candalas* of that of second class *sudras* is quiet natural and is the consquence of the improved culture and way of living they adopted. It was with the object of emphasising the fact that they were no longer *Candalas,* that they adopted the name-ending of *Sudra*, though they were originally called *Namas*. (O.G.C.I; Calcutta, Vol. II 1965; pp. 146-47. In the *Panchala* country Kashtriya prince do not hesitate to embrace a *Nishada* whom they call his friend and takes food from a *Savara* woman who has already served several sages (A.H. p. 78).

33. R.T. Vol.1 Book V. p. 201.
34. P.H.K. p. 113.
35. R.T. Vol. 1 Book V. p. 201.
36. *Ibid*. p. 202 **Note.** Soon after his accession, *Samakaravarman* has tried, in the words of *Asadha, 'to win the hearts of all the people'* by various measures of the facilities that is socio-economic and political.
37. *Ibid*. p. 203 **Note.** The Mohammedans have a story of that Mountain, which they say derives its name from *Panj*, five, and *Pir*, saints; five pious brothers, according to them, having settled on it and performed several wondrous feats around, but to me it seems more probable that the name came from *Pansal*, which, in the Kashmirian language, signifies a pass, and *Pir*, a devotee. The European and Persians call the whole mountain *Pir Panjal*, but the natives restrict this name to the pass. To them mountain chains after nothing remarkable, while the passes leading through them are of some importance. So also are isolated mountains, when they serve as land-marks, or are deemed holy as places of pilgrimage. In general they give no name to any other (Baron Charles Hugel, *Kashmir and the Punjab*, Jammu, 1972. p.114. Hereafter described as K.P). The same route followed by *S'amkaravarman* army. The verse contains a pun on the name *Prthivicandra*, 'the moon of the earth', which is cast in 'darkness' (*tamasi*) (R.T. Vol.1 Book V.P. 204). The Persian word ' pir' means an

old man or saint, and it has always been the common practive for *Fakirs* or *Pirs* to establish themselves in such positions for the sake of contemplating the works of the Creator and of receiving the *alms* of travellers; hence the word *Pir* in Kashmir has now acquired the secondary meaning of a mountain pass. It is rather a ugly zig-zags way. (T.M.E. P.409).

38. ***Ibid.*** P. 204 **Note.** The name *Gurjara* is preserved in that town of *Gujrat*, situated in the Panjab plain about five miles from the west bank of the Cinab, 74°- 7′ longitude and 32⁰- 34' latitude. It appears that the order name *Gurjara* had, at the time of the events here related, a much wider territorial application. Thus the kingdom of *Gurjara* the *Takkadesa* or land of the *Takkas*, which, as Hiuen-Tsiang's account clearly indicates (*Si-Yu-Ki*, p. 164. Sqq;, Life, p. 72), lay to the east of Chenab.

39. Term *Bhoja* mentioned 'independent' sovereign (*Paramesvara*), Arya, who is named as reigning in the Deogarh inscription, dated 862 A.D. In the *Pehoa* inscription of 882-883 (Alexander Cunningham; *Archealogical Survey* of India Report; Varanasi; 1966, p. 225 Hereafter described as A.S.I.R). This king *Bhoja* must have the political power in the early medieval period during the time of *Durlabhavardhana* of Kashmir. He was the ruler *Kanyakubja* or *Kanuaj* at that time. (B.N Puri, *Cities of Ancient India*, Delhi; 1966; p. 27. Thereafter mentioned as C.A.I.). While the kings of the middle country were generally contented with the title of Raja, rulers in the outlying parts of India preferred other designations the Eastern kings were styled *Samrat*, the southern *Bhoja*, those in the west *Svarat*, while the rulers of the Northern realms (*Janapadas*) were called *Virat*. These association of the *Samrat*, whose status was now regarded as higher than that of the *rajan*, with the east is important; It probably points to the growth of imperalism in the east *'Word'* a tendency that became more marked in the early days of Buddhism in Kashmir (A.H.I p. 43). The traditional meaning of the *Sastras* was subjected to critical examination and new conceptions of morality and religion remodelled the orthodox belief and habits. (Ibid. p. 812). And the founder of the line was a prince named *Lalliya Shahi* who flourished towards the close of the 9th century A.D. the fourth prince, *Bhima Shahi*, was the maternal grandfather of the celebrated queen *Didda* of Kashmir. His famous successor Jayapala came into conflict with the *Sultans* of *Ghazni*. (Ibid. p. 171). Alptigin was formally a slave of the *Samanid* rulers of Central Asia. This enterprising chief made himself independent in Ghazni and conquered a part of the Kingdom of Kabul. He died in 963 A.D. In 977 A.D. his sceptre passed into the hands of his son-in-law, Sabuktigin. About this time a large part of the territory from *Langhan* or *Laghman* to Kangra acknowledged the sway of *Jaipal* (*Jayapala*) of the Hindu *Shahiya* dynasty of *Wai hand* (*Udabhandapur*)

The Hindu king heard reports from travellers how the Sultan of Ghazni was encroaching on his dominions in the prosecution of "holy wars". To put a stop to his depredations, he advanced towards Ghazni and met his enemy near a place called Ghuzak between Ghazni and Lamghan.

A snow-storm compelled Jaipal to conclude a humiliating peace, but he soon broke his engagements and brought on his head the wrath of hte Sultan. The latter carried fire and sword into the territory of his antagonist and seized the districts in the neighbourhood of Lamghan. In 997 Sabuktigin died, and in the next year the crown went to his famous son,Mahmud. In 1001 the new Sultan inflicted a crushing defeat on *Jaipal* near the city of Peshawar. Unable to survive this disgrace, the defeated king burnt himself on a funeral pyre and was succeeded by his son, *Anandapala* (A.D. 1002 or 1003). In 1006 Mahmud took Multan, but the final subjugation of the city was postponed till 1010. In 1008 he routed the troops of *Anandapala*, led by prince *Brahmanapala*, at the battle of *Waihand*, and pursued the fugitives as far as Bhimnagar. *Anandapala* continued to offer resistance from the fastnesses of the Salt Range (*Nandana*). His successor, *Trilochanpala*, carried on the struggle with the assistance of *Samgramaraja* of Kashmir. In the end he was compelled to retire to the east and conclude an alliance with the *Chandella* ruler of Kalinjar and other princes of Mid India. But he was agains defeated on the river Ruhut (*Rahib*) identified by some with the *Ramganga*. He was assassinated in A.D. 1021-1022. With the death of his son and successor, *Bhima*, in 1026 the dynasty came to an end. Both Al-biruni and Kalhana bear testimony to the courage and magnanimity of this noble line of kings who poured out their blood like water in defending the north-western gates of their country against the invader. Mahmud did not remain content with the laurels he won in the Punjab. In 1014 he took Thanesar, and in the following years made an unsuccessful attempt to conquer the vale of Kashmir. He also burnt the temple of Mathura. In 1018 he sacked Kanauj and extinguished the once powerful empire of the *Pratiharas*. In 1022-1023 he received the submission of Gwalior and Kalinjar. His most famous expedition, that against Somnath in Kathiawar, was undertaken in 1025. The fall of the most celebrated Hindu shrine of the age in 1026 synchronised with the extinction of the Hindu Shahiya kingdom of the Punjab. Four years later the Sultan died. Mahmud's expeditions were mostly in the nature of plundering raids. The only permanent results of his arduous campaings were the annexation of the *Hindu Shahiya* kingdom and certain other districts in the Punjab and the north west borderland and the destruction of the morale of the Hindu armies. The raids of Mahmud must have made a profound impression on the minds of the great Rajput powers of Western and central India that sought to divid among themselves the imperial heritages of the *Pratiharas*. During the period 1030-1192 A.D., that is to say from the death of Mahmud to the arrival on the scence of Muhammad of *Ghur*, the princes of the Indian interior enjoyed comparative immunity from foreign attacks. The Ghaznavid Sultans and then harried certain territories, and on one occassion one of their generals advanced up to Benares and sacked the holy city. But on the whole, the invaders could not make much headway. The terror inspired by their ravages had, however, lasting consequences. (*Ibid* pp.182-184). The *Shahis* of *Uda bhanda*, politically, a more important *role* was played by the Kalachuri kings, *Gangeyadeva* and his son *Lakshmi Karna*. The former, as already stated above, assumed the title of *Vikramaditya* and took under his protection the holy cities of Allahabad and *Banaras*. *Lakshmi Karna* seems to have made himself master of the Southern *Doab* and did much to revive the glorious traditions associated with the empires of *Harsha* and *Bhoja*. He conciliated the rulers of Bengal by matrimonial alliances and pushed his conquests southwards as far as Kalinga. Had he lived longer he might have restored that shattered fabric of imperialism in nothern India and erected an effective barrier against the advance of the Turks. His career was cut short by a hostile combination of the rulers of Gujarat, Malwa, Bundol Khand and the Deccan. The *Kalachuria* still retained considerable power under his son and grandson, but the control of the *Madhyadesa* (Upper Gangas valley) soon passes into the hands of the famous house of *Gahadavala*. The founder of the *Gahadavala* dynasty was chandradeva who rose to power in the closing decade of the eleventh century. His grandson, *Govindachandra*, was the real, ruler of the *Madhya-desa* for half *a* century, first as crown prince (1104-1114) and later on as king (1114-1154). He founded an empire embracing the greater part of the present United provines and Bihar. He successfully defended Jelavana (in northern Oudh), *Benaras* and other holy places of Buddhist and Hindus alike against the Turks. But a rival empire was established in the west by the Chauhan Vigraharaja IV with seats at Ajmer and Delhi. The latter, city was probably founded by a *Tomara* chief tain about the middle of the 11th century A.D., and it was from the *Tomaras* that the *Chauhans* obtained possession of this famous capital (*Ibid* p.186) *Ballala Sena's* son, *Lakshmana Sena*, probably began to rule in 11-78-1179 A.D. or 1184-1885 A.D., though some scholars push the date his accession much further back and regard him as the founder of the lakshmana Sena era of 1119 A.D. He seems to have served his apprenticeship in the work of government as victory or military governor in charge of some district in *Kalinga*. On coming to the throne, he distinguished himself as a conqueror and a patron of learning. He claims to have pushed his conquests as far as the southern ocean, reduced *Kamarupa* to subjection and vanished the king of *Banaras*, who is no other than the Gahadavala king of Kanauj. Among the poets who graced his court, the most eminent were *Jayadeva*, the author of the *Gita Govinda*, and *Dhoyi*, the author of the *Pavanaduta*. The last mentioned work contains an interesting description of the Sena capital. The Senas, however, failed of stem the tide of Muslim invasion once the dyke erected by the *Gahadavalas* was broken. *Rai Lakhmanyia*, usually identified with *Lokshmana Sena* had to flee before the advancing arms of *Malik Akhtiyar-ud-din Muhammad Khalji* towards the close of the 12th or the early in the 13th century. His sons, *Visvarupa* Sena and *Kesava Sena*, maintained the struggle against the "Garga Yavanas", that is to say, the muslim invaders from the Kabul valley, and preserved their independence in Eastern Bengal till the latter half of the thirteenth century (*Ibid* p. 188).

40. To the north-west of Kashmir state, running upto and on the right of the Indus, was the Gilgit valley. it was a part and parcel of Dardistan

or *Darads*. There was, actually, no region known as *Dardistan* to its inhabitants. Dardistan appears to be simply a convenient, but somewhat misleading, name employed by the British Geographers to express a large tract inhabited by different Aryan races of somewhat similar type. It comprised, besides Gilgit, *Astore, Boonji, Hunza, Nagar, Punial, Yasin*, the independent republics of the Indus Valley such as *Gor, Darel* and *Tangir* and other countries south of the *Hindush* including *Chitral.* The ancient name of Gilgit its Hindu *Ras* or *Raj* (Kings) was *Sargin.* Later it was known as Gilgit, which the Sikhs and the Dogras corrupted into Gilgit. Gilgit was situated at an elevation of 4,890 feet above sea level in 35° - 55′ North and 74°-23′ East. The climate of Gilgit was dry and wholesome though the heat is summer, owing to the radiation from the anormous expanse of bare rock, was oppressive; but the mights were cool and fresh. There was no rainfall to speak of, it being almost intercepted by the neighbouring mountains. There was also practically no snowfall in Gilgit. The history of Gilgit, *'Sargin Gilgit'*, or the happy land of Gilgit, as it was known in its own *Shina* language, is lost in antiquity. The last ruler reputed to have been a Hindu was *Sri-Badat,* whose rule extended over all the neighbourhood from *Astore* to *Chitral*; he was a real person, but has become legendary on account of his reputed cannibalism. *Hunza* tradition has it that the daughter of the cannibal king married a *Hunza* prime *Shamsher* and it was this daughter who arranged her father's death. The dynasty which was founded by Shamsher was called *Trakhane,* from a celebrated *Ra* named *Trakhan*, who reigned about the commencement of the fourteenth century A.D. The previous rulers, of whom *Sri Badat* was the last, were called *Shahreis*. (Amar Singh Chohan; Historial Study of Society and culture in Dardistan and Ladakh New Delhi 1983). Thereafter explained as H.S.S'C. D.L. pp.1-2. According to these chronides king *Shahras or Sahiras*, son of Sahasi Rai ruled over an extensive kingdom bordering on Kashmir and Kanauj in the north and east, and extending as far as Makran in the west. When Yuen Chwang visited in Sind (629-45 A.D.) and found a Buddhist monarch of the *Sudra (Shu-to-lo)* caste identical with *Shahreis* or *Siharas Rai*, as is the most probable light on the origin of the Rais *dynasty*. The fact is that *Harsha-Vardhana* fought with the king of Sind lends some colour of probability to this account. The central part of these territories was under the immediate charge of the king, who had his capital al Alor, while the rest was divided into four provinces, each under a governor who is also described as a tributary ruler. This account agrees fairly well with that of Hiuen Tsang. King Sahiras lost his life in a fight with the king of *Nimruz*, a province of Persia, who had invaded his territory and entered *Kirman*. This took place probably at the beginning of the seventh century A.D. *Shahrais or Sahiras* was succeeded by his won Rai Sahasi II (C.A. Vo l. III. P. 165). Thus, *Trakhan* was succeeded as *Ra* or *Rai* of Gilgit by *Azar, Jamsher, Khisrau, Fardos, Habikan, Gauritham*, Muhammad Khan and Abas. Abas was the last of the *Trakhan* line; with him ended the independence of Gilgit; henceforward the valley was devastated by successive invasions of the neighbouring Rajas, who, each in turn, first acquired the country and then was defeated and killed by some other. In the twenty or thirty years ending with 1842, there were five dynastic revolutions in Gilgit, as follows:-

(1) *Suleiman Shah*, ruler of Yasin, of the *Bakhte* caste or family, who was a refugee in Gilgit and had been given protection by its ruler, killed *Abas* about 1805.

(2) *Azad Khan*, ruler of Punial, Killed Suleiman shah at *Char Kila* and ruled in his stead in Gilgit.

(3) *Tair Shah*, ruler of Nagar, displaced and killed *Azad Khan*; he himself died a natural death and was succeeded by his son, *Shah Sikandar*.

(4) *Gaur Rahman,* ruler of Yasin, conquered Gilgit and killed Shah Sikandar.

(5) *Shah Sikandar,* brother *Karim Khan,* having escaped to *Gor,* from there sent an agent to the Sikh Governor of Kashmir imploring aid against the invader. The appeal was responded to.

A couple of Sikh Regiments were sent under *Nathu Shah*, a Sayyid of Gujranwala, who was a capable commander and held the rank of a Colonel. This was about the year 1842. Up to this time the Sikhs had not occupied the intermediate country of Astore, but they had made it tributary to them; now on advancing they established a post there to make their communiation sure. In short, the Sikh Governor of Kashmir easily settled the whole country of Gilgit, was sent to supersede by giving a daughter to *Nathu Shah*, and peace was made all around. (*H.S.S.C.D.L.* pp. 3-4).

41. Term *Turuskas* is composed of three words *Tu+ru+skas* '*Tu*' means 'God' or 'Nama', '*ru*' means soul or 'light' and *skas* means 'friend'. Hence, '*Nam*' or '*Sabad*' is friend of every soul, when we surrender to the *Master*.

42. According to the early Buddhists records the *Rajmahal* Hills and the Western part of this area was known as the *Brahmarshi-desa*, and the entire region was roughly equivalent to *Aryavarta* as described in the grammar *of Pantanjali* (A.H.I. p. 5). On the one hand, the rise of a new empire on the ashes of Mauryan legemoney, which was successful in defending *Aryavarta* against the barbarian *outcastes* of the fronters. On the other hand, the dawn of the Brahmanical movement which reached its climax in the spacious days of Guptas. (Ibid p. 114). The subsequent passage of the inscriptions names along with *Achyuta* and *Nagasena* several other princes of *Aryavarta* or the upper Ganges valley and some adjoining tracts, who were violently exterminated. These include *Rudradeva, Matila, Nagadatta, Chandravarman, Ganapati Naga, Nandin* and *Balavarman*. The identity of most of the princes named in this list is still uncertain. *Matila* has been connected by some scholars with the *Bulandshahr* district in the centre of the Ganges and *Yumna Doad*, while *Ganapati Naga* seems to be associated by numismatic evidence with Narwar and *Besnagar* in Central India. *Chandravarman* is a more elusive but interesting figure (*Ibid* p.146). But petty then chieftains continued to rule over a circmscribed area in

North-West India and Malwa, waging a perpetual warfare with the indigenous princes till they were absorbed into the Rajput population. It is significant that the new aspiratns for imperial domunion in *Aryavarta*, *Yasodharman*, the Maukharis, the princes of the house of *Pushyabhuti*, and the *Palas* set much store on success against these outlandish barbarians who harassed their country as the *Yavanas* and *Saka-Pahlavas* did of old (*Ibid*. p. 154).

43. Term *Svamiraja* is consisted of two words *Svami+Raja, Swami* or *Swami* is the personality of the state manifested a will of his own. "A Swami Kautilya says' when endowed with rich qualifies enriches the Prakrtis with his own richness; of whatever character he is, of that character, the Prakrtis become, because their progress and decline arc dependent upon him." (M.V. Krishna, Rao; *Studies in Kautilya*; New Delhi; 1958 p. 120. Thereafter mention as *S.K.*). In addition to the title *Raja* or *Rajan* we came across the designation *'samrat'*, which in later times undoubtedly meant a paramount ruler. In the *Rig-Veda,* however, there is no trace of any terrestrial kingship of the Mauryan or Gupta type, though the idea of a universal monarch *(Visvasyabhuvanasya raja*) is met with (A.H.I. p. 29) 'He' is the lord of the people, did not govern without their consent. (*Ibid*. p. 30). The *raja* of the *Madhya-desa*, judging by the testimony of the epic, was not autocrat, (*Ibid*. p. 71). The title *Raja* or *Rajan* sometimes loosely applied to all the chief men of the state, for we hear of 7,707 Rajas among the *Lichchhavis*, though one document puts the figure at 500 and a Jaina text seems to limit the title to only *'nine'*. A Buddhist commentary seems to suggest that the *Rajas* ruled by turns.(*Ibid*. p. 75). Thus the duty of *Raja*, according to Hindu notions, was always please his subjects who were his *"Children"*. The virtuous royal lady found a shelter in the hermitage of *Valmiki*, where she gave birth of the twins, *'Kusa'* and *'Lava',* who subsequently returned to their ancestral home and succeeded to their heritage. (*Ibid;* p.93). H.G. Wells says that three great strucutral ideas ruled the mind of contemporary mankind; a clear vision of man in relation to the things about him; service of one universal 'God' of Righteousness whose temple is the whole world (*S.K*; p. 106).

44. According to H. Krishna Shastri, the Empire was divided into six principal provinces.Each province was under a viceroy, *nayaka* or *naik*, who might be a member of the royal house, or an influential noble of the state, or some descendant of the old ruling families (*A.H.I.* p. 380) *Naik* from the Sanskrit *nayaka*, a leader or chief. The title was given to provincial rulers or governors under the kings of Vijaynagar. See 'the History of the Naik kingdom of *Madura* (*Indian Antiquties*, 1914, pp. 1 follow); *Madura* mean sweet that is 'Word'.

45. In the world of 'light' and the earth lies the realm of the air, and the chief deities of this region are, besides Indra, the *Maruts* (Storm Gods), *Vayu* and *Vata* (the wind Gods), *Rudra* (the Howling God of strom and lighting), and *Parjanya* (the God of Rain). Of the terrestrial deties, the chief are *Agni, Soma* and *Sarasvati Agni,* or the Fire-God, received special homage because no sacrifice could be performed without

offerings to him. The libation of *Soma* was also regarded as speical sacred. *Sarasvata* was a river deity who came to be regarded later as the Goddess of learning. Of the three principle deities of the later mythology, Vishnu and *Rudra* (*Siva*) are, as we have seen already, know to the *Rig-Veda*, and Brahma, though not explicitly mentioned, has his precursors in *Vidhatri* (the Ordainer) *Hiranyagarbha* (the Germ of Gold), *Prajapati* ( the lord of Creatures) and *Brahmanaspati* ( the lord of Prayer). An important characteristic of *Vedic* Mythology is the predominance of the male elements; Goddesses like *Prithvi, Aditi, Ushas and Sarasvati* occupy a very subordinate position. In this respective the Vedic civilization presents a contrast to the pre-historic culture of the Indus valley, where the Mother Goddess is co-equal with her male partner. Another important feature of the Vedic religion is the tendency towards monotheism and even monism. The hymns foreshadow the idea of universal unity, and express the belief that God is One although he bears many names (A.H. p. 39).

46. It is possible that a recollection of the original name survived locally to the time of the glossator by the side of the customary designation of Pattana: *Patan,* though the latter must have already prevailed in *Karkota'* time. Term *Patan* soothed of two words that is 'Pa+tan', 'pa' means 'Father' & 'tan' means body. This body has been given by 'father' and erroneously thought he could recognise *S'amkaravarman's* town in the modern village of *Sankarpar* in the *'Shahabad'* or *'word'*, *'Kalma'*, Pargana (75° -14′ longtitude and 33°-37′ latitude. Neither the name of *S'amkarapura*, nor that of *Pancasastra,* can now be traced at *Patan*. Term *Pancasastra* is composed of two words *Panca+Sastra*, *Panca* means five, *'sastra'* in the first book of epic Mahabharta claims to be a *'anthoritative manual'* laying down rules of conduct for the attainment of *trivarga* or three great aims animating all human conduct, *Dharma* (moral and religions duties), *Artha* (material wealth) and *Kama* (pleasures of the flesh). Finally it claims to a *Moksha-Sastra* pointing the way of salvation to mankind. Manuals of a didactic character are chiefly found in the later books. Among the religious poems that form part of the epic, the most famous is the *Bhagavata Gita* or the *"song of the lord"*, which constitutes the bed-rock of Hindu theism (A.H.I. P.96).

47. *R.T.* Vol. 1, Book V. p. 207.

48. God gifted knowledge which is priceless. It is unlimit and upto the Master based on *Karma* theory of *Man*.

49. *R.T. Vol. I* Book V.PP. 207-209 **Note.** Regarding the proper meaning of the *parsad* means *par excellence* of *sainthood* gifted by *Guru* as the spirit of *'Nam'* or *'Sabad'*.

50. *Ibid.* p. 210. **Note.** It becomes evident that the *Diviras* were officials, who had to do with writing and accounts. *Lokaprakasa* mentioned the various classes of *Diviras* known as *ganjadiviras, nagaradiviras, gramadiviras, Khavasadiviras*. The word is derived from the Persian *dibir*, 'writer or secretary'.

51. **Note. *Lavata*** is evidently the same person as a load-carrier (*bharika*) by origin and term *S'akaca* having the similar meaning. Thus, the term

*ganjavara* is undoubtedly identical with the Persian *ganjwar* (treasure). In the list of officials mentioned above, the *ganjavara* is elaborated along with *Kasthahhipati* and *ganjadhipati*. It designated, perhaps, the village *headman*, the modern *Maqaddam or Lambardar*, who as the person directly responsible for the payment of the revenue, has since old days been an important factor in rural administration. Justice was often administered by the sovereign himself or a high official at the centre or in the provinces. Judges at the headquarters of a district had apparently the assistance of the chief Seths and *Kayasthas* of the locality, representative of the commercial and official classes.

52. *R.T.* Vol.1 Book V. pp. 210-212. **Note.** *Bhallata* is known as the author of the extant *Bhallatasataka*, a dictionary called *Padamanjari*, is repeatedly quoted by *Ksemendra*.
53. The king of *Darvabhisara* here mentioned is probably identical with the *Naravahana* who figures as the sone of the *Darvabhisara* king *Nara* in the pedigree *Lohara* family. But *Nara* is usually a wedded lace of about 2 meters in length, used for stringing *pyjama's* or *Salwars* and today we find that most of the people they used elastic. It shows that there is an indiscipline in the society having no manners. Therefore, it is also a duty of the King to check it out to creat a good atmosphere in the society.
54. **Note.** Term *dvaradhipa*, literally 'lord of the Gate' (or Gates) along with its equivalents meaning as *dvarapati, dvaresa, dvaradhisvara, dvaranayaka, dvaradhikarin*. This was indeed, the function of the officers and the charge of the *dvara* was hold by *Dvaradhikara*. Thus, in Kashmir, we find the valiant *Kandarpa* as the 'Lord of the Gate' engaged in expeditions against *Rajapuri* and other frontiers territories. Subsequently, when *Kandarpa* had resumed once again the charge of the *'Gate'* and pretender Bhuvanaraja will be inroad. The efforts of the *Vijaymala* will lead the road of Darad territory. There is another member of the royal family known as *Malla* will hold the post of *Dvarapati*, under *Kalasa* and also invade *Urasa*. One more lord of the Gate will exercise the power of the Commandant of a frontier fort, etc. It is interesting to note that 'Lord of the Gate' of the Hind period and the *Margesas* or 'guardians of the routes' called *margapa, adhvapa, adhvesa, margapesa* are generally referred to across the mountains routes. They are clearly meant for *Maliks* of Muhammadan times. They were the feudal chiefs known as *Pir Panjal*, discussed above. The official position of the *Dvarapati* must have been a very high and respectable. Such as the offices of the prime minister (*Sarvadhikara*), the commender-in-Chief (*Kampana*), cheif justice (*rajasthana*) and the *Padagra* post was superior to that of a *mandalesa* or governor. Hence, the post of the 'Lord of the Gate' is frequently referred under the name of *dvara*, 'dvara' is here an abbreviation for *dvarakarya* or *dvaradhikara* and the use of *Kampana* has already been explained in the note.
55. **Note.** *Samakaravarman's* expedition after the destruction of *Viranaka* lay to the north-west 'a seat of *Khasas*' produced in the 9th and

succeeding centuries a number of teachers who were reckoned among the greatest exponents of the Saiva doctrine and philosophy. No less important than the *Kashmir School* of Saivas were the Tamil and Kanarese saints and scholars known as the *Nayanars* or *naka* and *Vira Saivas* respectively. Foremost among the Tamil Saiva saints were *Tirujnana-Sambandar*, *Appar, Sundaramurti* and *Manikka Vasahar. Kanarese Saivism* found a Champion in the famous *Basava*, who has already been mentioned above. Basava was a minister of the Jaina king, *Bijjala* of the *'Kalachurya'* dynasty of *Kalyana*, who lived in the middle of the 12th century A.D. A distinguishing feature of *'Vira Saiva'* seat of *Karnata* to which *Basava* belonged was its zeal for social reform and special solicitude for the emancipation of woman fromt he thraldom of rigid custom (A.H.I. p. 203).

56. Term *Indus* is put together of the two words *In+dus*, 'In' means 'within' and 'dus' means 'absorve' the '*Words*' in the body like the *Panjshir* rivers northeast of Kabul. The district west of the river Indus became tributary to the Persians, and the name of Gandhara began to appear prominently among the subject nations in the early inscriptions of Darivs (522-486 B.C.), the most illustrious among the successors of Cyrus. Darius followed up the earlier successes of his house by sending a naval expendition to the Indus under the command of *Skylax*. This expedition paved the way for the annexation of the Indus Valley as far as the deserts of *Rajaputana*. It constituted the 20th and the most populous Satrapy of the Persian empire (A.H.I. p. 64). Thus, the young commander stormed Debal, captured *Nerun* and some other cities and strongholds, and pused on to the western bank of the Indus. His work was greatly facilitated by the treachery of certain Buddhist priests and renegade chiefs who desertged their sovereign and joined the invader. With the assistance of some of these traitors, Muhamad crossed the vast sheet of water separating his army from that of Dahir and gave battle to the Indian ruler near *Raor* (712 A.D.). *Dahir* offered a brave resistance, but was defeated and killed. The fort of Raor fell next after a heroic defence by the widowed queen. The invaders now pushed on to *Bahmanabad* and Alor, which submitted. The turn of Multan came next, the whole of the lower Indus Valley was now dominated by the Arabs. But the invaders had no mind to stop there. Already in the time of Muhammad-Ibn-Kasim minor operations were carried on in the neighbouring provinces. A later governor, *Junaid* or Junayd, pursued a more agressive policy and sent expenditions against Marmad (Marwar i.e. against *the man*, al-Mandal ) *Mandor* means *wandering man* near *Viramgam* i.e. the *way of 'happiness for mind*), Dahnaj, Barwas (Broach) Ujjain, Malibah (Malwa), *Baharimad*, al-Bal (*Vallamandal* means which *gives the power to mind*) and al-Jurz (Gurjaa). According to India inscriptions, the territories overrun by the invaders include sind, Cutch, Surashtra or Kathiwar, Chavotaka(some Chapa principality apparently of Gujarat or Western Rajaputana), a Maurya principality apparently in Southern Rajaputana or Maluca, and the Gurjjara territory apparently round Bhinma or Broach. The progress of the Arabs means A+ra+b+, 'A' stands for *'single'*, 'ra' means *'way'* or *'thought'*, 'b'

stands for 'bliss' and 's' stands for *sant* or *sainthood* was stopped by the Chalukyas in the south, the *Pratiharas* in the east, and the *Karkotas* in the North. But a new scene opened with the foundation of the kingdom of Ghazni by Alptigin in or about 962 A.D. *(Ibid.* P.182). The grandson of *Amir Timur*, early in 1398 A.D. Mir Muhammad besieged Multan and captured it after six months. Timur left samarqand in April, 1398, at the head of a large army, and having crossed the Indus, the Jhelam and the Ravi in September, appeared before *Talamba*, situated about seventy miles to the north-east of Multan, on the 13th October of the same year. He sacked *Talamba* and massacred or enslaved its inhabitants. After capturing several places on his way and massacring many of their inhabiants, he advanced to the outskirts of Delhi by the end of the first week of December, and butchered there about 100,000 adult male captives in cold blood. *Sultan Mahmud* and *Mallu Iqbal* endeavoured to oppose him there on the 17th December with a large army consisting of 10,000 cavalry, 40,000 infantry, and 120 elephants, clad in armour. But they were hopelessly defeated and took to their heels, Mallu fleeing to *Baran* and Mahmud to Gujarat (*Ibid.* p. 336). In the meanwhile, Afghan clans living there, they had the habits of highway robbery and of blackmailing the rich cities of the north-western Punjab. In order to keep the north-western passes open and the valleys at their foot safe, the government of *Aurangzeb* first tried to win over these hillmen by payments of money. But, "even political pensions were not always effective in securing obedience." Troubles began early in 1667 A.D., when the *Yusufzaiz* rose in arms under one of their leaders named *Bhagu*. A large number of them crossed the Indus above attack and invaded in Hazara district, while other bands began to ravage the western Peshawar and *Attock* districts. The Yusufzai, however, suppressed in the course of a few months. But in 1672, the Afridis rose in revolt against the Mughals under their chieftain Akmal Khan, who crowned himself king and summoned all the Pathans to organise themselves in a sort of national war. This victory increased the prestige and resources of Akmal Khan and lured more recruits to his side so that "the whole of the Pathan land from Attack to Qandahar" rose in arms. The *Khattak* clan of the Pathans also joined the *Afridis*, and *Khush-hal-Khan*, the poet and hero of the former, "became the leading spirit of the national rising and inspired the tribesmen with his pen and sword alike". In Februry, 1674, the Afghans assail an imperial force under *Shaja* at *Khan*, who was killed though the remnant of his army was rescued by a Rathor contingent sent by Jaswant Singh to support the Mughuls. This disaster convinced Aurangzeb that more serious efforts were necessary to restore imperial prestige in the north-west. He went in person to *Hasan Abdal*, near Peshawar, early in July, 1674, and by a clever combination of diplomacy and arms achieved much success. Many Afghan clans were brought over with presents, pensions, *jagirs,* and offices, while the more refractory ones were subdued by arms. When the situation had considerably improved the Emperor left the Punjab for Delhi by December, 1675. The success of Aurangzeb was confirmed by the wise policy of *Amin Khan*, the capable governor of Afghanistan from 1677 to 1698, was followed a tactful confiliatory policy under the wise advice of his wife, *Shahibji*, a daughter of 'Ali Mardan Khan'. Thus, the Mughal Emperor was able to suppress the Afghan risings and restore imperial prestige, in the north west. (Ibid. p. 494). In the meantime, lord Auckland's policy was proved indefensible from all points of view. As an independent ruler of Afghanistan, Dost Muhammad had every right to enlist Perso-Russian alliance on his side however prejudicial it might be British interests. It should also be noted that Dost Muhammad decided to accept Perso-Russian alliance after the failure of his efforts to secure British friendship. "We had ourselves", observes Kaye justly, "alienated the friendship of the *Barakzye Sirdars*. They had thrown themselves into the arms of the Persian king, only because we had thrust them off." Further, the poor excuse of Perso-Russian agression as a danger to British interests ceased to have any force whatsoever after the withdrawal of the Persians from Herat in September, 1838, thus "cut from under the feet of Lord Auckland all grounds of justification and rendered the expendition across the Indus at once a folly and a crime." Politically considered, the Governor-General's policy was ill-advised and inexpediant. Dost Muhammad, whom he wanted to depose, was an efficient ruler having sufficient control over the unruly Afghan tribesmen, whereas his nominee, *Shah Shuja*, though possessed of some capacity, had hitherto met with nothing but failure, and had no prospect of gaining popularity among the Muslims of Afghanistan by being reinstated through the assistance of the Sikhs, the old enemies of the Afghans, and of the Christian British power Shah Shuja was a man "whom the people of Afghanistan had repeatedly, in emphatic, scriptural language, spued out for these Barukzya (Barakzai) chiefs, who, whatever may have been the defects of their Government, had contrived to maintain themselves in security and their country in peace, with a vigour and a constancy unknown to the luckless Suddozye princes." In short, the Afghan war was launched, as Kaye pointed out, "in defiance of every consideration of political and military expediency and there were those who, arguing the matter on higher grounds than those of mere expediency, pronounced the certainty of its failure, because there was a canker of injustice at the core. It was,indeed, an experiment on the forbearance alike of God of man; and, therefore, though it might dawn in success and triumph, it was sure to set in failure and disgrace". Among the many contemporary critics of Lord Auklands policy, the Duke of Wellington Wrote to Mr. Tucker that "the consequences of crossing the Indus, once to settle a Government in Afghanistan, will be a perennial march into that country." His remarks was Prophetic. Regardless of these considerations, Lord Auckland largely influenced by his private advisers, *John Colvin* and *W.H. Macnaghten*, passed orders to assemble "the army of the Indus" to invade the Kingdom of Dost Muhammad. Owing to Ranjit Singh's objection to the passage of the British troops through his kingdom and certain other reasons, it was arranged that the main British force under the command of Sir John Keane and Sir Willoughby Cotton, accompanied by Shah Shuja, would advance from Ferozepore to Kabul by way of *Bahawalpur*, *Sind*, *Baluchistan*, and the *Bolan* and *Khojak* passes over a distance of one thousand miles, while the Sikh army, accompanied by Colonel Wade and Shah Shuja's son, Timur, would march from the Punjab through Peshawar and the Khyber pass. As Dr. Smith observes, "the plan violated all the conditions of '*Sound*' strategy and was that of a lunatic rather than of a sane statesman". (Ibid. pp. 753-754). The Afghan War was very closely connected with the conquest of Sind, which followed it. Sind embraced the lower valley of the Indus and was include within the empire of Ahmad Shah Durrani. But, during the closing years of the eighteenth century, it owed only a nominal allegiance to Afghanistan and was governed in practical independence by the *Mirs* or *Amirs* of the *Talpura tribe*, which, coming originally from Baluchistan, had overthrown the last of the *Kaloras* in A.D. 1783. The three important branches of the *Talpura* chiefs were seated at Hyderabad, Khairpur and Mirpur. The English had commercial interests in Sind for a long time; a factory established by them at *Thatta* in 1758 was abandoned in 1775 and their commercial mission to the *Talpura Mirs* in 1799 produced no important result. With a view to excluding French influence from Sind, the British Government concluded a treaty with the Amirs of Sind in 1809, which was renewed in 1820. The journey of Alexander Burnes in 1831 up the river Indus on his way to Lahore disclosed to the English the importance of Sind from the political as well as commerical point of view, and since then its absorption into the growing British Empire had been only a question of time. "Alas", observed a Seiad, "Sind is now gone since the English have seen the river." As we shall see, this proved wholly true as a Prophetic prediction of the 'Nam' during that period.

Sind had an ambitious neighbour in the Sikh ruler, Ranjit Singh, who coveted it as a natural sphere of expansion for his empire. But his attempts were thwarted by his friends, the English, who in their turn lost no opportunity of increasing their influence over that territory. Thus in 1831, Lord William Bentinck opposed Ranjit Singh's proposal for a partition of Sind. But the Amirs of Sindh had to conclude a treaty with the British Government, rather reluctantly, on the 20th April, 1832, which provided that "the rivers and roads" of Sind should be opened to the merchants and traders of Hindustan", but that no "military stores" and "armed vessels or boats" should come through these. As a sort of precaution against the apprehended absorption of their territory by the British, the Amirs took care to include another stipulation to the effect that "the two contracting powers bind themselves never to look with the eye of covetousness on the possessions of each other." This treaty was renewed in 1834. Up to 1838 Ranjit Singh often contemplated the incorporation of Sind into his empire, but was thwarted by the English, who now with a view to strengthening the ties by which the Amirs of Sind were "connected with the British Empire", proceeded to extort from them favourable terms as a reward for their protection against Sikh aggression. By a treaty concluded on the 20th Apri, 1838, Lord Auckland forced on them an accredited British Resident. In fact, Sind soon fell out of the frying-pan into the fire. Sikh ambition in regard to it could not be realised, but it was to pay a high price for the uncalled for British protection by being deprived of its independence through questionable means adopted by British officers. On the outbreak of the First Anglo-Afghan War, the English, in violation of the treaty of 1832, took an armed force through Sind, and informed the Amirs that "while the present exigency lasts *'Word'* the article of the treaty (of 1832) prohibiting the use of the Indus for the conveyance of military stores must necessary be suspended". Greater humiliation and loss were inflicted on the Amirs when Lord Auckland demanded from them a heavy sum as a price for unsolicited British mediation in effecting a commutation of the pecuniary demands of Shah Shuja on Sind. The Amirs, who had stopped the payment of any tribute to Shah Shuja during his thrity years' exile and had also been granted an exemption by Shah Shuja in 1833 from all claims, naturally hesitated to comply with Lord Auckland's demand. But they were given a warning to the effect that the British Government had the "power to crush and annihilate them, and *'Word'* will not hesitate to call it into action, should it appear requisite, however remotely, for either the integrity or safety" of the Empire, or its frontiers. The Amirs had no other option but to submit to the Governor-General's exaction. Further, the threat of Sir John Keane's march on the capital of Sind compelled them to accept fresh terms from Lord Auckland in February, 1839, by which they were bound to pay a sum of three lacs of rupees per annum for the maintenance of a British force in their territories, and Sind was "formally placed under British protection." This treaty was again revised by Lord Auckland and his advisers in theirown way and was sent back for final signature to the Amirs, who "objected implored and finally gave way, by affixing their seals to the revised documents." A worse fate was, however, in store for Sind. She had been intimidated and coerced by Lord Auckland; but his successor went further and imposed on her the yoke of British authority by Sheer force. During the critical years of the disastrous Afghan War, the province had been utilised as a base of operations by the British Government, and its Amirs had remained steadfastly loyal to their agreements with the English. But far from being duly rewarded for their attachment, the Amirs were unjustly charged with disaffection and hostility against the British Government by Lord Ellenborough, who sought a convenient pretext to give effect to his design of annexing Sind. To make matters easy for himself, the new Governor-General removed Major James Outram, the resident at Hyderabad, who had some experience of local affairs, and sent to Sind Sir Charles Napier with full civil and military powers as a representative of the Governor-General. Sir Charles Napier, a hot-headed and impulsive officer, acted on "the theory that the annexation of Sind would be a very beneficent piece of rascality for which it was his business to find an excuse-a robbery to be plausibly effected". He took it for granted that the vague charges against the Amirs had been proved,and , besides arbitrarily interfering in a succession quarrel at Khairpur, dictated a new treaty by which the Amirs were required to cede certain important territories in lieu of the tribute of three lacs, to provide fuel for British vessels navigating the Indus, and to give up the right of coining money in favour of the British Government. He did not stop with these demands, which amounted to an absolute surrender of national independence by the Amirs, but acted as if Sind had already become a part of the British Empire and "as though the right of the Governor-General of British India to parcel it out at his pleasure was unquestioned and unquestionable; and, moreover, as if it were desired to exercise this right in a manner as offensive as possible to those who were to suffer privation from the exercise". Thus before the acceptance of a fresh treaty by thc Amirs, he occupied the territory in question, and issued proclamations in strong language. Further, whilc talking of treaties, he sought to intimidate the Amirs by marching upon *Imamgarh*, a famous desert forttress lying between Khairpur and Hyderabad, without formally declaring war, and destroying it early in January, 1843 (*Ibid.* pp. 760-762). Henceforth, for several years the North-West Frontier policy of India was confined to relations with Afghanistan. The main problem was the position of the wild hill-tribes, which lived in the regions lying between Afghan and British territories and owed allegiance to neither. In pursuance of what has been termed the "Forward policy", the British Government desired to extend its power over them, so that the frontier of British India might be pushed far beyond the Indus. After some difficulties the two Governments came to an understanding regarding their spheres of influence. The Afghan Boundary Commission under Sir Mortimer Durand formally laid down the boundary-line. The Amir's subsidy was raised from twelve to eighteen lakhs a year, and he agreed nto to interfere with the tribes on the Indian side of the frontier line. The next problem was to deal effectively with these tribes. This proved no easy task, and punitive expeditions were necessary to quell the turbulent clansmen. A formal protectorate was declared over *Chitral* and *Gilgit* in 1893, but two years later the British officers sent to *Chitral* to help one of the rival candidates for the throne, was besieged by a large number of tribes who had declared *Jihad* or holy war against the British. The siege lasted for a month and a half, until a relieving army proceeded from Gilgit and another by way of the *Malakand Pass*. Again in 1897 there was a serious outbreak of hostilities. A large number of tribes, including the Mohmands and the Afridis, rose in revolt, and regular military expeditions, notably the Tirah *campaign*, were necessary to put them down. To prevent the recurrence of these outbreaks strategic roads and railways were built in the frontier districts and a redistribution of troops was made to cope with them more effectively and expeditiously. The frontier districts were separated from the Punjab and created into a North-West Frontier Province ruled over by a Chief Commissioner, immediately under the Governor-General, and subsequently by a Governor. These measures have not proved successful in keeping the region quiet and free from disturbances. Occasional raids into British territory and other disturbances by the hill tribes have come to be a permanent feature, and recently the British Government had to resort to bombing from aeroplanes to strike terror into them. In the light of these subsequent events we can appreciate the wisdom of Amir 'Abdur Rahman when he described the probable results of the British forward policy in the following terms, in a letter written to Lord Lansdowne (1888-94):

"If you should cut them (the hill tribes) out of my dominions they will neither be of any use to you nor to me. You will always be engaged in fighting or other trouble with them and they will always go on plundering. As long as your Government is strong and in peace, you will be able to keep them quiet by a strong and, but if at any time a foreign enemy appear on the borders of India these frontier tribes will be your worst enemies."

The advocates of the forward policy on the other hand support the intrusion of the British into these hill territories, as it gives them a better line of defence than the River Indus against any invasion from the west. This is perhaps correct from a strictly military point of view. But the enormous trouble and expense involved can be justified only if there is a real danger of a serious invasion from the west. Such danger was undoubtedly very remote when the policy was first adopted. But in the light of later events which no one could then have foreseen the threat could not be described as altogether an imaginary one. (*Ibid*. pp. 837-838).

57. R.T. Vol.1 Book.V. p. 215.
58. Term *S'vapaka* or *Suapaca* is equivalent to *Domba*, literally 'dog-cooker' is the designation of a despised low caste of *Sudra* family.
59. Life is a way of deeds, "as you sow show shall you reap."
60. Term *Prabhakaradeva* is composed of four words i.e., Prabha+ka+ra+deva, *Prabha* means Prefect 'Master', *'Ka'* means oblation of 'god' in later vedic literature *'Ka'* is a synonym for Prajapati, Brahma, Vishnu and other gods, (R.V.V.R. p. 92) *'ra'* means way or 'thought' and 'deva' in ordinary word in the Vedas for god is *Deva*, and the original idea of the word *Deva* is 'bright'. The Universal Indo-European word for 'god' or 'Nam' was *deivos*, which appears in very archaic latin as *deivos,* and later becomes *deus*. *Devos* in hte Gallic proper name *Devog-nata* is its caltic form. In Old Scandinavian *tivar* means 'gods'. In Lithuanian the form *devas* is found, which in Sanskrit *deva*. This noun is connected with the verb *'div'*, *dyu*, 'Shine', the shining of the sun and of the moon. Its use shows that the Indo-Europeans derived their first and most pervasive conception of divine power from the brightness of the sun. Max Muller explains picturesquely how this word came to be used to designate the gods, "*Deva* meant originally bright and nothing else. Meaning brights, it was constantly used of the sky, the stars, the sun, the dawn, the day, the spring, the rivers, the earth; and when a poet wished to speak of all these by one and the same word *Sabad* by what we should call a general term *'words'* he called them all *Devas*. When that had been done, *Deva* did no longer men 'the Bright ones', but the name comprehend all the qualities which the sky and the sun and the dawn shared in common excluding only those that were peculiar to each. (Ibid. pp. 52-53).

61. R.T. Vol.1 Book V.P. 217.
62. *Ibid.* p. 218.
63. *Ibid.* p. 219.
64. According to *Kulluka dharma* is based on revealed texts (*Sruti*); revealed texts are of two kinds, the *Vedic* and the *Tantric*. '*Sruti* is of two kinds viz. *Vaidiki* (consisting of the *Veda*) and Tantriki (consisting of *Tantra*). A vetern scholar like Dr. R.C. Hazra (in I.H.Q. Vol. 36 pp. 141-150) Tantrik deals with *Mantras*, secret practices and esoteric teachings of *gurus*. The word *Tantra* is a Vedic one. It occurs in Rg. Ved X. 71.9 (*Siris-tantram tanvate aprajajnayah*). *Tantra* here appears to mean 'loom' and the word is drived from the root 'tan' to spread or stretch. Panini in VII. 2.9 drives the word from the root 'tan' with affix 'tra' and in another sutra (V.2.70) states that *'tantraka'* means cloth recently taken off from a loom. The *Amarakosa* gives four meanings of 'tantra', on of which is *'Siddhanta'* (a system of thought or philosophy). *Harita's* idea appears to have been that a work dealing with the formulation of principles based on Veda (and hence called *'Tantriki'* from the word *tantra* meaning *Siddhanta*) might be designated *Sruti* (H.D. Vol. 1 p. 130).
65. Term *Ekangas* means belongs to one family either *Brahmans* or *Tantrins*.
66. R.T. Vol.1. Book. V. p. 220.
67. *Ibid.*
68. **Note.** It shows that *Kanyakusja* or *Kanauj* was not important power only in the early Medieval period during the rule of *Karkota* dynasty, but also had the political importance under the Utpala dynasty.
69. R.T. Vol.1 Book V. pp. 221-222.
70. *Ibid.* p. 223.
71. *Ibid.*
72. **Note.** The meaning of the term *S'ridhakka* is equivalent to *dranga* or the story of the *'Word'* or *'God' who is* supreme and destructive one. It is the story of the *Karmvarta* watched by God.
73. *R.T.* Vol.1. Book V. p. 225.
74. *Ibid.* p. 226
75. *Ranga* means 'way' of the mind for *'Goodness'* that is *'Nam' die to* Him and get solace for the mind.
76. **Note.** The exact application of the term *aksapatala* is that 'God' lives 'High' means above the material world. He knows every activities of the *man*.In various texts term has been differently interpreted and referring to *aksa*, 'law suit', gives the court of Justic or the 'office of the Accountant-General'. It is evident that the 'Superintendent of the *Aksapatala*' held an important office and post. Therefore, '*Nam*' or '*Word*' is Supreme, everybody has to pay his account to 'Him' according to the theory of *'Karma'* past and present. *'Nam'* is the only sources which leave us from the bad activities.
77. *R.T.* Vol. 1 Book V. p. 227.

78. Term *tilavadasi* means 'black minded' peoples those worship the idol which is made by the man not by the god. *Tila* is black colour oil grain having the shape of heart. It has also bad taste in taking. Therefore, mind or *man* is black, has the *Nilamata* means blue like Krishna colour *mata* is harmful for the society. As F. Bernier explains *Anil* was the old Portuguese name for indigo, from the Arabic *al-nil,* pronounced *an-nil. Nil* is common name in India, from the Sanskrit *nila* blue (T.M.E; p. 283). **Note.** It is a comparative study of the *mind* with the *Tiladvadasi*. But the mind or *man* belongs to *'God'*. He has the thirst of 'god' without 'him', he cannot satisfy. It is the only way to get rid of the material world.
79. *R.T.* Vol.1 Book V.P 229. **Note.** The lord of animate beings *Pasupati* or *Pasupata*. The term is composed of two words i.e, *Pasu+Pati*, *'Pasu'* means animal and *'Pati'* means *'Father'*. Befȍre the *'Nam'* or *'Word'* man has the qualities like animals when he obtains the *'Nam'* from the *'father'* or *'Pati'*, with the practise of *'Word'* or *'Nam'* he or she becomes *'Pati'*. It depends on the implementation of the man on *'Sabad'*. It is called *'Trisula'* means 'thirst' of the law of Nature that is 'love' which is very pious.
80. *R.T.* Vol. 1. Book V. pp. 229-230
81. *Ibid.* p. 230.
82. *Ibid.*
83. *Ibid.* p. 231.
84. *Ibid.* p. 232.
85. *Ibid.* pp. 232-233.
86. *Ibid.* pp. 233-235.
87. It is the fifth colourful note of the Kalhana *Rajatarangini* i.e. called *'Nam'* or *'Sabad'*.

# 4

# Advent of the Viradeva Dynasty

The exist of the *Utpala* dynasty from the active political scene of Kashmir ushered in a new era[1] with the advent of the *Viradeva* dynasty the inhabitants of Kashmir, they again found, a new ruler, *Yasakara* did not belong to any royal family no had be background of note[2], but was distinguished by good qualities, such as the pious performance of ablutions, etc., and having a knowledge of the *Aksaras*[3] (*'Words'*). His father, *Kamadeva*, had been a teacher in the house of *Meruvardhana*[4], an influential minister of the state[5]. His early life had been spent in a village homeland, but he was a learned man possessed head and heart qualities. His rule was not less efficient like the rulers of the *Karkota* and *Utpala* rulers. He was a capable ruler of the *Viradava* dynasty.

***Yasaskara* (939-48 A.D.)**

As noted earlier, *Yasaskara* had come to occupy the throne of Kashmir pecuilar circumstances and at a time when the country was devoid a political stability (*under Suravarman II*). But he vindicated his choice by the Brahmins, who had been chosen[6] is beaking of Kashmir, moon of the earth entered the royal palace, which resounded with the blessings and auspicious shouts of the woman, while his glittering Umbrella, which shone with a light equalling that of the sun, seemed to draw (around his head) the splendour of an *aratrika*[8] (illumination) performed with a silver vessel[9]. According to the Chronicle, there were certain political disruptions either external or internal nature, but king *Yasaskara* of Kashmir obtained the faith of the people through the power of his intellect. He restored the ordinances of former rulers which had fallen into abeyance, just as a great poet (restores) the methods of earlier poets. Through effective policies, he made the land free from the robbery, the doors of the stops were left open in the bazaars at night, and the roads were secured for the travellers. He exercised his power carefully for the promotion of agriculture and its functionaries. The Brahmans were persuaded to lay down their arms and devoted (solely) to their studies[10] about the *Vedas*. While Brahman *Gurus* did not drink the spirits of the *Nam* or God by singings and chants the Sanskrit words these were not seen house-wives figuring as divinities at *Guru*-consecration (*gurudiksa*[11]), and by shakes of their heads detracting from the distinguished character of the husbans. Kalhana again mentions that astrologer, doctor, councillor, teacher, minister, Purohita, ambassador, judge, clerk had not then without learning[12] the *'word'* or *'Sabad'*.

From the fact, we learn that a high fee had to be paid by the person, who were entitled only a small amount of embazzlement. It is well-known by the Master. 'He' is the marchent of the *sa* for a *'ra.'*[13]

**Story of the Brahmans**

Kalhana mentions that under the *Yasakara*, there had not been the partial attitude towards the Brahmans. But it was a great threat for the Brahmans, whose *manas* were wandering in the material world. It is not a bargaining of the sum, it the bargaining of 'love'. He (*Nam*) is free of cost, there is no need of money. One has to be trade of *Him* (*nam*). It is the duty of the man to distinguishing the right and wrong in his own life. Now, the *King* or *Lord* ever bent on exercising his supervision, it shows that again *Krta Yuga*[14] has been come back. Thus he has guided his people with ridicule and imprudent conduct. He is similar like a physician who prescribes wholesome food for another and eats himself what is bad[15].

**Administration of Yasakara**

*Yasakara* is noted for his judicial decisions that he was careful to perform his purifications of the world, like a Brahman versed in Vedic lore, yet he did not dismiss those attendants who had eaten the food-remants of the *Dombas*[16] *or Chamar.* He had honoured his princes by giving '*Word*' or '*Nam*' not swords to defeat the foot-soldiers who have not the basic qualification. In the beginning, he appointed four city-prefects (*nagaradhikrta*[17]), who helped themselves in turn to mony (revenue) as a source of income of the state, and were hanged each other's back. In the meanwhile, his eldest brother died after a long-continued joy with his own invention that is blind faith. When a *velavitha*[18] who raised the rank of a provincial governor (*mandalesa*[19]) intrigued by the queens to the king in connived manners. It becomes useless and inconvenient. In the court of *Yasakara*, a lady known by the name of *Lalla*, raised her love among ladies of his seraglio. King *Yasakara* completely came under her control due to her fascinating personaltiy because she had met secretly at night with a *Candala* watchman[20]. It shows that *Candala* watchman must have certaing good qualities, therefore, she caused an attraction of love and were also belonged the same family. The other officials known as *Hadis*, they are the intriguers of the 'love' committing sins round the clock not for the present, but for the future course of actions. In their blind faith, they did not kill her (soul), but they have imposed certain restrictions on their supposition imagination which became injurious or destroyer those who had taken the food of *Dombas* remnants for the sake of purity and made it impure, they had to pay the prices in case of leprosy through the touch of a leper[21]. The King *Yasakara* was anxious to secure royal dignity for his future births. His endowment policy built a piece of land which had belonged to his father, a *Matha* for students for *Aryadesa*, who were devoting themselves to (the acquisition of) knowledge. The superintendent of the *Matha* had the power to check the mint-dics (*tanka*) of the royal seraglio. He also granted fifty-five Agraharas land to the Brahmans at the bank of *Vitasta* to furnished with great implements[22].

**Varnata Abhiseka (948 A.D.)**

It appears from the Kalhana's *Rajatarangini*[23] that *Yasakara,* in his life time seized by an abdominal disease, *Varnata*, abdicated the throne and installed as his successor. He was the son of his paternal grand-uncle *Ramadeva*. Due to the lack of head and heart qualities, *Varnata Abhiseka* could not manage the office for a long time. After one day to the very next morning, he was dethroned and the son of *Yasakara* known by the name of *Samgramadeva* was descended on throne. In the meantime, *Yasakara* was died on throne. In the meantime, *Yasakara* was died after a short period of nine years rule (939-948 A.D.) at the age of twenty-four years.

**Samgramadeva (948-949 A.D.)**

*Samgramadeva*, yet had been a child crowned during the lifetime of his father. *Yasakara*, with the consent of the ministers headed by *Parvagupta. Parvagupta* managed to place the *Samgramadeva* under the regency of his grandmother, quite an old lady, with a view to wield real power from behind. No doubt, *Pravagupta* himself served the child-king by bring food[24] etc. but at the same time, he formulated a scheme to usurped the throne to destroy the child openly from the fear of powerful *Ekangas*. One day he heard at night a Supernatural Voice which said: "on the first day of *Caitra* the kingdom belongs legally to you and your race. If you proceed otherwise, there will be an early end for your life and family." *'Word'* or *'Nam'*, he recognised the futility of witchcraft, and still became more uneasy[25] . The hostile *Ekangas* threatened the King, he suddenly collected his troops on a day when people did not move outside on account of a heavy snowfall, and surrounded the palace. He slained in fighting his faithful minister *Ramavardhana*, who offered the resistance with the company of his son called *Buddha*. In the same time, he also tied a string with flowers which had been brought as an offering by his father's (*Yasakara*) *Velavitta,* round the neck of *Samgrama,* 'the

Crooked footed', (*Vakranghri-Samgrama*), and dragged him from the throne. He was at that time twenty-four year the role as an evil-doer to obtained the throne with sword and armour[26].

***Paravagupta** (949-950 A.D.)*

*Paravagupta* did not come to any royal background and was a common man. He became the ruler of Kashmir after the killing of *Samgramadeva*, was the son of *Samgramagupta*, who had been born in *Paravisoka* from a writer (*divira*) called *Abhinava.* On the appointment of *Parvagupta* as a king the malevolent princes, *Ekangas*, chiefs, ministers, officials, and *tantrins* were afraid of him, and showed nothing but treason[27]. But the angry king had his garment taken off, shaved off his hair and beard and became an ascetic. Yet among the ladies of the illustrious king *Yasakara's* seraglio, one pure-minded queen, like Gauri, removed all evil report. This virtuous woman cleverly practised a pious fraud upon *Parvagupta*, when with overconfidance, he constructed the temple within few days. Thus, the result of that was the king *Paravgupta* lost the royal power which he had to attained by treason, at the age of twenty-six (950 A.D.)[28].

**Kesmagupta** (950-958 A.D.)

*Kesmagupta* was the son of *Parvagupta*, he was equally ruthless as his father was. He had no discipline and character in his life, the royal assembly filled with whores, villains, idiots, and corrupt offiiclas, therefore, it was unfit to be visited by the wise persons. No doubt, he founded the (temple of Vishnu) *Phalgunasvamini*[29] and other shrines. Behind his back the king often laughed at his counsel, in order to kill the *Damara Samgrama,* who already entered into the famous *Jayendravihara*[30].

King *Simharaja*, the lord of the *Lohara*[31], in the meantime, along with strongholders of *Indra* (in power), decided to give him his own daughter (Didda) in marriage. This marriage had the political importance as *Didda,* the *S'ahis* daughter's daughter, wholly engrossed on the mind of *Kemagupta* and the king became humiliated by the appellation of *Diddaksema*[32]. The lavish *Ksemagupta* took thirty-six villages from the brunt *Vihara*, and gave them into the tenure of the *Khasa* ruler the maternal grandfather of Queen *Didda,* the illustrious *S'ahi*, built a high temple of Vishnu *Bhimakesava*[33]. The people of Kashmir when they saw the Ksemagupta ever roaming with dogs and surrounded by bands of *Dombas* carrying nets and jungle-folk[34]. He was shakened with fright at this movement and was seized by the *luta*-disease (accompanied) by fever, which caused his death[35] at the age of thirty four (958 A.D.)[36]. After the death of *Ksemagupta,* his minor-son *Abhimanya* became the ruler of Kashmir under the guy of Queen *Didda.*

***Abhimanyu (958-972 A.D.)***

*Abhimanyu* was the minor son of *Ksemagupta*, who ruled over the valley from 958 A.D to 972 A.D. He became the king under the guardianship of Queen Didda, whose character knew no marcy[37]. The officers who held the charge of foreign affairs and the royal administration, they mostly used to visit in the bedchamber of the queen without any hesitation. During the reign of *Abhimanyu*, there were also certain terrible conflagration from the side of *Tungesvara* shrine reached near *Bhiksukiparaka* near the shrine of Vishnu. The powerful *Vardhanasvamin* destroyed the great buildings with the limits of 'the Vetala's measuring line' (*Vetalasutrapata*[38]). This terrible fire purified the land by burning the great buildings touched by the *Dombas* and *Ҫandalas*[39].

***Didda's Enemity with Phalguna***

*Didda* had the enemity with *Phalguna* during the lifetime of *Ksemagupta*. He was the Prime Minister, or the lord of the Gate (*davarapati*) during his rule, who had given his daughter *Candralekha* in marriage to the king. On the death of her husband, she wished to become *Sati,* but in front of the funeral pyre she felt regret, and minister *Naravahana* at that moment, he prevented her for the self immolation. Then *Rakka*, who was malignant by nature, put into the embittered queen that apprehension are there that *Phalguna* would usurp the kingdom of Kashmir. *Phalguna* became aware of that[40], *Didda* and other ministers felt aversion and anger towards him, who distrusted from the palace and apprehended from the evil designed of his enemies. He resolved to stop at *Parnotsa* until his (sons) return. He felt the city followed by numerous troops and arrived near the vicinity of *Kasthavata*[41] together with his possessions. *Didda* on the instigation of *Rakka* and ministers had to resolve the misleading issue with the exit of *phalguna* from the active political scene. They had the feared of the attack and trembled. In short, he was recalled along with his troops from the *Parnotsa*, took the charge of the administration. In this way, *Didda* at night came out by a gameplan for the destruction of her enemies[42].

***Mahiman's and Patala Rebellion***

Before the *Phalguna*, when *Parvagupta* had the aim to become the crown, he married two daughters to the ministers known as *Bhoja* and *Bhubhata,* who had taken the oath by sacred libation (*Kosapithin*). The two sons who were born from them renowned as *Mahiman* and *Patala*. They were grown up in the palace of king as they were his own sons. These two were very keen entered into a conspiracy with *Himmaka*[43] to obtain the throne of Kashmir. Immediately, *Didda* turned out these two powerful persons from the royal palace.

And, they were going hither and thither from their own house with full of anger mood. In the meanwhile, she sent staff bearers in open hostility behind *Mahiman*, in order to banished him. Then, he had left the house of his father-in-law *S'aktisena*. He was joined there as a refuge like *Himmaka, Mukula, Eramantaka* a resident of *Parihasapura,* as well as by the famous *Udayagupta*, son of *Amrtakara, Yasodhara* and others, who came from *Lalitadityapura*[48]. No doubt *Mahiman* had a confederacy with huge troops at the time of political upheaval, but faithful minister *Naravahana* was the only one who, together with his relatives, did not abandon the side of *Didda* the opposite force with glittering weapons came near the vicinity of (the temple of) *Padmasvamin*[49], keen for the battle. *Didda*, thereupon, sent her son to the *S'uramatha,* for the averting of war. She quickly bought off the greedy Brahmans from *Lalitadityapura* by providing plenty of gold and thus, she broke up the league of her enemies that is Brahmans. The lame (queen) *Didda*, the widow of *Ksemagupta* rule became undisputed with *Mahiman*[50].

***Expedition against S'ahi Thakkana***

After crushing the *Mahiman* rebellion, *Yasodhara* the commander-in-chief of Queen *Didda* undertook an expedition against the *S'ahi* ruler that is *Thakkana*[51], captured by force. *Rakka* and other wicked persons of her administration instigated Queen *Didda* against the commander-in-chief that *Yasodhara* was betraying her and had taken money for keeping *Thakkana* (on his throne). She took this notice for the very truth. Consequently upon the glory of the commander-in-chief, had reached his house, *Didda*, immediately despatched staff-bearers with the evident intention of banish him[52].

**Rebellion Against Didda**

On the insult of *Yasodhara,* there was a rebellion led by *Himmaka, Eramantaka* and the others supporters of the commander-in-chief. The war was took place between the two group's near *Jayabhattarika*[53] to the vicinity of the *S'uramatha*. At that moment, *Rajakulabhatta* arrived there, scattered the enemy's force by the *'Sound'* of his martial music, and delighted by capturing *Yasodhara. Himmaka* was killed, *Eramantaka* was caught alive, and *Udayagupta* was fled away from the battle field. As soon as Queen *Didda* secured the victory against the rebels, she punished *Yasodhara, S'ub hadhara and Mukula,* together with their relatives. After destroying the treacherous ministers, she place the loyal *Rakka* and others on the royal posts[54]. Thus, the faithful *Naravahana*, the best among ministers, made the widow Queen (acquire power) over the whole land, and made her equivalent Indra (who rules over the whole heaven[55]).

**Rise and Fall of Naravahana**

During the political capricious, *Naravahana*, the able and faithful minister, had been a tower of strength and was the stunch supporter of the regent queen. In the council of ministers, she made an announcement for the faithful minister with the title of *Rajanka*. She had been remained with him in all the times. But there were also two sons of a litter-carrier *Sindhu,* and *Bhuyya* called *Kuyya*. The eldest , *'Sindhu'* had been previously a favourite in the house of *Parvagupta*, and obtained the charge of the treasury from Queen *Didda*. The newly created post known as (*ganjesa*) and the founder of this office called *Sindhuganja*. *Sindhuganja* told the queen with polished language that *Naravahana* had taken almost all the power of the royal house[56]. She noticed, it with a careful manners and adviced the *Naravahan* to leave this office. Subsequently, the mutual affection between *Didda* and *Naravahana* was removed (*niskrstasnehayoh*[57]) and sent word that she had got herself menses. It was the estrange between the two. Thus the foolish (Queen) who was unable (to use) her feet (*caranahina*), became, through her want of moral principles (*srutibahyata*), an object of reaproach, being in character just like the crow minded a stupid Brahman (who, being foolished and ignorant of the ritual (*Carana*), becomes an object of reaproach through his want of Vedic knowledge (*Sruti*)). Trusted *Naravahan*, who stood steadfast in his devotion towards Queen Didda in her difficult days. But he was publicly disgraced, could not withstand his insult and the result was that he committed suicide[58].

**Fearing of the Uprising of Damaras, and Didda recalled Phalguna**

Queen Didda had the fearing of rebellion in her mind when *Naravahana* committed suicide. A union was formed by the *Sthanesvara* and the Damaras chief against the Queen[59]. In the meantime, *Rakka* was died, Didda had in need a strong man. She recalled the *Phalguna* from the modern Poonch. He laid down the sword and took up the office of the crown. The eclipse of the rebellion led by Damaras, etc. they fled away in the battle field on the death of *Kayyaka*, the lord of the Gate, in their own place that is *Rajapuri*[60], Ultimately her *Ghosa* was cool down (*Uttara*) and (*Avaruddha*) lived with Queen *Didda*. The wicked *Jayagupta*, who was the favourite associate of *Udayaraja*, the queen's brother, he was the in charge of the *Aksapatala* (office) plundered *Kashmir*. *Abhimanyu*, whom the sins of his evil-conducted mother rendered miserable, fell into consumption. Thus, the noble character of Kashmir intercoursed with the wicked withered, just as the sun's heat (withers) the S'irisa-flower. The half-moon of the subjects was seizd by the eclipse of the fate at the age of forty-eight in 972[61] A.D.

***Nandi gupta (972-973 A.D.)***

After the death of *Abhimanya* his son *Nandigupta* became the ruler of Kashmir. No doubt, the heart of *Didda* (entered) in great sorrow for her (lost) child. Her cruel nature concealed by darkness, to cool down, she constructed the (temple of Vishnu) *Abhimanyusvamin* and (the town of) *Abhimanyupura*[62] on the merit of deceased son. Besides these, she further consturcted the (temple of Visnu) *Diddasvamin,* together with *Diddapura*, and a *Matha* for the residence of the people from *Madhyadesa*, *Lata* and *Saudotra*[63] means *fear of the pure thought.* In the memory of her husband, she also built a town at *Kankanapura*, decorated with gold showers called *'Kankavarsa'*, decorated with gold showers called *'Kankanvarsa'*. She also built a Vihara with a high quadrangle, as an abode for Kashmirians and foreigners (*dasika*). Under the name of her father, *Simharaja,* she erected the illustrious (shrine of Vishnu) *Simhasvamin,* and a *Matha* for the residence of foreign Brahmans. She alos repaired the ruined buildings (*Jirnoddhara*). *Valgamatha* was also erected, on the relic of *Valga*, a porter-woman-Timi-fish,[64] though living in sacred water kept in silence like a *Muni* in pretended meditation. After a single year unfaithful Queen Didda, lust for pleasures employed witchcraft against her little grandson, at the age of forty-nine[65], he was expired.

***Tribhuvana (973-975 A.D.)***

*Nandigupta* was nominally followed on the throne of Kashmir by his younger infant brother, *Tribhuvana,* the reins of governance was still controlled by the Queen *Didda*. But within a short period of two years, in the same fashion discussed above, she destroyed her grandson *Tribhuvane*. He was fifty one years of old at that time. The youngest son of *Abhimanyu* known as *Bhimagupta* was seated on the throne in 975[66] A.D.

**Bhimagupta (975-980 A.D.)**

After the death of *Tribhuvana, Bhimagupta*[67] was appointed on the throne of Kashmir. Then the cruel (queen) *Didda* put her last grandson, *Bhimagupta*, without hesitation on the path of death which bore the name *'throne'*. In the meantime, old *Phalguna* died, *Didda* had concealed her cruelty and malignity[68]. Thereafter, she openly extended her misconduct. Unfortunately, women of high origin abandoned themselves to the low[69]

***Rise of Tunga***

*Tunga*[70] was the son of *Bana*, belonged to *Buddivasa*[71] *in Parnotsa* native of a *Khasa* village. He had come as herdsman buffaloes. He reached in *Kashmir* with his five brothers known as *Sugandhisiha, Prakata, Naga, Attayika* and *Sanmukha*. He obtained the employment in the *Didda's* court as a letter-carrier *(Lekhaharaka)*[72]. He won the heart of *Didda* and was elevated on the post of foreign affairs[73] in the administration of *Kashmir*. She never felt the shame to love with *Tunga* and killed *Bhuyya* by poison. The *Velavitta Devakalasa, Rakka's* son, shameless wretched, who acted as a procurer, were placed by her in the office of *Bhuyya*. Beside these, *Kardamaraja,* the lord of the Gate and other (chief) officers were also accommodated in the same office. The minor-son *Bhimagupta*, after living four or five years in the palace, he learnt lot of about the affairs of the kingdom. He also noticed the way of behaviour of his grandmother and was interested to introduce certain reforms. Thus, the result was that the shameless queen imprisoned *Bhimagupta* on the request of *Devakalasa*. The doubt which clouded the mind of the people as to the mischief secretly done to *Nandigupta* and now she openly acted and dispelled it. In this way, she put all her grandsons out of the way, and ascended herself on the throne in 980 A.D[74]. *Bhimagupta* was fifty-six old at that time.

***Didda*** (980-1003 A.D.)

Attempt has been made in the foregoing pages to submit an historical background in reality for an assessment of the early career and reign of Queen *Didda*, who dominated the political scene of the *Kashmir* valley for nearly half a century. As cited above, she was the daughter of the powerful *Lohara* chief, *Shimharaja* and grand-daughter, from the mother's side of the illustrious *Shahi* king *Bhima*. Her career may be assessed in two broad phases: (1) From 958 A.D. to 981 A.D. and (2) From 981 A.D. to 1003 A.D. Immediately, after the death of *Ksemagupta*, the widow queen tackled the political upheavel with great sense. Her role as the regent of her son and the three grandsons has already been discussed in detail. Now career as a queen may be assessed herein detail:

During the rule of *Didda* as an independent queen, she appointed the *Tunga* on the post of prime minister (*Sarvadhikarin*) and was elevated above everybody. But his brothers, who were the ministers in the court of *Didda*, they were ousted, a discontent was raised in the kingdom. They met in council with the son of *Didda's* brother, *Vigraharaja*. He brought to *Kashmir* by the council of ministers. He had possessed strong head and heart qualities. As soon as, he arrived in the valley, he sensibly at once induced the Brahmans holding the chief *Agraharas* to enter upon a solemn fast (*Prdyopavesa*), in order to creat disturbance in the kingdom. At that time, Brahmans had been united and were ready to kill the *Tunga*. Queen *Didda* had the fearing of revolt in her mind for some days, she concealed him in the closed doors. She bribed the Brahmans with the presents of gold and then the fast was ended. In this way, *Vigraharaja's* power was scattered, *Tunga* again secured the power and strengthened his position and put to death *Kardamaraja*[75] and his supporters. Again this enmity led by the secret emissaries caused the Brahmans to begin a solemn fast (*praya*). *Aditya, Katakavarika* the favourite officers of *Vigraharraja,* who had secretly kept among them, they were fled away and some one killed. *Vatsaraja* was wounded and *Nyankotaka* was caught alive. *Sumanomantaka* and the Brahmans, who had taken the gold as bribe for the ending of fast (*praya*) from Queen *Didda*, All they were caught and put into jail by *Tunga*[76].

***Expedition against Rajapuri***

After the death of *Phalguna, Rajapuri* ruler, *Prthvipala* declared independent and attached over the *Kashmiri* force. Ministers known as *Sipataka* and *Ilamsaraja* were killed. *Chandra* and his other supporters on the distressed of their death and had to attain the relief[77]. *Tunga* and his brothers, they suddenly penetrated into the *Rajapuri* state and attached over the king *Prthvipala. Tunga* defeated the king *Prthivipala* and the town was burnt down entirely. He took legal action for the establishment of the peace. *Tunga* on his return to the city (Srinagar) after defeating the *Prthvipala* and received the command of the Kashmir army[78].

It is again visible that Damaras were secretly in legaue with *Prithvipala* and were interested to hurt the Kashmiri rulers. But their evil design was soon brought to an end by the *Tunga*[79].

***Appointment* of *Samgamaraja as Yuvaraja.***

It has been already recorded that there was no rightful claimant left to the throne of Kashmir after the death of last grandson of *Didda* that is *Bhimagupta.* During the last days of her life, she perposed the name of her brother's son *Samgramaraja* to the rank of *Yuvaraja* as her successor after testing him (as follows):

She assembled number of children for the test of intelligence before her, she threw down before them a heap of apples (*Palevata*[80]). While *Samgramaraga* held plenty of apples and was yet untouched. She declared him fit for the throne[81]. In the year 1003 A.D.[82], she had gone to heaven at the age of seventy-nine and *Yuvaraja* (*Samgramaraja*) became the ruler of Kashmir.

From the above written pages, we learn that *Viradeva* dynasty of Kashmir, dominated the political scene of the valley near about sixty-four years and ten kings enjoyed the pleasures of the earth. But the role of *Didda* was glaring and statesmanship of high order. During the last days of her life, she secured a change of the dynasty without any political resistance. Thus, being a woman, she showed the courage like a man and her name in the annals of Indian history is unforgettable.

## NOTES AND REFERENCES

1. P.H.K. p. 136.
2. *Ibid.*
3. *R.T.* Vol.1 Book V. p. 234.
4. *Ibid.*
5. P.H.K. p. 136.
6. *Ibid.*
7. *R.T.* Vol.1 Book V. p. 235.
8. ***Note***. *Aratrika* is the name of the ceremony in which burning lights, placed in earthen lamps, are swung around the head of a scared image. A similar site is still performed in Kashmir and Panjab on marriages, the lamps being swung around the bridegroom. It is also a comparative study of man and 'God' or 'Word' when marriage of the soul take place with the *'Nam'*. Similar kind of marriage happened to be there. It is also like remarriage in the day to day life. It gives contentment to the life.
9. *R.T.* Vol.1 Book V. p. 235.
10. *Ibid.* Book VI. p. 236.
11. *Ibid.* P.237 **Note.** *Gurudiksa* is a *Trantric* rite by which the pupil (*Sadhaka*) is initiated as guru or teacher. This *Diksa* is described, e.g. at the commencement of *Raghavananda's Paddhatiratnamala*, Jammu. Mss. No. 5293. *Gurudiksa* and the *Trantric* ceremonies, the *Guru* and his spiritual predecessors are worshipped by the sacrificers under their proper names coupled with those of certain deities. Muller says that there is not one single allusion in the hymns of the *Rigveda* to anything connected with writing. Pure Brahmans never speak of the *granthas* or books. They speak of their *Veda*, which means 'Knowledge'. They speak of their *Sruti,* which means what they have heard with their ears. They speak of *Smriti*, which means what their fathers have declared unto them. We meet with *Brahmans,* i.e. the sayings of Brahmans; with *Sutras,* i.e. the strings of rules; with *Vedangas,* i.e. the members of the *Veda;* with *Prava-chanas,* i.e. the preachings; with *Sastras* i.e. teachings; with *Darsanas,* i.e. demonstrations; but we never meet with a book, or a volume, or a page (R.V.V.R. p. 42).
12. *R.T.* Vol.1 Book VI. p. 237.
13. *Ibid.* p. 239.
14. *Ibid.* pp. 239-240 **Note.** The philosophers and sages of India have related with the formation of this earth differently, according to their own notions. Thirteen various accounts are given in the *Mahabharata* alone, not one of which is sufficiently satisfactory to induce us to addopt it in preference to another. The Hindus divided time into four Ages: Is, *Satyug*; 2nd, *Tritayug;* 3rd, *Duwapuryug*; 4th, *Kulyug;* and they assert, that the four ages continue in succession to all eternity; the present being the *kalyug*,

which when at an end, the *Satyug* will re-commence the earth, therefore, is by them, deemed eternal, without beginning and without end; and that a judgement day will come the *Sutyug* is said to have lasted during a period of 1,728,000 years; when virtue and truth prevailed, and man lived 100,000 years.

The *Traitayug* is a period of 1,296, 000 years; three parts of the creation, during that time, obeyed the word of God, and the life of man was 10,000 years.

The *Dwapuryug* is a period of 864,000 years; during which half of the creation was wicked; and man only lived 1000 years.

The *Kaliyug* is a period of 432,000 years; men, in this period, became sinful; only one quarter of the human race followed the dictates of God, and the life of man was curtailed to 100 years. According to the Hindu account, in the present year (1015 of the Hijra), 4684 years of the *Kaliyug* have elapsed.

It may be useful to state, that the *yuga* progress in an arithmetical ratio of 1,2,3,4, from the smallest to the greatest number, and are divisible both by the Indian cycle of 60 years, which is the usual divisor of time among them, as also by the figure 9, which is applicable both to time and things. These observations are intended to convey to the reader's mind the motion that the extravagancy of the Hindu calculations are not without method, and require only the key to become intelligible and within the limits of our belief. This is not the place to discuss a question which would fill a volume (R.M.P.1. pp. XLV-XLVI).

15. *R.T.* Vol.1 Book VI. p. 241.
16. *Ibid.* **Note**. Those who partook the food-remants of the *Dombas* or *Candalas*. They had their seats int he court, not only of *Cakravarman*, but of other subsequent kings (R.T. Vol.1 Book V. p. 227).
17. In the succeeding reigns of *Viradeva* dynasty one perfect of the city of Srinagar (*nagaradhiktra, nagardhikrta, nagaradhikpa*) was appointed. *Yasaskara* in order to increased the revenue, he appointed four perfects for the sake of fiscal advantages. The *Mayor* (*Nagarika*) or perfect of the city which was normally the *Sthaniya* or town proper it called *Nagarika*. (C.M.H.T.P.133).
18. The meaning of the *Velavitta* term is, when one has gone without the knowledge of God or *'Nam'*, one must have to repent, what it will take time according to theory of *Karma*.
19. **Note.** *Mandalesa*, *mandalesvara*, *mandelesitr* terms have been used for the word of governor in the Kalhana *Rajatarangini*.
20. *R.T.* Vol. 1. Book VI; p. 241.
21. *Ibid.*
22. *Ibid.*
23. *Ibid.*
24. *Ibid.*

25. *Ibid.*
26. *Ibid.*
27. *Ibid.*
28. *Ibid.* p. 246.
29. *Ibid.*
31. The original name of the state was *Parnotsa*, of which Punch is a derivation, and the original capital was a Lohara, the present Lohrin to the north-east of the town of Punch. The name *Parnotsa*, in its abbreviated form, has many variants. Cunningham uses *Punacha* or *Punach*; by the Kashmiris it is called *Punats;* Moorcraft spells the name *Prunch* or *Pruntz*. General court also has *Prunch,* but it is called *Punje* by Mirza Mogal Beg, who was wilford's surveyor, and *Punch* by Vigne (H.P.H.S. P.698) The identity of the latter name with *Prunts* is well-known to the Pandits of S'rinagar. Kashmiris represent a large percentage in the population of the town and territory of *Prunts*. This is evidently the result of the close political connection which has since old times existed between the latter Kashmir and *Parnotsa* (R.T. Vol.1 Book. IV. p.139).
32. *R.T.* Vol. VI. Book. VI. P. 249 **Note.** In the end of the *Utpala* dynasty, *Yasaskara* was followed by that of *Pravagupta*. In the time of *Ksemagupta*, son and successor of *Parvagupta,* the virtual ruler was his Queen *Didda*, daughter of her Lohara and descended through her mother from the *Shahis* of *Udabhandapura*. *Didda*, at first, ruled in the name of puppet kings and then seized the crown herself. She kept it till 1003 A.D. When she transmitted her sceptre to her nephew *Samgramaraja* of *Udayaraja*, the founder of the Lohara dynasty. A terrible invader now appeared on the scene. The *Shahi* kingdom of *Udabhandapura* fell after a heroic struggle, inspite of the assistance it received from the ruler of Kashmir. The kingdom of *Samgramaraja* fortunately escaped destruction at the hands of Mahmud of Ghazni, but was too much weakened by internal conflicts to interfere successfully in the general affairs of Northern India. It gradually sank to the position of a minor power and finally succumbed to the Muslims in 1339 A.D. (A.H.I. P.164).
33. R.T. Vol.1 Book VI . P.249 **Note**. *Bhima Shahi* erected a temple bearing his name in the adoptive country of his granddaughter. The shrine of *Bhimakesava* must also have been richly endowed. *Simharaja's* father-in-law, *"Bhima Shahi* and *Didda"* maternal grandfather is identical with king *Bhima,* whom *Alberuni* mentions in the list of the 'Hindu Shahiyas of Kabul', as the successor of *Kamalu or Kamaluka*. The Shahi ruler as already mentioned belonged to the Kingdom of *Udabhandapura*. By the latter name, the ancient capital of *Gandhara* is meant. To the end of the tenth century A.D. the task of defending the North-West Frontier of India devolved on their feudatories, the Hindu Shahis of *Udabhandpura* mention has already been made of this illustrious line of kings in connection with the history of Kashmir. The founder of the line was a prince named *Lalliyashahi* who flourished towards the close of the 9th

century A.D. The fourth prince, *Bhima Shahi,* was the maternal grandfather of the celebrated queen *Didda* of Kashmir. His famous successor *Jayapala* came into conflict with the Sultans of Ghazni. The struggle produced momentous consequents and it has already been discussed in the previous chapter. At present temple is supposed to be the resting place for the Muhammadans of the valley, who use to visit for pilgrim- age at Saint *Baba Bamadin Sakis*. Originally this place and shrine related with *Saint*, who had built this building for himself. The original character of the saint; *sad* is a common appellation of the Hindu ascetic in *Kashmir*. The *Mahatmya*, which is comparatively recent origin, knows nothing of *Bhimakesava,* but derives the name *Bhimadvipa* from *Bhima,* one of the *Saktis* of *Martanda*. Against this it must, however, be noted that the pilgrimage route of the *Martandatirtha* does not include a visit of *Bumazu*. This locality would scarcely have been omitted if an ancient tradition had connected the name of *Bumazu* with Bhima and the worship of *Martanda*. As far as our present knowledge of the history of Kashmir architecture goes, both this shrine and another small cella, situated a few steps to the South West of 'Bama-Din-Sahib's Ziarat', and also converted into a Muhammadan tomb, may well be attributed to the time of *Bhima-S'ahi*, or even a later period.

34. *R.T.* Vol.1 Book V. p. 2005.
35. *Ibid P.* 251. **Note.** In the meantime, in the country of king (Bhimasena) a plague caused by the *Luta*- disease, which much distressed his citizes (R.T. Vol.1 Book IV. p. 169).
36. *Ibid.*
37. *Ibid.*
38. *Ibid*. p. 252. The site of *Vardhanasvamin* temple shrines cannot ascertained now and marked on one side the extreme limit of Pravarasena's city. Its position is unknown, and so is that of *Bhiksukiparaka*. The term *Vetalasutrapata* contains clearly a reference of the legend of the demon which indicated to *Pravarasena* the site for his new city. The territory which was supposed to have been originally marked off by the demon's measuring line, might have borne the name *Vetalasutrapata*. Regarding the position of the oldest parts of the foundation of *Pravarasena's* town, can be correctly understood only in the connection with the topography of modern Srinagar. The most convincing proof is, however, furnished by the long list of buildings and localities which are mentioned by the Chronicle in the new capital, and which, beginning with *Pravarasena's* own great temple *Pravaresa*, can actually be identified within the modern S'rinagar or in its immediate vicinity. The term *Vetalasutrapata* contains clearly a reference originally marked off by the demon's measuring line which are disordered from the 'Word' or 'Nam'. Regarding the position of the oldest parts of *Pravaraspura*. From the fact, it is confirmed by the scholars that the name *Pravarapura* (for *Pravarasenapura* shortened *bhimavat*) can be traced

throughout the works of *Ksemendra, Bilhana, Kalhana* and later Chroniclers as the appelation of the city occupying the site of the present *S'rinagar.*

39. *R.T.* Vol.1. Book VI. p. 252.
40. *Ibid.*
41. *Ibid.* p. 253 ***Note***. Term *Kashthavata* is composed of two *words Kashtha+Vata* Sanskritized rather than a true Sanskrit word, and if taken literally can only mean a "garden of wood". The second member of the word *'Vata'* or *'Var'*, meaning "enclosure" or "garden". The name of the dried apricot *'word'* so commonly used in the hills *Mana* is *Kishta* in the local dialect: hence the derivation of the word Kishtwar, according to local etymology, meaning "the place of dried apricots." Another derivation is from the word *Kasht*, meaning "trouble" the next invasion of the *Chandrabhaga* Valley was from the south. Even at that early period there seems to have been a good deal of communication with the plains and in the annals, it is mentioned that a tribe named *Panjsasi,* who appear to have been a trading community from the *Panjeb* (*Sound*) called in Panjabi. The dealt in medicines and other hill products, such as dried apricots, which they received in exchange for goods. And, some of the *Panjsasi settled* down on the plateau and mingled with the other tribes, with whom for a time they lived on terms of friendship. But in consequence of some disagreement, a quarrel arose, and the *Panjsasi* being the more warlike, the Rotar and Ganai were subdued. But this did not end the strife, as the local tribes tried to recover their independence, and frequent encounters took place between the rival tribes. The *Panjsasi* lived near the Southern end of the plateau in the vicinity of the *Hoderi* spring, and being constantly in dread of an attack they did not lay aside their arms even engaged in field labour (H.P.H.S. p. 643).
42. R.T. Vol.1 Book VI. p. 254.
43. *Ibid.* **Note.** The *Tarikhs* of Haidar Malik and Narayan Koul give Himmaka's name as that of a Turk. Another Jahangir Mirza's servent Qaitmas *Turkman*. (This can be translated "He turns not back" or "He stops not". He is, of that character, the *Prakrtis* become, because their progress and decline are dependent upon him (*Babur Nama*; Tr. by A.S Bevaridge, Two Vols. Bound in one, Delhi, Reprint 1997; p. 237. Hereafter explained as *B.N.*)
48. *R.T.* Vol. 1 Book VI. p. 254 **Note.** *Lalitadityapura* is the same as *Lalitapura.* Its site is marked by the modern *Latapor* on the right bank of *Vitasta.* The local tradition of the place tells of a large town, which king *'Laltadit'* had built here on the adjoining udar.
49. *Ibid.* **Note.** *Padmasvamin* is a temple situated in *Padmapura* on the *Vitasta*, 74° 59′ longitude and 34° latitude called *Pampur* by *Panjabis.* The scanty remains of an ancient temple, situated in the centre of the town. So far, the literary meaning of the term is concerned, *'Nam'* or *'Word'* is the Master of the world. He is Perfect Master lives on the right

bank of the Bias. Panjabis called him *'Pure Father'* of the mind or man.

50. *R.T.* Vol.1 Book V. pp. 255.
51. *Ibid.* **Note.** *Thakkana* is the son of *Tanvanga* besides him, *Tanvanga* has the other two sons *Ajjaka* and *Dhammata,* who had returned from abroad and *Gunga's* sons, *Malla, Tulla,* the son of *Ajjaka* grandsons of *Tanvanga,* had the divisions of its disc(*Kala*) which are dripping with nectar *gives here the correct reading Tanvanga jams Thakka,* instead of the meaningless *Tanvangasthasthakka,* spoke to him these harsh words: "O you wretch, not of *Kayya* by kind *Kalasa* were you begotten. Your father was surely some coward, whoever he (may have been)." Prince addressed at that time, who knew no yielding in resolute conduct, he became like one over whom cold water had been poured in his sleep. (R.T. Vol.1, Book VII. p. 348).
52. *Ibid.* PP. 255-256.
53. *Ibid.* P. 256 **Note.** *Jayabhattarika*, only here mentioned, is possibly the designation of a temple, compare with *Simhadvara*, literally 'the lion' or 'the palace gate' which hung up great bells in all four directions, to be informed by their sound of those, who had come with the desire of making representations by the people from various nations presented themselves. All the riches countries seemed always to be pilled up. (R.T. Vol.1 Book VII, p. 336).
54. *Ibid.* p. 257.
55. *Ibid.*
56. *Ibid.* p. 258.
57. *Ibid.* **Note**. There is a double sense in *niskrstasnehayoh* which in connection with the simile would have to be rendered 'after the oily substance has been extracted.
58. *Ibid.*
59. *Ibid.* p. 259.
60. Its ancient name was *Rajapuri*, of which modern Rajouri is a derivation. It was bound on the north by the *Pir Panjal*; on the west by *Punch* and Kotli; on the south by Bhimbar and on the east by the Chinab. The entire area between the Jehlam and Chinab in the out hills, bore in former times the name of *Darvabhisara* before the time of Alexander's invasion, down to the 12th century A.D. and possibly a good deal later *Abisaras,* who first opposed Alexander on the advancement towards Indus, who is called "the king of the Indian mountaineers". After his capture *Aornos*, and passage of the Indus, *Abisares* seems to have got alarmed and sent envoys to Taxila, accompanied by his own brother and other notable men, to tender his submission. He had been in league with *Poros, Poros* is supposed to be the Greek rendering of Sanskrit *Paurava* meaning "descendent of (the race of) Puru." Our pilgrim goes on to relate that from *Punach* a journey south-east of above 400 li brought him to the *Ho-Lo-She-pu-lo* (*Rajapura*) country. This *Yuan-Chwang* describes as being above 4000 li in circuit its capital being above ten *Li* in circuit. It was a difficult country to travel in as it was very hilly with narrow valleys,

it was not fertile and it resembled *Punach* in products and climate, and like that country it had no sovereign of its own and was subject to Kashmir. There were ten Buddhist monasteries and the Brethern were few in number; There was one Deva-temple but the non-Buddhists were very numerous. The native annotar to our text here makes *Rajapura* to be in *"North India"*, but the annotator to the Fangehih representes it as a state outside of India (Y.C. p. 284). It is clear from the above statement that as early as the beginning of the eleventh century the town of *Rajapuri* was called *Rajawari,* which is evidently an intermediate form between *Rajapuri* and *Rajauri.* We may, therefore, assume that in ordinary usage the ancient form of *Rajapuri* had begun to be dropped before this time. The further change from *Rajawari* to *Rajauri* may have taken place gradually. In the later Chronicles down to Mughal times we find *Rajpuri* except once where *'Rajavira'* occurs (H.P.H.S. PP. 670-671)

61. *R.T.* Vol.1 *Book VI.* p. 260.
62. *Abhimanyapapura* is neither the temple nor the town. It is village known as *Bimyan* situated in marshly ground about four miles to the South-West of Srinagar at 34° 4′ latitude and 70°-49′ longtitude this village was founded by Queen *Didda.*
63. *R.T*.Vol.1-Book VI. p. 260.
64. *Ibid.* p. 261.
65. *Ibid* p. 262.
66. *Ibid.* **Note.** Only few coins bear the name as *Tribhuvanagupta* that he was a nominal ruler of Kashmir.
67. *Ibid.* **Note.** *Bhimagupta* is named as the reigning prince in the year of 976-77 A.D. when *Kayyata,* son of *Chandraditya*, composed his commentary on the *Devistotra* of *Anandavardhana.*
68. *Ibid.*
69. *Ibid.*
70. ***Note.*** The early career of *Tunga* finds its parallel in that of many *Paharis* area like that in particular Gujars of the present time. Coming to Kashmir from *Prunts* and the neighbouring hill-districts with thier buffaloes, they find ready employ as their buffaloes, they find ready employ as *Shikharis*, dak-carriers, etc: owing to their comparative energy and reliability.
71. Term *Baddivasa* identifies with *Bodol*, i.e. *Budil* composed of two wards *Bu+dil, 'Bu'* means having unpleasent smell, *'dil'* means 'heart'. Now at present unpleasent smell is coming out from the heart of the people which is below the *Pir Pantsal* or without *'Nam'*. It has given its name to a pass over the range and to a once much-frequented mountain route, as *Budil* lies a considerable distance from the territory now belonging to *Prunts* (*parnotsa*), and is separated from it by a high range of mountains. The same identification Cunninghan seems to have heard *(Ancient Geography of India, Vanaras, 1963.* p. 133), *'Badwal'* or *'Vaddiwasa'*, in the list of hill-states to the South of Kashmir. *'Badwal'* put together of two words 'Bad'+ 'wal', 'Bad' means, 'Bura' in Hindi, & 'wal' means

*Sakti* that 'Nam' is 'Bad power' when those who do not worshipp 'Him'. 'He' destroyes them. This is the challange of God.

72. Term *Lekhaharaka* is the *Khasid* means desire of modern Indian courts.
73. *R.T.* Vol.1. Book VI. p. 262.
74. *Ibid.* p. 263.
75. *Ibid.* p. 264.
76. *Ibid.*
77. *Ibid.*
78. *Ibid.* p. 265.
79. *Ibid:*
80. *Ibid.* ***Note*** *Palevate* is an '*apple*' as it has been believed by the Kashmirian Pandits the furit is discussed by *Srivara* together with *tanka* (pear, a yellowish-green or brownish-green edible fruit, narrow at the stalk and wider towards the tip. As phrases *go-pear shaped*, means *'go wrong'*, originated old English word) and *Cira* (appriot, an orange, yellow fruit resembling a small peach, originated from Portugese albricoque or Spanish albaricoque word), in the description of a *Kashmir* famine. It is also compared with the commentary of *Mankha Kosa*; *S.V. bhavya.*
81. R.T. Vol.1 Book. VI. p. 265.
82. *Ibid.*

# 5

# Establishment of the Lohara Dynasty

*Samgramaraja* son of *Udayaraja*, after testing him by *Didda*, he became the emperor of *Kashmir*, as noted earlier, came of the royal house of *Lohara*, a region which once formed part of the extensive empire of[1] the most famous dynasty of *Karkotas*. He was a nephew of the late Queen *Didda* and chosen by her as her successor, after her death in 1003 A.D. the empire was transferred to him without any hindrance or disturbance[2]. This was the third wonderful change in the royal dynasties which has been taken place through relationship by marriage[3]. Before the establishment of the *Lohara* dynasty in the Valley of Kashmir, had undergone a far-reaching change in mid-Asiatic regions that was to subsequently affected the political, social and cultural life of the people not only in Kashmir, but also on the Indian mainland[4]. While in the middle eastern Asiatic nations, lower eastern Europe, Egypt and large tracts of the upper African continent had 'bowed before the blast' with surprisingly little resistance, the Indian borderlands contrary to what is often averred, did not yield too easily[5].

After the death of the last *Rai, Sahasi* his Brahman minister, *Chach*, married the widow queen, and himself assumed the crown. During his long reign of forty years the Kingdom grew in extent and authority, and is described to have abutted upon the confines of Kashmir. His son, *Dahir*, who succeeded *Candra* or *Candar* (*Chach's* brother), had to face a serious *Arab* invasion because he did not chastise the people of Debul for having seized a vessel carrying rich presents from the King of Ceylon to *Hajjaj*, governor of Iran. *Muhammad-ibn-Kasim* led the expedition, he stormed Debul in H.93= A.D. 712, captured *Bahmanabad*, and reduced *Multan* in 723 A.D. Thus completed the conquest of Sind. This was the culmination of the *Arab* plundering raids, which began as early as H.15=636-37 A.D. during the *Khilafat* of *Omar*. Having got control of *Sind*, the *Arabs* initiated a vigorous policy of expansion, and *Junaid*, who was its governor under *Khalifa Hisham* (724-43 A.D.), was particularly active. He conquered *Al-Bailaman* (*Bhinmal*[6]) means, those who had not been involved in the material world called *Sudras*, *Jurz* (Gurjara Kingdom of Western India), and other territories, but against *Ujjain* he could merely make an incursion. In this direction he was perhaps repulsed by *Nagabhata* I. From this time onwards the Pratihara kings continued to be greatest foes of the Moslems and their faith, and this compelled the latter to see the alliance of the *Balharas* (*Vallabharajas*), *i.e.*, the *Rastrakutas* of *Manyakheta*. It is likely to *Arabs* might have achieved more successes in the interior of India, if the *Pratiharas* had not offered them a determined opposition. In Sind the conquerors followed a farsighted policy of toleration. No doubt, *Islam*[7] spread, but *Hindu*[8] temples were considered "inviolate like the *Churches* of the Christians, the synagogues of the Jews and the altars of the *Magians*". The Brahmans were even permitted to build or repair dilapidated temples. While the Arab garrisons were stationed at strategic centres, i.e., Sind, the internal administration was mostly left in the hands of the natives, who paid the land tax (*Khiraj*) and the poll tax (*Jeziya*). The Arabs also in certain respects yielded to the subtle influences of their Indian environments. For instance, they learnt Astronomy and Mathematics from the Hindus and translated into Arabic the work of *Caraka* and the fables of the *Panca-tantra*[9]. It was only in the beginning of the 11th century A.D. when *Samgramaraja* had laid down the foundations of the *Lohara* dynasty in the Valley[10], the internecine struggles, and the rise and fall of Arab princepalities like Multan and *Mansurah*. Thus, the Ghaznavides gradually displaced the Arabs in Sind, but it appears that the conquests of Mahmud Ghazni were not so thorough in lower plains of the *Indus* as in *Upper Sind*. Accordingly, soon after his death the former region virtually asserted its independence under the Hindu *Sumras*, who ruled there for about three centuries, and were followed by the *Sammas* in the middle of the fourteenth century A.D[11]. In this way, the kingdom of *Samgramaraja* fortunately escaped destruction at the hands of Mahmud of Ghazni, but it was too much weakened by internal conflicts to interfere successfully in the general affairs of Northern India. It gradually sank to the position of a minor power and finally succumbed to the Muslims in 1339 A.D.[12]. From the fastnesses of the Salt Range (*Nandana*), *Anandapala* continued to offer resistance, his successor, *Trilochanpala*, carried on the struggle with the assitance of *Samgramaraja* of Kashmir. In the end, he was compelled to retire to the east and conclude an alliance with the *Chandella* ruler of *Kalinjar* and other princes of *Mid-India*. But he was again defeated on the river *Ruhut* (*Rahib*) identified by some with *Ramganga*. He was assassinated in 1021-22 A.D. With the death of his son and successor, *Bhima*, in 1026 A.D. The dynasty came to an end. Both *Al-Biruni* and *Kalhana* bear testimony to the courage and maganimity of this noble line of things who poured out their blood like water in defending the north-western gates of their country against the invader[13] with the power of *'Nam'*.

**_Samgramaraja_ (1003-1028 A.D.)**

After the death of Queen *Didda*, *Sangramaraja* occupied the throne of Kashmir, his power of firm resolution was hidden by gentleness, supported easily on his arm the whole land, just as the lord of the snakes (*S'esanaga*[14]), while concealing the power of his breath under (his snake-hoods, which have) the charming appearance of a mass of lotus-roots, (supports the whole earth) on the mass of his hood[15]. In the Twilight (*Samdhya*[16]), he worshipped the daughter of the mountains (*Parvati*) and addressed the *Samdhya* with the following artful words : "(O *Parvati*), the adorable body of your mother has been created by Brahman in the spotless family of the *Pitrs*. When joined in my embrace in the twilight, you sportively play with my underlip, which is red like the China rose (*Japa*[17])." *'Word'* says, "(O *Samdhya*), Brahman has created the adorable body of you, the mother of the spotless family of the *Pitrs*. When you make your appearance in the twilight, you are again and again on my lip which is engaged in murmuring prayers (*japa*[18])".

At the death of Queen *Didda* most of the people had the views that the downfall of *Tunga* is nearby. But the queen (*Didda*) was so capable that before the point of death, she advised both *Samgramaraja* and *Tunga* and the rest take an oath by sacred libation (*Kosa*) that they would not harm to each other[19]. Anxious to secure assistance, he (*Tunga*) gave his daughter *Lothika* in marriage to the superintendent of the *Diddamatha*, *Preman* by name, who possessed wealth, courage and other (good qualities[20]). Therefore, there is great difference between the two that is *Chamar* and the Brahmans. *Chamar* is a king, who bent on Universal conquest and a Brahman of small mind whose hand is wet with offered of presents that is corruption, and gifts.

**Rising Against Tunga**

The chief minister, *Tunga*, who was distinguished himself, then the Brahman councillors in order to bring about the fall of rising *Tunga*, Brahmans and Purohitas made the sacred shrines (*Parisadya*) started a solemn fast (*Praya*) at *Parihasapura*. It was difficult for the king *Samgramaraja* to allay this revolt, which was caused by the common resolve of the Brahmans and the ministers, as fire and storm combined (to cause a conflagration[21]). But the Brahmans were adaments to dethrone the king. The *Samgramaraja*, *Tunga* and their people had agreed to this, those wicked-minded Brahmans in demanding something else. They said: "Let us burn this Brahman who has died through *Tunga*" violence in his (*Tunga's*) house". They are the evil spirit (*Krtya*) minded people used to perform a sacrifice of their hair (*Kesahoma*). It fells back upon them for the destruction of impure Brahmans. Thereupon the Brahmans will fled away and betook themselves in the house of *Rajakalasa*, who had been their secret instigator[22]. Those are disloyal of the *Rajakalasa*, they have to fight a long battle in their life, but the Brahmans have the different gate to go back their original homes. When *Rajakalasa* was defeated, the seven sons of *S'ridhara*, who were Brahmans councillors, came and fought for the same cause, and entered straight in the world of *Surya*. During the fighting, *Tunga* and *Rajakalasa*, who had been vanquished by *Sugandhisiha*, brought to his own house in fetters[23].

**Victory of Tunga**

*Tunga* also defeated his minister *Bhutikalasa* and his son *Rajaka*, compelled them for the *S'uramatha*. His another minister known as *Gunadeva*, he told *Bhutikalasa* without the ablutions in the *Ganga* one can not become a *Master*. But *Tunga* was aware of that, therefore, he again exiled *Bhutikalasa* and his son. No doubt, *Mayyamanataka*, the son of *Candrakara*, who for the time being had obtained *Candrakara*, who for the time being had obtained the position, but also died at the same time. Even the illustrious *Preman* too, the well-wisher of the king was also died after having a brief time his union with the King's daughter, and his friend like *Ganga* too has to die. Only *Tunga* and his brothers took enjoy[24] the moment. Thus, it is expected from the study that every occurence has to fall, but the life of the man is superior one must has to realise that why this opportunity has been given to man by the God. But *Tunga*, who had been eminently prudent[25] with his own misfortune that he took a low-born mean *Kayastha Bhadresvara* by name as his assistant[26].

***Rise of Bhadresvara***

*Bhadresvara* hereditary occupation was a gardener (*aramika*). He had to trade in night soil, act as a butcher and to sell fuel. *Tunga* made him as his assitant, but he did not know that due to his association, he brought about the destruction of (his own) fortune.He ousted the pious *Tunga* and appointed the *Dharmarka* in charge of the *Grhakrtya* office. But he was a wicked person. He cut off the sustenance of gods, cows, Brahman, the poor, strangers, and royal servants. Even wicked *Bhadresvara* did not allow his own people to live[27]. After this episode, *Tunga* made *Bhadresvara*, the master of the everything, and in the month *Asadha*, *Sugandhisiha* died[28]. *Tunga* at this moment was distressed that if his head had been cut off despatched against the illustrious *Sahi Trilocanapala*[29], the large army which has been attended by many *Rajaputras*, chief councillors, feudal chiefs, etc. They are capable to shake the earth, if they followed him[30]. This good counsel of *Trilocama* (*Pala*), he did not accept, but his troops were eagerly looking out for battle[31].

**Battle with Himmira**

*Tunga* acrossed the *Tausi* with a small troop and defeated the force of *Himmira* on the other bank of the *Tausi*[32]. Who just came for gaining the information of the *Tunga's* army. *Sahi* had the war experience, he repeated his request time and again, but did not accept the *S'ahi's* counsel because they have been blinded by desires[33]. Those, who do not act upon the advice of the *S'ahi*, their destruction is nearby[34]. In the morning a skillful battle was fought between the *Tunga's* and *Turuska* army, *Tunga* army was immediately defeated and *S'ahi* force became victorious, even *Jayasimha*, *S'rivardhana, Vibhramaka*, the Damara, of *Samgrama's* family[35] participated in this war. A terrible battle was fought by these three valiant person, but could not won the battle. The greatness of the *Trilocanapala* is that, he defeated them with natural calamities like floods, fire which burns the world at the end of the *Kalpa*[36]. It appears that when *Trilocanapala* had gone afar for a period of sometime, the whole country became overshadowed by hosts of fierce *Candalas* which (resembled like the clouds of) locusts. *Himmira* did not breathe freely even after obtaining the victory against the superhuman, and relying on his force to recover their victory[37].

**Destruction of S'ahi Kingdom**

Kalhana describes that the rapid and complete destruction of the powerful *S'ahi* kingdom must have deeply impressed the mind of all contemporaries. It seems to have been the last occasion on which the brave *S'ahi* opposed the invader within the *Panjab*. We can still feel this distinctly in the pathetic lines which Kalhana devotes to the memory of the vanished greatness of the *S'ahi* dynasty. They reproduce faithfully the very sentiments to which *Alberuni*, a witness of those great events, has given expression in his closing words on the Hindu *Shahiyas*[38]. At that time, *Kandarpasimha*, *Tunga's* son, who was full of pride on account of his wealth and strength, caused him uneasiness by behaving like a king[39].

**Intrigue against Tunga**

His brother *Vigraharaja*[40], too, who was waiting for an opportunity against *Tunga*. Within six months (it happened) by the will of fate that *Tunga* was called by the king along with his own company and by five to six attendants. He entered in the palace, *Parvasarkaraka* and others also followed *Tunga* there. Among the attendants of *Tunga* only *Simharatha* deserved praise, a descendant of *Maharatha* who had been a minister of *S'amkaravarman*. He, though unarmed, threw himself that very moment on the back of *Tunga*, at whom they were striking , in order to protect him[41].

**Murder of Tunga**

*Tunga* was murdered by wretched *Partha*, son of the Brahman *Dharma* who belonged to the royal council (*asthanabrahmana*[42]), and the foolish *Kanka*, were with *Tunga*. These two (persons) had their bowels moved, put their fingers into their months to protect themselves, as if they were cattle and dropped their weapons in terror. No doubt, *Canda* and others who were the followers of the *Tunga*[43], they were also frightened but they did not take the arms against the opponent group. They had seen their master's severed head's spirit and they displayed at this moment the character of a (true) servants. *Bhujamga*[44], the son of a Brahman feudal chief (*Samanta*[45]), killed twenty soldiers in the royal house when he opened his golden staff. Even *Trailokyaraja*, a treasure along with *Abhinava*, milk brother of *Kayyamantaka* were killed. Besides these, thirty brave *Ekangas*, who were the employ of *Tunga* were died left for heaven[46]. Only *Padmaraja* was escaped unhurt. *Canda*, who was the good fighter, a foreigner (*daisika*), *Arjuna* by name and the Damara *Helacakra* were also killed without weapons. Thus, one day *Tunga* along with his son treacherously murdered by the King when they entered into the royal palace[47].

**Affairs after Tunga's Death**

After the death of *Tunga, Samgramaraja* appointed his brother *Naga* as the commander-in-chief of the army. *Naga* had caused the death of his brother and nephew by corrupting the king's mind through secret calumnies. He was the destroyer of his own family and was branded with infamy[48]. The dark phase of *Samgramarja* rule was started when wicked *Bhadresvara*, who looted and plundered the treasury which belonged to the shires of *Bhutesvara*[49] and other gods[50]. It appears that low favourites rose to power and plundered the people, *Samgramaraja* at that time declared a true judgement, and did not establish even a drinking place (*prapa*), saying that the wealth he owned was unlawfully acquired, and died in the year 1028, after having had his son *Hariraja* consecrated[51] at that time.

**Hariraja (1028 A.D.)**

*Hariraja*, who ruled over the earth for less than a month approximately twenty-two days. His brief duration on the throne deserved to be praised among men, like the crescent of the young moon[52]. There was a general report, which was not contradicted, that the licentious queen-mother (*S'rilekha*) herself had used witchcraft against her son, who was dissatisfied (with her conduct[53]).

**King Ananta (1028-1063 A.D.)**

After the death of *Hariraja*, his milk brother, *Sagara* (*Ananta*) became the ruler of Kashmir, while the king's mother, *Srilekha*, who wished herself for the throne after taking a bath (where) the arrangements for the installation had been made and *'Word'* also assembled *Ekangas*[54]. Since the King's mother destroyed her son for the lust of throne, but at the same time the throne was taken by another the old paternal uncle[55], *Vigraharaja* of *Lohara*, who burnt down the 'Gate' (*dvara*[56]) after two and a half days unexpectedly entered the city[57]. He had been thrown himself into the *Lothikamatha*, and there the troops were sent by *S'rilekha* to killed him[58]. But his followers fired the place. Then lavish queen built two *Mathas* at the same time in honour of her husband and son, and started stressing on day and night of high treason[59]. Slowly and gradually, *Ananta* came out from the childhood. He was addicted of *extravagance* and other (Vices). The most dearer friends of *Ananta* were *Rudrapala* and *S'ahi* princes. They wasted the more revenues by drawing the excessive salaries from the kingdom for maintenance of *Ananta*. Unless and untill *Rudrapala* and *Diddapala* could not get rid from the money troubles, they could not sleep in peace at night[60].

*Anangapala*, (that) *Vetala*, who was the king's favourite, who broke up the golden status of gods, *Rudrapala* protected those property and lives which belonged to the *Candalas* and the like. *Kayasthas*, who were *Rudrapala's* intimates, oppressed the people among them, the famous *Utpala*, founded a *Matha* for the blind[61]. King *Ananta's* affection for *Rudrapala* is unforgetable. He had married the elder daughter to *Inducandra*, the lord of *Jalamdhara*, the moon-faced *Asamati,* on account of her beauty, the same who built a Matha called after herself at *Tripuresvara*[62]. He then married her somewhat younger sister, the Queen *Suryamati,* to the King. The campanion *Rudra* (*Pala*), who pleased his ears as *Suyodhana* through that of *Karna*[63].

***Rising of Tribhuvana and Invasion of Darads***

*Tribhuvana*, the commander-in-Chief of the *Ananta* king collected the *Damaras*[64], took the revolt against him to snatched the kingdom of Kashmir. Battle was started between the two, but *Ekangas* force of the king did not leave the side of the king. They knew the bravery of *Anantadeva*. King *Ananta* moved in the battle like a *Bhairava*, and made the earth shake[65]. King at every step saw the bodies of *Ekangas* were slashed with cuts and their names were reported by the attendants of the king relieved them for the *Aksapatal* office for the fixed assignment[66] as a 'law' or *Rita* with the beginning of the man (*Vilabdhisthavara*). Ultimately, *Tribhuvana* surrendered himself without any prior condition but the king was so kind, he received him affectionately. Moreover his relative *Brahmaraja* by name, superintendent of the treasury (*ganjadhipa*) having fallen in enmity with *Rudrapala*[67]. certain Damaras along with *Acalamangala*, King of the Darads, together with seven *Mlechcha* princes[68] reached at the village of *Ksiraprstha*, the most valiant *Rudrapala*, eager for battle, went to meet him. The battle was fought at the residence of a *Naga* called *Pindaraka*[69]. Thus, the *Mleccha* kings were captured and slain. Similar troubles (*avadalika*)[70] he had with his brother *Udayanavasta* and with Brahmans, who held solemn fasts (*praya*)[71]. *Rudrapala* and *S'ahi* princes died of the lutadisease, and blindness was created by the *Palas*. King *Ananta* found pleasure in a virtuous life and gave a chance to Queen *Suryamati*[72].

**Queen Suryamati's Pious Foundation**

Queen *Suryamati* also constructed the temple of Siva *Gaurisvara* named *Subhata* on the bank of the *Vitasta*. Besides these, she also two shrines of *Vijayesa* and *Amaresa*[73] under the name of her brother *Silhana* and of her husband (respectively[74]). Brahmans also took the advantage of the temple *Vijayesvara*[75] and *Amaresvara* at the same time for their own welfare. No doubt, new palace were built, but king *Ananta* left the royal palace after the death of *Rajaraja* and constructed his residence in the vicinity of the shrine of *Sadasiva*[76].

The foreigners like *Dallaka*[77], *Padmaraja,* who supplied betel-leaves which were favourite to the King *Ananta Deva*. The *Bhoja*, the lord of *Malava* was also invited in Kashmir. He constructed a round tank (*Kunda*) at *Kapatesvara* the gold which he sent to the king. In this way, King *Bhoja* got rid from the *Papasudana* Tirtha[78] *Nagarakhanda* also requested the king please give up almost the whole revence of the country into the credit of king and adorned the head with five resplendent crescents and the throne as a security will be vocate for him. In every month on the day of solemn reception, Queen *Suryamati* than put an end to the disgrace by *Padmaraja*. Even *Dallaka* was removed from the Whelm of the affairs and settled in the country[79].

**Suryamati's Ascendency**

It appears that for sometime, *Suryamati* took the *Anantadeva's* business in her own hands and she dominated her husband on the basis of chance and charity, as their behaviour towards each other was irreproachable. But at the sametime during the long rule of *AnantaDev* the light was passed from on servant to the other, like a maiden who has to choose her husband. *Ksema*, a barber(nai), filled the king's treasury by securing revenue from different sources as one-twelfth share (*dvadasabhaga*). Then *Kesava*, an honest Brahman from *Trigarta*, became minister, and threw lustre on the king just as the moon (throws her light) on a stuccoced terrace. Yet this very person was seen by the people (subsequently) going about alone and in poverty. Fortune, (which is like) a stroke of lightning from the cloud of fate, for whom is it lasting[80]? No. Keeping in view, the possessions are subject to fate, the pride which foolish people has taken in the greatness of their family and power is false and vain. No, this is the *'Ultimate reality'*. *Bhuti*, a Vaisya, who was watchman at the temple of *Gaurisa*, had (three) sons, *Haladhara, Vajra* and *Varaha*[81].

**Haladhara's Appointment as Prime Minister**

*Bhuti's* eldest son. *Haladhara* served the Queen *Suryamati* regularly and a day came, he obtained the prime-ministership (*Sarvadhikarita*[82]). Brave *Bimba*, son of his brother *Varaha*, who held the charge as lord of the Gate as the clouds at the end of the world (pour down water[83]). King *Ananta* was a powerful ruler, he won number of battles, now he started foreign expeditions.

**Foreign Expeditions**

King *Ananta*, no doubt, defeated the various kings of the adjoining areas, now, he extended his campaign towards *Campa*[84] and uprooted its king *Sala*[85]. Besides this, he also extended his campaign against *Kalasa*, the son of *Tukka*[86] on his return journey, *Ananta-deva* seems to have gone by *Vallapura*[87], which was evidently in revolt (at home[88]), and owing to his own rashness, he becmae involved in a difficult position, from which he was extricated by the sagacity of his minister, *Haladhara*. The Raja of *Vallapura*, at that time was, as Kalhana tells us, *Kalasa*, the son of *Tukka* whose reign began about 1050 A.D. He was still in power upto the period of 1087-88 A.D. He also visited *Kashmir* along with several other tributary hill *Chiefs* in the reign of *Kalasa*, the son of *Anantadeva* (1063-89 A.D.[89]). The illustrious *Rajasvara*, son of *Bhadresvara*, who was the lord of the Gate came under the possession of Damaras resided in *Kramarajya* and likewise a great many others[90].

**Haladhara's Downfall**

How can a person do service in the King's palace without suffering insults, even *Haladhara* became an object of slander on account of his continual attendance upon the queen, and was thrown into prison by *Asacandra* and others who were enraged against him[91]. Thus, *Haladhara* was deprived by the King from all of his property, he underwent the pains of imprisonment. Though wise persons like *Haladhara* endeavoured to dissuade him by referring the term regret (it). He ordered the Chamberlain *Ranaditya* to make the preparations for the coronation, though this (officer) warned him that he would feel regret[92].

There is no doubt from the study of the above pages we learn that with the establishment of the *Lohara* rule, there were certain rising agains the *Samgramraja* led by Brahmans and Damaras, supressed by him peacefully. He was succeded by his son, *Hariraja*, who ruled for less than a month, in a short period, there was an all-round improvement in the affairs of the state. After his death, *Hariraja* was succeeded by his younger brother, *Ananta*. As noted above, the king under the pressing influence of *Suryamati*, dominated the Kashmir politics about thirty-nine years (1028-1063 A.D.) against the various opposition, sometimes by *Vigraharaja*, *Damara,* etc. At last in 1063 A.D., his active rule came to an end and power was transferred to *Kalasa* his own son.

## NOTES AND REFERENCES

1. P.H.K. p. 160.
2. *Ibid.*
3. *R.T.* Vol.1 Book VI. p. 266.
4. *P.H.K.* p. 160.
5. *Ibid.*
6. *H.A.I.* pp. 337-338.
7. *'Islam'* is an Arabic term which is put together of three words *I+s+lam*, 'I' stand for 'ego','s' stands for *'sainthood'*, and *'lam'* means *'Word'* or *'Sabad'* or *'Nam' or Kalma*. Therefore, one has to completely surrender the *'ego'* before the *'God'* or *'Nam'* or *'Word'*, then one has to obtain the *'sainthood'*. Since the days of *Al-Biruni* many adherents of *Islam* has to be think that *laghu* does not mean a consonant without vowel nor *guru* a *consonant without vowel,* but that on the contrary, *laghu* means a consonant with a short vowel (e.g., *Ka,Ki,Ku*), *and guru* means the same with vowelless consonant (e.g., *kat, Kit, kut*), like an element in Arabic metrics called *'Sabad'*. (Two part in one volume; p. 138). This was the second great religion of India in point of numbers, have shown a profound interest in the science, philosophy and religion of their Hindu brethren, and to this day Hindu practices are not altogether a negligible factor in the village life of this country for the votaries of a different creed. *Islam* with its ideals of social democracy and imperialism has, in its turn, done much to counteract the fissiparous tendencies of caste and check the centrifugal forces in Indian politics by keeping alive the ideal of a pan-Indian state throughout the *Middle Ages* (A.H.I. p. 8). In the same times, the *Cholas* and Chalukyas were engaged in bitter feuds in the south, thrones and dynasties in Northern India were falling before the onslaught of the famous *Himmira,* Sultan Mahmud of Ghazni or Ghazna. The banner of *Islam* was unfurled in the land of the five rivers (Panjab) and the valley of the Twin rivers, the Upper Ganges and the Jumna. The arms of the Ghaznavid invader penetrated into the interior of Kathiawar and reached the temple of Somnath. Indian History enters on a new epoch. In the western part of Asia lies a vast

country called *Arabia,* a land of rocks and deserts with a few oases and fertile valleys, thinly peopled by a hardy and sturdy folk. In this country, at a short distance from the western sea coast, stands the hole city of *Mecca, 'Sabad'* where sometime in the year 570 was born the great Prophet, the founder of a religion that preached the unity of God, and roused the people to energy and unbounded enthusiasm. Under the successors of the prophet called *Khalifas* or *Caliphs*, who led the faithful from 632 A.D., the arms of the *Moslems* advanced in all directions, and the banner of *Islam* floated over many centuries from Iran to Spain. From the beginning, the Arabs had their eyes on the rich parts of Western India and the outlying parts of the north-west borderland. As early as the time of the great Pulakesin II, an army was sent to Thana near Bombay (637 A.D.). This was followed by expeditions to Broach, the Gulf of Debal (in Sind), and *Al-Kikan* (the district round Kelat). About the middle of seventh centruy, the Satrapy of Zaranj in southern Afghanistan fell into the hands of Arabs. The turn of Makran in Baluchistan came next. The Arabs now made repeated onslaughts on the Shah of Kabul, supposed to be descendent of the great Kanishka, and the *Ratbil* of Zabul in the Upper Valley of the *Helmud* river and some adjoining districts. The latter succumbed after a brave struggle (870 A.D.). The Turki Shahiya Kings of Kabul maintained a precarious existence till the closing years of the ninth centruy when they were supplanted by Kallar, usually identified with *Lalliya*, the founder of the Hindu Shahiya dynasty of *Udabhandapura* (Waihand, *Ohind* or *Und* on the Indus). Meanwhile, the Arabs had followed up their success in Baluchistan by the conquest of Sind. that province figures in the narrative of *Bana's* as one of the territories overrun by *Prabhakaravardhana* days of Hiuen Tsang the throne was occupied by a *Sudhra* dynasty that is *Rai* of Sind (*Ibid.* pp.180-181). It is well-know from the fact that the Indian religion spread to the western countries. Asoka sent Buddhist *missionaries* to western Asia, northern Africa and South-Eastern Europe, and claimed that the tenets of that religion were welcomed in these regions. We have no means of ascertaining the truth of this from independent evidence, but there is no doubt that even long after Ashoka people in Alexandria showed interest in Buddhism, and that both Buddhist and Brahmanical religion widely prevalent in several countries of western Asia before the advent of *Islam*. The knowledge of Indian philosophy and literature in the West is also an undoubted fact (Ibid. p. 212). Early in the fifteenth century A.D. a fugitive Hindu chief of Java founded the kingdom of *Malacca,* which soon rose to be a great political power and an important commercial centre. The conversion of its second king to *Islam* made *Mallacca* a stronghold of that power, which soon reacted on neighbouring territories. The new faith penetrated into Java (Soul), in the wake of trade and commerce, and even some members of its royal family were converted to it. By a concerted attempt of the votaries of the new faith, the ruler of *Majapahit* was driven from the throne at the beginning of the sixteenth of Majapahit, the whole of the island was converted to *Islam*. But the royal family and large element of the Hindu population took refuge in the island of Bali, which has been a Hindu colony for nearly a thousand years. With the exception of this island, where Hinduism flourishes even today, the rest of the *Malay Archipelagu*, generally speaking, adopted the faith and culture of *Islam* (Ibid. p. 222). The history of the colonies demonstrates the unsoundness of the popular belief that Hinduism can not be adopted by foreigners but is meant only for those who are bron within its fold. It shows the great vigour with which it could absorbs and vitalise foreign culture and could elevate even the most primitive races to a higher sphere of culture and civilization. If we remember that Indian culture and civilization played a similar role, though perhaps in a lesser degree, in western, central and eastern Asia, we can realise an aspect of the true greatness of India, not always sufficiently emphasised. The colonial and cultural expansion of India is one of the most brilliant, but forgotten, episodes of Indian history, of which any Indian may justly feel proud (*Ibid*. p. 223). With the decline of the *Caliphs* or *Khalifahs* of Baghdad supreme leaders and rulers of the greater parts of the Islamic world, the Muslim governor of Sind became virtually independent. In 871 A.D. the Khalifahas practically handed over the province to the famous *Saffarid* leader, *Ya-Qub-ibn-Lais*. On the latter's death, the Muslim territories in Sind were divided between two independent chiefs, those of Mansurah (near *Bahmanabad*) and *Multan*. Neither of these ever attained to great power, and both had to live in constant dread of their Indian neighbours, particularly the Imperial *Pratiheras* of *Kanay*. The Arab conquest of Sind did not immediately produce any far-reaching political effect, and it has been described by Mr. Stanley Lane-Poole as "an episode in the history of India and of Islam, a triump without results". But it is significant from the cultural point of view. Besides the exchange of ideas, it fascilitated the dissemination of the seeds of Indian culture in foreign lands. The Arabs acquired from the Hindus some new knowledge in Indian religion, philosophy, medicine, Mathematics, Astronomy and folk lore, and carried it not only to their own land but also to Europe. We know definitely from Mas'udi and Ibn *Hanqal* that *Arab* settlers lived side by side with their Hindu fellow-citizens for many years on terms of amity and peace, and *Amir Khusrav* mentions that the Arab astronomer *Abu-Ma,Shar* came to *Benares* and studied astronomy there for ten years. From the political point of view, the conquest of the Punjab by the Sultans of Ghaznbi, to which reference has already been made, was of far greater importance than the establishment of Arab principalities in the lower Indus valley (Ibid. pp. 275-276). But in spite of all this, to the historian of India, Sultan appears mainly as a n insatiable invader. He was neither a missionary for the propagation of religion in this country nor an architect of empire. The main object of his eastern expeditions seems to have been the acquisition of the *"Wealth of Ind"* and the destruction of the morale of its custodians. The annexation of Punjab was a measure of necessity rather than of choice. Nevertheless, it would be a mistake to assume that his invasions had no permanent political results in India. He drained the wealth of the country and despoiled it of its military resources to an appalling extent. The Ghaznavid occupation of the Punjab served as the key to unlock the gates of the Indian interior. Big cracks were made in the great fabric of Indian polity, and it was no longer a question of whether but when that age-old structure would fall. Neither the Arabs not the Ghaznavid (*Yamini*) Turks succeeded in adding India to the growing empire of *Islam*, but they paved the way for the final struggle which overwhelmed the Gangetic kingdoms some two hundred years later. The empire of Ghazni began to fall to pieces under the later successors of Sultan Mahmud, who were too feeble to maintain their position at Ghazni and in North-West India in the face of the rising power of the princes of Ghur, a small obscure principality in the mountainous region of Afghanistan to the south-east of Herat. The petty chiefs of Ghur, of eastern persian extraction, were originally feudatories of Ghazni, but, taking advantage of the weakness of their suzerains, they steadily rose to power and entered into a contest with them for supermacy. In the course of this contest, Qutb-ud-din Muhammad of Ghur, and his brother Saif-ud-din were cruelly executed by Bahram Shah of Ghazni (Ibid P.276). Muhammad of Ghur left no male heirs to succeed him, and his provincial viceroys soon established their own authority in their provincial viceroys soon established their own authority in their respective jurisdictions. *Taj-ud-din Yildiz*, Governor of Kirman, ascended the throne of Ghazni, while *Qutb-ud-din* Aibak assumed the title of *Sultan* and was acknowledged as the ruler of the Indian territories by the Muslim officers in India like *Ikhtiyar-ud-din* of *Bengal* and *Nasir-ud-din Qabacha,* Governor of Multan and Uch. *Qutb-ud-din Aibak's* rise excited the jealousy of *Taj-ud-din Yildiz*, who entered into a contest with him for the mastery over the Punjab. *Qutb-ud-din* defeated *Yildiz*, drove him out of Ghazni and occupied it for forty days. But the people of Ghazni, disgusted with his excesses, secretly invited Yildiz to come to their rescue. Yildiz did not fail to avail himself of this opportunity, and on his sudden and unexpected return to Ghazni, *Qutb-ud-din* fled away precipitately. This destroyed the chance of a political union between Afghanistan and India, which was not achieved till Babur's occupation of Delhi, and *Qutb-ud-din* became a purely Indian Sultan. He did at Lahore, early in November, A.D. 1210, in consequence of a fall from his horse while playing *Chaugan* or polo, after a short reign of a little more than four years. *Qutb-ud-din* was, remarks *Minhaj-us-Siraj*, a "high-spirited and open-hearted monarch." Endowed with intrepidity and martial prowess, he rarely lost a battle and, by his extensive conquests, brought a large part of Hindustan under the banner of *Islam*. His "gifts were bestowed by hundreds of thousands", and, for his unbounded generosity, he has been styled by all writers as *Lakh bakhsh*, or giver of lacs. *Hasan-un-Nizami*, the author of *Taj-ul-Ma*'asir, who is full of praise for *Qutb-ud-din*, writes that he "dispensed even-handed justice to the people, and exerted himself to promote the peace and prosperity of the realm". But the Sultan felt no hesitation in having recourse to stern measures in his conquests and administration when necessary. His devotion to *Islam* was remarkable. Thus Hasan-un-Nizami remarks: "By his orders the precepts of Islam received great promulgation, and the sun of righteousness cast its shadow on the countries of *Hind* from the heaven of God's assistance." He gave proof of his zeal by building one mosque at Delhi and another at Ajmer. On the sudden death of Qutb-ud-din at Lahore, the *Amirs* and *Maliks* of Lahore set up Aram Bakhsh as his successor with the title of *Sultan Aram Shah*, "for the sake of restraining tumult, for the tranquility of the commonalty, and the content of the hearts of the soldiery". The relationship of Aram with Qutb-ud-din is a subject controversy. According to some, he was Qutb-ud-din is a subject of controversy. Accoding to some, he was Qutb-ud-din's son, but *Minhaj-us-Siraj* distincly writes that Qutb-ud-din only had three daughters. Abul Fazl has made the "astonishing statement" that he was the Sultan's brother. A modern writer has hazarded the opinion that "he was no relation of Qutb-ud-din" but was selected as his successor as he was available on the spot. In fact, there were no fixed rules governing the succession to the Crown in the Turkish State. It was determined largely by the exigencies of the moment and the influence of the chiefs and the nobles. Aram was ill-qualified to govern a kingdom. The nobles of Delhi soon conspired against him and invited *Malik Shams-ud-din Iltutmish*, then Governor of Badaun, to replace Aram. Iltutmish responded to their call, and advancing with all his army, defeated Aram in the plain of Jud near Delhi. What became of Aram is not quite certain. Iltutmish belonged to the tribe of *Ilbari* in Turkestan. He was remarkably handsome in appearance, and showed signs of intelligence and sagacity from his early days, which excited the jealousy of his brothers, who managed to deprive him of his paternal home and care. But adversity did not mar his qualities, which soon opened a career for him. His accomplishments attracted the notice of *Qutb-ud-din*, then Viceroy of Delhi, who purchased him at a high price. By dint of his merits, Iltutmish raised his status step by step till he was made the Governor of Badaun and was married to a daughter of *Qutb-ud-din*. In recognition of his services during the campaign of Muhammad of Ghur against the Khokkars, he was by the Sultan's orders, manumitted and elevated as Amir-ul-Umara. Thus the choice of the Delhi nobles fell on a worthy man. But on his accession in the year A.D. 1210 or 1211, Iltutmish found himself confronted with an embarrassing situation. *Nasir-ud-din* Qabacha had asserted his independence in Sind and seemed desirous of extending his authority over the Punjab; and *Taj-ud-din Yildiz*, who held Ghazni, still entertained his old pretensions to sovereignty over the

Indian conquests of Muhammad. Ali Mardan, a Khalji noble, who had been appointed Governor of Bengal by Qutb-ud-din after the death of *Ikhtiya-ud-din* in A.D. 1206, had thrown off his allegiance to Delhi after Qutb-ud-din's death and had styled himseld Sultan 'Ala-ud-din. Further, the Hindu princes and chiefs were seething with discontent at their loss of independence; Gwalior and Ranthambhor had been recovered by their rulers during the week rule of Aram Shah. To add to Iltutmish's troubles, some of the Amirs of Delhi expressed resentment against his rule. The new Sultan, however, faced the situation boldly. He first effectively suppressed a rebellion of the Amirs in the plain of Jud near Delhi, and then brought under his control the different parts of the kingdom of Delhi with its dependencies like Badaun Oudh, Benares and Siwalik. The ambitious designs of his rivals were also frustrated. In A.D. 1214 Taj-ud-din Yildiz, being driven from Ghazni by Sultan Muhammad, the Shah of Khwarazm, fled to Lahore, conquered the Punjab up to Thanesar and tried to establish his independent power and even to assert his authority over Iltutmish. This was want Iltutmish could hardly tolerate. He promptly marched against his rival, and defeated him in a battle fought near Tarain in January, A.D. 1216. Yildiz was taken prisoner and sent to Badaun. Nasir-ud-din Qabacha, who had in the meanwhile advanced to Lahore, was expelled from that city by Iltutmish in A.D. 1217. He was completely subdued in February, A.D. 1228, and was accidentally drowned in the Indus, Sind being annexed to the Delhi Sultanate. About a year later, Iltutmish received a robe of honour and a patent of investiture from *Al Mustansir Billah*, the reigning *Caliph* or *Khalifah* of Baghdad, confirming him in the possession "of all the land and sea which he had conquered" as *Sultan-i-Azam* (Great Sultan) i.e 'God' or *'Nam'*. This added a new element of strength to Iltutmish's authority and gave him a status in the Muslim world. Further, "it fastened the fiction of Khalifat on the Sultanate of Delhi, and involved legally the recognition of the final sovereignty of the Khalifah, an authority outside the geographical limits of India, but inside that vague yet none the less real brotherhood of Islam." (Ibid. pp.281-283). This made him unpopular even with the Khalji nobles, who aspired after power and privileges during the rule of one of their leaders. One of them, Malik Ahmad Chap, who held the post of Master of ceremonies, told him plainly "that a king should reign and observe the rules of government, or else be content to relinquish the throne". There was only one unfortunate departure from this generous policy, when, by the Sultan's order, Siddi Maula, a *darvesh*, was executed on mere suspicious of treason. Such a ruler could not pursue a vigorous policy of conquest. Thus his expedition against Ranthambhor was a failure. The Sultan turned away from capturing the fort there with the conviction that it could not be accomplished "without sacrificing the lives of many Mussalmans". But he was more successful against a horde of Mongols, numbering about 150,000 strong, who in A.D. 1292 invaded India under a grandson of *Halaku* (*Hulagu*). Severely defeated by the Sultan's troops the invaders made peace. Their army was permitted to return from India, but *Ulghu*, a descendant of Chingiz, and many of the rank and file embraced *Islam*, settled near Delhi and came to be known as "New Mussalmans". This was an illadvised concession, which produced trouble in the future. The "New Mussalmans." Proved to be turbulent neighbours of the Delhi Government and caused it much anxiety. Even such a peace-loving king could not die a natural death on his bed. By a strange irony of fate he was done to death by his ambitious nephew in 1296. 'Ala-ud-din Khalji, nephew of Jalal-ud-din Firoz, was brought up by his uncle with affection and care. Out of excesive fondness for this fatherless nephew, Firoz made him also his son-in-law. On being raised to the throne of Delhi, Firuz placed him in charge of the fief of *Kara* in the district of Allahabad. It was here that seeds of ambition were sown in 'Ala-ud-din's mind. The "crafty suggestions of the Kara rebels", writes Barani, "made a lodgement in his brain, and, from the very first year of his occupation of that territory, he began to follow up his design of proceeding to some distant quarter and amassing money". It might be that domestic unhappiness, due to the intrigues of his mother-in-law, *Malika Jahan*, and his wife, also made him inclined to establish power and influence independent of the Delhi court. A successful raid into Malwa in 1292 and the capture of the town of *Bhilsa*, for which he was rewarded with the fief of Oudh in addition to that of *Kara*, whetted his ambition. At Bhilsa, 'Ala-ud-din heard vague rumours of the fabulous wealth of the kingdom of Devagiri, which extended over the western Deccan and was then ruled by Ram Chandradeva of the Yadava dynasty, and resolved to conquer it. Concealing his intention from his uncle, he marched to the Deccan through Central India and the Vindhyan region at the head of a few thousand cavalry and arrived before Devagiri. Contact of *Islam* with this part of India had begun much earlier, since the eighth century at the latest. *Ramchandradeva* was not prepared for such an attack, and his son *Sankaradeva*, had gone southwards with the greater part of his army. He was thus taken by surprise, defeated after a futile resistance, and compelled to make peace with the invader by promising to pay a heavy ransom. But as 'Ala-ud-din was about to start marching towards Kara, *Sankaradeva* hurried back to Devagiri and offered battle with the invaders, in spite of his father's request to the contrary. His enthusiasm brought him initial success, but he was soon defeated and a general panic ensued in his army, which led his followers to run away in different directions in utter confusion. *RamChandradeva* solicited the help of the other rulers of Peninsular India, but to no effect, and he was also greatly handicapped for want of provisions. No way was left for him but to sue for peace, whcih was concluded on harder terms than before. 'Ala-ud-din returned to Kara with enormous booty in gold, silver, silk, pearls and precious stones. This daring raid of the Khalji invader not only entailed a heavy economic drain on the Deccan, but it also opened the way for the ultimate Muslim domination over the lands beyond the Vindhyas. 'Ala-ud-din had no intention of sharing the wealth with the Sultan of Delhi. Rather it widened the range of his ambition with the throne of Delhi as its goal. In spite of the honest counsels of his officers, especially of Ahmad Chap, the most outspoken of all, the old Sultan, Jalal-ud-din Firoz, blinded by his affection for his nephew and son-in-law, 'Ala-ud-din, allowed himself to be lured into a trap laid by the latter. Urged on by a traitor at his court, he hurried on a boat to meet his favourite nephew at Kara without taking even the necessary precautions for self-defence, and this mistake cost him his life. The adherents of 'Ala-ud-din proclaimed him Sultan in his camp on the 19th July, 1296' (Ibid. PP.297-298). It would be, however, wrong to surmise from this outlook of 'Ala-ud-din that he disregarded the religion of *Islam*. Outside India, he was known "as a great defender of Islam". In India , there was a difference of opinion on this point. While the supporters of clericalism like *Barni* and his followers "emphasise his disregard of religion", Amir Khusrav, who was a man of culture and a shrewd observer of things, considered him to be a supporter of Islam. ' Ala-ud-din himself said to the Qazi: "Although I have not studied the Science or the Book, I am a Mussalman of a Mussalman stock." The inscriptions on 'Ala-ud-din's monuments also show that he had not lost faith in Islam. 'Ala-ud-din acted according to his conviction, and followed a policy of "thorough", calculated to help the establishment of a strong Government at the centre. The rebellion of Akat Khan, the revolt of the Sultan's sister's sons, Amir 'Umar and Mangu Khan, in Badaun and Oudh, the conspiracy of Haji Maula and the plots of the "New Mussalmans", all of which were effectively suppressed, led him to believe that there were some defects in the administrative system. After consulting his intimate advisers, he attributed these to four causes: (i) Disregard of the affairs of the state by the Sultan, (ii) the use of wine, (iii) intimacy and alliances among the nobles, which enabled them to organise themselves for conspiracies, (iv) abundance of money, "which engenders evil and strife, and brings forth pride and disloyalty" (Ibid. p. 307). The early years of the new ruler's reign were marked by success, and he rescinded the harsher edicts of his father. Political prisoners were set free, some of the lands and endowments confiscated by the late Sultan were restored to their original grantees and the compulsory tariff was removed. This no doubt gave of royal authority disappeared". Further, the Sultan soon plunged himself into a life of pleasure, which naturally made him indolent to the great prejudice of the interests of the State. His example affected the people also. "During (his reign of) four years and four months," writes Barani, "the Sultan attended to nothing but drinking, listening to music, pleasure, and scattering gifts." He fell completely under the influence of a *low-caste* (*Parwari*) convert from Gujarat, whom he styled Khusrav Khan and made the chief minister of his kingdom. This favourite shamelessly pandered to the low tastes of his master with the ulterior motive of seizing the throne for himself. Fortunately for Hindustan, the Mongols made no attention to invade it, nor was there any serious disturbance in any quarter, during this reign. There broke out only two rebellions, one in Gujarat and the other in Devagiri (in the Deccan). The Gujarat revolt was effectively suppressed by '*Ain-ul-Mulk*, and the Sultan's father-in-law, who had received from him the title of Zafar Khan, was placed as governor there. The Sultan marched in person at the head of a large army againt Devagiri. Harapala Deva of Devagiri fled away on the Sultan's approach, but he was pursued, captured, and flayed alive. Thus the whole kingdom of the Yadavas fell under the control of the Muslims and the Sultan appointed Malik Yaklaki governor of Devagiri. He also deputed Khusrav Khan to lead an expedition to Telingana, which was attended with success. After one year's stay at Devagiri, where the Sultan built a great mosque, he marched back to Delhi. These triumphs made Mubarak worse than before. Many members of the imperial family were killed. Mubarak made a departure from the practice of the preceding Sultans of Delhi by shaking off the allegiance to the Khalifat and proclaiming himself "the supreme head of the religion of Islam the Khalifah of the Lord of Heaven and Earth," and assumed the pontifical title of *'al-Wasiq-billah. (Ibid.* p. 312*). Mahmud Begarha* was by far the most eminent Sultan of his dynasty. The leading Muslim historian of his country observes that "he added glory and lustre to the kingdom of Gujarat, and was the best of all the Gujarat kings, including all who preceded, and all who succeeded him; and whether for abounding justice and generosity *'Chamar'* for the diffusion of the '*laws of Islam'* and of Mussalmans; for soundness in judgement, alike in boyhood, in manhood, and in old age; for power, for valour, and victory, he was a pattern of excellence". Ascending the throne at a comparatively young age, he at once took the management of the affairs of his kingdom into his own hands, and overpowered his hostile courtiers, who had formed a conspiracy to raise his brother, Hasan Khan, to the throne. He ruled vigorously, without the influence of any minister or of the harem, for about fifty-three years; and being a brave warrior, he gained success in all his campaigns. He saved Nizam Shah Bahmani from aggression on the part of Mahmud Khalji of Malwa, defeated the *Sumra* and *Sodha* cheifs of *Cutch*, suppressed the pirates of Jagat (*Dvaraka*), and reduced the strong forts of *Junagarh* and *Champaner*, the latter being named by him Muhammadabad. As a result of his conquests, the kingdom of Gujarat reached its extreme limits, extending "from the frontiers of *Mandu* to the frontiers of Sind, by Junagarh; to the *Siwalik Parbat* by *Jalor* and *Nagaur*; to Nasik Trimbak by Baglana; from Burhanpur to Berar and Malkapur of the Deccan; to Karkun and the river Narbada on the side of Burhanpur; on the side of Idar as far as Chitor and Kumbhalgarh, and on the side of the sea as far as the bounds of *Chaul*". Towards the close of his reign, he tried, in alliance with Qansauh-al-

Gharui, Sultan of Egypt to check the rising power of the Portuguese in the Indian Seas, who had within a decade, since the discovery of the Cape Route by *Vasco da Gama* in 1498, almost monopolised the lucrative spice trade from the *Red Sea* and Egypt at the expense of the interests of Muslim traders and the important sea-ports of Western India, like *Cambay* and *Chaul*. The Egyptian fleet, under the command of Amir Husain the Kurd, governor of Jedda, and the Indian contingent, under the command of Malik Ayaz, a Turk who had found employment in the court of Gujarat, defeated a Portuguese squadron commanded by Dom Lourenco, son of the Portuguese viceroy, Francesco de Almeida, near Chaul, South of Bombay, in 1508. But the Portuguese inflicted a crushing defeat on the allied Muslim fleet, near Diu, in 1509, and recovered their naval ascendancy on the sea-coast. Mahmud granted them a site for a factory at Diu. After the death of Mahmud Begarha on the 23rd November, 1511, the throne passed to his son Muzaffar II. He died 11th April, 1526 (Ibid. p. 352).

The result was that his kingdom was overrun by the Maghuls in 1600, but it was finally annexed to their Empire until 1633 in the reign of Shah Jahan. The Muslim kingdom of Golkunda grew up on the ruins of the old Hindu kingdom of Warrangal, which was conquered by the Bahmans in A.D. 1424. The founder of the *Qutb Shahi* dynasty was *Quli Shah,* a Turki officer of the Bahmani kingdom during the reign of Mahmud Shah Bahmani. He was appointed governor of Telingana by Mahmud Gawan and remained loyal to his master til, as a protest against the power and insolence of the Barids, he declared his independence in A.D. 1512 or 1518. He had a long and prosperous reign till he was murdered at the age of ninety in 1543 by his son Jamshid, who reigned for seven years. Jamshid's brother and successor, Ibrahim, fought against Vijayanagar in 1565 in alliance with the other Muslim Sultanates. He was a good ruler and freely admitted the Hindus to high offices in the State. After his death in 1611, the history of Golkunda was largely entangled with that of the Mughul Empire till it was annexed to it by Aurangzeb in 1687. When the distant provinces of the Bahmani kingdom declared their independence, the remnant of it survived only in name under the ascendancy of the Barids. In 1526 or 1527 *Amir Ali Barid* formally dispensed with the rule of the puppet Bahmani Sultans and founded the *Barid Shahi* dynasty of Bidar, which lasted till its territory was absorbed by Bijapur in A.D. 1618-1619. The five offshoots of the Bahmani kingdom had some good rulers, notably in Bijapur and Golkunda. The history of these Sultanates is largely a record of almost continuous quarrel with one another and with Vijayanagar. Each aspired to the supremacy of the Deccan, which was consequently turned into a scene of internal warfare, similar to what went on between the Chalukyas and the Pallavas in earlier days, or between Mysore, the Marathas and the Nizam in the eighteenth century. The disruption of the Bahmani kingdom, and the dissensions among the five Sultanates that rose on its ruins, seriously hampered the progress of Islam, political as well as religious, in the south, where the spirit of Hindu revival, that had manifested itself since the days of the Tughluqs, culminated in the rise and growth of the Vijayanagar Empire. (Ibid. p. 365). As on topics of Hindu life and tradition, as Malik Muhammad Jaysia did on Padmini; and Hindu writers wrote in the Persian language on Muslim literary traditions, as *Rai Bhana Mal* did in his chronicles. Numerous Muslim poets wrote in Hindi and Hindu poets in Urdu. Amir Khusrav is known to have been the author of some Hindi works. This assimilation between the two cultures led also to the springing up of new styles of art, architecture and music, "in which the basic element remained the old Hindu, but the finish and outward form became Persian and the urpose served was that of Muslim courts". Some Muslims of aristocratic Hindu origin, or living in a Hindu environment, assimilated the Hindu customs of *Sati* and *Jauhar*. Several intermarriages between the ruling members of the two communities helped this rapprochement and some again were the result of it. These inter-communal marriages, though sometimes tainted with compulsion as a condition of conquest, did much "to soften the acrimonious differences" between the two communities and assist the transplanting of the customs of the one to the fold of the other. The spirit of harmony and co-operation was not absent in the political field also. Besides retaining, out of necessity, the existing machinery of local administration, the Hindu headmen and accountants of the villages, the Muslim State employed a large number of Hindus, who became prominent in different branches of administration. Thus *Medini Rai* of Chanderi and his friends held high positions in Malwa; in Bengal, Husain Shah employed Hindu officers, most prominent amongst whom were *Purandar Khan*, Rup and *Sanatan*; the Sultans of Golkunda employed some Hindus as ministers; Yusuf Adil Shah of Bijapur entrusted the Hindus with offices of responsibility and the records of his state were ordinarily kept in the Marathi language. *Sultan Zain'ul'Abidin* of Kashmir anticipated Akbar in his pro-Hindu and liberal policy. The Muslim subjects of Ibrahim 'Adil Shah of Bijapur described him as *"Jagadguru"* for his patronage of the Hindus in his state. Examples of Rajput chivalry towards the Muslims are not rare. Thus the Rajput hero, *Rana Sanga*, was chivalrous enough to respect the independence of his vanquished foe, Mahmud II of Malwa; Qutlugh Khan after being defeated by Sultan Nasir-ud-din took refuge with *Rana Ban Pal* of Santur; and it is well known how *Hamir Deva* of Ranthambhor gave shelter to a rebel chief of 'Ala-ud-din Khalji at the risk of incurring the Sultan's wrath. Even the Vijayanagar Emperors employed Muslims in their military service from the time of Deva Raya II, and patronised "the cause of *Islam* in and outside their great capital". A famous Muslim general, Asad Khan of Bijapur, was once invited to Vijayanagar to witness the Mahanavami festival. Rana Sanga had a contingent of Muslim troops under him in his war with Babur and *Ravi*

*Dass*, both were *Sudras*, and Himu, a Hindu Benia, who rose to be the chief minister of '*Adil Shah Sur*, was the commander and leader of the Afghan troops in their last important fight with the Mughuls in A.D. 1556. These official appointments might have been due to political necessity than to any feeling of goodwill. But more can be no doubt that they facilitated the growth of amity between the Hindus and Muslims. In fact, in different aspects & life-arts and crafts, music and painting, in the styles of buildings, in dress and costume, in games and sports- this assimilation between the two communities had progressed so much that when Babur came to India he was compelled to notice their peculiar "Hindustani way". Sir John Marshall has very aptly remarked that seldom in the history of mankind has the spectacle been witnessed of two civilizations, so vast and so strongly developed, yet so radically dissimilar as the Muhammadan and Hindu, meeting and mingling together. The very contrasts which existed between them, the wide divergences in their culture and their religions make the history of their impact peculiarly instructive '*Chamar*'." Hinduism could not completely absorb *Islam* but was in turn influenced by it in two ways. On to one hand, the proselytising zeal of Islam strengthened conservation in the orthodox circles of the Hindus, who with a view to fortifying their position against the spread of the Islamic faith, increased the stringency of the caste rules and formulated a number of rules in the *Smriti* works. The most famous writers of this class were Madhava of Vijayanagar, whose commentary on a *Parasara Smriti* work entitled *Kalanirnaya* was written between A.D. 1335-1360; *Visvesvara*, author of *Madanaparijata*, a Smriti work written for king Madnapala (A.D. 1360-1370); the famous commentator of Manu, Kulluka, a Bengali author belonging to the *Benares* school by domicile and *Raghunandan* of Bengal, a contemporary of *Chaitanaya*. On the other hand, some of the religious systems of the Hindus, and led to the rise of liberal movements under some saintly preachers. With some differences in details, all these reformers were exponents of the liberal *Bhakti* cults, the message of which they sought to carry before the unlettered masses. They preached the fundamental equality of all religions and the unity of Godhead, held that the dignity of man depended on his actions and not on his birth, protested against excessive ritualism and formalities of religion *(Ibid. pp. 402-403)*. No doubt song and dance, a state of ecstacy could be produced in which the personal presence of God would be realised. His gospel was meant for all, irrespective of caste, colour and creed, and some of his disciples were drawn from the lower strata of Hindu society called 'untouchables' and from among Muslims. The influence of *Chaitanya's* teachings on the masses of the people has been wide and profound on the pattern of *Sufis*. In Maharashtra the religion of devotion was preached by *Namadeva*; all among his followers a few were Muslim converts to Hinduism. Namadeva, who belonged to a caste of tailors or calico-printers, flourished probably during the first half of the fifteenth century. With his faith in the unity of Godhead, he did not set much store by idol-worship and external observances of religion. He believed that salvation could be attained only through love of God. Thus he said:

*"Love for him who filleth my heart shall never be sundered,*

*Nama has applied his heart to the true 'Name'.*

*As the love between a child and his mother,*

*So is my soul imbued in the God."*

Kabir made the most earnest efforts to foster a spirit of harmony between Hinduism and Islam. His life is shrouded in a good deal of obscurity, and the dates of his birth and death are uncertain. He flourished either towards the close of the fourteenth century or in the first quarter of the fifteenth century. A legend tells us that he was born of a Brahmana widow, who left him on the side of a tank in *Benares*, and was then found and brought up by a Muhammadan weaver and his wife. He is represented by tradition to have been a disciple of *Ramananda*. Though, as Dr. Carpenter puts it, "the whole background of Kabir's thought is Hindu", he was also influenced to a great extent by *Sufi* saints and poets with whom he came in contact. Thus, he preached a religion of love, which would promote unity amongst all classes and creeds. To him "Hindu and Turk were pots of same clay: *Allah* and *Rama* were but different names". He wrote:

*"It is needless to ask of a saint the caste to which he belongs;*

*The barber has sought God, the washerman and the carpenter are Gods—*

*Even Raidas was a seeker after God.*

*The Rishi Swapacha was a tanner by caste.*

*Hindus and Moslems alike have achieved that*

*End, where remains no mark of distinction."*

Kabir did not believe in the efficacy of ritual or external formalities, either or Hinduism or of Islam; to him the true means of salvation was *Bhajan* or devotional worship, together with the freedom of the soul from all sham, insincerity, hypocrisy and cruelty.

Thus he proclaimed:

*"It is not by fasting and repeating prayers and the creed*
*That one goeth to heaven;*
*The inner veil of the temple of Mecca*
*Is in man's heart, if the truth be known.*
*Make thy mind thy Kaaba, thy body its enclosing temple,*
*Conscience its prime teacher;*
*Sacrifice wrath, doubt, and malice;*
*Make patience thine utterance of the five prayers.*
*The Hindus and the Mussalmans have the same Lord."*

Another great preacher of the time was Nanak, the founder of Sikhism and the reviver of the pure monotheistic doctrine of the *Upanishads*.

He was born in a *Khatri* family of Talwandi (modern *Nankana*), about thirty-five miles to the south-west of the city of Lahore, in A.D. 1469, and spent his whole life in preaching his gospel of universal toleration, based on all that was good in Hinduism and Islam. As a matter of fact, his mission was to put an end to the conflict of religions. Like Kabir, he preached the unity of Godhead, condemned with vehemence the formalism of both Hinduism and Islam. Thus he wrote:

*"Religion consisteth not in mere words;*

*He who looketh on all men as equal is religious.*

*Religion consisteth not in wandering to tombs or places of cremation, or sitting in attitudes of contemplation.*

*Religion consisteth not in wandering in foreign countries, or in bathing at places of pilgrimage.*

*Abide pure amidst the impurities of the world;*

*Thus shalt thon find the way to religion." (Ibid. pp. 405-406).*

Among the learned men of his time, the most eminent were Qazi 'Abdul Muqtadir Shanihi, Maulana Khwajagi, and Ahmad Thanesvari. Among the Lodhis, *Sultan Sikandar* of Kashmir was himself a poet, and gave considerable encouragement to learning. Most of the rulers of the Bahmani kingdom and other independent Muslim dynasties, like those of Bijapur, Ahmadnagar, Golkunda, Malwa, Jaunpur, Bengal and even Multan, were also patrons of letters during his period. The Muslims writers showed their skill in a branch of study which had been comparatively neglected by the Hindus. They wrote several first-rate historical books in elegant prose. Thus we have *Minhaj-ud-din's Tabaqat-i-Nasiri*, which is a general history of the '*Islamic world*' and was named after one of his patrons, *Sultan Nasir-ud-din Mahmud*. Amir Khusrav's historical *mesnevis* are full of valuable information, and his *Ta'rikhi-i- Alai* especially "contains an interesting account of the first few years of the reign of 'Ala-ud-din Khalji'. The most famous historian of the period was Zia-ud-din Barani, a contemporary of Muhammad bin Tughluq and Firoz Shah. Two other important historical works of the time are the *Ta'rikh-i-Firuz Shahi* of *Shams-i-Siraj* 'Afif, written during the reign of Firoz Shah, and the *Ta'rikh-i-Mubarak Shahi* of Yahiya bin Ahmad *Sarhindi*, which was written about eighty years after the death of Muhammad bin Tughluq and was largely used by later writers. It is inaccurate to describe the architecture of the period as "Indo-Saracenic" or "Pathan", as some scholars like Fergusson and others have done. Nor can it be regarded as entirely Indian in "soul and body", as Havell would ask us to believe. In fact, it represented a blending of Indian and Islamic styles, as did certain other aspects of the culture of the time. Sir John Marshall observed that "Indo-Islamic art is not merely a local variety of Islamic art", nor is it merely "a modified form of Hindu art '*Chamar*'. Broadly speaking, Indo-Islamic architecture derives its character from both sources, though not always in an equal degree". There is, no doubt, that there existed in India certain Brahmanical, Buddhist and Jaina styles, while Islamic influences were slowly entering into this land from the middle of the seventh century A.D. At the same time, we should note that what we generally call Islamic art was not of a homogenous and single type; but the followers of Islam, like the *Arabs*, the Persians, or the Turks, brought in their train the art of different parts of western and central Asia, Northern Africa and South-Western Europe (*Ibid* p.410). The history of India from A.D. 1526 to 1556 is mainly the story of the Mughul-Afghan contest for supremacy in this land. The previous Mughul (Mongol) inroads into India did not produce any tangible result except that they added, through the settlement of the "New Mussalmans", a new element to the Indian population and at times harassed the 'Turko-Afghan Sultans. But the invasion of Timur, who occupied a province of the Empire, the Punjab, accelerated the fall of the decadent Sultanate. One of his descendants, Babur, was destined to attempt a systematic conquest of Northern India and thus to lay here the foundation of a new Turkish dominion, which being lost in the time of his son and successor, *Hamayun*, in the face of an Afghan revival, was restored by the year 1556 and was gradually extended by *Akbar*. In fact, there were three phases in the history of the Mughul conquest of India. The first phase (1526-1530) was occupied with the subjugation of the Afghans and the Rajputs under *Rana Sanga*. The second phase (1530-1540) commenced with the reign of *Humayun*, who made unsuccessful attempts to subjugate Malwa, Gujarat and Bengal, but was expelled from India by *Sher Shah Suri*, which meant the revival of the Afghan power. The third phase (1545-1556) was marked by the restoration of the Mughul dominion by Humayun and its consolidation by Akbar. Babur, a Chaghatai Turk, was descended on his father's side from Timur, and was connected on his mother's side with Chingiz Khan *(Ibid.* p.425*)*. Hindukush range, separating Central Asia from Southern Afghanistan Baluchistan and India, becomes "much less forbidding" in the north of Herat, and through this vulnerable point an external invader from Persia or Central Asia may easily enter the Kabul valley and India. As the master of Kabul, the Mughul Emperor "must hold Qandahar or his dominions in unsafe. In an age when Kabul was a part of the Delhi Empire, Qandahar was our indispensable first line of defence". Qandahar was also an important trade centre, where merchants from different parts of Asia flocked together and exchanged their commodities. Through it goods were carried from India to other Asiatic countries more frequently than before, owing to the Portuguese domination of the Red Sea and their hostile relations with Persia. Further, the turbulent Afghan tribes of the frontier, such as the *Uzbegs* and the *Yusufzais*, were "very dangerous in their native hills, being democratic to a degree and fanatically attached to their liberty. Fighting in the fastnesses of their country which afford the best of natural defences, they were the *'Nam'* ever resisted any attempts to bring them into subjugation to any of the adjoining monarchies". Their attitude towards the Mughul Empire was far from friendly, but an imperialist like Akbar could hardly fail to realise the importance of effectively guarding this frontier. He was able to suppress the turbulence of the Uzbegs, whose leader, 'Abdullah Khan, remained friendly to the Mughul Emperor, and also to defeat the *Roshniyas*. The Yusufzais, too, were crushingly defeated by a large Mughul army commanded by Raja Todar Mall and Prince Murad. *Abul Fazl* writes: "A large number of them were killed and many were sold into *Turan* and Persia. The countries of Sawad (Swat), Bajaur and Buner, which have few equals for climate, fruits and cheapness of food, were cleansed of the evil-doers." Bhagwan Das and Kashmir, defeated its Sultan, Yusuf Shah, and his son, Ya'qub, in 1586. Kashmir was then annexed to the Empire, Mirza Haider Dulghat the *Chak* ruler. Sind and Baluchistan were conquered in 1590-1591 and 1595 respectively. Qandahar came into the possession of Akbar peacefully on the invitation *of Chak* rulers. Being harassed by his own relatives and also by the Uzbegs, the Persian governor of Qandahar, Muzaffar Hussain Mirza, surrendered it to Akbar's. (*Ibid.* p. 451).

Subsequently, the influence of his tutor, '*Abdul Latif*, impressed upon his mind the worth of liberal and sublime ideas and made him eager to "attains the ineffable bliss of direct contact with the Divine Reality". Lastly, his Rajput wives and his contact with Hinduism, and the reformation movements of his time, made an impression on his imaginative mind. Thus, "intelligent to an uncommon degree, with a mind alert and inquisitive, he was best fitted by birth, upbringing and association to feel most keenly those hankerings and that spiritual unrest which distinguished the century in which he lived. He was not only the child of his century, he was its best replica." It might be that Akbar's political aim of establishing an all-India Mughul Empire had some influence on his religious policy, as political factors largely influenced the religious settlement of his English contemporary, Queen Elizabeth. But there is no doubt that he had a yearning after truth and often "tempests of feeling had broken over Akbar's soul". We are told even by the hostile critic Badauni that "he would sit many a morning alone in prayer and melancholy, on a large flat stone of an old building near the (Fathipur) palace in a lonely spot with his head bent over his chest, and gathering the bliss of early hours". The conflicts of the different religious sects shocked his soul, and he devoted himself "to the evolution of a new religion, which would, he hoped, prove to be a synthesis of all the warring creeds and capable of uniting the discordant elements of his vast empire in one harmonious whole".

Akbar observed the external forms of the *Sunni* faith until 1575, when his association with Shaikh Mubarak and his two sons, Faizi and Abul Fazl, produced a change in his views. He then caused a building to be constructed at Fathipur Sikri, called the *Ibadat-Khana* or the House of Worship, with a view to discussing philosophical and theological questions. He first summoned there the learned 'Divines of Islam,' but their discussions soon took the shape of "Vulgar rancour, morbid orthodoxy and personal attacks" and they could not reply to some of the queries of Akbar to his satisfaction. In fact, their petty wranglings, of which Badauni gives a graphic picture, failed to satisfy his inquisitive sould, and led him to seek truth elsewhere. He therefore called to the '*Ibadat-Khana* the wise men of different religions and sects, notably Hindu philosphers like Purushottama, Devi and some others; some Jaina teachers, the most prominent of them being Hari Vijaya Suri, Vijaya Sen Suri and Bhanuchandra *Upadhayya;* and Parsi priests and Christian missionaries from Goa. He patiently attended to the arguments of the exponents of each faith, and went so far in relation to each religion that different people had reasonable grounds for affirming him to be a Zoroastrian, a Hindu, Jaina, or a Christian". But he was not converted to any of these faiths, and there is no reason to exaggerate the influence of Christianity over him more than that of any other religion. It seems that being dissatisfied with the bitter controversies of the Muslim divines, he was prompted to study "other religions by means of discourses and debates, which eventually resulted in his eclecticism" and in the promulgation of the *Din-i-Ilahi*. It was a new religion, "compounded", as the Jesuit writer Bartoli says, out of various elements, taken party from the Koran of Muhammad, partly from the scriptures of the Brahmans, and to a certain extent, as far as suited his purpose, from the Gospel of Christ". A firm believer in the policy of universal toleration, Akbar made no attempt to force his religion on others with the zeal of a convert or a religious fanatic, but appealed to the inner feelings of men. Akbar's conception of universal toleration was indeed a noble one, and is a brilliant testimony to his national idealism. Relying on the evidence of Badauni, an uncompromising critic of Akbar, and on the writings of the Jesuits, who must have been dissatisifed with the Emperor for their failure to convert him to their faith, Smith wrongly remarks that "the Divine Faith was a monument of Akbar's folly, not of his wisdom. The whole scheme was the outcome of ridiculous vanity, a monstrous growth of unrestrained autocracy". Von Noer, the German historian of Akbar, gives a correct estimate of the Divine Faith when he writes: "Badaoni certainly takes every opportunity of raking up the notion of Akbar's apotheosis for the purpose of renewing attakcs upon the great emperor. He however, was never in intimate relation to the *Din-i-Ilahi*; he repeats his misconceptions current among the populace, marred and alloyed by popular modes of perception. Akbar might justly have contemplated the acts of his reign with legitimate pride, but many incidents of his life prove him to have been among the most modest of men. It was the people who made a God of the man who was the founder and head of an order at once political, philosophic and religious. One of his creations will assure to him for all time a pre-eminent place among the benefactors of humanity-greatness and universal tolerance in matters of religion." *(Ibid. PP.458-459)*. Even *Shah Jahan's* last days were made highly tragic by the outbreak of a terrible war of succession among his sons. It broke out as soon as he fell ill in September, 1657, and subjected the old Emperor to extreme humiliation and agony till his exit from this world. Shah Jahan had four sons, all of mature age at that time *'Nam'* Dara Shukoh aged 43, Shuja aged 41, Aurangzeb aged 39, and Murad aged 33 were living master of mind and two daughters, *Jahanara*, who sided with Dara *Shukoh*, and *Raushnara*, who joined the party of Aurangzeb. All the brothers had by that time gained considerable experience in civil and military affairs as governors of provinces and commanders of armies, but there were differences among them in personal qualities and capacities. The eldest of them, Dara Shukoh, was in the confidence of his father, who desired him to be his successor. A man of election views, liberal disposition, and of scholarly instincts, Dara Shukoh mixed with the followers of other faiths i.e. '*Nam*' and '*Chamar*' and studied the doctrines of the *Vedanta*, the *Talmud*, the New Testament and the works of *Sufi* writers. He caused a Persian version of the *Atharva Veda* and the *Upanishads* to be made with the assistance of some Brahmana scholars and aimed at finding a *modus vivendi* among the apparently hostile creeds. For this he naturally incurred the displeasure of the orthodox members among his co-religionists, who went against him. But he was not a heretic. He never "discarded the essential dogmas of Islam; he only displayed the electicism of the *Sufis*, a recognised school of Islamic believers. If he showed contempt for the external rites of religion, he only shared the standpoint of many noble thinkers of all Churches, such as John Milton". His latest biographer has aptly remarked: "It is hardly an exaggeration to say that any one who intends to take up the solution of the problem of religious peace in India must begin the work where Dara had left it, and proceed on the path chalked out by that prince." But the excessive fondness of his father for him, and his constant presence at the court, prevented the growth in him of the qualities of an astute politician or the abilities of a brave general *(Ibid. p.481)*. Bahadur Khan, who brought the captives to Delhi on the 23rd August, 1659. On the 29th of the same month they were paraded throughout the city. "To complete his humiliation," writes J.N Sarkar, "Dara was seated in an uncovered *howdah* on the back of a small female elephant covered with dirt *Chams* exposed to the full blaze of an *August* sun, he was taken through the scenes of his former glory and splendour. In the bitterness of disgrace, he did not raise his head, nor cast his glance on any side, but sat like a crushed twig." His tragic plight excited pity in the hearts of the citizens. Bernier, an eye witness of the scene, writes: "The crowd assembled was immense; and everywhere I observed the people weeping, and lamenting the fate of Dara in the most touching language of the '*Nam*'. From every quarter I heard piercing and distressing shrieks of men, women and children wailing as if some mighty calamity had happened to themselves." But not a single hand could be raised to rescue the unfortunate prince, as he was girt round by cavalry and archers. Then a popular riot, directed against the traitor Malik Jiwan Khan, broke out on the 30th August. This riot hastened the end of *Dara*, whose life could no longer be prolonged by *Aurangzeb*. His case was placed before the 'Doctors of Muslim law', who condemned him on a charge of deviation from the Islamic faith. On the *night* of the 30th August the executioners snatched *Sipihr* away from his father's embrace and beheaded Dara. By Aurangzeb's order his corpse was paraded throughout the city to let the people know that their favourite was no more, and then buried in a vault under the dome of the tomb of *Humayun*. Thus the reign of *Shah Jahan*, which had begun with high prospects, came to a close in a series of dark tragedies. Shah Jahan was not essentially an unrelenting or excessively pleasure-seeking ruler, as European writers like *Roe, Terry, Bernier*, and *De Laet* considered him to be, and, as a modern writer, Dr. Smith also holds. There are, of course, certain instances of his severity. Stern as a conqueror and unsparing to his political rivals, *Shah Jahan* indeed acquired his throne by means that left unpleasant memories; but when we take into consideration the circumstances in which he had been placed through the ceaseless intrigues of *Nur Jahan*, "we lose", as Dow writes, "half our rage in the pressure of circumstances that drove him to such a ghastly step" *(Ibid. p. 487).*

Liberal Dara, he tried to enforce strictly the Quranic law, according to which it behoves every pious Muslim to "exert himself in the path of God", or, in other words, to carry on holy wars (*jihad*) against non-Muslim lands (*dar-ul-harb*) till they are converted into realms of Islam (*dar-ul-Islam*). This made him extremely puritanic in temperament, so that he took several steps to enforce "his own ideas of the morose seriousness of life and punctilious orthodoxy". He simplified the customary celebrations on his birthday and coronation day. From the eleventh year of his birthday and coronation day. From the eleventh year of his reign he discontinued the practice of *Jharoka-darsan*, a practice by which his predecessors appeared every morning on the balcony on the wall of the palace to accept the salute of the people, who then gathered on the ground in front. In the same year he forbade music at court and dismissed the old musicians and singers. But music, though banned from the court, could not be "banished from the human soul". It continued to be secretly practised by the nobles, and the imperial prohibition had some force only in important cities. In the twelfth year the ceremony of weighing the Emperor's body on two birthdays against gold, silver and other commodities was given up, and royal astronomers and astrologers were dismissed. But the belief of the Muslims in astrology was too deeply rooted in their minds to be removed by an imperial ordinance; it remained active till late in the eighteenth century. In order to avoid the *Kalima* (Muhammadan confession of faith) on the coins being defiled by men of other faiths, he forbade its use. He also abolished the *Nauroz,* which the Mughul Emperors of India had borrowed from Persia. He appointed Censors of Public Morals (*Muhtasibs*) *to* "regulate the lives of the people in strict accordance with the Holy Law." Aurangzeb personally practised what he sought to enforce on others. His private life was marked by a high standard of morality, and he scrupulously abstained from the common vices of his time. Thus he was regarded by his contemporaries as a "*darvish* born in the purple" and the Muslims venerated him as a "*Zinda Pir*" *or* living saint. To "promote general morality", he issued a number of regulations. He passed an ordinance prohibiting the production, sale and public use, of wine and *bhang.* Manucci tells us that the dancing girls and public women were ordered either to get themselves married or to leave the kingdom. The Emperor also passed strict orders against singing obscence songs, and stopped the burning of faggots and processions during certain religious festivals. It is mentioned in the official "guide-books" of Aurangzeb's reign that he forbade *Sati* (December, 1663), but "the evidence of contemporary European travellers in India shows that the royal prohibition was seldom observed". The Emperor, however, did not rest satisfied with these regulations only. He issued other *firmans* and ukases, which marked the inauguration of a new policy in regard to important sections of the people. The year 1679 saw the reimposition of the *jizya* tax on "unbelievers". The new regulations and ordinances must have produced a deep impression on the people affected, and added much to the difficulties with which the imperial government had to deal. No one can deny the Emperor Aurangzeb the credit of being a sincere and conscientious exponent of the faith that was in him. But it is also true that his ardour and zeal made him oblivious of the fact that the country over which destiny had placed him to rule was not inhabited by a homogeneous population but included various elements rich in their religious traditions and ideals, which needed tactful and sympathetic understanding. Aurangzeb certainly made a mistake in identifying the interests of the State with those of his faith and in offending those who differed from it. The policy generated feelings of discontent among certain sections of the people, which by distracting his energies during the remainder of his reign proved to be one of the most potent causes of the decline and fall of the Mughul Empire. The first serious outbreak of anti-imperial reaction took place among the *Juts* of the Muttra (Mathura) district, where the imperial *faujdar*, '*Abdun-Nabi,* had oppressed them greatly. In 1669 the sturdy Jat peasantry rose under a leader, *Gokla, zamindar* of Tilpat, killed the *faujdar,* and kept the whole district in disorder for a year, till they were suppressed by a strong imperial force under Hasan 'Ali Khan, the new *faujdar* of *Muttra. Gokla* was put to death and the members of his family converted to Islam. But this did not crush the *Jats* permanently. They rose once again in 1685 under the leadership of Raja Ram and plundered Akbar's tomb at Sikandra in 1688. Raja Ram was defeated and slain and the principal stronghold of the Jats was reduced in 1691. But they soon found a more formidable leader in Churaman, who welded the disorganised *Jats* into a strong military power and organised an armed resistance against the Mughuls after Aurangzeb's death. *(Ibid pp. 496-97).* The establishment of the Mughul administration, on ideas and principles different from those of the Sultans of Delhi, was mainly the work of Akbar. Of his two predecessors, *Babur* and *Humayun*, the former had neither time nor opportunity, and the latter neither inclination nor ability, to elaborate a system of civil government. While gifted with political genius of a high order, Akbar was indebted in certain respects to the Sur example of administrative organisation. The Mughul government was a "combination of Indian and extra-Indian elements." It was, more correctly speaking, "the Perso-Arabic system in an Indian setting". It was also essentially military in nature and every officer of the Mughul State had to be enrolled in the army list. It was necessarily a centralised autarchy, and the king's power was unlimited. His word was law, and his will none could dispute. He was the supreme authority in the state, the head of the government the commander of the State forces, the fountain of justice, and the chief legislator. He was the *Khalifah of God*, required to obey the scriptures and Islamic traditions, but in practice a strong king could act in defiance of sacred law if he so liked. There was nothing like a cabinet of ministers in the modern sense of the term. The ministers could not claim to be consulted as a matter of right; it was entirely a matter of the Emperor's pleasure to accept their advice or not. Much depended, indeed, on the personality of the Emperor and his ministers. A wise ruler like *Shah Jahan* wanted invariably to consult a *Sa'dullah Khan*, while a minister like *Hussain 'Ali Khan* would have little regard, even open contempt, for his crowned puppets. The first six Mughul rulers of India possessed, however, a strong commonsense, and their autocracy did not, therefore, degenerate into an unbearable tyranny trampling on the rights and customs of the people. Endowed with the spirit of "benevolent despots", these rulers worked hard for the good of their subjects, in one way or another and extended his power towards *Kashmir*. (Ibid. p. 554).

However, the Persian or other foreign artists Akbar's court were few in number, the most famous of them being 'Abdus Samad, Farrukh Beg, who was of Kalmuck origin, Khursau Quli and Jamshed. The Hindu artists predominated in number. Of the seventeen leading artists of Akbar's reign, no less than thirteen were Hindus. *Abul Fazl* thus refers to the standard of their art: "More than a hundred painters have become famous masters of the art, while the number of those who attain perfection, or of those are middling, is very large. This is specially true of the Hindus, their pictures surpass our conception of things. Few indeed in the whole world are found equal to them." They worked in collaboration and excelled in portraiture, book illustration and illumination and animal painting. Chief among them were *Basawan, Lal,*

*Mukund, Haribans* and *Daswanth*. The last-named belonged to the *Kahar* or palanquin-bearer caste, while the rest belonged to the *Kayastha, Chitera, Silavat* and *Khatri* castes and were drawn from different parts of the country.

Akbar, who shared with others of his race "an intense appreciation of the wonder and glory of the world", encouraged pictorial art in every possible way and gave in a religious outlook in spite of the Islamic injunction regading the representation of living forms. "It appears to me," said he, "as if a painter had quite peculiar means of recognising God; for if a painter in sketching anything that has life, and in devising its limbs, one after the other, comes to feel that he cannot bestow individuality on his work, he is forced to think of God, the Giver of life, and will thus increase his knowledge." In this way he sought to remove the discontent of the orthodox Muslims, who were opposed to the art of painting. "Bigoted followers of the letter of the law," writes *Abul Fazl*, "are hostile to the art of painting, but their eyes now see the truth." The school of art that grew up under Akbar continued to flourish in the reign of *Jahangir* through the enthusiastic support and patronage of the latter. Jahangir was an excellent connoisseur, who paid high prices for any pictures that satisfied his aesthetic taste, and an art critic who could tell the names of individual artists in a composite piece. The famous Muslim artists of his court were *Aga Reza* and his son, *Abul Hasan*, of Herat; *Muhammad Nadir* and Muhammad Murad from Samarqand, who were among the last foreign artists to come to India; and Ustad Mansur. Among the Hindu painters of this reign, Bishan Das, Manohar and Govardhan were the most eminent. (Ibid. p. 599). Certain Brahmana ministers, wearing sacred threads, should not be allowed to preach from the pulpits. Instead of allowing the Samaj to be drawn away from the old Hindu lines laid down by *Raja Rammohan Roy, Devendranath*, by virtue of his position as the sole trustee of the Samaj, dismissed *Keshab* and his followers from all offices and positions of trust and responsibility. *Keshab* took up the challenge and started a separate organization which included most of the local branches. Thus by the year 1865 the *Brahma Samaj* was divided into two camps, the conservatives and the progressives. The former included men who believed in one God and discarded the worship of images, but did not want to sever all connection with Hindu society, while the latter consisted of those who regarded popular Hinduism as too narrow and chafed at the use of Sanskrit texts and the performance of social practices which symbolised that religion. After the great schism, the Adi Brahma Samaj, the organisation of Devendranath, quietly followed the pure monotheistic form of Hinduism, setting its face deliberately against social reform or propaganda of any kind. But it soon passed into obscurity. The period of reformation ushered in by Raja Rammohan Roy was over and a revolution was now in progress. The newly started "Brahma Samaj of India" had a triumphant career under the guidance of *Keshab Chandra Sen*. The missionary exertions all over Bengal and even far outside its boundaries led to an increase in the number of local churches. The inclusion of women as members and the adoption of a moderate programme of social reform formed a new feature of the rejuvenated society. It was chiefly due to its efforts that the Government passed the Act III of 1872, which abolished early marriage of girls and polygamy, and sanctioned widow marriages and inter-caste marriages for those who did not profess any recognised faith such as Hinduism and Islam. Another striking feature was the adoption of the *Samkirtan* in the *Vaishnava* style for the purpose of propaganda. At first "Jesus was the inspirer and teacher of Keshab and now came *Chaitanya*. The two streams combined and made a confluence which soon produced novel and striking results". The passion of *Bhakti* (devotion) seized the members, and in true *Vaishnava* style many of them prostrated themselves at each other's feet and especially at the feet of Keshab. Reverence for the leader grew apace and he gradually came to be regarded by some as a prophet or a divine incarnation. This practice of "main-worship" led to a fresh discord in the *Brahma Church*. Progressive and rationalists strongly protested. *(Ibid. p. 879)*. The Arya Samaj has not, however, escaped the rationalism of the present age. Already there is a growing section among it which present age. Already there is a growing section among it which recognizes the value of English education and is inclined to a more liberal programme. Its chief exponent is Lala Hansraj and its visible symbol the Dayananda Anglo-Vedic College of Lahore. As a countermove to this we may point to the famous Gurukul of Hardwar, founded in 1902, which seeks to revive the Vedic ideal in modern life. It may be noted, in conclusion, that Dayananda, at the beginning of his career, tried to come to terms with the Brahma Samaj and a Conference was held in Calcutta in 1869 with that end in view. Nothing, however, came of it, and the Arya Samaj ultimately overwhelmed and absorbed the Brahma Samaj movement in the Punjab, where, in Lahore, a Brahma Samaj had already been started in 1863. The synthesis of the two great forces, the ancient or Oriental and the modern or Western, marks the Ramakrishna Mission, the last great religious and social movement which characterises the nineteenth century. *Ramakrishna Paramahansa* (1836-1886), after whom the Mission is named, was a poor priest in a temple near Calcutta. He had scarcely any formal education, Eastern or Western, worthy the name, but led an intense spiritual life in his splendid isolation. He had a deep faith in the inherent truth of all religions and tested his belief by performing religious exercises in accordance with the practice and usages not only of different Hindu sects, but also of *Islam* and *Christianity*. His broad catholicity, mysticism, and spiritual fervour attracted a small number of occasional visitors, mostly from Calcutta. He lived and died as a secluded spiritual devotee, unknown except to a comparatively small group of people. To them he expounded his views in short pithy sayings and admirable parables. Most of these were collected and published before his death and many other works about him and his sayings have been published since them. The most famous among his disciples, and the one most beloved of the *guru*, was a young graduate of the Calcutta University named *Narendranath Dutta*, afterwards famous as *Svami Vivekananda* (1836-1902). It was he who carried the message of Ramakrishna all over India. His learning eloquence, spiritual fervour and wonderful personality gathered round him a band of followers whcih included both prince and peasant. With their help, and after untold sufferings, he attended in 1893 the famous "Parliament of Religions" at Chicago, and at once made his mark. *(Ibid. p. 884).* On the death of the Amir, 'Abdur Rahman, who had concluded a friendly treaty with the British Government, in September 1901, Lord Curzon had some trouble with his successor, Amir Habibullah, over the renewal of the treaty. Habibullah claimed that it was an agreement between the two countries and did not require renewing on the death of the *Amir*; but Lord Curzon argued that the treaty with the late Amir was a personal one and insisted on its renewal. For some years all communications with the Government of India were stopped by Amir Habibullah, who refrained from drawing his subsidy and claimed the title of "His Majesty". He was undoubtedly encouraged by the anti-English activities of Russia. But in November 1904, during Lord Curzon's absence from India, the acting Viceroy, Lord Ampthill, sent a mission to Kabul under Sir Louis Dane. A treaty was concluded in March, 1905, by which all the engagements between the British Government and 'Abdur Rahman were renewed and Amir Habibullah's claim to the title of "His Majesty" conceded. The tables were, however, turned two years later after the signing of the Anglo-Russian convention in August, 1907. According to this Russia agreed to treat Afghanistan as outside her sphere of influence and equal commercial facilities were provided for England and Russia in that kingdom. The Amir, who "regarded this union of the two great neighbours with natural suspicion", refused to give his consent to the clauses of the Convention. But this counted for nothing, as Russia stood by the agreement. Hence forth Habibullah remained aloof, but during the First World War he rendered England valuable service by maintaining a policy of strict neutrality in spite of the incitement of hostile parties. The combination of the European powers, and their attempts to introduce Western civilization in Afghanistan D. gave an impetus to Pan-Islamic forces in that country, which became formidable after the fall of the Tsarist Government in Russia in 1917 and the consequent disapperance of Anglo-Russian friendship. Amir Habibullah made himself unpopular with the orthodox and anti-British party in Afghanistan by his attempts to introduce European manners and customs into his land and was assassinated on the 20th February, 1919. A short struggle for the throne ensued in which Amanullah, a son of the murdered Amir, came out successful. Party under the pressure of internal torubles, and partly under the influence of the war party, Amanullah decided to embark on a war with the English. Thus began the Third Anglo-Afghan War (April-May,1919). *(Ibid p. 904)*. The Zoroastrian Conference which inaugurated in 1910 at the instance of a Pari priest named Dhala who had visited America and studied in Columbia University under the renowned Zoroastrian scholar, Professor Jackson, has rendered beneficial services to the community. The *Chief Khalsa Diwan*, with its headquarters at Amritsar and branches in different parts of the country, advocating liberal reforms in society and culture, and the Khalsa College at Amritsar, gave eloquent proofs of Sikh awakening. Largely through the 'Aligarh Movement, the history of which has been already traced, Islam in India was roused to a new life. The chief exponents of this "New Islam" were Maulavi Chiragh 'Ali, the Rt. Hon. Syed Amir Ali, Sir Shaikh Muhammad Iqbal, Prof. S. Khudabakhsh and Prof. A.M. Maulavi. A number of *anjumans* or societies, and a powerful Muslim press, sprang up for the service of the Muslim community. The Ahmadiya Movement, started by Mirza Ghulam Ahmad of Qadian in the Gurudaspur district of the Punjab for the restoration of the "true and unpolluted faith of Islam to the followers of the Prophet", also gained a number of followers in different parts of the world.

Under the influence of the general awakening of the country, a spirit of reform permeated various classes of Indian society and profoundly modified their ideas, habits and customs. The most striking change in Indian social life of to-day is in the position of women. Women are not only coming out of their *purdah* and receiving education, but are also taking active interest in social and political matters and are claiming their rights as citizens. As a matter of fact, the women's movement in India, which started largely under the inspiration of Ramabai Ranade, has "succeeded with a swiftness and to a degree that would have seemed fantastic even a few years earlier."

Attempts have been made by the State and reformers to do away by legislation with the evil of early marriage. In 1901 the Gaikwar of Baroda passed the Infant Marriage Prevention Act, which fixed the minimum marriageable age in the State, for girls at twelve and for boys at sixteen. The Age of consent committee met at Simla in June, 1923, to enquire into the question of marriage reforms. After its report appeared, Rai Saheb Harbilas Sarda's Child Marriage Bill was passed in 1930. The Act evoked much opposition among the conservative sections of the people and did not prove very effectual in actual working. The Widow-Remarriage Movement, which had many notable Indian social reformers as its advocates, has also made some progress *(Ibid., p. 957)*.

8. **Note.** The name "India" was applied to the country by the Greeks. It corresponds to the "*Hi (n) du*" of the old Persian epigraphs. 'Hi' means greating to high fidelity of *'Sound'*, 'n' stands for 'zero' or *'nadir'* an Arabic word, and *'du'* means *'two'* composed of two English alaphbets

d+u, 'd' stands for 'destruction' or destroyer or injurious that the *man* and 'u' stands for *'unique'* that is *'Nam'* or *'Sabad'* or *'Word'*. Like *"Sapta Sindhavah"* and *"Hapta Hindu"* (A.H.I. P.4). *Satta* or *sapta*, for seven, rather than the Iranian word *"Hapta"*, where the initial 's' has been changed to 'h'. considering the language, it is clearly an Indian dialect because initial 'v' by 'b', while medial becomes the semi-vowel 'W'. Like Middle Indio(Prakrit) in *'Sapta'* becoming *'Satta' (Ashvini Aggrawal; In search of Vedic-Harappan Relationship; New Delhi; 2005: pp. 88-89)*. *'Word'* the appellations of the country of the Aryans in the *Veda* and *Vandidad*, *'Sabad'*, it is derived from the *Sindhu* (the Indus), the great river which constitutes the most imposing feature of that part of the sub-continent which seems to have been the cradle of its earliest known civilization. Closely connected with *"Hindu"* are the later designations *"Hind"* and *"Hindusthan"* as found in the pages of mediaval writers. (A.H.I. P.4).

9. **Note:** This ethical compositions of *Santideva* and treatises on polity written by *Kamandaka* and *Somadeva* may be mentioned in this connection. In one domain, that of historical literature, the post-gupta period produced works the like of which had not been seen in earlier ages.
10. P.H.K. p. 160.
11. H.A.I. p. 339.
12. A.H.I. p. 164.
13. *Ibid.* p. 164.
14. *S'esanaga*, the King of the serpents, supports the earth on his thousand heads. Therefore, on account of their intertangled mass and relatively small size, are compared to lotusroots.
15. R.T. Vol.1 Book VI. p. 266.
16 **Note.** The words put into the mouther of Siva may by a series of puns be understood as referring either to his consort *Parvati* or referring either to his consort *Parvati* or to *Samdhya*, the personification of the twilight and of the prayer recited at twilight. *Mena*, the mother of Parvati and the wife of *Himavat*, belongs to the race of the *Pitrs* or *Manes*. *Samdhya* figures as the mother of the *Pitra*. In the above statement both interpretations have been given.
17. Term *Japa* is soothed of two words *'Ja+pa'*, 'Ja' means living man's *mana* and *'pa'* means *'Father'*, Thus, the country like China had made the *father* of the living *manas* and forgotten the *ultimate reality* that is *'Nam'*. As *Bhai Tara Singh* stood the ordeal bravely, reciting the words of the *Japji* and calling on the name of God. After a few day's torture, he surrendered his soul on the Ist of July, 1747. His torturer too had died a few hours before him, not without suffering, because he had been attacked by a disease which had stopped his urine. (Teja Singh & Ganda Singh, *A Short History of the Sikhs,* Vol. one, Patiala (New Delhi); Third Edition; 1999; p.124. Thereafter mentioned as S.H.S.)

18. R.T. Vol.1 Book VII; p. 267.
19. *Ibid.*
20. *Ibid.* p. 268.
21. *Ibid.*
22. *Ibid.*
23. *Ibid.*
24. *Ibid.*
25. *Ibid.*
26. *Ibid.* p. 270.
27. *Ibid.*
28. *Ibid.*
29. *Ibid.*
30. *Ibid.* p. 271.
31. *Ibid.* p. 273.
32. Term *Tausi* is probably connected with Sanskrit word *'tusara'* meaning 'snow', and etymologically 'a river coming from the snows'. *Tausi* is the ancient form of the appellation *Tohi* which is now barne by several mountain-streams joining the *Vitasta* and *Chenab* from the south slopes of the Pir Panjal Range. The name '*tohi*' is drived from the joint name of two streams that is *Vitasta* and *Chenab* in the north and the South of the Kashmir city= (*Mahajanapada*) states powerful. Term *'tohi'* also indicates that God is great and powerful *'To+hi'*.
33. R.T. Vol.1. Book VII. p. 272.
34. *Ibid.*
35. *Ibid.*
36. *Ibid.* **Note**. The cutt of the trees and of water deities like the Ganges is noted by Curtius and Strabo, and the idea of the *Kalpa-Vriksha*. The tree which will give a man all he wants, occurs prominently in literature, including that of the *Jainas*. Most of the deities are now thoroughly anthropomorphised and become quite human in dress, talk and action. With the growth of anthropomorphism came the increased use of images and the construction of temples for daily service. Icons were know to the ancient people of the lower Indus Valley, and stray allusions to images have been traced in some Vedic texts. But the first undoubted historical reference to image-worship by an Aryan Tribe occures in a passage of curtius, who states that an image of *Herakles* was carried in front of the *Paurava* army as it advanced against Alexander. *Patanjali* refers to the exhibition and sale of images of *Siva*, *Skanda* and *Visakha* by the *Mauryas* who rose to power at the end of our period (A.H.I. p. 82). Till a short time ago, perhaps even at present, the popular belief among Hindus as the origin of the *Vedas* was that they were eternally existent in the mide of the supreme, and made manifest by him in each *Kalpa*. The *Kalpas* here referred to are the periods into which, according

to Hindu reckoning, the time is divided. Such a *Kalpa* is a 'day of Brahma', and a 'day of Brahmn' consists of a thousand *Yugas* or *ages*, amounting altogether to four hundred and thirty-two million years of mortals. At the beginning of each *Kalpa* all the existing universe is created and the *Vedas* are supposed then to be revealed by Brahma through the *rishis*. At the close of the *Kalpa* all the existing universe is destroyed and then there is a new creation and a new revelation in the new *Kalpa*. (R.V.V.R. pp. 38-39)

37. *R.T.* Vol.1 Book VII. p. 273.
38. *Ibid.* Section V. pp. 107-108.
39. *Ibid.* Book VII. p. 273.
40. **Note.** Prince *Vigraharaja* was the son of *Didda's* brother.
41. *R.T.* Vol. 1. Book VIII, p. 274.
42. Term *asthanabrahmana* indicates rank of a *Durbari* in modern India.The term has the same significance as the *asthapradhan* whose functions were (*i*) the *Peshwa* or the Prime Minister, who had to look after the general welfare and interests of the Kingdom, (*ii*) the *Amatya* or the Finance Minister, whose duty was to check and countersign all public accounts, (*iii*) the *Mantri*, who had to preserve a daily record of the King's acts and the proceedings of his court, (*iv*) The *Sachiva* or the superintendent, who was in charge of the King's correspondence and had also to check the accounts of the *mahals* and *paraganas*, (v) the *Sumant* or the Foreign Secretary, (vi) the *Senapati* or the commander-in-chief, (vii) the *Pandit Rao* and *Danadhyaksha* or the Royal Chaplain and Almoner, and (viii) the *Nyayadhisa* or the Chief justice. All the ministers, excepting the *Nayaadhisa* and the *Pandit Rao*, held military commands besides their civil duties, and at least three of them were placed in charge provincial administration as well. The ministers were no less than thirty in number. *Shivaji* divided his kingdom into a number of provinces, each being placed under a viceroy, who held office at the king's pleasure and was assisted like him by a staff of eight chief officers. The viceroy of the *Karnatak* had a position somewhat different from that of the other provincial governors, and he exercised more power and discretion. (*A.H.I.* p. 518)
43. *R.T.* Vol.1. Book VII. P.274 **Note.** *Tunga* was the commander-in-chief of the army, but he was the brother of *Naga*.
44. *Ibid.*
45. *Ibid.*
46. *Ibid.* p. 275.
47. *Ibid.*
48. *Ibid.*
49. *Ibid.* **Note**. The worship of Siva *Bhutesa*, 'the Lord of the beings', localized near the sacred sites of *Mount Haramukuta*, has played an important part in the ancient religion of *Kashmir*. The legend relating

how *Siva* came to take up his residence in that neighbourhood in the form of *Bhutesa*, is given in the *Nilamata Purana* and is closely connected with the of *Nandinksetra*. The name of *Nandinksetra* and *Haramukuta Mahatmyas* has been given to a high alpine valley at the foot of the east Glaciers of the Haramukh peaks which contains the sacred *Kalodaka* lake popularly known as *Nund-Kol*. This lake, situated in circular shape at 75° longitude and 34° 25′ latitude, at an altitude of about 13,000 forms one of the cheif stations on the pilgrimage to the sacred *Ganga Lake* (*Uttaramanasa*), which lies a short distance above it. According to a legend told at length in the *Nilamata*, *Nandin*, born as son of *Silada*, performed in the *Kalodaka* a great penance, where upon Siva took up his permanent abode there by the side of his faithful attendant. The inner portion of the lake, showing a deep blue colour, is supposed to mark the residence of *Kala* or Siva; the outer portion, of a light green colour, that of *Nandin*. Siva is worshipped there under the name of *Nandisa*. In the narrow gorge of the *Kankanai* River (*Kanakavahmi*) which flows past the south foot of this spur, and some two miles above the hamlet of *Vangath* (*Vasisthasvama*) 75° 2′ longtitude 34° 21′ latitude are found the ruins of some seventeen temples of various age and dimension. These ruins are now almost hidden by the luxuriant vegetation of the forest. Their identity with the buildings which Kashmirian Kings had at different periods raised in honour of *Siva Bhutesa Jyesthesa*. Jalauka, Asoka's son, is said to have erected to *Bhutesa* a stone temple with rich endowments. Gifts at the sacred site are recorded of *Narendraditya* and *Lalitaditya*. *Avantivarman* also appears as a benefactor of *Bhutesvara* and one of his visit was the occasion of the interesting episode. In the disturbed reigns of the later period *Bhutesvara* shared the calamities of other Kashmirian shrines. Under *Samgramadeva* its treasury was plundered by a powerful minister *Bhadresvara*. *Bhutesvara* seems to have escaped the sacrilegious confiscations of *King Harsa*, but under his successor *Uchchala* it suffered greatly by a conflegration. During the rebellions under *Jayasimha* the temples were sacked by maruding hillmen. Of the later fate of the shrine no record is left in the chronicles. *Abu-L-Fazl* does not refer to it, but Haidar-Malik, in reproducing our passage, correctly renders *Bhutesa* by *Bhutisar* i.e Buthser. The pilgrims route on their return from the sacred lakes on the *Haramukuta* still leads past the site. But no attention is paid to the temples, which, to judge from their condition, must have long ceased to be places of worship. The fine spring now called *NaranNag* which lies at the North East corner of the ruins and which forms now the final stage of the *Haramukuta* pilgrimage. It has been assumed that *Mlechchas* here referred to are, perhaps the Greeks.

50. *Ibid.*
51. *Ibid.* p. 277.
52. *Ibid.* p. 278.

53. *Ibid.*
54. *Ibid.*
55. *Ibid.*
56. *Ibid.* **Note.** By term *dvara* is meant here the watch-station on the Tosamaidan pass is open, to do the distance between *Loharin* and Srinagar in the short time indicated by the text and route properly known as *Karkotadranga*. The place where the route passes the scrap of the Tosamaidan plateau before descending to the village of *Drang*, is still closed by old watch-towers marked on the map. This locality is now called *bar-bal* i.e 'the place of the Gate'. In Sanskrit called *dvara* in Kashmiri called *bar.*
57. *Ibid.*
58. *Ibid.*
59. *Ibid.*
60. *Ibid.*
61. *Ibid.*
62. *Ibid.*
63. *Ibid.*
64. *Ibid.*
65. *Ibid.* p. 280.
66. *Ibid.*
67. *Ibid.* p. 281.
68. *Ibid* .
69. *Ibid.* **Note.** It is curious that this *Maga* name, which is well-known to the Epics and Puranas, does not occur in the long lists of Kashmirian sacred springs given by the *Nilamata* and the *Mahatmyas.*
70. *Ibid.* **Note.** The word *avadalika* seems otherwise unknown. Its apparent etymology from *dal, lit*; *'rupture'*, and the context, justify the above interpretation.
71. *Ibid.*
72. *Ibid* p. 282.
73. *Ibid.* **Note.** It is probable the name of *Amaresa* or *Amaresvara* to a shrine situated at the site now marked by the village of *Amburher*, about four miles to the North of *Kashmir* (*Srinagar*) on the road towards the *Sind Valley*. This place, the modern name of which is clearly derived from *Amaresvara* composed as *Kother* to *Kapatesvara* and *Jyether* to *Jyesthesvara*. All these passages describe fights in the immediate vicinity of Srinagar. It is also mentioned as *Amaresapura* by *Jonaraja*, *Sahibram* in his *Tirthas* gives correctly *Amaresvara* as the old name of the village, and refers to an *Amaresvara* Linga worshipped there. In 1895, *M.A. Stein* visited there and found considerable remains of an old temple built into the Ziarat of Farrukhzad Sahib. A little to the wonder of the latter, on the shore of the Anchar Lake, are two *Nagas,* one of which, named

*Ganga*, is still annually visited by the pilgrims proceeding to the *Tirthas* of *Mount Haramukuta*. Now the popular Tirthas of *Amarnath* or *Amburnath* situated at a great altitude above the sources of the *Lidar* river at 75° 34′ longitude 34° 5′ latitude. It is popularly known by the name of *Sesanaga,* and forms one of the stations of the great *Amaresvara* pilgrimage. The legend told in Chapter VI. of the *Amaresvaramahatmya*, it is true, identifies the lake with the serpent *S'esanaga*. But in the same chapter the lake is also designated by the name of *Susrama Naga,* which evidently reproduces the older form *Susravas* in the Kashmiri pronunciation of *'Susram'*. As *'SusramNag'* the lake is still known among the older *Purohitas* of *Amaresvara* and under this name it is also referred to in the appropriate gloss which gives on our passage. The white colour of the lake's water is noticeable, and is possibly due to the surrounding limestone rocks. A narrow inlet of the lake opening to the south towards the glacier of the *Kohenhar* peak, is popularly known by the name of *Zamatur Nag,* 'the son-in-law's Naga', and corresponds to the *Jamatrsaras* of our narrative. It is mentioned as *Jamatrnaga* along with the *Susramanaga* in the route directory of the *Amaresvara*-pilgrimage as given in the *Tirthas*. The *Amaresvara-Amarnath* or *Amburnath* situated at a considerable altitude, 75$^0$ longitude 34° 13′ latitude Siva *Amaresvara* is believed to have manifested himself to the gods who entreated him for protection against death. The god is worshipped in a linga-shaped ice-block. For a description of the locality and the route leading to it. This pilgrimage, notwithstanding its hardships, now ranks amongst the most popular in Kashmir and attracts in great numbers pilgrims from other parts of India. In old times, however, this Tirtha can scarcely have claimed such importance, if we may judge from the scanty reference made to it in the *Nilamata* and in the *Rajatarangini*.

74. *Ibid.*
75. *Ibid.*
76. **Note.** There we find *Sadasivapura*, that is the quarter near *Sadasivapura,* that is the quarter near *Sadasiva*, repeatedly mentioned as a part of the city of Srinagar. There are two place *Sadasivapura* on the left river bank and opposite to the quarter of *Samudramatha* in which the partisans of the *Cakkas* (Tsaks) posted on the river bank in the *Samudramatha* fired across at their opponents who occupied *Sadasivapura*. It has been described that great fire was broke out at *Sadasivapura*, and subsequently crossing the *Vitasta,* destroyed the *Samudramatha* with the neighbouring parts of the city. By *Samudramatha* (called *Samudramatha* by *S'rivara*, IV, 121, 169) is meant certainly the present *Mahalla* of *Sudarmar* composed in Kashmir, *Sudar*, 'sea' in Sanskrit *Samudra*). This quarter is situated on the right bank of the river, immediately below the second bridge. Opposite to it on the left bank lie the quarters of *Zaindar Mahal, Purusayar Karaphal* Mahal, Malikyar, all belong to the Zilla *Tasavan*. Here, then, we have to assume,

was situated the shrine of *Sadasiva* and the royal residence of Kalhana's time. As the *Kutakul* flows in this neighbourhood parallel to the *Vitasta*, and at a distance of scarcely more than 400 yards from the latter, the above quoted passages of the *Rajatarangini* which speak of the palace as close to the *Ksiptika* or *Kutakul*, fully supported our identification. With the evidence above recorded curiously agrees a local tradition which has survived in this neighbourhood. An ancient Linga, which was standing until a few years ago on the Ghat (Yarabal) of *Purusayar* about fifty yards below the second bridge, has been known to the old *purohitas* living in these quarters by the name of *Sadasiva*. It has recently been placed in a small temple erected close to its original position on the left river bank. It is possible that we have in the traditional name of this old linga the last surviving trace of the ancient designation of the locality. The "old palace" (*Puranarajadhani*) is mentioned and its position has not been identified. We may safely assume that, with the rest of the city founded by *Pravarasena,* it was situated on the right bank of the river (R.T. Vol.1 Book VII. p. 283).

77. *R.T.* Vol.1 Book VII.p. 283 **Note**. Term *dallaka* means draw the people from the material world to the *daisike* that is heavenly world.
78. *Ibid.* p. 284.
79. *Ibid.* p. 285.
80. *Ibid.*
81. *Ibid.*
82. *Ibid.*
83. *Ibid.* p. 286.
84. **Note**. *Champa (Annami)* is the modern hill state of *Camba*, which comprises the valleys of all the sources of the Ravi or '*Ravidas culture*' and some adjoining valleys draining into *Cinabs* as described by (Cunningham, *Ancient Geography*; p. 141). King *Sala* has been rightly identified by Prof. Kielhorn with *Salavahana*, who has mentioned as King *Somavarmadeva's* predecessor in the *Camba* grant. The latter was executed in the reign of *Asata*, whose name occurs as the ruler of *Champa* under *Kalasa* (1087-A.D.). (Alexander Cunningham pointed out in the Archealogical Survey Report India Vol. *XIV.* p. 114 that Kashmir had the relation with *Campa* between the period of 1083-1443 A.D. they were in agreement with the traditional list of the *Camba* Rajas as preserved in the family which still rules that hill-state. No doubt, the supermacy of king *Ananta* was being acknowledged in *Campa*, *Darvabhisara, Trigata* and *Bhartula* (*Vartula*). But does not give his authority for these dates, As (Cunninghan, *Ancient Geography*; *p. 141)*, places the invasion of *Campa* by king *Ananta-Deva* between 1028-1031 A.D. It deserves to be noted that our text shows everywhere the spelling *Campa*, whereas the name (in its alternative form) is written *Canpaka* in the grant above quoted the latter spelling with *n* is regularly adopted in all *S'arada MSS* for the name of the *Campaka* flower, compares with

the name of Kalhana's father; written *Canpaka* throughout in A. Regarding the character ascribed to the inhabitants of *Campa,* According to Hieun Tsiang there were 20 *Aramas* or Buddha shrine and Vihars at Kangra where he stayed during the spring month of 635 A.D. The king of the state was an ally of *Harsh* of *Kanuja* and had the Buddhist influence (D.K. P.2)(A.C Katoch *Discovery of Kangra*, Gurgaon; 2004, p. 2, Henceforth described as D.K.). However, with the passage of the time untouchability developed and with the better understanding of the kings or Rajas not mixed up with *Harijan*, particularly the *Chamar* even today (*Ibid. p. 26*). The *Nains* are the barber. This being a barber, he was a true village menial and he shaved and shampooed the villagers (Ibid. p. 85). He was one of the impure castes standing much on the same level as the washermen, for above the *Chamar* and somewhat below the *Lohar* for his occupation as a barber proper was considered degrading. The outcaste tribes had their own *Nais* for a *Nai* who had shaved a *Chura* (sweeper) or *Chamar* would not be permitted to touch a Rajput (Ibid. p. 86). The *Bhats* were often, called, like the *Mirasi* (Ibid) in Champa district.

85. R.T. Vol.1 Book VII. p. 286.

86. *Ibid.* p. 287.

87. **Note**. The *Balor* or *Basohli* State, the original capital was at Balor (*Vallapura*), which was the ancient name of the state, twelve miles west of Basohli, situated on a plateau overlooking the Bhini River, a tributary of the *Ujh*. The state was bounded on the north by *Bhadrawah*, on the east by Chamba and Nurpur, on the South by *Lakhanpur* and *Jasrota*, and on the west by *Bhadu* and *Mankot*. The principal source for the history is the *Tawarikh-i-Rajputan*. The *Vansavali* unfortunately is very unreliable. Two manuscripts of this are in the possession of the *parohits* or family priests of the Rajas of Balor; they are from the same source, but differ slightly in some of the details. Both are in the Vernacular, but have evidently been rendered by an ignorant person from the original in Sanskrit, which has now been lost. The first portion of the *Vansavali*, which is mythological, is omitted in this history. It traces the descent of the Balauria Rajas from the *Pandavas*, and they are therefore of the *Chandarbansi* or Lunar race (H.P.H.S P.587). According to the *Vansavali* the change of capital from Balor was made several generations before the first historical notice in the eleventh century. This is improbable as in the *Rajatarangini* the state is invariably referred to under the name of *Vallapura* (Balor). We know, moreover, from *Alberuni* that in his time (1017-1031 A.D.), Balor was situated on the road from Kanauj to Kashmir, which seems to have followed the route through the outer hills in ancient times, as it did at a much later period. The original site of Basohli, however, is said to have been close to the right bank of the Ravi, where ancient remains still exist; and an older town stood there in early times, where the Rajas occasionally resided, though

the capital was at *Vallapura* (Ibid. p.589). On the other hand a 'chief of *Vallapura', Brahmajajjala*, is named in the list of faithful Rajaputras from abroad who stood by *Sussala* in his greatest straits. Here probably a scion of the *Vallapura* family is meant. *Sussala* also had a wife *Jallala* from *Vallapura*. Finally, we are informed that King *Jayasimha*, after a successufl expendition, replaced *Vikramaraja* by *Gulhana* in the rule of *Vallapura*. *Kalasa*, the Lord of *Vallapura*, is mentioned again as one of the hill Rajas who presented themselves at the court of *Kalasa* of Kashmir in the winter of 1087-88 A.D. *Subsequently* in Sussala's reign we find *Padmaka* of *Vallapura* together with his son *Anandaraja*, joining the league of hill chiefs which supports the Kashmirian pretender *Bhiksacara*. This prince is at a later data brought from *Vallapura* to *Rajapuri* by Sussala's enemies (R.T. Vol.1 Book VII. p. 287).

88. R.T. Vol.1 Book VII. p. 287.
89. H.P.H.S. pp. 588-589.
90. R.T. Vol.1 Book VII. p. 287.
91. *Ibid*. pp. 287-288.
92. *Ibid*. p. 288.

# 6

# Kalasa (1063-1089 A.D.)

As soon as *Kalasa* (*'Pure-thought'*), became the ruler of Kashmir Valley; *Ranaditya* was then presenting the princes in the King's assembly, he had been filled with the thought of the greatness of the royal dignity, and being blunt in his manners, put his neck on the king's neck and introduced him with these words: "Your Majesty, this is prince (*Rajaputra*) *Ananta*[1]." It appears from the study that in the very beginning, the ministers had been against the *'Pure-thought'* or *Sudhra* or *Kalasa* assumption of regal office and, by bringing *Ananta* again into active politics, scored a great diplomatic victory over the supports of the former[2].

When the king turned round and looked at him in anger, he openly laughed, and thus spoke to him bluntly: "Why the rulers of *Kanyakubja* and other (countries) are introduced in this manner, not even a *Muni* can abandon his pride[3]." As soon as the king heard these words which went into the mind and heart of the far-seeing ministers, he was unable to give an answer. On the next day wise *Haladhara* saw the new king attended by a regal court, and the old one accompanied only by a few followers, he reproached the king in aptly feigned anger, and thus induced him to resume the (royal) dignity.[4]

**Ananta Resumes the Royal Power**

By such words the (old) king *Ananta* had resumed the royal power, and thus king *Kalasa* defrauded by his diplomatic skill. Henceforth *Kalasa* was king merely in name, taking even his meals, etc., regularly in the presence of his parents. King *Kalasa's* cousin *Ksitiraja*, the son of his uncle *Vigraharaja*, on account of his son *Bhuvanaraja*, who was lusting for his throne[5]. He was the ruler of *Nilapura* and was preparing an expedition against his father with the forces of that (ruler[6]). To the impious minded, who had given the names of (certain) *Bhagavatas* whom his father honoured, to dogs, which he invested with the Brahminical thread. But this issue was placed before the Brahmins by *Ksitiraja*. He piously resolved to see the nectar of complete renunciation which would remove the pains of his soul, even his wife was not interested into it. But he was determine to say something about the nectar[7].

**Utkarsa Installed at Lohara**

*Ksitiraja* bestowed quickly his kingdom upon *Utkarsa*, the second eldest son of *Kalasa*, who was born from the queen *Ramalekha*, though he was (still a child) at the breast. Then this royal *Rsi* set out to visit *Tirthas* in the company of wise men. After enjoying the blessings of quietism for many years, king *Ananta* entrusted his young grandsom (*Utkarsa*) to keeping of *Tanvangaraja*, who was the son of his father's cousin (*Jassaraja*)[8] strengthened his position at *Lohara*, and returned to *Kashmir,* then died at *Cakradhara* the members of the royal family in this (land) enjoyed all possessions in common, and their relationship was not stained by treachery. *Buddharaja,* who begot the brave *Madanaraja*. The latter's son, named *Jinduraja*, a most arrogant man disliked by the king but liked by the queeen and was appointed as a minister. He attacked over *S'obha*, the one-eyed Damara of *Degrama*[10], who had caused great trouble to the king, and executed him[11]. *Utkarsa* along with the chief army officer compelled the *Rajapuri* ruler to pay the tribute. No doubt, *Haladhara* was the supporting staff to king *Ananta* at this moment declared do not take the foreign expedition recklessly and avert your disaster in *Vallapure* by cunning.

Only beware of the *Jinduraja* who has raised himself to the highest position and *Jayananda*[13] will created dissension between you and your son[14]. But king *Utkarsa* had the powerful *Jinduraja* thrown into prison by *Bijja*[15], as soon as he lay down his arms.

**Kalasa's Evil Conduct**

During this course of time king *Kalasa* accompanied with his four arrogant princes (*rajaputra*) from the *S'ahi* family, *Bijja, Pittharaja*, *Paja* and *Jayananda*, the son of the treasurer *Naga*. But an excellent Brahman, *Arnara Kantha* had obtained absorption in Siva, the king became the pupil of his son *Pramadakantha*[16]. No doubt, *Kalasa* was evil-diposed by nature in wicked practices, but who made the distinction between the those (women) who are approachable and those who are not[17]. This theory of distinction made by evil-minded persons not by the *'Ultimate reality'* that is *Guru* or *Word*. Those honourably called th .nselves learned men (*Bhattapada*). They also believe on the great rites and ritual without fear because they grimly conscious of their power. Deceitful in their ignorance and vaunting themselves (learning) as a physician and Guru. They had gradually established their position as a Guru of dyers and other craftsmen. Now they have been made "cat-merchent" and were putting at ease (again) and *Assafoetida* (*hingu*) on their heads. In this way, they are worthless though they were in character. But at that time *Kalasa* will lead into darkness to light, just as the day by the (thundering) clouds.

There was a strolling player, *Camaka* by name, who knew how to play on the flute, a persistent corrupter of women. In a drunkern freak, *Kanaka*, a son of *Haladhara*, had become angry with him, had him bound to a post, and his nose cut off by his servants. This parasite, whose disfigurement foreboded evil, gradually acquired the new kings attachment by acting as procurer. At the same time, a man (*nrkukkura*) obtained as the King's favourite a place even among the councillors, and received the title of *Thakkura*[19]. He cut off his family relation (*Vamsa*) which was caused his humiliation and a nose bridge (*nasavamsa*) was made. He was captivated by the wives of others, even he did not forbear to enjoy the king's sister *Kallana* and her daughter *Naga*[20]. As soon as, king *Kalasa* and his wife came to know, they refrained to express this shameful act, but concealed his anguish. Thus, he was most dear to the dissolute young king[21]. It appears that king *Kalasa* has the authority to take the sins for virtues. He puts those five or six procurers at work, the king once proceeded at night to the house of *Jinduraja* lusting for illicit love. There, in her own house, the daughter-in-law of *Jinduraja,* a very licentions woman, had given an appointment at night to king *Kalasa*[22]. As soon as *Jinduraja* entered the gate of the house, the barking dogs betrayed him, and the *Candalas* (watchmen) were be labouring by telling them: "Stop, this is king *Kalasa*[23]. First come from darkness to light without prior any condition then inherited self-respect as good comes from doubtful for a tenure of life. What does not change for the worse when that *philosopher's stone*[24], 'honourable character' dissolves into heavenly life.

**Rupture Between Ananta and Kalasa**

Both *Ananta* and *Kalasa* wept a long at night by putting on the throne to their grandson *Harsa,* (Queen) *Bappika's* son, who was the embodiment of all sciences. *Bijja* and *Jayananda* conducted the trembling *Kalasa* with his wife Dilha[25] in the apartments. This clever (woman) announced that her husband suffered from headache, and rubbed oil on the head of the frightened (*Kalasa*). Thus, Queen (*Suryamati*) then relinquished her devouted meditation after saying harsh words to the king, went to her son under the pretext of inquiring regarding his health. He was only admitted singly by *Bijja*[26].

**Ananta Proceeds to Vijayesvara**

King *Anantadeva* was angered by the non-admission of his followers, and thereupon, in the excitement of his rage, set off to proceed to *Vijayaksetra*. As soon as, *Ananta* and his wife arrived at *Avantipura* on their way, *Vissavatta* and other local Brahmans approached him and said[27]. There is tormented in their minds by their son's misconduct, caught sight of (the shrine of) *Vijayesvara*, their hearts were cheered as by the (sight of) a beloved relative[28]. They passed there certain days along with all belongings (necessary) arrangements[29] that is, food, clothing, and shelter.

**Establishment of Ananta at Vijayesvara**

During the short stay of *Ananta* at *Vijayesvara* the princes of this locality, who were the sons of *Tanvangaraja*, *Gunga*, and other relatives, followed *Anantadeva*; (so did also) *Suryavarmachandra* and other *Damaras*. The illustrious king *Ananta* abandoned all cares by posting *Ksirabhupa*[30], *Naunagara*, etc. and other *Damaras* on respective places at *Vijayesvara*. He left *Srinagara* in the month *Jyaistha* in (1079 A.D.); and found the delights of heaven on reaching *Vijayaksetra*[31]. On the other hand, king *Kalasa*, on the departure of the king *Ananta* found that the land had lost its wealth when its guardian-snake has gone. King *Ananta* consulted *Bijja* and others respect officers, appointed the *Jayananda* on the post of prime minister (*Sarvadhikara*), *and Varahadeva,* who was a native of the town of *Vitastatra*, in charge of the 'Gate'. *Vijayamitra* was promoted from the superintendent of clothing to king's commander-in-chief, and *Jinduraja* was inducted on the route of *Simika* by the request of the king. In this way, the whole ground of *Vijayesvara* was shaded by the (royal) parsol, forest (*Chattracchayatavi*) became narrow with the troops of horses which were playing with the balls (*guda*)[32] put down (before them). *Suryamati, Mayya* and other Brahmans who she fully trusted sent secret message to her beloved son: "lead away your troops. While I live, there is no fear for you from your father. But rather you should appease him, straight forward as he is, by conciliatory words"[33].

**Retreat of Kalasa**

The son of *Kalasa* had heard the request of his mother the retreat of the troops from all directions to their own (residence). Because the character of an enmity was entered in the heart time and again, even though allayed (*Samdhiyamanam*), just as a wet garment rends (again and again even though repoured[34]). The pure-minded (king) *Kalasa* was thus getting excited (Lit. heated up) every day and cooling down every night, he resembled a pool (of pure water) which is reduced by the autumn (and in this condition gets warm in day time and cools down at night). The son destroyed the houses and other (property) of those who were on his father's side, went the hen-pecked father did nothing to those of the son's faction[35]. It was vexed by the rough words of the queen who was blined by affection of her son, and by those of his harassed followers, the king felt very miserable. He wished to take back the royal dignity from his son, as he knew his force to be lacking brave men, and as he held (but) a low opinion of *Jinduraja's* prowers. Due to the deposing his son he had offered the royal dignity to the sons of *Tanvanga,* who were averse to (taking) it, the queen, fearing evil for her own descendants, talked him over at night and called *Harsa* through messengers in order to make him king[36]. *Harsa* joins *Ananta.*

*Harsa* was called by the messengers of his grandparents, he prepared daring feat, though he was guarded by guards who were in attendence in the outer court[37]. King *Kalasa* for a brief time seemed to follow, to some extent, his mother's advice, though the hostility (between him and his father) was growing[38]. On the request of *Kalasa*, the commander-in-chief had to wish to proceed to *Khasali*[39], in the meantime the Brahman held a solemn fast (*praya*) against both father and son, in order to put a stope to their hostility which caused ruin to the country. They learned that their son, by the advice of *Jayananda* and others were put behind the bar, the left in dismay and went once more to *Vijayesvara*[40]. Though the enmity was thus growing, enslaved by her (maternal) affection, kept back her husband from reprisals. There was then a woman of easy virtue belonging to the fishermen's caste, *Ludda* by name, and her lover was a bold Damara called *Thakka*, over whose mind she had the complete control. The face of the wicked (*Kalasa*) was always lit up by an amused laugh when he heard his attendants mentioning his parents by the names of those two[41].

**Destruction of Vijayesvara**

The town of *Vijayesvara* was laid down in ashes by fire along with all the stores of the king. The distressed queen, who from the grief at the last of everything was seeking death. She was dragged with great difficulty from the burning of the house by the sons of *Tanvanga*[42]. The king with his followers resided their in the town which was shadded by umbrella-shaped roofs made of seed-matting which had to become (like) a deserted forest[43]. The old king endeavoured to restore that town, the new king being left unchecked through his mother's favour, was always causing pain to his father by various evil communications[44].

**Ananta leave the Kashmir**

*Kalasa* now wished to make his father leave the country, and persisted in ordering him repeatedly to go to *Parnotsa*. His masterful wife urged him again and again with taunts to effect this project. He spoke to her in private (only) *Thakkana, Tanvanga's* son, being present[45]. *Harsh* words such as he had not uttered "People hold women to be a useless accessory for men, but in the end, men are (but) an instrument of play for women[46]. "Wives proud of their high-swelling breasts (*payodharaunnatyat*) destroy the land (of their royal husbands) by (substituting) sons born from another race, just as the rivers (overflowing with rain on the rise of the clouds (*payodharaunatyal*) destroy land) by the stones (they bring down[47]).

"Wives foster the childern, but destroy the husbands (thinking): 'those are a support to the end. What is the use (on the other hand) of such worn out (husbands[48])?".

"Now the often repeated story appears true to my mind that this (son) *'DeepitRaj'* has sprung from another stock, and has been substituted by her".

"One should know that a son who differs in looks and manners, who is at enemity with his relatives and without affection for his father is born from another's seed[49]"

Because there was a rumour that *Kalasa* was the son of a *Mahattama*[50] called *Prasasta*, and that she had substituted him on the death of her own child[51].

"It might be said: 'He is useless, past his time, turned out of the country by his son: (now) his wife, too, leave him.' This, indeed, is what I am afraid of [52]. No, you are the *"ultimate reality."*

**Ananta's Suicide**

*Ananta* was reeling, *Thakkana* with tears in his eyes. His wife noticed that king is going to suicide with a knife into his anus[53]. But he made his death proud with the spirit of law. As soon as , he sacrificed his life as if in atonement for his breach of courtesy, his wife in gratitude became the guardian (of his interests). To all followers, from prince to *Candala*, she gave the daily allowance due to them, just as if she were at ease, in order to fulfill her husband's obligations. When her grandson crying touched her feet with his head, as she handed (him) the sacred libation, she kissed him on the head, and told him: "Do not trust your father[54].

**Ananta's Funeral and Suryamati becomes Sati**

*Ananta's* wife *Suryamati* ordered a hundered mounted soldiers to watch there over her grandson; then she sent forth her husband placed on a litter. After passing the one day and half a day, this devoted wife paid her reverence to (Siva) *Vijayesana* (Vijayesa) and proceeded outside seated in a litter[55], which mixed with the vibrating sounds of the funeral music[56]. Along with the troops, she reached the burning ground as the day was sinking[57]. After this the queen abandoned the hope of seeing her son, and asking for water from the *Vitasta*, recited the following verse: "But those who die with *Vitasta* water in their body, obtain for certain final deliverance, just like those who proclaim sacred learning[58]. Thus, *Gangadhara, Takkibuddha* and the litter-carrier *Dandaka*, and of the female servants *Udda*[59]. *Nonika* and *Valga*, followed her. Moreover, *Senata,* and *Kremata,* of the families of *Bappata* and *Udbhata*[61], who had been the king's favourities, renounced the world (and stopped as mendicants) at *Vijayesvara*. He attained sixty one years age, along with his wife, the union with Pura's enemy (*Siva*) and with *Gauri*[62].

**Reconciliation of Kalasa and Harsa**

As soon as reconciliation of *Kalasa* and *Harsa* took place, king *Kalasa* proceeded to *Vijayesvara* to fetch his son, his eyes were tormented by the charred ruins and his ears by the reproaches of the people[63]. After taking an oath by sacred libation (*Pitakosa*) he came (back) to the city[64]. In the meantime, there arose in the king a righteous disposition and a legitimate care for wealth which altogether removed his poverty. *Jayyaka* who was the clever son of a house holder at *Selyapura*[65], called *Mayana* had gradually attained the position of a Damara[66]. As snake keeps himself alive by feeding on air; he lies in a hole of blinding darkness; being naked, he requires at sexual intercourse that another should give him a screen to remove his embarasment; exhibiting such miserliness, he guards the treasures for another's sake. Nobody else is great in doing good to others except only the greedy one[67].

**Administration of Kalasa**

Though *Kalasa* could not have much time to look after the administration ever since his father handed the reign of government till a reconciliation of *Harsa*[68]. Thereafter through a rise in the subjects (fortune caused by their previous) merits, *Kalasa's* mind was ever profitably (occupied), just like that of a father, (with plans) for the kindly protection of the people[69]. He took up the present and future income and expenditure department under his personal supervision worked like a clerk. Living in comfort he divided his administration into three fold (objects)[70]:-

1. He had to watch on the acts of his own people and of strangers by means of a spies system, only the dreams of his subjects remained unknown to him[71].
2. He looked after the country just as a householder after his house, no one among the people every felt misery[72].
3. The king had dreaded slander and was conciliatory policy towards his enemies, never meted out punishment openly, even to thieves[73].

It appears from the study that under the *Kalasa's* administration, the people were always seen cheerful and happy, occupied with hundreds of marriage feasts, sacrifices, pilgrimages and other great festivities. Among the foreigners, he established his ascendency through a prudent policy, could not even take their food without his superintendents[74]. So far as his relatives are concerned, who were in his service (namely) *Thakkana* and the other two sons of *Tanvanga,* who had returned from abroad, and

*Gunga's* sons, *Malla* and the others, who were the younger brothers of one who had died, he delighted with splendid gifts, just as the mood (delights) the gods and *Pitrs* with the division of its dise (*Kala*) which are dripping with nectar. Though the King had reached a mature age, he did not get rid of his vice and the evil habits which the wretched foreigners had taught him[75]. He also used to go with the ladies of his seraglio. Moreover, he was eagerly bent on the celebration of the great rites (*mahasamaya*[76]). He took great cups in the company of his *Gurus*, without regard for moderation[77].

**Kalasa's Pious Foundation**

King *Kalasa*, whose doings were thus of a mixed character, built afresh town and Siva temple at *Vijayoksetra*, which had been burned down before. He founded a permanent endowment (*Vyayastbiti*) and a temple of *Siva*, the *Amalaka* ornament of gold shrine *Kalaservara* at *Tripuresvara*,[78] and the stone temple of which had a roof (adorned) with innumerable goldens cups (*ghati*[79]). The artist from the *Turuska* country also come in Kashmir to built the Siva temple. He remained for several days enjoying the king's hospitality, till the minister *Nanaka*[80], who had a very sharp intellect, discovered his art by means of inference King *Kalasa*, whose magnificance exceeded that of Indra, consecrated a *Banalinga*[81] called *Anantesa* and numerous other sacred images[82].

**Expedition of Kalasa to Rajapuri**

After the death of king *Sahajapala*, his son *Samgramapala* had been placed on the throne of *Rajapuri*[83]. At the same time, child-king's uncle *Madanapala*, who possessed great power and had full of pride, exerted himself to usurp the throne, and *Samgramapala's* sister took refuge with the king as did the Thakkura *Jassaraja*[84]. King *Kalasa* received two favourable supporter that is *Jayananada* and *Bijja* from the cabinet of the *Rajapuri*[85] rulers. No doubt, king *Kalasa* was an intelligent ruler of Kashmir, had a deep insight into the affairs of mind[86]. In this way, he secured the *Rajapuri*, and told the *Jayananda* in secret when he was fell into a fatal disease, and *Bijja* was kick out under the pretext of having take cut betel from his mouth[87]. Though *Jayananda* had the relation at *Rajapuri* with king *Kalasa* and spoke to him thus: "Clearly the kingdom does not belong to you, since *Bijja* has come to power[88]."

**Bijja's Exile**

King *Kalasa* before the returning to Kashmir, he talked in a low voice with *Bijja*, *Bijja* departed abroad with smile, just as *Haladhara* brought about the fall of *Jinduraja*[89]. At the point of death *Jayananda* ousted *Bijja* from his position and had the fear in his mind from the attack of *Bijja*. As soon as, he returned after his departure from *Surapura*[90], their king

*Kalasa* freed from his fear. Innocent *Bijja* had risen his importance and kept his faith forever swore by the feet of *Kalasadeva* as if he was a diety[91] or *God. Bijja* and others at the time of exile, *Jayananda* died for the time being *Suryamati* holding the charge of the state. As a result of the exile that most of the supporters of *Bijja*, one after the another incident, they were killed and *Vamana* was appointed as Prime Minister[92].

**Vamana as Prime Minister**

*Kalasa* appointed the *Vamana* as the Prime minister (*Sarvadhikarin*), who had been *Jayananda's* assistant and was the Guardian of his children[93]. In the cabinet of *Vamana* wonderful ministers and officials were corporated in the gatherings of thoughtful people. King confiscated the properity of the *Avantisvamin* temple and set up a (revenue) office (*Karmasthana*) called *Kalasaganja*[94]. It was difficult to guard (the interests of) his subjects, but he did not give the *Padagra* office to the minister *Nanaka*, though he was expert in raising revenue, as he was afraid of his cruelty. *Prasastakalasa* and other sons of *Rajakalasa* obtained the great favour before the king as ministers[95]. In the meantime lord of *Rajapuri* was again attacked by *Madanapala*[96], King *Kalasa* sent the commander *Bappata* for his support and *Madanapala* was defeated, and sent to Kashmir in fetters. *Varahadeva's* brave brother *Kandarapa* whome the king made him the lord of the Gate to crushed the Damaras[97]. This diplomacy and bravery, he had learned from the *Jinduraja* became victories in *Rajapuri* and elsewhere[98]. *Madana,* whom the king made commander-in-chief, killed *Bopa* and other Damaras[99]. In this manners, he rose up his power and falconer *Vijayasimha* as town prefect destroyed all thieves[100]. *Kandarpa, Udayasimha* and others sent at the same time to *Lohara,* king forced *Bhuvanaraja* to retreat for away. As soon as he had received (in marriage) *Bhuvanamati*, the daughter of *Kirtiraja*, Lord of *Nilapura*, he got rid of the trouble (caused) by this enemy[101]. *Vijayasimha*, the master of the city prefect, along with the king bestowed the *Mallu*[102], the son of *Gunga* in order to give him practive in the discharging of official work. Subsequently, he was made the lord of the Gate[103].

**Urasa Invasion**

During the invasion of *Urasa*[104], *Malla* revealed the proud of his bravery same as the story of the son of *Pratha*, who recovered the cows without hesitation. He crossed the *Krsna*[105] with five or six horses, in this way, *Malla* carried off king *Abhaya's* kingdom along with horses.

***Assembly* of *hill Rajas* (1087-1088 A.D.)**

As soon as king *Kalasa* versed in his policy, there came eight kings brought the earth under his supremacy in the year 1087-1088 A.D.[106]

They appeared in the presence of king *Kalasa* from the different areas: *Kiriti*[107], the ruler of *Buddhapura* (*Chamar*); *Asta*, king of *Campa*, and *Kalasa*, *Tukka's* son, lord of *Vallapura*, king *Samgramapala*, too, lord of *Rajapuri; Utkarsa*, *Lohara's* ruler; *Sangata* (*Candala*), king of *Urasa*, *Gambhirasiha*, Chief of *Kanda*[108], and the illustrious *Uttamaraja*, the ruler of *Kasthavata*. This important assemblage of the differenet rulers could not be noted in the closely packed mass of people till the flood of the rain gradually increase in sound from river into the ocean[109]. This event was took place during the winter at that time the water of the river *Vitasta* has been frozen as hard as a rock but the kings enjoyed full comfort. Whatever the rulers could imagine in their mind, they found before their eyes, since *Vamana* obtained it. The skill of this minister was splendidly revealed as, without confusion, he made the arrangements for this occasion which others could not have met, just as if it had been an ordinary one[110]. After the kings departure *Malla* displayed himself disinclined to (keep his) office, *Kandarpa* again appointed by the king as the incharge of the "Gate". This minister had full of pride, undertook an expedition at his own expense and also took the strong castle called *Svapika* by stratagem[111]. As soon as he returned to the city, he resigned from his office though the king requested him (to retain it) thereupon *Prasastakalasa*, who had continually to carry the messages (between the king and *Kandarpa*) and had been angred by *Kandarpa's* haughty words, plucked up his self-confidence, collected a large number of soldiers with his own money, of which he had a great deal, and obtained *Kanadarpa's* place for his own brother *Ratnakalasa* though the latter had purchased a great position with money, but he was not in any position with money, but he was not in any respect equal to *Kandarpa*[112]. It is difficult to a painted lion do the acts of a real one[113] that is '*Word*' or '*Nam*'. There is another difficulty for the king that there should be an excellent servent to accept the charge of the *Rajasthana*[114] in the city. He severely beatened the thief of man having died, the kind-hearted (minister) left in dismay this office and proceeded toward *Ganga*[115]. King who introduce this (country) the taste for charal songs (*upangagita*) and a careful selection of female dancers, as customary in other lands[116] He also founded a town of his own name near *Jayavana*[117] and a huge buildings with fine tanks and gardens were also built by the thousand[118] of Ruppes.

**Conduct of Prince Harsa**

It appears from the conduct of prince *Harsha*[119] that he was a man of accomplishments, knew several languages, a great poet and a good artist in the field of classical music[120]. Once he was singing in the assembled crowd, who were enjoying the moment, king *Kalasa* got up and wept outside to attend a call of nature. *Harsha* thought himself that due to the interruption of king his dignity has been dash to the ground[121]. All the courtiers of the ruler, they inspired the *Harsha* against the disregard displayed by his father. *Vissavatta*, a parasite of his father, told him as if in jest; "kill him and rule the kingdom[122]". Thereupon *Vissavatta* urged him again after a very long time as a repeated efforts using *Dhammata's* an intermediary[123].

**Harsa's Conspiracy**

Displeasure of *Harsa* arose from his growing treacherous desire. A conspiracy was started by him along with his courtiers to kill his father. He posted everywhere bravos (*tiksna*) to obtain the position of confidants (with *Harsa*), *Vissavatta* had the fear in his mind to betrayal[124]. He quickly reported the matter to the king. As soon as prince heard this news, he alarmed and did not go that day for his meal to his father, even though he was invited by the messengers[125]. The messenger whom his father sent, he told in embarrassment and misfortune: "I wished to do that at the instgation of others[126]," *Word* (then) went home.

**Attack on Harsa**

*Kalasa* beatened his head with his hands, and exclaiming: "O son of a *Ksattriya* woman, even the (deities which are the) prime causes (*Karana*[127]), after having lived for ever so many world-periods, must by necessity follow the will of Fate". Then he called out to the *Rajasthaniya* from the window: "the prince is safe here. Do what is proper for you[128]!"

**Harsa's Imprison** in (1088 A.D.)

In the year sixty-four (1088 A.D.), the riot was took place by the rogues, who had sown enemity between father and son[129]. Young prince owing to the thoughtlessness, he acquired in the company of wicked person[130]. He was thrown into imprisonment and the proud Queen *Bhuvanamati*, who had been made a party to the covenant[131] (between fahter and son) as a surety, committed suicide by cutting her throat. *Nanaka* advised the king that he should take his life or eyeshight, either himself or through others intrigues. Among these intriguer, *Sugala* the grand-daughter of the king *Tukka*, endeavoured when she had secured her father-in-law's favour to kill her husband[132]. Both *Nanaka* and *Sugala* consulted together, and induced a wicked cook to mix poison into *Harsa's* food[133]. Subsequently, though his father had to decided to change the cooks, the prince ate nothing but what *Prayaga* brought. He took every day food which he passed in that (prison) as a gain[134].

**Kalasa's Illness and Death**

*Kalasa* suddenly afflicted with vital disease by over-indulgence in sensual pleasures. He was suffering under a curse to prepare for the consecration of sacrificial cups in a Siva temple and blood from his nose was dropped into the cup of *Mahakala*[135]. This sudden bad omen could not in the least be stopped by the application of remedies, but on the contrary increased[136]. In the meanwhile, *Utkarsa* was brought from *Lohara* hills in order to bestow the crown on *Harsa*[137]. But the sounds of the kettle-drums drowned the walls of the people, he set out by the waterroute in boats, alongwith his ministers and seraglio[138]. During his illness, *Kalasa* or *Sudhra* king had requested that gifts be made to the people and to his eldest son, while he was giving instructions to *Utkarsa,* his tongue became heavy[139]. *Nanaka* pretended to mistake the name of *Harsa* for the word *adarsa,* in order to conceal (the king's) real thought before him[140]. At the last breath, he was forty-nine years (1089 A.D.) he called the ministers by gesture along with *Mammanika* and six other wedded queens, as well as a concubine called "*Jayamati,* follow him (into death[141]). From the whole of the woman kind his favourite concubine named *Kayya* was disgraced; because in the whole seraglio, she was of *low origin*. Subsequently, she resided near *Vijayaksetra* and became shame upon women of lowly mind[142] i.e. Brahmin.

**Utkarsa (1089 A.D.)**

The circumstances under which *Utkarsa* occupied the throne of Kashmir have already been discussed above. Though he had the backing up by the concil of ministers behind him, but he did not stay long at the whelm of affairs partly because of the conditions[143], King *Utkarsa* promised the same daily allowance which his father *Kalasa* had granted to *Harsadeva*[144]. The result was that he had soon to yield place to *Harsa,* who had been thrown into a fresh prisonbars and watching the state of affairs which were prevailing at that time[145].

**Early Troubles of Utkarsa**

As soon as *Utkarsa* being enthroned from the affairs of Kashmir his step-brothers who were maintaining themselves on the allowances from the state-treasuries came into opposition[146]. King *Kalasa* had many sons of whom, Vijayamalla from Queen *Padmasri, Jayaraja* from *Keyya*[147], deserve special notice. There was a political rivalry both in *Kashmir* and *Lohara* on the issue of the appointment of *Utkarsa*. Though it was the day of his advent to the throne, it did not appear to the people as such, being spoilt by the absence of joy, just as a festive day does not appear as such to a person suffering from illness[148]. It appears from the account of Kalhana that *Utkarsa* had the commitment with his father *Kalasa,* before the cremation of his deceased father[149]. But it became difficult by the requests of the *Thakkuras*[150] to take food without *Utkarsa*, while keeping a fast, at the *Utkarsa's* elevation to the Kashmir throne, who holding *Lohara*, once the glory of *Ksitipati* freed far and wide the earth from the footprints of the *Mlechchas*[151]. he had been brought from the *Lohara* hills in order to inaugurate to bestow the crown on *Harsa*. Therefore, *Thakkuras* of *Lohara* and the step-sons of *Kalasa* opposed the coronation of *Utkarsa* that he did not deserve to rule both kingdoms in his single hand. While with his flowing tears he was, (as it were); offering handful of water as an oblation (to the *pitrs*), his younger brother and the opposition group, who were prevented from attending their parents' funeral, are required to bathe on receiving the news of the latter, just like those who return from the burning ground[152]. He refused to take meals and dismissed his message to be set free with a commitment on his part to remain exile and not to oppose the sacred libation (*Kosa*) by king *Utkarsa*. *Utkarsa* made a false promise on the sacred libation and refused to take food, went on strike. *Harsa* now managed secretly *Prayagaka* to approach *Vijayamalla*, after placing in his hand own ear-ring in (token of his) trust[153]. But there was no royal interest between them. *Vijaymalla* took keen interest on this political issue, keeping in view, the protection of life among the brothers. *Utkarsa* regulated all his state affairs to his ministers, prominently to *Kandarpa* as discussed above that he was of greedy nature. Therefore, *Utkarsa's* state state of affairs appears in disorder and proved false in reality, because he had to inspect only the treasuer of the state[154].

**Revolt of Vijayamalla**

*Vijayamalla* who was forced by the greedy king to leave the country. He left the country among those who had been stood sureties readily to accompany him[155]. During his journey from the city, he stopped one night at *Lavanotsa*[156] along with the sureties personal. This small troops of the force impressed upon *Vijayamalla* to secure the freedom of *Harsa* from the prison bar. In this way, they set free the *Harsa,* then prince turned back and marched toward the capital to gain in their scheme. Some Damaras also took up the advantage of the situation and joined with him[157]. Besides these, *Madhuravattu* and his son *Naga* escorted the king's side, but the route to see the king was *Padmapura*. He was late to see the king. Thus, the good omens of prince *Harsa* burnt the houses along with troops, even the prince *Jayaraja* left the battle field and joined with the side of *Vijayamalla*[158]. By this way, *Vijayamalla* force was strengthened in comparison with *Utkrsa* and they declared that they would not leave the place until *Harsa* was freed and was crowned by the citizens with great honour and said: "Let *Harsadeva* be crowned, who showers gifts like the cloud which is to drown the world. Let this avaricious *Khasa*[159], who is like a shopkeeper, be turned out of the kingdom". At the same *Harsa* despatched the *Thakkuras*, with the defeated guard of the *Utkarsa* as a neutral force[160]. *Thakkuras* frightened then on the act of *Harsa,* who got open the door himself[161]. He also came across with the sixteen soldiers of the guard (*Varika*[162]) who came from *Lohara* to kill him, despatched by *Utkarsa*[163]. *Nanaka,* time and again adviced the *Utkarsa* that *Harsa* has acrossed all the dangers of mind and free from the imprisonment of the life. (It was for this) that sixteen soldiers of the guard from *Lohara*, they declared that we did not strike the *Harsa* at once after relieving the *Thakkuras*[164]. *Harsa* called each of them one by one offered them betel[165]. They felt ashamed at this welcome and surrendered their weapons from their hands and murdered from their minds[166]. In this way, they were set free from the previous blunders and sins, and lived together with love. Before that they were the equivalent like the cow[167] (animal). It was their misfortune that they were not put on right tract. Therefore one must have to take the advantage of the time relating to the story of *Haris candra* and it is better than the goddess *Kali*[168], who time and again made a plans for the royal Fortune. This idea also came into the mind of *Utkarsa* that *Harsa* should be free from the cycle of birth and rebirth at the time of execution. Unfortunately, his security personnel did not carry out the messages what has been told by the messangers of *Utkarsa.*[169]

**Execution of Harsa**

During the time of *Harsa's* execution the arrangement which was made by the *Utkarsa* it was totally based upon the Rajaputra *S'ura,* son of *Satya*[170] *that* is *'Nam'*. At the same time *Utkarsa* put the token of respect into the hand of *Harsa* to get rid of from the rings of lies and illusions. Those had become the lord of the *Sindhu-land*[171] *(Jayadratha)* and his supporter *Vrddhaksattra*, it feels that their heads had been cut off from the benefit of the request and obtained the advice of same. Therefore King *S'rutayudha* took up the decision to wage a war through divine mace. Protection depends upon the service of the Master otherwise there is destruction[172]. Is it possible for a ruler of the areas that he can secure the destruction of the masses which at one time has been given by the god as a token of love and forgotten him[173]. Now the time has come to replace the other force. The same story between *Harsa* and *Utkarsa* was repeated. But *Vijaymalla* had to believe that *Harsadeva* has been killed. He set to fire the palace of the king and his followers but a voice came and calling out: "Your elder brother lives"[174]. King *Utkarsa's* immediately despatched *Harsa's* wife *Sugala* to make assure to *Vijayamalla* by putting earring with her husband[175] In this way, *Harsa* was liberated, and danger was removed, and royal palace was also abstained from fire. *Vijayamalla* along with his force and citizens celebrated this victory with grandeur[176]. *Utkarsa* left the scene of fighting[177], and went back to his residence (of the king), before it *Vijayasimha*[178] became barrier for him. *Harsadeva* immediately ascended the throne and all the powers of kingdom were invested his hand. *Utkarsa* was distressed on hearing this news[179], and committed suicide in 1089 A.D. He ruled 22 days.

In short, from the study we learn that the rule of the *Kalasa* from 1063 to 1089 A.D. was a commenable in the history of Kashmir, there was a peace and prosperity in all walks of life. The people of that areas were used to live with mutual love and affection and help to each other in every odd hours. So far as administrative machinery of *Kalasa* is concerned, he appointed trustee people on the key posts, having the love for the public interest. No doubt, *Vijaymalla* took revolt against him, but it was effectively suppressed by his capable son *Harsa,* as soon as, he became the ruler of Kashmir.

## NOTES AND REFERENCES

1. R.T. Vol.1 Book. VII. p. 288.
2. P.H.K. p. 180.
3. R.T. Vol.1 Book VII. p. 288.
4. *Ibid.* pp. 288-289.
5. *Ibid.* p. 289.
6. *Ibid.*
7. *Ibid.* p. 290.
8. *Ibid.*
9. *Ibid.*
10. **Note.** Term *degrama*, mentioned only here is in all probability the modern hamlet of *Degam*, situated about one and a half miles to the western of *Supiyan* on the left bank of the *Rembyara* about 70° 53′ longitude 33° 43′ latitude. A few hundred yards of the south of *Degam* lies the well-known sacred spring of *Kapalamocana* (marked as *Nagbal*' on the map). In the *Mahatmya* of the Tirtha, the place bears the name of *Dvigrama*, and a fanciful legend is told to account for this name. Pandit Sahiram also writes the name *Dvigrama* in his special antiquity for this Tirtha. (R.T. Vol. 1. Book VII. p. 290).
11. R.T. Vol.1 Book VII. p. 290.
12. *Ibid.* p. 291.
13. *Ibid.* **Note.** The author of *Chaitanya Bhagavata*, which besides being a standard work on the life of Chaitanya Deva, is a store-house of information concerning the Bengali society of his time; *Jayananda* (born in 1513 A.D.), The author of *Chaitanya Mangal*, biographical work giving some fresh information about Chaitanya Deva" life. (A.H.I. p. 582).
14. R.T. Vol.1 Book VII. p. 291.

15. *Ibid.*
16. *Ibid.*
17. *Ibid.*
18. *Ibid.* p. 292.
19. *Ibid.* **Note.** *Thakkura* is a title applied in the Chronicle only to the small nobility, presumably Rajputs from the hill territories to the South of *Kashmir*. At present the name *Thakur* is borne in those regions by the chief cultivating class, which ranks next below the Rajputs. Thus, they are the *Bhaiya-Bhayin*, the first parents of the Oraons, having been born of the blood of the chest (*Sanskrit, Uras or Ur*) of the holy ascetic, their descendants came to known as *Uragon Thakur* or *Uraons* . And in those olden days they were quite as respectable as the Brahmans, and wore the sacred thread. When, later, the *Oraons* fell from their high state, and began to eat indiscriminately whatever food, clean or unclean, that came to hand, they forfeited their claims to the name of *Uragon Thakurs*, and came tobe called *Oraons* (*T.H.I.* p. 31).
20. R.T. Vol.1 Book VII. p. 292.
21. *Ibid.* p. 293.
22. *Ibid.* p. 294.
23. *Ibid.*
24. *Ibid.* **Note.** *Ravidas* despite his poverty, he was well-known for his hospitaltiy to saints, sadhus and the poor. Once a holy man visited his place, and Ravidas as usual offered him the warmest hospitality and gave him all comforts, seeing *Ravidas's* utterly impoverished condition and being pleased with his hospitality and devotion, the holy man offered him a *philosopher's stone,* which could immediately transform his shoemaking iron tools into gold and remove his poverty once and for all. Ravidas politely declined the gift. Thereupon the holy man demonstrated the capability of the *philosopher's stone* by actually transforming one of Ravidas's iron tools into gold and insisting that he accepted this gift. But Ravidas remained adamant.Being a true saint, he would not accept gifts from anyone for his personal use. The holy man put the stone in the thatched roof of Ravidas's hut and went away, saying that Ravidas should make use of it without hesistation. It is said that man returned after thirteen months and seeing him in the same impoverished state, asked about the stone. Ravidas thereuopn replied that it must be in the same place where it had left it. Seeing the utter contentment and detached attitude of Ravidas, the holy man was dumb-founded. According to Priydas, God himself in the guise of a holy man, had come either to relieve Ravidas of his poverty or to test his contentment. Ravi das's attitude in this regard is well expressed in the following verses:

    *Not the slightest liking have I for the Philosopher's stone;*
    *It causes entanglement in the world.*
    *Giving up all cravings, I fix my mind.*
    *On the holy feet of the lord alone, says Ravidas*
    *If you aspire to the highest bliss, They you must inculcate contentment in your mind.*

*Where there is contentment,*
*No blemish can stand, says Ravidas.*
*True happiness lies in realizing true holiness;*
*No happiness is there in accumulating wealth.*
*The accumulation of wealth is the storehouse of miseries;*
*Realize this fact in your mind, O Ravidas.*

For Ravidas, the real philosopher's stone is the *Name* of God, which transforms sinners into saints and makes mortals immortal; As he puts it:

*How can iron (human life) be transformed into gold.*
*If the philosopher's stone touches is not?*
*People donot understand, says Ravidas;*
*Like those gone mad, they have lost their way.*
*God's name alone is my support;*
*It alone is my life, my vital breath and my wealth.*

Ravidas's growing fame as a devotee of God enraged the brahmins of Kashi, and there is a story that they approached the king with a request to prevent this low-born *'Shudra'* means *Pure thought*', this menial worker, from worshipping God. In the court of the King, Ravidas was challenged to explain this outrageous action of offering devotion to God despite being only a cobbler by birth. Ravidas humbly explained that caste and creed are man-made distinctions that constitute no barriers to offering devotion to God. Finally, the king descided to leave the decision to God himself. An image of God was placed in the middle of the royal court, and the Brahmin priests and Ravidas were asked by turn to physically draw the image to themselves through the power of their devotion. The priests tried their best to attract the image of God through recitation and chanting, but to no avail. When Ravidas's turn came, he fervently prayed to God as follows:

*Act not in such a way, O my lord, that my work may go wrong,*
*As you merely watch, sitting at a distance*
*Kashi is crowded with a multitude of people,*
*Who have come to witness this assembly to devotees.*
*Keep or give up your reputation as the saviour of the lowly,*
*prays Ravidas, the cobbler*
*I have come to your shelter, O God of allgods.*
*Have mercy on me, considering me as your own.*
*With faith in your Name, I have give up expectations of help from others;*
*My mind derives no comfort from worldly of servances*
*Accept the service of your slave, Ravidas, O Lord,*
*And manifest your Name, the purifier of Sinners.*

At this morning prayers, it is said, the image of God was seen seated in the lap of Ravidas. In another version of this story it is further added that the Brahmins, with a view to humiliating Ravidas in public, had attached a condition to this trial of devotion. The defeated party would have to carry the victorious person in a palanquin through the main streets of the city. In accordance with this condition, the Brahmins had to carry Ravidass in a litter through the main streets of Varanasi amidst the people's applause for Ravidas. (K.N Upadhyaya; *Guru Ravidas The Philospher's Stone; Punjab* (India). Reprint, 2005, pp. 12-14. Henceforth discussed as G.R.P.S.)

25. R.T. Vol.1 Book VII. p. 295.
26. *Ibid.*
27. *Ibid.*
28. *Ibid.* p. 297.
29. *Ibid.*
30. *Ibid.*
31. *Ibid.*
32. **Note**. Term *guda* seems to be meant balls made up of crushed sugar with an admixture of certain condiments such as are commonly given in India to horses on occasions when greater exertion is required from them. These balls are still known in the Panjab by the name of *'gud'* (*god* in Kashmiri)
33. *Ibid. Vol.I.* Book VII. p. 299.
34. *Ibid.*
35. *Ibid.*
36. *Ibid.* pp. 299-300.
37. *Ibid.* p. 300.
38. *Ibid.*
39. *Ibid. Note* An old name of *Khasalaya* is probably *Khasali*. Finally we have evidence of the latter's settlements in the valley of *Khasalaya* which is several times referred on the map of Kashmir, which leads from the Marbal pass in the South East corner of Kashmir down to *Kistwar.*
40. *Ibid.*
41. *Ibid.* p. 301.
42. *Ibid.* p. 301.
43. *Ibid.* p. 302.
44. *Ibid.*
45. *Ibid.*
46. *Ibid.*
46. *Ibid.*
47. *Ibid.*
48. *Ibid.*
49. *Ibid.* p. 303.
50. ***Note.*** Term *mahattama* seems to designate an office of the politician, but the character of the latter is not clear. They are also called *Baharupa Sahelaka*, an important person, is spoken of as *mahattama*. The last named passage shows there could be more than one *mahathama* at the same time. Regarding *mahattara,* which is different title called *'Word'* or *'Nam'*. The *Lokaprakasa*, i, mentions in its list of officials a *rajamahattama* this duties, as defined in an unfortunately corrup passage of the IV; *Prakasa*, seem to have had some connection with the regal court of justice.
51. R.T. Vol.1 Book VII. p. 303.
52. *Ibid.* p. 304.
53. *Ibid.*
54. *Ibid.*

55. *Ibid.*
56. *Ibid.*
57. *Ibid.*
58. *Ibid. p. 306* **Note.** This verse actually occurs, with a slight variation in the second half (*Sarve moksam gamisyanti yatha te brahmavadinah*) in the *Vijayesvaramahatmya*, alleged to belong to the *Adipurana*. It is very probable that Kalhana has quoted the verse from this text. Like modern Pandits he is likely to have been familiar enough with the Mahatmya of so popular a Tirtha. The general habit of Indian authors to quote from memory accounts for the difference of the text.
59. **Note.** Sometime term *Uddha* for *Udda* and as *Candaka* opposite to *Dandaka*.
60. **Note.** *Bappata* is scarcely the person, who sent by the king *Kalasa* as a commander to support the lord of *Rajapuri* on the attack of *Madanapala*.
61. **Note.** The learned *Bhatta Udbhata* was probably meant king *Jayapida*'s *Sabhapati* (chief Pandit), and received a daily allowance of one lakh Dinnaras.
62. R.T. Vol.1 Book. VII p. 307.
63. *Ibid.*
64. *Ibid.*
65. **Note.** *Selyapura* is in all probability the modern *Silpor*, a large village in the *Dunts*, *Pargana*, situated in circulation 74° 45′ longtitude 34′-1 latitude. It has been wrongly spelt '*Shalipoor*' on map. This identification is supported where *Selyapura* is mentioned in connection with *Sussala's* march from *Lohara* to Srinagar. *Silpor* lies on the direct route connecting the Tosamaidan pass, and thus Lohara (*Loharin*) with the capital.
66. R.T Vol.1 Book VII. p. 307.
67. *Ibid.* p. 308.
68. *P.H.K.* p. 186.
69. R.T. Vol.1 Book VII. p. 309.
70. *Ibid.* **Note**. The *triad* of *Dharma*, *Artha* and *Kama* is meant. The threefold division of a ruler's time is prescribed in ancient Indian literature.
71. *Ibid.*
72. *Ibid.*
73. *Ibid.*
74. *Ibid.*
75. *Ibid.* pp. 309-310.
76. *Ibid.* **Note.** Kalhana refers, as the following lines show, to a trader became tradition who by his quack practice and other swindling acquired reputation as a Guru in the *Tantra* line which means fear of the body. That the rites and ritual of the latter are meant here, is shown by the expression of the term *samaya* in the minds of intellectual, often used in *Tantra* works in the sense of 'observance' rite. *Tantric* rites connected with the drinking of spirits seem to be alluded to regarding the expression of *Mahasamaya* and *Somayacara* faithfull healing by means of *Mantra* for the human being is still commonly practised in Kashmir by persons who are versed in *Tantra* or fear of the body or pretend to be so.

77. R.T. Vol. 1. Book VI. p. 310.
78. *Ibid.* **Note.** The position of the sacred site of *Tripuresvara* (or *Tripuresa*) can be fixed with great probability near the modern village of *Triphar*. The expression of the *svarnamalasara* recurs in the description of temples. *Amalasara*, the more exact expression employed by Kalhana, means literally 'Kernel of the *Amala* (fruit). Hiuen-tsiang to knows *Amalaka* (*O-mo-lo-kia-ko*) *as an* architectural term mentions in the *Si-ya-ki*. Vol. II, pp. 95, 136. The *Amalaka* device, which might roughly be described as having the shape of a melon longitudinally divided by strongly pronounced ribs, is a constant and apparently very ancient feature prevailing through Northern India. It must have been regularly used also for the decoration of the high roofs of Kashmir temples. It is found on the Payech temple that the gold used in its decoration exposed it to serious risks already in Harsa's time.
79. R.T. Vol.1 Book VI, p. 310.
80. The movement began with *Guru Nanaka* (1469-1539 A.), who was born on April 15, 1469 (Vaisakh Sudi3, 1526 BK), in the Kashtriya clan at Talvandi *Rai Bhoey*, now called *Nankana Sahib*, about 40 miles to the South-West of Lahore. His father, *Mehta Kalu*, was a *Patwari* or village accountant to the *Bhatti* landlord named *Rai Bular*. At the age of seven *Nanaka* was put to the village school under a Brahmin teacher from whom, he learnt artithmetic and book-keeping, besides reading and writing in *Devnagri* that was the script of the God. He soon exhausted the stock of learning that the village teacher possessed, and went to a local Maulvi for the study of Persian and Islamic literature. When he grew up, he supplemented his knowledge by associating with saints and hermits. (S.H.S. p. 2). In Chronological order, they are *Jai Dev* of Bengal; *Farid* of the Punjab; *Nam Dev, Trilochan* and *Pramanand* of Maharastra, *Sodhna* Sindhi, *Beni and Ramananda* of Utter Pradesh, *Kabir*, and *Ravidass* of Utter Pardesh, *Mira Bai* of Rajasthan, *Bhikhan* of Utter Pardesh; and *Sur Das* the blind poet of Oudha. (Khushwant Singh; *A History of the Sikhs;* Vol.1. 1963; p. 306). Hereafter referred as H.S.). Ten Sikh Gurus (1469-1708) (1) *Guru Nanaka* (1469-1539), (2) *Guru Angad* (1504-1552). (3) *Guru Amar Das* (*1479-1574*), (4) *Guru Ram Dass (1534-1581)* (5) *Guru Arjun Dev* (1563-1606). (6) *Guru Hargobin*(1595-1644), (7) *Guru Har Rai* (1630-1661). (9) *Guru Tegh Bahadur* (1621-1675). (10) *Guru Gobind Singh* (1666-1708). *Nanaka* was deeply interested in *Indian* lore in general and in the writings of the contemporary *bhagats* in particular, whose teachings he compared with his own and criticized in passing. His scholarly attainments were considerable as shown by his erudite compositions like the *Japji, Asa-di-var, Sidh Gosht* and *Onkar.* During his long tours he visited different centres of Hindu and Muslim faiths, and acquainted himself with their systems. He often referred to ancient writers *Asa-di-var,* XIII.1.2; XIII. 2. 1. *Japji*, XXII. 2.3; *SriRag Ashtpadi, VII,* 6; *Gauri Guareri, Xii* 1; *Basant Ashtpaid,* III.2. made apt use of classical stories, and had philosophical discussions with learned *Yogis, Pandits* and *Sufis*, whom he was always able to convince by his deep learning and hard commonsense. The architectural design of his compositions and his

epigrammatic style, closely packed with reflective thought on great problems of life, bear ample witness to his being a scholarly writer. From the beginning, he had a protestant and critical frame of mind. At the age of nine, when he was asked to go through the ceremony of *Yajnopavitam*, he refused to wear the sacred thread, saying that he would rather have a thread that would 'neither break, nor get soiled, nor be burnt or lost' (*Var Asa, XV.*1). His mind was so fixed on God that, for sometime, he would do nothing but sing '*His*' praises and meditate of *his name.* His father, suspected that he must be suffering from some physical disease, and brought in a physician to treat him. Nanaka laughed at this misconception and said:

*"Physician, go the way;*
*My body groans, because my soul is crying;*
*It is not a case for they medication.*
*The creator alone who has given me this pain can remove it."*

His father was bent on putting him to some profession or trade, but all his attempts failed to take him out of his spiritualistic mood, which was growing intenser everyday. Egoism is a great disease, but its remedy also lies with itself.' 'God pervades all nature by an art that is artless' (*Var Asa*). He was sent to *Chuharkana*, a neighbouring town, with some money to buy goods of common use and sell them at profit. He, however, spent the money in feeding a party of holy men whom he met on his way to the market. He considered it a *profitable business,'* and returned home. The place is still called *Sacha Sauda* (or 'good bargain'). There are many stories of a similar nature designed to show Nanaka's other worldliness, but most of them seem to be only settings provided for the word-pictures drawn by him in his verses. Mehta Kalu, not satisfied with his son's conduct, allowed him to be taken to Sultanpur, where Nanaka's sister, *Bibi Nanaki,* was married. Her husband, Jai Ram, had some influence with the local Governor, Daulat Khan Lodhi, and secured a respectable post for Nanaka, whom he presented as an educated man. Nanaka was put in charge of the state granary, where the corn collected as a part of the land revenue was stored and sold out to people. *Nanaka* discharged his duties efficiently and removed the wrong impression which his previous conduct had given to his parents. He even married (he was eighteen then), and had two sons, *Sri Chand* and *Lakhmi Das.* But in spite of his good management of business his love for God was as intense as ever. When, in the course of weighing out grain to customers he came to the number 13, which is pronounced as *Tera* and which also means *'thine'*, he would enter into a trance and go on repeating *Tera Tera* (*Thine, Thine*) until his attention was drawn back to the mathematical meaning of the word. At night, he would sing the praises of God, in which *Mardana,* a Mohammdean drummer, would accompany him on his rebeck (S.H.S.; pp. 2-4).

81. **Note** *Banalingas* are linga-shaped pebbles brought from the bed of the *Narmada* which are used in Kashmir as in other parts of India for the purposes of worship their name is derived from *Bana,* the Asura, who worshipped Indra. Another designation is *Narmadesvara* (R.T. vol.1 Book VII; p. 283).

82. R.T. Vol.1 Book VII. p. 311.
83. *Ibid.*
84. *Ibid.*
85. *Ibid.*
86. *Ibid.*
87. *Ibid.*
88. *Ibid.* p. 312.
89. *Ibid.*
90. **Note** The Journey from Srinagar to *Surapura* a quarter mile above the present *Hurapor,* where the level ground of the valley is reduced to a gorge by rocky spurs projecting from the hill-sides. It is nowadays put at two and a half daily marches. A local tradition relates that at this spot there once stood an ancient wall and gate, closing the route which leads along the right bank of the *Rembyara* river to the *Pir Pantsal* pass. This gives for *Bijja's* march to *Surapura*, and the return journey of those who so far accompanied him, a total of five days.
91. R.T. vol.1 Book VII. p. 313.
92. *Ibid.*
93. *Ibid.*
94. *Ibid.*
95. *Ibid.*
96. **Note.** Under *Lalitaditya* and *Vinayaditya* Kashmir had come into conflict with the arms of *Ganda*, which was the name applied to a people of Western and North-Western as well as to their country. A confederacy of indigenous chieftains revolted against the king. *Divvoka*, a *Kaivarta*, held sway in North Bengal which was temporarily lost to the *Palas*. Sometime after *Divvoka* his nephew Bhima became king. The latter was overthrown by *Rampala*, the youngest brother of *Mahipala* II, mainly with the help of his *Rashtrakuta* relations. The new king once more restored the fortunes of his family. *Ramapala* was followed by his son *Kumarapala,* a grandson, *Gopala* III, and a second son *Mandanapala*. In the end *Pala* supremarcy in Bengal was destroyed by *Vijayasena*, who belonged to a family that came from the *Kanarese* country in the Deccan. The Sena power was firmly established in almost the whole of Bengal by the middle of the twelfth century A.D. The *Pala* dynasty produced the last great Hindu emperor whose commands were issued from the historic city of *Pataliputra*. Like Mauryas and the Guptas, the *Pala* sovereigns raised a kingdom in Eastern India to a position, of pre-eminence in *Aryavarta*. Like their illustrious predecessors they maintained relations with the distant potentates of the world as known to them, and not only did much to foster religion and culture in India by encouraged their spread to foreign lands. (A.H.I. P.168). In the one hand, the proselytising zeal of *Islam* strengthened conservatism in the orthodox circles of the Hindus, who with a view to fortifying their position against the spread of the *Islamic* faith, increased the strigency of the caste rules and formulated a number of rules in the *Smriti* works. The most famous writers of this class wre *Madhava* of *Vijayanagar*, whose commentary on a *Parasara Smriti* work entitled *Kalanirnaya* was

written between 1335-1360 A.D.; *Visvesvara* author of *Madanaparijata,* a *smriti* work written for king *Madanapala* (1360-1370 A.D.). The famous commentator of *Manu, Kulluka*, a Bengali autor belonging to the *Benares* school by domicile and *Raghunandan* of Bengal, a contemporary of *Chaitanya*. On the other hand, some of the democratic principles of Islam made their way into the social and religious systems of Hindus, and led to the rise of liberal movements under some saintly preachers. With some differences in details, all these reformers were exponents of the liberal *Bhakti* Cult, the message of which they sought to carry before the unlettered masses. They preached the fundamental equality of all religions and the unity of *Godhead,* held that the dignity of man depended on his actions and not on his birth, protested against excessive ritualism and formalities of religion and domination of the priests, and emphasised simple devotion and faith as the means of salvation for One and all (Ibid. pp. 403-404).

97. R.T Vol.1 Book VI; p. 314.
98. *Ibid.*
99. *Ibid.*
100. *Ibid.*
101. *Ibid.*
102. **Note.** *Malla's* father, *Gunga*, was the brother of *Tanvanga*, and the grandson of *Kantiraja* of *Lohara*. *Tanvanga* had also other two sons known as *Ajjaka* and *Dhammata*. The genealogical table of *Malla's* family obtained the Kashmir throne through his sons *Uchchala* and *Sussala*.
103. R.T. Vol.1 Book VII. p. 314.
104. **Note.** *Urasa*, given as a local name in the *gana* to *Panini* is undoubtedly the ancient designation of the hill region which lies between the upper course of the *Vitasta* and the *Indus*. Its greatest part is now comprised in the British district of *Hazara Lassen* was the first to recognize in *Urasa* the territory of *"Apoa or Ovapoa"* which Ptolemy, VII, i.45, places between the *Bidaspes* and *Indus*. Hiuen-Tsiang, describes it as the *'Kingdom of Wu-La-Shi'*, situated to the North West of Kashmir, and dependent on the latter, *Si-yu-ki*, p. 147; life, p. 68. In *Mahabharata, Urasa* is probably meant for *Uraga,* a country mentioned between *Abhisari* and *Simhapura* (Salt Range). The king of this region figures under the name of *Arsakes* in the account of Alexander's Panjab campaign. The whole hill-tract was known in Muhammadan times generally as *Pakhli*. It is also worthy of notice that the northern portions of the tract were governed from Kashmir to *Pakhli* even during Sikh rule. 'Kalhana's references to *Urasa* fully confirm the show that the close connection with Kashmir which existed in Hiuen-tsiang's days, continued later times. Under *Kalasa* or *'Pure-thought'*, *Urasa* was occupied by a Kashmirian force which crosses the *Krsna* river that is *Krsnaganga*. The direct route from Kashmir into *Hazara* at present crosses this river above its junction with the *Vitasta* at Muzaffarabad. *Abhaya*, king of *Urasa*, the son of *Munga* subsequently appears with other dependent princes at the court of *Kalasa*. The daughter of Abhaya was married to *Bhoja*, the

son of king *Harsa*. Payment of tribute by *Urasa* is mentioned in the reign of *Sussala*, and a victory of *Jayasimha* over *Dvitiya,* king of *Urasa,* alluded to Kalhana's own time. It took the Kashmirian troops six days to reach the frontier of Kashmir territory at *Bolyasaka*, from the place where *Samkaravarman* was wounded. This locality has been identified with the present *Buliasa* on the right bank of the *Vitasta* about four miles below *Kathai*. From the latter place exactly six daily marches are still counted to Abbottabad, the modern administrative centre of the Hazara District. It has always been considered the easiest line of communication between Kashmir and the regions to the west. It may, therefore, safely be assumed to have been used also by the Kashmir army on its return from the Indus. In view of this, and the close agreement of the distances, it seems probable that the encounter with the inhabitants of *Urasa* in which *Samkaravarman* was mortally wounded took place somewhere in the hills about *Abottabad*. It is to be noted in this connection that *Mangali*; where popular tradition, locates the ancient capital of the country, lies on this route between Abbottabad and *Mansahra*.

105. **Note.** The *Krsna* is the *Kisanganga* river which on the route, discussed above.
106. *R.T.* Vol. 1 Book VII. p. 315.
107. **Note.** Term *Kirti* is an abbreviation of the name of *Kirtiraja,* who was the lord of *Nilapura*. After the marriage mentioned in the latter passage it is strange to miss *Kirtiraja* in the list of princes assembled at *'Kalasa's* court, when he followed the Prakrit word *Buddhapura* i.e. *Nam*.
108. **Note.** A Raja of *Kanda* is referred for Bhadrawah Proper, in the picturesque of the *Niru* means *'Light'* in (Sanskrit Nira=water), of which the ancient name was *Bhadravakasha* as found in the *Rajatarangini* meaning literally "Happy Region". The lower portion of the valley, from *Kaleni* to the Chinab, is called *Khasali*. It is separated from Balor by the Chatar Dhar Range in which situated the *Kund Kaplas* mountain farther west the same range, there called Dodhara divides Bhadrawah from Chanehni. The interesting myth of *BasakNag* is not only regarded as the presiding deity of *Bhadrawah*, but as the first Raja of the valley. In Sanskrit literature he occurs under the name of *Vasuki* and often figures as the king of the *Nagas*. The attendents of the *Naga* shrines are a Brahman *pujari* and a *Chela* or disciple in Sanskrit called *Cheta* who belongs to the agricultural caste of the *Meghs*. They are a low caste tribe in the outer hills. The temple of Baski Naga at *Bheja Uparla* has two *Chelas,* one of whom is a *Megh* and the other a *Thakkur*. According to popular notions the *Chela* is a more important personage than the *Pujari*, for it is he who, at the time when rain is needed, becomes possessed by the deity, who is supposed to prophesy through his mouth. The state of feigned or real ecstasy, in which such predictions are uttered, is indicated by the word *nachna*, "to dance". The *chela* is very prudent in the wording of his prophecises so that it never can be said that they have not come true. The same institution is found in connection with Devi worship. (H.P.H.S. pp. 617-618).
109. R.T. Vol. 1 Book. VII. p. 315
110. *Ibid.*

111. *Ibid.*
112. *Ibid.*
113. *Ibid.*
114. **Note.** The *Rajasthana* office simply called *rajasthanadhikara*. It has been repeatedly evident that a high post of judging mentions along with the great official charges of the *Kampana* and *dvara*. Regarding the functions attached to this office, Kalhana tells us as to the employ of the *'Rajasthaniya'* Alamkara in Jayasimha's reign. Our passage shows that the *Rajasthanadhikara* was connected with the administration of justice. If we assume that its holder was discharging duties equivalent to those of Chief-Justice, we could account for the literal meaning of the title that *rajasthana* is used as the equivalent of *Rajagrha*, or 'royal palace', is proved by the indifferent use of the titles' *Rajagrha* and *Rajasthaniya* in the case of *Alamkara.* The administration of justice has always been regarded in India as a direct function of the king, who is to hold court, according to the *smritis,* in a separate building within his own palace. The delegation of this regal duty to a locum tenens, i.e., a Chief Justice, is equally well-known to Indian tradition. This delegate, who in the *Dharma* texts figures under many different names. He may well have taken his title from the royal palace in which his court was held. In support of this explanation we may refer the same *Alamkara*, is described as holding charge of the duties of the outer palace (*bahyarajasthan-adhikarabhak*), and to the *Lokaprakasa's* note on the *rajasthaniya*. The list of great officers given at the commencement of *Prakasa* iv, describes him as looking after the protection of the subjects (*prajapalanartham udvahati raksayati sa rajasthaniyah*). That judicial functions are mentioned here, becomes evident from the passage immediately following, which mentions a fourfold division of courts: *pratisthita, apratisthita, mudrita* and *sasita*. The third designation is exactly that applied to the court held by the king's judicial representative. Sub ordinate judicial officers may be meant where *rajasthaniyamantrinah* are mentioned, as well as where several *rajagrhyas* are referred to the term *rajasthana* seems to be used in a more several sense, 'royal court'. In the latter passage the account-office called *S'eda* is described as a 'Rajasthana'. *Rajasthaniya* is found as an official title also in inscriptions of the Gupta period, but its mention there throws no light on the character of the office.
115. R.T. Vol. 1. Book VII, p. 317.
116. *Ibid.*
117. **Note.** *Jayavana* is the modern village *Zevan* about six miles to the South East of Srinagar. The *Taksaka Naga* is worshipped to this day in the large pool of limpid water situated close this village. It has been happily described by tne pest Bilhana, who was born in the neighbouring village of *Khonamusa* (*Khunamoh*) in his *Vikramankadevacarita,* XVII; 70 (as translated by Prof. Buhler): "At a distance of a *gavyuti* and a half from *Pravarapura* (Srinagar) lies a place with high-rising monuments called *Jayavana* (Zevan), where a pool filled with pure water, and sacred to *Taksaka,* lord of snakes, cuts like a war-disc the head of Kali bent on the

destruction of Dharma." From the Taksaka Naga the cultivation of the saffron flowers which flourishes in this neighbourhood, is supposed to have originated *Tirthas*. The *Mahatmya* of the neighbouring *Harsesvara* Tirtha, mentions the Taksaka Naga and indicates Jyaistha Purnima as the day on which he is to be visited in connection with *Harsesvara* pilgrimage. Sculptured stones are found at the Mukammadan burial grounds and also in the houses of the place but not in sufficient masses to justify the belief that the buildings referred to by Kalhana were of really of great extent or massive construction. No reference is found elsewhere to a *'town of Kalasa'*. The Mathas which Harsa is said to have plundered, are perhaps those referred to in our passage. The Mathas and other buildings which *Kalasa* began to erect at *Jayavana* might be meant here.

118. R.T. Vol.1 Book VII. p. 317.
119. **Note.** Poet Bilhana also praises *Harsa* in *Vikramankadevacarita*; XVIII 64-66 for his personal bravery in battle, and for his skill as a poet, by which he surpassed even *S'riharsa*. He also refers to his power of composing sweet songs in all languages (*sarvabkasakavitva*). Prof Buhler, *Vikram*, *Introduction*, p. 19, has rightly pointed that this very passage, by its reference to an earlier royal author, *S'riharsa*, makes the suggested attribution of certain compositions, like the *Ratnavali*, to *Harsadeva* of Kashmir very doubtful. It is uncertain also whether we have in any of the verses which the authologies ascribe to *Harsadeva* in compositions as the prince of Kashmir.
120. R.T. Vol.1 Book VII. p. 317.
121. *Ibid.* p. 318.
122. *Ibid.*
123. *Ibid.*
124. *Ibid.* p. 319.
125. *Ibid.*
126. *Ibid.* p. 320.
127. **Note.** By *Karana* are meant here five deities recognised as such in the *Saiva Sastra*: *Brahman, Visnu, Rudra, Isvara and Sadasiva.*
128. R.T. Vol.1. Book VII. P.321.
129. *Ibid.* p.322.
130. *Ibid.*
131. *Note.* The convenant made between *Kalasa* and *Harsa* on *Ananta's* death seems to be alluded to daily allowance, the father promised to the son safety for the treasures of his grandparents and for his own person.
132. R.T. Vol.1 Book.VII . p. 323.
133. *Ibid.*
134. *Ibid.*
135. **Note.** Siva in the form of *Mahakala* was worshipped at a famous shrine in *Ujjayini*, the capital of Avanti in *Malava*. The verses alludes to the belief that the tusks of elephants are split by the moonrays.
136. R.T. Vol.1. Book VII. p. 323.
137. *Ibid.* p. 324.
138. *Ibid.* p. 325 **Note.** The usual route from *Vijayesvara* (*Vijabror*) to the temple of *Martanda*, lies by the *Vitasta* to below *Anantang* (Islamabad), and hence across the alluvial plateau for a distance of about five miles.

139. *Ibid.*
140. *Ibid.*
141. *Ibid.*
142. *Ibid.* p. 326. **Note.** Those become high in the home of god, they must have to surrender the 'ego' without any condition otherwise she (soul) has the stigma on her life. It is very clear from the 'Law of Nature'.
143. *P.H.K.* p. 195.
144. *R.T.* Vol. 1 Book VII ; p. 326
145. P.H.K. p. 195.
146. R.T. Vol.1 Book VII; p. 326.
147. *Ibid.*
148. *Ibid.*
149. *Ibid.*
150. **Note.** The *Thakkuras* refer to *Lohara*, which by *Utkarsa's* elevation to the Kashmir throne had become united with the latter kingdom.
151. R.T Vol. 1 Book VII ; p. 290.
152. *Ibid* ; p. 327.
153. *Ibid.*
154. *Ibid.*
155. *Ibid.* p. 328.
156. **Note.** The position of *Lavanotsa* is uncertain, though the place is several times mentioned by Kalhana. It appears from the study that Srinagar could be reached by a single forced march from *Lavanotsa,* and that *Padmapura*, or *Pampar*, lay on the route. It is also mentioned that *Lavanotsa* a siege of *Vijayesvara* in connection with it, we can only conclude that the distance between these two places was not great. Finally, it was situated near one of the high road leading to Srinagar from abroad.
157. R.T. Vol. 1 Book VII. p. 328.
158. *Ibid.*
159. **Note.** Term Khasa has been applied to the rulers of *Lohara*. It appears that the name *Khasa* has been used since early times in Sanskrit literature for the designation of tribes settled in widely different parts of the Himalaya regions. It can be shown from a careful examination of all the passages that their seats were restricted to a comparatively limited region, which may be roughly described as comprising the valleys lying immediately to the South and West of the *Pir Pantsal range*, between the middle course of the *Vitasta* in the west and *Kastavata* (*Kistwar*) in the East. Queen *Didda's* father, *Simharaja*, the ruler of *Lohara* is designated a *Khasa*. The position here indicated makes it highly probable that the *Khasas* are identical with the modern *Khakha* tribes to which most of the petty hill-chiefs and gentry in the *Vitasta* valley below Kashmir belong. The name *Khakha* is the direct derivative of *Khasa*, in Sanskrit being pronounced since early times in the *Panjab* and neighbouring hill-tracts. The *Khakha* chiefs of the *Vitasta* valley retained their semi-independent position until Sikh times, and alongwith their neighbours of the *Bomba* clan, have ever proved troublesome neighbours

for Kashmir. Of the maranding inroads which the *Khakha* made during the troubles of the *Pathan* rule, and later still, in Shaikh Imam-ud-din's time, 1846, popular tradition in Kashmir has retained a vivid recollection. That the *Khasas* already in earlier times deserved the character of expert plunderers. Fredric Drew, in his book *Jammu and Kashmir Territories,* suggests that the *Bambas* and *Khakhas* of the Jhelum valley might be classed under the head *Chibhali*. Very little is known as to when these people migrated into *Muzaffarabad* and *Uri* districts, or whence they came; but it is generally admitted that they had a foreign origin. It is probable that the *Khakhas* have occupied the country on the left bank of the Jhelum for 300 years or more and that the *Bambas*, who live on the right bank of the river, came in yeat earlier. The *Khakhas*, who enjoy the proud title of Raja, are, like the *Chibs, Musalman* Rajputs, and trace their descent to Raja Mal Rathor. They regard themselves as belonging to the Janjuah tribe. The *Bambas*, who are styled *Sultans*, deprecate a Hindu origin. They claim to belong to the *Kureshi* tribe, and say that the name Bambas is a corruption of Bani-Hashim, and that they are descended from Ali, the son-in-law of Muhammad. The *Khakhas* and Bambas have a privileged status in the Jhelum valley, and their power has varied according to the weakness or strength of the central authority under the Afghans, the *Khakhas* and Bambas paid little to their overlord, and were practically independent. The Sikhs tightened their hold over the Jhelum valley, but the *Khakhas* and *Bambas* retained certain privileges (P.G.K. p. 34).

160. R.T. Vol.1 Book VII; p. 329.
161. *Ibid.*
162. **Note**. The meaning of the term *Varika* is drived from *Vara,* fixed time; i.e. 'turn of duty.'
163. R.T. Vol. 1 Book VII. p. 329.
164. *Ibid.*
165. *Ibid.* p. 330.
166. *Ibid.*
167. **Note.** Sanskrit word 'go' is intended to be taken here also in its usual meaning of 'cow' in English. The verse must be understood as referring equally to the latter (Also see in detail the meaning of the term in my book '*History of the Brahmans*').
168. *R.T. Vol.1 Book VII; P.330.* ***Note*** *Goddess Kali,* a form of Durga, is here put into the relation with *Kala* that is *mana* or *Brahmana,* the god of the death.
169. *Ibid.*
170. *Ibid.* P.331 **Note.** Term *Satya* as *Satva*, which can scarcely be 'right' that is '*Sabad*' or 'Nam'.
171. **Note.** English official society in his midnight studies, be it as it may, when Colebrooke, fifteen years after his arrival in India, after completing the compilation and translation of the *Digest of Hindu Law* begun by Sir William Jones, came out in the same year (1797) with a study of his own 'Father', *Essays on the Religioun Seremonies of the Hindus,* Brahman's work "showed very clearly that he had found excellent

instructors, and had been initiated in the most sacred literature of the Brahmans," even had he not explicitly testified in his writing that Brahmans had proved by no means averse to instruct strangers, and that they did not even conceal from the sacred texts of the *Veda*. Sir William Jones, infounding the Bengal Asiatic Society, became the initiator of systematic and consecutive research in the newly opened quarry. His friend and fellow labourer, Charles Wilkins, lived to be greeted in his native land, at the close of an unusually long and well-filled life, with the title of "*Father of Sanskrit Studies*". And well earned was the recognition, since he often had sacrificed the tastes which drew him to purely scholarly pursuits in his chosen field, in order to devote himself to the drudgery without which the establishment of the society must have remained barren of practical result (V.I. p. 100).

172. R.T. Vol.1 Book VII; p. 331.
173. *Ibid.*
174. **Note.** From the 'Voice of God', a message came that there is a need of emenclation, the time has come to end the Brahmin script and to start the mirred which easily explained in *Sarada* characters. Sarada alphabet is the direct descendant of the Brahmi alphabet of north western India of the sixth, seventh and the eighth centuries as found among others in the Nirmand (district Kangra) plate of Mahasamanta Maharaja *Samudrasena*, the Hatun (Gilgit) rock inscription of Patoladeva Sahi, the Gilgit manuscripts, coins of Pravarasena, *Toramana* and of the *Karkota* rulers of Kashmir and Bharamaor and Chattrahi inscriptions of Meruvarman (Chamba, H.P). The earliest known records in which the Sarada characters appear for the first time are the coins of the Utpala dynasty of Kashmir (9th century) and a brief record incised on the fragment of a broken jar discovered from the precinets of the Avantisvami temple and containing the name of Avantivarma (855-883 A.D.), the founder of the temple. Of about the same date is the Sarahan *Prasasti* of queen Somaprabha, Spouse of Satyaki, a ruling Chieftain of Sarahan opposite Saho in ancient Chamba. Among the other records of slightly later date, mention may be made of the Dewai (Pakistan) inscription of the Shahi King *Bhimadeva* (10th century) the Srinagar (now Lahore Museum), and the S.P.S Museum inscriptions of the reign of queen Didda (A.D. 980/1-1003), the Bharamour and *Sungal* (District Chamba) copper plate inscription of king Yugakaravarman and his son Vidagdhadeva, Barikot and Hund (Pakistan) inscriptions of the Shahi king Jayapala and a few other inscriptions from Hund including that of the queen Kamesvaridevi. Sarada is the alphabet of Kashmir par excellence and remained in use for several centuries in an extensive area of north western India including Gandhara or north western Pakistan, Ladakh, Jammu, Himachal Pradesh, Panjab and Delhi. The alphabet continued to be used in Himachal Pradesh and Panjab upto the 13th century when it was replaced by its descendant the Devasesa which in turn gave rise to the modern alphabets of Gurumukhi and Takari. In Kashmir, however, its use continues to this day though it is confined to the older generation of the priestly class. Considering the extent of the region over which the Sarada alphabet remained in use for a long time, the number of Sarada

epigraphic records discovered so far is by no means very large. In all 98 inscriptions have been discovered so far, 13 in north western Pakistan, 34 in Kashmir, 6 in Jammu, 5 in Ladakh, 36 in Chamba, 3 in Kangra and one in Delhi.

On the basis of the Sarada characters used in these records, three successie stages of development of the Sarada alphabet can easily be discerned. The earliest phase is represented by the inscriptions and coins of 9th-10th centuries, the second by those of the 11th-13th centuries and the third and final by the epigraphic and literary records of the 14th and the subsequent centuries. While the use of the Sarada alphabet in the inscriptions dates from the 9th century A.D its use in the manuscrips, however, is not known until the 12th century when we find it first used in a manuscript discovered from the village Bakhshali in the Peshwar district of Pakistan. The manuscript which tonains an important work on Mathematics bears no date but on palaeographic grounds can be assigned to the 12th century. Next in date is an old birch bark manuscript of *Munimatamani-mala* which is the earliest known Sarada manuscript discovered so far in Kashmir and assignable on paleographic grounds to the 14th century. The other early known manuscripts are the birch bark manuscript of *Sakuntala,* birch bark manuscript of the Adi and Sabha Parvan of the *Mahabharata* and the birch bark manuscript of *Kathasarita Sagara*, all assignable to 16th century.

As pointed out above, about a dozen Sarada inscription have come to light from ancient Gandhara or north western Pakistan so far. Most of these are either fragmentary or defaced and now lying in the Lahore and Peshawar Museums. The earliest known inscription is the Dewai inscription of the Shahi King Bhimadeva. The other important inscriptions are those of the Shahi King Jayapala discovered from Barikot in upper Swat and Hund ancient *Udabhandapura* dated 146 and of queen Kamesvaridevi dated 154-157. The last known inscription from the region is the stone inscription of certain Vanhadaka now preserved in the Peshawar museum and dated Laukika 538 or A.D. 1461.(B.K. Koul; History and Culture of *Ancient Gandhara and Western Himalayas* , New Delhi 1990; P.I-3. Hereafter, described as H.C.A.G.W.H)

The Sarada inscription from Gandhara, though very brief and fragmentary, constitute an important source of information regarding the Shahi rulers of Kabul and Gandhara and help us solve some of the problems connected with the history of this famous dynasty i.e. '*Chamar*' an account of which has been preserved for us by Al-Biruni in his *Kitab-ul-Hind.* Considering the fact that the Sarada alphabet has been in use in Kashmir from the 9th century A.D. to this day and also taking into account the explicit statement of Kalhana that he studied and made use of all types of inscriptions including the land grants for writing his Chronicle, the number of Sarada epigraphic records discovered so far in the valley is by no means large and surprisingly not a single copper plate inscription registering the grant of land has been discovered so far. The earliest specimens are the legends on the coins of the Utpala (or Varman) dynasty and the fragmentary inscription mentioning the name of Avantivarman referred to above. Next in date are the two inscriptions of the reign of Queen Didda (A.D. 980/110030) referred to above, one incised on a stone slab discovered from a private house in Srinagar dated (*Laukika*) 68 or A.D. 992 and the second on the pedestal of an image of Budhisattva Padmapani dated (Laukika) 65 or A.D. 989 preserved in the S.P.S Museum Srinagar. The other important inscriptions are: Tapar stone Lintel inscription of the reign of Paramandadeva, (Laukika) 33 or A.D. 1157 Arigom stone slab inscription of the (Laukika) year 73 or A.D 1197.The Kotihen (district Anantnag) inscription of the reign of Shahabadena (Shihab-u-Din), dated (Laukika) 45 or A.D. 1369, the Khonamuh stone slab inscription of the reign of Jayanola-Uadena Shaha (*Zain-ul-abidin*) dated Kali 4530 or A.D. 1428.The last known inscription from Kashmir belongs to the end of the 18th century. It has been discovered at Digom or Kapala *Mocha*n in the Pulwama district and is dated (Vikram) 1846 or A.D. 1789.

The inscription of Kashmir mostly preserved in part do not add much to our information regarding the history and culture of Kashmir but they are usually dated and help us verify the correctness of the chronology as given by Kalhana and his successors. They also contain at times very useful information about the contemporary culture of ancient and mediaval Kashmir. A few inscriptions in Sarada characters were noticed in the Ladakh area by Vigne, Cunningham, and Francke. Two of them discovered at dras contain mention of the Budhisattva Maitreya. One of them is dated in the 7th year probably of the *Laukika* era. In the Jammu province a few inscriptions in Sarada characters have come to light. Two of them were discovered at Dacchan's and Zaji-Nai in the Doda district. That of *Dachhan* is dated in the reign of Sri Nanta-deva who may be identified with the king Ananta of Kashmir (A.D. 1028-1063). It is dated in the year 12 presumably of the *Laukika* era and corresponds to A.D. 1036. The other is comparatively of a late period and on paleographic grounds can be assigned to the 16th century A.D. Two more inscriptions were noticed by Vogel, one is a ruined temple on the ancient site of Babor,ancient Babapur 17 miles each of Jammu and the other on a stone linga at Kishtwar. Both the inscriptions are now to much defaced to be deciphered. Chamba is the only place in the western Himalayas which has yielded a pretty large number of Sarada inscriptions of diverse types consisting of rock and stone inscriptions, image inscriptions, copper plate inscriptions and the fountain stone inscriptions. The earliest Sarada record as noted above is a beautifully executed inscription from Sarahan which contains a lovely poem in praise of the beauty of Somaprabha, the wife of Satyaki, a hill Chieftain, in an elegant and well-embellished Kavya style. The most important and the well preserved inscriptions are the copper plate characters issued by the rulers of Chamba like *Yugkaravarman, Vidagdhadeva, Somavarman* and *Asata*. These charters are not only important for constituting an important source of information regarding the ancient history of Chamba but are important for their geographical contents as well. They contain mention of some ancient districts and villages of Chamba and thus throw some light on the ancient geography of the state as well. They are also valuable source of information regarding the system of administration as it prevailed in ancient Chamba since they contain mention of several administrative titles and designations. Their value is still more enhanced by the fact that they constitute the only specimens of this type of epigraphs that have come to light in the entire north western hill region of the country so far. A very important group of Sarada records and unique of its type is formed by those engraved on the elegantly carved fountain slabs discovered from different parts of Chamba and now preserved in the Bhuri Singh Museum in Chamba and town. These slabs were erected at springs by the pious donors for earning religious merit. The inscriptions on these slabs are particularly important from historical point of view. While the copper plate inscriptions are dated only in the regnal years of the kings, these often contain dates both in the regnal years of the kings and in the Sastra era the local designation of the Laukika or Saptarsi era commonly used in Kashmir and the hills.

This no doubt helps to a certain degree to build up the chronology of the ancient rulers of *Chamba* on more or less sound basis. The records are again historically very important for they show that the state was divided into small principalities ruled by Chieftains called *Rajanakas* who, however, owed allegiance to the rulers of Chamba or sometimes to the rulers of the neighbouring hill states of Vallapura (Balor) in whose regnal years they dated their records.

Only a limited number of Sarada records has come to light in Kangra so far. The most important and the well preserved inscriptions are the well known Baijnath Prasastis incised on two large stone slabs in the famous temple of Baijnatha at Baijnath (ancient Kiragrama) in the Kangra district of Himachal Pradesh. The *Prasasti* No.I gives an account of the construction of a temple in honour of lord Vaidyanatha (Baijnath in vernacular) by two merchant brothers Manyuka and Ahuka and records the donations made to it by some pious individuals. It is dated in the year 80 of the reign of Jayacandra, the lord of Trigarta to whom the ruling chief of *Kiragrama, Laksamana-candra* owed allegiance. The date of the *Prasasti Sam Jyestha Sukla Pratipat* corresponds to 2nd of May, 1204 A.D. The Prasasti No.11 contains a brief account of the baronial house of Kiragrama to which *Laksamana candra* belonged. Itis dated in the Saka year 1126 corresponding to A.D. 1204.

Another record worthy of note from Kangra is a brief inscription engraved on the pedestal of a statuette of Jain Tirthankara Parsvanatha dated (Laukika) samvat 30 corresponding to A.D. 1254.

The use of the Sarada alphabet in Delhi is attested to by a stone slab inscription discovered from a well at Palam 12 miles South West of Delhi. Only the concluding portion of the inscription is in the Sarada, the rest is in Nagari.

It is dated Vikram-Samvat 1337, Sravana Va Ti 13, Wednesday, corresponding either to the 26th June, 1280 A.D. on to 13th August 1281 A.D in the reign of Sultan Ghiya Thud-din (Ghayas-u-Din) Balban (*Ibid.* pp. 3-6)

175. R.T. Vol. 1 Book VII. p. 331.
176. *Ibid.* p. 332.
177. *Ibid.*
178. **Note.** *Vijayasimha* was appointed by the king *Kalasa* as a captain of the thieves or called as town prefect. He was taken into the service to destroy all the thieves. It was his accomplished duty to stop the enter of the wrong doer and he did his job.
179. R.T. Vol.1 Book VII; p. 333.

# 7

# Harsa (1089-1101 A.D.)

The rule of *Harsa* was a high watermark in the history of Kashmir for several obvious reasons. At the commencement of his reign *Harsa* displayed wise forbearance in retaining many of his father's officials and trusted servants, notwithstanding their former conduct towards himself. It was probably due to his prudent policy that when his brother *Vijayamalla* became disaffected and conspired against him, no dangerous rising followed *by Vijayamalla* had to seek refuge across the mountains in *Dard* territory, where he was soon after sometimes killed by an avalanche. This event seems to have consolidated *Harsa's* position, and Kalhana gives us a glowing account of the splendour of the Kashmir court during the period immediately following[1]. The circumstances in which *Harsa* occupied the throne of Kashmir have already been described above and the suicide committed by *Utkarsa* went into an inner appartment with the concubine called *Sahaja*[2]. For this reason wise men, remembering that love may vary in the end, should not for certain blame or praise, women. (thus it came) that while their origin, social position and their love for their (respective) lords were alike, the conduct of *Kayya* and of *Sahaja* deserved blame and praise (respectively)[3]. She to had been a dancing girl attached to a temple[4], just as (if it were) gold by entering the pyre after smearing thickly over her lover, (which resembled) liquefied red chalk (*gairika*[5]).

**Description of Harsa's Character**

King *Harsa* exhibited from the very beginning, who young as he was had attained the royal power after experiencing so many changes of fortune, is undoubtedly the most striking figure among the later Hindu rulers of Kashmir. His many and varied attainments and the strange contrasts in his character must have greatly exercised the mind of his contemporaries. We see these impressions duly reflected in the elaborate description, which Kalhana gives us of *Harsa's* character, and which was no doubt based on first hand information, such as that given by his own father *Canpaka*[6]. Kalhana displays to us king *Harsa* as a youth of powerful frame and great personal beauty, courageous and fond of display. He was well versed in various sciences and a lover of music and arts[7]. He regulated all the settled plans and policies, which displays (assertion of the) ruling power and yet has witnessed excessive disregard of orders; which (tells) of excessive abundance of liberality and of (equally) excessive persistence in confiseation; which gives delight by an abundant (display of) compassion and shocks by the superabundance of murders; which is rendered charming by the redundance of pious works and soiled by the superabundance of sins; which is attractive on all sides and yet repulsive, worthy of praise and deserving of blame; which sensible men must magnify and deride, regard with love and yet feel aggrieved at; which is to be blessed and to be condemned, worthy of memory and yet to be dismissed from the mind[8] and went up to *'Nam'* that is called *'Chamar'*.

The atoms of 'light', we learn from his carriage which flashed like the reflected image of the sun; on his round, broad head-dress was fixed a high diadem. He used to look around like a pleased lion; his bushy beard was hanging down low; his shoulders were like those of a bull, his arms great, and his body of a dark-reddish complexion; he had a broad chest with a narrow waist, and his voice was deep like thunder. Thus even superhuman beings would have lost (before him) their presence of mind[9]. In the palace, councillors, chamberlains and other (attendants) had to adorne with golden chains and bracelets[10]. As a new sovereignity, king *Harsa* regarded the opinion of *Vijayamalla* just as that of a *Guru*[11]. He bestowed his interest to the state offices as his father *Kalasa* has given[12].

**Administrative Reforms**

The first and foremost task of *Harsa* was to bring the administrative machinery into some semblance of order. During the long drawn-out family feuds, it had been subjected to dispute among officers, both high and low, took active part in court-intrigues and neglected their duties towards the people[13]. About this period *Harsa* succeeded also in asserting his authority outside Kashmir. From the mountains of the *Lohara* territory which since *Utkarsa* had become attached to Kashmir by a kind of 'personal union'. *Harsa* sent *Kandarpa*, the 'lord of the Gate', on an expedition against *Samgramapala*, the chief of *Rajapuri, Kandarpa* after a severe contest in which two hundred Kashmirians are said to have fallen, carried the town of *Rajapuri* and forced its lord to pay tribute[14]. He placed, *Madana* in chief command of the army (*Kampana*), and others like *Vijayasimha* and the rest, each in his own (previous) post[15]. He also set free *Prasastakalasa* and employed him in his own (former) posts[16]. Minister *Nanaka* and his milk-brother, *Vissavatta* was put to death on the pale by the king's servants, after cutting off his ears and nose in the presence of his wife[17]. In his prosperity, *Harsa* elevated the *Sunna*, the son of *Vajra* and grandson of *Ksema*, who was a descendant of *Rakka,* was together with his younger brother raised to the chief rank among the ministers[18].

**Conspiracies against Harsa**

Evil counsellors, soon began to stir against the king, *Jayaraja,* a half-brother of *Harsa,* from a concusine of *Kalasa*, engaged in a dangerous conspiracy. *Harsa*, however, proved to be on his guard on this occasion. With *Macchiavellian* skill he made *Jayaraja* surrender to *Dhammata*[19], a relative from another branch of the *Lohara* family, who had himself been concerned in the conspiracy. After cruelly executing *Jayaraja* in the year of 1095 A.D; he then turned from *Dhammata* and had him, as well as his four brave sons, killed by the sword and the hangman. Similarly he put out of the way other near relatives though they had given no cause for suspicion[20].

**Rising of Vijayamalla**

Inspite of *Harsa's* sincere efforts to overhauled the administrative machinery and his pains for efficiency, he could not rule peacefully in the valley. *Vijayamalla*, at the instigation of evil-minded persons had to make a plan to murder of his elder brother that is *Harsa* on the issue of divided regal power (with him[21]). In this battle, *Vajayamalla* attacked the king's horeses from the stables[22]. It was the fighting with might hastened to leave the city, while his wife with him on his horseback[23]. But it was the superhuman fight, just as unseasonable cloud sent down torrents of rain, and the land seemed everywhere flooded. The prince was enveloped by the shower of rain, and by the arrows and winds will produce a noise (similar to that) of many kettle drums[24]. He was crushed along with force by the sons of *Candaka*[25]. Thus, the bridge of *Vitasta* and *Sindhu* had been broken by the flood, but he crossed by swimming, along with his wife, after descending from his horse[26]. In this way, brave (Vijayamalla) disappeared from the view of the enemies, and proceeded towards the country of the *Darads*[27] by the route of *Lahara*. Though *Kandarpa*, the lord of the gate', had closed everywhere the routes of the town of the *Darads* (*Daratpuri*[28]) hidden in the mountains. He was received with warm welcome by the illustrious *Vidyadhara Sahi*[29], the *Darad* (ruler). It appears that king *Harsa's* royal power, which for sometime was reduced by the fear of a struggle for the crown, began than again to expand. At that time the title *'Raja'* could not applied to any *saint*, not to the other kings, because they were[30] to serve the society with the blessing of nature that is *'Nam'* or *Sabad.*

**Harsa's Innovations**

*Harsa*, who was liberal and broad-minded, introduced elegant fashion trends in his land just as the spring (brings flowers) into the forest[31]. He broke the age-old customs and traditions that had taken the roots in the social life of the people of the valley during the preceding millenium of tyrannical monarchical rule[32]. He asserted with the single exception of the king, worn their hair loose, had carried no hand-dress and no ear-ornaments. In this land where the commander-in-chief *Madana*, by dressing his hair in braids, and the prime minister *Jayananda*, by wearing a short coat of bright colour, had incurred the king's displeasure, there this ruler introduced for general wear a dress was fit for a king[33]. When some of his ministers had got themselves up in brilliant finery, he, without feeling jealous, got his own female attendants to swing lights (*aratrika*) around them[34]. As he was interested in his amusements of the *Daksinatya* (*Dekkan*) fashion. He also issued a coin-typed (*tanka*[35]) copied from that of *Karnata*. People appeared in his assembly hall with waving palm-leaves, adorned with big forehead-marks of sandal ointment, and wearing splendid long daggers[36]. Whereas the ladies wore long garlands formed by their-braids into which were (woven) golden *Ketaka*-leaf (ornaments); the pendants which they wore over their forehead marks made the latter unsteady; they joined the corners of their eyes with their ears by a line drawn with collyrium; into the ends of their locks which were not veiled, were twined gold strings; with the hanging-down train of their lower garments they kissed the ground; their breasts were dressed in jackets which also covered the half the length of their arms. Their smiles seemed to spread (the perfume of) camphor as they moved about; when dressed in man's attire they wore a delusive likeness to the god of love[37]. It seems that *Harsa* was addressed by the prayers, even at that times beggers were also come out to support each others, just as the cloud's shower take the help of a big ocean then become capable of refreshing all beings[38]. Due to the soft approach of king *Harsa*, all bands of the musician came to vie with kings. It shows that *Harsa* was a man of art and learning. He provided equal footing to litters, horses, parasols, etc[39].

*Bilhana*[40], the fellow-countryman of Kalhana, who had left Kashmir in the time of king *Kalasa*. He had been made by *Parmadi*[41], the lord of *Karnata*, his Chief Pandit (*Vidyapati*), who travelled on elephants through the hill track of *Karnata*, and his parasol was depicted aloft before the king. As soon as he heard the liberal attitude of *Harsa*, he thought everything is false without him[42]. It shows that the house of *Harsa* was very high and beautiful having golden *Amalaka* ornaments like the buildings of clouds[43]. So far his *Nandana*[44] grove is concerned, there were all trees, but only the wishing trees (*Kalpadruma*) are absent then he put them to shame by his liberality[45]. He made the lake called *Pampa*[46], which was full of water and different kinds of birds and animals extended to its curved and horizon shores[47]. He was more competent in all the sciences than *Brihaspati*[48]. The songs which *Harsa*, has composed, they had the melodic sense, if his enemies will listen, they might be have tears roll on the eye-lashes[49].

**Harsa's Royal Court**

Study reveals that, from the very beginning the rule of *Harsa* was very active to raise and maintain the dignity of the royal splendour court. He had been instilled by a sense of discipline amongst his officers, and towards their duties, dresses, etc., in routine business, he had to slept twice time in a day and kept awake at night, when he held his assemblies[50]. Normally he passed his nights in the assembly-hall with the illumines of thousand lamps. Meetings were also attended by the learned men with dances and musical performances[51]. It appears that *Harsa* had a long discussion at night with his courtisans, *Rsis* and its singers like Gandharvas for the bound up the ladies locks into a knot for the placement of the *S'ephali flowers*. It was the fixed meeting-place of Kubera and Yama that a common-man could seek liberality from the reign of terror[52].

No doubt, during Harsa's reign, gold and silver coins[53] were plantiful in circulation in this land, but copper were rare[54]. At that time majority of the people was greedy of material things like *Sunna*[55] (gold), but they had forgotten the prefect of police (*dandanayaka*[56]), and was exalted above all[57]. So far *Harsa's* Mathas are concerned, at *Jayavana, Suryamulaka*[58] and *Vijayesvara*, which were left empty for their maintenance, is attested from his real properity. Now the royal fortune of *Patta* has been found its proper object in the relief of the sufferings of those who were hungry, sick, helpless, poor or otherwise (distressed[59]). *Canpaka* the father of Kalhana had to spent every year seven days at *Nandiksetra*[60] during the whole time (intervening between *Harsa's* visits) to turned his wealth to overhaul. *Harsa* also supplimented the Brahmans by providing skins of black antelopes, cows with calves, and other natural gifts[61]. Moreover, *Vasantalekha*, the wife of *Harsa*, who belonged to the *Sahi* family also founded Mathas and *Agraharas* in the city and at the holy place *Tripuresvara*[62].

It shows from the above mentioned facts that *Harsa* had the long devotion towards Saiva and his courtiers. It was the noble transactions during his rule in Kashmir[63]. It is the amusement of fate that the strong are deceived by the weak, and those who hold all affairs in their hands are confused by those without power[64]. Confused in his senses therefore, king *Harsa* placed three hundred and sixty women of doubtful character in his seraglio[65]. He only left the women of the *Domba*[66] and *Candala* class from this group. In the meantime, *Harsa* made a secret plan with *Bhuvanaraja*[67] to once again to seize *Lohara* on the instigation of his foot soldiers (*Kotapadati*[68]). As soon as *Harsa* reached at *Darpitapura*[69], he heard about *Kandarpa*, 'the lord of the Gate', who had already left to fight against the *Lohara*. Thus, *Harsa* disappeared[70].

**Expedition against Rajapuri**

*Rajapuri* was a vassal of Kashmir for a long time ruled by *Samgramapala*. The kingdom of *Samgramaraja* fortunately escaped destruction at the hands of Mahmud of Ghazni, but it was too much weakened by internal conflicts to interfere successfully in the general affairs of Northern India. It gradually sank to the position of a minor power and finally succumbed to the Muslims in 1339 A.D[71]. The Hindu king heard reports from travellers how the Sultan of Ghazni was encroaching on his dominions in the prosecution of "holy wars". To put a stop to his depredations, he advanced towards Ghazni and met his enemy near a place called Ghuzak between Ghazni and Lamghan. A snow-strom compelled *Jaipal* to conclude a humiliating peace, but he soon broke his engagements and broughts on his head the wrath of the *Sultan*. The latter carried fire and sword into the territory of his antagonist and seized the districts in the neighbourhood of Lamghan. In 997 Sabuktigin died, and in the next year the crown went to his famous son, Mahmud. In 1001 the new *Sultan* inflicted a crushing defeat on *Jaipal* near the city of *Peshawar.* Unable to survive this disgrace, the defeated king burnt himself on a funeral pyre and was succeeded by his son, *Anandapala* (1002-1003 A.D.). In 1006, Mahmud took *Multan*, but the final subjugation of the city was postponed till 1010. In 1008, he routed the troops of *Anandapala*, led by prince *Brahmanapala*, at the battle of *Waihand*, and pursued the fugitives as far as *Bhimnagar*. *Anandapala* continued to offer resistance from the fastnesses of the Salt Range (*Nandana*). His successor, *Trilochanpala*, carried on the struggle with the assistance of *Samgramaraja* of Kashmir[72]. In the meanwhile, *Kandarpa* was engaged in bringing the discontented foot-soldiers (*Kotabhrtya*) under his control. Thus, annoyed *Harsa* sent the prefect of police (*Sunna*) against *Rajapuri*[73]. He unwisely delayed for one and a half months on the outskirts of the castle (of Lohara) with great forces[74]. He did not show any determination (to start) an expedition against the *Lohara*, but it was the ardour of the enemy[75]. Thereupon *Harsa* again addressed to *Kandarpa*, who was keeping inactive to conquered *Rajapuri* though had no supply[76]. On the six day which *Kandarpa* passed fasting in the depth of the mountains, *Rajapuri* at (a distance[77] of) more than one Yojana to stop the the enemy's forces from the froces of the prefect of police only one leader followed him, *Kularaja*, a descendant of the family of *Buddharaja*[78]. When he laid down in the outer court of (the palace of) *Rajapuri*, after having slain a host of opponents, the enemy thought from his white parasol that *Kandarpa* was killed[79]. But at the mid-day the mighty *Kandarpa* penetrated into the royal palace of *Rajapuri* with twenty or thirty soldiers. Three hundred his own foot-soldiers stopped before *Rajapuri* with twenty or thirty soldiers three hundred his own foot-soldiers stopped before *Rajapuri* and thirty-thousand of the opponent camp could not turn to flight[80]. In this battle, a large force of the enemy was killed. Thus, a brave man, who appeased his master's reproach which was (troubling him like) a *Vetala*. The life which has been given by the master for the purpose of realization of *reality* at the time of birth, but the soul has accompanied with mind or *man* and trapped into the material life committing violence on the deadly field of battle[81] i.e. earth. In the same day, a huge rally was organised by the irritents who were defeated in the attack by *Kandrapa*[82]. Be wilderness was took place at this moment, *Kandrapa* then took tribute from the lord of *Rajapuri*, who paid homage, and returned within a single month to his own country[83]. *Harsa* welcomed the *Kandrapa* with great honour along with the perfect of police and others. The hard-hearted *Ananda*[84], who was acting as an administrator at that time at *Parihasapura*. He had made his name in the priest corporation (*Parsad*) called *Vataganda*. He had also been put by the *Harsa*, upon the advice of councillors who were won over by a large bribes. He was the incharge of the *Padagra* and other (offices) after ousting *Vamana*. At that time, he was aspiring to the office of 'Lord of the Gate', and was greatly supported by the ministers who were *Kandrapa's* enemies[85]. In this way, *Kandrapa* became the governor of *Lohara*[86], and has taken to himself *Utkarsa's* son as a Lord of *Lohara*[87]. King *Harsa* agreed on this proposal and immediately, he sent *Patta* and a *Takka*, *Asidhara* by name, with a great force to kill that relatives[88]. *Kandarpa*, who heard that *Asidhara* tried to seize him. Thereupon *Kandrapa* drew out his hand, in the meantime judgement came from *Harsa* and addressed by *Patta*, that his relatives, whom they brought and handed over to him. The result was that the minister left his post and proceeded to *Varanasi*[89]. By slaying one chief, appointed another, who freed from the tax on S'raddhas at *Gaya*[90] to the *Kashmirians*[91]. *Harsa* also killed the capitan of penis robbers along with his men on a very critical way and freed the eastern region from the enemies for movements[92]. Moreover, he removed and destroyed the tiger at *Varanasi*, and embellished the eastern area with Mathas devoted to pious uses[93]. On the other hand, the evil councilors badly perturbed by their mutual jealousy, in a few days the king comes totally to grief like a post between (them)[94].

**Dhammata's Conspiracy**

*Harsa*, however, was not destined to rule in peace and prosperity after the departure of *Kandarpa*, just a conspiracy was started against *Harsa* to obtain the throne by killing him[95]. *Dhammata, Tanvanga's* son instigated *Jayaraja*, engaged for king's murder from the village of *Bilava*[96], and drew two or three women from the (king's) seraglio into the plot[97]. In the meantime, plot was executed by *Harsa*, *Dhammata* was despatched as envoy to *Rajauri* with great honour, while stopped at the house of *Sahasramagala* (to which he had gone) for the sake of a auspicious day, *Jayaraja* was detained to see him[98]. At the same time, a servant of *Prayaga* was listening behind the wall secretly and prohibited *Dhammata* to leave. *Jayaraja*, however, was failed (in his design) and summoned the two brave Damaras from *Samala*, called *Vaga* and *Paja*[99]. As soon as *Harsa* heard the news of betrayed from the servants of *Jayaraja* deserted, he prepared to leave him[100]. *Harsa* placed the guards at night in all directions. In the morning *Tanvanga's* son (*Dhammata*), send out all the excuse worship the '*Nam*' *or* '*Sabad*' otherwise *Jayaraja* has to come time and again in the cycle of birth and rebirth[101]. In this regard *Prayaga* by order of the king placed the guards outside the assembly hall, and informed the *Dahammata*, in a low voice, to seize *Jayaraja*[102]. Thereupon, *Tanvanga's* son (*Dhammata*) assured the king *Harsa* that he went up to *Jayaraja* and boldly spoke to him: "The king is dissatisfied with you. If you indeed free from guilt, at once give up your sword to show your innocence[103]"

**Jayaraja's Execution (1095 A.D.)**

It appears from the study that *Jayaraja* was expert to handle the sword and bow,but when he accompanied with *Dhammata*, he left the sword and used to live like a common man. It is the weakness of the *Jayaraja*, he did not taste '*Him*'. At this juncture, *Tulla*, the son of *Ajjaka* and grandson of *Tanvanga,* spoke to him with these harsh words: "O you wretch, not of *Kayya* by king *Kalasa* were you begotten. Your father was surely some coward, whoever he (may have been[104])". When *Jayaraja* was asked to give an account of his treason by the *Dharmraj* then what, you will be torture by the Yamas, but not *Dhammata*. It has been determined that his death is certain at night by a rope round his neck. Therefore, in the house of the God, *Jayyaka* had to kill with the *Nam,* and his body might be thrown into the water of *Bhattarranadvala* for the food of fishes. Ultimately, *Jayaraja* was killed in the month of *Bhdrapada* at the age of seventy-one (1095 A.D)[106].

Now, *Harsa* made a plan, who to kill the *Dhammata*. In order to execute this, he secretly gave orders to a valiant *Thakkura* of *Lohara*, to call *Kalasaraja*, the best of his soldiers[107]. He also expressed his fear at the presence of *Kalasaraja*[108]. In his agony he struck the elder son of *Kalasaraja*, who was badly wounded because of his ill-luck, and left there as food for the dogs[109]. While king himself came into the court-yard and shielded, *Ralhana* and *Salhana*, the grandsons of *Tanvanga*, who had laid down their weapons[110]. *Tulla* and others who were preparing a plan to fight against *Harsa*, cunning *Udayasimha*[111] deceived this plan tactfully, who came and said: "you are my sons[112]". They laid down their arms. Accepting his advice, they spoke to him with a laugh: "O grandson of *Tanvanga*, you have forgotten what you said before to *Jayaraja* : 'O you wretch, not of *Kayya*, etc[113]." After saying this, a bloody battle was fought, as it were, the impurity of his origin. In the meanwhile *Tulla*[114] and others went for resolving before the king, they were (arrested and) thrown into the prison by the *Harsa's* men. But wicked *Takka*, *Bimbiya* by name were also prevailed upon the king for execution at night[115].

**Execution of Tanvanga's Grandsons**

*Tulla, Vijayaraja, Bulla* and *Gulla*, these were the four grandsons of *Tanvanga,* rolled in death at the place of execution by *Harsa*. The beauty which remained with them even in death is described to this day by those of great age[116], *Harsa* uprooted his own family, put to death by secret execution, *Domba*[117], the elder of the two sons of *Utkarsa*, whom he had been (himself) brought up. Their story is related with love and affection from the core of the heart and flow of tears appear for a long time as if a neclace of rubies had been scattered[118]. *Harsa* also destroyed *Jayamalla*, the son of *Vijayamalla* because, he killed the relatives of the kings who preserve the dignity of the house. The foolish *Asvatta*[119] tree (Caladala), in order to make well-grown comb of honey in the dense thicket of its numerous high branches easy to approach and seize by any lucky person, by fate's instigation to shaking spontaneously, and puts the bees which guard that (honey) well out of the way by killing them with the blows of its (falling) leaves[120.] The king, whose mind was perverted by the most sinful perfidies against his relatives[121], *Ksema*, the son of *Vamana*, knowing that he hated his father. Therefore, *Harsa* removed the duplicate parasol and placed over the (Shrine of Siva) *Kalasesa*[122], there came to him an artist from the *Turuska* country[123]. The pious *Prayagaka* cunningly stopped this plan[124] along with the wretched *Lostadhara,*

*Haladhara's* grandson, who was as clever in insinuating himself as a *Vetala* in getting into (motionless) corpses, conducted (*nastacestanam*), spoke in scret to the king and said: "Let the villages, the gold, and other (property) bestowed upon the (temple of Siva) *Kalasesvara* be taken away. With the stones of that temple I shall build you a bridge over the *Vitasta*." "I paint a picture on the sky; with lotus threads I weave a dress; I procure the gold seen in dreams; I build a wall with snow." A king of obtuse mind takes verily even such and similar sayings for truths. That (king) who in bewilderment has nothing to say to such things, has not maturity (of mind), and can only be deceived[125]. But *Prayaga* was the attendant of the Lord (*Nam*), a sick person of time as his food[126]. Then *Lostadhara*, once at a time of gesting and asked the king *Harsa* to set a god free from his captivity. He thus spoke to him with a smile: "there was once at the town of *Udabhanda* the *S'ahi* called *Bhima*[127]". "The *Bhimakesava* (temple) which he founded, was on account of a quarrel among the members of the *Purohita* corporation (*Parisadya*[128]) locked up for a long time int he reign of *Kalasadeva*[129]." He reflected upon the mighty temples as a wealth in the desert shrine to the local *Purohita* corporation then induced the king by a solemn fast (*praya*[130]) to grant (them) in compensation exemption from the forced carriage of loads (*rudhabharodhi*[131]) In order to get hold of the statues of gods, the treasures (of the temples) had been carried of, *Harsa* appointed *Udayaraja* 'prefect for the overthow of divine images' (*devotpatananayaka*[132]). It shows that divine images made of gold, silver, and other (materials) rolled about even on the roads, which were covered with night soil, as (if they were) logs of wood[133]. Only two chief divide images were respected by him, the illustrious *Ranasvamin*[134] in the city, and *Martanda*[135] (among the images) in townships[136]. There was not one temple in a village, town or in the city which was not despoiled of its images by that *Turuska,* king *Harsa*[137]. Among colossal images, two statues of *Buddha* were saved through requests addressed by chance, namely the one at *Parihasapura* by the singer *Kanaka,* who was born there, and the other in the city by the *Sramana Kusalasri*[138]. Those who are anxious to build up over time fortunes do not afraid of evil actions, though in this universal they may have been enlightened with the 'truth' which is wonderful for all. Thus, the elephant, though he is on the pleasure-seat of the (Lotus-born goddess) Laksmi, yet somehow falls into the criminal tank that is avrice world by the desires cannot obtain the lotus born goddess. However, *Harsa* possessed this treasure from his forefathers, those who started this journey from *Lohara* to household confiscated the temples with endeavour to secure (more) wealth for the future course of action[139]. On the choice of *Harsa* certain ministers were appointed, they corrupted the system for the sake of their own interest forgotten the purpose of life to serve the other, even the *Gauraka* of the minister, though a respectable man from the very beginning, now he has been distrusted, and become the master of 'perfect of property' (*arthanayaka*) (and with it) the function of plundering the property of all temples and villages has been started[140]. Moreover, *Sahelaka*, of the Purohita corporation (*parsada*) at the temple of *Samarasvamin*, who was the adviser of the *Vijayamalla*, now became the enemy of the king by obtaining the double revenue of both the 'perfect (*nayaka)*[141]. of night and day soil[142]. Owing to his senselessness (*jadya*), which was only hidden by the appelation (given tohim)' he who is pregnant with riches' (*srigarbha*[143]), the employ of these treasures (*Kosa*[144]) corresponded to their manner of acquisition. All this becomes insignificant by the side of *Harsadeva's* senselessness[145]. *Bhimanayaka*, who could play with charming music, first he has to please the public with his performance on a drum like *Doma*. Therefore, on this account, *Kanaka*[146]*, a* younger brother of *Canpaka*, became (*Harsa's*) own pupil in singing and dancing in practising certain songs of the nature[147]. His reward is high in this connection. When he saw a picture of *Candala*[148], the beautiful wife of *Parmandi*[149], the lord of *Karnata*, he was struck by the god's love.

**Harsa's Love for Candala**

*Harsa* had low-natured parasites urged to the senseless princes to take the incitements as ridiculous jealousy, as (if they were) dogs[150]. He shamelessly vowed before his court to secure *Candala* and to overthrow *Parmandi*. As he had taken a vow not to use unboiled camp[151] (until then), wandering poets thus ridiculed while pretending to praise him: "The king of brilliant lustre has renounced the chewing of *Potasa*[152] embraced *Candala*; effected his entry into the town of *Kalyana*[153], saw the *Pimmala*[154] and was satisfied his curiously about the great treasures (hidden) in the ground of the king's park[155]." Unfortunate *Madana*, the commander-in-chief, pleased the *Harsa* byaccepting the post of Chamberlain to that (queen) in effigie[156]. Inspite of the decoration of temples, she is decorating her body with dresses and ornaments to please the *Harsa*. Therefore, one has to pay the allowance for her. In this story *Madana* is also shameproof but *Harsa* is stupid in this regard, like (gold) on the touch-stone[157]. Whereas other parasites have been plundered by him and saying. "There, we have brought you and your mother *Bappika*[158] from heaven", and others brought slave girls before him and said they were goddesses. *Harsa* worshipped them and taught them, but in discussion, they confused his mind[159]. *Harsa* then desired to give magic perfection to his body (*pindasiddhi*[160]) and some *Domba* made swallow a drink which he had pretended to obtain the power[161]. At present persons of little faith whose minds are doubtful in regard to the miraculous deeds of *Meghavahana*[162] and other (ancient kings), so there will be surely in time people who will not believe these astonishing misdeeds which *Harsa* relates[163]. Then there occured somehow serious misconduct among the women of his seraglio, which foreboded the fall of the king, who himself was the embodiment of all that is immoral or the sinfulness of his subjects[164]. Even his father's wives, who had brought him up on their arms, he took in his arms, kissed them, and continually disported himself with them, by a harsh word he punished and violated *Naga*, the daughter of his father's sister[165]. It shows that *Nagas* have been spoiled the purity of earth dire to their misconduct with the company of political leaders and the wisemen, they are considered as animals. Therefore to achieve the success against the evil doer, *Harsa* started his expedition against *Rajapuri*, with all his collected forces[166].

**Harsa's Expedition Against Rajapuri**

After the collection of large force, *Harsa* started his expedition against *Rajapuri*, sieged the fort of *Prthvigiri*[167] by placing his troops at the foot-hill (of Rajapuri[168]). *Harsa* also with his force remained there for more than a month to gain the power. However, the supplies which king *Samgramapala* offered in order to save the garrison was cut off by the *Harsa's* force[169]. Moreover, he bribed the prefect of police (*Sunna*[170]). Thereupon, these (men), who were mostly of low character began under ironical sayings a solemn fast (*praya*), and as the king's treasury was far away. In this way the army of *Samgramapala* fell into disorders[171]. From that time onwards towards the glory of the king was vanished and his epithet of *Pratapacakravartin* (' the glorious rule of the universe') faded away together[172]. At this occasion he only praised *Kandarpa*, who had accomplished (alone) that enterprise in which he with all his servants had failed [173]. It was the same scene, as *Karna* and the rest (stirred up) the descendant of *Kuru* (*Duryodhana*[174]), after he had been defeated on the expedition against the hardsmen (*ghosa*[175]). The disputant who has been defeated by getting the king into trouble, Sahela, the Mahattama[176], was in apprehensions on account of embezzlement.

**Expedition Against Dugdhaghata**

After the conquest of *Rajapuri*, *Harsa* undertook an expedition against *Dugdhaghata*[177] fort along with the *Lavanyas*[178] of *Lahara* or *Lohara*, after the Damara *Lakkanachandra*, who held it, had been previously executed on king *Ananta's* order by *Janaka*[179], the lord of the Gate, *'Word'* or *'Nam'* had been offered (*to Kalasa*) *by the Janaka*[179], the lord of the Gate, *'word'* or *'Nam'* had been offered (to Kalasa) by the (Damara's) wife, who was fasting before the (king's) door. At that time king *Kalasa* refused it and the king of the *Darads* took the possession of it[180]. Due to the natural calamities, *Harsa* repeatedly pressed the king to seize this (fort), and the latter undertook the attempt, when *Canpaka*, who was in charge of the Gate by the king's order, the *Vataganda*[181] *(Ananda*) endeavoured to get the better of him[182]. This latter, since the *Harsa* had withheld (from him) as the incharge of the 'Gate' and had been appointed as a governor (acting) as lords of 'Gate[183]'. Though *Ananda* caused confusion in the army, the lord of the Gate (*Canpaka*) crossed the *Madhumati* river and invested the fort with his troops[184]. On the other hand, *Kashmirians* force fought with the *Darad* soldiers, who threw down big boulders and other (missiles). It would be difficult to defeat on account of shelter which the fort has been given to them[185]. Because *Malla*, *Gunga's* son, kept with his sons at the place of attack, called *Prajimathika,* and caused (to the enemies) alarms which they withstood with difficulty[186]. In this connection, *Harsa's* two brave sons, *Uchchals* and *Sussala* had been already informed about the royal power on account of that ambition. The elder of the two, who was already in difficult position to control them and hated the throne, on the condition of that he had to start the expedition for the coming events along with his force[187]. Therefore, it would be difficult for the *Darad* soldiers to obtain the fort[188].

**Retreat from Dugdhaghata**

At the time of retreat from *Dugdhaghata,* then there will be again a heavy rain to turn the (whole) ground into one (sheet of) water, and displayed an order of the *New Fate* effacting *Harsa's* lustre. Fate has already displayed itself the favourable and infavourable conditions of the life which enveloped it entirely, like armour[190]. Thus, the whole force of the *Darads*, which is rushing forward like the ocean to flood, will be stopped by these two, who resembled two mighty rocks on the coast[191]. Therefore, from that time onwards all the people will think that these two proud (princes) deserved the crown, but not the cowardly king as (it, she were) a girl choosing for herself as her husband[192]. In this regard, all people, in anticipation of coming events, compared the two as brother like *Rama* and *Laksmana*, while the king was likened to *Ravana*[193]. The barking dog in mighty will bite the stone from the distance, but not the person[194].

**Execution of Madana**

As soon as, *Harsa* returned from the *Darad* territory, being pleased with his services, *Madana,* who had made commander-in-chief, will talk openly of his defeat[195]. In his anger *Harsa* wished to kill him because *Madana* had neglected a written order which was sent by the queen[196]. While the people will feel tribulation and *Harsa* imposes heavy fines which shall be take away their breath, just as if a boulder has been thrown on an old bullock which is similar to the worn out ploughing system[197]. When *Madans*, at the same time will turn up from *Madavarajya,* not received by the king *Harsa* because he has been already frightened by them and went to the house of the councillor *Laksmidhara*, who was a *Takka* (by birth)[198]. Besides, *Laksmidhara*, one more minister will be placed for execution with his son, while the troops looked on laughing. Those who had the self-confident by great favours and do not care for the service of the master. They will find their end like those (snake-Charmers[199]) who boasting of their familiarity with a great snake (die) violently owing to their charm (failing[200]). Pro-blessing of *Suryamati* will assert itself among the band of intriguers until (it brought about also) the death of *Madana*[201]. *Harsa* believed, we will tremble at the sight of valour, which the *Kalasaraja* had placed in fetters in the house of *Laksmidhara*[202]. In order to insult him, king *Harsa* will sent his enemy *Udaya,* under the pretext of making an inquiry[203]. The proud (*Kalasaraja*) on seeing the other sparkling in his luck, he will flame up in anger and seized the weapon from some one who struck him down and kill him[204]. Thus, the evil-minded king along with servants will be ended[205]. On this land which suffered wounds, as it were, of the king's infliction, there will be series of calamities one after the another like famine, plague,[206] etc. During that moment in broad daylight people will be kill by the robbers, it would be the compulsion for them to take a golden bowl from the king's apartments[207].

**Famine In Kashmir (1099 A.D.)**

In 1099-1100 A.D., famine was took place in Kashmir due to the heavy flood and there arose an extreme scarcity of all wares[208]. At this moment, a *Khari*[209] of rice was bought at the rate of five hundred *Dinnaras*, and two *Palas*[210] of grape-juice having the cost of one *Dinnara*. Of salt[211], pepper, *Assafoetida*[212] (*hingu*) *and other (articles)* it was difficult to hear the name[213]. *Harsa* tormented the people through Kayasthas, and did not even let alone the earth in towns, villages or elsewhere, owing to the heavy fines which he inflicted[214].

**Persecution of Damaras**

*Harsa's* first attack was took place against the numerous Damaras of *Holada*[215] in *Madavarajya*. They were killed just like birds in their nest. Since he impaled even travellers he left in *Madavarajya*[216] not even a Brahman[217] alive, but certain *Lavanyas* have been frightened and fled in all directions[218]. Some of them, whom ate cow's meat in the lands at the *Mhchchas,* they were the worker of water-wheels, hand-mills[219] etc. At the Gate of *Harsa's* (palace), there would be seen in every row of *Lavanyas* heads, who had qualified arches (*torana*), which appeared like cups (*ghati*[220]). Indeed, it will be decide at that time on the basis of qualification that is *'Nam'* or *'Chamar'* and the Brahmans will hang at the gate of the royal palace of *Harsa*[221]. So far the outskirts of *Balerakaprapa*, as far as *Lokapuriya,*[222] is concerned, governor has formed one avenue since the time immorial and fixed with the *Damaras* on pales or colourless[223]. When *Harsa* exterminated the Damaras in *Madavarajya*, he hurried to *Kramarajya* to follow up the same procedure[224]. Therefore, the resident of Damaras is in *Kramaraja.* Certainly they have collected a large force in *Laulaha*[225] for fighting and committed great slaughter. They have been watched by the governor for a long time. In the meantime, the younger son of *Malla*(*Sussala*) intoxicated by youth which was comforting the heart of *Laksmidhara's* wife[226]. She was attracted by that prince who was her neighbour, and felt no love for her husband, whose look was like that of monkey[227].

**Designs against Uchchala and Sussala**

It can safely be concluded from the above discussion that *Harsa's* power and prestige was on the wane. He did not take up any subjects during the time of natural calamity. On the other hand, he insisted on strict revenue exactions through his unpopular *Kayastha* officials. Politically, *Sussala* and *Uchchala* were gaining power and popularity both in the army and the masses, because of their heroic stand during the misadventure of *Harsa* at *Dugdhaghata*[228]. *Harsa* had naturally jealous of the two and was further instigated by his minister, *Lakshmidhara*, to kill both of them[229] on the issue of secret love-affair with his young wife. This evil design of the king was then reported by a courtezan, *Thakkana* by name, who was secretly connected (with them[230]). At the sametime *Darsanapale* had removed their doubts of the matter, they left at night by the two attendents[231].

**Flight of Uchchala and Sussala (A.D. 1100)**

*Uchchala* and *Sussala* left the city secretly in the month of November (Margasirsa) (A.D. 1100), and reached the seat of the Damara who is living at *Utrasa*[232]. Thus, treacherous *Lavanya's* chief Damara *Prasastaraja*[233], however, prevailing his conduct abroad with his own younger brother named *Sillaraja*[234]. Whereas his elder brother had proceeded to *Rajapuri*, and the younger had already taken the position himself in the court of *Kalha*, the ruler of Ka*linjara*[235]. As soon as two will left the country, no confidence was left behind by any one in

(*Harsa's*) reign, and he himself alarmed the evil omens of the time[236]. *Harsa* asked *Samgramapala*, (*King of Rajapuri*) through *Laksmidhara*" to kill the *Uchchala*, and offered him money (for this) i.e. *'Nam'* or *'Sabda'*[237]. *Samgramapala* at this juncture did not pay much attention towards the *Malla's* son. He displayed great respect on account of his fear from the *Chamar* or *Harsa*[238], who served the society from the very *low profile*. It is the past practice in this world, those believe on fate, raises his enemy whose success is approaching a great importance[239]. It appears that *Rajapuri* people had always existed inimical relationship with the *Kashmiri* rulers[240].

**Uchchala at Rajapuri**

*Uchchala's* stay at *Rajapuri* had played a very diplomatic role with the *Damaras* to disgruntte their league[241] . *Damaras* again persecuted the king and compelled him to land in Kashmir as a messenger with offers of presents[242] that is *'Nam'* or *'Sabda'*. Besides these, Raja *Janaka* father of *Sita, Suryavarmacandra's* son also made an additional efforts by despatching an artistic messengers[243]. As soon as *Samgramapala* witnessed the messengers of the Damaras. He gave up the fear of mind, and openly paid honours to *Uchchala*[244]. Wavering, *Samgramapala* was assured his safety when camphor was broken over (*Uchchala's*) head as a gift of Nature which wished to let him start with great affectation[245]. At that time *Kalasaraja* was the chief *Thakkura* of the *Rajapuri* territory, who had been bribed by *Harsadeva*, and said to him: "Put the (*Uchchala*) in the fortress of *Rajagiri*[246]. He (*Harsa*) will then fear from the desire whatever he had with his friend[247]. In this way it was addressed to the weak ruler of *Khasa*, who had the fear in his mind from the side of *Harsa* on the accumulation of wealth as a lust[248] and illusion in this world.

**Intrigue against Uchchala**

And he replied that I am unable to capture the resolution of *Uchchala*, but he was detained by tricks[249]. After these words he dismissed his own house, and then he spoke to Uchchala: "In the morning you ought to visit *Kalasaraja*[250]. When *Kalasaraja* heart that *Uchchala* had gone back to the kingdom of *Khasa*[251]. It appears that it was a diplomatic game against the *Uchchala*. *Uchchala* understood that *Harsa* had come to attack with efficient soldiers[252]. In the meanwhile, the lord of the *Khasas* tried to make help to settle the issue, stayed with *Kalasaraja* and asked the *Uchchala* please come to his own assembly-hall[253]. As soon as the discussion in the hall was completed, *Uchchala* with great dignity addressed the role of *Khasa* who tried to reconciliate the relation between the two, while anger gave harshness to his speech: "Long ago there lived a king of *Darvabhisara*[254] *Nara*, a descendant of

*Bharadvaja*. his son was *Naravahana*, who begot *Phulla*[255]." "The latter (begot) *Satavahana*[256] from him sprung *Canda*; his son was *Chanduraja* who also had two sons called *Gopala* and *Simharaja* "*Simharaja,* who had many sons, gave his daughter *Didda* to king *Ksemagupta* in marriage. She being left without a husband or male children, placed *Samgramaraja*, the son of her brother *Udayaraja*, on the throne . (Another) brother of her, *Kantiraja,*begot *Jassarja*[257]." "*Samgrama* (raja) was the father of *Ananta*, *Jassa*(raja) that of *Tanvanga* and *Gunga*. From *Ananta* was born king *Kalasa*, and from *Gunga* (was born) *Malla*". "From *Kalasa* were born *Harsadeva* and the rest, and thus from *Malla*[258]. Then, when this is the pedigree how can foolish person ask: 'Is this one (of the princes of Kashmir [259])'? Answer No, only *'Nam'* or *'Words'* remains. From the genealogy of *Uchchala* we learn that earth is destructive one, even our own body, then quesion rises whohelps the soul that is *'Nam'* as *History* reveals. Therefore, we thank the God, who withdrew us from the illusion of *Maya,* which disgraced us as the race of *Kashmir* kings[260]." Who won the beauty of *Nature*, it appears that he conquered the whole world. No doubt, *Uchchala* wad distressed at *Rajapuri*, after leaving *Samgramapala*, who was in his camp, the queens of the latter cheered him up[261].

**Uchchalas's fight at Rajapuri**

Study reveals that a war was took place between *Uchchala* and *Kalasaraja* at night in *Rajapuri*. *Lostavatta* and his armed force was killed in the fight[262]. In the meantime *Somapala* wife of *Uchchala* along with cheiftains prevented the war of *Rajapuri*[263]. It was the full-moon day of *Caitra* (March-April) when this event was took place. *Kalasaraja* started his expedition on the fifth day of the bright half of *Vaisakha*[264]. He despatched his force under the commander-in-chief of *Vattadeva* and raise the revolt in respective route, and later on, he started to invade *Kashmir* through *Kramarajya*[265]. At that time, *Kapila*, the son of *Ksemaraja* was the ruler of *Lohara*, after the death of *Udayasiha*[266]. He allowed him to pass this territory[267]. He marched all over the heads, with sword and shield, and told the (Kapila's) soldiers, first you have to flee at *Parnotsa*[268] (Punch).

**Uchchala's Kashmir Invasion**

After the fighting of *Rajapuri, Uchchala* marched toward Kashmir invasion, just like a falcon lusting after flesh[269]. He captured the commandant of the 'Gate' (*dvaresa*), *Sujjaka* by name. As soon as they arrived at *Kashmir, Damaras* and *Khasikas*, the enemies of the king came from all walks of life joined with him down to the mountains[270]. King *Harsa* was frightened on the surprise visit of *Uchchala* when he dropped from heaven or been thrown forth from the womb of the earth[271]. He then became perplexed that he might have got a firm footing who obtained in his *Kramarajya* assigned by God[272]. No doubt, since the prefect of police (*Sunna*) delayed in collecting troops, he despatched in hurry *patta* by providing a large number of officers[273]. But *Uchchala* had obtained a firm footing at that time. He also caught a horse of auspicious marks which came from the enemy's camp, representing the royal Fortune, as soon as he arrived at *Varahamula*[274]. Thereupon, *Mahavaraha*[275] was took place by a girl, and his head was garlanded, just as if the earth, which rested on his shoulders like that of (god)[276]. During the period of fighting road was blocked, *Kaka*[277] and his family was also abandoned at *Huskapura*, and left the things on the direction of *Kramaraja*[278]

**Rising of Damaras**

From the *Kashmir History,* we learn that Damaras time and again created the problem in the way of life by obtaining the power in the administration and threw the governor into a panic condition[279]. No doubt, they defeated many noteable soldiers, such as *Yasoraja*, etc. but his authority in most of the times had been gone in vain[280]. It appears that he gradually disappeared, and occupied *Taramulaka*[281], where his apponents, joined by *Uchchala* and also followed him[282]. He collected there a large force for sometimes, who resembled like clouds, rainfall, etc. for the destruction of earth at the end of the *Kalpa*[283]. It is a struggle for victory between the two forces, just as two jealous elephants for one female[284]. Then *Ananda*, too, a material uncle of *Uchchala*, collected the Damaras and raised a rebellion against *Madavaraja*[285]. During the rebellion *Damaras* came from all regions, just as bees from the holes come out (in the ground) when the snow melted[286]. At that time the Mahattama *Sahla*, the Kayastha, was commander-in-chief of the unfortunate King's army, as well as the lord of the Gate, though attacked by *Ananda* in frequent fights[287]. Ultimately *Uchchala* surrendered his army in the battle field which was surrounded by the Governor[288]. Governor urged the *Uchchala*, kindly proceed towards the destination after this there is little opportunity for you[289]. As soon as *Uchchala* marched from the battlefield, *Ananda* plundered the various towns, villages, in this way *Uchchala* kept his dignity intact[290].

**Uchchala at Parihasapura**

During this process, *Ananda* on the other side allowed the *Uchchala* to occupy *Parihasapura*. It was the difficult place which had the steep slopes and the water (around[291]). *Ananda* ordered his people awake up early in the morning for the worship of the '*Nam*' otherwise you do not come out from the troubles[292]. It is the enterprise of the God with the theory of mind[293]. Those do not enterprised the God they will dragged in the battlefield of the life that is birth and rebirth[294]. Those die in the living life, they win the victory of life. They free from the worries of life[295]. It appears that *Uchchala* had already covered the distance to reach at *Bharatasetu*[296] and routed the enemy's force without any resistance[297]. Now the king's army had come to the agitated occan, but the army of governor destroyed almost half of the force of the enemy[298].

**Uchchala's Defeat**

After a short period; *Uchchala's* force was broken up, and the *Damaras* will come by running for their own safety and some one who tried threw themselves into the *Rajavihara*[299]. At the very moment a Damara will call the *Trillasena,* they set afire to the Vihara, and then think it was *Uchchala*[300]. Thus, the proud *Uchchala*, who had long fought with *Somapala,* the paternal uncle of *Darsanpala* was in trouble induced by *Janakacandra* in the middle of the opponents cavalry, and some one betray in the battlefield took the shelter at *Parihasapura* to face the death[301]. After acrossing the *Vitasta* with his own horse from the village of *Gaurikabala*[302], again he proceeded with the Damaras to *Taramulaka*[303]. The lust of the limited victory, King will return to his capital, bestowing praises upon (the governor) *Ananda*[304]. As it appears that he did not follow inpursuit by his opponents[305]. It will took a fresh courage. Despite of these, *Uchchala* again made an effort in the month of *Jyaistha* to collect the scattered force from all the sides with due care[306]. During the time of natural calamities, prouded prince will become the friend of everybody with the blessing of 'God'[307].

**Destruction of the Parihasakesava Image**

In the study it is expressed that *Harsa* fractured the glourious image of Vishnu which had been obtained from the sixth century A.D at *Parihasakesava*[308]. This event was took place during the time of midst famine *Uchchala* became helpless at that time and went for regaining of his power. After this happening,heaven and earth became lull till the death of *Harsa*[309]. It appears that it was a story among the people before the sixth century A.D.; there had been the age of darkness, even at daytime. With the installation of *Parihasakesava* image; which spread daylight by its silver, it happened again for a month and a half after the destruction of that (image[310]). After a little relaxation, *Harsa's* opponents became encouraged, in the meanwhile *Sussala* appeared from the direction of *Surapura*[311] . As soon as *Harsa* came out the relaxation to regaining the power from his *'Father' Sussala* was stopped by him at *Avanaha*[312] he praised his elder (brother)[313] that is *'Nam'* or *'Chamar'*. No doubt, he received certain horses which were presented by the king *Kalha*. It was the story of the class struggle, where from it was started and came to end with an artistic manners at the same place. It shows that politness defeated the enemy[314] that is *mana* or mind, who is the commandant of the *Kaliyug*. (*Manikya*) *Harsa* secured the victory of *Surapura* the watching station (*dranga*[315]) with ample means[316]. It is the story of the great luck, who obtained such kind of wealth which displayed a wonderful world[317]. At this juncture *Harsa* disregarded *Uchchala*, sent his own governor known as *Patta* to fight against *Sussala*, whose movements were rapid at that time[318]. Thus, in this battle the troops of the (prince) were routed at *Surapura*. Most of them were drowned in the water of the *Vaitarani*[319] and found their end[320]. In this way, *Susala* became victorious at *Surapura*.

**Sussala's Victory at Surapura**

In this war goddess was badly defeated by *Sussala at Surapura* which could not touch the body of the brave *Darsanpala*; since he was not true to his mastery.[321]. It appears on the following day, the flying troops has escaped with their fortune joined with *Sahela*, who stopped at *Lokapunya*[322]. No doubt, during the attack of *Sussala, Sahelaka* had the fear in their mind, now the end of the world is going to take place,and the defeated troops get into the city[323]. With this approach *Sussala* had at *Taramula*, obtained again a firm stand[324]. The opposite force that is *Damaras,* who were existed themselves mostly bare foot, were defeated by the (King's) cavalry. It appears that the mountain route of *Lahara* or *Lohara* was difficult one[325]. *Harsa* appointed *Udayaraja* as the lord of the Gate, sent as a governor to *Lahara* to fight against *Uchchala*[326]. Thereupon the maternal uncle of the sons of *Malla* (Ananda) had already there at *Padampura*, in the cabinet of the King, ministers were frightened to take the charge of the army as a commander-in-chief because it was the difficult task to handle[327]. In that helpless situation, *Chanraraja* voluntarily accpeted the duty from the king's hand and decorated his office (*adhikarasraj*[328]). He was descended from the illustrious *Jinduraja* on the desire of his forefather (*pitar*), who had displayed noble conduct and behaviour in this universe[329]. It reveals that *Chandraraja* took the charge of the force at the time of desperation, like the son of *Drona*[330]., who drove the hostile force from *Padmapura*[331]. *Sussala* gradually occupied the territory of *Padamapura,* and on the ninth day of the bright half of *S'ravana* killed the enemy's general (*Kampanesa*) insided *Avantipura*[332]. The latter separated from his troops which were fighting near *Govardhanadhara*[333]. There were only few attendants who can listen the music. At that time the cavalry of the enemy was walking by road along the bank of *Vitasta* and put him to a sudden death. Luck will not favour those who are careless in the efforts to see the *'ultimate reality.*[334]

When *Harsa* saw the headship of *Chandraraja*, he hoped afresh victory as it was (a sign of) fate's victory, just as the lion (while moving away) turns back to his glances [335]. After *Chandraraja*, who showed energy in his efforts, had collected an army in its eighteen fold division moving towards *Vijayaksetra*[336]. The Creator Power i.e. *'Nam'*, resembling a person holding a balance, did not allow at that time the equilibrum between the two forces to be disturbed just as (if they had been) the double scales[337]. Thus, this incident was took place on the third day, there was no seasonal rainfall, but the force of *Chandraraja* was demoralized and ran away from *Lohara* or *Lohara*[338]. In this rainfall, no doubt, soldiers felt the pain of cold wind left all the belongings (equipment) of the army, as (if they had been helpless) animals[339]. Then *Janakachandra* and his officials, they put the governor to death, though *Uchchala's* feeling, he kindly protected[340]. In this victory it appears that *Janakachandra* was the only one, who purchased the glory of 'God' within the body among king *Harsa's* servents, who were characterized by double-dealing[341]. Beside him, *Devasarman*[342] and others must have been the models of convincing victory[343]. No doubt, certain had followed the same game (against me) for having inverted (the order). It would also depend on fate in the battlefield, when result will come out from the destruction of the *Lavanyas*[344]. Now the confusion has been created in the enemies camp. The time has come to streamline the truth by operating the warship under the sea for a long period, because all the properties of the living man belongs to ocean. Therefore one cannot call the ocean as a fool[345]. *Gajja*, his mother, who is praise worthy and has noble character, has borne great sons for the devotion to thier *Lord's* service[346]. In every risky time king always deputes her sons because she has been over burden by the maternal affection[347]. In this victory it appears that faithful sons of the *'Father'* and the *'mother'* virtuous of a life[348]. In the meanwhile, *Uchchala* arrived at *Hiranyapura*[349], majority of the Brahmans assembled there and consecrated him as a king[350]. During this event most of the minister advised the king, who was greatly depressed, because there was the majority of enemies belongs to the mountain of *Lohara*. After sometime, people will recall you as a new ruler[351]. He replied: "It is not easy to start a thing, leaving behind the ladies of seraglio, treasures, the throne and other precious things of life[352]". No doubt, certain trust worthy servents, they will help to consolidate the treasurers and other basic needs of life[353]. Beside this, there is also the loss of dignity if throne on which a lover of a *Svapaka* woman was (seated) or occupied by another[354], let it will be depend on the 'Father's decision or put into the mouth of the ministers on the judgement of day.

**Ministers' Advice to Harsa**

On the very day of the Judgement, *Harsa* was adviced by ministers whom the king had cherished, must have been beasts in human form that they did not remove his misfortune when had reached such a pitiable state[355]. As soon as success will be achieved by the mere sacrifice of the body that would be end of the one *Yugas*[356] and started the another. Those who looked upon their master's sorrow, fear, misery, and other afflictions as if they were an actor's (exhibition), make this earth unholy, though it is (hallowed) by sacred places[357]. *Harsa* who did high acts though he had fallen into errors as if possessed by demons, addressed once more those beasts of men[358]. At that time death and *Kubera* sit upon the lips of kings', this saying was proved in this *Kali Yuga*[359]. Henceforth, people generally would not be blame on this success whether it was justified (by the attending circumstances[360])." Since the churning (of the ocean) has succeeded, does anyone blame the churning-mountain (*Mandaradri*) for the unfavourable circumstances (attending the enterprise), namely that hte destroyer of the wings (of the mountains, i.e Indra), an enemy, was the helper, and that he whose juice causes death (*Vasuki*), was the churning-cord[361]." *Harsa* had also the problem to maintain the people's 'ego' or I, by determining the scientific study, affected to be (solely) a producer of riches (*srigarbha*[362]), this has been the cause of my confusion[363]." On this account *Harsa* have been fallen into a helpless state[364]. Hence, he study the verses of king *Muktapida*[365], who had been shining at the heads of the kings, was caught by his enemies in a difficult situation, and reduced to great straits[366]. When he marched in the northern region with his few followers, he concealed his troops on different routes. Therefore, he was blocked by the enemy on a difficult path[367]".

**Tale of king Muktapida's Death**

The brief story of king *Muktapida's* death is that he could not keep his honour intact[368]. He always busy with pretends in the meanwhile attacked were launched by the *Nature* like epidemic disease called *dandakalasaka*[369]. On the pretention of *Muktapida, dandakalasaka* became illness and wept with motionless eyes and shouted from the one senses[370] out of nine. Strong-minded (kings), they passed the resolution on the adire of their councillor's on the request of disgrace which fate wrought (for them[371]). *Harsa* closed his lips after saying few words. His ministers advised him to send *Bhoja*[372] and his son to the castle (of *Lohara*[373]) to preserve his lineage[374]. The same king of whom in the time of his good fortune it is held on account of his wisdom, courage and other qualities that he might be attack by Indra[375].

**Disaffection of Harsa's Servants**

In the closing reign of *Harsa*, all the servants of the king became *Tantrin*, a disaffection was started against him by this troop[376]. A dancing girl from the family of the female dancer *Kanasravati*, had adopted a girl of unknown family called *Jayamati*. The latter after losing her virginity was as a young woman *Uchchala's* mistress, and became subsequently from greed of money the concubine of the governor. *Ananda*. When latter died she, devoid of shame, went to *Uchchala*. This very person through the will of fate was destined to become the chief-queen (of Uchchala[377]). The king (*Harsa*) in his hatred of the family of *Malla* had *Vyaddamangala,* the son of *S'rilekha*[378] nephew, attacked and killed[379]. His wife, who was a daughter of the maternal uncle of *Malla's* sons (*Ananda*), and her mother-in-law set their house on fire and burned themselves[380]. From the study it indicates that during the closing days of *Harsa* reign only two or three follower he had not the desire to join the enemy camp that is *Tantric*.

**Attack on Malla**

During the times of disaffection in *Harsa's* court *Sahi* princesses alert him: "*Malla* is an accomplished hypocrite who makes (your) court disaffected, while hiding his ferocious nature, like another yama, under the observance of the vow of silence and other (austerities). Therefore, let him, as an enemy and anxious to see his sons on the throne, be killed without fear[381]". *Harsa* himself proceeded towards the attack on *Malla* to fulfill his desire[382]. He however, had remained in his house and had given *Salhana*[383] and (two) other half-brothers of the two future kings (Uchchala and *Sussala*) as hostages, in order to assure the king[384]. It shows that *Harsa* has worn the sacred cord, holding in his hands the rosary, with his fingers rendered brilliant sacrificial grass, with his forehead smiling, as it were, with its mark of ashes, he (appeared) like another *Jamadagnya* (*Parasurama*[385]). At the time of death he seemed to carry on his head the water of *Prayaga* under the guise of his moving locks which were wet from the bath, and partly white partly black. His hero's band (*Virapatta*) seemed like an (ordinary) headdress, his shield like a parasol; carrying his sword like-blade (*asidhara*[386]) he seemed as if on the way to the *Dharatirtha*, and his sword as if it were his staff[387]. In this war two Brahmans were also involved known as *Rayyavatta* and *Vijaya*. They were the superintendent of the kitchen *Kosthaka* and the soldier *Sajjaka* distinguished themselves by falling in that fight[388]. Even the doorkeeper *Udayaraja,* though wounded and his agent *Ajjaka*, escaped with their lives, as their time had not yet come[389]. It appears that when the gate closely beset from all sides by the hostile soldiers, *Malla* put his hand fearlessly at their head[390]. Now the time has come for the death of *Malla*[391].

**Death of Malla**

*Harsa'* first enemy was *Malla*, he was seen pierced by hundreds of sharp-pointed arrows, and asleep on his couch of a hero like another *Bhisma*[392]. He cut off his head at that time *Malla's* princely consort *Kumudalekha* and his wife's sister *Vallabha,* immolated themselves in a fire kindled in their residence[393] Besides these, *Asamati* and *Sahaja, Malla's* dauther-in-law, who were the wives of *Salhana* and *Ralha,* and the daughter of Raja and *Avakalya* (respectively), also burned themselves[394]. In addition to this number, six more female attendents of the ladies of his household, who had been in the enjoyment also burned on the same pyre[395]. This event was took place on the left bank of the *Vitasta*, the water of which became warm by the conflagration of the great house and by the tears hot with grief. On the other side of the *Vitasta, Nanda* the mother of the future kings, who was of noble birth, was in her own seraglio and was eagrly looking from a high terrace towards the camps of her sons, distinguishable in the north and south by the smoke of their kitchen-fires. This virtuous lady burned herself in her house together with her nurse *Chandri*, who left unable to see the water which was to be offered at the funeral libations of her whom she had brought up as a child with her own milk. She (*Nanda*) had not yet seated herself in the flaming fire, but was (already) surrouned by the flames which were playing around, as (if they were her) female companions, when she uttered the following curse against the king: "May you, O sons, before many days do to the family of your father's enemy what the son of Jamadagni (*Parasurama*[396]) did" *Darsanapata*[397], though the king was preparing to kill him[398], or it may be that he was spared by malice for only one other year to suffer humiliation and to rot away by disease[399]. As soon as *Malla's* sons heard the news of their father's murder on the ninth of the dark half of *Bhadrapada* (August), their grief became absorbed in rage[400].

**Sussala's Attack on Vijayesvara**

Due to his burning ferocity, the villages as far as *Vahnipuraka*[401], *Sussala* marched immediately towards *Vijayaksetra*[402]. Thereupon *Candraraja*[403] marched out to meet his attack *Patta, Darsanapala* and others deserted him together with their troops[404]. In that battle two *Rajagrhyas Aksotamalla* and *Malla*, a descendant of *Cacara*, were received in the embraces of the celestial maids[405]. It appears that darkness has been created by the dust. Now the time has come to settle the dust with the help of *Parasol. Chandraraja* embraced in the arms of the divine maids as well as his follower *Induraja*[406]. Due to the death of this hero, it shows that his fate has been torn up, as it were to their very fibres, the roots of the lotusplanatation of king *Harsa's* hopes [407]. As soon as *Sussala* captured the place of *Vijayesvara,Patta* and rest of them, they were fled away due to fear in the temple of *Vijayesa* and closed the gate[408]. There were only one councillor (*asthaniya*[409]) known as *Padma* remain, who felt that it is fighting of the outside. In this battle *Laksmidhara* was died which was captivated by the Damaras[410]. At the same time *Sussala* was ascended at the roof of the treasury (*ganja*) of the *Vijayesvara* (temple) and rest of the masses assembled below as the frightened animals[411]. No doubt, cleer *Sussala* had given a confidential assurance of gaiety, first among them the two, *Patta* and *Darsanapala* in his presence[412]. As they could not get up[413], *Sussala's* followers dragged them up by a rope, under some (strange) impulse, must verily thrill even the body of the creator of the Universe[414]. He opened the door and stepped quite alone[415],the place where *Sussala* held his assembly, being covered with heaps of gold and silver sword-hilts and decked with arms appeared as if decorated with strewn flowers[416]. Creator handed them over to the Damaras to guard it for three days[417]. As soon as *Sussala* reached in the village of *Suvarnasanura*[418], he then discharged *Patta* and *Darsanapala*, who wished to go abroad. But unlucky *Patta* went to his wife at *Surapura* and forgot to go abroad[419]. The same kind of role has been played by the treacherous *Darsanapala*, who was counteracted by his friendship for *Patta*[420]. In this struggle it appears that *Sussala* was anxious to capture the throne of Srinagar even though he was prevented by his elder brother [421].

**Sussala's attack on Srinagar**

During the campaign of *Sussala* at Srinagar his younger brother *Uchchala* did not imply any precedance, as they were almost of the same age and at all times they were equally arrogant[422]. Within two or three days *Sussala* occupied number of places even, in the neighbourhood[423]. He set fire to '*Word*' or '*Chamar*' *Bhojadeva*, the king's son, whose other name was *Buppa*, went forth to fight with him[424]. His father had the fear in his mind and kept himself powerless. But now he was set free (to act) as there is no alternative[425]. This prince was born to surpass his adversary, whose power was excessive, just as the *Timimgala* ('Swallower of the Timi') (Surpasses) the large see-fish (timi[426]). Father of *Sussala* displayed ingratitude (*Pittha*), the wicked son of *Devesvara*, though raised by the king to a high position, has yet joined the enemy's camp. In this struggle of war, king asked his (*Pitthai's*) son *Milla* for his horse. *Sussala* proudly washed off the insult in the battlefield with the streams (of blood) that flowed from the sword-blades[427]. Thus, the ruin of everything did not cause such great pain to the king's heart, of that grate pain to the king's heart, of that grateful man at that time when they honoured it solely by words[428]. In this precipitated war the army of *Sussala* was routed twice time by *Bhoja* and fled away to *Lavanotsa*[429]. *Bhoja* in this stretching heat returned to his father's side in the garden[430].

**Uchchala's move in Srinagar**

During the *Uchchala's* invasion toward Srinagar in the north from the bank opposite to the royal palace[431]: "The elder son of *Malla* has arrived. Break off the bridge[432]!" At the same time prefect of police (*Sunna*) had sent the (Uchchala) *'Word'*: "The throne is in *Sussala's* power, if you do not reach today[433]" Thereupon he marched very quickly in the battlefield, and killed the *Devanayaka*[434] first, then proceeded toward the (temple of the) god *Narendresvara*[435]. Whereas, the *Naga* the town-prefect, who has encamped (*Sthanastha*[436]) alongwith troops, marched forth with a force of horsemen to meet him[437], emerged from the fight with *Sussala* and felt no fear from *Uchchala*[438]. It appears that *Naga* might have been liked by the governor (*Ananda*) to go to his own house[439]. The reward which this gentleman got for his double-dealing would be seen in his present life[440]. He died before to live in this very universe. As soon as *Uchchala* reached on the bank of river, he saw that there is a great bridge between the two city i.e. *Earth* and *Heaven*. It appears that this universe is burning by a forest fire[441] the body of *Janakacandra* is the central place, who wore the white armour like that of the planet venus in the darkness[442]. In this connection *Harsa* had already constituted the *'Great Bridge'*[443] (*mahasetu*) with boats for his own benefit, by the will of fate it served in the end with enemy's advantage[444]. At that time *S'ahi* princesses and other queens will eagerly to die, and also ascended with fire-brands to the four—pillared pavillion (*Catuskika*[445]) of the 'Palace of hundred gates' (*Satadvara*[446]). On such occasion people will look on with indifference as their lord fought with his rivals at the bridge-head, without feeling affectively, just as (if it were mere) horseplay on the *Asvayuji* day[447]. Now, king *Harsa* took up the fight with bridge-head, time and again held back by his wives to set fire in the palace, but the victory was yet in store[448]. It is very right that *Mallaraja's* residence was very close to the royal house. It would be fired by *Janakacandra* after crossing the river[449]. It appears that *Bhoja* flamed the fire towards the palace and took to flight in the kingdom of lost[450]. Moreover, it will opened the gate of the enemies which has been covered by mere reeds. Suddenly, they came out from the courtyard into the open[451]. From the majority of the enemies five to six horsemen having the intention of reaching *Lohara*, after crossing the bridge in front of the

*Simharajamatha*[452]. Whereas, king will ride with some horsemen outside the buildings and with tears (in their eyes) looked in the direction where his son had disappeared from the sight[453]. At the very moment the various servants of the king's wives were battering the four-pillared pavilion (*catuskika*[454]) in order to save (their mistresses) who were seeking death[455]. Even this massages did not listen by the *Sahi* princesses that the enemy of the four-pillarad pavillion had broken from the heart[456]. During that movement citizens and Damaras will strike to each other with upraised weapons plundered the valuable treasures in the burning palace[457]. Some will found their death there, some will got rid of their poverty; some of them became ridiculous by obtaining things which they had never set their eyes upon before[458]. *Harsa* sacked the palace, one put camphor into his mouth thinking it was white sugar. As soon as it burned his mouth, he will throw the pot into the river[459]. In the meantime some *low-caste* people eager to obtain gold burned clothes which were painted with gold and someone anxiously will search into the ashes[460]. At certain places *low-caste* were also found grinding unpierced pearls choosing from the white rice corns[461]. The goddess of wealth known as *Laksmi* will be seen residing in this earth, if there is ill-treatment, she did not exist anywhere once again[462]. At such occasion, wild *Damaras* would be seen at every moment carring ladies of the king's *seraglio* who wore dresses, ornaments and hairstyles resembled fairies[463]. While seventeen queens with *Vasantalekha*[464] at their head, including daughters-in-law (of the king) burned themselves there and rest will leave the hall[465]. At the same time crackling noise will listen from the burning buildings that it was the bubbling of the aerial stream[466] boiling under intense heat[467]. King *Harsa* will view this (spectacle) standing close to the drinking fountain (*Prapa*) of the illustrious *Padmasri*[468], recite time and again ancient verses of the *'Nam'* or *'Chamar'* which he remembered in his anguish: "the fire which has risen from the burning pains of the subjects, does not go out, until it has consumed the king's race fortune and life[469]." In the last, *Uchchala* acrossed back to the other side (of the *Vitasta*) river along with the Damaras, when he saw his opponent had the armed force, he left the palace burning[470]. It appears that the opponent force is coming bare-footed and death is lurking in their mind. They remained into the confusion at every moment[471]. It is very sure, those do not believe on the *'Word'* or *'Nam'*. They might have to face the *Anantapala*. These are the words of the prefect of police[472]. At this juncture *Canpaka* advised him either to fight or to go to *Lohara*. Therefore, *Prayaga*[473] was the second course, but not the first[474]. *Harsa* did not receive the news of his son, during that condition he told *Canpaka* to follow up his track. *Canpaka* spoke to *Harsa* in the following verses: "O king, in a short time you will have no one else to follow you *Prayaga*. Hence you ought not to send me away also[476]." *Harsa* replied touch with *'Words'* of the *Master* which contained a reproach, he bent his downwords in embarrassment and started to follow up the prince[477]. It appears that he started his journey with fifty horsemen, including his brothers, servants, etc. Out of the fifty horsemen, he found himself only with four (to follow him) who acrossed the other side of the river[478]. Now the two brothers of the same father i.e. *Sesaraja* had fallen on the road after having their horses have been killed, they suggested follow the way of *Dhanaka*[479]. In pursuit of this moment *Canpaka* is wandering by the river-way though without obtaining the news of the prince, he came at the close of the day to the confluence of the *Vitasta* and *Sindhu*[480]. In the same way King *Harsa* despatched other trustee persons to search out his son, and others again used this pretext to leave his side[481]. *Canpaka*, the prefect of police[482] , who had taken bribes and shown himself disaffection in the war against *Rajapuri*.Those, who were unable to tolerae efficient officers (by his side), had rendered the army worthless, who had made the king object to his son's departure to *Lohara*. It depicts that they had brought the enemy into the City While the king was taken up by another fight. *Harsa* or *'Nam'* had brought about the ruin of everything, also prevented the king at that time from taking the proper course of action[483]. There was a complete dejection from the side of the manifold advice, and week-minded king could not focus upon any single action[484], that is *"Dalit Voice"*. *Dalit Voice* does not give a sound, it gives secret message to the listener in their holes during the time of counselling in different directions to the (opinions) different people till date we do not reach at any resolution[485]. Therefore, it is our duty to ask even a mean person, without asking them we can not advice them boldly as it is the part of the human character[486]. At the same time king *Harsa* went for fighting, an equery (*Suta*), *Trailokya*[487] by name, laid hold of his reins and extolling the prefect of police. He again adressed him in the following lines," your grandfather once won a victory with the *Ekangas*[488] and the mounted men. Therefore, let us go to the *Aksapatala* (office), in order to collect them[489]. "Joined by them we fall from behind upon the enemies, whose force consisted chiefly of foot soldiers, and destroy them as falcons (destroy) the brids.[490]"

**Dessertion of Harsa's Troops**

After the defeat of enemies, *Harsa's* troops will move in all directions, just like people caught by a down-pour while watching a theatrical performance[491]. At that time the sons of *Seyaraja*[492], who came from *Heaven Parevitasta*[493]. They will provide him jewelled necklace (ornaments) for the journey to spread the *"Radha Soami"* mission in aborad. During that period regal ornament was in the hands of market gardeners; at that time king will be distinguished by his his lustre appeared to the people deprived of his royal dignity[494]. No doubt, his soldiers deserted at every step, because he has been moved from the *Aksapatala* and other offices, but no one can match with him[495]. After retiring from the mission at late in the evening looked like a refuge among the houses of his ministers, but no one let him in when he stood at the door of public[496]. Whereas, the (Brahmans) who are clever till date in solemn fasts (*Prayopavesa*), are thoroughly useless in the end. Vain is the reliance which kings put on wretched Brahmans[497]. *Deepit Raj* son of Dr. *Raj Kumar* is anxious in wandering among the houses of all those who were (of note) in this land, hoping to be received by the minister of *Kapila*[498]. *Loharakotta* will always keep himself away to spread the mission, and his wife will ask the King to stop him, but he will proceed on boats one after the another, and could not deceived by fate, will carry on the mission[499]. Study reveals that sons of ministers like that of their father, concealed themselves from the unfortunate (king), just like poor debtors from their creditors[500].

**Harsa's Attack from S'rinagar**

During the attack of *Harsa* from Srinagar most of his trustee and followers gave up his side when he had to pass the (hill of ) *Pradyumna*[501]. The people themselves are called *Rajaputras*[502], *Anantapala* and the rest, who claim descent from the thirty six families and who in their pride would not concede a higher position to the sun himself, they to left him step by step, and their houses disappeared in the dense darkness[503]. In the very moment *Harsa* descended from his horse after approaching the *Johilamatha*[504], the perfect of the police with his younger brother also deserted him[505] . "Here is my father-in-law" house", he said ," after looking for a place there for you to pass the night, I shall return." Under this pretext he departed. During his departure, *Prayagaka* asked his younger brother for his bracelet in order to procure provisions; instead of this he gave him barley[506]. In the last moment *Harsa* left his property cosisting of a single garment, with his bare life and with the single *Prayaga* as follower[507]. At the time of death (*Mukta*), the cook of *Canpaka's* attendent *Jalaka*, accompanied with the king as a trustee friend[508] . From that period, they were wandering hither and thither, a woman came from a den called out to them that the ground in front has been hard on account of breaches made by the flood[509]. *Harsa* then set down on the bank of *Vitasta,* and *Prayagaka* called some boatmen to proceed to the castle of *Jayapura*[510]. He had already arranged with the soldiers stationed there to conduct the king to the residence of *Bhimadeva*[511]. *Bhimadeva,* supported by *Uchchala*, had told him that he would attached himself to the king if he were to come to his seat[512]. As soon as, the boatmen brought a boat, the king did not get into it. It appears that he was condemned and confused by the dangers, who had come close under his eyes[513]. At the close of the function, the lamp of their intellect was drawn quickly, as if it noticed the snake in the hand of approaching death[514]. King at that time was seeking shelter, did not remember *Bimba,* even the Damara of *Nilasva*[515] too, did not join the his enemies. While treason was ripe, this honorable man had alone kept faithful, life a true wife never turned his eyes towards anyone else (but his lord[516]). At the same times cloudes started to let flow their waters, as tomake the earth cleansed from the evil doers[517]. O Shame! the name of the evil-doers, though unworthy of remembrance, now it has been openly mentioned in the sequence of the narrative[518].

**Harsa Became Refuge**

At a burning-ground, *Harsa* became refuge, he took permission from certain divinities known by the name of *Somesvara,* who worshipped (there) by a magician called *Somananda*[519]. During this period in the courtyard of *Somananda*, there was a hut of *low-class* begger named *Guna*[520], and was (surrounded) by a garden shaded by high trees[521]. This man used to live in the company of prostitute whose (real) name was *Bhisca,* generally known as *Virahabhujamgi*[522]. *Chinna* (beggar) who used to live in the neighbourhood of the shrine of *Pratapagaurisa*[523], *Mukta* took the king to pass the night[524]. No doubt, *Harsa* was held by *Mukta* and *Prayagaka*. Thus, they proceeded time and again to see the ground by the flashes of lighting[525]. From hut to *Prayagaka* and *Mukta* brought with great difficulty the stumbling king who had no headdress, emotionally wore the soaked clothes[526]. *Harsa* has the knowledge of distress *Kandarpa* in what way wicked councillors, they ousted him, who was the responsible off his ruin, just as *Utpala* (had remembered) the demon *Rudra*[527]. As soon as *Mukta* got the charge of the four wall, king first entered in the courtyard of the hut and found beggar was absent[528]. During his entrant his right foot struck against a stone and bled; by this he knew evil omen has been prevailed and hut was locked[529]. He sat down in the courtyard late at night, which the terrible masses of clouds made fearful[530]. Keeping in view the damaged reputation, he stood on the muddy bare ground and passed that night of terrible rain, his body was covered by a woollen cloak of a slave[531]. At one time, he was slave according to the commitment with mind and now awoke up. But he has forgotten the interval period of his misfortune[532]. Now, the 'ego,' I, is disturbing me time and again[533]. Then *Harsa* thought: "My kingdom is lost; my wives are burning; my son has disappeared; I am alone, without friends and provisions, rolling about in the courtyard of a beggar." When he thought of each one of these misfortunes he could not even in stories find any one else who had sunk (so) low and was afflicted with sorrow equal to his own.[534]

**Murder of Bhoja**

Now, *Bhoja* left the city along with the two or three horsemen wandering here and there, and reached *Hastikarna*[535]. He thought during the wandering: "Surly, in five or six days I must win back the throne, even if Indra were my enemy[536]". As a man of valour, restless, like the embryo (moving) in the womb, as (if it were) the breath of (former) actions touching (the child as it leaves the womb). Who completed this process[537]. His servant *Nagesvara* had to think that who sent for the journey of his mother and who stopped inside the *Rangavata*[538] (grove). It appears that his servant *Nagesvara* constrúcted empty temple called *mandir* and staying uselessly. Even he unnecessarily imposed the duties to *Ksathriyas* for his own exaggeration[539]. As soon as his conspiracy was leaked out itself. *Ksathriyas* will attack over him like a lion and destroyed the self styled hero[540]. At this moment his maternal cousin *Padmaka* and his favourite *Khela*[541], who showed unmeasured strength in fighting[542]. When *Sussala* and *Uchchala* heard the news of *Bhoja's* murder, at that time only *Harsa* was there for the protection of throne. He was removed from their mind, but one edge was remained[543]. Therefore, his royal fortune regained the life from the exile after a long period, but sometimes it appeared that he did no gain it[544]. As soon as *Harsa* heard the news of Bhoja's death from the wife of a beggar in the presence of *Prayaga*[545]. *Harsa* told the *Prayaga*, it was a false (report) require the actual condition of his body[546]. During his grief striken period it delineates that his son (*Bhoja*) had fallen in the combat of great heros and had been murdered as a baby in their arms [547]. He fenced his childhood while decorated with precious ornaments[548] that he could not feel humiliation by the thought: "The youth who ought to have been spared, is killed , I, however, who an old, prolong my life by such unseemly means"[549]. As per the enquiry of *Prayaga* he had been proceeded to the *Bhagavamatha*, but he deprived of thought by his *Bhagavanmatha*, but he deprived of thought by his grief. He said it will be revealed at night not even a wish (to do this[550]). In this judgement it looks that night had been covered by the heavy dew-drops which rained like tears from the down-turned face of the moon and by the wailing cries of the ruddy geese[551]. In the morning mendicant (beggar) said that he brought a householder beast for sacrifice, *Prayage* told[552]. "Look, O king, how happy the people are when they have lost their lord". He replied with a smile: "Why do you talk as if you were simple-minded[553]?" *Prayaga* had given back those two pots which contained cooked food in a sauce[554]. Mendicent (begger) again urged secretly to *Harsa* to obtain (proper) food. The latter said: "the amount left me after yesterday's expenses is no sufficient. Yet I will try" and then we have to proceed ahead[555].

**Betrayal of Harsa**

*Harsa* leave no stone unturned in secret for the small-minded people during his lecture, even it is very soft for a very fragile persons[556]. No doubt, *Manoratha*, the relative of a Brahman ascetic, heard the tale from that mendicant (beggar) who was his friend[557]. *Harsa* told the beggar: "We shall obtain wealth from king (*Uchchala*) by delivering his kinsman", and thus lead him as a traitor[558]. Beggar definitely believed to have been born from some despicable foul servent, since good and bad actions are indicated by a corresponding birth[559]. Between the two *Illaraja* learned the fact and reported to *Uchchala*, who ordered him to act himself in this matter[560]. His other friends, however, discussed that it was the Kayastha *Bhutabisca* who got the report of mendicant and the Brahman to approach *Illaraja*[561]. If they made this statement false then it will be prove that they are the dishonest people of *Bhutabhisca*[562] and traitor[563]. No doubt, *Harsa* will punished him like a died man after having been carried on the back of a *Svapaka* and faced severe humiliation[564]. At that time, *Harsadeva* will suddenly came in painful emotions, and at the repeated request of *Prayaga, Harsa* will make up his mind to take more food, thought his grief over his son was fresh[565]. Thinking at all time that the *beggar* had arrived bringing food for *Harsa*. He looked out through a window as a young bird (looks out) from its nest[566]. At that occasion, *Harsa* witnessed that hut had been entirely surrounded by soldiers who had come up, and heard the noise of the bolt being withdrawn from the gate of the courtyard[567]. He understood that he had been conspired against the villains of a beggar in the association of the soldiers, as he called from the courtyard to the *Mukta* to come out[568]. *Harsa* requested the *Mukta*[569] please leave me, as you havebeen constituted by me, opened the door without fear grasped the small knife he had by his side[570]. One of the sadistic soldier, spurred on by bold assurance, then stepped up to him with draw sword and wearing armour[571]. No doubt, King was expert in athletic exercises, threw this man down to the ground, though hindred are there in his movements by the narrow space of the hut, but mercy will not kill him[572]. At that moment he said that this world is full of false pride: " To kill this wretch who is on the ground does not help me[573]". Two soldiers will be fell to the ground in ups and down after removing the roof due to the fear of upraised weapon[574]. For a moment he had to be seen standing like a soldier in the staff carried by a soldier whoentered first, just as *Camunda*[575] (stood) over *Ruru*[576]. At the last stage, war was not rendered glorious by lion-like roars (of brave men), nor by the sound of kettle-drums, nor the furious noise of (clashing) arms of king[577]. Contrary to this, armed Damaras will get punished without noise in their huts, as cats (get round) a mouse which is inside a pot[578]. At the same time a foot-soldier had to enter through the roof attacked the king after striking *Prayagaka* on the shoulder and head. This soldier will hit the king which his weapon repidly twice with a dagger in the breast and killed[579] on spot.

**Death of Harsa A.D. 1101**

*Harsa* was killed in 1101, A.D. after uttering twice the word: "O Mahesvara", he laid down the ground, just like a tree which has been cut down at the root[580]. From the death it expresses that he was a thief who entered in a house like a flight[581]. Study reveals that *Harsa* was a powerful king, nor of any other (King) has been seen shameful[582]. During the time of battle *Harsa* announced the grandeur of this high-minded (King) with all its attending happiness[583]. His fault was that he want of independent judgement, and all errors which brought about his complete ruin (may have been those of his ministers[584]). At that time *Harsa* was forty two years and eight-months, when he was expired on the fifth day of the bright half of *Bhadrapada* in the year 1101 A.D.

At the age of seventy seven[585]. In short, it appears from the above statement that *Harsa"s* native force was interested to extint his race like (another) *Duryodhan*[586]. As it has been stated by the great author of *Samhita*[587], *Kuru* descendanted from the *Moon*, now they are maligning the character of the stars and planets[588], as they were the destoryers of their own family[589]. There is, no doubt, that there are numerous people on this earth who cut off the head of their lord and carried it, just as (if it were) that of a robber, before his opponent[590]. During that period, earth and oceans were shocked, sky became cloudless and sent down heavy rain[591]. Those people penetrated against his head, they became the staff of his secretariat after the natural calamity. A new era, will be start which is known as *'Rule of the Nature' or 'Rule of the law'* in Sanskrit called 'Rita' or 'word', just as the destruction of divine images (had been commenced in *Harsa's* reign[592]). It displayed, *Uchchala* did not look at the head when he was brought from the murder[593], result was that soul had the long tears when she was burned there called as Gaurha. Therefore, the story of *'Harsa' or 'Chamar'* in Sanskrit called *'Charmkara'* is surprising like a story of *Ramayana*[595] or *Mahabharata*. It is a flash of the new light,' whose souls have been struck by delusion. After seeing and watching such want of affection on the part of the people whose minds have been absorbed by their own comfort, the heart (of men), O shame, still does not renounce the world and seek its (role) pleasure in (a residence in) the forest[596]. It is not a properity of individual who assured nothing in the beginning and nothing in the end, suddenly goes for a moment, in the interval, through the condition of happiness and again of misfortune, resembling an actor without head of feet. Where he goes, when hidden behind the curtain of mundane existence (*Sanasara*) we do not know[597]. At any time royal fortune abandoned its seat in the family of *Udayaraja,* and proceeded to that of *Kantiraja*, (while keeping) within the race of *Satavahana,* as the daylight, after having the *Himalaya* summit when it is deserted by the gods or 'Nam', (proceeds) to the celestial slopes of the mount *Meru*[598].

In this way the rule of the seventh (7th) *Taranga* of the 'Nature', composed by Great Kalhana son of Kashmiri Lord *Canpaka* is closed and proceeded towards the next which begins with the name of *Uchchala.* Thus, the rule of *Harsa* from 1089 to 1101 A.D. had a significant development in the field of life in the Kashmir History. There was high rate peace and prosperity, people love to each other, they were low-caste people of the *'Nam'* or *Chamar* race called *Sudras.*

## NOTES AND REFERENCES

1. R.T. Vol.1 Section V. p. 112.
2. *Ibid.* Book VII. p. 334.
3. *Ibid.* p. 335.
4. *Ibid.*
5. **Note.** Red Chalk (*gairika*) is used in melting gold to give it greater brilliancy. The reason behind this silence of the texts about the yellow ochre is hard to explain. This may, however, be suggested that the law-makers on painting covered both yellow ochre and red ochre by the word *gairika,*, and to them the earthen colour producing a yellow shade was, possibly, only a variety of *gairika* (A.K Bhattacharya; *Technique of Indian Painting*; Calcutta; 1976; p. 7 Hereafter explained as T.I.P.)
6. It is for Kalhana's work alone that we can gather some facts regarding his origin and person, ascribe its composition to "Kalhana, the son of the great Kashmirian minister, the illustrious Lord-*Canpaka*" There is no reason to doubt the authenticity of the information conveyed to us in the colophones. Kalhana wrote the introduction of his Chronicle in the year 1148-49 A.D. and completed his work in the year following. Considering this date and the significance of the above titles, the identity of Kalhana's father with the*Canpaka* who is repeatedly mentioned in the

Chronicle itself. In the several passages which mention *Canpaka*, we find the later invariably spoken of with evident respect for his character and activity. We first meet him as lord of the Gate (*dvarapati*) or commandant of the frontier defences in the latter part of *Harsa's* reign. On the occasion of the king's expedition against the castle of *Duguhaghata* on the Darad frontier, shortly before 1099 A.D., *Canpaka's* success ineffecting the investment of that mountain stronghold notwithstanding the intrigues of official rivals is specially eulogized. When relating Harsa's desperate struggle for his crown and life, Kalhana mentions *Canpaka* amongst the last few officials who loyally held out by the king's side. He is careful to explain *Canpaka's* absence at the final catastrophe by a detailed account of the special mission which the doomed king entrusted to him. The dialogue which *Kalhana* puts into the mouth of king and minister, bears, every appearance of historic truth. Reference every appearance of historic truth. Reference is made in it to a particular incident which, from the nature of the case, could not have well been rembered by any one except *Canpaka* himself. Its special record and that of the whole dialogue becomes intelligible in the light of the fact that Kalhana was the minister's son. This connection, too, explains the exact and graphic account which Kalhana is able to give us of the flight of the unfortunate king from the capital and of his tragic death. The only companions of Harsa on his flight and during the few days of his hiding were his faithful chamberlain *Prayaga*, and *Mukta*, a menial servent of Canpaka's household. The former was killed in fighting together with his royal master. *Mukta* alone escaped death under circumstances which Kalhana takes special care to explain and justify. It is evident that he had received his account of Harsa's last days from this sole surviving witness who belonged to his father's household. Kalhana describes *Canpaka* as a fervent worshipper at the *Tirthas* of *Nandiksetra*, the present Buthiser. This accounts for the intimate acquaintance he himself displays with that sacred site. As Canpaka's son he was likely to have accompanied his father on his regular and annual visits to the *Tirthas*. From a reference to the latter it appears that *Canpaka* was yet living about the year 1136 A.D. Incidental notices of the *Rajatarangini* enable us to trace yet another close relative of Kalhana. The Chronicle relates among many extravagant acts of *Harsa* that the music loving king presented one lakh of gold coins to *Kanaka*, a younger brother of *Canpaka*, who had gained his favour by taking lessons in singing from him. The same *Kanaka* is subsequently praised for having proved himself grateful to the memory of his royal patron. He retired, after the latter's death, to *Benares* and ended there his days in pious resignation. If this younger brother of *Canpaka* was in reality Kalhana's uncle, as there seems every reason to assume, we can account for *Harsa's* extravagant present by the family's high position. Kalhana also mentions as another meritorious act of *Kanaka* that by his timely intercession he saved the colossal *Buddha* image at *Parihasapura*, his birthplace, from destruction by king *Harsa*. The saving of the only other *Buddha* statue, which escaped the king's clutches, is ascribed to the *Buddhist S'ramana Kusalasri*. In view of this company it is difficult to avoid the conclusion that *Kanaka*, too, was personally connected in some way with Buddhist worship. The abrupt manner in which *Canpaka* is introduced to us in the first-named passage, appears to me a further indication of his identity with the Chronider's father. Kalhana when first mentioning new personages in his narrative, ordinarily particularizes their origin and position. The omission of such particulars in this case of *Canpaka* is significant. Kalhana, who seems never to have troubled himself about making his narrative intelligible to other than contemporary readers called *Champa* (*Annami*) of his father in Sanskrit language, a member from the Hindu colony of that place.(R.T. Vol.1 Section 1. pp. 6-7)

7. *R.T.* Vol.1 Section V. p. 112.
8. *Ibid.* Book VII. p. 336.
9. *Ibid.*
10. *Ibid.*
11. *Ibid.*
12. *Ibid.* p. 337.
13. P.H.K. p. 201.
14. *R.T.* Vol. 1 Section V. p. 113.
15. *Ibid. Book* VII. p. 337.
16. *Ibid.*
17. *Ibid.*
18. *Ibid.*
19. **Note.** *Dhammata* had been protected by *Thakkana* and his other brother. The two elder sons of *Tanvanga* seem to have died in exile.
20. *R.T*. Vol.1 Section V., p. 113.
21. *Ibid.* Book VII, p. 338.
22. *Ibid.*
23. *Ibid.*
24. *Ibid.*
25. *Ibid.*
26. *Ibid.*
27. ***Note.*** The upper valley of the *Kisanganga* is meant, which is to this day inhabited by *Darads*. The *Daradas* are the modern *Dards* regarding whose territory and ethnography may be consulted. Their seats, which do not seem to have changed since the times of Herodotus, extended from *Citral* and Yasin, across the *Indus* regions of *Gilgit, Cilas*, and *Bunji* to the *Kishanganga* valley in the immediate north of Kashmir. The tribes inhabiting the latter valley are meant in most of the passages in which the chronicle mentions the *Daradas or Darads*. It can be reached by several mountain tracks from the Sindh valley i.e *Lahara* (*Lar*). The name of *Lahara* survives in the designation of the modern district *Lar;* which comprises the whole of the territory drained by the sind and its tributaries. This identification is correctly indicated by crossing the *Vitasta* at its

confluence with the *Sindhu* (opposite *Shadipor*), *Vijayamalla* avoids the necessity of crossing subsequently the latter river on his way to the *Dard* country.

28. **Note.** The 'town of the *Darads*' (*Daratpura*), mentioned here, situated probably in the *Kisanganga* Valley. It is, perhaps, meant the modern *Gurez,* the chief place of the upper *Kisanganga* Valley. The epithet *girigupta* 'hidden in the mountains', would well apply to that place. *Gurez* lies in a valley whose level ground is nowhere more than about one mile broad; all around rise high mountain ranges.
29. **Note.** The title *Sahi* of the *Dard* ruler is indicated by *Law* or *Rita*, which fills the locuna here shown in *Above*. The title *Shah* has been borne for centuries back by the *Dard* rulers of *Citral* and Yasin. Whether it is of pre-*Muhammadan* origin and connected with the royal title of the *Sahis* of the *Kabul* Valley, is doubtful.
30. *R.T* Vol.1. Book VII. p. 339.
31. *Ibid.*
32. *P.H.K.* p. 204.
33. *R.T.* Vol.1. Book VII. p. 339 **Note.** Can the change of fashion trend here referred to have had something to do with the spread of customs from the Muhammadan West to the East. It is only the theory of mind which took the shape of fashion trends into the society as an disorder of the nature. Therefore, displeasure has been permeated in the society itself, because mind is a *Satan* thinker.
34. *Ibid.* p. 340.
35. **Note.** Term *tanka* means here, as well as living *man,* simply 'coin-type' or 'die' and does not designate a coin of 'fine gold' here given to *tanka* to *tankapati*, 'mind-master' *tankasala* 'mint'. It has been described the actual coins to which Kalhana refers here. They are of gold, and bear *Harsa's* gold. Their type is quite different from that maintained through the whole of Hindu coinage of Kashmir. The facts of the coins are being made in imitation of those of *Karnata* is fully corroborated by the coins of that country. It may be noted that these coins are extremely rare, while the ordinary copper (or brass) coins of *Harsa* are quite common to the present day.
36. R.T. Vol 1. Book VII, p. 340.
37. *Ibid.* **Note.** The smile is compared to the camphor on account of its brightness.
38. *Ibid.*
39. *Ibid.*
40. *Bilhana* the author of *Vikramankadevacarita* written about the eight decade of the eleventh century, may be consider as certain. The available data regarding the life and works of *Bilhana* have been set forth exhaustively in Chapter 1. of Prof. Buhler's ***Introduction.*** Kalhana notice that Bilhana left Kashmir during the reign of *Kalasa*, is of importance for the poet's biography. With reference to the weighty reasons shown by Prof. Buhler, we must assume that the period between 1063-1081 is

meant here when *Kalasa* was nominal ruler after his father's death.

41. *Parmadi* is the well-known surname or *biruda* of the *Calukya* king *Vikramaditya Tribhuvanamalla* whose family history and exploits form the subject of *Bilhana's* above mentioned poem. He ruled at *Kalyana* in the year 1076-1127 (See. L.C.P.20). Kalhana's statement as to the honours paid to Bilhana at *Parmadi's* court, agrees closely with what the poet himself tells in his work. "There the lucky poet received from the *Calukya* king, the terror of the Colas, the dignity of chief pandit, distinguished by the grant of a blue parasol and a mast elephant." Buhler.
42. R.T. Vol.1 Book VII. p. 341.
43. *Ibid.*
44. **Note.** Term *Nandana* is the name of Indra's grove. *Harsa* might have given this appellation to a pleasure garden.
45. *R.T.* Vol.1 Book VII. p. 341.
46. The Lake (*Saras*) here referred to is in all probability the lagoon called now *Pamba Sar*. This lies to the East of *Patan*, and extends as far as *Gund-Ibrahim* at 70° 39′ longitude and 34° 10′ latitude, and the stream marked *Adin* on the map.
47. R.T. Vol.1 Book VII. p. 341.
48. The bands of the Aryans marched under their leaders, who had banners. The would sing or shout the prowers of their ancestors, and boast of the aid which India or *Brihaspati* granted them. Conches were blown as horns. Sometimes the leader drove in a war-chariot covered with cowhides; some warriors used bows and arrows; others had darts. The bands often slew all in the villages they conquerred. Sometimes they were contented to carry of the plunder. When an invader attacked an Aryan settlement, ramparts were thrown up, trees were made into barricades, and the gods were called to aid. The 'weapon-song' is a hymn that echoes with the clamour of the strife. (R.V.V.R. P.17). In the *Rig-Veda Brihaspati* and *Brahmanspati* are equivalent and mean 'Lord of Prayer'. *Brihaspati* is a deity, in whom the action of the worshipper upon the gods is personified. He is the suppliant, the sacrificer, the priest who intercedes with the gods on behalf of men, and protects them from the wicked. He represents the priests and the priestly order. He is also designated as the *Purohita* of the gods. He is the lord and protector of Prayer. He is described as destroying the demon *Vala* and driving forth the cows i.e causing the clouds to yield their rain. He is also described as the father of the gods; and creator of the gods like a black-smith; to have a hundred wings; to be armed with an iron axe. In some passages he is identified with Agni, but this opposed by others. (Ibid. P.92). He sharpens and carries the great iron axe of *Brahmanaspati* and forges the thunderbolts of Indra. He forms husband and wife for each other. He has given to the heaven and earth and to all things their form. He is master of the Universe, the first born protector and leader. He bestows long life puts speed into the legs of a horse, gives blessings and is possessed of abundant wealth (Ibid.P.94). Be pleased with our oblations thou loved

of all gods, *Brihaspati*:
*Give wealth to him who brings thee gifts.*
*At sacrifies, with your hymns worship the pure Brihaspati that 'Word' or 'Nam'.*
*I pray for power which none may bend for 'Word'.*
*The Bull of men, whom none deceive, the wearer of each shape at will.*
*Brihaspati most excellent. (Ibid. p. 185).*

49. R.T vol.1 Book VII. p. 341.
50. *Ibid.*
51. *Ibid.*
52. *Ibid.*
53. **Note.** The fact underlying this poetically *extravagant* statement is that *Harsa* is the later Kashmiri king of whom authentic gold and silver pieces have hitherto be found in the *Medieval India* also noted above. Of copper and brass coins *Harsa* appears to have struck a very large quantity, these pieces being far more commonly met within the *Bazars* nowadays than those of any other Kashmiri ruler. His gold and silver coins are, on the contrary, extremely rare.
54. R.T. Vol.1 Book VII. p. 342.
55. **Note.** Term *Sunna*, here we meant that the temple of the god is empty without *'Nam'* or *'word'* which god has given to us for the purpose of the realization of 'Him'.
56. **Note**. Term *dandanayaka* is found only for those official (people) which has the designation of *Sunna*. Its literal meaning is 'prefect of punishments'. The term as well as *sarvadandanayaka*, is found in Nepal and Canarese inscriptions.
57. *R.T.* Vol.1 Book VII. p. 342.
58. *Suryamulaka* religion was normally aniconic, and in their pantheon the female element was subordinated to the male, and the place of honour was given to deities like *Indra, Varuna, Mitra*, the *Nasatyas*, *Surya, Agni* (Fire) and other supernatural beings who seem to have been quite unknown to the originators of the "Indus" culture (A.H.I. p. 24). It is certain that the tablets belong to a period in the evolution of the Aryan religion when *Indra, Varuna*, and the other gods associated with them, still retained their early Vedic pre-eminence and had not yet been thrown into the shade by the Brahmanic *Prajapati* or the epic and Puranic *Trimurti* (Ibid. p. 25). Other important deities of the upper realm of light are *'Surya'*, the illuminator,; *Savitri,* the Enlivener; *Pushan,* the Nourisher; Vishnu Urukrama, the wide striding Sun; the *Asvina* or the *Nasatyas,* perhaps the morning and evening stars, later the gods of healing, parallel to the *Dioscuri*; and *Ushas*, the lovely Goddess of the Dawn. Between the world of light above and the earth below lies the realm of the air,and the chief deities of this region are, besides *Indra*, the *Maruts* (Storm Gods), *Vayu* and *Vata* (the Wind Gods), *Rudra* (the Howling God of Storm and Lighting), and *Parjanya* (the God of Rain). Of the terrestrial deities, the chief are *Agni, Soma* and *Saraswati*. *Agni*,

or the Fire God, received special homage because no sacrifice could be performed without offerings to him. The libation of *Soma* was also regarded later as the Goddess of learning. Of the three principal deities of the later mythology, *Vishnu* and *Rudra* (Siva) are, as we have been already kown to the *Rig-Veda*, and *Brahma*, though not explicity mentioned, has his precursors in *Vidhatri* (the ordainer), *Hiranyagarbha* (the Germ of Gold), *Prajapati* (the Lord of Creatures) and *Brahmanaspati* (the lord of Prayer). An important characteristic of *Vedic Mythology* is the pre-dominance of the male element.Goddesses like *Prithivi, Aditi Ushas* and *Sarasvati* occupy a very subordinate position. In this respect the vedic civilization presents a contrast to the prehistoric culture of the Indus valley, where the mother Goddess is co-equal with her male partner (*Ibid. p. 39*).

59. R.T. Vol.1 Book VII. p. 342.
60. *Canpaka*, repeatedly mentioned as a chief official of *Harsa*, cannot be anyone else but Kalhana's father, who in the colophons bears the title *'Prabhu'*, 'Lord'. Any doubt on this point is removed by the evident, care shown by Kalhana in his account of *Harsa's* end to justify *Canpaka's* conduct in those critical circumstances, and of a servant of the latter, *Jelaka*, is of interest, as it indicates the probable source from which Kalhana gathered his detailed account of the last days of *Harsa*. It might be concluded that *Canpaka* had ultimately retired to *Nandiksetra* i.e the Tirtha of *Bhutesvara*. It has been already shown above that we have a recognise in this *Kasvira* the original Prakrit form which Ptolemy's *Kao^eipa, Kao^eipia* (Pronounced *Kaspira, Kaspiria*) are intended to transcribe. Linguistic science can furnish no clue to the origin of the name nor even analyze its formation. This fact however, has not saved the name from being subjected to various etymological guesses which for curiosity's sake may receive here a passing notice. It must be held to the credit of Kasmirian Sanskrit authors that their extant writings are wholly innocent of this display of etymological fancy. If the *Unadisutra*, P.472, *Kaser mut Ca,* is to be applied to the word *Kasmira*, the latter would have to be dissolved into *Kas-m-ira* according to the traditional grammatical system. No less illustrious a person than the emperor *Babar* opens the list. His suggestion was that the name may be derived from the hill-tribe *'Kas'* living in the neighbourhood of *Kashmir*. We easily recognize here the reference to the *Khasas* of the lower hills. Their name, however, in its true form has, of course, no connection with Kashmir. Another etymology, first traceable in Haider Malik's chronicle and hence reproduced by other Muhammadan writers, derives the first part of the name from *'Kashap'*, i.e, *Kasyapa*, and the second either from Ks.*Mar* i.e, *Matha*, '*habitation*', or *a* word *mir*, supposed to mean 'mountain'. It was, perhaps, a belief that this whimsical etymology represented some local tradition, which induced even so great a scholar as Burnout to risk the conjectural explanation of *Kashmira* as *Kasyapamira*, i.e. 'the sea of Kasyapa'. There is neither linguistic nor any other evidence to support

this conjecture. It would hence scarcely have been necessary to refer to it had it not, on the authority of a great name, found its way also into numerous works of more general character. Now, however, *Cakradhara* is no longer visited as a *Tirtha*, though the *Purohitas* of *Vijayesvara* still retain a recollection of the former sanctity of the site.

61. *R.T.* Vol.1 Book VII. p. 342 *Note* .The skin of the black antelope is required at religious ceremonies for the seating of the *Purohita.*
62. *Ibid. Note.* Regarding the Tirtha of *Tripuresvara,* a striking confirmation of this surmise is afforded by the only passage of the Sanskrit Chronicles which mentions the *Pir Pantsal* pass by its proper name. *S'rivara*, iii, 433, when relating the return of a Kashmir refugee 'by the route of *S'urapura'* in the time of *Hassan Shah* (1472-84 A.D), tells us of a fatal chill he caught 'on the top of the *Pancaladeva*'. It is clear that the name here used corresponds exactly to the modern *Pir Pantsal*, 'Pir' being the nearest Muhammadan equivalent for *'Deva'*. Dr. Bernier's has already shown us that popular superstition had not failed to transfer also the supernatural powers of the *'Deva'* to the *'Pir'* who acted as his representative on the Pass called '*Nam*' or '*Sabad*'.
63. *Ibid.*
64. *Ibid.* p. 343.
65. *Ibid.*
66. **Note**. Term *dana* corresponding with the Latin word '*domus*' or '*Domba'* is ued in Sanskrit for a single house or home (John Wilson; *Indian Caste*, New Delhi; 1976; Vol. II. P.109. Hereafter referred as *C.I.*). Prof. Wilson gives "race" as the supplied word, but this seemingly on the authority of *Sayana* (Ibid. P.108).
67. **Note.** The context clearly requires here emendation of *Lohara* for *Lahara* as of *Preryamano* for *Puryamano* compared with *Prahitair* and as *Bhuvanaraja* had the lust of power. The identical clerical error has also occured in the name *Lohara* or *Lahara*. We have seen that *Hiuen Tsiang* and Ou-K'ong coming from the ancient Gandhara and *Urasa*, followed it on their way to Kashmir, and that it was well-known to Alberuni. But it seems probable that its importance, military and commercial, was then for smaller than that of the *Pir Pantsal* and Tosamaidan routes. It is only in modern times that this western route has attained real prominence. The originated in the time of the Afghan rule over Kashmir, when the route along the *Vitasta* to Muzzaffarabad and have through *Hazara*, afforded the shortest and least it lay in the *Vitasta* valley and just on the border of Kashmir territory. Kalhana have been able to trace the position of *Viranaka* at the modern hill-village of *Viran*, near the left bank of the *Vitasta* and only a short distance above *Buliasa*. The valley below the old frontier thus marked is now known as *Dvarbidi*. Its ancient name is supplied to us by an old gloss of the *Rajatarangini* which speaks of *Bolyasaka* as situated in *Dvaravati*. Local inquiries have shown that even to the present day popular tradition indicates a ridge a short distance above *Buliasa* as the eastern limit of *Dvarbidi*. In the account of

*S'amkaravarman's* above mentioned expedition six marches are counted from the capital of *Urasa* to *Bolyasaka*. This agrees exactly with the present reckoning which also counts six marches from the vicinity of *Buliasa* to *Abbottabad*. Near this place, the modern headquarters of the Hazara District, the old capital of *Urasa* was in all probability situated.

68. **Note.** The 'soldiers garrisoning the castle' (*Kotapadati or Kotabhrtya*) are repeatedly mentioned in connection with *Lohara*. *Salhana* and *Lothana* had been sent to *Lohara* as prisoners in 1112 A.D. They correspond to the *Killahdar* troops kept up in small detachments until a few years ago for the garrisoning of the numerous small forts in the hill-regions around Kashmir. These troops were permanently settled in particular forts, and generally held land in their neighbourhood.
69. Term *Darpitapura* here we meant *Harsa* was in the world, and the world was made by him, and the world knew him not.
70. *R.T.* Vol. 1 Book VII ; p. 343.
71. *A.H.I.* p. 164.
72. *Ibid.* p. 183.
73. *R.T.* Vol.1 Book VII. p. 343.
74. *Ibid.*
75. *Ibid.*
76. *Ibid.* p. 344.
77. The distance from Lohara (*Loharin*) to *Rajapuri*, i.e. the town of *Rajapuri*, Via *Surankote* and *Thanamandi* ,may be estimated at four marches. *Kandrapa* took, perhaps, a more difficult track across the mountains.
78. *Buddharaja*, the son of *Induraja*, a member of *Kularaja*.
79. *R.T.* Vol.1 Book VII. p. 344.
80. *Ibid.*
81. *Ibid.*
82. *Ibid.*
83. *Ibid.* p. 345.
84. **Note**. It is not certain what is meant here by the expression of *Paripalyam Kurvan*. From the reference made to the corporationof priests at *Parihasapura*, it might be concluded that *Ananda* had some something to do with the administration of the property of the corporation, and of the shrine to which the latter was attached. The expression of *parsad* is used throughout the *Rajatarangini* to designate the corporations, formed by the *Purohitas* of individual temples and *Tirthas*. Their members are called *Gurparisadya,* also *parsada*. The ancient divisions of *Kramarajya* and *Madavarajya* are separated by a line drawn through Srinagar. This fact, as well as the great historical interest attaching to Srinagar as the capital of the country, make it a convenient starting-point for our survey. The history of Kashmir has always been reflected as it were in that of its capital, and in particular the characteristic passage the emendation *parisadyanam* is confirmed which shows the *Gurparisadyas* of a temple in common ownship of its property. Such corporations exist to this day

at all greater Kashmirian pilgrimage places, such as the *Tirthas* of *Sarikadevi* on the *Haraparvat, Jvalamukhi* at Khruv, *Vijayesvara, Anantanaga, Vernag, Tulamulya, Kotitirtha* (Varahamula), wherever there are several families of resident of Purohits. The latter called *Thanapati* in Kashmir. In Sanskrit called *Sthanapati* and in Kashmiri called *sthanapala* easily explained in *S'arada* characters, place the fees and *daksinas* received from the pilgrims in a common fund from which after meeting the expenses on temple buildings, etc., each family receives its proper share according to a fixed rate of participation. Some of these corporations receive now from the state benefices in kind (rice) which are subject to the same rule of partnership. This system evidently applied also to the land-grants which these corporations enjoyed in old times. Notwithstanding to loss of *Samdhimat's* alleged endowments the position of the *'parsada'* must have been a comfortable on even in Kalhana's time, if we may judge from the frequent references made to their political influence during the Brahman assembly to come to a decision regarding the future king. The *Parisadyas* seem often to have adopted this procedure, and thus to have played an important part in political complications. In the latter interesting passge they are represented as bringing the sacred images and paraphernalia of their shrines along with them to the city when proceeding *en masse* to their fast. In all modern corporations of this kind. M.A. Stein come across in *Kashmir* and the *Panjab*, there is a kind of manager usually called *Darogha,* who realizes the income of the corporation from grants, pilgrims' donations, etc., and distributes it among the individual *Purohita* families. This munager takes for himself a respectable share of the revenue, and at the greater *Tirthas* is a person of considerable influence and means. He holds his office generally by inheritance but care is taken that he should not be a *Purohita* himself or connected with any of the local *Purohita* families. *Ananda* may have been an administrator of this sort at one of the temples at *Parihasapura.* Regarding the site of *Parikasapura* and the identification of its shires with ruins on the *Paraspor* Udar. *Ananda* himself is called *Vataganda* and *Canpakam* regarding the term *Padagra* equivalent to *Nanaka.*

85. *R.T.* Vol.1 Book VII. p. 345.
86. **Note.** The office of governor (*mandalesuara*) is mentioned in connection with *Lohara* the latter, as governor, seems to have held charge of Kashmir proper.
87. *R.T.* Vol.1 Book VII. p. 346. **Note.** The reading of *Utkarsaputram* is preferable to that of (*Putrav*), because the following verse speaks only of one relative of *Harsa.*
88. *Ibid.*
89. *Varanasi* was the capital city of *Kashi* which, according to the *Jataka* was the chief city in All India. The name *Varanasi* or *Baranasi* is drived from the joint name of the two streams *Varan* and *asi*, in the north and the South of the city = (*Mahajanapada*). These states were powerful. (Rajendra Pandey; *Kashi Through The Ages*; New Delhi; 1979; p. 20).

90. **Note.** Here reference is made to a certain tax which pilgrims performing S'raddhas at *Gaya* had to pay, and from which *Eramantaka* had freed *Kashmirian* visitors of the Tirtha, perhaps by means of a great donation. Exemption from this tax is mentioned again by appointing one after slaying another chief. The 'freeing of Gaya', which is recorded in an inscription of *Samvat* 1516, translated by Cunningham relates probably to a similar act of munificence. Now, a pilgrims tax has been levied at *Gaya* until quite recently for municipal purposes.
91. *R.T.* Vol.1 Book VII. p. 346.
92. Kanishka's rule lasted for twenty-three years. His immediate successor was *Vasiskha*, who had a short reign and was succeeded by *Huvishka*. The empire of *Huvishka* was not less extensive than that of the traditional patron of *Asvaghosha*. It may have spread farther to the west, as a regard of his reign has been unearthed at *Wardak* to the west of Kabul. Mathura was now a great centre of *Kushan* power and it was adorned with monuments by *Huvishka* as the city of Peshawar had been embellished by the greatest of his predecessors. For some time *Huvishka* had apparently a colleague or rival in *Kanishka* of the Ara inscription, who is described as a son of *Vajheshka*, possibly the same as *Vasishka*, and receives in addition to the titles of great king, the king of kings, son of heaven (*devaputra*) assumed by his predecessors, the novel title of *Kaisara,* "Caesar". In Kalhana's Chronicle we have a reference to the rule of "*Huṣhka, Jushka* and *Kanishka*" apparently identical with *Huvishka, Vajheshka* and his son. They were the reputed founders of three cities in Kashmir named after them. *Kanishka* of this passage may have reference to the predecessor of *Vasishka*, but it is more probable that the king referred to by Kalhana is identical with its namesake mentioned in the *Ara* inscription. The last great king was *Vasudeva*. I, who ruled from about the year 67 to 98 of the *Kanishka* era. Most of his inscriptions have been found at or near Mathura, and his coins usually bear the god Siva and rarely any Iranian deity. It is not improbable that he gradually lost touch with the north-west was hastened by the rise of the *Sassanian* dynasty of Persia. In the third century A.D. We find references to four separate kingdoms all dependent on the Yue-chi. This possibly suggests territorial disintegration through the nominal suzerainty of the "son of heaven" may have continued to be acknowledged by all these states. The rule of the Kushans in part of the Jumna valley seems to have been supplanted by that of the *Nagas*. The latter are represented as ruling over *Mathura, Padmavati* (*Padam Pawaya*) and a few other places in *Mid-India* contemporaneously with the Guptas of *Prayaga* (Allahabad), *Saketa* (Oudh) and *Magadha* (South Bihar). About the middle of the fourth century A.D. the *Nagas* were reduced to subjection by the Gupta emperors. The "Son of Heaven" continued to rule in diminished glory over an obscure corner of the Indian borderland where he soon felt the irresistible might of Gupta arms. (A.H.I. pp. 122-23).
93. *R.T.* Vol.1 Book VII. p. 347.

94. *Ibid.*
95. *Ibid.*
96. *Bilava*, only here mentioned, is probably the present village of *Bilau*, situated in the *Chirath* Pargans at 74° 55′ longitude 33° 51′ latitude (*'Belloh'* on map).
97. *R.T.* Vol.1 Book VII. p. 347.
98. **Note.** The suspicious time for the commencement of a journey astrologically falls earlier than the time by which the person concerned finds it convenient to start he may *proforma* leave his own residence and proceed to the house of a friend or other conveniently situated in the same place. He can then begin his real journey whenever convenient. The innocent ruse is still commonly practised by Kashmiri *Brahmans.*
99. *R.T.* Vol.1 Book VII. p. 347.
100. **Note.** From the study we learn that the first *Naga* dynasty was established in *Kali Samvat* 653 A.D. The first ruler of this dynasty is known *Gonanda* 1. This dynasty had thirty five kings. There were known as *Lava, Kusa, Khagendra, Surendra,* etc.
101. **Note.** Judging from the *Satadvara*, it seems to have been the designation of a separate building in the palace. Possibly a large quadrangle is meant from which a hundred doors opened. By *Catuskika* or *Catuska* (Pavilion) is meant probably an open pavilion attached to the palace, and having four pillars. At the time, on the enter of queens *'Catuskika'* had blocked its door, and the servants who wish to prevent them from buring themselves, have first to force an entrance. *Janakacandra* and *Bhimadeva,* alongwith their men, then drew swords in the pavilion to stay each other. In the morning, he stepped out into the pavilion (*Catuskika*) to reassure the citizens, and despatched mounted men to search for the troops. He (*Mallaka*) got away even from these three assailants and ran towards the king, whom he had sighted entering the door of the pavilion (*catuskika*) to worship.
102. *R.T.* Vol.1 Book VII. p. 348.
103. *Ibid.*
104. *Ibid.*
105. **Note.** The name *Bhattaranudvala* survives in that of the *Brarinambal*, a logoon fed by the *Mar* (*Mahasarit*) and situated between the south-eastern quarters of Srinagar in front of Dilawar Khan's Bagh. (*Brari* is an oblation case of *bror*, the Kalhana's derivative of *bhattaraka* Kalhana's *nambal* < Sanskrit *nadvala* is a term commonly applied to lagoons and marshes)
106. R.T. Vol.1 Book VII. p. 349.
107. *Ibid.*
108. **Note.** then *Prayaga*, by the king's order, despatched a messanger, and the murder (*titsna*) *Kalsaraja* came up along with his two sons.
109. *R.T.* Vol.1 Book VII. 349.
110. *Ibid.*
111. *Udayasiha* is probably the same person who is named *Udayasimha*, sending *Kandarpa* and others at the same time to *Lohara.*
112. *R.T.* Vol.1 Book VII. p. 350.

113. **Note.** When (prince) addressed the crowd, who knew no yielding in resolute conduct, he became like one over whom cold water had been poured in his sleep.
114. *Tulla*, the son of *Ajjaka* and grand son of *Tanvanga.*
115 *R.T.* Vol.1 Book VII. P.350.
116. *Ibid.*
117. **Note.** Term *Domba*, we have an example of an opprobrions name given for the superstitions reasons fully explained here. A small tribe allied to the *sheranis.* They are divided into two main branches, *Mahsand* and *Ghora Khel.* The former are sub-divided into four and the latter into eight sub-divisions. The *Babars* are a civilized tribe of Domba and most of them can read and write. A *Babar*, the *Amin-ul-Malik*, *Nur Muhammad Khan,* was *Diwan-i-Kul-Mamlakat* to Taimur Shah and gave a daughter to *Shah Zaman Abdali.* Four *Babar* families are also settled in Multan. They are deovted to commerce and are the wealthiest quietest and most honest tribe of the sub-*Sulaiman* plains. Edwardes called them the most superior race in the whole of the trans-Indus districts, and the proverb says. 'A *Babar* fool is a *Gandapur* sage'. Intensely democratic, they have never had a recognized chief, and the tribe is indeed a scattered one, many residing in *Kandahar* and other parts of *Khorasan* as traders. A few are still engaged in the *powinda* traffic.The *Babars* appear to have occupied their present seats early in the 14th century A.D., driving out the *Jats* and Baloch (means theory of *mind* and God) population from the plains and then being pushed northward, by the *Ushtarani* proper. Their centre is *Chandwan* and their outlay villages are held by *Jat* and *Baloch* tenants, as they cultivate little themselves. *Domba,* female *Dombani, Dum*, or less correctly *Dom*: female *Dumni*, dim. *Dumra,* according to Ibbetson the *Dum* is to be carefully distinguished from the *Dom* or *Domra*, the executioner and Corpse-burner of Hindustan, who is called *Dumna* in the hills of *Hashiarpur* and Kangra. But the *Chamba* the *Dumna* is called *Dum* and in the hill states about Simla he is a worker in bamboo. In Maya Singh's *Punjabi* Dictionary. *Dumna* is said to = 'a species of bee'. Again Ibbetson mentions the *Dum* of the plains is identical with the *Mirasi,* the latter being the Muhammadan, Arabic name for the *Hindu* and *Indian Dum.* But though the Dums may overlap the *Mirasis* and be in common parlance confused with them, they appear to be, in some parts of the *Punjabi* at least, distinct from them and Mirasis are beyond all question inextricably fused with the *Bhats.* In Gurgaon the *Dum* is said to be identical with the *Kanchan,* and to be a *Mirasi* who plays the *tabla* or *sarangi* for prostitutes; who are often *Mirasi* girls. Such *Duma* are also called *bharwa* (pimp) or *Sufardai. Dum* women as well as men ply this trade. But another account from the same District says that the *Dum* is the, *Mirasi* of the *Mirasi*; and that he gets his *alms* from the menial castes, such as the *Jhiwar, Dakaut, Koli, Chamar, Bhangi, Julaha* and *Dhanak.* In Lahore too they are described as quite beyond the *Mirasi* pale, as the true Mirasis will not intermarry with them

nor will prostitutes associate with them, though, like the *Bhands*. The Dum ranks below the *Bhand* also. The latter are skilled in *bhandar* a practise of which the *Dum* is ignorant. It consists in absorbing all the water in a large bath and ejecting it through the ears, nostrils or month. They sing and play for them when they dance or sing professionally. In fact, they rank below the *Chuhra*. So too in *Ludhiana* they are distinct from and lower than the *Mirasi*. In Dera Ghazi Khan the *dum* or *Langa* are said to be an occupational group of the *Mirasis* and to be the *mirasi* of the Baloch tribes. In other words they are identical with *Dom* or *Domba*, whose name means minstrel in Balochi. The *Dumna*, called also *Domra*, and even *Dum* in Chamba, is the *Chuhra* of the hills proper, and is also found in large numbers in the sub -mountain tracts of Kangra. Hoshiarpur and Gurdaspur. Like the *Chuhra* of the plains, he is something more than a scavenger; but whereas the *Chuhra* works chiefly in grass, the *Dumna* adds to this occupation the trade of working in bamboo, a material not available to the *Chuhra*. He makes sieves, winhowing pans, fans, matting, grass, rope and string, and generally all the vessels, baskets, screens, furniture and other articles which a re ordinarliy made of bamboo. When he confines himself to this sort of work and gives up scavengering, he appears to be called *Bhanjara*, at any rate in the lower hills, and occasionally Sarial. The *Dumma* appears hardly ever to become Musalman or Sikh, and is classed as Hindu, though being an outcast he is not allowed to draw water from wells used by the ordinary Hindu population. The *Dumna* is often called *Dum* in other parts of India, as in *Chamba*; and is regarded by Hindus as the type of uncleanners. Yet he seems once to have enjoyed as a separate aboriginal race some power and importance. Further information regarding him will be found in Sherring (1,400) and Elliot (1,84). He is, Sir Denzil Ibbetson considered, quite distinct from the *Dum-Mirasi*. *Dumna*, a low sweeper caste, also called *Bhanjra* in the hills and in Gurdaspur, Jullundar and Hoshiarpur. They make *Chiks*, baskets, etc of bamboo and do menial service. Apparently the term is a generic one, including *Barwalas, Batwals, Daolis* and *Sansois*. But in *Lahore*, where the *Dumna* is also found, he is described as distinct from the *Batwal*, and as a Hindu who is yet not allowed to draw water from Hindu wells. Some of the *Dumnas* will eat from a Muhammadans hands. Their clans are *Kalotra, Manglu, Pargat, Drahe, Lalotra*. The word is probably only a variant of *Dum. Dumra, Domba,* dim of *Dum* in the hills term is applied to any low caste which works as tailors, masons or carpenters or in bamboo. (G.T.C.P.N.W.F.P. PP. 249-51). The Dogras are also the great Aryan race settled in and has become the main population of India, those of that race who spread into the mountains. The settlers in the hills that edge the *Panjab*, all events those of them who have retain their Hindu faith. The origin of the name is this Near Jammu are two holy lakes, *Saroin Sar* and *Mansar*, which will in course be described; from this came Dugar, and from the Dogras. The hightest is of course the *Brahman* illustrates both the processes. Beyond all question the scholarship or a holy life, but when the status became hereditary all inducement to attain its qualification disappeared.The caste next in standing is the Rajputs, including *Thakurs Rathis* and *Rawats*, etc. Next below inestimation come some castes whom have been bracketed together; their occupations are various, but in rank they are near equal. These are *Banya, Krar, Nai and Jiur* with some others. They include the lower class of traders of different kinds, shopkeepers for the most part small and petli fogging; they included the *barbers* and others whose business it is to minister to the wants of those above them, especially the carriers, called *Kahars* in the plains; but here called *Jiurs*, whose occupations are the carriage of loads on the shoulders, including the *Palankin*, and the management of the flour mills worked by water. Last come those whom the Englishmen generally called "Low Caste Hindu" but who in the mouth of a Hindu would never bear that name; they are no recognised as Hindu at all; they are not allowed even a low place among them the names of these castes are *Megh* and *Dum* and to these must one called *Dhiyar,* whose occupation is iron-smelting and who seem to be classed generally withothers. These tribes are the descendants of the earlier, the pre-Aryan, inhabitants of the hills, who became, on the occupation of the country by the Hindus, by the Aryans, enslaved to them. They were not necessarily slaves to one person, but were kept to do the low and dirty work for the community still their position; they are the scavengers of the towns and villages. *Dhiyars* have also the low employment though they seem ethnologically allied to the *Meghs* and *Dums*. *Dums* and *Megha* are in large scale at Jummu. They have been also scattered all over the country, both the outer hills and the next higher mountains. They get a scanty living by such employments as brickmaking and charcoal burning, and by sweeping. They are liable to be called on at any time by the authorities for work that no others will put their hand to. A result of this class of labour being done by them is that they are reckoned utterly unclean, anything they touch is polluted. No Hindu would dream of drinking water from a vessel they had carried, even if they had brought it suspended at the end of a pole. The *Meghs* and *Dums* have physical characters that distinguish them from the other castes. They are commonly darker in colour, while the others of these parts have a moderately light brown complexion; these people are apt to be as dark as the natives of India below Delhi. The *Meghas* seem to hold a position as regards the *Dums*. Somewhat like that of the Brahmans among Hindus. Of those, in all probabilty are the *Julahs,* that is, weavers, whom form a large proportion of the Muhammadans of Jammu so much so that one word of the town is called "the weavers quarter". (Fredric Drew; *The Jammoo and Kashmir territories,* Reprint; New Delhi 1999 PP.55-57. Hereafter referred as J.K.T.) Low down the Jhelam river, west of *Kotli* and of *Mirpur,* there is a caste or tribe called *Gakkars or Kokkars,* these, with other high castes, would be classed as *"Sahu"* (Ibid.P. 59).

Beginning with lowest of the four, we find the *Dums* acting as musicians, like the low caste *Mirasis* of the Panjab and *Domas* of other parts of India, and like also the *Bems* of Ladakh and the *Batals* of *Kashmir* (Ibid. P. 426). Such names are still common throughout the whole India, and are usually given to children born after the death of their elder predecessor.

118. R.T. Vol.1 Book VII. p. 350.
119. **Note.** According to the author of the *Samaranguna-Sutradhara,* there are five type of brush, viz, *Kurea, hastakurca, bhasakurca, callakurca* and *Vartani*. Of these five types the first one is shaped like the sprout of a banyan tree, the second like the sprout of as *asvattha* (*Ficus religiosa*), is called *Caladala* because its leaves are every dropping, the third one like the sprout of an Indian fig (*plaksa-sucinibha*), and the fourth like the sprout of an *udumbara (Ficus Glomerata)*. It is enjoined that the broad lines are not to be drawn with a brush having the shape of the sprout of a banyan tree i.e. *Kurca*, and fine lines are not to be executed with the help of a brush shaped like the sprout of a *plaksa* tree i.e. *bhasakurca*. The application of white priming i.e. *Lepyakarma*, should be made with a brush having the shape of the sprout of an *undumbara* tree, i.e. *callakurca*. It is, however, difficult to arrive at any clear conclusion on the basis of the data gleaned from severely damaged verses of the *Samarangana-sutradhara*. Nevertheless, this much can be known that the Indian painters were habituated in the use of various types of brush. From the etymological consideration of the terms like *Callakurca* and *bhasakurca*, it is also possible to surmise that the brushes with different names played distinctive roles in the process of making a painting. As reards the materials used in preparing them, it is advised that the fibres of bark and the hard hairs are good for the purpose. Experts in painting, however, favoured brushes made of hairs of the ear of a bullock. For a brush used in anointing colour, fibre is said to be the best material. It is further known that bamboo-sticks generally served as handle. Classification of the brushes on the basis of their thickness and thinners, and the role they play in delineating a painting, may also be found in the *Manasollasa*. (T.I.P. p. 50).
120. *R.T.* Vol.1 Book VII. p. 351.
121. *Ibid.*
122. *Ibid.*
123. *Ibid.* p. 311.
124. *Ibid.* p. 351.
125. **Note.** During the time of *Harsa* a *'Great Bridge'* (*Brhatsetu*) was built on the *Vitasta*. Only since then is such construction of boat-bridges (*nausetu*) known. *'Brhatsetu'*, 'the Great Bridge', must be taken in all probability as a proper name. It is certainly used as such in term Brhatsetu designating probably the 'chief bridge' in the Srinagar of Kalhana's time. The same term is used for the boat-bridge which *Pravarasena* II. is said to have constructed. As this boat-bridge was evidently the first of its kind

in the country, the name might have clung to the bridge which continued to be maintained in the same locality. Where this locality was unable to ascertain. Keeping in view, the position occupied by the old parts of Srinagar founded by *Pravarasena* himself. It inclined to look into the vicinity of the present. Fourth or Fifth Bridge as a likely place for *Pravarasena's* bridge. Up to the fourth bridge the river forms an almost straight reach, and the smoke rising from *Maksikasvamin* is probably the old name for the island of *Mayasum,* lying between the *Tsunth Kul* and the *Vitasta*. It could be easily seen from this point. It is certain that *Maksikasvamin* was the name of a part of S'rinagar or a suburb immediately adjoining the capital. Therefore, *Maksikasvamin* can be safely identified with the island of *Mayasum,* which lies at the South East corner of Srinagar between the *Vitasta* and the two branches of the Tsonth Kul or *Mahasarit*. The western-most point of *Mayasum* lies almost opposite to the southern extremity of *Kathul,*and the fire could easily have been carried across the river there by a high wind. The legendary account which these verses give of the foundation of *Pravarasena*' town, can be correctly understood only in connection with the topography of modern Srinagar. At the latter, it has already been correctly fixed the site of *Pravarsena's* capital. In the support of this identification he referred to the general agreement of the description given above with the situation of the present capital and to the testimony furnished by Hiuen-Tsiang. The latter names as his quarters in the capital of Kashmir that very *Vihara* of *Jayendra* which we know that the pilgrim on his arrival at the Kashmir capital stopped at the convent (Vihara) of *Che-ye-in-to-lo* or *Jayendra*. There he received instruction in the various *Sastras* from the chief of the priests of the establishment and probably spent most of his two years stay in the country (631-633 A.D.) that this establishment was identical with the *Jayendravihara* of our text. *Jayendra's* 'Great Buddha' was probably a colossal statue like the *Brhadbudda* which king Lalitaditya erected in copper at *Parihasapura* and reached upto the sky. In order to kill the Damara *Samgrama*, who, when attached by assassin, had entered the famous *Jayendravihara,* he (*Ksemagupta*) had the latter burned down without marcy and its Buddha-statue melted down by king *Ksemagupta,* who used its brass for the consturction of the *Ksemagaurisvara* temple. Another colossal Buddha statue in the city is mentioned under *Harsa* and *Sussala*. For a *Brhaetbuddha* which survived to the 14th century A.D., to have been built by *Pravarasena* II's maternal uncle in the new city. Subsequently, called attention to designations surviving for parts of the modern city, such as *Didamar* (*Diddamatha*) *and Bradmar* (*Bhattarakamatha*), which prove its identity with the town of *Pravarasena* II. It is confirmed by the fact that the name *Pravarapura* (for *Pravarasenapura* shortened *bhimavat*) can be traced throughout the works of *Ksemendra, Bilhana,* Kalhana and the later Chroniclers as the appellation of the city occupying the site of the present Srinagar. To the present day it has also continued to be used in this sense in colophons of *Janmapattras* and other documents of the study. The most convincing proof is, however, furnished by the long list of buildings and localities which are mentioned by the chronide in thenew capital, and which beginning with *Pravarasena's* own great temple *Pravaresa*, can actually be identified within the modern S'rinagar or in its immediate vicinity. Looking then within the precincts of the present Srinagar for the local names mentioned in our legend, we can in the first place identify that of the river *Mahasarit*. It had previously not been recognised as a name at all, but a series of passages proves that if was the ancient appellation of the stream which issues from the Dal Lake and joins the *Vitasta* at the South East extrmity of Srinagar. *Tejahsena* by the King's order was impaled and also *Marica,* the son of the commander of horse, *Lavaraja* Kalhana narrates that the body of King *Uchchala* who had been murdered in his palace at Srinagar, was hurriedly cremated by a few faithful servants at the burning place which lay 'on the island situated at the confluence of the *Mahasarit* and *Vitasta*'. A reference to the map of Srinagar will show that the only island in or near the capital which can be said to be situated at the meeting of the *Vitasta* with another stream. The name *Mayasum* can be traced back without difficulty to *Maksikesvamin* through intermediate *Apabhramsa* forms in which the first part of the name, *Maksika*, was turned, perhaps, into *Mahiya, Mahya Maya*. For the identity of *Maksikasvamin* with *Mayasum* speaks the mention of the former inconnection with a great fire which arose in *Kasthila*, the modern Kathul, a quarter of Srinagar situated nearly opposite to *Mayasum*. Long before the island of *Mayasum* was taken up for the modern European quarters, there existed a thickly populated suburb at its western extremity near the first city bridge. A *Maksikasvamin* Naga is mentioned by the *Nilamata-Purana*. The conclusion to be drawn from this regarding the identity of Kalhana's *Mahasarit* is further confirmed by the fact that close to the place where the western brance of the Dal stream joins the *Vitasta* (a little below the present first bridge, there existed till the times of Maharaja Ranbir Singh a Hindu burning Ghat. In the fifteenth century A.D., an identical locality can be safely assumed that it marked the site of the burning ground referred above and alluded to in our own passage. *S'rivara* gives to the place the more modern name *Marisamgama*, which from a passage of the *Vitastamahatmya*, can be proved with cerainty to apply to the junction above indicated. Though *Tilaka* stood at *Vijayesvara,* yet the Damaras resident in (the districts) *Khaduvi* and *Holada*, marched on and made an attack on the bank of the *Mahasarit*. Thereupon all the Damaras from *Madavarajya* marched on and occupied the bank of the *Mahasarit*. On one occasion the Damaras, upon a given signal, fell together upon the city in a combined attack after crossing the *Mahasarit. Yasoraja, Bhiksu, Prthvihara* and the rest eager to break into the city stood on the bank of the *Mahasarit* where was nothing to obstruct them. *Trillaka* and others counted upon reaching the banks of the *Mahasarit,* and the Damaras of

Nilasva were to make an attempt for *'Nam'* or *'Sabad'* as *Visa* on the centre of the city. In them stream is spoken of as on the line of attack upon the city, in particular for forces coming from the East. A reference to the map will again show that the shallow stream coming from the Dal forms actually the South-Eastern boundary for that part of Srinagar which lies on the right bank of *Vitasta* and contains the greater portion of the city. Protected as it is on the East and West by the lakes of the Dal and Anchiar, and on the South by the *Vitasta*, this part of Srinagar can be attakced with advantage only over the narrow neck of land in the North or across the stream issuing from the Dal in the South-East this stream, now known by the nameof *TsunthKul*, 'the apple-tree canal', is bounded along its right or North bank by an old embankment about one and a half miles long, which stretches from the rocky foot of the *Takht* hill in the East close to the high-lying bank of the *Vitasta* antiquity of this embankment. Without its large portions of the city which are built along the low-lying shores of the Dal and the numerous channels stretching from the latter to the west, would along with all the 'floating gardens' of the lake be exposed to annual inundations from the river. A further proof of its antiquity is furnished by the fact that this embankment bears along with the quarter built on it merely the general name of *Suth*, from Sanskrit *'Setu'*, *'dyke'*, whereas all the other numerous embankments and causeways about S'rinagar have distinctive appellations. Several topographical considerations combine to prove that it was this old dyke or *'Setu'* which the popular legend related by Kalhana represented as the leg and knee of the demor who helped *pravarasena* to cross the *Mahasarit*. In the first place we can see from the map that the dyke described actually turns sharply at an angle of 90 degrees opposite to the camping-ground known as the Chinar Bagh. It thus curiously resembles a bent knee. Still more convincing is the fact that we find the name of *Ksurikabala*, which according to verse the modern name *Khudabal* to which it corresponds. The Kashmiri's word *bal*, meaning 'place', is frequently found as the final part of local name in Kashmir *Yarabal* ('friends meeting place') *Marabal, Pokhribal*, etc. shows the great part these embankments play in the daily life of the people marked the spot where *Pravarasena* reached firm ground, still attaching in its Kashmir derivative *Khudabal*, to the city quarter situated at the west end of the embankment. (For the phonetic connection of *Khudabal* and *Ksurikabala*, compare with Kashmiri *Khur* < Sanskrit *Ksura*. A new popular etymology which saw in *Khur* the word *Khud,* "hollow", might have helped in the change of *Ksurikabala* > *Khudabal* ). Finally it should be noted that Kalhana's description of the *'Setu'* dividing the water of *Mahasarit* (*mahasaritovari, setusimantitam, (iii).* 345) is exactly applicable to the *Suth*, if we assume that the various channels and marshes which lie immediately to the North of the dyke, and are like the *Tsunth Kul* fed by the waters of the Dal, were also comprised under the name of *Mahasarit*. That this was indeed the case, is rendered highly probable by the fact that the whole network of these waterways to the North of the *Suth* has retained to the present day the name of *Mar*, which we have encountered above in the form *Mari* as an earlier appellation of *TsunthKul*. The question whether we have to see in this form *Mar* a phonetic derivative of Sanskrit *Mahasarit* or *Vice Versa* in the latter form a Sanskrit adaptation of some earlier Kashmiri name, cannot be settled from our present materials and its decision would not affect the topographical conclusion above indicated. Long after the name of the village *Saritaka*, where the demon showed to *Pravarasena* the site for his new town, can no longer be traced , but its position is sufficiently indicated by the mention of the goddess *Sarika*. The latter, a form of Durga, has been worshipped since ancient times on the North-West side of the hill which lies immediately of the North of the central part of Srinagar and is called after her *Sarikaparvata* or Kashmir *Haraparvat*. The distance of the hill from *Khudabal* is about one and three-quarter miles. The legend told at length in the *Sarikamahatmya* related to Durga, taking the shape of a *Sarika* bird (*Maina*), carried in her beak the hill from Mount Meru to its present place in order to close a gate of the Daityas dwelling in hell. Subsequently, she took up her abode on the hill to make sure of their not escaping. This story is also briefly referred to in the *Kathasar*. For another name of the hill, *Pradyumnapitha,* in honour of this magician who was the very image of Brahman and the foremost of the philosophers (*brahmavid*) the queen caused the exceedingly splendid (hall called) *Brahmanandapa* to be erected. A modern popular etymology, generally accepted by Panjabis and European, has turned the Hill S'arika into the 'Hill of Hari' or 'the Verdant mountain" *Harsa* discovered that (measuring line) which the *Vetala* had laid down, at village *Saritaka* at which the goddess *Sarika* and the demon (*Yaksa*) *Atta* resided. It is possible that he figured merely in the popular etymology of the name *Saritaka* which that verse evidently alludes to. But it may be noted that another translation is also possible. *Attena* might be taken as an instrumental from the word *atta*, tower, which would be a poetic designation of the hill, called *srnga* in the Mahatmya. We should then translate: " '*Word*' at the village *Saritaka,* at which the goddess *S'arika* with her towering (hill) and the Yaksa resided." The demon of the legend whom Kalhana calls alternately bhuta, *raksas, vetala*, might well be designated also as *Yaksa*. *Sarika* renders to *S'aritaka* by *Haratath*. If this gloss is intended for the name of the village *Haratrath,* in the Paraspor Pargana, $74^0$ 41' longitude, $34^0$ 9' latitude, no value can be attached to it, as the distance of the latter place from Srinagar precludes all thought of its being meant in the legend here related. The term *Vetalasutrapata* contains clearly a reference to the legend told of the demon which indicate to *Pravarasena* the site for his new city. It appears that the locality where the *Vetala* was supposed to have laid his measuring line, was known by the name of *Vetalasutrapata*; but its position cannot be clearly gathered from that passage. It is curious that of the numerous permanent wooden bridges over the *Vitasta,* whose peculiar construction has attracted the notice of all modern travellers in Kashmir, none can be traced back to an earlier date than the *Zaina Kadal,* one of the seven bridges of Srinagar, built by Zain-ul-abidin in the 15th century A.D. Were the engineers of hte Hindu period who showed such skill in stone architecture less versed in bridge construction than their Muhammadan successors, who built chiefly in wood? the passage shows that the building of stone bridges over greater rivers was unknown in Kashmir during the Hindu times.

126. *R.T.* Vol.1 Book VII. p. 351.
127. *Ibid.* p. 352.
128. **Note.** For the term *Parisadya*, the revenue of the great villages which he gave as endowment for each Linga, has through the lapse of time become lost now-a-days to the Purohita corporations (*Parsad*).
129. *R.T.* Vol.1 Book VII. p. 351.
130. *Ibid.*
131. **Note.** The term *rudhabharodhi*, corresponding to the modern *Begar*, has been explained probably the first reference to the system of forced labour, which under the name of *Kar-begar* has remained to this day one of the most characteristic features of Kashmir administration. The nature of the country, and the absence of proper roads, renders it necessary to use load-carriers in preference to all other means of transport. The system of *Corvee* entailed hereby opens the way for much oppression. The manifold abuses connected with *'Begar'* in Kashmir. In the absence of a special labouring class, the whole demand for transport labour falls on the villagers. Expeditions outside the valley have at all times been dreaded by the agriculturists, on account of the hardships implied by the increased requisitions for carriage. Until the recent road to Gilgit was constructed the rumour that transport was required for troops going in, or coming from, that direction, would cause a general stampede among the villagers. It has been already pointed out that the system of forced carriage by villagers or *Begar,* has in old days as up to the present time been the only means available for military transport in and about Kashmir. The system is not likely to have been worked with greater leniency in Kalhana's days than in modern times. We may safely conclude from the author's discreet allusion that the success of *Dhanya's* commissariat arrangements was attained at an expense of human life and human suffering, perhaps not smaller than that which accompanied generally the annual transport of stores for the Gilgit garrison until the construction of the *'Gilgit Road'* a few years ago. *Samkaravarman* was certainly not the first levy *Begar* for transport purposes, but he seems to have given in this *Corvee* a systematic organisation (*rudhabharodhi*), and to have used it also for fiscal extortion. Villagers, it appears, who did not turn up to carry their allotted roads, wee fined by the value of the latter at enhanced rates and the same fine was levied the following year a second time from the village as a whole. The thirteen kinds of the *Corvee* referred

above cannot be specified. The term *rudhabharodhi* recurs, where exemption from this impost is mentioned as a privilege from this impost is mentioned as a privilege granted to the Purohitas of a temple. Possibly the term included, like the modern *Kar-begar,* the various requisitions for village produce, until recently free of payment, which could be made by officials. The context requires the emendation *Krtaprayaih* for *Krtaprayopavesa*: "I then began a *Prayopavesa*, but somehow the different judges decided against him, giving on each occasion judgement in favour of the defendant", who held solemn fasts (*Praya*) and immolating themselves in fires. The term *sthanapala* (temple-purohitas) corresponds to the modern Kashmir *thanapati* in Sanskrit *sthanapati*, and designates, like *Parisadya* or *parsada*, the members of the Purohita-corporations at sacred shrines, and *sthanapati, Samayan,* all the other friends of the king, like *Ganga* and the rest, died also. Only *Tunga,* with his brothers, remained to enjoy pleasures.

132. **Note**. It is doubtful whether the word *devanayaka* is really a proper name, or only an ironical designation of '*Udayaraja* whom *Harsa* is said to have appointed as 'prefect for the overthrow of divine images' (*devotpatananayaka*). No mention is made subsequently of *Udayaraja*. Kalhana refers here to the image of *Parihasakesava* placed by Lalitaditya at *Parihasapura*. According to the pure-minded king, the *pala*, which according to the authorities corresponds to 4 *Karsa*, each of 16 *masa,* must be taken as =4 *tolaka*. The *tolaka*, the modern *Tola*, is in Kashmir still as in Abu-I-Fazl's time (*Ain-i-Akbari*, Vol.II. PP. 354, 366) =16 *masa* = 96 *raktika* (*rats*). This *prastha* is usually estimated at 16 *pala*. The term *pal* is still used in Kashmir for 1/20 *Ser*. This image contained 84,000 *Palas* of silver, which, accepting the calculation given in the note on that passage, would correspond to a weight of 336,000 *Tolakas*, or approximately as many rupees. The currency value of this mass of silver in the Kashmir of *Harsa's* time cannot be estimated with exactness. But it must have been far greater than that of the equivalent amount of rupee coinage at the present times. Regarding the term *dinnara* (*dinara*) *spoke by Kalhana* we cannot fail to note that they range themselves under two heads. *Either* Dinnaras are mentioned in a general way without any particular amount or quantity being specified. *Or* we have exact statements of cash amounts, coupled with the term *dinnara* had to be taken in the general sense of 'coin' or 'money', was made quite evident by the passage which mentions under king *Harsa*, 'Dinnaras of gold, silver and copper'. Here we have clearly the word *dinnara* in the sense of *mudra*,' coin', distinctly given to it by the *Unadikosa*. The latter word is commonly used to this day in the sense as 'money', in particular, 'coined money' or 'cash.' It is evident that according to the interpretation of the glossator *dinnara* is not the designation of any particular monetary value, but term of much more general significance, corresponding somewhat ot our 'cash' or 'currency'. This, however, occurred only in the year preceding *Harsa's* death, and at a time when he must have been

reduced to great financial straits by *Uchchala's* rebellion.

133. R.T. Vol.1 Book VII. p. 353 **Note.** The gloss of the word gives the meaning of Kalhana's *ganyar* (plural *ganya*), 'log of wood'. The meaning of this word is a tropical grass with tall thick stems from which sugar is extracted. It has the comparative study of the 'Nam' that one can extract from this god gifted body.

134. **Note.** From the legend related by Kalhana, it can be concluded that the shrines of *Ranesa* and *Ranasvamin* were within or near the city of Srinagar and at no great distance from each other that of *Ranasvamin*, however, appears to have enjoyed greater celebrity, and some of the references permit us to trace its approximate position. When *Svapaka* woman of *Dombas* ruler *Cakravarman* went, on the festival of *Tiladvadasi*, to visit the (temple of Visnu) *Ranasvamin,* only the proud Damaras among the chiefs did not follow her. Kalhana mentions the queen of *Cakravarman* paid a visit to *Ranasvamin* in the month of *Magha,* which is the time for the greatest snowfall in the valley and, therefore, least suitable for travelling shows that shrines must have been within easy reach from the palace. In *Srikanthac*, iii. 68, *Mankha*, Kalhana's contemporary, refers to his father's worship of *Ranasvamin,*and *Jonaraja* in his commentary distinctly describes the latter as *'Sripravarapura-pradhanadevata.'* Jonaraja in his own chronile, 872, has further left us the notice, that *Zain-ul-abidin* carried the canal called *Jainaganga* on which his new 'town' *Jainanagari* was built, 'as far as *Ranasvamin'*. As *Jonaraja* indicates in verse 870 with laudable accuracy the *Pradyumnagari* and *Amaresapura*, i.e the Haraparvat and *Amburher* i.e. *Amaresvara*, about two and a half miles to the south of *Ranyil*, it is clear that this last named place is meant by *Hiranyapura.* Similarly, when *Uchchala* marches from *Lohara*, i.e., the Sind valley, to the siege of the capital, he has his *abhiseka* ceremony performed *en route* by the *Brahmans* of *Hiranyapura*. As the extreme limit of *Jainanagari,*it is clear that this canal is identical with the one now called *Lacham Kul* in Sanskrit called *Laksmikulya* which brings the water of the Sind river via *Amburher* into the quaters of *Naushahra* and *Sangin Darwaza.* The latter lies immediately to the West of the *Haraparvat.* The canal continues hence its southerly direction to the *Jama Masjid* and ultimately emplies itself into the *Mar* canal near the bridge *Kadi Kadal.* It could be proved that the present termination of the *Lacham Kul* is the same which *Jonaraja* knew in the time of Zain-ul-abidin 1459 A.D., inclined to identify with the *Ranasvamin* the ruin of ancient temple which lies in the corner formed by the Mar and *Lacham Kul.* It owes its partial preservation to the fact that it has been utilized by the Muhammadans as the Ziarat of Pir Haji Muhammad Sahib. Besides the walls of a raised octagonal cella and the stairs leading to its two doors, the enclosing walls and the gateways of the ancient courtyard are yet standing. The building has not been noticed in any of the papers dealing with the remains of the ancient architecture of Kashmir. If the Lacham Kul ended in old days

further North in the branch which flows into the Dal lake near the *Butakadal,* we might took for the *Ranasvamin* among the numerous ruins of ancient temples found about the mosque of Madin Sahib in the North part of Sangin *Darwaza*. Pt. Sahibram in his *Tirthas,* briefly refers to the *'Ranasvamivisnu',* as situated to the west of the Haraparvat without giving any further hint as to its position.

135. The ruins of the temple of *Martanda,* here mentioned, form the most striking remains which have survived of the ancient architecture of Kashmir. They are situated near the North edge of the alluvial plateau (Udar) of *Matan*, 75° 17′ longitude and 33° 45′ latitude. About one mile to the North-West of the temple, and at the foot of the Udar, lie the sacred springs of the *Martanda Tirtha*. The name given to the temple and its site leaves no doubt as to its having been erected in honour of Visnu Surya, who has evidently been worshipped since early times at the above *Tirtha* under the form of *Martanda*. The Tirtha has remained to the present day one of the most celebrated pilgrimage-places in the valley, and annually attracts crowds of visitors from all parts of India. The legend related in the Martandamahatmya connects the springs with the story of the production of the sun from the lifeless egg (*mrtanda*), which Aditi, the wife of *Kasyapa*, had brought forth as her thirteenth child. The Tirtha of *Martanda* is already mentioned in the *Nilamata*, 1036, among the places sacred to Surya. The ruins of Lalitaditya's temple have on account of their size and architectural beauty been more frequently described than any other ancient building of Kashmir. They consist of a lofty central edifice, with a small detached shrine on either side of the entrance, and of a quadrangular courtyard of imposing dimensions surrounded by colonnader. To this magnificent enclosure Kalhana refers in the expression *prasadantar*. It is said that this temple had been built by *Ramaditya*, and that Lalitaditya had only added the enclosure. The interior of the quadrangle was once filled with water, and the temple thus 'placed more immediately under the protection of the Nagas'. There are no Nagar or springs anywhere on the arid plateau, and the water brought to it once by an ancient irrigation canal from the Lidar river could never have taken their place according to traditional notions. The temple of Martanda is mentioned again by Kalhana in the time of King *Kalasa,* who died there. The usual route from *Vijayesvara* (*Vijabror*) to the temple of *Martanda,* lied by the *Vitasta* to below *Anantnag* (Islamabad), and hence across the alluvial plateau for a distance of about five miles. The shrine escaped being plundered under *Harsa*. Subsequently it appears to have been fortified position by a rebel force in Kalhana's own time, on which occasion the temple enclosure (*prangana*) is specially mentioned, those who fall bravely in battle are received after death in the world of the sun. All allusion is intended also to those who after the defeat sought refuge in the temple of *Martanda.* Jonaraja mentions the temple among those which Sultan Sikandar of Kashmir, ' the Idol breaker,' destroyed, but refers also subsequently to the locality under the

name *Martanda*. The temple as well as the Tirtha bears now the Kashmiri name *Matan* (from Martanda), found already in *Ain-i-Akbar*, II, p. 358, whereas the village round the springs is popularly known as *Bavan* in Sanskrit *Bhavana*). The ancient temple is no longer a place of pious interest for the pilgrims, no longer a place of pious inerest for the pilgrims, who visit instead the modern temple dedicated to Martanda by the side of the Naga. The *Mahatmya* and Nilamata also read throughout *Martanda*.

136. R.T. Vol. 1 Book VII. p. 353.
137. *Harsa* on account of his procedure against sacred images, may well be called a *Turuska,* i.e. a Muhammadan. But may not the use of this epithet, alongwith the fact of his iconoclasm, be taken as an indication of *Harsa's* leanings towards Muhammadan? Formerly people in this country had, with the single exception of the king, worn their hair loose, had carried on headdress and no ear-ornaments. It can scarcely be doubled that Kalhana is alluding here to Muhammadan troop-leaders in *Harsa's* service. By eating pork, which the latter would not touch, the king puts himself lower even than the *Mlechchas*. May be recognise in the mention here made of '*Turuska*' officers, another indication of *Harsa's* propensity towards Muhammadanism? i.e. theory of mind or *mana* called *Brahmans.*
138. R.V. Vol.1 Book VII. p. 353 **Note.** The great *Buddha* statue at *Parihasapura* is certainly the one which king Lalitaditya erected in the *Rajavihara*. The statue in the city is evidently identical with the *Brhadbuddha* mentioned as still standing in Srinagar in the time of *Sussala*.
139. *Ibid.*
140. *Ibid.* p. 354.
141. **Note.** The term *Nak*, the contraction of *Nayaka* is the common epithet (of respect) used by the lowly *Mahars* of the Maratha country. From the abundance of *Naka* connected with the Bhills of the *Baria* jungles, east of Barola, they are called *Nakadas*. (I.C. Vol. II; P.99)
142. *R.T.* Vol.1 Book VII. P.354 **Note.** The important part which the night soil of the city plays in Kashmir horticulture, Kalhana evidently means by *aramika* the market-gardener, the modern *maliar* of Kashmir the work of the latter is invariably connected with the use of night soil or *Poudrette* as manure, and is, therefore considered degrading. An agriculturist who takes up the work of a market-gardener, cuts himself off from agriculture Muhammadans. Butchers too, in Kashmir, now exclusively Muhammadans, are esteemed men of low occupation, and it is clear that in Hindu times a still stronger taint must have attached to their calling. This virtuous (king), after he had prohibited the slaughter of living beings in his country, helped the butchers and others to a sinless livelihood (by grants) from his own treasury. From the curious account given in our passage of *Bhadresvara's* career, we may conclude that plasticity of the social system in Kashmir which at present strikes the observer coming from other parts of India, is not a development of modern date. The

peculiar elasticity of social organisation in Kashmir has been duly noted and illustrated with remarkable facts. (Walter R. Lawrence; *Kashmir Valley;* New Delhi, Reprint, 1985. P.306. Hereafter explained as K.V.).

143. **Note.** By *Srigarbha* an epithet of *Harsa* seems to be alluded and its possible significance "that for the sake of maintaining the people 'I' (ego), though versed in a combination of sciences, affected to be (solely) a producer of riches (*Srigarbha*), this has been the cause of my confusion." So far *Ksemagupta's* appellation *Kankanavarsa* is concerned, for *Abhimanyu's* epithet or nickname *Kankanavarsa,* ' Rainer of bracelets,' and pleased themselves by making him often shower bracelets on their arms. *Kankanavarsa* is found as the name of a magician. At that moment there arrived *Rajakulabhatta*, scattering the enemy's force by the sound of his martial music, and delighting his own (side). *Kankanapura* is, perhaps, the modern *Kangan,* a village on the right bank of the Sind river at the 74° 57′ longtitude and 34° 16′ latitude.

144. **Note.** Perhaps a pun is intended upon the word *'Kosa'*, which might also be taken in the sense of 'Calyx of the lotus'. The words of the first half verse might be interpreted also as referring to the lotus. The lotus, on account of its growth in the water, *jala*, is often credited with the quality of being *jada,* 'dull'. Brahman is born from a lotus and is seated on a lotus; *Jadiman* means both coldness and dullness. In *Jalaja* an allusion is intended to *Jadaja*, 'born from a fool'. This strong-armed king, whose glory (*pratapa*) tormented his enemies, which rivalled the city of *Indra.* Why, is there not the moon to defeat the (Ocean's) hell-darkness? Is there not the poison (of *Kalakuta*) to frighten that (ocean), which swallows up the waters? Is there not *Dhanvantari* to destroy the (*Submarine*) fire in its interior? Though all these (properties of the ocean) together have proved without avail, yet the ocean should not be called a fool those who consider that success is dependent on fate, will show their perception of (the truth of ) things just by praising him. The *Ganga* is represented in Puranic legends as having come forth from the *Brahmanda* or mundane egg, when Vishnu, after his strides over heaven and earth, touched it with his toe. Before descending to the earth the sacred stream passes over Siva's head. The word *Jadu* contains an allusion to the water (*jala*), which forms the subject of the preceding simile.

145. **Note.** The recollection of *Harsa's* mad proceedings still lives in the Kashmiri phrase *Yi Kyaho, Hars'divhyu, 'why, he is like Harsadeva!* It is applied to persons who commit foolish and extravagant acts.

146. **Note.** In the absence of any contradictory evidence we must assume that this *Kanaka,* brother of *Canpaka,* whom *Harsa* rewarded so magnificantly for taking singing lessons from him, was Kalhana's own uncle. The high position of the family would explain in some way the extravagant present. The values which can be shown to have been actually used in reckoning, are given in the following table with their Sanskrit and modern designation:-

12 Dinnaras = 1 *Dvadasa* ("Twelver"), *Bahagani.*

2 Dvadasa = 25 *Dinnaras* or 1 *Pancavimsatika* ("Twenty fivers"), *Puntshu*
4 Pancavimsatika = 100 *Dinnaras* or 1 *Sata* ("Hundreder"), Hath
10 Sata = 1000 Dinnaras or 1 Sahasra ("Thousander"), *Sasun*
100 Sahasra = 100, 000 *Dinnaras* or 1 *Laksa* ("Lakh")
100 Laksa = 10, 000, 000 *Dinnaras* or 1 *Koti* ("Crore")

In using the designations here indicated it was usual, but not necessary to add the word *dinnara* in the general sense of "money" (modern dyar), in order to mark their character as monetary terms. The equivalent values for Akbar's time, calculated on Abu-1-Fazl's estimate, are shown in a separate. column

| *Value in Dinnaras* | *Designation* | *Early Hindu coins (Upto 855 A.D)* | *Later Hindu coins (from A.D 855 on wards)* | *Muham madan coins* | *Equivalent values on Abu-l-fazl's estimate* |
|---|---|---|---|---|---|
| 12 | *Dvadasa* (*Bahagani*) | 00000 | AE 45 grs | 000 000 | 1/8Dam or 1/320 Rupee |
| 25 | *Pancavimsa tika* (Puntshu) | AE 110 grs(?) | AE 91 grs | AE 83 grs | 1/4 Dam or 1/160 Rupee |
| 100 | *Sata* (Hath) | 000 000 | 000 000 | 000 000 | 1 Dam or 1/40 Rupee |
| 500 | 000 000 000 | 000 000 | AR 23 5 grs | 000 000 | 5 Dams or 1/8 Rupee |
| 1,000 | Sahasra (Sasun) | 000 000 | 000 000 | 000 000 | 10 Dams or 1/4 Rupee |
| 2,000 | 000 000 000 | 000 000 | 000 000 | AR94 grs | 20 Dams or 1/2 Rupees |
| 2,500 | 000 000 | AR 120 grs | 000 000 | 000 000 | 25 Dams or 25/40 rupee |
| 12,500 | 000 000 | 000 000 | AN 73 grs | 000 000 | 125 Dams or 3 1/8 rupees |
| 100,000 | Laksa (Lakh) | 000 000 | 000 000 | 000 000 | 25 rupees |
| 10,000,000 | Koti (Crore) | 000 000 | 000 000 | 000 000 | 2500 Rupees |

The table of the coinage of Kashmir as far as it can throw light on the old monetary system of the country, it will be useful to summarize here briefly the results of our inquiry concerning this system. It shows that only denomination of coins which can be traced throughout, is the copper coin representing 25 *Dinnaras.*

147. *R.T.* Vol.1 Book VII. p. 354.

148. **Note.** *Candala*, female *Candalani,* one of the low caste in Punjabi Dictionary, *Nishadas, Panlasa.* Hence the statement of the *Dharmsastra* that issues of such detestable unions became *Chandalas.* (O.G.C.I p. 91) *Chanal*, or probably *Channal,* from *Chandala*, whom all Sanskrit authorities represent as begotten by a *Sudra* on a Brahman. His occupation is carrying out corpses, executing criminals, and other object offices for the public service. The menial class of Kangra and Mandi, corresponding to the Dagi in Kulu and the *Koli* in the Simla Hills, the *Chanals* in Kangra appear to be inferior to the Kolis of that District, and some of them atleast will not touch dead cattle, or mix on equal terms with those who do. On the other hand, in Kulu Saraj some of the

*Chanals* rank below *Kolis*. *Dagi-Chanal* is a very common term for the caste: and in Kulu it appears to inclue the *Nar.* Yet a *Chanal* of Mandi State will not intermarry with a Dagi of Kulu. The *Chanal* is also found in *Chamba*, where the proverb goes: *Chanal Jetha, Rathi Kanetha,* 'the low caste is the elder and the *Rathi* the younger brother, doubtless pointing to a tradition that the*Chanal* represents an earlier or aboriginal race. (G.T.C. P.N.W.F.P. pp. 151-52).

149. **Note.** *Parmadi* is the well-known surname or *biruda* of the *Calukya* king Vikramaditya-*Tribhuvanamalla* whose family history and exploits form the subject of *Bilhana's Vikramankadevacarita* poem. He reigned at *Kalyana* in the years 1076-1127 A.D. His wedding with *Candralekha* or *Candaladevi*, the daughter of the *Silahara* prince of *Karahata*, is described in the vii and viii. Cantos of the *Vikramankadevacarita Bilhana* gives a lenghty account of the charms of the princes whom the king is said to have won in a *Svayamvara.*
150. *R.T.* Vol.1 Book VII. p. 355.
151. **Note.** Camphor is prepared as a crystalline substance, deposited on cooling, from a decoction made from chips of certain kinds of wood. 'Unboiled camphor' is, therefore, a nonentity. *Harsa's* vow is as ludicrous as his boast to invade *Karnata.*
152. **Note.** *Potasa* is given in the *Rajanighantu* as the name of a kind of camphor.
153. **Note.** *Kalyana,* the old capital of the Western Calukyas, is identical with the modern town of that name in the Bidar district of Haidarabad. The *Gauda-Vaho* first describes Yasovarman's conquest of *Magadha* and *Vanga*, and then proceeds to narrate a conventional *digvijaya*, which covered the end of the peninsula. Of these Yasovarman's invasion of Bengal may have been a fact, at least his suzerainty over Magadha is corroborated by an inscription, but the rest of his *digvijaya* seems to be imaginary. Yasovarman, however, has been tentatively identified with 'King of north India' defeated by the Calukyas king *Vinayaditya* about 695 A.D. The Calukyas of course claim victory, and from the inscription it appears that the battle was fought in the Ganga-Yamuna doab, not during a *digvijaya*. It is however, evident that the Calukyas did not gain any significant victory in north India, and it is quite probable that Yasovarman repulsed Calukya invasion of north India (C.H.A.I. p. 299).
154. **Note.** From the term *pimmala* or *primmala* is here meant that it is such kind of river, which mind has to across through the master as a bridge, ship or boat to see the 'Father' and become 'Father'.
155. *R.T.* Vol.1 Book VII. p. 355.
156. *Ibid.*
157. *Ibid.*
158. **Note.** *Bappika* was a princess from the *Campa* family. She was the mother of *Harsa*. It shows that there were the relations between the royal houses of *Kashmir* and *Campa*. *Campa* is the modern hill-state of *Camba* or *Chamba (Annam),* which comprises the valleys of all the sources of

the Ravi and some adjoining valleys draining into the Chenab. King *Sala* has been rightly identified by Prof. Kielhorn with *Salavahana,* who is mentioned as king *Somavarmadeva's* predecessor. The latter was executed in the reign of *Asata*, as the ruler of *Campa* under *Kalasa* (1087 A.D). Cunninghan has rightly pointed out that the reference made by *Kalhana* for *Kalasa* of *Vallapura,* with the old chiefship of *Ballavar,* situated in the lower hills to the East of Jammu. The petty *Rajas* of *Ballawar,* sometime before their territory was swallowed up by the State of Jammu, had transferred their seat to *Basaul or Basohli* of the Ravi. But the small town of *Ballavar,* 75° 40′ longtitude, and 32° 37′ latitude still remains in the ruins marks of its former importance. *Kalasa*, the lord of *Vallapura*, the son of *Tukka,* whose reign began about 1050 A.D.; and he was still in power in 1087-8 A.D. When he visited Kashmir along with several other tributary hill chiefs in the reign of *Kalasa*, the son of *Tukka,*was fifteenth in succession from Bhog-Pal, the founder of the state, and allowing twenty two years to a reign, we concluded that the state came into existence in the first half of the eighth century. The first historical mention of *Vallapura* occurs in the *Rajatarangini* in the reign of *Ananta-deva* of Kashmir (A.D. 1028-63). *Ananta-deva* invaded *Chamba,* probably about 1055, deposed the ruling Raja, and set up another in his place. This expedition was mostly likely the result of a revolt among the hill chiefs against Kashmir supermacy, which had been more or less in force for several centuries. On his return journey *Ananta-deva* seems to have gone by *Vallapura,* which also was evidently in revolt, and owing to his own rashness, he became involved in a difficult position, from which he was extricated by the sagacity of his minister, *Haladhara*. Moreover, from Alberumi, that in *Samgramapala* and *Utkarsa* (*Harsa's* brother) had been placed on the throne of *Rajapuri*, when king *Sahajapala* was died. Balor at that time was situated on the road from *Kananj* to Kashmir, which seems to have followed the route through the outer hills in ancient times, as it did at a much later period, as one of the hill *Rajas* who presented themselves at the court of *Kalasa* of Kashmir in the winter of A.D. 1087-88. Subsequently in Sussala's reign we find *Padmaka* of *Vallapura*, together with his son *Anandaraja* joining a league of hill chiefs which supports the Kashmirian pretender *Bhiksacara* (removal) to the court of *Naravarman* of Malava. *Naravarman* here referred to is mentioned in the genealogical lists of the later *Paramara* rulers of *Malava* as contained in their copper-plate grants. From the Nagpur stone inscription, it appears that *Naravarman* was on the throne in the *Vikrama* year 1161, i.e. A.D. 1104-5, having succeeded his brother *Laksmadeva*, son of *Udayaditya*. *Bhiksu,*being the synonym of the name *Bhiksacara,* is used indifferently with the latter. This prince is at a later date brought from *Vallapura* to Rajouri by *Sussala's* enemies. When that (ruler) had become convinced that the king's enmity could not be appeased by any measures, he called *Bhiksacara,* his enemy, from *Vallapura*. On the other hand, a chief of

Vallapura' *Brahmajajjala* is named in the list of faithful *Rajaputras* from abroad, who stood by *Sussala* in his great straits. Here probably a scion of the *Vallapura* family is meant. *Sussala* also had a wife *Jajjala* from *Vallapura* might have been a daughter or near relation of *Brahmajjala*. It is probable that most, if not all, of the partisans of the partisans of the king who are named here, belong to *Rajput* families of the hill-regions to the south of Kashmir. It appears that the members of the ruling family of *Campa* or *Chamba* and their relations with Kashmir, are in agreement with the traditional list of the *Chamba Rajas* as preserved in the family which still rules that hill-state. An interesting reference, probably to the people of the state occurs in two *Chamba* copper-plate deeds of the eleventh century A.D; relation to events which happened in about A.D. or 930 *Chamba* was invaded by the Lord of Durgara (Jammu) assisted by the *Saumatikas",* evidently a people near the *Chamba* border'. evidently a people near the Chamba border; and that the allied army was defeated by *Sahila-Varman*, the *Chamba* chief . Bilhana, *Vikram. XVIII* , speaks of king *Ananta's* supermacy being acknowledged in *Champa, Darvabhisara, Trigarta* (Kangra), *Kuluta* (Kulu) and *Bhartula* or *Vartula* or the story of *Nature* or God. Whereas the places of the invasion of *Campa* led by *Ananta Deva* between A.D. 1028 and 1031, does not give his authority for these dates. It deserves to be noted that our text shows everywhere the spelling of *Campa,* whereas the name (in its alternative form) is written *Canpaka* in the grant above quoted. The latter spelling with *n* is regularly adopted in all *Sarada* script for the name of the *Campaka* flower; compares also the name of Kalhana's father, written throughout in A. Regarding the charateristic of the inhabitants of *Campa,* the territory of *Trigarta* is identical with the modern hill district of *Kangra* situated between the mountains of *Chamba* and the upper course of the *Bias;* compares *Vishnupur*. With reference to the ancient stronghold and capital of the district, *Kot Kangra* or *Nagarkot*, renders *Trigarta* by *Nagarakotta*, and its famous old fortress, can be traced from the time of Mahmud of Ghazna to the present day (*Alberuni India* Vol. II, p. 11). As *Trigarta* formed, in ancient times part of the kingdom of *Jalamdhara* (Jalandhar), *Inducandra*, who is identical with the *Indracandra* of the genealogical list of the Katoch *Rajas* of Kangra, is called *indumukhim* immediately after him, king of *Jalamdhara*. Even the gods have no pity in *Trigarta,* no morals in *Campa*, no generosity in the *Madra-* land, and no good-will in *Darvabhisara*. The combined names of the *Darvas* and *Abhisaras* are mentioned in various ethnographical lists, furnished by the *Mahabharta,* the *Puranas* and *Brhatsamhita*, along with those of tribes belonging to the Panjab. From the evidence available it appears that *Darvabhisara* as a geographical term comprised the whole tract of the lower and middle hills lying between the *Vitasta* and *Candrabhaga*. The *Candrabhaga* seems to mark the eastern limit of the territory in the passage of the *Vishnupur*. The topographical point *Ghoramulaka*, which is only here mentioned, was probably situated to the north of *Rajapuri* in the direction of the *Ratta Pir* range. It is clear that the hill state of Rajapuri (Rajapuri) was included in *Darvabhisara*. *Madradesa* is an old name of the central Panjab between the *Bias* and the Jehlam (or *Chenab*). The verses probably reproduces a proverbial saying of Kalhana's time. *Rajapuri* is clearly included in the judgement passed on *Darvabhisara*. It must, however, be noted here that *Bhimbher Danagale*dese, would restrict the application of the term to the lower hills between the limits above indicated. *Bhimbhar,* the first locality named by the glossator, lies at the foot of the outer hills, in the centre of the tract between the *Vitasta* and the Chenab and was the centre of little hill-state. The name *Danagal* appears to survive in that old *Ghakkar or Kokkhar* fort in the lower hills near the *Vitasta*. *Uttambya* is probably only a clerical error for *Uttambhya;* seems to show *Darvabhisara* as subject to Kashmir in the time of *Utpalapida*. But *Samkaravarman* has again to conquer this territory before he proceeds against *Gurjara*, the modern *Gujrat* to the South of Bhimbhar. The name *Gurjara* is preserved in that of the modern town of *Gujrat,* situated in the Panjab plain about five miles from the west bank of Chenab at 74° 7′ longitude and 32° 34′ latitude. The name of the modern town is also used in an extended sense for the designation of the neighbouring territory, comprising the upper portion of the Doad between Jehlam and Chenab rivers to the foot of the *Bhimbhar* hills. In this sense the term is well-known in Kashmir. It appears that the older name *Gurjara* had, at that time of the events here related, a much wider territorial application Kalhana represents as *Takkavisaya* called *Vulliya* bought from *Turuskas,* an ethnic designation, *Takka* is used in connection with the names of certain persons such as *Asidhara, Bimbiya, Madana*. Cunningham has rightly connected the name *Takka* with that of 'the kingdom of *Tseh-Kia*', which Hiuen-Tsiang reached after travelling to the South East of *Rajapuri* or Rajapuri. The Kingdom of *Tseh-Kia* is described as bordening in the East on the *Vipasa* (Bias), and in the West on the Indus. Its capital was in close proxmity to the old city of *She-Kie-Lo*. The latter place is undoubtedly identical with the ancient *Sakala,* famous in Brahmanical and Buddhist tradition. *Sakala* is mentioned in *Mahabharata,* as the capital of *Madras* or *Bahikas,* tribes settled in the modern Panjab, and with the *Bahikas* we find the Takkas actually identified in *Hemacandra's* synonymic Lexicon (*Abhidhanacintamani*). The position of *Sakala* has not yet been fixed with certainty, though it has been the subject of much speculation with speical regard to the supposed identity of *Sakala* with the *Eayyaha* of Arrian and the *Eayaha* (or Euthydemia) of Ptolemy. It is, however, probable that the ancient city was situated somewhere between the Chenab and Ravi. There we should them have to took for the seat of the *Takka* tribe, which in Hiuen-Tsiang's time appears to have ruled the greatest part of the Northern Panjab. Towards the end of the 9th century its power must have been considerably reduced, as in our passage the term *Takkadesa* is evidently used in a far more restricted sense than Hiuen-Tsiang's 'Kingdom of

*Tseh-Kia*'. Cunningham has rightly traced out the term *Takka* the name *Takeshar* which Alberuni gives to a region situated to the South of the Pir Pantsal Range and neighbouring on the region of *Lauhawar* (Lohara). Cunningham thought to have recognized the name *Takka* also in Urdu *Taqin*, the designation used for an Indian territory by *Ibn Khordadbeh* and *Ibn Rosteh*. Now modern glossator sees in *Takka* the name of the 'Atak river' , i.e the Indus, and identifies *Takkadesa* with *Skardo* ! For the custom here alluded to cutting of a finger as a sign of unconditional surrender is repeatedly mentioned in the chronicle, who acknowledge their guilt and ask for marcy,as we learn from the *Mallarjuna's* conduct. It appears that the person who had been made a prisoner could claim the victor's mercy by presenting to him his cut-off finger as a mark of submission. Cunninghan, who refers at length, to genealogical lists preserved by the descendants of the 'Kangra Rajas, does and *Bhuvanacandra* actually occur in them. He, however, justly points out that the word *'Candra'* which forms the second in all the names furnished by the family rolls. These names, from the 14th century downwards, can be checked by coins and other documentary evidence. It can, therefore, be safely assumed that the use of such names goes back to the ancient period. *Chandra*, composed by *Chandra,* one of the red-robe-wearing sect, the fowller of *Buddha.* (Alberuni's India Vol. 1. p. 135). It is evidently due to the tradition connecting the *Katoch* Rajas of Kangra with the *Chandrvamsa*. The verse contains a pun on the name *Prithivicandra,* 'the moon of the earth', which is cast in darkness (*tamasi*). The later ruler of this family was *Inducandra.* It makes clear from the study that the expedition of *Samkaravarman*, son of *Avantivarman,* was extended the boundaries of Kashmir in several directions. He seems to have come into conflict with the emperor *Bhoja* I of Kanauj and *Lalliya Shahi* of *Udabhandapura* or *Und* on the Indus and wrested a portion of the Punjab from *Gurjaras* (A.H.I.P.163). He also extended his power northwords as far as *Pehoa* and southwards as far as the *Vindhyas,* but his further progress was stopped by *Samkaravarman* of Kashmir and *Dhruva Dharavarsha* a *Rashtrakuta* chieftain of Broach. He was more successful in the east. The *Gaudas* (of Bengal) were defeated and the *Pratihara* empire in the time of his successor stretched as far as *Paharpur* in North Bengal. The empire of *Bhoja* was visited by the merchant *Sulaiman* who spoke highly of the strength of his cavalry and of the peace that reigned in his kingdom. (Ibid. p. 170). Kangra lies far away to the East of the route which Kalhana seems to indicate when making the King proceed Via *Bhimbhar* (*Darvabhisara*) to Gujrat (Gurjara), and hence to the west towards the upper Indus. In explanation hereof, it will be sufficient to refer to the very numerous instances, both ancient and modern, in which Indian kingdoms were designated by the name of the capitals for the time being (e.g., the use of the name Lahore for the whole Panjab in the reign of Ranjit Singh). Finally, we are informed that king *Jayasimha,* after a successful expedition, *Vikramraja* was uprooted by *Gulhana* at *Vallapura*. Cunningham also states that *Kalasa* name was very much corporated in the genealogical lists of the *Ballavar* family.

159. *R.T.* Vol.1 Book VII. p. 356.

160. **Note**. The term *pindasiddhi* is composed of two words *pinda+siddhi*; *pinda* nevertheless the path of the 'Fathers' is distinct from that of the gods, for it is that of death (See X, 18, 1, and 88, 15), by which all men are to follow. It is as the representatives of this same spiritual power that the *Pitris* have so much to do with ordering or producing natural phenomena. Therefore the oblations offered to both should also be different. So, while the Fathers are Soma-lovers and Some-drinkers of *'Word'* or *'Nam'* and have a general invitation to come and partake of it at sacrifices with the gods, special offerings are reserved for them at their own particular commemorative festivals *'Sabad'* the *Shraddhas, mana* or *Brahmana* principally a kind of wheat cake or dumpling called *pinda,* one of which is provided for every *Pitar* invited. Hence the name: *Pinda-pitriyajna* '*Word*' or *'Nam'* "Cake oblation to the Fathers". For there were different kinds of *Shraddhas* on different occasions and anniversaries. Some were sacred to the memory of one departed relative, and some to that of the family dead generally, and some to that of all the pious and glorified dead *'Sabad'* a sort of All Saints' Day (Vol. pp. 365-66). The daily *pitriyajan,* or ancestor worship, is one of the five sacrifices, sometimes called the great sacrifices which every married man ought to perform day by day. (R.V.V.R; p. 101). Term *Siddhi* hardly any other *Dharmasutra* deals with *Yoga* and its technical terms *ike Pranayama, pratyahara, dharana* at such length as *Devala* or the '*law of nature or 'Nam, 'Sabad'* does (Vide H.of Dh. Vol.V. pp. 1380-81, notes 2263-64) for *Sankhya* technique, p. 1409 n.2314 on definition of *Yoga,* P.1435 note 2356 (on *prana* and *apana*), p. 1439 note 2363 (on *Pranayama*); p. 1445 n.2375 (on *pratyahara*), p. 1447 note 2380 (on *Dharana*)*, 1453* (n.2390 on *Siddhis)*, p. 1458 note 2398 (on *ahankara* and *mamatva*). (H.D. Vol.1. p. 283). It may be noted that prose quotations from early in the christian era, if not before, there was a theoretical classification of the various schools of thought looked on as orthodox, and the *Saddassana* or 'Six Doctrines' or *'the six system of Salvation,* became a regular feature of Hinduism. The six schools were actually of differing origin and purpose, but all were brought into the scheme by being treated as equally valid ways a salvation. They were divided into three groups of two, which were thought to be related and complementary. These were: *Nyaya* and *Vaisesika* ; *Sankhya* and *Yoga*; and *Mimamsa* and *Vedanta* *Nayaya* ("*Analysis*") was rather a school of logic and epistemology than of theology. It looked back to a teacher, *Aksapada Gautama,* the *sutras* or aphorisms attributed to whom are probably no earlier than the Christian era. Logic was forced into the scheme as a means of salvation by the contention that clear thinking and logical argument were essential means to the highest bliss and thus a religious basis was given to what

was essentially a system of reasoning (W.T.W.I. p. 323). Logic was not, however, confined to this school, but was utilized and adapted by Hindu, Buddhist and Jaina alike. One of the most important topics of Indian thought in this field was the question of *Pramana*, which may be translated "means of reliable knowledge". According to the later *Nyaya* schools there were four *pramanas*, perception (*Pratyaksa*), inference (*anumana*) inference by analogy or comparison (*Upamana*) and "*Word*" (*Sabda*), the pronouncement of a reliable authority, such as the Vedas. (Ibid. P.501). The word *'Veda'* means 'Knowledge, Knowledge, *par excellence*, i.e., the sacred, "spiritual knowledge". It does not signify either any individual literary work as the "*Koran*", or even a collection of definite number of books arranged at a particular time, such as the Bible or the *'Tripitaka'*, it is mass of literature. (R.C Majumdar, A.I. p. 33). Thus the *Vedas* are called *apaurusheya* (not made by man) and *nitya* (existing in all eternity while the *Rishis*, or sacred poets to whom they are ascribed, are known as *mantradrashta*, i.e inspired *seers* who saw or received the *mantra* by right directly from the Supreme Creator (Ibid. p. 34). The history of India is mainly that of the Aryans of India. It source is the *Rigveda* i.e., '*Nam*' "*Word*" *'Sabda' 'Kalma'* etc Which is the earliest book not merely of Indians but of the entire Aryan race. It thus throws light not merely on Indo-Aryan history but on general Aryan origins, on pre-historic phases of Aryan religion, culture and language (in respect of inflexion, accent and metre). Common Aryan home and languages have been discovered that the language of the *Rigveda* bears affinity to languages like Persian, Greek, Latin, Teutonic, Celtic and Slavonic in regard to both roots of verbs and certain grammatical forms. They have also in common words expressive of the primary relationships or experiences of life: such as the words for father, mother, son, daughter, God, heart and trees, axe and tree, dog and cow; e.g. Sanskrit *Matar* =Latin *Mater* = English *mother*; Sanskrit *Sunu*= Lithuanian *Sunu*= Old High German *Sunu*= English *Son*. (R.K Mookerji; A.I. P.48). We may instance the following names of gods: *Avestan Indra* = *Vedic Mithra* = Vedic *Mitra*, *Avestan Naonhaithya* = Vedic *Nasatyas*, Avestan *Verethnaghna* = Vedic *vritraghna* also Avestan Stanza *Tat thwa* = Vedic *Tut tva*. (Ibid. PP. 51-52). That the age of the *Rigveda* is not later than that of the Indus civilization of about 3250 B.C. has been already explained on the basis of the links of connection between the two culture. The India as known to the *Rigveda* is indicated by the rivers *Kubha* (Kabul), Krumu (Kurram), *Gomati* (Gomal), *Suvastu* (Swat), showing that Afghanistan was a part of Rigvedic India. The *Rigveda* also mentions the five rivers of the Punjab, viz. Sindhu (*Iravati* or Ravi), *Vipas* (Beas), as also *Sutudri* (Satlej) and Sarasvati (*Sarsuti*). It also mentions the Ganga and the Yamuna and the *Sarayu* and minor rivers like the Sushoma (*Sona*), the *Marudvridha* (*Maruwardwan*). Rigvedic, India is also called by the Rigveda (VIII, 24, 27) as the land of the seven rivers, *Sapta-Sindhavah*. The *Rigveda* also gives some indications of the scenery of its country. A part of it consisting of hymns to *Usha* is inspired by the splendours of dawn in the dry tracts of Western Punjab. It also contains many hymns described thunder and lighting, rain bursting from the clouds, as also mountains which are not seen in the Punjab, but in the region called *Brahmavarta* watered by the Saraswati, the *Drishadvati* and the Apaya where the bulk of the *Rigveda* must have been composed (Ibid. PP.52-53). The division of the *Rigvedic* peoples was took place into two groups. One included the *Srinjayas* and the Bharatas settled on the *Drishadvati*, Sarasvati and Apaya, and worshipping Agni. The other group comprised the five peoples-Yadus, Turvasas, Druhyus, Anus and Purus. On account of their alliances with aboriginal peoples, the Yadus and the Turvasas are once branded as *Dasas* or non-Aryans, while the non-Aryan epithet *mridhravach* is applied to the Purus. The first clash was between the Turvasas allied to the *Vrichivants* on the *Hariyupiya* (Harappa means absorb the '*Nam*' in the body) and the Srinjayas arrayed with 30,000 mailed warriors on the *Yavyavati*. The *Vrichivants* were extreminated in the battle. The Bharatas were at first "robbed of their possessions by their enemies. But they soon prospered under Vasishtha under whom the struggle between the two warring groups was brought to a head in what is known as *Dasarajna* or the Battle of Ten kings (Ibid. PP.53-54). It is very interesting to note how this figure corresponds with, and to a certain extent explains, the later conception of Siva. As is well-known, Siva is regarded as a *Mahayogin*, and is styled *Pasupati* or the lord of beasts, his chief attributes being three eyes and the *Trisula* or the trident. Now the apparent *Yoga* posture of the figure in *Mohenjo-Daro* justifies the epithet *Mahayogin,* and the figures of animals round him explain the epithet *Pasupati.* The three faces of the figures may not be unconnected with the later conception of three eyes, and the two horns with the tall head-dress might have easily given rise to the conception of a trident with three prongs. (A.H.I. pp. 20-21). The *Vedanta* school added intuition or presumption (*arthapatti*) and non-perception (*anupalabdhi*), the latter an unnecessary scholastic refinement. The six categories overlapped somewhat, and the Buddhists generally included all forms of knowledge under the first two categories, while the Jainas usually allowed only three, perception, inference and revelation. The materialists allowed only perception, and their opponents made short work of their efforts at proving by inference that inference could not give reliable knowledge. It was probably in the study of the process of inference that schools of true logic arose. From the necessities of metaphysical discussion false arguments were analysed and classified; of these logicians recognised the chief fallacies of classical logic, such as *reduction ad absurdum* (*arthaprasanga*), circular argument (*cakra*), '*infinite*' regression (*anavastha*), dilemma (*anyonyasraya*), and *ignoratio elenchi* (*atmasraya*). A correct inference was established by syllogism, of which the Indian form (*Pancavayava*) was somewhat more cumbrous than the Aristotelian. Its five members were known as proposition

(*Pratijna*), reason (*hetu*), example (*udaharana*), application (*Upanaya*) and conclusion (*nighamana*). The classical Indian example may be paraphrased as follows:

1. There is fire on the mountain,
2. because there is smoke above it,
3. and where there is smoke, there is fire, as for instance, in a kitchen,
4. such is the case with the mountain,
5. and therefore there is fire on it.

The third term of the Indian syllogism corresponds to the major premiss of that of Aristotle, the second to Aristotle's minor premises, and the first to his conclusion. Thus the Indian syllogism reversed the order of that of classical logic, the argument being stated in the first and second clauses, established by the general rule and example in the third, and finally clinched by the virtual repetition of the first to clauses. The "example" (in the above syllogism the kitchen) was generally looked on as an essential part of the argument, and helped to strengthen its rhetorical force. Evidently this elaborate system of syllogism is the outcome of much practical experience in discussion. Three membered syllogism were admitted by the Buddhists, who rightly rejected the fourth and fifth members of the orthodox syllogism as tautological. The basis of the generalization (for example "where there is smoke there is fire") on which every inference rests was believed to be the quality of universal concomitance (*Vyapti*). The nature and origin of this quality was much discussed, and its consideration led to theories of univerals and particulars, which are too recondite for consideration in this book. No treatment of Indian thought is complete without a brief reference to the remarkable epistemological relativity of Jainism. Jaina thinkers, and some other heterodox teachers also, explicity rejected what in classical logic is called the law of the exclused middle. For the Jaina there were not merely the two possibilities of existence and non-existence, but seven. Thus we may affirm (1) that an object, say a knife, exists as a knife. We may further say (2) that it is not something else, say a fork. But it exists as a knife and does not exist as a fork, and so we may declare of it (3) that in one aspect it is and in another it is not. From another point of view (4) it is indescrible; its ultimate essence is unknown to us and we cannot posit anything final about *"Word"* it is inexpressible. By combining this fourth possibility with the three former ones we obtain three further possibilities of predication of *'Word'* (5) it is , but its nature is indescrible, and (7) it both is and is not, but its nature is indescribable. This system of seven aspects of predication is known as *Syadvada* ("the doctrine of 'may be') or *saptabhangi* ("the sevenfold division"). The Sanskrit terms for the seven aspects are : (1) *Syadasti*, (2) *Syannasti,* (3) *Syadastinasti,* (4) *Syadavaktavya*, (5) *Syadastyavaktavya* (6) *Syannastyavaktavya,* and (7) *Syedastinastyavaktavya*. As well as *Syadvada* the Jainas had another sevenfold system of predication known as *nayavada*, the theory of standpoints, or ways of approaching an object of observation or study. The first three of these are connected with the object itself (*dravyarthika*), and the latter four with its modifications and the words used to describe it (*paryayarthika*). *(1)* A mango tree may be considered simultaneously as an individual having a definite size and shape and as a member of the species "mango tree", (2) it may be treated merely as a representative of the "universal" mango tree, and as corresponding to the general concept of a mango tree, without taking its individual qualities into account, or (3) it may be considered merely as an individual, without taking note of its specific qualities. Further it may be thought of (4) as it is at the present moment, for instance as bearing ripe fruit, without any regard to its past as a sapling or its future as firewood. (5) We may think of it from the point of view of its name 'Mango', considering all the synonyms of that name, and their implications. These synonyms may be subtly differentiated, and (6) we may consider their nuances and connotations. Finally (7) we may consider an object in its relation to a given epithet; thus by referring to a hero as a "lion" we mentally abstract all his un-lion like qualities and think of him only as a being of strength and courage. The Sanskrit names of the seven *nayas* are : (1) *naigama,* (2) *Sangraha* (3) *Vyavahara* (4) *rjusutra* (5) *Sabda* (6) *Samabhirudha,* and (7) *evambhuta*. Soma Jaina schools rejected that last three standpoints, which are hardly consistent with the first four, being rather Semantic in character than epistemological. Modern logicians might make short work of these rather pedantic systems of ontological and epistemological relativity, but they have a fundamental quality of breadth and they have a fundamental quality of breadth and realism, implying a full realization that the world is more complex and subtle than we think it, and that what is true of a thing in one of its aspects may at the same be false in another. (W.T.W.I. PP.501-503). *Vaisesika* (" the school of Individual characteristics") was complementary to *Nyaya*, and perhaps older, and in medieval times the two merged into what was virtually a single school. While *Nyaya* specialized in logic, *Vaisesika* was rather interested in physics than theology. The earliest text of the school is the *sutras* of the legendary founder, *Uluka Kanada,* which had numerous exponents and commentators, the greatest of whom was *Prasastapada* of the 5th century. The basic tenet of *Vaisesika*, held in common with Jainism and some schools of Buddhism, was that nature is atomic. The atoms are distinct from the soul, of which they are the instrument. Each element has individual characteristics (*Visesas*), which distinguish it from the four other non-atomic substances (*dravyas*), which the school recognises — time, space, soul and mind. The atoms are eternal, but in the great dissolution at the end of the life of Brahma. They are separated one from another, and all things are destroyed. The new Brahma utilizes the old atoms to create the world afresh. *Vaisesika* thus postulated a dualism of matter and soul, and declared that salvation depends on fully recognizing the atomic nature of the universe and its difference from the soul. (Ibid. PP.323-24). Ancient Indian ideas of physics were closely linked with religion and theology, and differed somewhat from sect to sect. As early as the time of the Buddha, if not before, the universe was classified by elements, of which all schools admitted at least four :- earth, air, fire and water. To these orthodox Hindu schools and Jainism added a fifth, *akasa*, which is generally translated "ether". It was recognized that air was not of 'infinite' extension, and the Indian mind, with its abhorrence of a vacuum, found it hard to conceive of empty space. The five elements were thought of as the mediums of sense impressions:- earth of small, air of feeling, fire of vision, water of taste, and ether of sound. Buddhists and Ajivikas rejected ether, but the latter added life, joy and sorrow, which were thought of as in some way material, making a total of seven elements. Most of the schools believed that the elements other than ether were atomic. India atomism was certainly independent of Greek influence, for an atomic theory was taught by *Pakudha Katyayana*, an older contemporary of the Buddha, and was therefore earlier than that of Democritus. The Jainas believed that all atoms (*anu*) were identical, and that differences of the character of the elements were due to the manner in which the atoms were combined. Most of the schools, however, maintained that there were as many types of atom as there were elements. The atom was generally thought to be eternal but some Buddhists conceived of it not only as the minutest object capable of occupying space, but also as occupying the minutest possible duration of time, coming into being and vanishing almost in an instant, only to be succeeded by another atom, caused by the first. Thus the atom of Buddhism in some measure resembles the quantum of Planck. The atom was quite invisible to the human eye; the orthodox *Vaisesika* school believed the single atom to be a mere point in space completely without magnitude. A single atom had no qualities but only potentialities, which came into play when the atom combined with others. The *Vaisesika* school, which specially elaborated atomic dectrines and was the school of atomism *par excellence*, maintained that, before combining to form material objects, atoms made primary combinations of diads and triads. This doctrine of molecules was developed differently by Buddhists and Ajivikas, who taught that in different proportions in a molecule (*Samghata, Kalapa*). Every molecule contained at least one atom of all four types, and obtained its character from the predominance of a given element. This hypothesis accounted for the fact that matter might show characteristics of more than one element: thus wax might melt and also burn, because its molecules contained proportions of water and fired. Accoding to the Buddhists the molecules cohered by virtue of the atoms of water in each, which acted as adhesive. Indian atomic theories were not based so much on experiment, as on intution and logic. They were not universally held. (*Ibid.* p. 497) ***Sankhya*** (" the count") is perhaps the oldest of the six systems, being mentioned in the *Bhagavat Gita* and occuring in a primitive form in the upanisads. Its legendary founder was the ancient sage *Kapila,* but the earliest surviving text of the system is the *Sankhya* resembles Jainism in its rigid dualism and fundamental atheism. It teaches the existence of twenty-five basic principles (*attva*), of which the first is *'Prakrti,' Sabda'* or *'Word'* a term usually loosely translated "matter" (1) Creation, or rather evolution, is not due to the operation of a divinity, but to the inherent nature of *Prakrti.* From *Prakrti, Prakriti* develops (2) Intelligence (*buddhi,* also call *mahat* "the Great one"), and hence is produced (3) Self-consciousness (*ahankara*). *Prakriti* has in fact evolved into an active divinity. Through self-conciousness emerge the five subtle elements (*tanmatra*), invisible matter in its most ethereal form; the five are (4) "ether" (*akasa*), *(5)* air, (6) light (7) water and (8) earth. From the subtle elements the material elements (*mahabhuta*) emerge (9-13). Working on this material Self-conciousness then produces the five organs of sense (*jnanendriya*)*: (14)* hearing , *(15)* touch, (16) sight, (17) taste and (18) smell, and the five of action (*Karmendriya*) *(19) speech,* (20) grasping, (21) walking (22) evacuation and (23) procreation. Each of these organs corresponds to an element, in respective order. Finally self-consciousness produces the twenty-fourth of the basic components of the world, mind (*manas*), looked on as a sixth sense, which acts as intermediary between all the ten organs and the outside world. This remarkable and fantastic doctrine of cosmic evolution, interpreted in simple terms, implies that bodies, and indeed the whole cosoms, are products of the ago (*ahankara*), conceived as basically material. But there is another *tattva,* the twenty-fifth. This is *Purus,*literally "the person", the soul. As in Jainism, there is an *infinite* number of souls in the universe, all equal, eternally inactive spectators of the evolution of *Prakrti. Purus* is not dependent on *Prakrti* nor *Prakrti* on *Purusa 'Sabda'* or *'Word'* a universe is conceivable completely devoid of soul and yet evolving in the same way as the universe we know, for intelligence, personally and mind are not parts of the soul. Yet the souls in some way become involved in matter, and their salvation lies in realizing their difference from it. A very important feature of *Sankhya* metaphysics is the doctrine of the three constituent qualities (*guna*), causing virtue (*Sattva*), passion (*rajas*) and dullness (*tamas*). In its undeveloped state cosmic matter contains these three in equilibrium, but as the world evolves one or other of the three preponderates in different objects or beings, and the proportions account for the values of the universe. *Sattva guna,* the quality of virtue, is present in all things tending to truth, wisdom, beauty and goodness, the quality of passion inheres in all that is fierce, violent, energetic, forceful or active, while dullness is found in what is dark, stupid, gloomy, wretched or unhappy. This three fold classification affected many aspects of Indian life and thought and its influence reached far beyond the *Sankhya* school which made it its own. The dualism of soul and matter' and the fundamental atheism of *Sankhya* were somewhat modified in the middle ages as a concession to the prevalent monism and theism. *Purusa* literally means "person" or "man", and *Prakrti* is of feminine gender. It is not surprising that the latter was personified as the wife of the former, especially by the trantric sects. The inactive *Purus* of the earlier system became a generator, and the cold and rather pedantic *Sankhya* in a much modified form, became the common property of popular Indian religion of later times. *Yoga,* the well -known in the west, and is connected etymologically with the English word "Yoke". It may be freely translated "spiritual discipline" or " application. The term is loosely used to imply all the religious exercises and acts of self-mortification of Indian religion, the earnest follower, of such practices being a *yogi.* In his broad sense *Yoga* has been part of the teaching of every Indian sect, but it was also the name of a distinct school, which emphasized psychic training as the chief means of salvation. The basic text of this school is the *Yoga Sutras* of Patanjali; this teacher was traditionally identified with a famous grammarian believed to have lived in the 2nd century B.C, but the *Sutras* in their present form are pobably several centuries later. The metaphysical ideas of the *yoga* school were originally closely akin to those of *Sankhya,* but they differed in that they brought a deity into the picture (Ibid. pp. 324-25). As in olden days there was a pious king named *Bhayajit.* Under him, all the subjects were happy and prosperous. Once a *Brahmin* came to him crying "Oh! king, there is certainly sin in your kingdom, or why my young son will die untimely? Please get my son back from the other world". The king accordingly demanded the return of the Brahmin's son from the God *Yama,* on whose refusal a fight ensued. Yama was defeated. then came *Brahma,* the Creator, who told the king: "life and death follow *Karma.* Yama has nothing to do with them. You rather draw a picture of the Brahmin son". The king did son *Brahma* put life to that picture and told the king : "As you have conquered the *nagna Pretas* (naked ghosts) you will be, henceforth, known as *Nagnajit,* you could draw this picture in this world. You got to the divine *Silpin Visvakarman i.e 'Nam'* who will teach you everything regarding *Citravidya* or paintings or picturesques." (D.N. Shukla; Royal Arts; Faizabad (U.P) India 1967. pp. 75-76. Hereafter described as R.A.) The God (*Isvara*) of Yoga was not a creator, but a specially exalted soul, which has existed for all eternity without ever being enmeshed in matter. Thus the God of Yoga resembled the Buddha of the lesser vehicle, or the glorified *Tirthankara* of Jainism, never coming in contact with his worshippers, but invaluable as an example. He was specially symbolied in the sacred syllable *OM,* which in the Yoga school was much revered as giving insight into the sublime purity of the soul and thus aiding meditation. A *Yoga* theism soon developed, however, and the God of later Yoga texts differs little from that of other schools.

The limbs of yoga has been divided into eight stages, reminding us of the eight fold path of Buddhism but far less practical:-

(1) Self-control (Yama), the practice of the five moral rules: Non-violence, truthfulness, not stealing, chastity, and the avoidance of greed.

(2) Observance (niyama), the regular and complete observane of the above five rules.

(3) Posture (asana), sitting in certain postures, difficult without practice, which are taught to be essential to meditation. The most

famous of these is padmasana, the "Lotus Posture", in which the fact are placed on the opposite thighs, and in which gods and sages are commonly depicted.

(4) Control of the Breath (pranayama), whereby the breath is held and controlled and the respiration forced into unusal rhythms, which are believed to be of great physical and spiritual value.

(5) Restraint (Pratyahara), whereby the sense organs are trained to take no note of their perceptions.

(6) Steadying the mind (dharna), by concentration on a single object, such as the tip of the nose, the navel, an icon, or a sacred symbol.

(7) Meditation (dhyana), when the object of concentration fills the whole mind.

(8) Deep meditation (Samadhi), when the whole personality is temporarily dissolved (W.T.W.I. pp. 325-26).

According to Swami Prabhavananda, *Yoga* aptly compared to a tree bearing luscious fruit. The seed of the Yoga-tree is nourished by *Yama* and *naiyama*, as its begins to germinate its further fed by posture and *pranayama* "the mind diseased" (S.H. p. 248). *Yoga* was sometimes developed in special and rather dobious ways, especially by the *tantric* schools of the Middle Ages. The course of training outlined above was known as 'Royal Yoga' (rajayoga), but other Yoga systems developed, such as the "Yoga of spells" (*mantrayoga*), which taught the continual repetition of magic syllables and phrases as a means of dissociating the consciousness; the "Yoga of Force" (*hattayoga*), which emphasized the importance of physical means such as special acrobatice exercise and very difficult postures, and sometimes advocated sexual union as a means of salvation, and the "Yoga of Dissolution" (*Layayoga*), often identified with *hathayoga*, based on certain ancient Indian physiological notions, which play a big part in the form of Yoga sometimes taught by Western practitioners (W.T.W.I. p. 326). There are some special features in the British *Yogi-Yajnavalkya*. Most early and medieval works on *Yoga* do not dilate upon the prescribed daily duties (such as bath, *sandhya, suryopasthana*), while this work attaches importance to them and dilates upon them. Another outstanding feature is that it upholds the view called '*Jhanakarmasamuccaya*'. One reaches the Highest self by the union of knowledge and actions, one would not secure perfection by treating the two as distinct from one another, therefore one should have recourse to both. *Jnana* is predominant but not so when bereft of actions, activity (actions) is predominant, but not when devoid of knowledge. Therefore, perfection results from both only; just as a bird cannot fly on one wing. (To hold) that *moksa* (release from bondage) follows from knowledge is a sign of indolence. Unwise people desire no activities for "fear of trouble to the body" (B.Y.Y.IX. 28,29,34). Another noteworthy matter is that the Br.Y.Y.arranges the list of the eight *angas* of *Yoga* as *pratyahara, dhyana* and *dharana* and departs from the order stated in *yogasutra* II.28. The *Br. Y.Y.* holds that even a householder by performing the prescribed duties, by thoroughly understanding the nature of *Atman* and by the thorough knowledge of Vedanta passages secures *moksa*. (*H.D.* Vol.1 p. 455). *Yajnavalkya I* 10 states that *Brahmanas, Ksatriyas* and Vaisyas are *duijas* and all rites for them from *Garbhadhana* to *Antyesti* are to be performed with Vedic *mantras*. So a *Vaisya* could take to the order of forest hermits if he chose to do so. But the *Yoga-Yaj* (II. 30 and 35 expressly states that Kastriya can resort to three *asramas* (i.e. he cannot become a *Sanyasin*). *(Ibid. p. 456)*. As a matter of fact, both Hindus and Muslims had mutual admiration for each other's culture, since the early days of the advent of *Islam* into India, and one of the sources of Muslim mysticism was India. Famous Muslim scholars and saints lived and laboured in India during the Medieval period, and they helped the dissemination of the ideas of Islamic philosophy and mysticism in the land. The wholesome spirit of mutual toleration found expression in the growing vaneration of the Hindus for the Muslim saints, and a corresponding Muhammadan practice of venerating Hindu saints; and it ultimately led to the common worship of *Stayapir* (the true saint). It was probably due to this feeling of friendliness that conversion of the Muslims into the Hindu fold and reconversion of the Hindus to their original faith, could be possible during this period and later on. It was out of the desire for mutual understanding that Hindu (Sanskrit) religious literature was studied and translated or summarised in the Muslim courts like those of *Zain-ul-Abidin* in Kashmir and Husain Shah in Bengal. Further, Muslim courts and Muslim preacher and saints were attracted to the study of Hindu Philosophy like *Yoga* and *Vedanta* and the sciences of medicine and astrology. The Hindu astronomers similarly borrowed from the Muslims technical terms, the Muslim calcutions of latitutdes and logitudes, some items of the calendar (*Zich*) and a branch of horoscopy called *Tajik* ; and medicine the knowledge of metallic acids and some processes in iatro-chemistry. The growth of Urdu, of the mingling "Out of Persian, Arabic, and Turkish words and ideas with languages and concepts of Sanskritic origin, is a proof of the linguistic synthesis of the Hindus and the Muslim". (*A.H.I.* p. 401). The period was not entirely barren of important compositions in Sanskrit religious as well as secular, though in this respect it suppers in comparison with the preceding two or three centuries. About A.D. 1300 Parthasarathi Misra wrote several works on the *Karma Mimansa*, of which the *Sastra Dipika* was studied most widely. Some works which expounded the doctrines of the *Yoga*, *Vaisesika*, and *Nyaya* systems of philosophy were produced during this period. The more important were produced during this period. The more important dramas of the time were *Hammirmada-mardana* by Jay Singh Suri (A.D. 1219-1229), *Pradyumnaabhyudaya* by the Kerala prince *Ravivarman, Pratap Rudra Kalyan* by Vidyanath (A.D. 1300), *Parvati Pariyana by Vaman Bhatta Bana* (A.D. 1400.), *Gangadasa Pratapa Vilasa*, celebrated the fight of a prince of Champaner against Muhammad II of Gujarat, by Gangadhar, and the *Vidagdha*

*Madhana* and the *Lalita Madhava,* written about A.D. 1532 by *Rupa Goswami,* minister of Husain Shah of Bengal, and author of no less than twenty-five works in Sanskrit. *Smriti* and grammatical literature flourished during this period in *Mithila* and Bengal the most famous writers being *Padmanabha Datta, Vidyapati Upadhyaya* and Vachaspati of Mithila and Raghunandan of Bengal. It was also marked by the production of a mass of Jaina literature, secular as well as religious. The Vijaynagar rulers extended considerable patronage to scholars like *Sayana*, his brother, *Madhava* Vidyaranya, and others, and there was consequently a wide Sanskrit culture. We find instances of Muslim scholars possesing a knowledge of Sanskrit. (Ibid. p. 408). The Chain of arrangements in Creation's work-shop, which is a truth-showing exhibition of evidences, and an illustration of self-existent power, needs to be linked to the sway of a lofty soul which may, be help of the Divine arm, sustain the burden of the universe, and can, by the strength of its perfect intelligence, supply both substance and system to the work of the terrene and terrest rials (The *Akbarnama, Abu-i-Fazl.* Tr. by H. Beveridge (I.C.S); First Indian reprint 1973, 2nd, 1979 vol.II New Delhi; P.1. Hereafter explained as A.N.). As the *Caliph* was the head of the Church as well as of the state, so Akbar as the Caliph of the age might read his own coronation sermon. He did once try to do this inimitation of Timur and Ulugh Beg. Badauni, Lowe, p. 276 (Ibid. p. 3). His Majesty, from religious motives, dislikes the name *Banda,* or slave, for he believes that mastership belongs to no one but 'God' or 'Nam' or 'Sabda'. He therefore calls this class of men *Chelas,* which Hindi term signifies a *faithful disciple.* The word *Chela* is the same as the Arab, *murid,* a disciple who places implicit belief in his *murshid* or *pir,* the head of the sect. "Any many of this Majesty's special disciples, in 991, called themselves *Chelas* in imitation of the use of this term among *Jogis"* Badauni II, p. 325 (The *Aini Akbari,*, Abul-Fazl-Allami, Vol.1 Tr. by H. Blochmann, M.A 2nd Edition revised by Lt. Co.D.C Phiuott; New Delhi 1889; p. 263. Hereafter mentioned as *A.A.*). Various meanings attach to the term *Slave*, in as much as such a man blindly follows his *Pir. Yoga*, a word with many connotations, is a method frequently taught by the *Guru* for attain divine knowledge, and inner peace through harmony with reality. Common features of all *Yogic* routines are the adoption of a meditative posture (*asana*), controlling the breath and body from the outer world, and concentrating the mind on a *mantra.* (W.Owen Cole, *The Guru In Sikhism,* London; 1982. P.6. Hereafter wrote as G.S.). The chief vein of the body, known as *Susumna,*runs through the spinal column. Along it at different points are six "Wheels" (*Cakra*) or concentrations of psychic energy. A the top of the vein *susumna* within the skull is *Sahasrara* a specially powerful psychic centre symbolically referred to as a lotus. In the lowest "Wheel", behind the genitals is the *Kundalini*, the "serpent power", generally in a quiescent state. By *Yogic* practices the *Kundalini* is awakened, rises through the vein *Susumna,* passes through all the six "Wheels" of psychic force, and unites with the topmost *sahasrara*. By awakening and raising his *Kundalini* the yogi gains spiritual power, and by uniting it with *Sahasrara* he wins salvation. The awakened *Kundalini* gives to the *Yogi* superhuman power and knowledge and many yogis have practised *Yoga* rather for this than for salvation. Some adepts of this form of *Yoga* have developed powers which cannot fully be accounted for by European medical science and which cannot be explained away as subjective, but the physiological basis of *laya-* and *hatha-yoga* is certainly false; there is no *Kundalini, susumna* or *sahasrara*. The ancient mystical indologists, but by open-mined biologists and psychologists, who may reveal the true secret of the *yogi*. For whatever we may think about his spiritual claims there is no doubt that the advanced *Yogi* can hold his breath for very long periods without suffering injury, can control the rhythm of his own heart-beats, can withstand extremes of heat and cold, can remain healthy on a starvation diet, and, despite his austere and frugal life and his remarkable physical contortions, which would ruin the system of any ordinary man, can often survive to a very advanced age with full use of his faculties. **Mimamsa** ("Enquiry"), differed in origin from the other systems in that it was not so much a school of salvation as of exposition. Its original purpose was to explain the *Vedas*, and it was virtually a survival of *Brahmanism*. The earliest work of the school is the *Sutras* of *Jamini* (Perhaps of the 2nd century B.C.), which set out to show that the *Vedas* are eternal, self-existent, and wholly authoritative, and to defend their authenticity against all comers. This led to some development of logic, dialectics and semantics in the school *Sabarasvamin* (? 6th century) the greatest of *Mimamsa* scholars, had much to say on law. It was only in the 7th and 8th centuries that the school developed a full philosophy of salvation, according to which respect for the *Vedas* and observance of their rules were essential first steps on the road. By the time of Kumarila (8th century) the *Mimamsa* school was beginning to merge with the *Vedanta* (W.T.W.I. pp. 326-27). In the sixth and seventh centuries A.D. *Saivism* seems to have been replaced *Vaishnavism* as the imperial religion of Northern India. It counted among its votaries supreme rulers, foreign as well as indigenous, such as *Mihiragula, Yasodharman, Sasanka* and *Harsha*. Among renowned *Pasupata acharyas* of the age was the famous *Udyotakara*, the writer of a gloss on *Vatsyayana's* commentary on the *Nyaya Sutras*. In the eighth century the country Kerala on the Malabar coast produced a teacher who, though not an adherent of any form of sectarian saivism, did much to popularise devotion to Siva among the teeming millions of India. This was the *Sankaracharya*, one of the post-gupta period. *Sankara* came of a Brahmana family of *Kaladi*. He was an ardent *Vedantist* and the most powerful exponent of the doctrine of pure monism (*advaita*) which he elucidated in his commentaries on the classical *Upanishads*, the *Bhagavad Gita* and the *Brahma sutras* of *Badarayana*. He was not only a great thinker but an able organiser.

Among the most durable monuments of his organising zeal are the famous monasteries at Sringeri in Mysore, Dwaraka in Kathiawar, Puri in Orissa and Badrinath on the snowy heights of the Himalayas. He died at a comparatively early age, and his memory is held in affectionate reverence by millions of Hindus throughout India (A.H.I. p. 203). The earliest among the Tamil Vaishnava saints were the *Alvara*. The most renowned among them seem to have flourished in the seventh and eighth centuries A.D. The *Alvars* represented the emotional side of *Vaishnavism*, and they were followed by a line of *acharyas* who represented its intellectual side. Foremost among the *acharyas* were *Nathemuni, Yammunacharya* and *Ramanuja*. The last-mentioned teacher was the son of a Brahmana who lived in a village near Madvas. Ramanuja made Kanchi and *Srirangam* the chief centres of his activities, but the hostility of the Chola government compelled him to seek shelter at the *Hoysala* court in the Mysore country. He died in twelfth century A.D. he combated the absolute monism of *Sankara* and laid emphasis on *Bhakti* as a means of salvation. The school of philosophy that he established was known as *Visishtadvaita* or qualified monism. His followers are known as *Sri Vaishnavas*. Many of the great medieval reformers of India drew their inspiration from his teachers. Shortly after Ramanuja lived Madhva, a famous exponent of the dualistic school of the *Vedanta* (Ibid. p. 205). It is known to us that in the Muslim courts the philosophy of Hindu saints on *Yoga* and *Vedanta* was not only popular, but it was also preached by the Muslim saints. For example, the illness of *Shah Jahan* and the consequent scramble for the throne among his sons, and subjected the old Emperor to extreme humilation and agony till his exit from this world. *Shah Jahan* had four sons, all of mature age at that time-*DaraShukoh* aged 43, *Shuja* aged 41, *Aurangzed* aged 39, and *Murad* aged 33 and two daughters, *Jahanara,* who sided with Dora Shukoh, and *Raushnara*, who joined the party of *Aurangzeb*. All the brothers had by that time gained considerable experience in civil and military affairs as governors of provinces and commanders of armies, but there were differences among them in personal qualities and capacities. The eldest of them, Dara Shukoh, was in the confidence of his father, who desired him to be his successor. A man of eclectic views, liberal disposition, and of scholarly instants, Dara Shukoh mixed with the followers of other faiths and studied the doctrines of the *Vedanta* Talmud, the *New Testament* and the works of *Sufi* writers. He caused a Persian version of the *Atharva Veda* and the upanishads to be made with the assistance of some Brahmana scholars and aimed at finding a *modus vivendi* among the apparently hostile creeds. From this he naturally incurred the displeasure of the orthodox members among his co-religionists, who went against him. But he was not a heretic. He never "discarded the essential dogmas of Islam; he only displayed the eclecticism of the *Sufis*, a recognised school of Islamic believers. If he showed contempt for the external rites of religion, he only shared the standpoints of many noble thinkers of all churches, such as John Milton." His latest biographer has aptly remarked: "it is hardly an exaggeration to say that any one who intends to take up the solution of the problem of religions peace in India must begin the work where Dara had left it, and proceed on the path chalked out by that prince." (Ibid. p. 480). *Vedanta* ("the End of the *Vedas*"), also called *Uttara Mimamsa* ("Later Mimamsa"), is the most important of the six systems, and, in its many sub schools, it has produced the characteristic features of modern intellectual Hinduism. The basic text of the system is the *Brahm Sutras* of Badarayana, written early in the Christan era, which have been commented on by many scholars of all ages, down to the present day. *Vedanta* is still a living school, and modern theologian and mystical teacher such as Vivekananda and Aurobindo Ghose, and philospher such as Sir S. Radhakrishna, are all Vedantists. The dectrines of *Vedanta* were based on the *Upanisads*, and gave logical and organised form to their many mystical speculations. The classical *Vedanta* is that of the great philospher *Sankara* (1788-820), a South Indian Saivite Brahman, who in a short lifetime composed extensive commentaries on the *Brahm Sutras* and the Chief Upanisads, travelled all over India preaching his dectrines, and founded an order of Hindu monks. *Sankara* was an orthodox *Brahman*, for whom all the *Vedic* literature was sacred and unquestionably true. To harmonize its many paradoxes he had recourse to an expedient already known in Buddhism. (W.T.W.I. p. 328). Quite early in the history of the Great Vehicle feminine divinities found their way into the pantheon. One such was *Prajnaparamita,* the perfection of Insight, the personification of the qualities of the *Bodhisattva,* later, the Buddhas and *Bodhisattvas*, who were thought of as male, were, like the gods of Hinduism, endowed with wives, who were the active aspect, the "force" or "Potency" (*Sakti*) of their husbands. The god was thought of as transcendent and aloof, while the goddess was active in the world, thus the god might be best approached through the goddess. The productive activity of the divine was thought of interms of sexual union, an idea as old as *Rig-Veda*. With the spread of these ideas sexual symbolism, and even sexual intercourse as a religious rite, were incorporated into the teachings of some schools of both Hinduism and Buddhism. (Ibid. pp 279-80). It was also a double standard of truthy. On the everyday level of truth the world was produced by Brahma, and went through an evolutionary process similar to that taught by the *Sankhya* school from which *Sankara* took over the doctrine of the three *gunas*. But on the highest level of truth the whole phenomenal universe, including the gods themselves, was unreal-the world was Maya, illusion, a dream, a mirage, a figment of the imagination. Ultimately the only reality was *Brahman,* the impersonal World soul of the Upanisads, with which the individual soul was identical. As in the Upanisads, salvation was to be obtained by recognition of this identity through meditation. *Sankara's* Brahman is not really different from the "void" or the Nirvana of Mahayana

Buddhism (Ibid. p. 328). The Body of Essence eternally penetrates and permeats the universe; it is the ultimate Buddha, of which the other two bodies are emanations, more or less unreal. The Body of Bliss exists in the heavens and will continue until the final resolution of all things into the Body of Essence. The created body was a mere emanation of the Body of Bliss. This reminds us of the Docetic hereby in Christianity, and it has been suggested that Docetism and the doctrine of the three bodies owe much to a common gnostic source. The Buddha's body of bliss is the presiding deity of the most important Mahayana heaven, Sukhavati, the "Happy land," where the blessed are reborn in the buds of lotuses, whise rise from a lovely lake before the Buddha's throne. This divine Buddha is usually called *Amitabha* (Immeasurable Glowry), or *Amitayus* (Immeasurable Age). He too shares the compassion of the *Bodhisattva* for, though he enjoys endless and infinite bliss, he maintains an interest in his world, and especially in his heaven. At his touch the lotuses open, to give birth the blessed, who are nourished and grow through the food of his word. According to some Chinese and Japanese sects whoever calls on his name, however, sinful he may have been, is assured of rebirth in his heaven. *Amitabha* is, infact, a Father in heaven. He, the historical Gautama Buddha, and the Bodhisattva Avalokitesvara are closely associated, and play a bigger part in Mahayanist thought than do other Buddhas and Bodhisattvas, because they are chiefly concerned with this region of the universe and this period of cosmic time, but there are many other heavenly Buddhas, presiding over other heavens and other universes. All are emanations of the primal Body of Essence, which is no other than the Brahman, the world soul or Absolute of the Upanisads, in new guise. The Body of essence is sometimes referred to in later Buddhist writings as *Adi Buddha*, the Primeval Buddha, and is also described as the void (*Sunya*), the true (*Tattva*), wisdom (*Bodhi*), or the womb of those who attain the Goal (*Tathagatagarbha*). Moreover it is Nirvana. The final state, which the *Sthaviravadin* school found so difficult to describe in words, was, for most sects of the Great vehicle, not really different from the mystical union with the absolute Brahman of the Upanisads. The wheel turned full circle, and the mystical monism which early Buddhism so strongly opposed found its way into later Buddhism, but with a new terminology. (Ibid. p. 277). A fact is well recognised by *Sankara's* opponents, who called him a crypto-Buddhist. Sankara's greatness lies in his brilliant dialectic. By able use of logical argument, and, we must admit, by interpreting some phrases very figuratively, he reduced all the apparently self-contradictory passages of the Upanisads to a consistent system which, though no unchallenged has remained the standard philosophy of intellectual Hinduism to this day. The comparison of Sankara in Hinduism with St. Thomas Aquinas in the Roman Catholic Church is a very fair one. The doctrine of Sankara is often known as *advaita* ("allowing no second", i.e monism) or *Kevaladvaita* (strict monism). (Ibid. P.328). A widespread Vaisnavite school known as the *Pancaratra* ("Five nights", of uncertain significance), give a cosmological basis to the myths of *Vasudeva-krsna*, by identify him and his family with cosmic emanations and thus building a system of evolution similar to those of the more orthodox six systems, of which we have described the *Sankhyam* as a typical example. From Vasudeva, identified with Vishnu, the ultimate personal godhead, developed *Sankarsana* (another name of *Krsna's* brother Balarama) at the beginning of time; this emanation was identified with *Prakrit*, or primal matter. The two produced *Pradyumna* (Krsna's son) identified with *manas* or mind, thence arose Aniruddha (Krsna's grandson) who was self-consciouness (*ahankara*). Only then did the three *gunas* evolve, and with them Brahma the demiurge. (Ibid. P.329).

161. *R.T.* Vol.1 Book VII. p. 356.

162. **Note.** *Aryaraja's* abdication which was followed according to Kalhana by a restoration of *Gonanda's* family to the rule of Kashmir. *Meghavahana*, the first prince of the restored dynasty, is said to have been the son of *Gopaditya*, a great grandson of Yudhisthira, living in exile at the court of the king of Gandhara. *Meghavahana,* who is supposed to have taken possession of the throne of his forefathers at the invitation of the Kashmirian ministers, is described as a strong but pious ruler. Various acts attributed to him, like the prohibition of the killing of animals, even in sacrifices and the building of numerous Viharas by his court seem to show *Meghavahana* in the light of a patron of Buddhism. Apart from several legendary anecdotes which are intended to illustrate the spiritual greatness of the king and his command of supernatural powers acquired thereby, Kalhana relates of him a 'digvijaya or conquest of the world. *Meghavahana* is supposed to have undertaken it in order to impose his prohibition of slaughter on the whole earth, and to have subjected in the course of it even *Vibhisana*, the mythical demon king of Lanka or Ceylon. It needs scarcely to be demonstrated that no historical value can attach to the record of such fabulous conquests. That popular belief in Kashmir gave them full credence is shown by the fact that certain royal banners, used still in Kalhana's time, were alleged to have been presented on that occasion by the lord of Lanka. Kalhana himself acknowledges some embarrassment at having to relate "of this king of recent times, acts which cannot be believed by common people". But among these extravagant tales it is yet possible to discern some date which seem historical. The report of *Meghavahana* having come from *Gandhara* acquires significance in view of the unmistable numismatic evidence which points to Kashmir having been founded by *Amrtaprabha, Meghavahana's* chief queen, was known already to On-kong. The attribution of a Stupa known by a Tibetan designation (*Loh-Stoupa*) to the *Guru* of this foreign queen, seems also to rest on genuine tradition. Of *Meghavahana's* son and successor *S'resthasena*, who is said to have borne also the names of *Pravarasena* and *Tunjina*, we are told only that he built various sacred structures at

*Puranadhisthana,* 'the old capital', the site of which is marked by the modern *Pandrethan. S'resthasena* is said to have two sons, of which the elder, *Hiranya*, succeeded him, while the other, *Toramana*, acted as *Yuvaraja. Taramana* presumed to strike coins in his own name, whereupon *Hiranya* threw him into prison for the remainder of his life. During his long captivity a son was born to him, who was brought up in disguise and in humble surroundings, but ultimately ascended the throne as *Pravarasena* II of *Hiranya's* historical existence we do not possess at present independent evidence. But the name of *Toramana* is found on a species of Kashmir copper coins of which remarkably large quantities have been preserved to this day. The connection of this coinage with Kalhana's notice cannot be doubted; but the interesting historical questions which are raised by it, and which have been fully discussed elsewhere, do not admit at present of a certain solution. By the evidence of the characters of their legend the coins bearing the name of *Toramana* must belong to their earliest issues to the fifth or sixth century of our era. They are undoubtedly the oldest representatives of that peculiar type which the copper coinage of Kashmir exhibits throughout the whole of the Hindu period. The fact of this type making its first appearance of the coins of *Toramana* and the abundance of their issues suggest that these coins were first struck b y some powerful conqueror. It has accordingly been supposed that the *Toramana* of these coins is identical with the Epthalite king *Toramana*, the father of *Mihirakula,* of whom it can be shown that he ruled over the Panjab and probably also Kashmir towards the close of the fifth century (R.T. Vol.1. pp. 81-83). Epic poetry and the drama in the period after the great Guptas did not always reach the level of *Bharavi* and *Bhavabhuti.* But the later age still produced poets and playwrights of ability like *Magha*, Sri *Harsha, Bhattanarayana, Kshemisvara,* and *Krishna Misra.* Lyric poetry flourished long after *Bhatrihari*, and the twelfth century saw the composition of *Jayedeva* of the *Gita Govinda,* one of the sweetest of the Sanskrit song-books. Works of merit continued to be produced in other field of learning and literature. The prose romance of *Dandin,* the later versions of the didactic fables of the *Panchatantra*, the ethical composition, of *Santideva* and treatise on polity written by *Kamandaka* and *Somadeva* may be mentioned in this connection. In one domain, that of historical literatue, the Post-Gupta period produced works the like of which had not been seen in earlier ages. The msot notable among them were the *Harsha-Charita* of Bana, the *Rama-Charita* of *Sandhyakara,* the *Vikramanka-Charita* of Bilhana and the *Rajatarangini* of Kalhana. *Sankara, Ramanuja* and other eminent philosphers of the epoch under review do not suffer by comparison with the great masters of the days of *Kanishka* and the *Satavahanas.* In astronomy, the period of *Yadava* rule produced the great *Bhaskara*. We have towards the close of the age under review a number of polymaths like *Bhoja* of *Dhara*, *Somesvara* III of *Kalyana* and *Kshamendra* of Kashmir who showed their interest in such diverse subjects as poetry, rhetoric, polity, philosophy, astronomy, architecture, medicine, alchemy, music and painting. (*A.H.I.* p. 210). If this argument is correct, we should, indeed, have to charge Kalhana with having placed the father some seven hundred years after the son. But it must be remembered that as far as our present knowledge goes, Kashmir may well have known another and later ruler bearing the name *Toramana;* the name though unusual and probably of *Turkish* origin, can be show from Kalhana's narrative to have been borne by a Hindu narrative to have been borne by a Hindu Sahi prince of Gandhara as late as the tenth century. However, the question as to the real issuer of the *Toramana* coins may ultimately be decided, it will be difficult to explain why he should appear in Kalhana's narrative as an ill-fated pretender. According to Kalhana, *Toramana* died in captivity, and his son *Pravarasena,* who had grown into a youth by that time, left Kashmir for a tour of pilgrimages. *Hiranya* himself is supposed to have died shortly afterward, after a rule of thirty-one years. (*R.T.*Vol.1. p. 83).

163. R.T. Vol.1 Book VII. p. 356.
164. *Ibid.*
165. *Ibid.* p. 357. **Note.** It is doubtful whether the *Naga* here mentioned is identical with the princess of that name referred *Kallana*. *Kallana*, the mother of the latter, is there described as an aunt of *Kalasa*, not as his sister, as our passage would represent her as his mother.
166. *Ibid.*
167. **Note.** Term *Prithvigiri* which is composed of two words i.e. *Prithvi* + *giri*, *Prithvi* according to the poets, the thinkers, and contemplatives of all nations have been attracted to what lay beyond the experience and testimony of their material senses called fort, and have conceived the universe as divided into several "Words", visible and invisible. Obviously the oldest of such speculations, the starting-point for all subsequent ones, is the conception of "The two worlds" *"Word"* Heaven and Earth. Many names are given to each in the *Riv-veda,* but in their special connection as a divine couple, who between them and by their union have given life to all creatures and are ever supplying them with means of preserving that life, they are addressed, jointly and inseparably, as *DYAUS AND PRITHIVI* (V.I. p. 136). Father *Dyaus* (Zeus, Diespiter), the Shining God of Heaven, and mother *Prithive,* the Earth Goddess, are among the oldest of the Vedic deities, by the hymns scarcely reflect their former greatness. They have been cast into the shade by *Varuna,* the encompassing sky, and Indra, the God of thunder and Rain. *Varuna* is the most sublime deity of the early *Vedic* pantheon. He bears the epithet *Asura* (Avestan *Ahura*) and he is the great upholder of physical and moral order, *Rita*, the idea of which is at least as old as the fourteenth century B.C, as we learn from the inscriptions mentioning the names of the *Mitanni* kings. To *Varuna* people turned for forgiveness of sin just as they did to Vishnu in the later age. (A.H.I. p. 38). The latter name is singularly direct and unimaginative; it means simply "the Broad", and if it offeres any interest,

it is from the suggestion of antiquity it contains, since that is scarcely the epithet which would be chosen, out of many, as specially distinctive, in a land of towering peaks and steep-sided ridges, and therefore it does not seem too unlikely that the name, as the conception, may have been familiar prior to the Aryan descent into the *Penjab,* carrying the mind back to the period (Indo-Eranian ?) of dwelling of flat, boundless plains and steepes (V.I. pp. 136-37).

168. *R.T.* Vol.1 Book VII. p. 357.
169. *Ibid.*
170. *Ibid.*
171. *Ibid.* p. 358.
172. *Ibid.*
173. *Ibid.*
174. **Note**. As we know *Prtha's* son is meant *Arjuna*. The story how he recovered the herds of cows in *Virata, Uttara's* father, which Duryodhana had carried off, is fold at length in *Mahabharata.* IV; Adhyayas XXXV. Sqq. *Dhritarashtra* had more than a hundred children, of whom the eldest was *Duryodhana*.
175. *R.T.* Vol.1 Book VII. p. 358.
176. **Note.** *Mahathama,* one who has attained the highest degree in the order of the *Jogis*.
177. **Note.** *Dugdhagahata*, the name of the hillfort here mentioned as *Durgaghata,* but can be safely restored as *Dugdhaghata* with reference to the form found in other passages, the frontier fort on the route to the Darad territory. We find the name in two division is given as *Dugdha* and *ghatta*. But quite erroneously has been given *Satta* against *Dugdha*. Both these passages agree with our own in placing this fort on the border of the Dard territory to the North of Kashmir. The *Daradas* are the modern *Dards* regarding whose territory and ethnography may be consulted. Their seats, which do not seem to have changed since the times of *Herodotus,* extended from Citral and Yasin, across the Indus regions of Gilgit, Cilas, and Bunji to the Kishanganga valley in the immediate north of Kashmir. The tribes inhabiting the latter valley are meant in most of the passages in which the Chronicle mentions the *Daradas* or *Darads*. It must be assumed to have followed in Kalhana's time, as it does at the present day, the mountain range which forms the watershed between the *Vitasta* and Sindh rivers on the one side and the Kisanganga on the other. A closer indication as to the position of *Dugdhaghata* is furnished by the mentioned river *Madhumati*. This *Madhumati* can be no other than the stream of the *Bandapor Nala* (Marked '*Budkool*' i.e. *Budkol*, on the map) which flows into the Volur lake from the North near the village of Kulus, and is to this day known by that name to the Brahman population of the valley. The several *Sangamas* of this stream are still visited as pilgrimage-places by the Brahmans of the neighbouring districts. This accounts for the mention made of this *Madhumati* as a sacred stream in the *Nilamata* Purana, *1261 sqq.* 1398. The other stream of this name

which flows into the Kisanganga at the *Sarada* Tirtha. The *Tirtha* here referred to is the ancient shrine of *Sarada*, traced by M.A. Stein in September, 1892, at *Sardi* in the upper Kishna Valley, circ. 74° 15′ logitude and 340 48′ latitude. The shrine of *Sarada* is situated on a small hill, above the junction of the Kishanganga River with a small stream known to this day as *Madhumati,* which flows from the mountain range to the South East. Almost opposite to *sardi* a large stream, coming from the snowy range towards Cilas, meets the Kisanganga from the North. It is called *Kankatori* on the map, but designated as *Sarasvati* by the *Saradamahatmya* and local tradition. Our verse contains an allusion to the union of these three streams, the Kisanganga which is also called simply *Ganga* or *Sindhu* in the Mahatmya, being represented by *Sarada,* a form of Parvati-Ganga. Kalhana has occasion to mention the shrine of *Sarada (Saradasthana,* in connection with *Jayasimha's* siege of the fort of *Sirahsila*, traced by him some miles below *Sardi.* The pilgrimage to this shrine must have enjoyed considerable renown in old days, as even ALBERUNI heard of it. "In inner Kashmir, about two or three days journey from the capital in the direction twoards the mountains of Bolor, there is a wooden idol called *Sarada* (Sic) which is much venerated and frequented by pilgrims", (See India, Vol.1. p. 117). Abul-Fazl, *Ain-i-Akbari* also mentions the shrine of *Sarada*, adding a story according to which the temple begins to shake on the 8th *Sudhi* of each month (Vol. II. p. 366). The upper Kishanganga valley was practically independent territory or Yaghistan during the Moghul and Pathan rule. This circumstance, in connection with the distance of *Sardi from Kashmir* proper and the difficulty of the paths leading to it, explains why the *Tirtha* has become practically unknown among the Brahman families living in the neighbouring *Parganas* of the *Kamraj*. For the convenience of the worshippers a substitute of the ancient shrine of the goddess has now been provided in the close neighbourhood of Srinagar. At the time prescribed for the *Sarada* pilgrimage, a *Naga* called *Saradakunda*, near the village of *Tsatsa,* some four miles to the North of the Dal lake, is visited by numerous pilgrims. The shrine of *Sarada* is indicated as the northern boundary marked of Kashmir in the *Desavyavastha*. It cannot be thought of inconnection with *Dugdhaghata* on account of its position outside Kashmir. During the visit of M.A Stein in August 1894, at *Bandapur Nala*, he ascertained that a pass leading over the mountains in the North in the direction of Gurez (map '*Goorais*') bears the nameof *Dudakhut*. The close similarity of the names, incombination with the topographical details given below, makes it highly probable that the name of the old fort has survived in that of the pass. In Kashmir *dud* (milk) is the phonetic representative of Sanskrit *dugdha*. In the second part of the modern name, *-Khut*, we have, perhaps, a popular etymology, Kashmiri *Khut,* means a cutting, a narrow passage. Or *Vice Versa,* Kalhana's *-ghata* may be taken as Sanskritized rendering of an earlier Kashmiri form of *Khut*. The pass of *Dudakut* which subsequently ascended, lies at the head of the side valley shown as *Minimarg* on the map. Its position may be fixed approximately at 74° 49′ longitute, and 34° 35′ latitude, and its height at about 11,500. Its immediate approach from the south or Kashmir side is formed by an open valley which for about three miles ascends very gradually with grassy slope. This valley bears the name of *Vijje-Marg*, and may possibly correspond to the *Prajimathika*. The route leading up to the *Dudakhut* pass from the village of *Atavuth* is all along practicable for laden animals, and was, until the construction of the 'Gilgit Transport Road' over the neighbouring *Tragabat* pass, often used by the *Dard* traders of *Gurez*. It was also, according to the information supplied to me, used regularly by the Sikhs for military transports, until a disaster which befell a convoy through an avalanche lower down in the valley, led them to change the route to the *Tragabal* pass some seven miles to the South East. The latter pass has been adhered to ever since, through it is higher than the *Dudakhut* Pass, and owing to its communication. The watershed on the *Dudakut* pass is formed by an almost level plain about a quarter of a mile broad. To the east of it rises abrubtly an isolated rocky hillock about 150′ high, which shows precipitous walls to the South and West, and is also on the other sides accessible only with difficulty. The tope of this hilllock forms a small plateau about 100 yards long, and half as broad, which commands a complete view of the approaches of the pass both from South and North. On this plateau M.A. Stein was able to trace scanty remains of walls which seemed to have belonged to polygonal towers such as are found to this day near the *Pir Pantsal* and Tasamaidan Passes. The military position afforded by this hillock is excellent, and it is possible that we have in these remains that last traces of the fort of *Dugdhaghata* referred to in the chronicle. The details furnished by the narrative of the siege of *Dugdhaghata* seem to support this assumption. The configuration of the hillock and the hardness of its rock would make the construction of atank very difficult. Hence we can understand the curions expedient of storing snow and water for the garrison's use *nirhrasa*, which is an easily explained clerical error for *nirhrade*. Of the high elevation at which the for *Dugdhaghata* must have been situated, we have an unmistable indication in the heavy snowfall which put an end to the siege. Fate lets some fall as they rise, and throws up others while they fall, and thus seems to play with (men if they were) balls. After what is stated previously about the drought and the warm weather, which had reduced the fort's snow-supply. It is clear that this snowfall must have occured at the close of the summer or atleast early in the autumn. And in this connection it may be noted that heavy snow-storms have more than once been experienced in recent years on the neighbouring Tragabal Pass as early as September. Notwithstanding this elevation, and the consequent severity of the climatic conditions, a fort erected at the *Dudakhut* pass would have remained in habitable for a small garrison throughout the year. This is proved by the fact that the block huts built on the even more exposeded *Tragabal* Pass have been inhabited through recent winters by employes of the Dak and telegraph service of the Gilgit Road. Finally, we may point out that the narrow gorges of the *Madhumati* and its northern tributary, through which the route to the Dudakhut pass leads above and below the village of *Atavuth*, correspond exactly to the whole army abandoned its stores, threw away the treasure, left its valuables and dropped its arms, thinking of nothing but flight. Thus the route followed by the Kashmirian force on its disastrous retreat from *Dugdhaghata*.

178. **Note.** The *lavanyas* mentioned here for the first time, play a great part in the internal troubles. They must have formed at that time an important tribal section of the rural population of Kashmir, and their name, like that of the *Tantrins*, survives in a modern *'Kram'* name of very frequent occurance, viz, *luni*. The numerous passages in which the Lavanyas as a body or individuals are referred to, tell us nothing about their origin, but show that many of them must have held a position of influence as land-owners or tribal headmen. Then furious, like another god of death, he ordered the governor (*Ananda*) to slay all of the Damaras who had become over powerful. Where we read of a prosecution of the *Lavanyas* in *Madavaraja*, they are repeatedly designated as *Damaras*, the designation *Luni*, as other 'Krams' in Kashmir, is nowadays a mere name, there being nothing to distinguish those who bear it from other Muhammadan agriculturists in regard to customs, occupation, etc. *Lunis* are found throughout the valley. According to a villagers statement, they are popular supposed to have come from Cilas.

179. **Note.** King *Janaka* held assemblies of learned men for discussion. One *bandin* (i.e. *Suta* at his court used to argue with learned men, defeated them and plunged them in water. *Uddalaka* had a pupil *Kahoda*, who married the daughter of his *guru*. She conceived and the child in the womb rebuked his father when he committed mistakes in repeating *Veda*. The father cursed the foetus that he would be defective in eight limbs. *Astavakra* defeated *bandin* and those who had been thrown into water (including *Kahoda* who had been defeated by *Bandin*) were revived by *Varuna* and then *Kahoda* recited a verse set out in the note below (*H.D. Vol.1* p. 394). The most distinguished among the tribes of the period were at first the *Kuru* and the *Panchals* with their capital at *Asandivat* and *Kampila* (*Kampilya*) respectively. The former occupied *Kurukshetra 'Word'* or *'Sabad'* the tongue of land between the *Sarasvati* and the *Drishadvati* (*Chitang-Rakshi*) *Brahmans* as well as the districts of *Delhi* and Meerut. The latter occupied the *Bareilly, Budaun* and *Farrukhabad* districts of the united Provinces and some adjoining tracts. The *Kuru* nation was probably formed by the amalgamation of several small tribes including the *Panchalas* sprans from an obscure *Rig-Vedic* tribe known as the *Kruvis*, with whom were associated the *Srinjayas* and the *Turvasas*. The later *Vedic* texts mention powerful *Kuru* kings like *Balhika-Pratipiya*, *Parikshit* and *Janamejaya*, all of whom figure prominently in epic legends. *Parikshit* is the hero of a famous song of praise found

in the *Atharva Veda*. It describes him as a Universal King (*raja visvajanina*) and his kingdom as flowing with milk and honey. His son *Janamejaya* is credited with having gone round the earth, completely conquering on every side. His successors were not so powerful as he was. They sustained disasters and were finally obliged to fly from *Kurukshetra*. According to later tradition a scion of the *Kuru* race transferred his residence to *Kausambi* (*Kosam, near Allahabad*) and ruled over a powerful kingdom which survived till the rise of Buddhism. The *Panchalas* also produced conquering kings who engaged in wars and alliances with the *Kurus*. But their chief title to fame rests on their land being the home of theologians and philosophers like king *Pravahana-Jaivali* and the sages *Aruni* and *Svetaketu*. In the time of the Upanishads the fame of the land of the *Panchalas* as a centre of Brahmanical learning was eclipsed by the country of the *Videhas,* who king *Janaka*, the patron of *Yajnavelkya,* won the proud title of *Samrat*. He gathered the celebrities of the *Kuru-Panchala* countries at his court "much as the intellects of Athens gathered at the Court of Macedonian princes." The *Videhan* monarchy fell shortly before the rise of Buddhism, and its overthrow was followed by the rise of the *Vajjian* Confederacy. (*A.H.I.* p. 42). Of the two ancient Sanskrit epics the *Ramayana* is alluded to in, and was probably completed before, the *extant Mahabharat*. But while the *Mahabharata* was known to *Asvalayana* and Panini, there is no similar early reference to the *Ramayana*. The latter who upraised a mountain with his hands," i.e. probably *Krishna*. The latest books refer to Vasudeva of the Yadu family and his close associate, the incarnation of *Nara*, i.e. Arjuna. The nucleus of the *Ramayana* is the story of *Rama,* the eldest son of *Dasaratha,* a prince of the Ikshvaku family of Ayodhya in Fyzabad district of Oudh. The prince married *Sita*, the daughter of *Janaka*, King of *Videha* in North Bihar-owing to a palace intrigue, the *Ikshvaku* prince had to leave his home and go into exile for a period of fourteen years. He repaired to the *Dandaka* forest in the Deccan with the wife and faithful half-brother *Lakshmana*. He dwelt for some time on the banks of the *Godavari* in *Panchavati*, which is usually identified with Nasik. Here he came into conflict with the *Rakshasas* or cannibal chieftain who were a source of disturbance to the peaceful hermits of the locality. Among the hostile chieftains were some persons closely related to *Ravana*, the mighty King of *Lanka* (Ceylon). That potentate sought to avenge his injured relations by carrying off *Sita,* wife of *Rama*, to his inland home. In their distress, the *Ikshvaka* princes allied themselves with *Sugriva, Hanuman* and other monkey chiefs of *Kishkindhya* in the Bellary district of South India and crossed over the Lanka. They killed the *Rakshasa* king with most of his clan and rescued the princess *Sita*. As the period of Rama's exile was now over, he returned with his wife and brother to Ayodhya where he was warmly received by his half brother *Bharata* in whose favour he had been made to relinquish his rights. Meanwhile people came to question the propriety of taking back a princess who had long been kept confined by a *Rakshasa* King. To silence the unreasonable clamour of the multitude, *Rama* had to banish his faithful consort, the ideal of Indian womanhood. The duty of a *Raja,* according to Hindu notions, was always to please his subjects who were his "Children". The viruous royal lady found a shelter in the heritage of *Valmiki*, where she gave birth to the twins, *Kusa* and *Lava*, who subsequently returned to their ancestral home and succeeded to their heritage (Ibid. pp. 92-93).

180. R.T. Vol.1 Book VII. p. 360.
181. **Note.** By *Vataganda* here is meant *Ananda*, who had himself aspired to the office of lord of the Gate. It is not certain what is *Kurvan.* From the reference made to the corporation of priests at *Parihasapura,* it might be concluded that *Ananda* had something to do with the administration of the property of this corporation, and of the shrine to which the later was attached. The name of *Parihasapura* is preserved in that of the Pargana *Paraspor* which, as indicated on the survey map, comprises the well-defined little tract lying between the marshes on the left bank of the *Vitasta* immediately to the South West of *Shadipur.* The identity of the names *Parihasapura* and *Paraspor* is evident on phonetic grounds, and was known to the authors of the Persian Chronicles (Haidar Malik, Muhammad Azim, Birabal Katser). Under King *Harsa* the colossal Buddha image of *Parihasapura* is mentioned among the few sacred statues which escaped being seized and melted down by that king. This colossal image is referred to as *Brhadbuddha,* in connection with the *Rajavihara.*
182. *R.T.* Vol.1 Book VII. p. 361.
183. *Ibid.* **Note.** The expression of *dvaradhikaribhih* does not indicate that there were several 'Lords of the Gate'. It appears that there is only one Gate to see the God that is *'Nam'* or *'Sabad'* but that the disappointed *Ananda* intrigued against all those who were successively holding the office.
184. *Ibid.*
185. *Ibid.*
186. *Ibid.*
187. *Ibid.*
188. *Ibid.*
189. *Ibid.*
190. *Ibid.*
191. *Ibid.* p. 362.
192. *Ibid.*
193. *Ibid.*
194. *Ibid.* p. 363.
195. *Ibid.*
196. *Ibid.*
197. *Ibid.* p. 364.
198. *Ibid.* p. 363.

199. **Note.** This festival, which comes round towards the end of July, is of a decidedly propitiatory character. Pilgrims flock to the *Naga*-shrines which abound in certain districts; the cities teem with snake-charmers, whose weird charges eagerly crawl around the pans with milk placed at intervals on the ground in all the principal. Thoroughfares, before the admiring eyes of a devout and festive throng. It is worthy of notice: Ist, that temples dedicated to serpents are not found in the North of India; 2nd, that the priests of such temples are never Brahmans, but belong to the lower castes. Indeed, the old Aryan spirit is so much alive still in the noble castes, that they hold-the serpent to be of evil omen and a Brahman, if he happens to see one in the morning, will give up for that day whatever work or errand he may have on hand. (V.I. pp. 294,296).
200. R.T. Vol.1 Book VII. p. 363.
201. *Ibid.*
202. *Ibid.*
203. *Ibid.*
204. *Ibid.*
205. *Ibid.*
206. *Ibid.*
207. *Ibid.*
208. *Ibid.*
209. **Note.** The ancient measure of the *Khari,* mentioned already in a hymn of the *Rig-veda* (IV. 32.17), and known toPanini, has remained to the present day the standard of weight in Kashmir. It is called *Khar* in Kashmir, but has been known in the official language for centuries past by the Persian designation of *Kharwar* (for *Khar-bar,* 'ass's load'). The latter term, evidently substituted by a kind of popular etymology for the Kashmir one, is found already in Abul-Fazl's account (*Ain-i-Akbari*, ii, p. 366). In the *Lokaprakasa* the measure is still named as *Khari* or *Kharika*. The division and weight of the *Khar* does not appear to have changed since the time of Akbar, as the table of weights in actual use, as given by (Mr. Lawrence, K.V. P.243) agrees with statements recorded by *Abul-Fazl* (L.C) and Moorcroft, *Travels*, ii. P.135, in making the *Khar* (*Kharwar*) the equivalent of 1920 *pals* (Sanskrit pala). Taking the latter measure as equal to 3/3/5 *Tolas*, the Khar corresponds to 177/129/175 Ibs. avoirdupois (Lawrence). The *Khar* is divided into 16 *Trakhs*, the Trakh again into 4 *manuths* (Abu-L-Fazl's *Man*) of 30 *pals* each, or into 6 *Sers* of 20 *Pals.* Owing to the ancient custom, until quite recently in force in Kashmir, of estimating and paying salaries, etc in grain instead of cash, the term *Khar* came to be used also as the designation of a mometary value. The *Lokaprakasa* according speaks in several passages (ii. Pr). of a *dinnarakhari* or *suvarnakharika*, crossponding to Abul-Fazl's distinction between the 'Kharwar in Kind' and the 'Kharwar in money' (*Kharwar-i-naqdi*); Similarly since early times, to designate that area of land under rice-cultivation which is supposed to require a *Khar's* weight of rice-seed; compared *bhumikhari* in *Lokapr* ii with *Kharika*, Panini,

v.i.45, and (Lawrance, K.V. p. 243). During the time of *Avantivarman*, Kalhana gives 200 *Dinnaras* as the price of a Khari of rice for years of good harvest previous to Suyya's drainage operations, and 36 *Dinnaras* as the reduced price after the execution of the latter. Subsequently we read of 500 *Dinnaras* being paid for a Khari in the reign of *Harsa* during a famine. For prices of later famines, where 1500 and even 10,000 *Dinnaras* are mentioned, respectively. Estimated by this standard the 100,000 *Dinnaras* daily pay which *Udbhata, Jayapida* chief pandit was lucky enough to draw, was a very respectable remuneration indeed, corresponding in value to 500 *Kharis* of grain. Calculated at the rate indicated by *Abul-Fazl*, and increased by 12 percent in accordance with the greater intrinsic value of the earlier copper coinage, the Lakh of Udbhata's daily pay would amount to 28 ½ rupees. This daily allowance, though acceptable enough even for a Pandit of the present day, would scarcely excite the attention of a modern Chronicler. But if we convert the sum named by Kalhana into its equivalent in grain, and estimate the present value of the latter according to the commutation rate of ¼ rupee for the *Khari*, we arrive at the sum of 625 rupees as representing approximately for the present day the same purchasing power which *Udbhata's* 100,000 *Dinnaras* had in his own times. (R.T. Vol.II. p. 327).

210. **Note.** The *Tolaka,* the modern *Tola*, is in Kashmir still as in *Abul-Fazl's* time (*Ain-i-Akbar*; ii, pp.354, 366) = 16 *masa* = 96 *raktika* (rats). The *Pala*, which according to the authorities corresponds to 4 *Karsa*, each of 16 *masa,* must be taken as = 4 *tolaka*. The *prastha* is usually estimated at 16 *pala*. The term pal is still used in Kashmir for 1/20 ser and also called 'moment' in Dogri language.

211. **Note.** Salt is not found in Kashmir, but it was imparted from the Panjab and Ladakh. The increach in the import of salt is especially satisfactory, as in 1892, it was shown that the annual average of consumption in Kashmir was exactly half of that prevailing in the Punjab (P.G.K. p. 69).

212. **Note.** Nor is Assafoetida produced within the limits of Kashmir; see ib. p. 68.

213. R.T. Vol.1 Book VII ; p. 364.

214. **Note.** With *na mrd apyavasesita* compared with the Kashmiri saying, mits ti *thavunas na* ( not even the earth has been left).

215. **Note.** Holada is the modern *Vular* Pargana, which comprises the valley opening to the North East of the *Vitasta* between the Parganas of Dachunpor and Vihi. Its present administrative centre is Tral, 75$^{0}$-11' at longitude and 33$^{0}$-56' at latitude. There remained (faithful) three Damaras from Lohara, *Devasarasa* and *Holada* and one Damara-lady from *Nilasva*. The position is still more distinctly indicated by two officers of king *Jayasimha* being besieged by the rebel Damaras of *Holada* within the temple of *Avantisvamin* at *Avantipura*. The latter place belongs still to the *Vular* pargana. The above identification is further supported by the passage which mentions the Damaras of *Holada* along with those of *Khaduvi* i.e. *Khruv* in the neighbouring *Vihi* Pargana. The written

passages holding the name as *Holala*, using the latter 'क' (which in Kashmir is called *bud rakara* the big r') to mark the pronunciation of 'd' as 'r'. This as well as the reading *Holara* brings *Holada* still nearer to the modern representative of the name. In view of the above passage quoted above, Kalhana considered the correction *Holadayam* for *holalayam* is of indispensable. The Damara from *Holada* is probably *Trillaka*. The position of the latter's residence is nowhere clearly indicated, but it shows that it could not have been far from Martanda. Perhaps it was in the upper Lidar valley which adjoins *Holada* or Vular. The circumstances in this connection has already been suggested that *Trillaka's* seat was in *Holada*.

216. **Note.** Kashmir from ancient times to the present day has been popularly divided into two great parts, whose modern *Kamraz* and *Maraz* are derived from the terms *Kramarajya* and *Madavaraja* used by Kalhana and his successors. According to the generally prevailing notion *Kamraz* comprises the *Parganas* on both sides of the *Vitasta* below Srinagar, and *Maraz* those above. This boundary of the two divisions can be traced out clearly in *Abul-Fazl's* list of *Parganas* (*Ain-i-Akbari*, II. P.368). For an examination of all passages in the *Rajatarangini* shows that it existed already in Kalahana's time. It has been correctly indicated the general meaning of the modern terms, but it was wrongly informed when placing the boundary at the junction of the *Vitasta* and *Sindhu* rivers. The term *Kamraz* is occasionally used also in a more restricted sense for the designation of seven Parganas in the extreme of North West of the Valley (*Khuyahom, Zainagir, Lolan, Uttar, Machapur, Hamal, Kruhin*). This explains the varying accounts referred to by (Prof. Buhler, Report P. 11). The identity of *Madavaraja* with *Maraz* is known to some of the Srinagar Pandits, and the designation of the eastern portion of the valley.

217. **Note.** From the *Shrimad Bhagvad Gita* it has been noted that 'I' and 'Mine' 'becoming a Brahman'. (An article written by P.K. Joseph Dhar; Daily Excelsior, Jammu, August 16, 2006. p. 6).

218. R.T. Vol.1 Book VII. 364.

219. **Ibid. Note.** The working of water wheels and hand -mills still offers a means of subsistence for the poor in towns of Northern India. *Vattadeva* and other exiled Damaras left off turning water wheels, hand mills and the like, and joined him on the march.

220. *Ibid*. p. 365.

221. *Ibid*.

222. **Note.** *Lokapunya* identified with *Lokabavan* in Sanskrit called *Lokabhavana* a fine spring or Naga situated near the village of *Larikpur* $75^0$-12' at longitude and $33^0$-38' at latitude, in the bring Pargana. Near the basin formed by the spring, are the ruins of a small summer house erected by one of the Mughal Emperors, apparently with materials of some earlier building. Fragments of ancient stone images lie in the water near the spring, which is visited by the Brahmans of the neighbourhood.

223. R.T. Vol.1 Book VII. p. 365.

224. *Ibid.*
225. **Note.** *Laulaha* is in all probability the old name of the present *Lolab* Pargana to the North West of the *Vular* lake. The proper Kashmiri pronuciation of the modern name is *Lolav.* Compared for a phonetic parallel *Karnaha, Karnav. Karnadha, or Karnaha, is* the present *Karnav*, a hill district which lies immediately to the West of *Kamraz*. It comprises a portion of the Kisanganga valley above Muzaffarabad, and the several valleys drained by the Karnav river. The latter joins the Kishanganga from the south at $75^{0}$-51' longitude and $34^{0}$-23' latitude. The form *Karnaha* found in the second passage is perhaps, preferable in view of the modern pronunciation ;'ह' and 'ढ' as written in *S'arada* do not differ much. The district seems to have been held in Hindu times by petty chiefs who were, at least nominally, subject to Kashmir. Its habitants were *Khasas* (*Khasakas*) stood prepared to kill *Dhanya,* thinking that under these circumstances he was in *Bhoja's* power. *Lothana,* who appears to have intended an invasion of Kashmir proper, by one of the easy passes which lead from *Karnav* into Uttar or *Hamal* Parganas, is forced by *Udaya's* energetic action to retire into the upper Kishanganga Valley. The *Lokaprakasa* ii, has metamorphosed *Lolav* into *Lulavaka,* and Pt. Sahibram in his *Tirthas,* makes up the form *Lolava* (*i*).
226. *R.T.* Vol.1 Book VII. p. 365.
227. *Ibid.*
228. *Ibid.* p. 366.
229. **Note.** The lacuna of two syllables which the text shows, may conjecturally be filled by reading *tayor ghate.*
230. *R.T.* Vol.1 Book VII. p. 366.
231. *Ibid.*
232. **Note.** *Utrasa* is undoubtedly, the modern village *Vutarus* (map 'Watoassoo') , situated close to *Sangas* in the *Kutahar* Pargana which is at 75°-22′ longitude and 33°-43′ latitude. Pt. Sahibram reproduce the name as *Uttarasa* in his *Tirthas.*
233. **Note.** *Prasastaraja* , the *Labanya,* is the Damara of the preceding verse in the Kashmir history. Term *DAMARA* is one of the common occurence in Chronicle, and the persons whom it designates play a prominent part in the later portions of the narrative. It is, hence, important to ascertain its significance with as much precision as our materials will permit. The word *Damara*, in the sence in which it is used in the *Rajatarangini* and the later Chronicles, has not yet been traced outside Kashmir. Neither Kalhana nor his successors have thought it necessary to define or explain the term. It cannot, therefore, surprise to us that its true bearing has not been recognised by earlier interpreters that it is a destructive part of the life. One has to be leave it. Therefore, it is requested to everybody, kindly choose the construstive part of the life that *'Nam', 'Word', 'Chamar', 'Candala', 'Sudhra',* etc. From the reference made here, we can see clearly that Kalhana has seen in reality of his own times the behavour of the *Damaras.*

234. *R.T.* Vol.1 Book VII. p. 366.
235. **Note.** Term *Kalinjara*, more correctly spelt the same word. He then underwent much grief on account of the death of *Kalha,* the lord of *Kalinjara*, and of *Malla*, the mother of his chief queen. *Meghamanjari* was propably the chief queen at that time, who had been his beloved consort, and whose fortune had been his support. *Kalha* is mentioned, visited *Sussala* at *Attalika* must have been died in the meanwhile. It shows that *Kalha* was the lord of *Kalinjara* at that period. It cannot be the same place as the well-known *Kalanjara,* 'a city of the *Kalachuri* Kings of Central' India, now represented by the *Kalanjari* hill fort in the *Banda* district of the North West Provinces. The context of the passages where *Kalha* and *Padmaratha,* a later ruler of *Kalinjara*, are mentioned. It shows that some hill territory to the South of Kashmir is meant. To this territory refers clearly also the notice found in *Ferishta's* history (tr. Briggs, Vol.1 pp.89, 99) of 'a hill fort called *Kalunjur* on the frontier of 'Kashmeer'. The fort is mentioned by *Ferishta* as the place where Mahmud of *Ghazna* imprisoned one of his high officials.
236. R.T. Vol.1 Book VII. p. 366.
237. *Ibid.*
238. *Ibid.*
239. *Ibid.*
240. *Ibid.*
241. *Ibid.*
242. *Ibid.*
243. *Ibid*
244. *Ibid*
245. *Ibid.* **Note.** The breaking of camphor is evidently referred to as a custom assuring protection to a stranger.
246. **Note.** The fortress of *Rajagiri* is mentioned under the name of *Rajagiri* in an interesting passage of Alberuni's India, i, p.208. The position of the fortress *Rajagiri* (*recte Rajagiri*), which is referred by Kalahana as in possession of the Raja of Rajouri or *Rajapuri* must be looked for at some point of the upper Suran valley, i.e to the south of the Mount *Tatakuti*. Finally, the 'fortress Lahur', which Alberuni places west of Mount 'Kularjak', can be no other than our *Lohara*. The entrance of the Loharin valley lies almost due west of *Tatakuti*, at a distance of about thirteen miles as the crowflies, the highest peak of the *Pir Pantsal Range*, at the elevation of $74^0$ -32' longitude and $33^0$-44' latitude. The position indicated by Alberuni for *Rajagiri*, and the fact that he saw the fortress on Mahmud Gazani's expedition against Kashmir, suggest that this stronghold was situated in the valley of the *Prunts* Tohi (*Tausi*), which forms the approach to the *Pir Pantsal Pass*. M.A. Stein have listen of the existence of several ruined forts between *Bahramgalla* and Suran valley, but have never been able to visit the latter. A close examination of the local traditions and of the topography of that hill region will probably enable us to fix the positionof *Rajagari* with as much accuracy as that of *Lohara*.
247. R.T. Vol.1 Book VII. p. 367.

248. *Ibid.* p. 368.
249. *Ibid.*
250. *Ibid.*
251. *Ibid.*
252. *Ibid.*
253. *Ibid.*
254. ***Note.*** From the pedigree of the *Lohara* family detailed in this book and compare the genealogical table in Appendix.
255. *R.T* Vol.1 Book VII, p. 368.
256. **Note.** It appears from the study that *Satavahana* the ancestor of the *Lohara* family. The name *Satavahana* has been corrected here after in place of *Sarthavahana*. The name is found in the alternative form *Salavahana* also as that of a Raja of *Campa* grant (edited by Prof. Kielhorn, *Ibid* Ant; XVII. p.8) King *Sala* has been rightly identified by him with *Salavahana*, who is mentioned as King *Samavarmadeva's* predecessor in *Campa* grant. The latter was executed in the reign of *Asata*. The southern potentate who put an end to the rule of the *Sungas* and the *Kanvas* is described in the Puranas as an *Andhra*, a name applied to the people of the Telugu speaking tract at the month of the *Godavari* and the *Krishna*. In contemporary epigraphic records, however, kings of this line are invariably referred to as *Satavahana* and a "district of the *Satavahana*" has been proved to lie in the neighbourhood of *Bellary* in the *Kanarese* are of the Madras presidency. The memory of the dynasty lingers in the story of the king *Salivahana* famous in Indian folk-lore. This legendary hero seems to have appropriated to himself the glorious deeds of several distinguished members of long line of emperors of the Deccan. The founder of this family was *Simuka* but the man who raised it to eminence was his son or nephew *Satakarni* I. The latter allied himself with the powerful *Maharathi* chieftains of the western Deccan, and signalised his accession to power by the performance of the horse-sacrifice. Sometime after his death, the *Satavahana* power seems to have been submerged beneath a wave of *Saythian* invasion. But the fortunes of the dynasty were restored by *Gautamiputra Satakarni*, who took pride in calling himself the destroyer of the *Sakas* (*Saythians*), *Yavanas* (Greeks) and *Pahlavas* (Parthians). *Gautamiputra* built up an empire that extended from *Malava* in the north to the *Kanarese* country in the south. His son, *Vasishthiputra Pulumayi* ruled at *Pratishthana* of *Paithan* on the banks of the *Godavari*, now situated in the *Aurangabad* district of the *Nizam's* dominions. Two other cities, *Vaijayanti* (in North *Kanara*) and *Amaravati* (in the *Guntur*) *district* attained eminence in the *Satavahana* period. A king name *Vasisthiputra Satakarni*, who may have been a brother of *Pulumayi*, married the daughter of the contemporary *Saka* Satrap (Viceroy) *Rudradaman* 1, but this did not prevent the latter from inflicting crushing defeats on his southern relation. The power of the *Satavahanas* revived under *Sri Yajna Satakarni* but he was the last great prince of the line, and after him the empire began to fall to pieces

liek the *Bahmani* kingdom of a later age. The most important among the succeeding powers in the Deccan were the *Abhiras* and the *Vakatakas* of *Nasik* and Berar in *Upper Maharashtra*, the *Ikshvakus* and the *Salankayanas* of the Krishna and west Godavari districts, the *Pallavas* of *Kanchi* (near *Madras*) and the *Kadambas* of *Vaijayanti* or *Banavasi* in North *Kanara*. (A.H.I. pp.115-16). The satraps of the upper Deccan and part of Western India belonged to the *Ksheharata* race, probably a branch of the *Sakas*. They carved out a principality on the ruins of the early *Satavahana* empire and attained great power under *Nehapana*. But they were finally overthrown by *Gautamiputra Satakarni* who restored the fallen fortunes of the *Satavahana* family. The satraps of Ujjain traced their descent from the Lord (*Svamin*) *Chashtana,* the *tiastanes* of Ptolemy the geographer. *Rudradaman*, grandson of *Chashtana,* ruled from about A.D. 130 to 150, and was one of the greatest Saka rulers of ancient India. He entered into a matrimonical alliance with the *Satavahana* dynasty, but this did not prevent him from inflicting defeats on his southern neighbour. If his court poet is to be believed his sway extended from the Konkan in the south to sind and Marwar in the north. The successors of *Rudradaman*, were not so strong as he was. Internal feuds were common. Power gradually *fell into* thehands of the Abhire chieftains. The death-knell of Satrapal rule in Malwa and Kathiawar was sounded when a new indigenous empire rose in the Ganges valley in the fourth century A.D and the arms of Samudra Gupta and Chandra Gupta II swept through the tableland of Malwa and involved Saka and Abhira in common ruin (Ibid. p.119). One of the most important changes related to the system of provincial government. The system of government by hereditary officials with the Persian title of Satrap was introduced in Taxila, Mathura, Ujjain and a few other places and we have references even to functionaries with the Greek titles of *meridarch* and *strategoes*. A body of counsellors (*mati sachiva*) seems to have been associated with some of the provincial rulers, but the rule of others was often of a purely military character. The influence of the system of military governors (*strategos*) is clearly seen in the appointment of *Satrvahama* kings of district officers styled *mahasenapati*. In spite of the prevalance of military rule in certain areas the old self-governing institutions did not wholly perish. Town councils (*nigama sabha*) *and* officials styled *nagarakshadarsa* (city judges) are mentioned in several records and these correspond to the municipal commission and the *nagala viyohalaka* of the Maurya period. The affairs of the village continued to be controlled by the village functionaries led by the head-man. The village assembly afforded a field for co-operation between kings and villagers (Ibid. p.131). There is no reason to doubt that the Greek writer described the actual conditions as witnessed by him as opposed to the theory of the law books. The restoration of the fourfold division of caste (*Chaturvarna*) was sought by the great *Gautamiputra Satakarni*, who referred to *dvijas* (Brahmanas) and *avaras* (lower orders) as objects of his special care and to the *Kshatriyas* as a conceited class whom he did much to repress. The cause of *Gautamiputra's* hostility to the warrior caste is not clear. It is possible that the ranks of the latter were being swelled of the *Manava-dharma-sastra* (Institutes of Manu) as regarded Kshatriyas. It is well-known that the the wrath of the great *Satavahana* was specially directed against the latter. Caste rules could not, however, be rigidly enforced. The *Satavahanas* themselves intermarried with *Sakas*, and Brahmanas figure as generals and kings like Drona of old (Ibid. p.132) *Vats*, where it is mixed (technically "cleansed" with water and milk to sweeten it. (R.C. Majumdar; *The Vedic Age; Reprint, Bombay*, 1988. p.378. Hereafter cited as *V.A.)* In the times of emergency they had to pay benevolences. But such imposts were levied on rare occasions and a *Saka* ruler specially notes the fact that he carried out certain works without resorting to forced labour, extra case or benevolences. In parts of India the lot of the rural population was probably a little harder. Some idea of the burdern borne by the ordinary villagers in these tracts may be gathered from the immunities (*Parihara*) that were granted, according to certain records of the *Satavahanas* and their successors, to *Vatakas* and *Kshetras*, this is, gardens and fields, conferred on privileged individuals or communities by royal personages. Such plots were "not to be entered by royal officers, not to be touched by and of them, not to be dug for salt, not to be interfered with by the district police." A fuller list of various kinds of immunity is given in a *Pallava* record which says that a garden which belongs to the Brahmanas is to be "free from *Kara* (extra cess), free from the taking of sweet and sour milk, free from the taking of the onen in succession, free from the taking of grass and wood, free from the taking of vegetables and flowers." (Ibid. p.135). During the period of *Satavahana* sacrifices are very much in evidence. Of the occasions on which the *Maurya* king, according to *Strabo,* went out in times of peace, one was for the performance of sacrifice. Sacrifices were also offered by private persons and the services of "philosophers" were requitioned for the purpose. The people of India, generally sober, freely indulged in drink when these ceremonies were performed. Asoka tried to put a stop to the killing of living creatures on such occasions. *Vaishnava* reformers made an attempt to spiritulize sacrifices by giving them a new ethical meaning. But a great Brahmanic revival followed the rise of the houses of *Pushyamitra, Simuka-Satavahana* and *Siva-Skandavarman* Pallava. Rites like the *Asvamedha* and *Vajapeya* came to be celebrated by princes on a grand scale. (Ibid. p.139). The Scythian conquerors of India had received their first great check in the Deccan. *Gautamiputra Satakarni* of the *Satavahana* dynasty had entirpated the *Kshaharata* race and dealt crushing blows to the *Sakas, Yavanas,* and *Pallavas.* The power of the invaders was, however, still unsaken in the north where the "Son of Heaven" ruled in undiminished glory in the first part of the second century A.D. Even in Western India there was a *saka* revival under the great Satrap *Rudradaman* I. Chinese evidence shows that Yue-chi power was still for from being broken in A.D. 230. The rise of the Nagas in the Jumna valley pushed to North Sythians furthers towards the north-west borderland of India, but the descendants of Rudradaman continued to rule over the fair provinces of *Malwa* and *Kathiwar.* The later scythian rulers proved to be tyrants. A Brahmana historian of the seventh century A.D. refers to one of them as *Parakalatrakamuka* "Coveting the wife of another." An epic poet makes the prophecy that *Sakas* and other *Mlechcha* (barbarian) kings will rule unrighteously in the evil age to come. The members of the four orders will not adhrere to their duties and country will become a desert. Harassed by barbarians the earth in an earlier epoch had taken refuge in the strong arms of *Chandragupta Maurya.* She now found shelter in another line of *Chandraguptas* (Ibid. p.144). *Gautamiputra Sri Yajna Satakarni,* who probably ruled towards the close of the second century A.D., was the last great King of his house. After his death, the *Satavahana* empire began to fall to pieces. The Nasik region in *Maharashtra* seems to have been lost to the *Abhira* king *Isvarasena.* The *Vakatakas* rose to power in Berar and some adjoining tracts. The Western *Kanarese* districts fell into the hands of a line of *Satakarni* who received the epithet of *Chutukulananda* and are sometimes referred to as *Chutusatakarnis* to distinguish them from the *Satavahana Satakarnis* of the Imperial line. They had their capital at the famous city of *Vaijayantipura* or *Banavasi* in north *Kanara.* The old imperial line continued to rule for some time longer in the Andhra country at the month of the Krishna till they were supplanted by the *Ikshvakus,* the rulers belonging to *Ananda gotra*, the *Brihatphalayamas*, and the *Salankayamas.* The latter were succeeded by the *Vishnukundins.* The *Salankayanas* already ruled as petty chieftains as early as the second century A.D. They must have asserted their independence shortly after the fall of the Imperial *Satavahanas.* They came into conflict with the northern emperor *Samudra Gupta* in the fourth century A.D. Meanwhile another power had risen in the far south of India with its capital at *Kanchi*, modern *Conjeeveram* near Madras, by exercising control over some of the Kanarese districts and the south part of the Andhra country at the mouth of the river Krishna. This was the *Pallava* power. At the time of famous raid of *Samudra Gupta*, the most important dynasties in trans-*Vindhyan* India were the *Vakatakas* of the upper Deccan and the *Pallavas* of Kanchi. The Gupta conqueror does not appear to have come into direct contact with the *Vakatakas.* He vanquished, however, a chief named *Vyaghraja*, who may have been identical with a *Vakataka* feudatory named *Vyaghraraja.* (Ibid. p.172). Both he and *Vakpatiraja* enjoyed the patronage of *Yasovarman* of *Kanauj.* Towards the end of the ninth century A.D. the court of *Kanaya* was adorned by *Rajasekhara.* (Ibid. p. 210).

257. R.T. Vol.1 Book VII. p. 369

258. *Ibid.*

259. *Ibid.*
260. *Ibid.* **Note.** *Uchchala* compliments himself in these words at not having been put under obligations by the *Rajapuri* chief. These would have placed him in the humiliating position of being the client of his inferior.
261. **Note**. Among *Samgramapala's* wives, there might have been relatives of *Uchchala*. A daughter of *Uchchala* known as *Saubhagyalekha* endeavoured to slay by (the hands of) her own servants those who carried her uncle's head. At the length, after *Rajapuri* had thus been thrown into disturbance, the head came before *Somapala,* her husband, who was stopping at a distance. He was the son of *Samgramapala.*
262. R.T. Vol.1. Book VII. p. 369.
263. *Ibid.*
264. *Ibid.*
265. *Ibid.*
266. **Note.** *Udayasiha* is probably the same person who is named *Udayasimha.* The route followed by *Uchchala,* from *Rajapuri* via *Lohara* and the Tosamaidan pass into *Kramarajya.* The early season at which *Uchchala* forced the pass accounts for the surprise of the Kings officers as described in the following verses.
267. *R.T.* Vol. I Book VII. p. 370 **Note.** Most probably the watch-station of *Karkotadranga* on the Tosamaidan route is meant here.
268. *Ibid.*
269. **Note.** *Khasika* or *Khaśaka* is another form of the ethnic name *Khasa.* It has been frequently mentioned in the Kashmir Chronicles. It can be shown from a careful examination of all the passages that their seats were restricted to a comparatively limited region, which may be roughly described as comprising the valleys lying immediately to the South and West of the *Pir Pantsal* range, between the middle course of the *Vitasta* in the Western and *Kastavata* (*Kishtvar*) in the East. In the numerous passages of the *Rajatarangini,* we find the rulers of *Rajapuri*, the modern Rajauri, described as 'Lords of the *Khasas*, and their troops as *Khasas.* proceeding from Rajapuri to the East we have the valley of the upper Ans River, now called *Panjgabbar,* referred under the name of *Pancagahvara*, as a habitation of *Khasas.* Further to the East lies *Banasala,* the modern *Banahal*, below the pass of the same name, where the pretender *Bhisacara* sought refuge in the caste of 'the *Khasa Lord' Bhagika.* The passages show that the whole of the Valley leading from *Banahal* to the *Chandrabhaga,* which is now called *'Bichlari,'* and which in the Chronicle bears the name of *Visalata,* was inhabited by *Khasas.* Finally we have evidence of the latter's settlements in the valley of *Khasalaya*, which is several times referred in the Kalhana's *Rajatarangini. Khasalaya* is certainly the valley of *Khaisal* (marked on the map as '*Kasher*'), which leads from the *Marbal* pass in the South East corner of Kashmir down to Vistvar. An old name of Khasalaya is probably *Khasali.* Turing to the West of Rajapuri, we find a *Khasa* from the territory of *Parnotsa* or Prunts mentioned, *Tunga* was the son of

*Bana*, a *Khasa* whose native village was *Baddivasa* in *Parnotsa* modern Poonch, who rose from the position of a cowherd to be Queen Didda's all-powerful minister. The queens own father, *Simharaja,* the ruler of *Lohara* or *Loharin,* is designated a *Khasa*. It is known to us that his descendants, who, after Didda, occupied the Kashmir throne, were looked upon as *Khasas*. Of this locality it has been shown that it was situated in the ancient *Dvaravati,* the present *Dvarbidi,* a portion of the *Vitasta* Valley between *Kathai* and Muzaffarabad. The position here indicated makes it highly probable that the *Khasas* are identical with the modern *Khakha* tribe, to which most of the petty hill-chiefs and gentry in the *Vitasta* Valley below Kashmir belong. The name *Khakha* (Pahari, in Kashmir Singular *Khukh*, plural *Khakhi*) is the direct derivative of *Khasa*, Sanskrit's being pronounced since early times in the Panjab and the neighbouring hill-tracts as *Kh* or *h*. The *Khakha* chiefs of the *Vitasta* valley retained their semi-independent position untill Sikh times, and along with their neighbours of the *Domba* clan, have ever proved troublesome neighbours for Kashmir. Of the marading inroads which the *Khakha* made during the troubles of the Pathan rule, and later still, in Shaikh Imam-ud-din's time, 1846, popular tradition in Kashmir has retained a vivid recollection. That the *Khasas* already in earlier times deserved the character of expert plunderers. In the Kashmir Census Report of 1891, p. 141, the *Khakhi* are entered with 4046 souls as a subdivision of the Muhammadan hill-Rajputs.

270. R.T. Vol.1 Book VII. 370
271. *Ibid.*
272. *Ibid.*
273. *Ibid.*
274. **Note.** By *Varahaksetra* is designated the site and vicinity of the ancient *Varahamula* which is marked by the present town *Varahmul* (Vulgo *Baramula*) at the western entrance of the Valley. This locality has enjoyed great sanctity since early times as the dwelling-place of Vishnu in his incarnation of *Adivaraha* or 'Primeval Boar'. The legends connected with the sacred site and the various localities in its neighbourhood are related in the *Varahaksetramah*, and often alluded to in other Mahatmyas as well as in the *Nilamata Puran* (1180, 1348 sq). *Kalhana* uses here the expression *Varahaksetra* for the whole neighbourhood including the site of *Huskapura* on the left river bank. In the later Chronicles, and in the Mahatmyas, we find *Varahaksetra, Varahaksetra, Varahatirtha* used indifferently in the same sense. The ancient temple of *Varaha* was situated on the narrow strip of ground between the foot of the hills and the right river bank. The town which occupied the same position as the present Varahmul, is named *Varahamula. Huskapura* which as shown the modern *Uskur*, had the advantage of being situated in an open plain, and was evidently in old times a larger place than its sistertown *Varahamula. Hiuen-Tsiang* refers only *Huskapura* as a religious foundation at *Huskapura* (Life, p. 68), but Alberuni knows both '*Ushkara*

and *Baramula* at the entrance of the valley (India, p. 204). Subsequently *Huskapura; Uskur* has dwindled down to a small village, while *Varahamula* has remained a town of importance and the trade emporium to the west. The position of the two Mathas founded by Ksemagupta at *Huskapura* can no longer be traced.

275. **Note.** The earth which Vishnu in his farm of *'Varaha'* or 'Primeval boar', had raised up from the ocean, is compared to a girl who chooses her husband at a *Svayumvara.*
276. *R.T.* Vol.1 Book VII. p. 371.
277. **Note.** The *Kaka* family is frequently mentioned in the *Rajatarangini. Tilaka, Sobhaka* and others, who held high posts and *Uchchala* and his successors, belonged to it. There is no mention made elsewhere of the *Kakas* being physicians. For *'Vaidya'*, a later hand in A has corrected *'Vaisya'* which would turn the families here mentioned into *Vaisyas.*
278. *R.T.* Vol.1 Book VII. p. 371.
279. *Ibid.*
280. *Ibid.*
281. **Note.** Though term *Taramulaka* is repeatedly mentioned in this book that is 'Nam' which is feed of the mind.
282. R.T. Vol.1 Book VII. p. 371.
283. *Ibid.*
284. *Ibid.*
285. *Ibid.*
286. **Note.** In his prosperity, *Harsa* bestowed priceless gifts of captivity just as the tree blossoming in *Caitra* (gives rich food) to the balck bees which merge from the holes of the ground.
287. R.T. Vol.1 Book VII. 371.
288. *Ibid.*
289. *Ibid.*
290. *Ibid.*
291. *Ibid.*
292. **Note.** The quadrangles (*Catuhsala*) which enclosed *Lalitaditya's* temples and *Vihara* at *Parihasapura.*
293. *R.T.* Vol.1 Book VII. p. 372.
294. *Ibid*
295. **Note.** Neither *parair* nor the reading adopted in the text, *parair,* gives a satisfactory sense. In the above statement according to the conjectural emendation *paurair.*
296. **Note.** *Bharatasetu* means 'story of the love', its position is unknown perfectly.
297. *R.T.* Vol. Book VII. p. 373.
298. *Ibid.*
299. **Note.** There are named in the Chronicle, *Parihasakesava, Muktakesava, Mahavaraha, Govardhanadhara,* and *Rajavihara*. The first four were temples dedicated to the worship of Vishnu. The last *Rajavihara* as its name shows, was a Buddhist convent. Under king *Harsa* the colossal

*Buddha* image of *Parihasapura* is mentioned among the few sacred statues which escaped being seized and melted down by that king. This image was evidently the one mentioned that king, who was free from passions, built the ever-rich *Rajavihara,* with a large quadrangle (*Catuhsala*), a large Caitya, and a large (image of the) *Jina* (Buddha) (R.T. Vol.1 Book IV. p. 142).

300. *R.T.* Vol.1 Book VII. p. 373.
301. *Ibid.*
302. **Note.** Term *Gaurikala* here is meant that '*Nam*' or *'word'* is the meat of soul.
303. *R.T.* Vol.1 Book VII. p. 373.
304. *Ibid.*
305. *Ibid.*
306. *Ibid.*
307. *Ibid.*
308. **Note.** Kalhana refers here the image of *Parihasakesava* placed by *Lalitaditya* at *Parihasapura*. According to this image contained 84,000 *Palas* of silver, which accepting the calculation given in the note on that passage, would correspond to a weight of 336,000 *Tolakas* or approximately as many rupees. The currency value of this mass of silver in the Kashmir during the time of *Harsa* cannot be estimated with exactness. But it must have been far greater than that of the equivalent amount of rupee coinage at the present time.
309. **Note.** In this curious and somewhat involved passage, Kalhana seems to refer a natural phenomenon which lasted for some time during the last year of *Harsa's* reign (A.D. 1100-1101) and which was attributed by popular superstition to the destructionof *Parihasakesava* image. This coincidence might have given rise to the legend that the great silver image had originally been erected for the purpose of removing a similar phenomenon.As regards the phenomenon itself in *Harsa's* time, we can gather two points from Kalhana's account. Firstly, dust of pigeon-grey colour is said to have filled the atmosphere from the time of the removal of the image (after *Jyaistha*, i.e 27th April-26th May, before 9 Sudi *S'ravana*, i.e. 18th July of the year 4976, A.D. 1100); to the death of *Harsa*, 5 Sudi *Bhadrapada* 4177, i.e. August 31st, A.D. 1101. Secondly, after the destruction of the image there was darkness for one and a half months. Combining these two facts, the assumption seems justified that what really took place at the time indicated was a phenomenon of atmospheric dust which manifested itself with great intensity for a month and a half at its commencement in the summer of A.D. 1100, and which lasted until the summer of the next year. It is characteristic that the story about the alleged phenomenon which preceded the erection of the *Parihasakesava* statue, is not even alluded by Kalhana, though he gives there a lengthy account of all the images and temples erected by *Lalitaditya* at *Parihasapura.* The guarded language in which this part of the story is referred to in our own passage also deserves notice.

310. R.T. Vol.1 Book VII. p. 374.
311. *Ibid.*
312. **Note.** *Avanaha* is identified with *'Paudupavagrama'*, i.e the hamlet of *Padapavan* situated about five miles below *Hurapor* at the point where the routes to the latter place and to Sidan separate; 74°-52′ 30″ at longitude and 33° 42′ 15″ latitude. The place is correctly marked as *'Pad Pawan'* on the larger survey map. The connection in which *Avanaha* is mentioned the proposed identification very doubtful and correct one.
313. R.T. Vol.1 Book VII. p. 374.
314. *Ibid.*
315. **Note.** The term *dranga* is given by the commentator of *Mankha's Kosa* as the equivalent of *raksasthana,* 'watch-station', S.V. *Gulma.* The terms *drangika drangika, drangika, drangika* which are frequently found as designation of officials in copper-plate grants of the *Valabhi* dynasty are evidently derived from *dranga* in the mention significance. This spot, which is covered by dense fire forest, is now known by the name of *Ilahi Darwaza,* 'the gate of God'. But the father of the present *Muqaddam,* or village headman, a man of great age, distinctly remembered to have heard in his youth also the designation of *Drang* i.e. *dranga.* Ancient coins are frequently found in this locality, and some traces of old Walls can still be followed through the thick undergrowth which covers the ground. A relic of ancient art is found some 330 yards higher up on the right bank of the stream, where a large rock shows in three richly ornamented niches elegantly carved relievo representations of temples of the Kashmirian style. A local tradition relates that at this spot there once stood an ancient wall and gate, closing the route which leads along the right bank of *Rembyara* river to the *Pir Pantsal* Pass. The *Drangesas* figure in frequent passages of the later Chronicles under the name of *Margesas* or 'Lords of the passes'. Their duties were entrusted in Mughal times to hereditary *Malika.* The descendants of the latter, shorn after the Sikh conquest of their power and *Jagirs,* are to be found still at *Supiyan* (below *Hirapor*), Shahabad and other places along the great routes leading over the mountains. (Vigne; *Travels;* ii, p. 270, Hugel *Kaschmir* ii. pp. 167 sqq; i.p. 347).
316. **Note.** *Sussala* seems to have secured for his use the revenue of the customs station at *Surapura.*
317. *R.T.* Vol.1 Book VII. p. 374.
318. *Ibid.*
319. *Ibid.* p. 375 **Note.** *Vaitarani* is the name of the river which has to be crossed to reach the world of the god of death. The name seems to have been applied to one of the streams which join the *Vitasta* above *Vijayesvara.* But the passages of the *Nilamatapuran*; 1319, and the various Mahatmyas (*Vitastamah, Gangodbhedamah, Kedaramah,* etc.) in which this name occurs, do not permit of a certain identification. The only river near *Surapura* is the *Rambyara* or *Ramanyatavi* (i, 265), and it is curious that the tradition of the *Vijayesvara* purohitas, as

communicated by Pt. Vasu Bhoyu of that place, actually takes the name *Vaitarani* to be the appellation of the *Rambyara* in its course near and below Supiyan.

320. *Ibid.*
321. *Ibid.*
322. *Ibid.*
323. *Ibid.*
324. *Ibid.*
325. *Ibid.*
326. *Ibid.*
327. *Ibid.*
328. **Note**. The expression of the term *adhikarasraj* is fully explained by Jonaraja's comments on *Srikanthae* iii. 50, which inform us that it was the custom in Kashmir to put a garland of flowers on persons newly appointed when receiving charge of their office. The king granted the garland (*Sraj*) of the office of chief justice (*rajasthana*) to *Dhanya,* that of the commander-in-chief to *Udaya*, and the charge of *Kheri* to *Rilhana.* He had offered to *Sujji,* by the king's direction, the garland of office (*adhikarasraj*) for the commander-in-chiefship and the other (high posts), excepting, however, the garland for the post of chief justice (*rajasthans*), without thus satisfying him (*Sujji*).
329. R.T. Vol.1 Book VII; p. 375
330. **Note.** *Asvatthaman*, the sonof *Drona*, is meant, who commanded the surviving *Kauravas* after their last great battle.
331. *R.T.* Vol.1 Book VII. p. 375
332. *Ibid*
333. **Note.** Pt. Sahibram refers in his *Tirthas*. to a *Naga* called *Govardhana* situated in the vicinity of Anantanaga (*Anatnag*). In the *Gangodbhedamah*, 99 sq, reference is made to a *Govardhanadhara* Vishnu, apparently worshipeed in close proximity to the Tirtha of *Bhedadevai*, i.e. *Budabror* in *Sukru*. The distance between this locality and *Avantipura* is, however, considerable.
334. **Note.** It appears from the study that *Maya* is the illusion of attentions, God with draw the man from it. Therefore, *'Nam'* is the source of it, who free the man from attentions and illusion.
335. *R.T.* Vol.1 Book VII. p. 376.
336. *Ibid.* **Note.** The numbers here given refer to the conventional division of an army, as indicated e.g. *Amarakosa,* ii. pp. 8,79,81.
337. *Ibid.*
338. *Ibid.*
339. *Ibid.*
340. *Ibid.*
341. *Ibid.*
342. **Note.** Kalhana wishes to say that *Ananda*, the governor, might fitly be placed even before *Devasarman* and other models of faithful servants while he was (kept) in this state, the self-respecting *Devasarman,* alone among the ministers, remembered the honours (received) from the king, and felt grieved day and night.

343. R.T. Vol.I Book VII. p. 376.
344. **Note.** While the *Harsa's* army came on like the agitated ocean, the governor destroyed the enemy's force throwing himself into its midst time.
345. R.T. Vol.1 Book VII. p. 377.
346. *Ibid.*
347. *Ibid.*
348. *Ibid.*
349. **Note.** *Hiranyapura* has been founded at *Ranyil,* a village situated at the elevation of $74^0$ 51 longitude and $34^0$ 12' latitude, close to the high road with leads from S'rinagar to *Gandarbal* and the Sind Valley. A Naga near this village, which is visited by the piligrims proceeding to the *Haramukuta* Tirthas, is referred to in the *Tirthas* and the *Suresvarimahatmya* as *Hiranyaksanaga*, and in the *Haramukutamahatmya* as *Hiranyaganga.* It is certain that Kalhana himself saw in this *Vikramaditya-Harsa* of Ujjayini the king whose supposed victory over the *S'akas* he believed; according to the theory, he can scarcely be meant for the great *Harsa* of Ujjayini, also called *Vikramaditya*, whose relations with Kashmir in the times of *Matrgupta*, i.e. 208 years later according to his own reckoning, and whose real date fell in the first half of the 6th century A.D. If *Harsa* of Kanauj, the *Harsavardhana* of Hiuen-Tsiang and the inscriptions (Circ. 606-650 A.D.), is intended, the chronological aberration is quite as great as that already noted in the case of *Mihirakula.* It is to be commemorated by the commencement of the *Saka* era, 78 A. by destroying the *S'akas* he made the task light for Siva who is to descend to the earth for the extermination of the *Mlechchas;* and by the close approach of the above data to A.D. 106, the data wich Kalhana's chronology assigns to the death of *Hiranya.* Kalhana himself helps us to correct the great chronological error implied by this view, when stated, *Siladitya Pratapasila* can be identified with *Siladitya* of Malava, whom Hiuen-Tsiang (*Si-Yu-Ki*, ii.p. 261) mentions as having flourished sixty years before his own time and apparently indicates as the successor of *Vikramaditya* (L.C, i. p. 108). Prof. M. Muller, *India*, p. 289, assigns to *Siladitya* hypothetically a reign from 550 to 600 A.D. As it is indicated *Siladitya* ruled about 580 A.D. in Malava, we must conclude in accordance with the arguments first set forth by Dr. Bhau Daji (J.Bo.Br.R.A.S, 1861, p. 208 Sqq.), that Kalhana's *Vikramaditya-Harsa* was in reality the same as the *Vikramaditya* who is mentioned by Hiuen-Tsiang as the predecessor of *Siladitya.* The reign of this Vikramadity may be placed with Prof. M. Muller (India, pp. 286 sqq.) in the first half of the sixth century A.D. It has been identified that present village *Ranyil* on the way from Lar (Lahara) to Srinagar.
350. R.T. Vol.1 Book VII. p. 377.
351. **Note.** The text shows here a lacuna which probably extends over four *padas.* It may be concluded that the missing *'words'* contained also a request for advice addressed to the ministers by the king.

352. *R.T.* Vol.1 Book VII. p. 377.
353. *Ibid.*
354. **Note.** *Cakravarman's* conduct is alluded to the low caste of the singers, and takes *Hamsi* and *Nagalata* into his seraglio.
355. *R.T.* Vol.1 Book VII. p. 378.
356. *Ibid.*
357. *Ibid.*
358. *Ibid.*
359. *Ibid.*
360. *Ibid.*
361. **Note.** When the gods churned the Ocean to recover the fourteen *'Ratnas'* the greatserpent *'Vasuki'* was twisted round the mountain which served as the churning stick, and *Indra* directed the operation.
362. **Note.** The meaning of the term *Srigarbha* is not quite certain. By this an epithet of *Harsa* seems to be alluded 'Ksemagupta's appellation *Kankanavarsa*. For *Abhimanya's* epithet or nickname *Kankanavarsa,* Rainer 'of bracelets'. *Kankanavarsa* is found as the name of a magician. He brought from the *Tuhkhara* land the brother of the magician *Kankanavarsa* ('he who rains gold'), who bore the name of *Cankuna* and excelled by his great qualities. *Kankanapura* is, perhaps, the modern *Kangan,* a village on the right bank of the Sind river at the elevation $74^0$ 57' longitude and $34^0$ 16' latitude.
363. R.T. Vol.1 Book VII. p. 379.
364. **Note.** The King refers to the death at this servants hand for which he has asked and replied to them: "I am unable to kill myself, therefore you should slay-me when misfortune has arrived."
365. **Note.** The story told as an episode in verses represents one of the version in which the legends of king *Muktapida-Lalitaditya's* death in popular tradition. Indeed, just as most wonderful deeds are related of this king, so the reports about his end are also very astonishing. The particular version here related with himself (*Muktapida-Lalitaditya*) in order to preserve the foremost position which he head long held among kings.
366. R.T. Vol.1 Book VII. p. 379.
367. *Ibid.* p. 380.
368. *Ibid.*
369. **Note.** According to passage from the *Carakasamhita* quoted in N.p. W, the illness here named is a kind of dysentery.
370. *R.T.* Vol.1 Book VII. p. 380.
371. *Ibid.* pp. 380-81
372. **Note.** *Harsa* was anxious to die in fighting, but paralyzed by his misfortune could not nerve himself for a resolute step. As swayed by the conflicting counsels of his confidants, he moved about helplessly, more and more of the remaining troops deserted. Others who were faithfully attached to him, *Harsa* himself despatched to follow up his son *Bhoja*, who had previously fled with a few attendants. Among those sent on this futile erranet was also the faithful *Canpaka,* Kalhana's father,

whose departure at this critical time the Chronicler has taken special care to explain to us. Curiously enough *Uchchala*, after seeing the palace burned, had retired again to the right bank, and by this want of prompt resolve had left *Harsa* another chance of escape. But the doomed king failed to make use of it. His soldiers dispersed, and after he had vainly endeavoured to find a refuge in the houses of various grandees, he found himself desorted by all but his devoted personal attendant *prayaga,* and *Mukta*, a cook of one of *Canpaka's* followers. While in hiding there, next day *Harsa* suffered the fresh grief of hearing the news of the death of *Bhoja* who had been deliberately murdered on his flight by his own faithful servents.

373. *Lohara* or *Loharakotta,* ' the castle of Lohara', has played an important part in Kashmir history as the ancestral home and stronghold of the dynasty whose narrative fills the last two cantos of Kalhana's work. In view of the very frequent references which Kalhana makes to this locality, its correct identification is essential for the full understanding of the events related in the portion of the Kashmir Chronicle.
374. R.T. Vol.1 Book VII. p. 381.
375. *Ibid.*
376. *Ibid.*
377. *Ibid.*
378. *Srilekha*, the queen of *Samgramaraja,* daughter of the illustrious *Yasomangala*, as her husband was a feeble power indulged in licentious conduct.
379. R.T. Vol. 1 Book VII. p. 382.
380. *Ibid.*
381. **Note.** *'Harsa'* wives from the *Sahi* race are mentioned between the kingdom of the Darads on the north and the *Turuska* power on the south is fairly accurate. We know from the Chinese Annals that in the middle of the eight century A.D. Udyana or the modern *Swat* with the neighbouring hill regions was united with Gandhara under the rule of 'the King of Ki-pin', who belonged in all probability to the dynasty of the Turkish Shahiyas' of Kabul. If the dominions of *Lalliya Shahi* extended equally far to the north, they must have bordered on the territories held to this day by the Dard tribes inhabiting the Kohistan on the upper Indus, Cilas and Citral.
382. *R.T.* Vol.1 Book VII. p. 382.
383. *Salhana, Lothana* and *Ralha* were born from *Sveta*, of the three sons, *Salhana* and other (two) who had been born to *Mallaraja*, the middle one had died. The eldest and youngest who remained, *Salhana* and *Lothana*, had from fear, when *S'ankharaja* searched for them in order to kill them betaken themselves into the *Navamatha* (R.T Vol.II. Book VIII. p. 32).
384. *R.T.* Vol.1 Book VII. p. 382.
385. **Note.** Post *Vedic* Brahmanism, however, retains a vivid memory of a bitter struggle for supermacy between the Brahman caste and that of the

*Kshatriyas*. It is given in the form of a story both in the *Mahabharata* and the *Puranas*: The *Kshatriyas* had become so arrogant and oppresive that the interference of Vishnu himself was needed to repress them. The god took human form and was born in the family of the Bhrigu, a priestly race of divine descent, as Parashu-Rama ("Rama with the axe") who became the exterminator of the *Kshatriya* race and filled five lakes with their blood" '*Word' after which he gave the earth to the Brahmans!* (V.I. p. 278)

386. **Note.** The various comparisons and puns, which can in part only be paraphrased, account for the remark made in the preceding verse, viz that *Malla*, when going out to fight, seemed yet to retain the dress of a *Muni* or silence. Thus the term *asidhara* is drived *dhara* in the north and the south of the city = (*Mahajanapada*). As waters of the Ganga and Yamuna meeting at Prayage are supposed to be white and black respectively. For the sacred bathing-place *Dhara.*
387. *R.T* Vol.1. Book VII. p. 382.
388. *Ibid*. p. 383.
389. *Ibid.*
390. *Ibid.*
391. *Ibid.*
392. **Note.** The *Kuru* host, led by *Bhishma, Drona, Karna* and other mighty warriors, was destroyed. The *Pandus* with their allies, the *Panchalas* and *Srinjayas*, who suffered terrible losses, but they successed in gaining back their kingdom. Although there is no clear reference in the extant Vedic texts to the battle of *Kurukshetra,* we have distinct hints in some of the *Brahmanas, Upanishads* and *Srauta Sutras* of the hostility between the *Kurus* and the *Srinjayas* the disasters threatening the *Kurus* and their final expulsion from *Kurukshetra*. The name *Pandu* is mentioned in *vedic* literature, but we have references to *Arjuna, Parikshit*, and *Janamejaya* and the first two have already been deified in some of the later Vedic texts. That the *Pandus* were a historic tribe or clan is proved by the testimony of Ptolemy in whose time they occupied a portion of the Punjab. *Bhisma,* the *Kurava,* was wounded to death by numberless arrows.
393. *R.T.* Vol.1 Book VII. p. 383.
394. *Ibid.*
395. *Ibid.*
396. **Note.** *Parasurama* revenged the murder of his father by exterminating the whole Ksatriya race.
397. **Note.** *Darsanapala*, though keeping by *Harsa's* side, was a secret supporter of the pretenders mentioned above.
398. *R.T.* Vol.1 Book VII. p. 384.
399. *Ibid.*
400. *Ibid.*
401. **Note.** *Vdhnipura* is nowhere else mentioned. *Durgapura* has proposed to amend *avahnipuraka* into *Avantipuraka*. But this expression

*Krodhavahnina* contains clearly an illusion to the name *Vahnipura*. The place meant might be the present village of *Vampor*, situated about two miles to South West of *Vijabror*: *Vijayesvara*.

402. *R.T.* Vol.1 Book VII. p. 384.
403. **Note.** The original reading of this statement is subsequently corrected *Induraja* as the son of *Candraraja*.
404. *R.T.* Vol.1 Book VII. p. 384.
405. *Ibid.*
406. *Ibid.*
407. *Ibid.*
408. *Ibid.*
409. **Note.** Term *asthanabrahmana* recurs and seems to indicate a certain rank which, perhaps, corresponds to that of a *Durbari* or *asthanadvija* for *Citraratha*, could also mean "holding the position (of a Brahman councillor)" in modern India. Thus the term *asthaniya* has probably the same significance. Kalhana seems to allude to the ancient Indian custom according to which persons in danger of their life put grass into their mouths to implore mercy. By symbolically representing themselves as cattle, they became inviolable. The Kashmirian heroes of our narrative have no grass at hand, and use their fingers as a substitute. It must, however, also be kept in view that the cutting off of a finger is repeatedly referred in the *Rajatarangini*, as a mark of submission.
410. *R.T.* Vol.1 Book VII. p. 384.
411. *Ibid.*
412. *Ibid.*
413. *Ibid.*
414. *Ibid.* p. 385. **Note.** It is corrected with *Durgapura or 'pyangam'*.
415. *Ibid.* **Note.** *Sussala* had the eighteen divisions conventionally counted in any army.
416. *Ibid.*
417. *Ibid.*
418. **Note.** *Suvarnasanura* is probably identical with the present village *Sunasamil*, situated in the Sukru Pargana at the elevation of 75⁰ 56' 15" logitude and 33⁰ 50' 40" latitude (marked on larger survey map). This identification is supported by the month of *Pausa* he (*Prthvihara*) sent from *Suvarnasanura Tikka* of *Devasarasa 'Word'* to stay the wife of *Garga* (*Chudda*), where the place is mentioned in connection with *Kalyanapura*. *Kalyanapura* is repeatedly mentioned in the text. *Tarapura* can be identified with certainty with the present village of *Kalampor*, situated in the *Sukru* Pargana at 74° 54′ longitude and 38° 48′ latitude, close to the high road leading from *Supiyan* to Srinagar. This identification is proved specially by *Srivara*. The position of *Kalganapura* is clearly indicated in the lastnamed passage by the reference to *Drabhagrama*, the modern *Drabagam*, about two miles the North West of *Kalampor*. It is very probably that the gloss *Kalamapuram*, which has written above *Kamalakhyam puram* in the following verse,

and was only by a mistake of copies in the wrong place called *Surapura*. In Sanskrit *Suvarna* appears in Kashmir as *Suna*.

419. *R.T.* Vol.1 Book VII. p. 385.
420. **Note.** The text of the first verse as found does not give proper sense. *Samsrstamano* is an impossible form, and has probably to be corrected with Durgapure into *samsrjyamano*. The following verse also displays that *pyasmarsid* cannot be correct. It has been translated above according to the conjectural emendation *Vyasmarsid.*
421. *R.T.* Vol.1 Book VII. p. 386.
422. *Ibid.*
423. *Ibid.*
424. **Note.** The text here a lacuna which though only of one syllable, renders it impossible to ascertain the meaning of the preceding word *'Kalasa', 'Chamar', 'Nam',* etc. It might have been the name of a building (temple of *Kalasesa*?) or the designation of a portion of the palace.
425. R.T. Vol.1 Book VII. p. 386.
426. *Ibid.*
427. *Ibid.*
428. *Ibid.* p. 387.
429. **Note.** The position of *Lavanotsa* is uncertain, though the place is several times mentioned by Kalhana. From the study it appears that Srinagar could be reached by a single forced march from *Lavanotsa,* and that *Padmapura,* or Pampar, lay on the route. From the passage discussed above which mention *Lavanotsa* in connection with a siege of *Vijayesvora*, we can only conclude that the distance between these two places was not great. Finally, Brahman pointed out the king that man standing among the inhabitants of *Lavanotsa,* who had been summoned by messengers. It shows that *Lavanotsa* was situated near one of the high roads leading to Srinagar from abroad.
430. R.T. Vol.1 Book VII. p. 387.
431. **Note.** The 'old palace' (*Puranarajadhanai*) must be meant here the royal residence which existed before *Anantadeva* built his new palace near *sadasiva* temple. We may safely assume that, with the rest of the city founded by *Pravarasena*, it was situated on the right bank of the Vitasta river. It must be noted, however, that *Puranarajadhanyagree*, as printed in the text, is an emendation for *purani raja* of the MSS. The site once occupied by the royral residence and abandoned on the construction of the new palace by *Avantadeva.* This site has already been mentioned as *puranarajadhanai,* for the meaning of *sthandita*.
432. *R.T.* Vol.1 Book VII. p. 387.
433. *Ibid.*
434. **Note.** Word *devanayaka* is really a proper name, or only an ironical designation of *Udayaraja* whom *Harsa* is said to have appointed as 'prefect for the overthrow of divine images' (*devotpatananayaka*) no mention is made subsequently of *Udayaraja.*
435. **Note.** The shrine of *Narendresvara* is nowhere else mentioned. It might have been erected by, or named in honour of king *Narendraditya-*

*Lahkhana.* The name *Lahkhana* which writes with the *Jihvamuliya* before *Kh,* can be read clearly in the latter spelling on the observe of a silver coin described by General Cunningham, later Indo-Scythians, pp. 97, III and Plate VII, Fig.12. It shows the legend (*Ra*) *Ja Lahkhana Udayaditya,* read by C. '*Raja Lakhana* ('Word') *Udayaditya* Cunningham, though not recognising the name as occuring also in our passage, had rightly ascribed this coin to Kashmir, on the ground of the striking resemblance it bears 'in type and size and general fabric' to the unique coin of *Deva Sahi Khingila* (represented L.C, Plate VII. II). The latter ruler has been identified with the *Khinkhila* or Narendraditya I. The type of this coin is unmistakably that of an Ephthalite ruler, and closely resembles that of the coin of *Lahkhana.* Two coins bearing the legend *Sri Narendra* (figured *coins of Medieval India,* plate III, Fig. 5) show the *'Kidara'* type, and seem to belong to another later ruler, but the legend is scarcely certain. There is a close connection between the type ('*Sassanian Bust'*) of these two coins and that of others bearing the name of *Jabula, Mihirakula, Hiranyakula* (*'Word'*). Cunningham was thus fully justified in assuming that they all belong to rulers of the Ephthalites or *White Hune.* As the dominions of the latter included also Kashmir, it appears very probable that by *Lahkhana-Narendraditya* of the *Rajatarangini* is meant the same king who calls himself *Lahkhana-Udayaditya* on the coins. As in the case of *Khinkhila*, so we have here an Indian appellation used by the side of the foreign name *Lakhana.* Why this Indian name should have been differently recorded by Kalhana, is a question which our present materials do not permit us to answer. But it is certainly curious that copper coins closely resembling in type the coins of the above mentioned Ephthalite rulers actually show the name *Narendra (*Cunningham, L.C. p. 118 and Plate IX, Fig. 12).

436. **Note.** Here the rendering of the term *sthamastha* is conjectural. The word, which clearly has a military significance, recurs though he (*Uchchala*) went into camp like the other ministers, he did not do anything worthy of himself in the fighting, but remained like (a mere) on looker. Some indication as to its meaning is furnished by certain passages of *Srivara's* Chronicle, where the simple *sthaman* seems to designate the 'camp' or 'contonment', and *sthamastha* or *sithamasthita* the troops occupying it. He declared: 'Hear, O king, the reason why we, though guardians of the quarters, receive even in the present fourth *yuga* your command with reverence". We read of a dislocation of troops according to which one divisions is to form the centre by occupying the city and two other divisions to form the wings by giving into *'sthaman'* . When he asked his ministers for means of crossing the waters, *Cankuna,* who stood on the bank, threw a charm (*mani*) *into* the water, which was very deep. It is mentioned a distribution of the forces by three routes, 'according to their separate *sthamans.* He again announce: "But on my impregnable firmness certainly even such an effort of yours breaks down, as the iron on the diamond." As a leader he spoke as *'sthamasthita'* i.e. encamped

at the outskirts of the city, and he was asked by him about this, she told him with a bright smile: "There is a very large lion here which attacks and kills living beings." It is said that he used another part of his troops for guarding the routes and dismissed another *'sthamartham'* as it is understood to their standing quarters. The meaning here conjectureally proposed for the word *sthaman*, agrees with its etymology and the interpretation given for it in Vedic passages, viz. 'station', 'place'.

437. *R.T.* Vol.1 Book VII. p. 387.
438. *Ibid.*
439. **Note.** The stratagem of *Ananda* is alluded that excellent (governor) though captured in this fashion, thought (only) of what was of help to his lord. Devotion to the master does not change in self-respecting men, even at the close (of their life).
440. *R.T.* Vol.1 Book VII. p. 388.
441. *Ibid.*
442. *Ibid.*
443. **Note.** *Brhatsetu,* 'the Great Bridge', must be taken in all probability as a proper name during the time of Kalhana in Srinagar. The same term is used for the boat-bridge which Pravarasena II is said to have constructed unfortunately the latter passage does not furnish a clear indication of the bridges position, though it shows that the latter was at some distance from *Maksikasvamin* (*Mayasum*) . Boat-bridges are mentioned by Kalhana in the time of *Harsa.* As this boat-bridge was evidently the first of its kind in the country, the name might have clung to the bridge which continued to be maintained in the sama locality. Where this locality was, it is difficult to ascertain. Keeping in view the position occupied by the old parts of Srinagar founded by *Pravarasen* himself. It would be inclined to look to the vicinity of the present Fourth or Fifth Bridge as a likely place for Pravarasena's bridge. Up to the Fourth Bridge the river forms an almost straight reach, and the smoke rising from *Maksikasvamin-Mayasum* could be easily seen from this point. Then another wife of the king, called *Indradevi, Meghavahana*, queen. The *Indradevibhavana Vihara* is mentioned again in the account of the troubles following *Bhiksacara's* usurpation. Its position is not known. Disastrous fires have also in modern times frequently visited Srinagar. The last occured in 1892, when a great part of the city was laid in ashes. The prevalent use of wood in the construction of all private buildings, and the narrowness of the streets, assure a rapid spread for such conflagrations (Lawrance, K.V. p. 204).
444. *R.T.* Vol.1 Book VII. p. 388.
445. **Note.** By *Catuskika* is meant probably an open pavilion attached to the palace, and having four pillar.
446. **Note.** *Satadvara* seems to have been the designation of a separate building in the palace. Possibly a large quadrangle is meant from which a hundred doors opened.
447. The text of this passage is restored by reading with *asvayujigalim* for *Yujilagim* of which gives no sense. The old custom mentioned in the *Nilamata* of indulging in mutual jokes and playful abuse on the last day of the *Asvayuja* mouth. Allusion is made here to the story told in the *Milamate*, according to which Kashmir was occupied in consequence

of curse of '*Kasyapa* for six months of each year by the *Pisacas,* who forced the human settlers to retire from the country from the full-moon day of *Asvayuja* to that of *Caitra.* The kings who followed each other in rapid succession are compared to the kings of that legendary age who had to abandon their country each year on the *Asvayjui* day. Connected with this legend is the old custom prescribed for the *Asvayuji* day in *Nilamata.* People had to amuse themselves by throwing mud at each other, by indulging in abuse and playing jokes in order to frighten away the *Pisacas,* who attempt to enter the homes of men at that date. This custom, how entirely forgotten, is referred by Kalhana as *asvayujigali* and appears also to have been in the mindof the author of the gloss on our passage. However, itis unable to make out what the latter meant by *Cascaryartham* and *heyarayah.* With this expression *asvayujigali* in our passage are to compared the words of the *Nilamata purana Kardamenanuliptamaih Kriditavyam* tutha *naraih Suhrdah Kardamenapi lepayadbhir itas tatha*) ('*Word*' or '*Nam*' *aslilam Vadamanais ca hyakrosadbhis tatha dvija.* It is probably that Alberuni, *India*, ii. p. 180, refers to a custom somehow related to that indicated by the *Nutamata*, when speaking of a festival celebrated on the 15th day of *Asvayuja* ('when the moon stands in the last of her stations, *Revati*', i.e. on the Asvayuji day). At that festival 'they wrangle with each other and play with animals.' Can the strange name recorded for this festival,'*Puhai*' having anything to do with the *Pisacas?*

448. R.T. Vol.1 Book VII. p. 388.
449. *Ibid.* p. 389
450. *Ibid.*
451. *Ibid.*
452. *Ibid.*
453. *Ibid.*
454. **Note.** The queens on entering the *'Catushika'* had blocked its door, and the servants who wish to prevent them from burning themselves, have first to force an entrance.
455. *R.T.* Vol.1 Book VII. p. 389.
456. *Ibid.*
457. *Ibid.*
458. *Ibid.* pp. 389-90.
459. *Ibid.* p. 390.
460. *Ibid.*
461. *Ibid.*
462. *Ibid.*
463. *Ibid.*
464. **Note.** Give an estimate of the life to the 'nature' why the *'nature'* has given the life. It will be asked at the time of death, what you have did for the life to answer the god. Those did something they must be relief from the destruction. It is only '*Nam*' or *'Chamar'* can help you during this period otherwise hell is always ready for you. It depends on your labour in this spiritual field. Here needs piousness not cleverness of the mind for his own benefit. It is a deal of *'Truth'* as Nanaka says: *"Sacha Sauda"* or good bargain.

465. *R.T.* Vol.1 Book VII. p. 390
466. **Note.** The Ganga in its flew through the air (*Akasaganga*) is alluded to the statement.
467. *R.T.* Vol.1 Book VII. p. 390.
468. **Note.** Term *Padmasiriprapa*, is only here mentioned, might have been a drinking fountain or well constructed by *Padmasri* the queen of *Kalasa*.
469. **Note.** This verse is found, according to *Bohtlingk, Indian Spriiche,* 4206, with slight textual variations in the *Yajnavalkyasmrti*, the *Pancatantra* means 'five fears of the mind', and in numerous didatic texts and anthologies.
470. R.T Vol.1 Book VII; p. 390.
471. *Ibid.*
472. *Ibid.*
473. **Note.** *Harsa* left his trustee servants *Prayage* for intrigues to go to *Lohara*
474. *R.T.* Vol. 1 Book VII. p. 390.
475. *Ibid.* p. 391.
476. *Ibid.*
477. *Ibid.*
478. *Ibid.*
479. **Note.** Term *Dhanaka* here we means that *'Nam' 'Kalma'* which is priceless, it is free of cost obtain from the *'Prefect Master'*, like *Baba Gurinder Singh Ji.* Therefore, it is requested to every body, Kindly seek the *'word'* live in Heaven. Besides this, there is no alternative.
480. ***Note.*** It is noted that without *Durgaprasada,* son of *Vrajalala,* Kalhana *Rajatarangini*, Bombay Vols.I-II, 1892-94, Hereafter mentioned as Durga prasad, emendation *Varvartmana* for the meaningless *Va Vartmana* of the text.
481. *R.T.* Vol.1 Book VII. p. 391
482. **Note.** *Harsa* displayed firmness and did not accept those gifts that he bribed the prefect of police (*Sunna*).
483. *R.T.* Vol.1 Book VII. p. 391
484. *Ibid.*
485. *Ibid.* p. 392.
486. *Ibid.*
487. *Ibid.* **Note.** Term *Trailokakhya* which occurs in *Vansavali* requires correction. These are :*Gunakhya* or *Gun-Rai*, *Trailokakhya* (i.e. *Trailokya*). *Akhya* is evidently no part of the name, but must be the Sanskrit *Akhya*, meaning "an appellation" "a name" and, as the second member of a compound, "called", "named" "*Trailokakhya*" Therefore *'means' 'Word'* or *'Chamar'* called *Trailoka* (or better, *Trailokya*). With *Trailokya* we reach firmer ground. Though nothing but his name is recorded in the *Vansavali*, there are two inscriptions in *Churah*, the northern province of *Chamba* state, which almost certainly refer to him. We have been seen that previous to the founding of most of the Hill states the country was portioned out into small baronies under rule of

*Ranas* and *Thakura*, who perhaps acknowledged a nominal subjection to one or other of the greater kingdoms in the hills or on the plains. *Churah*, the province just referred to, was originally held by many such petty rulers, and our records point to their having been subject to *Vallapura* before coming under the supremacy of *Chamba*. The records to which reference has been made consist chiefly of inscribed slabs which the *Ranas* erected at fountains, in memory of their deceased relations and for the sake of their bliss in the next world. In these inscriptions it was customary to mention the name and regnal year of the Raja to whom the Rana owed allegiance: and also the Sastra year in which the inscription was carved. In the *Tisa* and *Sai parganas* of *Churah,* three such slabs have been found, each bearing the name of a Raja, named *Trailokya-deva.* No such name occurs in the genealogical roll of the *Chamba* chiefs, but we find it in that of Balor, and the conclusion seems justified that T*railokya* of *Vallapura* is the Raja referred to. The date of the most legible of the inscriptions is S.17=A.D. 1041, and by its help the second inscription is found to be dated in S.4=A.D. 1128-29. It is, therefore, probable that *Trailokya-deva* of Balor (*Vallapura*) ruled over *Churah* in the first half of the eleventh century. We may also conclude that *Chamba* had not then acquired any footing in *Churah,* which had been under the supermacy of *Vallapura* from the earlier period. According to the *Vansavali, Trailokya* was succeeded by his son, *Kalas-Pal,* who in his turn was followed by *Tung-Pal.* The name of *Kalas-Pal* occurs twice in the *Rajatarangini* where he called "*Kalasa* the son of *Tukka,* lord of *Vallapura.*" We must assume that the *Rajatarangini* is correct and that a mistake has occured in the *Vanasavali. Tung* and *Tukka* are doubtless the same, and this name and that of *Kalasa* have been reversed in copying. *Trailokya* probably died soon after A.D. 1041, and was succeeded by *Tung* or *Tukka,* who reigned till about A.D. 1050, and was then followed by his son, *Kalasa* or *Kalas-pal.* It was, as we have already seen, during the reign of *Kalasa* (probably about A.D. 1055) that *Vallapura* was invaded by *Ananta-deva* of Kashmir. Apparently, as the result of that invasion, the state had to acknowledge the supermacy of Kashmir: for we find the same *Kalasa* mentioned among the hill chiefs, who visited Srinagar in A.D 1087-88 in the reign of Raja *Kalasa*, son and successor of *Ananta-deva.* We are also told that *Harsa,* the son of *Kalasa* of Kashmir, had married a grand-daughter of Raja *Tukka of Vallapura,* named *Sugala,* who tried to poison her husband when he was thrown into prison by his fahter, in A.D. 1088. From this it follows that *Kalasa* of *Vallapura* must have reigned in the second half of the eleventh century, probably from A.D. 1050 to 1090. The *Rajatarangini* refers to some other ancient rulers of *Vallapura* whose names are found in the second *Vansavali* as *Karam Rai* and *Takht Rai* , between *Trailokya* and *Kalas*, almost certainly due to interpolation. There are : *Padmaka* and his son and heir-apparent *'Word'* or *'Chamar'*, the *Yuvaraja, Ananda*; both of whom espoused the cause of *Bhikshuchara,* grandson of *Harsa* of Kashmir, when he was attempting to recover the throne which had been usurped by the *Lohara* princes, *Uchchala* and *Sussala*; also *Jajjala* who supported *Sussala*. It, therefore, appears that *Padmaka* may have been a son or grandson of *Kalasa,* and *Ananda* and *Jajjala* his sons, whose names have been omitted in the process of copying. The events with which these names are associated in the *Rajatarangini* occurred in A.D. 1113 and later. There events may here be briefly detailed as throwing an interesting light on contemporaneous history. *Harsa,* the son of *Kalasa* and grandson of *Ananta-deva* of Kashmir had aroused bitter feeling against himself by his confiscation of temple property and his persecution of the Damaras or great landlorders, many of whom he caused to be massacred. A rebellion, favoured by the Damaras, who supported the *Lohara* princes, *Uchchala* and *Sussala*, resulted in *Harsa* and his son, *Bhoja* being killed and in the accession of *Uchchala* to the throne. *Bhikshachara,* the infant son of *Bhoja*, was spared and was afterwards conveyed by his relative, the princess *Asamati* to the court of King *Naravarman* of Malava (Malwa), where he was brought up and educated. *Uchchala* took steps to prevent his return by concluding treaties with the princes through whose territories he must pass. This precaution, however, was futile Uchchala was murdered in A.D. 1111, and was succeeded by his brother, *Sussala,* but the disorder then prevail in Kashmir encouraged the supporters of the old dynasty to invite *Bhikshachara* to return. At *Kurukshetra* (Thanesar) he fell in with five hill chiefs, who were performing in company the pilgrimage to that place. Three of them : *Jasata* of *Champ, Vajradhara* of Babbapura (Durgara) and *Sahajapala* of *Vartula* (Batol?) '*Word*' or 'Nam' were ruling chiefs; while two others: *Balha* of *Trigarta* (*Kangra*) and *Ananda* of *Vallapura* (Balor). *Nam* or *Chamars* were *Yuvarajas* or heirs-apparent and co-rulers. *Bhiskshachara* was nearly related to the *Champa* chief, being his nephew on the mother's side, and by him he was received with favour and distinction. The other chiefs also treated him with like honour. From *Kurukshetra* he proceeded to *Vallapura* where Raja *Padmaka,* at the instance of *Ananda*, the heir-apparent, and *Jasata* of *Champa*, gave him a cordial reception and bestowed on him a daughter in marriage. There he remained for some time. An attempt was made to raise troops to assist in the invasion of Kashmir, the principal coadjutor being a *Thakur,* named Gayapala, who possibly has his residence at *Mulkihar* in *Chamba*. It failed, however, as *Gaya-Pala* was murdered by some of his own relatives; while *Daryaka*, one of *Bhikshachara's* chief supporters, also fell in an expedition against *Gaya-Pala's* murderers. Meantime the princess *Asamati* died; and the funds provided by the Raja of Malwa having become exhausted, less attention was shown to the royal claimant, and he, therefore, retired to *Champa*. There he remained four or five years under the protection of Raja *Jasata* his maternal uncle; but the interest in his fortunes had declined, and Kalhana tells us that he had difficulty in obtaining even food and clothing. He, therefore, left *Champa* and retired to *Vartula*, a small state on the bank of the *Chinab,* the ruler of which, named *Denga-Pala*, received him kindly and gave him a daughter in marriage. There he remained for some time. In A.D.1118, having now reached manhood; he seems to have again returned to *Vallapura* and from there he was invited to *Rajapuri* (Rajauri) by *Som-Pal* (Somapala), the Raja of that place, who favoured his succession to the Kashmir throne. After many vicissitudes, *Bhikshachara*, in A.D. 1120, succeeded in regaining the throne, but held in only for six months, when, through his own folly, he was again driven into exile. By this time he had been entirely abandoned by the chiefs of *Champa* and *Vallapura*, owing probably to Kashmir intrigue, and these chiefs had made peace with *Sussala*, the Raja of Kashmir. In A.D. 1122, *Jajjala*, lord of *Vallapura,* assisted *Sussala* in the defence of Srinagar, and the Kashmir Raja had inter-married with the *Vallapura* royal family, for one of his queens, who became *sati* with him, was a princesses of the *Champa* family. The only chief who stood by *Bhikshachara* to the last was *Denga-pala*, his father-in-law. After many adventures he was at last, in A.D. 1130, killed by Kashmiri troops in a fort at the south end of the *Banihal Pass*, and the war of succession came to an end. (H.p. H.S. pp. 593-96).

488. **Note**. Regarding the *Ekangas* and their share in the victory of *Ananta* is equivalent. No doubt, *Aksapatala* had its connection with the *Ekangas*. Unfortunately, they have been divided into two parts that is *Right* and *Left*. It is a class struggle theory. Those struggle with the life they will attain the fruite .
489. R.T. Vol. I Book VII. p. 392.
490. *Ibid.*
491. *Ibid.*
492. **Note.** The person referred tohere as *Seyaraja* is possibly identical with the *Sesaraja* which one can see the person.
493. **Note.** Term *Parevitastam* formed by prefixing *pare* one has to across the neuter river. It appears further that the locality called *Parevitasta* must have been situated a considerable distance above Srinagar. As neither *Bhoja* nor the king proceed up the river, the accusative ending of *Parevitastam* would be inexplicable. In this way we proposed to emend *Parevitastat*.
494. *R.T.* Vol.1 Book VII. p. 392.
495. *Ibid.*
496. *Ibid.*
497. *Ibid.*
498. *Ibid.*
499. *Ibid.* p. 393.
500. *Ibid.*
501. **Note.** *Pradyumnal* is probably an abbreviation of the name *Pradyumnapitha* or *Pradyumnasikhara* given to the 'hill of *Sarika*' or *Haraparvat* in Srinagar. As the greatest part of old Srinagar law on the

right back of the river and around that hill, *Harsa's* visits to the Houses of various ministers, etc., may have taken him beyond the *Sarika* hill. The latter text does not furnish an explanation of the name. But *Somadeva* in the *Kathas.* ixxiii. 109 alludes to a story which would connect the hill with the love of *Usa* and *Aniruddha,* the son of *Pradyumna.* The east slope and foot of the hill is now covered by extensive buildings, including *Sarais,* connected with the famours *Muhamadan* shrines of *Muqaddam Sahib* and *Akhun Mulla Shah.* These probably occupy the sites of earlier Hindu structures such as the *Matha* referred to in our verse. The text leaves it doubtful as to whether the two temples mentioned here were also situated on this hill or elsewhere.

502. **Note.** It is known to us that there were certain *Rajaputras* families in the area of *Basohli*, for among them it was everywhere reckoned as one of the seven wonders of the hills. As already stated, *Bhog-Pal* was the founder of the state, and was, therefore, the first of the *Balauria Rajas.* After him ruled the following *Rajas*, of whom we know nothing but the names: *Nag-Pal, Singh-Pal, Soj-Pal, Satyadik-Pal* and *Radhik-Pal.* A younger brother of the last Raja is said to have founded the *Bhadrawah* state. This may possibly mean that from an early period *Bhadrawah* was fief under the suzeranity of *Balor*, though it did not become an independent state till a much later period. Next in succession come to names of *Laksman-Pal, Sakya-Pal, Man-Sakya* (or *Sakat*). Here an interesting note occurs in the *Vansavali* to the effect that *Som-Pal*, the younger brother of the last-named Raja, settled at *Sumaria* and became the ancestor of the *Sumarta* (or *Sumata*) was a separate state, and probably the original name of Balor state, and also the name of the territory of which at a later time *Bhadu* became the capital. Another note states that *Man-Sakya* himself removed the capital from *Vallapura to Basohli,* after having killed a *Rana,* named *Bisu,* who apparently had previously been in possession. Such traditions are found all through the hills, and tend to confirm the popular belief that the *Ranas* and *Thakurs* were the original rulers in the hills. As already suggested, the note regarding the conquest of *Basohli* may, only mean that *Man-Sakya* added it to his kingdom, and founded a town on the *Ravi* where he occasionally resided, though the capital was at *Vallapura.* The next names are : *Dev-Sakya, Bhog-Sakya* and *Apar-Sakya,* but the names ending in *Sakya* look suspicious. The designation of certain exclusive family groups by a term indicating the original number of houses counted within the group, is still customary among the *Dogra Rajputs.* Thus a section of the *Mians* is known as the *'Yaran Ghar,'* 'eleven houses'.

503. *R.T* Vol.1 Book VII. p. 393

504. **Note.** According to the law of Nature *"Harsa"* assigned his duty to *the mind or mana* called *Brahmana* as an his younger brother.

505. R.T. Vol.1 Book VII. 393.

506. *Ibid.*

507. *Ibid.*

508. *Ibid.*

509. **Note.** The river banks for some miles below the city now also show numerous breaches through which the water in flood-time passes into the low-lying marshy tracks on both sides.

510. **Note.** The description given here of the twin towns *Jayapura* and *Dvaravati*, which *Jayapida* founded, has been fully discussed by Prof. Buhler, who, in the course of his tour in 1875, succeeded in tracing their site and remains near the village of *Andarkoth* situated on the *Sambal* lake at the elevation of $74^0$ 42' longitude and $34^0$ 13' latitude. Refering for all details as regards the topography and ruins of the place to the exhaustive and accurate account given by Prof. Buhler, *Report,* p. 13 sqq; it will be sufficient to notice here the following points directly bearing on the identification. *Andarkoth* is the name given to a village which lies partly on an island rising from the *Sambal* lake, and partly on the low-lying strip of land separating that lake from the *Vitasta* numerous temples, which the tradition of the villagers distinctly attribute to a king *'Jayapida'*. This tradition, which verified on the spot by M.A. Stein at several occasions fully agrees with the one current among the Pandits of Srinagar, who all look up *Andarkoth* as the site of *Jayapida's* capital. We can attach all the more importance to this tradition as it is borne out by the old gloss which explains *abhyantara Kotta* by *'Andarkot'*. Its survival is sufficiently accounted for by the fact that the place was still known in the time of *Srivara* i.e towards the close of the 15th century, by the name of *Jayapidapura* or *Jayapura. Dvaravati,* which was built in the water and called after *Krsna's* town, was popularly known in Kalhana's time as *bahyakotta*, the 'Outer castle', and *Jayapura* as *abhyantara Kotta*, the 'Inner castle'. The latter name is undoubtedly preserved in the modern *Andarkoth*, which in Kashmir has the same meaning. The term *Bahyakotta* Prof. Buhler thought to have recognised in the name *'Bahirkut'* which according to the information obtained for him by his Kashmirian assistant (Report, p. 15) was applied to the village situated on the above mentioned island. Careful inquiries made by Stein on several occasions, both at the village and in its neighbourhood, have shown that this supposed name *'Bahirkut'* is wholly unkonwn, and that both portions of the village are called *Andarkoth*, as indeed Prof. Buhler's himself had been rightly told by his boatmen. The name *'Bahirkut'* is thus, in all probability, due only to some misunderstanding on the part of Prof. Buhler's inforormant. As a Kashmiri village name it would have been all the more curious as Kalhana's does not know the word *'bahir'*, but uses *'nebar'* as the contrast to *andar.* With *Bahirkut* we must abandon also Prof. Bhuler's proposal of placing *Dvaravati* on the island and *Jayapura* on the opposite lake-shore. All the buildings which Kalhana specially mentions, three *Buddha* image, four Vishnu as *Samkarsana, Aniruddha, Vasudeva, Pradyumna* known as *Vishnupura* and five (offices designated) by the word 'Great'(*pancamahasabda*), such as the *Vihara*, the temples dedicated to *Jayedevi, Brahman* and *Kesava*, the *Matha* of

*Jayedatta*, are distinctly placed at *Jayapura*. Ruins corresponding to such structures can be traced in for greaters number on the island plateau of *Andarkoth* than on the opposite shore, and it is, therefore, more probable that the former was the site of *Jayapura*. The largest ruin situated at the North Western corner of the plateau has already by Prof. Buhler been rightly recognised as a temple dedicated to *Vishnu*, on the evidence of a large sculptured block bearing representations of that deity. This ruin may now be assumed to correspond to the temple of *Kesava* referred by *Kalhana Sesa* (Serpent). The epithet *Kotta*, which Kalhana gives to *Jayapura*, which equalled heaven (in beauty) i.e. 'Great' (*Pancamahasabda*) , which is reflected also in *Srivara's* expression *durga*, receives its proper significance if we take into account the strong position occupied by the plateau of *Andarkoth*, surrounded as it is on all sides by water. *Jayapura* served also later times as a royal residence, but its buildings were already in ruins in the time of *Zain-ul-Abidin*. Of *Dvaravati* no further mention is found either in the *Rajatarangini* or in the later Chronicles. We may conclude from this circumstance that the place had lost its importance already at an early date. This again accounts for the comparative insignificance of the ruins extant at the probable site of *Dvaravati*. The latter is indicated by a few detached hamlets, all belonging to *Andarkoth*, which stretch in a semicircle along the edge of the lake to the North of the *Andarkoth* island. During a short visit paid to the site in May, 1896. Stein traced the remains evidently taken from ancient structures in the ruined *Ziarat* of *Saiyid* Habibulla, and in the foundations of an old building known as the Qazi Hamam. From the central hamlet at which the latter is situated, a causeway (*Suth*), about 400 yards long, leads across the *'Sar'* to the island of *Andrakoth*. It is built entirely of old stone-material. The tradition of the villagers attributes the ruins here named, like those on the island itself, uniformly to king *'Jayapida'*.

511. **Note** Neither a person nor a locality of the name *Bhimadeva* is known. It is a conjectural emendation might be suggested *preryasrayam* for *preyasrayam* of *'Nam'* or *'Sabda'*.
512. *R.T* Vol.1 Book VII. p. 394.
513. *Ibid.*
514. *Ibid.*
515. **Note.** *Nilasva* must be the name of a territorial division in Kashmir proper, which, however, cannot be identified now. The *Lokaprakasa* shows the name as *Nilasa* in the list of Kashmir parganas given at the commencement of IV. *Prakasa*. The deceitful king at *Garga's* order had *Bimba*, the Damara of *Nilasva*, who was hateful before the latter, thrown into the *Vitasta* with a stone bound (to him). All the Damaras of *Nilasva* and his soldiers made common cause with the enemy, and went to attack his forces. The passages mention, Damras of *Nilasva*, without giving any clue as to the position of the tract. *Srivara* speaks of an assembly of people from *Nilasva* at *Dugdhasrama*, i.e. *Dudarham*, at the lower month

of the Sind Valley. The Fourth Chronicle seems to place *Nilasva* in a westerly direction, as a force is collected there to oppose an enemy encamped about *Pratapapura,* i.e. *Tapar. Abul-Fazl's* list of Parganas contains no name bearing the slightest resemblance to *Nilasva.*

516. *R.T.* Vol.1 Book VII. p. 394.
517. *Ibid.*
518. *Ibid.*
519. *Ibid.*
520. **Note.** It gives the name of this mendicant (beggar) as *Chinna*. He was the forefather of the writer.
521. R.T: Vol.1 Book VII. p. 394
522. *Ibid.* p. 395. **Note.** *Virahabujamgi* is a nickname *'Brahman'* 'a snake, when without a lover'.
523. **Note.** The position of this temple cannot be traced, and hence the locality where *Harsa* found his death, is also uncertain. From the preceding account of *Harsa's* flight, it must be concluded that it was some distance below Srinagar near the right bank of the river.'
524. *R.T.* Vol.1 Book VII. p. 395.
525. *Ibid.*
526. *Ibid.*
527. **Note.** One account is that at the *Daksha* sacrifice *Rudra* knocked out his teeth while he was eating the *Purodasa* offering. *Pushan* is adored in eight hymns of the *Rig-veda.* There are the sons of *Prishni,* the cloud-cow, and of *Rudra,* rather a subordinate deity in the *Veda,* though undoubteldy very old, but who, in later Brahmanism and especially Hinduism, rose to the highest rank. *Prishni,* "speckled," from the roof *Prish,* which, however, also means 'sprinkle" (the connection between the two is obvious) a play on homonyms or *pun* quite in the taste of all ancient ethical poetry, and a liberal source of stories, riddles, and puzzles. (The *Rig-Veda*, Vol.III. p. 320) quoted from *V.I.* p. 209.
528. *R.T.* Vol.1 Book VI. p. 395.
529. *Ibid.*
530. *Ibid.*
531. *Ibid.*
532. **Note.** It has been translated according to *punah, svabhre; manahsvabhre.* Term *put-kr* is used here, in the sense of the *Panjabi* and *Pahari pukarna,* 'to shout to a distance; to call to a far-off person.' It is a vital wound at the neck-bone and incapable of action, he rolled on the ground, covered with blood. "Whom shall we call to help? who knows of us to drag us up from here, as a leader of the elephant-herd (would drag out) two young elephants sinking in the quagmire?" while *'Nam'* or *'Chamar'* stood there, *Bhoja* heard in the evening shouts coming from a distance, (one did not know) whence, and expressed his alarm.
533. *R.T. Vol.*1 Book VII. p. 395.
534. *Ibid.* pp. 395-96.
535. **Note.** *Hastikarna* is placed by the gloss at *Vyaghrasrama-Vagahama,* i.e the modern village *Vagahama* situated in the *Dachumpor Pargana* at the elevation of 75$^0$ 10' longitude and 33$^0$ 5' latitude, not far from

the right bank of the *Vitasta*. A spring which issues in this village, is still at present known as *Hastikarnanaga,* and is mentioned by this name in the *Vijayesvaramah. xi,* 182, *Amaresvaramah* i.9, and *Tirthas*. This spring is probably meant also in *Haracar.* XIV. 43, and *Nilamata*, 985. The *Hastikarna* mentioned by *Srivara* in connection with *Mari* stream or *Mahasarit,* must be a different locality and in the vicinity of Srinagar at *Prayagaka*.

536. *R.T.* Vol.1 Book VII. p. 396.
537. **Note.** The unborn child is supposed to remember the actions done in its former existences, and to form plans accordingly for the new life. As it leaves the womb these reminiscences and plans are forgotten, and newly-born individual become subject to the consequences of its preceding existence (*Karman*).
538. **Note.** It takes meaning from the term *Rangavata* for the name of a sacred enclosure (*vata*) or grove at *Hastikarna*. The same name in Kashmir called *Rangavor,* is given to this day to an old grove of walnut trees at Gus. By *Uttaraghosa,* Kalhana means evidently the present village of *Gus* in the *Uttar* Pargana elevated at 74° 17′ longitude and 34° 31′ latitude· The place is mentioned under the name of *Ghosa* in the *Saradamah*. 124, and its Naga is probably referred to under the name of *Gosa* in the *Nilamata Purana*, 939. The *Uttar* Pargana in the extreme of North West of *Kramarajya* (*Kamraz*) is mentioned *as Uttaraka* in*Lokapura*, ii.
539. *R.T* .Vol.1 Book VII. p. 396.
540. *Ibid.*
541. **Note.** There is emend in term *Lalitakas Caiva*, with reference to *Lalitascaiva* is here in place of *Lalitavacaiva* and can scarcely be distinguished in *Sarada* characters. Though living among favourities of low character, and still in his boyhood, he did not acquire bad habits.
542. *R.T.* Vol.1 Book VII. p. 396.
543. *Ibid.*
544. *Ibid.*
545. *Ibid.* p. 397.
546. *Ibid.*
547. *Ibid.*
548. *Ibid.*
549. *Ibid.* p. 398.
550. *Ibid.*
551. *Ibid.*
552. *Ibid.*
553. *Ibid.*
554. *Ibid.*
555. *Ibid.*
556. *Ibid.*
557. *Ibid.* p. 399.
558. *Ibid.*

559. *Ibid.*
560. *Ibid.*
561. *Ibid.*
562. **Note.** 'He' turned the *Mahattama Sahela* and many others out of office, and made them wear clothes of hamp of Jail. *Bhanga, 'hemp'*, in Kashmiri called *'banga'*, grows plentifully in Kashmir, and 'furnishes an excellent fibre from which strong and durable ropes are made. Therefore, this material is as far as, could nto ascertain for a long period in the content of cloth. *Harsa* made *Bhutabhisca,* in order to ridicule him, act like a strolling player together with the wife, and run about like a *Domba* soldier.
563. *R.T.* Vol.1 Book VII. p. 399.
564. *Ibid.*
565. *Ibid.*
566. *Ibid.*
567. *Ibid.*
568. *Ibid.*
569. **Note.** It is interesting to note that why *Mukta* escaped from the treacherous *Harsa.* It permits us to assume that Kalhana had his account of *Harsa's* flight and death directly or indirectly from this surviving witness, who was connected with his own family of *Canpaka* and *Jolaka.* Perhaps this expresses also the favourable colour put upon *Mukta's* department at the catastrophe.
570. *R.T.* Vol.1 Boo VII. 399
571. *Ibid.*
572. *Ibid.* pp. 399-400
573. *Ibid.*
574. *Ibid.*
575. **Note.** The story of the fight in which *Camunda,* a form of *Durga,* with her attendants, the *Saktis,* defeated and killed the Daifya *Pura,* is told e.g in the *Padma* pura, v. XXVI. 59-95
576. *R.T.* Vol.1 Book VII. p. 400
577. *Ibid.*
578. *Ibid.*
579. *Ibid.*
580. *Ibid.*
581. *Ibid.*
582. *Ibid.*
583. *Ibid.*
584. *Ibid.*
585. **Note.** Kalhana explains here to the fact that in the year of *Harsa's* death (*Lokakala,* 4177, A.D. 1101-2), the luni-solar calendar had an intercalary month which fell into the month of *Bhadrapada,* two months of that name being thus counted for that year. The tables given by Canningham, *Indian Eras,* p. 173, and in Messrs. Sewell and Dikshit's *Indian Calendar.* p. iii, actually show *Bhadrapada* as the intercalary month for

that year, and thus Kalhana's statement is proved to be correct. *Harsa's* death according to *Bhadrapada Sudi* 5. As Kalhana designates there the month simply as *Bhadrapada*, we may assume that the day meant was the fifth day of the bright half of the proper (*nija*) *Bhadrapada*. This half, according to the rule of the *Suryasiddhanta* still observed in Kashmir, follows after the intercalated month, in this case called *dvitiyabhadrapada* (compared, *Indian Eras*, p. 91 and *Indian Calendar*, p. 30). This date of *Janakachandra's* death must accordingly have been *Karttika Vadi* 5. Kalhana mentions of the intercalary mouth of this year furnishers interesting evidence as to the general accuracy of his chronology for the later reigns.

586. **Note.** According to the story of *Mahabharata,* king *Vichitravirya* of *Hastinapura,* in the *Kuru* country, identified with a place in the Meerut district, had sons named *Dhritarashtra* and *Pandu. Dhritarashtra* was born blind and hence *Pandu* succeeded to the throne. He died in the life time of his elder brother, leaving five sons, *Yudhisthira, Bhimasena, Arjuna, Nakula*, and *Sahadeva. Dhritarashtra* had more than a hundred children, of whom the eldest was *Duryodhana*. The sons of *Pandu* married *Draupadi*, daughter of the king of *Panchala*. The third prince, *Arjuna,* married also *Subhadra*, sister of Krishna who belonged to the powerful. Yadava confederacy of Mathura and *Devaraka* (in *Kathiawar*). The *Pandus* claimed a share of their paternal kingdom. They were given the *Khandava* forest to the south of the *Kuru* kingdom, where they built the stately city of *Indraprastha* near modern Delhi. At the instance of Krishna they overthrew *Jarasandha*, the powerful king of Magadha, who was seeking to establish his own supermacy. The Magadha ruler had carried off hundreds of princes as prisoners to the fastness of *Girivraja* with a view to offering them as victims in a horrid rite. The *Pandus* now effected conquests in all directions and laid claim to the rank of paramount rulers, performing the *Rajasuya,* which was now a sacrifice of imperial inauguration. The prosperity of their rivals roused the jealously of the sons of *Dhritarashtra*.

587. **Note.** During the early Vedic age trade probably consisted mainly of barter. The chief articles trade, judging by the evidence of the later *Samhitas,* were clothes, coverlets and skins. The standard unit of value was the cow, but necklests of gold (*nishka*) also served as a means of exchange. Whether *nishka* in the early period possessed all the characteristic marks of a regular coinage, is a highly debatable question. No gold coin of the old indigenous type was yet been discovered in India, but the transition to the use of coined money was clearly prepared by the *nishka*, which was a piece of metal that came to possess a definite weight, if not the hall-mark of state authority (*A.H.I.* p. 35). Before the closing of the Vedic period, the Aryans possessed an extensive literature handed down in the Brahmanical schools by memory. Some idea of the vide range of subjects in which the people interested themselves may be obtained from several lists given in the *Upanishads*. One such list

makes mention not only of the *Vedas* but of *Itihasa-purana* (legend and ancient lore), *Pitrya* (the science relating to the manes), *Rasi* (mathematics), *Daiva* (knowledge of portents), *Nidhi* (Chronology), *Vakovakya* (dialectics). *Ekayana* (ethics), *Deva-Vidya* (etymological interpretation of divine names), *Brahmavidya* (knowledge of the Absolute), *Bhutavidya* (Knowledge of the Absolute), *Bhutavidya* (demonology, or science of elements), *Kshatra vidya* (the military science), *Nakshatra vidya* (astronomy), *Sarpa vidya* (the science of snakes), and *Devajana* vidya (dancing and music or mythology). Another list mentions the *Vedas*, phonetics (*Siksha*), ritual (*Kalpa*), grammar (*Vyakarana*), etymology (*nirukta*) metrics (*Chhandas*) and astronomy (*Jyotisha*). If all the subjects mentioned in the former list were dealt with in special treatises, most of them have not come down to us. A brief account of the extant works of Vedic literature included in the second list is given below.

The word *Veda* comes from the root *vid,* to know. It means knowledge in general. It is specially applied to a brance of literature which has been handed down from time immorial by verbal transmission and is declared to be sacred knowledge or divine revelation (*Sruti*).

The Veda consists of four different classes of literary composition:

1. The *Mantra* (saying, song, formula) constitutes the oldest division of vedic literature, and is distributed in four *Samhitas* or collections known as the *Rik, Sama, Yajus* and *Atharva Samhitas*. The first three are sometimes spoken of as the *Trayi* or threefold knowledge, being alone recognised at first as cannonical scriptures. The *Rik-Samhitas* is a collection of lyrics in praise of different gods. These were recited by the priest styled the *hotri*. Most of the songs belong to an age anterior to what we have called the later vedic period, but the collection as a whole may not be as old. The *Samhitas* of the *Samaveda,* or the *'Book of Chants'*, contains hardly any independent matter, all its verses except seventyfive being taken directly from the *Rig-Veda*. It songs were meant to be sung at the Soma sacrifice by a special class of priests called *Udgatri.* The *Samhita* of the *Yajurveda,* or Book of sacrificial Prayer, consists not only of stanzas taken from the *Rig-veda,* but also of original prose formulas to be uttered by the *Adhvarya* priest who performed the manual work involved in a sacrifice. The collection has two divergent texts, viz, (a) the *Samhita* of the Black *Yajurveda* preserved in the *Taittiriya, Maitrayani* and *Kathaka* recensions, and (b) the *Somhita* of the white *Yajurveda* preserved in the *Vajasaneyi* recension.

   At a time considerably later than the *Samhitas* mentioned above, a fourth attained to cononical recognition, the *Atharva Veda*, or the Book of magic formulas. Though its recognition came later, much of the matter contained in the collection is old. Some of the Atharvan *hymns* were of popular rather than priestly origin and may be as old as the earliest parts of the *Rig-veda*. The *Atharva-Samhitas* is, in the main, a collection of songs, spells and incantations for the healing of disease, the restoration of harmony, the exorcism of evil spirits, etc. But there are certain hymns of rare beauty that celebrate the power and omniscience of God and the beneficence of Mother Earth.

*May Earth pour out her milk for us,*
*a mother unto me her son.*
*O Prithvi, auspicious by the woodlands,*
*auspicious be thy hills and snow-clad-mountians.*

2. The second class of Vedic works are known by the name of *Brahmanas* i.e. treatise relating to prayer and sacrificial ceremony. They are mainly prosetexts containing observations on sacrifice. They also contain cosmogonic mythes, old legends and *gathos* or verses celebrating the exploits of kings famed in priestly tradition.
3. Next come the *Aranyakas* or forest texts, books of instruction to be given in the forest or writings meant for wood-dwelling hermits, which are found as appendices of the *Brahmanas.* These treatises resemble the *Brahmanas* in language, style and even content, but they are concerned more with the allegorical signification of rites, and the mystic meaning of the texts of the *Samhitas* than with elaborate rules for the performance of the great sacrifices. The bulk of the *Aranyaka* literature is old, but certain portions may belong to a date posterior to the period under review.
4. Lastly, we have the *Upanishads,* " secret or esoteric dectrines". The name is derived by some from the root *'upa-ni-sad'* which means *'to sit down near some one"* and is applied to doctrines that may be imparted to son or a trusted pupil *seated near the teachers.* The Upanishads are either imbedded in the *Aranyakas* or form their supplements. They are also found an independent works. The contain deep speculations of a philosophical character which "revolve around the two conceptions of *Brahman* and *Atman*," i.e. the universal soul, the absolute and the individual self. The oldest Upanishads are usually regarded as pre-Buddhistic, but some of the treatises bearing the name "Upanishad" certainly belong to a much later period. The classes of literary works named above are alone classed as *Sruti,* or Revelation, and constitute the vedic literature proper. But closely connected with them as auxiliary treatises, though not regarded as a part of the Revelation, there exist a class of compositions called *Vedanga,* "members or limbs of the Veda". They are regarded as less authoritative then the *Shruti,* and are styled *Smriti*, memory or tradition, as handing down only the tradition derived from ancient sages to whom the *Vedas* were "revealed". The originated mostly in Vedic schools (*charanas*) and their contents are often expressed in an extremely condensed style of prose intended for memorisation, to which the name *Sutra* (thread, clue, guide, rule aphorism) is given. Some of the treatises were versified in later times. The *Vedangas* are six in number, viz, *Siksha* (phonetics), *Kalpa* (ritual), *Vyakarana,* (grammar), *Nirukta* (etymology), *chhandas* (metrics), and *Jyotisha* (astronomy). These subjects are already mentioned in some of the *Upanishads*, though the extant manuals may belong to a much later period. The manuals of *Siksha* deal with the correct pronunciation and accentuation of the Vedic hymns. The productions of the *Siksha* school include the "connected text" of thc *Rig-veda* as well as the "Word-text" which gives the text of the

verses in a complete grammatical analysis. But the most remarkable compositions of the *Siksha* class are the *Pratisakhya Sutras* which contain the rules by the aid of which the *Samhita-patha (*connected text) can be formed from the *Pada-Patha* (*Word-text*). (*Ibid.* pp. 51-53)

588. **Note.** The astrological houses in *Harsa's* horoscope are to be counted from cancer, and thus correspond to the Zodiacal sign, Scorpion, Sagittarius, capricorn and Aries. The positions of the planets are correctly indicated in the diagram of the horoscope drawn and reproduced in the Education. Regarding the terms by which the astrological houses are referred to in the text compared with Varahamihiran *Laghujataka* i. The quotation from the *'Samhita'* refers probably to Varahmihira's *Brhatsamhita* mentioned above. The 'malignant' planets (*papah*) are the Sun, Moon, Saturn, and Mars compared with *Laghujataka* ii. 4. According to Prof. Jacobi, "the horoscope of *Harsa*, as given in the text and correctly explained by the drawing in the gloss, does not suit the king's (presumable) birth date *Lokakala* 4134 (Kali 4159, A.D. 1058) 9 months. For at that time Saturn was in Taurus, not in Scorpion, and Venus in Scorpion, not in Captricorn. The places of the three remaining planets (Mercury, Mars and Jupiter) square with our text. The error in Saturn's position is such as to exclude the possibility of any conjectural correction."
589. *R.T.* Vol.1 Book VII. p. 401.
590. *Ibid.*
591. *Ibid.*
592. *Ibid.*
593. *Ibid.*
594. *Ibid.*
595. **Note.** The nucleus of the *Ramayana* is the story of Rama, the eldest son of *Dasaratha,* a prince of the *Ikshvaku* family of Ayodhya in the Fyzabad district of Oudh. The prince married *Sita,* the daughter of *Janaka*, king of Videha in North Bihar. Owing to a palace intrigue, the *Ikshvaku* prince had to leave his home and go into exile for a period of fourteen years. He repaired to the *Dandaka* forest in the Deccan with his wife and faithful half brother *Lakshmana.* He dwelt for sometime on the banks of the Godavari in *Panchavati*, which is usually identified with *Nasik.* Here he came into conflict with the *Rakshasas* or cannibal chieftains who were a source of disturbance to the peaceful hermits of the locality. Among the hostile chieftains were some persons closely related to *Ravana,* the mighty king of *Lanka* (Ceylon). That potentate sought to avenge his injured relations by carrying off *Sita,* wife of *Rama*, to his island home. In their distress, the *Ikshvaku* princes allied themselves with *Sugriva,* Hanuman and other monkey chiefs of *Kishkindhya* in the Bellary district of South India and crossed over the Lanka. They killed the *Rakshasa* king with most of his clan and rescued the princess *Sita.* As the period of Rama's exile was now over, he returned with his wife and brother to Ayodhya where he was warmly received by his half-brother *Bharata* in whose favour he had been made to relinquish his rights. Meanwhile people came to question the properity of taking back a princess who had long been kept confined by a *Rakshasa* king. To silence

the unreasonable clamour of the multitude, *Rama* had to banish his faithful consort, the ideal of Indian womanhood. The duty of a *Raja*, according to Hindu notions, was always to please his subjects who were his "children". The virtuous royal lady found a shelter in the hermitage of *Valmiki*, where she gave birth to the twins, *Kusa* and *Lava*, who subsequently returned to thier ancestral home and succeeded to their heritage. It is difficult to say if there is any kernel of historical truth underneath this tale of a princes adventures in the land of cannibals and monkeys. *Rama* and *Sita* are names met with in the vedic literature, though not always as appellations of human beings. They are, however, in now way connected in the Vedic texts with the illustrious lines of the *Ikshvakus* or the *Videhas*. The name of Ravana is absolutely unknown to Brahmanical or non-Brahmanical literature till we come to the epics themselves or to works like the *Kautilya Arthasastra,* which show acquaitance with the epics. It is, however, possible that *Ikshvaku* princes played a leading part in the colonisation of the Far South of India, as names of *Ikshvaku* kings figure prominently in the early inscriptions of Southern India. Whether the name of *Ikshavku* was first popularized in the south by princes from Ayodhya or by followers of the *Sakya* teacher of *Kapilavastu,* who also claimed *Ikshvaku* descent, must remain an open question (*A.H.I.* p. 93). In the history of Indian art and literature flourished in *Java* to an extent unknown elsewhere. There are still hundreds of temples in ruins, and an extensive literature, in manuscripts, based on Sanskrit. The *Ramayana* and the *Mahabharata* were most popular in that island, and even to-day furnish the theme of their popular shadow-play, called *Wajang,* and theatrical performances. With the fall of Majaphit, artistic activities came to an end in *Java* (Ibid. p. 222). The patronage of the princely courts also considerably helped the growth of literature. *Vidyapati* was the court poet of a Hindu chief named *Siva Simha.* The Muslim rulers of Bengal engaged scholars to translate the *Ramayana* and the *Mahabharata* from Sanskrit into Bengali, which they understood and spoke. Thus *Sultan Nusrat Shah* of Gaur had the *Mahabharata* translated into Bengali. *Vidyapati* says much in praise of this *Sultan* and also of Sultan *Ghiyas-ud-din. Krittivas*, whose Bengali version of the *Ramayana* has been regarded by some as the Bible of Bengal, enjoyed the patronage of a "king of Gaur". *Maladhar* Vasu translated the *Bhagavata* into Bengali under the patronage of Sultan Husain Shah and received from him the title of *Gunaraja Khan.* Husain Shah's general, Paragal Khan's son, *Chuti Khan,* governor of Chittagong, employed *SrikaraNandi* to translate the *Asvamedha Parva* of the *Mahabharata* into Bengali. We have already noted what great encouragement was given to the development of *Telugu* literature by the *Vijayanagar* court. (Ibid. pp. 407-8). The Persian literature of Akbar's reign may be considered under three heads: (i) historical works (ii) translations, and (iii)poetry and verse. The well-known historical works of the reign are the *Ta'rikh-i-Alfi* of Mulla Daud, the *Ain-i-Akbari* and *Akbarnamah* of Abul Fazl, the *Muntakhab-ul-Tawarikh* of Babauni, the *Tabaqat-i-Akbari* of Nizam-ud-din Ahmad, the *Akbarnamah* of Faizi Sarhindi, and the *Ma'asir-i-Rahimi* of *'Abdul Baqi'*, complied under the patronage of Abdur Rahim *Khan-i-Khanian*. The most accomplished writer (in Persian) of the reign was Abul Fazl, a man of letters, a poet, an essayist, a critic, and a historian. By order of the Emperor, many books in Sanskrit and other languages were translated into Persian. Different sections of the *Mahabharata* were translated into that language by several Muslim scholars and were compiled under the title of *Razm-Namah*. After labouring for four years, Badauni completed the translation of the *Ramayana* in A.D. 1589. Haji Ibrahim Sarhindi translated into Persian the *Atharva Veda*. Faizi the *Lilabati*, a work on mathematics; Mukammal Khan, Gujarati the *Tajak*, a treatise on astronomy; 'Abdur Rahim Khan-i-Khanan the *Waqiat-i-Baduri*; and Maulana Shah Muhammad *Shahabadi* translated the *History of Kashmir*. Some Greek and Arabic works were also translated into Persian. A number of famous poets or versifiers produced works of merit under the patronage of Akbar. The most famous among the verse-writers was Ghizali. Next in importance to him was Faizi, a brother of Abul-Fazl. Other Prominent poets were Muhammad Husain Naziri of *Nishapur*, who wrote *ghazals* of great merit, and Sayyid. Jamaluddin Urfi of *Shiraj*, the most famous writer of *Qasidas* in his days (Ibid. p. 580). Among the writers of the *Rama* cult, the most illustrious was *Tulsi Das* (A.D. 1532-1623), who lived in *Benaras* "unapproachable and alone in his niche in the temple of "Fame". He was not merely a poet of a high order, but a spiritual *teacher* of the people of Hindustan, where his name has become a house hold word and his memory is worshipped by millions. The most famous of his works, known as *Ramcharitamanasa*, or "The Pool of Rama's life", not of the land has been described. Sir George Grierson explained as "the one Bible of a hundred millions of people" of Hindustan. Growse also observed in his translation of the *Ramayana* of Tulsi Das that "his book is in every one's hands, from the court to the cottage, and is read and heard and appricated alike by every class of the Hindu community, whiter high or low, rich or poor, young or old". This period was also marked by "the first attempts to systematise the art of poetry itself", made by writers like *Keshava Das* (A.D. 1580), a Sandhya Brahmana of Orcha, *Sundar Senapati* and the Tripathi brothers, who flourished during the reign of *Shah Jahan* (Ibid. p. 582).

596. R.T. Vol.1 Book VII. p. 402.
597. *Ibid.*
598. *Ibid.* **Note.** In the above passage it has been discussed (the reigns of ) six kings the family of *Udayaraja* (who ruled) for ninety-eight years less three days". Thus the total length of the reigns for those six kings is correctly given, the dates for the deaths of *Didda* and *Harsa* being *Lokakala* 4079 *Bhadrapada* Sudi 8 and 4177 *Bhadrapadasudi* 5, respectively have been explained in the text.

# 8

# UCHCHALA (1101-11 A.D.)

The assassination of *Harsa* brought to an end the rule of the family of *Udayaraja*, who ruled nearly a century, i.e., for ninety-eight years less three days[1]. *Uchchala*, the new king, who became the ruler of Kashmir after the death of *Harsa,* just as the ocean before the churning had brought to light neither its poison nor its nectar[2]. His accession, therefore, marked the beginning of the rule of the second branch of the same family[3]. In the race of *Harsa's* crown, *Uchchala,* the elder of the two sons of *Malla,* had proved successful. But his position at the commencement of his reign was very precarious[4].

**Trouble by the Damaras**

In the beginning, the rule of *Uchchala* was thoughtless in his actions[5] and the leaders of the Damaras, to whose rebellion he owed the throne, behaved as the true rulers in the land, and *Sussala*[6], his ambitions younger brother, was ready to rise against him. In order to secure safety from *Sussala*, he ceded to him the *Lohara* territory[7] as an independent chiefship. Against the great feudal landlords, *Uchchala* protected himself by a drexture use of *Macchiavellian* policy. By fomenting among them jealousy and mutual suspicion, he secured the murder or exile of their most influential leaders, without himself incurring the odium. Then, reassured in his position, he openly turned upon the Damaras[8] and forced them into disarmament and submission[9]. As he arrived (there), he carried all belongs with his councilors, while his elder brother out of tender regard did not creat any problem[10]. *Uchchala* had the doubt for the resistence of certain soldiers (*Kottabhrtya*) at the time of entrant, he had accompied with a son of *Utkarsa,*' *Pratapa* by name, and thus addressed them[11]; "I want to make this (prince) king, acting (myself) as his doorkeeper." The neighbouring chiefs stood humbly before the king, as it they were his own servants[12]. The road will be blocked for somedays by his followers, but his siner *Kanaka* got an opportunity to spread the *'Radha Soami'* mission abroad[13]. He gave his life at *Varanasi*[14] in weariness of the world, (being the only one) among *Harsa's* servants who displayed honour in this respect[15]. Sincere *Uccala* or *Uchchala* at that time conducted *Janakacandra* that the king and other Damaras seemed to lose all importance. Besides these, *Bhoja* son of *Harsa* had the daughter of king *Abhaya*[16] of *Urasa*[17], a male child from the Queen *Vibhavamati*. As he was born after two or three other sons had died (in childhood), the *Gurus* anxious (to assure him) a long life, had given him the ignominious name of *Bhiksacara*[18] ('beggar'). Though this kid is of two years, should have been treated as an enemy, as he continued the enemy's stock, yet the king had the advice from the side of *Janakacandra* preserved him and entrusted him to his own queen[19]. At the same time *Janakacandra* was calculating that the Damaras they submitted equality before the *'Law'* or *'Word'* that enemity should not be created. No doubt, *Uchchala* had already displayed great honour and sincereity in this context[20]. He also alluded his intention of giving to him charge of the 'Gate'. Thereupon, there arose ill feeling (against *Janakacandra*) in *Bhimadeva* and all the other (Damaras[21]). It was the question of jealousy between them and his risen high, and their respective followers challanged each other to fight for a stake[22]. During the condition of choes and confusion *Arjuna, Kalapasa's* son, a violent follower of *Bhimadeva* struck with his knife the body of *Janakacandra*[23]. Latter, they knocked the door of the king's apartment, thinking that king had arranged this conspiracy. At the sametime, fast was took place in the house of the common (*Snanadroni*[24]), *Bhimadeva* ran towards him with a dagger drawn to kill him[25].

**Murder of Janakacandra**

During the time of lawlessness the accountant of *Bhimadeva's* household, who had been hidden behind a pillar, she cut down the body of *Janakacandra* into two pieces[26]. Without any information she wounded his younger brothers Gagga[27] and *Sadda*[28], they will flee[29] immediately towards Bias. The lightening lord will strike down the enemy which had been lurking in their mind for a long period and being them in low deeds[30]. It will be appear that there is a colossal change in their living and will felt we are betraying our lord. 'He is always in check. Even though *Bhimadeva* is getting enjoy of the *'Inner voice'* why not others, while *Gagga* trusted him[31], and will sent to *Lahara*[32] to recover his wound after defeating the Damaras, who were frightened, to their mounted and (respective) territories[33]. In this way one has to proceed *Madavarajya* and other executed the *Kaliya*, then it became a strong force[34]. Due to the deep judgementof the *'Word'* or *'Nam'*, *Gagga* became more affectionate towards the King as great as (if he had been) his son[35]. It is understood by Lord that king, who cared for his subjects and did not tolerate even a word of the opposition group, and never displayed an kind of resistance against *Gagga* when he committed lot of offences.[36] It is well known by the *Bhimadeva* that he had two dirty councillors at that time who always misguided him again the King. Do not worry, God will listen our request[37].

**Administrative Reform of Uchchala**

After ascending the throne, *Uchchala* went outside (his inner apartments) in the morning and occupied himself in the outer courts (of the palace) till the evening, in order to learn what the people said[38]. It appears from the statement that he was extremely conscious of the difficulties and problems of his subjects, in accordance with the other he, being ever ready for exertion, would, if he heard but the (mere) word ' opponent', start (at once), even though it was a midnight, he will crushed the rebolt[39]. King had possessed great firmness and wisdom among kings. His conduct was without stain not even damaged by avarice kind of material. Study revealed that his reign will be cleared off by the *'Master's Song'* that is 'Nam' on the basis of his virtuous conduct (which is purifying like) Ganga water [40]. No doubt, during his administration he had the less resources (*anga*), but he removed almost entirely the dense darkness on the mind, like another *Anuru*[41]. There was a commitment between the ruler and the king, first you have to vow before the *'Nam'* or *'Word' or 'Chamar'* (*Prayopavesa*). He judged the persons in proper manner[42]. During the rule of *Uchchala,* he was not ready to listen any kind of grievances of the public because it was his pain, even he would not spare himself from the punishment[43]. It is also expressed that king did not even spare his own relatives and officials on their carelessness in public business[44]. It was his prime duty to look after the state business and help the weaker sections of the society[45].During his rule, he visited on horseback to listen the grievances of the people[46], did not bother that 'I am a king'. Whosoever approached king had followed, but his presence of mind will proved fruitful to the public as a wishing tree[47]. His words were the shower of gifts during the time of his visit along with attendants for the public even in the places of his relaxation[48]. Those will do work hard in their respective professions, they might be given high reward of reverence[49]. *Uchchala* was always ready at any time to listen the problems, just as a father (relieves) of his sons[50]. He provided the food-grain to his public at cheap-rate from his stores to stop the rising famine[51]. Due to his tender-heart, he freed the food-grain to the robbers, please plunder it as a basic need of the life and, lead a blameless life by giving them employment as the guardians of treasuries[52]. Hence, to suppliments the cry as, "Give, give to me", so this liberal *Uchchala* was heard saying, "Give, give to him".[53] No need of the gift, it was the magnanimity of the soul, who had given the gift of the messengers who are (concerned with it[54]). He stressed on those words, "unlike a tree (which is merely) painted (and hence gives no fruit[55])." Moreover, on the day of *Sivaratri* and other festive occasions like marriage, etc. he flooded the presents to his people, just as Indra (floods) the earth with rain at the conjunctions of planets[56]. It displayed from the study that *Uchchala* introduced effecient administrative reforms in every walks of life in comparsion with the *Harsa*. Though it was a regal seat, when he obtained it[57]. But it was nothing more than a clod of earth. He showed excessive liberality such as even *Kubera* would find difficult to practise[58] it. By birth he was *Kashmiri*, but he did not ready to waste the soil by erecting *Mandir* and *Masjid*[59], or purchasing horses[60] . It was the wonderful idea of the *Uchchala* that he threw his soul in every direction in everywhere in everything. It proves from the study that he had acquired a complete knowledge of the soul of his people[61]. The food which had been given by the king to the Brahmans, was sufficient for their disease as a medicine, and those who had no livelihood, the means of subsistance[62]. At the time of *Sradh* [63] sacrifices, when propitiatory rites (had to be performed to avert) bad omenus (connected with eclipses, comets and the like *Uchchala* also betowed thousands of cows, horses, gold, gifts, etc to the *Brahmanas*[64].

**Construction Works of Uchchala**

Study reveals that first of all *Uchchal* paid a special attention to built the new temples during his reign which were suddenly burned in the whole town at *Nandiksetra*[65] as it were constructed in the very ancient period[66]. No doubt, this pious (king) also restored the decayed (buildings) of Vishnu *Cakradhara*[67], *Yogesa*[68], *Suayambhu*[69], etc. Besides this, he also carried off king *Harsa's* work at *Parihasapura*[70] the illustrious (image of Vishnu) and parrot house which gives solace that is *'Nam' (Sukavali*[71]). In addition to this, *Uchchala* also decorated the (shrine of vishnu) *Tribhuvansvamin* without jealousy. He also renovated the throne of *Harsa* which had been damaged by burning in the memory of the royal power which *Jayapida* acquired from *Harsa*[72]. King had also the attachment with *Jayamati*[73] because she secured the rare (privilege of) occupying half of the share of the throne, and did not disgrace in this universa, though she had the common birth[74]. She is different in character, charm of manners, liberality, fraternity, wisdom, equality as well as other good qualities, and also helpfulness for those who were without support and distressed[75]. No doubt, she had the attachment with the King, even though she had the charming beauty within the body, but she has been tempered by the demons[76] and forgotten the king.

**Actions of Uchchala against his Officials**

*Uchchala* took wonderful action towards his faithful servants, first of all he uprooted the *Kayasthas* or money lenders. He was the king of poor people, who every kept free from greedy, and had another merit which he stood foremost among all his virtures. He ever recited to himself the verse: "officials in truth are eager to kill, desirous of evil, robbers of others property, rogues and demons; he (the king) should protect his subjects from them[77]." It is also appeared that certain officials are plagues for the people, and not only cholera colic, and exhaustion, rapidly destroying everybody[78]. So far as the crab is concerned, it will kill his father, and the white ant destroys her mother, but some ungrateful Kayastha, they will creat certain problems, but as soon as he became powerful in the spiritual thought, he will destroy everything[79]. Slowly and gradually, he will come out from the material world and gives himself a distinction to those who are *vetala*[80]. Moreover, the official belong to him, like a poison-tree, makes, O wonder, the ground upon which he rises up without any unapproachable methods[81]. He will try to suppress all the rogues as a king leave all the official work as an imprisonment of the *Schedule caste* in the politics[82]. Those who were not in a mood to go by teachings of Dr. B.R. Ambedkar, they will make a laughter by (seeing) him with his long body, with his beard bound up, wearing an extravagant headdress, with a spear in his hand, and with his knees and thighs (joined) together[83]? Besides the *V.T. Rajshekar,* Editor of *'Dalit voice',* one more official will be found in the courtezan, he made dance and sing in his presence with (pantomimic) movements of the head, in the company of musicians, courtezan, and parasite[84]. In addition to this, another will be bound naked to a cart, with half his head shaved and the (remaining) hair covered with lumps of vermillion[85]. So far the disgraced officials are concerned, they became known everywhere by nicknames from their (having had to) play on earthen pots and to decorate their heads (in a ludicrous fashion[86]). One who dismissed from the era of *'Light'*, he had to pay the prices of the life in cyclical manner as a routine matter of the life[87]. Those who had grown up and old one, they must be admitted in the school of learning (*bhurja*[88]) as (if they were) the children[89]. Some of them known as street-beggars, they would be seen chanting hymns loudly along with the company of the children to amuse the people in the morning and evening movement[90]. Some of them will be appointed on the dignified posts[91]. Whereas Brahmin will remain live in puzzling contents as the prisoners of the bar, time and again due to his 'egoness', and recite hymns (*stotra*) of Sanskrit such as *Stavarajas*[92] contained in the *Mahabharata*, etc. and to mumbling the (spell called)

*Durgotharinividya*[93]. In this manner, most of evil-minded Kayasthas will be seen in misfortune condition. Because they could not cheat the Master, after this event they will follow the policy of reconciliation with rulers. But they must be control by appointing honest and capable superintendents[94] . During the time of learned *Sivaratha* had to recite the verse at the *Sivaratri* festival, chief-superintendent of the King *Uchchala* will insisted on them[95]. It is sure from the side of *Uchchala* that he will not take part in this righteous actions in the *Krta yuga* till the realization of their crimes[96]. It is up to the Master to punish them according to their merits of crimes. So far as the duty of *Uchchala* is to think about the future course of action about the royal dignity that he understands his former birth[97]. Therefore, *Uchchala* had noticed to the enemy of God to free from the clatches of the material life as his duty to aware the poor people in this field [98]. It is a duty of the husban towards the faithless wife who alway betrayed her real husband i.e. *'Nam'* or God. It makes clear from the study that King must have obtained the 'Power' from the 'Father' who knows every wit of the world[99]. 'His' theory is based on 'law of marketing' or law of commerce as described by the various scholars of the world in their thesices as between a merchant and his customer, but the blind man has suppressed this thought by judging themselves and has taken the load of others[100]. But he could not understand that he had deposited priceless amount in his own body which is his true character to realize within the body as a real friend of God[101]. Now the time has come to furnish the balance of payment (*arthamatra*[102]) to met out the expenditure[103]. Those who had passed twenty to thirty years of their life, what they had to deposit (*nyasadharin*[104]) in their account and what they had drawn from the theory of Master i.e. give and take policy[105]. It appears from the statement that wicked soul which trapped by mind had embezzled in the saving account with deceitful manner in delay tactices by making various pretexts[106]. It is a comparative study of the life in comparsion with stream and ocean; but a thing deposited in the merchant's hand is never recovered again [107]. It is the punishment of the *'Nature'*. No doubt, theory of mind displayed a very negative role in the possession of amount, but at the time of embezzlement, she displayed gentle appearance and oily talks[108]. She does not know about her life where from she started and where from she will be ended, but she has been judged with smiles from the former friend that is 'God[109]' No doubt, courtezans, the official (*kayastha*), the clerk (*divira*) and the merchant, being (all) deceitful by nature, but certain trained teachers have been sent by the 'God' to perform their duty, but in return she (soul) has given a poisoned arrow[110]. Brahmin is a *Kirata* on this earth, always displayed themselves as a superior person on this universe by symbolizing identification marks, sometimes mark of sandal-ointment and in dress, ears and heart,[111] etc. They take their life in a moment, just as a dangerous scorpion would which is marked in six places[112]. Such kind of people, they are eating the flesh of man or trading of it, just like a gourd, and resembles it, being white and black in colour the vibration of life, sweating from the smoke of the fire, having a mouth (narrow) like a needle and a very capacious belly[113]. Therefore, how they demonstrate their (depositor) from their pretexts account, they always displayed anger and frown the their saving account (and said[114]). That word *sreyase*[115] (' to profit' i.e. '*Word*') which was put at the opening (of the account), has turned into *asseyase* (' to loss') by man or mind. Six hundred (*Dinnaras*) have been taken by those who acrossed the bridge[116]." Whereas " a hundred (Dinnaras) were given to the leather-worker for the repairing of a torn shoe and of a whip. For fifty (your) servant girl took ghee against a blister on the foot[117]." Three hundreds were given to the potter-woman[118], one hundred brought from the market mice and fish-juice to feed tenderly the kittens of that cat[119]. Seven hundred were brought from the feet as well as rice-flower, ghee and honey on occasion of the baths of the *Sraddha*[120] fornight. Three hundreds should be given to the obstinate beggar who are expert in assaults[121]. For the incense (*dhupa*[122]), the roots of the *Sanda*[123] plant and the onions (presented) to the Gurus[124] at an average (estimate) of the whole cost one hundred or two must be counted[125]. Keeping in view the total tele of the (merchant) must be deducted from their account what they have deposited, but interest they had to be paid since the life has been given to him along with the original sums (*mulagrahana*) at the time of his death. Please take this thorne (from my side[126]). Take the deposit, but the amount of this debt (*ujjamadhana*[127]) which was advanced to you on trust, you should give (back) honestly together with its interest[128]." At the meantime (customer) must fell assured. But subsequently we recognised that (the merchant offer) was like to a knife smeared over with honey[129]. Therefore, it is essential to sue those in court of the Master, who had displayed cruel-hearted and dishonesty (merchant) in the embezzlement by knowing the 'word'. Such kind of cases could not be taken into consideration[130] .

**Judgement of Uchchala**

It appears from the study during the time of judgement the cases will be judged by the judges if they had not been able to arrive at a decision, produced before the King, King decided it in the following manner, saying to the merchant:-

"If the deposited money (*dinnara*) is to this day still (available), then let some small portion of it be produced. Then we shall pronounce the judgement[131]." After doing this, he (*Uchchala*) looked at the money and spoke to the ministers: 'Do kings use (for their money) the coin type (*tanka*[132]) of future kings?" "If not, then how come there to be on money deposited in king *Kalasa's* time, also coin types which show the name[133]? i.e. *Chinna* "For this (it follows that) the merchant here has used for his purposes the deposited lakh, just as also this (customer has used) the goods which he had taken from time to time from the merchant[134]." "Therefore, if the plaintiff has to pay to this merchant interest on what he has taken from him, from that time to the present day, then this (merchant) too ought to pay to him interest on the full lakh from the time of its being deposited, what need be said of the original amount [135]? "Compassinate persons like '*Baba Guriender Singh Ji*' can settle only this much. But for such persons (as the merchant) a harsh treatment would be right like that (employed) by the illustrious *Yasaskara* [136]." Whereas in a law-suit a merciful order is appropriate in the case of a person who has been under a mistaken notion. But severity ought to be used against him who has employed fraud[137]." It will take time to settle the account at the right time. First we have to care of our race which required no stimulation. It is our duty to realize the friends from the commanding power to free from the arrogance which is stigma on your character[138]. Therefore, first we themselves free from the jealousy and other sinful acts[139]. During the noble bearing, *Uchchala* destroyed the honour and life of numberlessmen. On the other hands; men of high honoured will be crushed and humiliate during the time of lecture[140]. Besides this, the living men, like sleeping snakes did not dare to say in laud voice[141] . There should be a good moral conduct and one cannot blame the other. The Creator of the universe (Brahman[142]), who had claimed his birth from (the lotus) which grows in the mud; his body is covered with a reddish-brown colour; his dignity is to destroy by imperfections (such as are implięd) by the loss of his immaculate character (consequent) upon the cutting of his head, and by other (defects) and so on[143]. Whereas the king did not reflect upon this and every day discussed openly the defects of his servants descent, conduct, personal appearance and the like[144]. Besides this, he (*Uchchala*) will take an excessive pleasure in fights and caused numberless men of valour to fall in duels by raising mutual enemity between them[145]. On the monthly report, at Indra festivals and on other auspicious days he presented riches to those soldiers who joined in single combats[146]. In addition to this, there was not at that time any festival when the ground in the court of the palace was not drenched with blood, and lamentation not be heard[146]. Soldiers of the noble race who had left their homes, as if in exultation, were carried away mutilated from the palace court by their relatives[147]. At the same time king saw his soldiers, were killing who had glistering black hair, fine beards and splendid apparel, and felt delight instead of pain[148]. Moreover, certain women and their husbands who went in the royal palace returned safe, they had to think that they had taken the profit in a day[149].

**Ministers of Uchchala**

From the study it indicates that certain ministers of *Uchchala*, they proudly used to say: "Let that be done we want", and will not allow any contradiction by force on various servants to act as ministers[150]. Therefore, he has to spoil the character of those who had gone out of the control put them in disgrace[151]. During the commander-in-chief *Danchaka, Uchchala* had shown anger during his powerful position, but at the same time he had to fly high to *Visalata*[152] where from the *Khasas* came down and killed him[153]. Whereas, little *Rakkaka* whom he will himself raised the dignity of 'Lord of the Gate', when he will be grown up, will deprived from the office to spread the *'Radha Soami Mission'* in abroad[154]. Parallel to him, general *Manikya* will be suddenly dismissed from the service of the 'Gate', devoted himself in his affliction to austerities at *Vijayaksetra*[155]. Moreover, *Tilaka*[156] and other excellent men from *Kaka's* family, who held chief command of the army (*Kampana*) and other officials of the office will remain live in displeasures by their pliant nature[157]. Due to his devotional services, he will give the office of Chief Justice (*rajasthanadhikara*) to *Bhogasena* though he had not attendants[158]. It appears from the statement that *Bhogasena* was a powerful man than the *Gaggachandra*[159], when the terrible fight was took place at a festival of *Indradasdevi* whereas, *Radda, Chudda* and *Vyadda*, they were the sons of the common soldier of the name of *Sadda,* were the ministers of *Uchchala*[160]. In addition to this, *Tilaka*[161] and *Janaka*, the sons of *Vijayasimha* will remain with the company of *Uchchala* during the time of terrible scene as the serving servent, and were received as his councillors[162]. They will be named as, *Yama, Aila, Abhaya, Bana,* and the rest will also remain held the charge of *'Gate'* and other offices. But their fortune in conpensatory obtained 'Light' from the Master[163]. To company with them, two or three old (officers), like *Prasastakalasa*, who were amongest them, appeared like decayed trees in the midst of young ones[164]. Master will also recalled the *Kandarapa* on his request to hold the office but he could not accept it, because he knows that the nature of *Uchchala* is intolerent[165]. It appears from the study that under *Uchchala*, there will be new things under the new rulers of the land[166]. The goddess of fortune, as if she were a courtezan covered by a magic spell and subdue the strong-minded persons and to make them trespass[167]. Thus, the regal dignity will remain intact, just as if they were in the spirit of death. Therefore, most of their enemies and relatives will lose the relationship[168] in the regard of the establishment of '*Chamar* dynasty in Kashmir'.

**Sussala's Invasion**

Study indicates that king *Sussala*, though in possession of all that gives happiness, planned a sudden attack on his brother in the hope of wresting the kingdom for him[169]. It was the abrupt change as fast as a falcon, had arrived (in Kashmir) and had got beyond the place called *Varahavarta*[170]. *Uchchala* made a plan suddenly and attack with a strong force, before he had secured a firm stand to defeat him[171]. He left the place without the consent of parents[172]. He started his journey before the king had started to return after accomplishing this deed, he heard that (*Sussala*), whose valour was formidable, had returned with grace[173]. Therefore, *Gaggacandra* will start his journey by order with a strong force and defeated certain troops of *Sussala*[174]. Besides this, certain troops of *Sussala* which could not stand before him in the battle field. Therefore he will found certain relief from the celestial maids (*Apsaras*[175]). There are two Rajaputras known as *Sahadeva* and *Yudhisthira*, they will also pay back something in the battle of *Mahabharata* in the favour of Lord [176]. In this battle, Gagga will capture certain excellent horses which had been slipped away from *Sussala's* army. This was the excitment scene in the favour of King (*Uchchala*) that he owned many horses who are wandering without any direction[177]. As soon as king heard this news *Sussala* will encamped his army on the route of *Selyapura*[178] and later on, he will follow the same route as followed by *Kramarajya*[179]. On the foot-step of the *Kramarajya, Sussala* also proceeded with a small unit of the army towards *Darad* land[180]. In between, king had the duty to executed the Damara *Lostaka* near *Selyapura,* who had opened the way for him to proceed the city[181]. No doubt, act was harmful, but his brother with tender nature seized the *Lohara* mountains with no efforts[182]. At the same time, the illustrious king *Sussala* had already married the spotless *Meghamanjari,* the daughter of king *Vijayapala*. (She was) the daughter's daughter of *Kalha,* lord of *Kalinjara*[183], who being himself without a son had brought her up, who she lost her father, with tender love in place of a son and in his own palace[184]. Due to the greatness of the *Uchchala* no body will raise any revolt[185]. Samethings will be happened during the time of bold king *Sussala*, two left (the Darad Land) by routes hard to pass and after many months reached his own territory by a difficult mountain-track[186]. Keeping in view, certain events which we have averted, slowly and gradually, they will be tackle by the king *Uchchala* in phase manner[187]. Besides these, there are certain other pretenders who will rise soon to see the *Bhimdeva* had the good hold on *Bhoja*, who was the son of King *Kalasa*. He will call on the assistance of *Jagaddala*, king of the *Darads*[188]. Besides him, there were other supporters known as *Salha,* the son of one of king *Harsa's* concubines, and *Sanjapala*, the brother of *Darsanpala*[189]. Whereas, the shrewd king will come back in diplomatic manners from the lord of the Darads to refrain from agression, then he will be proceeded to his own country as a routine matter[190]. In the same way, *Salha* will also followed him; *Bhoja* went secretly to his own country, and *Sanjapala* will also took service in favour of king *Sussala*[191]. In a very brief period, *Bhoja* had been betrayed by his own servant, who had already been crroupted by power as a robber like executed king[192]. Moreover, *Pitthaka*, too, *Devesvara's* son, who aspired to the ruler and had to flee into another world then again a political system was started by the Damaras to see him[193]. It will again we see that politician were rely on notoriety, and move here and there without aimlessly like animals. It appears that they deserve to be laughed at[194]. Inspite of these factors, certain bazaar-cook who were very cunning like fox, they were the intriguer as the son of *Malla, Ramala* by name[195]. There were also preferred presents, honours to appricate the 'ego' whereas, his neighbouring chiefs, they were also disturbed by this dirty politics and were seen that they are cheating themselve by keeping 'Him' away[196]. During the time of blistering heat 'ego' will distrubed him (*Uchchala*) then in the same fashion as today he came alone to *Kashmir* and on being his own *Karma*, soul will be recognised and the servants of the king, they will punished her like her past action[197]. The same copy of the same hero will be repeated for the people's amusement in the royal camp, and same kind of people will be replaced of the same caste, in selling articles of food[198], etc. It is the wonder of the nature that we are the same person in the same drama. Most of the people, they use cunning story of the mind in life and raise their position high in destructive manners, the result will that they cannot change their fate, and time and again they came in the cycle of birth and rebirth, and could not get rid from this world by life[199]. Therefore, mans effort is similar to a fire in the grass, which by the wind it becomes more flame up in one place to another in copy manner[200]. But he or she cannot get away by running from his or her destiny; otherwise they are always attach with fire[201]. There is no other sources which leads the life of the man to his destiny[202], except *'Nam'* or *'Word'*.

Due to the *Uchchala's* order even *Bhiksacara* cannot be condemn to die. He was also taken at night by the executioners from *Jayamatis* apartments to the place of execution[203]. Whereas Brahman is bound by his *Karma* theory that he will be thrown immediately into the *Vitasta* river by winds. His breast is still palpitating. But after some times, he will recovered his consciousness and was given the title of *Asamati*[204], which was the relative of *Shahi* princesses name *Didda*. She was the clever woman, who took her sons and grandsons secretly from *Kashmir* to *Dekhan*[205]. The ruler of *Malava* known as *Naravarman*[206], who was aware of this story like a real son of the *'Father'*, had trained in the field of army personel and in the sciences of the *nature*[207]. Some of the people have the opined that *Jayamati* herself had preserved an option for another child of the same age killed in his place[208]. As soon as *Uchchala* listen this news, who had returned from abroad, he ceased thereafter to show affection for this (queen)[209]. *Uchchala* did not disclose an course of action with the princes whose (lands) lay on the route to prevent his (*Bhiksacara's*) entry (into Kashmir[210]). The foul playing persons they also disturbed in an open way as to his wife's (faithfullness) and it is his foolishness to invite another enemy for the sake of danger[211]. This event is related with Queen *Didda*, who killed her sons and grandsons one after another by witch craft, whether it was true or false, but *Bhiksacara* could not obtain it as important that it could effect on his fate[212]. Because it is the wonder of the *Nature* who created the man which depends up the former actions or deeds i.e. *'Nam'* or *'God'*. It is called the imagination of man which he deals[213]. *Bhiksacara* rose his power secretly for the ruin of the people, as the fire (rises) in a thicket to burn down towns, villages and others (habitations) of the areas[214]. Besides this fact, certain poison-trees must be to plant *Prativisa* (antidote) as a part of nature, but at the same time when pure water of the raining season will spoil it[215], and makes itself felt. It is an idea of far-sightedness of the *'Creator Power'* which indeed will be examine during the time of threat given by the *Nature* for the destruction of creation, and the *'Nam'* will counteract this problem in phase manner[216].

**Birth of Jayasimha(1105-06 A.D.)**

During the birth of *Jayasimha*[217] king *Sussala* became a powerful king of the world, but his power slowly and gradually became decline[218]. Since the birth of *Jayasimha* ('Lion of victory') he was everywhere victorious in his life[219]. He (*Sussala*) at that time has possessed the title of *Sarvarthasiddha*[220], the name of *Buddha* due to his supernatural powers in all matters of the life. Therefore, his son *Jayasimha* was appropriate at that moment, but it was not in conventional use (*rudhi*) *and (*restricted to this particular King[221]). As soon as, King *Uchchala* saw the sign of saffron (coloured[222]) foot of this (son), he gave up his anger against his brother[223] i.e. Brahman. Besides this the enmity between father and uncle will be remove and gave peace to both the kingdoms[224] i.e. earth and the heaven.

**Pious Foundation of the Uchchala Kingdom**

From the study we learn that King *Uchchala* had the duty to increase the merits of his forefather, who had gone to heaven for a long time. It is his duty to built a Matha under his name on the site of the paternal (house[225]). It is also the duty of the liberal king to celebrate this moment with great consecrated ceremony by providing basic need of the life that is *'Nam'* or *'Word'* to the poor people of the *'Father'*[226.] Due to this act most of the great kings they were astonished to know from the distant that what kind of presents of great value has been delivered by the (ruler) to them as a wealth of praiseworthy[227]. According to this delivery queen *Jayamati* will compel to built Vihara of *Matha* in order to put a noble use that she became rich by wealth and sing a song in the favour real *husband* or *Father*[228]. No doubt, king had certain demerits in his life due to his former (birth); but now he had to built (*'the new Matha'*) known as *Navamatha*[229]. The *Vihara* which *Uchchala* had built in honour of his sister *Sulla*[230] or *'Rani'* on the site of the other paternal (house), did not acquire proper renown[231]. Indeed, *Uchchala* did not think of death which was hanging over his head. He did not settle his account on the foundations to lay down his kingdom (when he was died[232]). Because, he depends on the Master's statement.

**Uchchala's Adventure**

Once upon a time King *Uchchala* went for the adventure of *Varhatacakra*[233] to the hill-village like *Goa*, Bombay, etc. to see the *Svayambhu*[234] fire, while stopping his own work of *Kramarajya*[235]. As soon as *Uchchala* started his journey from the village of *Kambalesvara*[236], in the mean time, there suddenly came the force of *Candalas*, robbers of that locality, and surrounded him to lead the tour[237]. On the other side, the opposite force was interested to strike him down, though he had a very small force with him, yet his *'word'* courage arrested their weapons, and they did not strike 'Him'[238] . During this adventure, path being blocked, he passed one night in the deep mountain-gorge moving about with a few followers[239]. At the same time, evil rumour was widely spread in the camps. It was difficult to stop and causing commotion, that the king was no more[240]. No doubt, this bad report which was a small affair when it started from the camp, became important in the city, like the wind from a hillgorge when it reaches the forest[241]. On the arrival of prefect of the city one of the soldier of *Chudda*[242] known as *Kamadeva* the brother of *Radda* and the rest[243] were ready to agitate in the city, but failed in his plan, and addressed the king as a simple man (*Sadda*), but he was an intriguer among the householders[244]. In this way,

King *Uchchala* "Having got hold of the kingdom thus without rivals, you should yourself rule it, since the number of your friends, relatives and servants makes you invincible[245]. After this adventure, *Uchchala* had thus spoken to them, the company of the villains felt the desire to become rulers, and were quickly preparing themselves to seat the *Uchchala* on the throne[246]. The report which was submit by them to the principal, they honoured the race of the illustrious king *Yasarkara* put into all of their family the aspiration to the throne[247]. Even though, who were dishonest in course of their life, they turned their ambition by sayings disaffection. Why this wicked procedure was not recommended in the favour of *Sadda*, because he belongs to the family of the load-carrier *Lavata*[248]*? i.e 'Nam'*. No doubt, he was the only son of a small official called *Ksemadeva*, who had a ferocious character, as befitted a person given to desperate actions[249]. At the same time, when he snatched a golden pitcher from the royal palace, he was suspected owing to (certain) indications; but yet not recognised (as the thief) on account of (his) cunningness[250]. As soon as, *Uchchala* will carry a dagger, bareheaded who makes laugh and insluted him time and again even though his attitude towards them very positive and he (behaved himself) like a *Rajaputra* and they never thought that he has the power of third worlds which is a very small things i.e. *'infinite'* (compared with himself[251]). Now *Uchchala* is swinging his fingers to and fro, but he can (ever) occupied by a thought of the throne, which was seen to bear an evil fruit[252]. Whenever *Chudda,* etc; were eager to grasp the royal power both owing to his advice and by their own desire, but when they heard that the king was alive, they lost their hopes[253]. As soon as, this project will be over; ambition was ever (present) for a long time before the birth with *'Chinna'* as a fast friend in the world. It is the *'inner message'*, now the time has come that without (openly) displaying itself, we shall never close our eyes nor sleep[254]. During this moment even the *Satsangi* who do not have the respect of king, they always in a position to let down him even though he instructed them about the right path. They will be removed from (their posts in) the royal court, please go for the politics (i.e. the place of *rajasthana*[255]). *Uchchala* who by nature used at all times harsh words against the politician. He cut their nose at the very moment and then they start to cry in vain like dogs[256]. Even though they lost their '*Father* in the time of king *Harsa,* from that period, they were living in the house of widow mother who was (yet) young and hot-blooded[257]. At that time she killed a soldier called *Mayyamattaka*. Who was the neighbour and intimate friend of the paramour of their mother[258]. At the due course of time king asked himself why they did not punish her to cease the victory of Master or *Sant*. She was self-style master, then king angerly ordered cut off their nose[259] in the presence of king and used to inquire after them with the words: Where are the sons of the woman with the cut nose[260]?" *Uchchala* who was like death to the Kayasthas, had removed *Sadda* too from his official position after having (previously) employed him as the superintendent of the 'Chief Treasury' (*brhadganja*) and other (treasuries[261]). No doubt, *Sadda's* own accountant whom had violently maltreated, then she denounced to the king that there is an embezzlement in the revenue of treasury[262].

**Conspiracy against Uchchala**

It appears from the study that a conspiracy has been started against *Uchchala* thereupon in indignation took (from him) the post of *pravesabhagika*[263] (cashier of Manas), this ferocious man urged *Radda, Chudda* and the rest to (follow up) their former plan[264]. After this, they decided to kill the King, and waiting for an opportunity put themselves into communication with other evil-minded persons, *Hamsaratha*, and the like[265]. Those were interested in the favour of king, they will took an oath by sacred libation (*pitakosa*), but for four or five years they never found an opporunity[266]. They were conscious that the secret design will not betray him, though it was planned for a long time and by many persons who were much divided (amongst themselves[267]). They discussed themselves: "It is to you that the king ever uses words which cut to the quick," and thus fomented disaffection towards the ruler[268]. Intriguers protecting her by put the hands to her breasts, sides and back with hidden armour. but she continually followed the king in a bad manner[269]. *Uchchala* had already been unable to support separation from *Jayamati,* though (king) would do anything to please her; just as she was an ordinary lover, now after two years a permanent dislike for her (which was due) to a change in his character foreboding his end[270]. No doubt, king attributed this to her before a warning that he protected *Bhiksacara,* others again to the inconstancy of love and passions which resembles that of the lightening[271]. In the meanwhile, *Bijjala*, the daughter of the lord of *Vartula*[272] means 'war of love' (Smt. *Amrita Devi*), whom the king had married with her in the heaven as an affectionate son[273]. At the same time *Samgramapala*[274] wad died and his son, *Somapala* was died and his son, *Somapala* by name ascended the paternal throne[275]. As soon as, *Uchchala* listen that the intriguers had given the crown of hatred to him. It has been understood by the *Gaggachandra,* why we imprisoned the elder brother, who was right at that moment and became enraged against *Rajapuri*[276]. *Uchchala* gave the hand of his daughter (*Ramiyan*), who was a surety of lasting good fortune. At length, after *Rajapuri* had thus been thrown into disturbance, the head came before *Somapala*, her husban, who was stopping at a distance[277]. It shows that it will be the greatest feast of celebration with splendour and great expense by the lover of all his subjects from different field of thought as a magical thought gem to supplicants[278]. As soon as, *Uchchala* son-in-law will leave the spot, king will turn out the employ (words) to all the *Tantrins* for some slight displeasure, but now let the conspirators go free[279]. At the same time *Bhogasena,* too, whom the king will removed in anger from the charge of the Gate, became his enemy[280]. It displays that he was the powerful man since the time immemorial and suppressed all the Damaras.[281]

The remaining material of Lohara will be settled by king *Sussala*[282], who is still in awaiting position. Keeping in view, the hostile attitude (against his brother) was mixed with tenderness. King ordered him go back, whereupon *Bhogasena* had spoken in a derogatory way to me. It makes clear from the study that 'history repeat itself' on hearing this news. The anger will remove on spot without any obtacle.[283]

**Bhogasena Joins the Conspirators**

Study also indicates that king was insulted by the brave *man* who was his best friend known as *Radda, Chudda* and others then took him into the secret[284]. *Uchchala* at one time he was anxious to gain Yama" land (i.e. death) did not exile those who had be insulted the king. They were full of aspirations, who formed a league and had lost their subsistence[285]. In the meanwhile crooked minded *Sadda* will reproached them, kindly trust him and judge him that he has straightforward character and never tolerate them during the execution[286]. He informed: "The king must be killed to-day, even if its costs our lives. Otherwise *Bhogasena* with his shallow mind will betray (the conspiracy[287]). Study discloses that the words of *Saddha* were not untrue, because *Bhogasena*, anxious to open the account of (the conspiracy), told the king that he wished to say something in secret[288]. king replied: "What are you going to tell? I shall not give you (back) the charge of the 'Gate'. By this insult he led him to join the conspirators[289]. King has been already free from the birth and rebirth. He hates those who do not act upon his instructions, just like a person who forgets himself in deep sleep on a day at the end of the hot season[290].

**Attack of Conspirators**

Keeping in view, the above passage, it delineates that certain *Tantrins* who came as the security personnel of the King in his palace to attack on him[291]. But certain *Candalas* entered into the hall of the palace who had given a sign, and told them: "Strike at him at whom we strike to-night [292]. After delivering the lecture, King will take the food with them, standing in the outer hall. He turned out the servants by saying that the king was in an angery mood[293]. They do not know that King was already prepared to go to *Bijjala*' apartments, and dull armour sensations came out from the inner hall, with lamps lit to guide us[294]. At the same time, king got into the central hall with a few followers, *Sadda* blocked the hall and left with followers[295]. Whereas the opposite door already blocked by others and the conspirators will surrounded the king do something for us to seek the *'Nam-Dan'*[296]. In the meanwhile, one (of them) will try to stop them why we ask him in this context, he is just making fool us. He is known as Brahman *Teja,* the son of *Dinna*. He hold his hair and struk him with a dagger[297]. With the grace of God, many daggers will penetrate into his limbs, yellow-coloured by his golden ornaments appeared like great snakes (moving) in the cliffs of Mount Sumerill[298]. There will be the crying "Treason, treason", he freed his hair which they had seized, and tore off with his teeth the leathering-string which held back the hilt of his toy-dagger[299]. Certain attendant of the *Uchchala,* known as *Sujanakara* who carried *Katar*[300] (*Kattarka*) fled from the field to his side when certain enemy, they attacked on him[301]. *Uchchala,* at the same-time, withdrew the small knife, fit for a boy. It was difficult to secured the hit[302]. There are certain internal organs which *Uchchala* has been bound up to attack holding the dagger between his knees[303]. *Manmukh* Teja who was talking with loud voice, *Uchchala* struck him with full strength and fell down to the ground (at once[304]). After this *Uchchala* struck *Radda* from the behind and lion-like roar turned round and tore open *Vyadda*[305]. *Uchchala* cut down the various army personnel and soon he breathed his last, writing in (agony[306]). After some times, he get out the hall, but the hall door was kept closed by the guards who did not know that he is the King[307]. King moved by another door, *Chudda* stepped in his way and saying: "Where are you going?" struck at him with his sword[308]. As soon as he saw the *Bhogasena,* who was standing at the end of the doorway with his face turned away, and appeared like a wooden brush on the wall[309]. As soon as, king went to the past history of the man, said "*Bhogasena,* why do you look on?" In his same he replied something indistinct[310]. *Rayyavatta*, a lamp-bear, who was unarmed, had taken up the fight with a brass lamp, and fell under their strokes[311]. It appears from the statement discussed above that *Somapala*, a Rajaputra from *Campa* did not fall into disgrace when after slaying assailants he succumbed to their strokes[312]. Keeping in view, the journey of king dominated the *Ajjaka,* the grandson of the illustrious *Surapala* and a son of *Rajaka,* ran away like a dog, hiding his dagger just as (if it were his) tail[313]. As soon as, king took the flight was endeavouring to scale the railing, the *Canadalas* cut his knees and fell down the ground[314]. In the meanwhile a faithful *Kayastha, Srngara* by name, threw his own body over him but it was removed by the enemies after their strokes had lacerated his body[315].

**Death of Uchchala (1111 A.D.)**

Study reveals that *Uchchala* ruled for ten years, and died on 1111 A.D. due to his sharp struggle in the life, he strucked down the number of attack with his numerous weapons like dagger and the *Tantrins,* which seems like a garland of dark-blue lotuses (bestowed upon him) by *Kali* (as a mark) of her choice[316]. Even though his brother *Sadda* was ready to cut his throat, He says: "this rogue may perhaps simulate death thought yet not dead[317]." Because he uses to 'die to live' in *'Nam'*, which is very difficult to attain for an ordinary man. It is the message of the heaven, only those can listen who surrenders their life in this material world to the Master. These people are the agent of the *'Words', 'Word'* was in the begining of world with God and God was the *'Word'*. It is unending dialogue between the present and past as E.H. Carr, mentions in his book, *'What is History? Uchchala* cut off his fingers with the help of his pen, and drew his jewelled rings, exclaiming: "It is 'I' who turned out of office (by him)[318]." The long armed (king) *'Nam'* has been seen on the ground as if asleep, with his face covered by the locks from which the garlands had fallen, and with one foot yet shod[319]. It has been appeared from the study that (king) had displayed a great interest towards the people at a large extent as a role signed to him by the nature, as a servant of the *'Nam'* known as *'Surata'*, who had gone out to alarm the people through the documents, but cut down by the enraged *Bhogasena[320]*. *Uchchala* started his journey from the apartments as the beloved wife of the husband did her job as a housewife. It was felt by the *Uchchala* that it was the mistake to visit the residence of Kali as the wastage of time[321]. Kings who in their kingdom went eagerly and obtained enjoyments for a moment, and please their mood with a multitude of various dresses of the *Lamas,* resemble like bees which are flying in the garden seek eagerly the stamina (of the flowers) and please thereselves with a multitude of various blossoms. Alas, they (both) somehow disappear as soon as they have been seen; those (kings) are thrown down by their destiny set in motion by fate, and these (best) by the creeper (set in motion) by the wind and the system will be changed[322]. Even though the lord of Lanka (*Ravana[323]*) who had vanquished the three worlds, was defeated by animals and the *Kuru* lord, the foremost of numberless kings against the *Pandevas.* They will received a kick from the foot with the help of *'Nam'* which is known as *'Dr. Raj Kumar'*. Thus every (great person of the Indian History conference of 2006, December 28-31 will find) in the end a humiliating defeat, just as (it he was) of an ordinary background i.e. called 'infinite' by nature or *'Chamar'*. Who then would keep up his pride and think. 'I am great?. No, it is only *'Nam'* or *'Word'*. Which feeds to everybody in everytime in this universe[324]. It appears that king had number of enemies at one time, now they are dead, and will carried naked paper without lace due to his parasol-power[325] which only given by God to the *Sudhra rulers* who are attached with the *'Dhamma-Dana'* or *'Nam-Dan'* mentioned by king Asokha in his life time as the *'Asokha the Great'* or *'Akbar the Great'* or *'Neoplean the Great'* of the universe. From the nature they were very poor or have-nots like Karl Marx and Engel in their life[326]. It reveals from the study that *Uchchala* had the same powers like the king *'Siva'* had the arms powers to his neck, and another instrument of power he had in his down feet. Thus, they dragged the King *Uchchala* whose neck hung down, hair was waving, body was drenched with blood, and wounds emitted a faint whistling sound which is coming of the *'Royal Palace of the Nature'* i.e. *'Nam'*[327]. It has been carried by him in naked manner like a pauper to the burning-ground of the *'Nature'*. Sometime it was frightened and cremated by the theory of mind called *'manmukh'* on this ground of island which is trapped by the *Mahasarit*[328] and *Vitasta* in so many time in this universe by the *'Cosmic order'* that is '*Word*' or *'Nam'*[32]. No body can imagine when it was constituted and where from it was born out, it appears it is flowing like a stream which never stop unless and untill, there is no natural calamities like flood rain, earthquake, etc[330]. So far the death of *Uchchala* is concerned; it is said that he was forty first years of old who he was died in the year (of the Laukika era four thousand one hundred) eighty-seven (A.D. 1111) on the sixth day of the bright half of Pausa[331].

**Radda-Sankharaja (8-9th December, 1111 A.D.)**

As soon as, *Uchchala* disappeared from the throne of Kashmir, *Radda* and *Sankharaja* had a sharp struggle to obtained the throne. In this sharp struggle, *Radda* killed the *Sankharaja* with the help of sharp sword and armour, placed himself on the throne, (where he appeared) like a *Vetala* on a stone of the burning ground[332]. that traitor (*Radda*), who had taken the name of *Sankharaja,* went the way of the evil-doers, after having reigned for one night and one day[333]; he watched the scene of nature. It has been rightly expressed by Kalhana that *Radda* occupied the throne during the night which followed by *Uchchala's* murder, and during the next morning, he ascended the throne. His relatives and followers fought bravely in his presence to shield him and (dying) adorned the battle field as a matter of honour[334]. Besides the relatives, two *Tantrins, Vatta* and *Patta*, and *Katta surya* and others soldiers fell, after fighting for a long time, and died at the main gate of the palace (*Simhadvara*[335]). *Radda* won this battle with the help of sword and shielder were seen in the palace court yard dancing, as it were, like an actor on the stage of the combat and striking his opponents[336]. No doubt, he cut down many by his strokes of power, time and again victory was rendered to his enemies, and he was fell at last in the combat[337], due to the cruel struggle of *Garga* against (*Radda*).

***Conspirators Defeated by Gargacandra***

In this sharp struggle to eliminate the *Vyadda, Gargacandra* played a very predominent role to defeat the conspirators with the help of *Diddamath* by the citizens, who poured ashes and stones (upon him), and his head was thrust into a privy drain[338]. Those who betrayed him, he will dragged them by ropes (bound) to their ankles, and at once he will received honour from the every quarter of their family deeds which they had lost during the dark period of the history[339]. Besides this, *Hamsaratha* and others who fled from the joint family of *Sadda* somewhere, no doubt, they will suffered for sometimes due to the lurking threat of the *'Word'* on their head which is very unbearable then the death[340]. Because this life is for the *Bhogasena* and they have been strongly mixed into it. *Radda* turned back with his desire of offering resistance, after examining his soldiers, he retired in fear somewhere, followed by some of his own people[341]. In this business, *Gargacandra* had already the armed man. He will killed those who are the leaders of conspirators[342]. We have never listen such kind of people who loved with desperate skill of business as this illustrious (man) displayed, like *Bilo*, etc. because as a simple man of the *'Nam'* or *'word'*[343]. It is very difficult to understand the (Raddh) as a traitor. He is the 'Father' of the *Sankharaja,* as soon as he took the charge of the reign from the night (*rat*), a new era will be started on that day[344]. These traitors will also claimed that we are also from the descended of the *Yasakara's* family, and, therefore, they will held like king *varnata,*[345] the royal power only for a moment[346].

The evil-doers or *Kiratas* always move in the story of the birth and rebirth, no body destroy the lion i.e. *'Nam'* and other (wild beasts) by raising jungle-fires and by constructing shops to trap the people for their personal benefit, they will find their end by the accidental fall of rocks. All people, in deed, will rushed forward by the one path of death. 'I am the slayer and he the slain' *'Word'* this means a difference but for a brief time[347]. Those who hear the winds of the higher music, they enjoy the auspicious acclamations of the woman folk at their own wedding. They never listen the distress of the life. Those are worried with the lamentation of their wives, the cannot librate their life from the illusion of the *Maya*[348]. Those live in heaven, they rejoic for a moment even to-day and tomorrow. They are player of the enemies, excited them with joy. It shows that it is their blind faith which never removed from them. No doubt, they are the problem Creators but not '*Creator*[349]'. The evil-doers or traitors due to their desperate act, they will be thought in the evening, which war we have launched at night did not give us any signal about the attack. But they are illetrate about the signal, when it will be launched after few days. This signal will be listen in the world over and will give a direction to the world[350]. As soon as, *Garga* he accomplished his task and appease his master by throwing himself, down to the throne, against for a long time, 'He' will be lamented with his 'Lord'[351]. He shedded tears of lamented along with his followrs to free from the fear of minds, which always trapped the man and king who was dear to every body[352].

**Burning of Uchchala's Queens**

*Uchchala's* cunning Queen *Jayamati* who was eager to live in this worldly affair, but her treasuer *'Nam'* will not allowed her to live their. She will raise compassion on the request of *Garga* and spoke to him: "Brother, make an arrangement with me." He, however, as a 'Pure-thought' called *'Sudhra'*. We have taken these words in the purely convention, and prepared, her (soul) on the funeral pyre, this is the outcome of *'Nam'* which is also known as 'existing power' in everybody, but it depends on the right implementation of it, otherwise it is same as the illetrate man[353]. It is the matter of strong devotion towards the master not in a duplicate manner; but in a strong manner. It is very difficult to understand the status of the women in comparsion with the minds, it is not a joke like the worldly life of a couple, who are measuring their characteristic as waviness of her ample locks, eveys of almonds, etc. But she should be faithful to her husband at the right track[354]. It is natural those women are unfaithful of their husbands, they might be traped by the fire. Therefore, there is also a law for them to judge the *'husband'*, i.e. *'Nam'* or *'Word'*. Otherwise, they must burn by the Brahmins as their tradition[355]. As soon as, *Jayamati* listen this music, she immediately ascended on the pyre, no doubt, her limbs were hurt, but robber was eager to decorate her with ornaments which was moving in the form of *'Churi'* or *'Chura'*. It is such kind of *'Ornament'* which always gives sound to everybody at every moment[356]. It makes clear, from the study at the same times two queens seen by the peoples were unbearable, but they were consumed by the flames together with their chowries and parasol power[357]. They were also raised lamentations and their eyes were as if burning with pain. *Garga* displayed immediately his noble character in full purity, he requested his wife, do not trap me in the illusion, he did not seat himself on the throne for some time[358]. In a move, he, looked out eagerly for certain persons who had the arms of their own desire to place King *Uchchala's* son, in order to have the consecrated as a King[359].

Now a day, they are laughing on the real character of the King even his brothers-in-law. They do not undersand themselves; we are the real beggers in the forms of beautiful dress. They are called modern beggers working under the theory of mind, but king had the higher status which is equivalent to the *'infinite'*[360]. Three sons of the *Uchchala* which were born from the *Mallaraja* from the princess called *Sueta*, the middle one had also died in the *'Nam'*. The eldest and youngest who remained in fear known a *Salhana* and *Lothana,* they must have to go in the destruction of *'Nam'* called *'die to live'*. after this *Sankharaja* will search out the food for them to kill out the enemies of the *Navamatha*[361] *i.e. 'Nam'* or *'Word'* in order to settle the remaining score.

**Salhana (1111-12 A.D.)**

In the gap arrangement period, shameless intriguer *Tantrins,* collected their bare-footed soldiers again try to defeat the *Salhana* as they uses the traditional way of conspirators, brought up the elder of the two, *Salhana'* remaining force. When *Garga* who had not found anyone fit for the throne after watching this moment. They will think that he is a consecrated King of the time[362]. It will be very shameful for those, who always neglected us in a (single) day and night within four watches, three kings who ought to have been seen within the same generation[363]. It will also be displayed that certain royal attendents will served in the evening to King *Uchchala*, in the morning to *Radda,* and at mid day *Salhana*[364]. Now-a-day, King *Sussala*, who is at *Loharakotta*, heard the news of his brothers death at that time one-and-a-half days had been passed away. He will feel into great emotion[365]. Messenger were also depatched by *Garga* threw himself crying to the ground, which made *Sussala* clear certain doubts (as to his brother's death), and break out in lamentation[366]. In the roaring events, messenger of *Garga* first did not listen the (coronation) of *Salhana's* because at that time his brother mind or *man* on death bed, and requested was made to come to the point[367], otherwise account will be settled at the right moment on the right day. Do not become the 'cheater of the Reservation'. 'Father' is watching the activities of the sons and daughter very minutely what kind of assignment was alotted to them and what they are doing[368]. In the meanwhile, *Garga* already despatched a (messenger) to their houses to left their houses march towards the *'Nam'*, but they do not believed that he is accomplished man equivalent to *'Nam'*[369], It is very difficult for them to suppress 'Him', because he knows the activities of the enemies. If the enemies do not believe *'Him'*, will call *Sussala* for them[370].

**Sussala's Journey towards Kashmir**

As soon as, fiends of darkness will be over, (*Sussala*) the advancement of period will be displayed towards the *Kashmir,* just as to watch the movement of the *Earth*[371]. In his march, he will met with the second messenger of the *Garga,* and will report of all the activities of the movement which were happened in the past, and spoke to him: "Assuredly, do not come.[372]" We are sufficient to crush the conspiracy in your absence, your younger brother, *Salhana,* has already been made as a 'King of the Universe'. What is the use of your coming on this earth to direct the people follow the 'Right track' i.e. *'Radha Soami'* as an abstract of all religion[373]. As soon as *'King Baba Gurinder Singh'* listened the message of *Garga,* keep impatient in his anger, spoke them in the laughing manner, it is very difficult to proceed in the political platform, because politician, they do not understand the original concept of the politics which is derived from the Sanskrit word *'Rajniti'* or very original to the term called Rig-veda or *'Word'* in ancient time by the Indian rulers. Terms were changed with the advancement of the mankind from one civilization to another civilization. Therefore it is very difficult to understand without the study of *'Nam'* in the present form [374]. The crown does not come to us from the father. If (even it were so) the next born is heir. "But (in truth) my elder brother and I have conquered it with our arms[375]." "We two took the kingdom, and noboday gave it to us. Are the means no gone by which we gained it before? as *'Words'* of the *'Word'*[376]. After addressing the *Uchchala* by saying this the message of *'Nam'* or *'Word'* which is unbrakable in the life, will always moves in the same direction, in the same fashion as a fast friend of the refine race[377]. *Baba Gurinder Singh* will send one after the another to *Garga* (Dr. Raj Kumar' Professor of History, Department of History, Govt. College for Women Parade, Jammu) (J&K) to win him over with the help of *'Nam'* or *'Word'*. He always do 'His' *Kasthavata*[378] at the same time at the same place, but in different form. While *Gargacandra* always visits as a *'beggar'* of the 'Lord', who was there in the past on *Salhana's* side; and remain take his position at the same place known as *Huskapura.*[379] by different names as our fore-father did. During the closing of the day, his messengers who had gone for rest for a while, returned on the request of *Garga,* because he had the attitude of counciliatory disposition, but enemies had evil intentions[380]. Besides this, king (*Sussala*) again entered into the business of *Garga* to his own foster-brother *Hitahita*[381]. At the same time *Bhogasena,* whom their fate had been deluded, but has come in the presence of the King. Certain *Khasakas* employed by *Bilvanana*[382] as intercessors[383]. *Salhana* sent the cavalier *Karnabhuti* to the king, and efforts were made to entice him, but *Bhogasena* would defeat *Garga*[384]. It was wrong to say that *'Sussala'* was waiting for an opportunity to stay the betrayer of his brother, who deserve (to be put to death) without temporizing[385]. *Garga* again approached him by messengers saying: "How can I join you by whose side are the betrayers of your brother[386]?" i.e. *'Nam'*.

**Bhogasena killed by Sussala**

Study shows that *Sussala* was a *'Powerful'* man. He is merely delaying that his race *Bhogasena* may leave the path of darkness. As soon as, he will attack on the earth at night all will kill together with his brother[387]. *Karnabhuti*, who is brave in fight having different characteristic of the life. He did not played less role with his step brother *Tejahsena*, but they are thankless, Let them free, will find its result as they did[388]. Keeping in view, certain order's of the King were impaled by the *Marica,* who was the son of the commander of horse *Lavaraja*[389]. They do not know, the courage of the King and his reward. His force was so (small) in object, but it will function to maintain his position with it.[390] *Sanjapala* he had already despatched with King (*Sussala*) and will joined with him later on after sparing certain days and, will bring horses for riding[391]. As soon as, they arrived, his force will be strengthened and become power. He will be the commander of *Garga,* with numerous troops[392].

**Sussala's Fight with Surya**

Study disclosed that *Sussala* was the key player who fought with *Surya* alongwith tursted advisers. He saw those bent on harming the King in difficult period, who was obstinated due to his self-confidence, to mount his horse and to put on his armour[393]. *Sussala* struck the enemies with shower of arrows which was everywhere of unbrokeable and made the sky clear with flight of locusts[394]. Keeping in view, the stroke of the arrow, enemies acknowledged the request of the *'Nam'* and keep down their weapons.[395]

**Escape of Sussala**

For sometimes King was desperate, when his soldiers were slain by the enemies, fled in hasty and wounded treacherously[396]. It appears that his horse crossed a bridge as below which roared as the river flow in ups and down, which is very difficult to pass, even for birds of the sky[397]. Two or three, among them *Sanjapala* also managed to follow him, and kept a sharp edged weapon on the back of the enemies to kill them at every step[398]. It has been known to the *'Master'* that brave (King) had already killed twenty or thirty enemies with the piece of paper, who the *Khasa* seat called *Viranaka*[399], why the enemies keep a distance from him[400]. At the same spot, there are certain few men who are naked from clothes, food and shelter as the basic need of the life, 'O wonder' fearlessly attacked and punished the *Khasas*[401]. After sometimes, he will be killed by the will of fate, he will again reached in *Lohara*, as soon as he acrossed the snow valley of *Kashmir* and watch the station which is equally difficult *(Samkata)*[402] and easy one in the sense of realization of

God. No doubt, in the beginning, he had faced death at every step and had been preserved (only because he was destined) to live longer, yet he made a plan to conqueror the *Kashmir*[403]. The long standing enemity with *Garga* will become poor *Hitahita*. He will be compelled to bound his hands and feet, when he will be thrown into the *Vitasta* river from the head of the bridge at the 'Gate' (*dvarasetu*[404]). As soon as, *Salhana* was thrown into the cold water, *Ksema,* a servant of his, threw himself down before him, and rose higher by his very fall level to the *'Nam'* or *'Infinite*[405]*'*. In the meanwhile, *Garga* then joined king *Salhana* to obtain exceptional power (over him), having given by him to defeat his opponent. This King who had secured the crown without possessing advisers or resolution. It has been seen that he was in confusioning state of mind all (around to him); because he had the lust of power without doing anything[406]. It is very clear from the study that one can use his political wisdom nor any kind of muscle power or greedness of the cunning mind *Rajniti* nothing was prominent in the mentioned King as (Character[407]). It was his ignorance, exploited in the hands of *Bhogasena*[408]. During his reign robbers will plundered the *'Nam'* from his palace even at midday. What need not to speak more that there should be the traffic on the roads? for the *'Nam'*[409] seekers. Even though lame woman Queen (Didda) will have to maintain herself alongwith her husband for rising the throne in the previous spirit as their mind had been distracted by fears of *'Nam-Dan*[410]*'* Slowly and gradually, the woman which *Salhana* enjoyed today and *Losthana* enjoyed next day as a marks of respect. In this context, they will share in common, the pleasures of the throne[411]. As this (King) *'Sat Paul'* had no knowledge of the character of men; and never displayed his duties and all actions of thoughtful persons, because he realized the real duty of the man to learn a lesson from the past[412]. Moreover, he put *Ujasuha, Lothana*[413] brother-in-law, who was well-fitted for assembly of ascetics, into the office (of lord) of the Gate which required rude valour[414]. During *Ujasuha,*at the time of holding counsel, declared that he would ward off the dangerous *Sussala* by muttering his own magic of spell and more than hundred thousand will approached to him at that times[415]. But a deceitful king of *Garga's* order will be *Bimba,* the Damara of *Nilasva*[416], who was dangerous before the latter, and was thrown into the *Vitasta* with a stone, he bound (to him[417]).

**Gargacandra's Role as a King**

From the above study we also learn that the role of *Gargacandra* was predominance in making the King, while at the same time, he destroyed his various enemies and killed many Damaras of *Halaha*[418] by his poisoned food, he gave them at the proper time at the proper moment which is unforgetable to the enemy due to the mere shadow of the King, (all) whether of the outer or inner (court), whether small or great were dependent on *Garga* for their life and death[419]. As soon as, *Garga* came from *Lohara* during the presence of King all the people in the city were agitated and distressed by fear of his wonderful power[420]. Because at that time the report spread that *Garga* had arrived in anger to kill all the members who were employed in the king's family by impaling them on boats[421]. It will be visible with two or three days that all the members of the family will feel shaken by fever, in consequence of such a terrifying news that a women who made pregnant will miscarry[422]. In this context, *Tilakasinha* and others will boldly attacked on *Garga's* residence, without asking for the King's orders[423]. Keeping in view, the majority of the people in great excitement will rushed along with weapons, but *Gargachandra* had received them all without dismay[424]. Besides these, *Dilhabhattaraka, Lakkaka* and others will be seen riding on horse without any fear in the streets near *Garga'* residence[425]. It was the duty of the king to control them according to their wish, but on the contrary sent *Lothana* to encourage the assailants, when their energy became decline, kind had to be answer[426]. As soon as, *Garga's* soldiers will bar on the road, *Lothana* will be seen neither surrounded (*Garga's*) house nor could be burn it down, though he (attempted to) set it on fire[427]. There is only one *Kesava* who was superintendent (*mathesa*) of the *Lothikamatha*[428], skilled in the use of a bow, and harassed the (Garga's) soldiers by shooting them with arrows[429]. It will also appeared in the evening when the Kings men had become scarce with (waning) light, *Garga* had to start on horseback with his followers[430]. Without any resistance, he will encounter at *Lahara*, and carried off as his prisoner *Ujasuha,* who was staying in ill-health at *Tripuresvara*[431]. On the following, day he set him free from saying: "What is the use of this mendicant?" The King will not be dethrone, as *Sussala* was also (his) enemy[432]. After this event, in the town there was a great terror in every where in return of *Garga* will find barricading their houses in shift manner[433]. No doubt, there will a problem to conciliate *Garga* as a King, whereas certain Mahattama like *Sahala* had to act as his envoy in *Lahara*[434]. *Salhana* persuaded *Garga* to agree to give his daughter (in marriage to the king) *Somapala*, but (*Garga's*) of his daughter to the king who was like a (mere) ghost[435]. After this a league was formed with king *Sussala*, will not allow an alliance (with *Salhana*), though he was already pressed (for it) and later on follow by the same rule[436]. At the same time, kingdom will be shattered into pieces, and king *Sadda* was killed,

*Hamsarath* and *Nonaratha*, whom he was secured by spies.[437] Certain *Yamas* which were tortured by sparks of fire,needles, and other means of talk, *'Word'* made them undergo terrible sufferings, before that their life have been already fled away from sufferings[438]. It was the right decision of the King when *Malla, Bhogasena's* wife, who was working in hid, to follow her husband to death[439]. King in his alluded way, he suppressed the weakness(on his part), meanwhile he destroyed *Dilhabhattara* by providing slow posion of killing[440] . It has been assessed that *Dilhabhattara* was neither of royal blood nor of such fierce prowers which the wicked (King) have obtained from the master[441]. He cut out all the ways in secret manner, therefore, *Dilhabhattara* could not put him out of the answer[442], A same kind of treatment his sister manliness, followed the fit answer of the question and could not fire on the king[443].

In brief, from the above passage, we learn that king *Salhana's* reign was rendered unbearable by terror of darkness which had been long drawn from the evil dream i.e. living *man* which shattered the glimpse of the light is going to compile[444].

**Sussala Enters Kashmir**

Study reveals that *Sussala* was a capable rule, he knows the moment of the attack, but there is little bit distrusted by *Garga* because he is very simple man notwithstanding their league which he has formed. It has been observed that *Sussala* was concentrating on *Kashmir* and *Sanjapala* ahead of the point[445]. *Lakkaka* to whom king *Salha*[446] (*na*) had given the charge of the 'Gate' together with (ample) means, had to set out the march with some difficulty and reach *Varahamula*[447] to fix the point of *'Gate'*. *Garga* knows the nefarous design of *Lakhaka* that he will marched behind him. His troops were defeated and plundered during the visit at the town of *Varahamula*[448]. *Salhana* was fled away from the field as soon as his soldiers arrived with their mortal bodies i.e and their heavenly bodies were band by the *Apsaras*[449]. As soon as, *nayaka* appeared, and earth was disappeared and covered by *Uppa, Chudda* and other brave men of noble lineage. Who were fallen, just as pearls of the string and central pearl (*nayaka*) is looking hanging from the string[450]. At that time *Lakkaka* had no support, joined with the side of King *Sussala*, after having been relieved from his fear then both has to approach to *Sanjapala*[451]. In the meanwhile King (*Sussala*) *and Sanjapala* had gone far away to attack on the enemy, came closer, and being urged the citizens please come to the point, but the *Damaras,* they had taken their support[452]. Even *Sahelaka* also came to his side, after having informed by *Salhana* that they would make peace for the theory of *'Nature'* with King *Sussala*[453]. Besides these, only his younger brother *Uchchala* made a contract with

King *Salhana,* who established his relation as long as the *Cataka* (birds long) for the cloud to rain[454]. No doubt, *Chudda, Garga's* wife (soul) has been presented before him; and also brought two daughters for them to make marry as Queens of the King[455]. Between the two, one is called *Rajalakshmi* which has been chosen by king for his own bride, the younger one called *Gunalekha*[456] by name, he has been accepted as his daughter-in-law[457].

**Salhana Encompassed in the Palace**

Study also highlights, as soon as *Salhana* was surrounded by the enemies, *Sanjapala* had already marched in this direction; and his younger brother *Uchchala*; and King (*Sussala*) were already there at the main gate of the royal palace[458]. Even though, one of his opponent, who was the followers of *Radha Soami Sect,* were already there at the Gate and could not hit him, and proved as a useless effort against his enemies[459]. No doubt, his opponent at that time were remained with his soldiers in the barricaded palace, *Sussala's* troops were trembling from fear of an attack from *Garga*[460]. It appears King (*Sussala's*) soldiers do not trust in *Garga,* though he had given his two daughters (in marriage), and stayed because they had to stay; and trembling whenever a leaf shook[461]. While the whole day has already been, exhausted, the soldiers were also feeling fear and King was prevented by family affection from setting fire to the strong building occupied by his enemies. *'Word' Sanjapala* effected an entrance by breaking the shutters of a window with a stone, opened the door and attacked on those who were in the courtyard[462]. The footsoldier of *Lakkaka* was followed by him, his feeling was assured that (by rushing) into the great mass of the enemy, whereas *Sanjapala* was acting like a moth (which flies into the fire[463]). This soldier who like him had been at the invasion of the *Darads,* was in desperate contest of *Kasthavata* and had to keep her image. *'Word'* the Matha-superintendent *Kesava* followed him, just as the son of Sini (*Satyaki*) *and* the son of the wind *(Bhimasena)* (followed) the house of Partha (*Arjuna*) when he demanded the horse from the *Indus* region[464]. As soon as, they got out of the hall, and had with difficulty to opened the gate of the courtyard by their blows. Brave King (*Sussala*) at that moment entered in person[465]. It shows that the war was took place between the two forces continued undecided in the courtyard. No doubt, number of soldiers were found dead there[466]. Moreover, Brahman *Ajjaka*, a native of *Patamgagrama*[467], who was the minister of *Salha*. He became victorious in the war according to the celestial maidens[468]. Whereas, *Kayastha Rudra* who had been promoted to the post of superintendant of the treasury. He was rewarded by his lord to sacrifice his body in the war[469]. Just as a tree in the evening covered by the birds to settled down in their houses and make noise in the surrounding; but after sometimes there is quite silence, as (if merely) painted the threatening of King *Sussala* on horseback[470]. Before ascending the throne of *Kashmir*, he was yet in the court yard, where he heard the shout, "Victorious is (King) *Sussala*", and the sound was a large drums[471]. It is noticed from the study that no one else in *Mallaraja's* house has felt the humiliation as such received by *Salhana* and *Lothana*. They suffered lot there[472]. Moreover, *Sussala* was very cunning to know that two persons who were in armour and on houseback and saying: "You are boys" they gave up their swords.[473]

From the aforesaid study, we learn that *Uchchala* was a wonderful ruler, he played the predominance role in the one hand and others, for the survival of *Chamar* Dynasty. He was well versed with the politics which dominated the Kashmir throne with false propaganda and notions as evil dominated the truth. He will fight with the full strength to obtain the throne of Kashmir as *Pandevas,* killed the *Kurus* in the *Mahabharata* for their rightousness. It was the such kind of war against the enemies as it was fought by *Ram and Laxaman* in the *Ramyana*. No doubt, after the death of *Uchchala,* there was a sharp struggle for the throne of Kashmir one year ruled by *Salhana* and then occupied by *Sussala.*

## NOTES AND REFERENCES

1. R.T. Vol.1. p. 402.
2. *Ibid.* Vol.II. p. 1.
3. *p. H.K.* p. 227.
4. *R.T*. Vol.1, p. 117.
5. *R/T.* Vol.II. p. 1 **Note**. The source of trouble of *Uchachala* was his kindness and overbearing by his brother.
6. *Ibid.* p. 1.
7. *Ibid.* p. 2.
8. **Note.** By the 'robbers' (*dasyavah*) *the Damaras* are meant here, the honest *Uchchala* from kind-heartedness allowed robbers (*dasya*) to rise to high (posts) in remembrance of their (past) services, just as sandalwood tree allows the snakes (to climp up on it). After having got his kingdom clear of the robbers (*dasyu*) by diplomacy as well as by open acts of repression. King *Uchchala* gradually gained assurance. The robbers (*dasyu*) resembling a dense mass of goblins, tasted in the City, as it were, the pleasures of heaven, (though they were) fit only for rustic fare. When the latter had treated, he brought *Bhiksu* back again and proceeded to the territory of the Damaras (*dasya*) in *Madavarajya* in order to win them over. While *Prthvihara* was organising any army at *Vijayaksetra* by collecting the Damaras (*dasya*) of *Madavarajya*, the king, ready for a bold enterprise. The spirits of the robbers (Damaras) rose to their throats, the ministers minds to uncertainty, and the love desires of the celestial maids to the highest pitch, while the murders (climed) up the hill. Some Damaras robbers who had his confidence, kept near him in order to kill him by deceit, and awaited for an

opportunity to carry out their treason.

9. *R.T.* Vol. I p. 117.
10. *Ibid.* Vol. II, Book VIII. p. 2.
11. *Ibid.*
12. *Ibid.*
13. **Note.** *Kanaka* was the pupil of *Harsa*, he was interested to spread the mission of *'God'* or *'Nam'* or *'Radha Sowmi'*.
14. **Note.** *Varanasi* in ancient literature it is called *Baranasi,* universally known as *Benares*, is a large city situated between the two rivers, the *Barna* and the *Asi*. The *Asi* is a mere brook and the city is situated on the left bank of the Gangas, between the *'Barna Nadi'* on the North East and *Asi Nala* on the South West. The former rises to the North of Allahabad and has a course of 100 miles. From the joints names of the two which bound the city, North and South the Brahmans drive *Varanasi* the Sanskrit form of *Benaras* (Cunningham; *Ancient Geography of India*; p. 437).
15. R.T. Vol.II. Book VIII. p. 2.
16. **Note.** *Abhaya* was the King of *Urasa,* has to be crossed above the present Muzaffarbad in order to reach *Urasa*, the modern *Hazara*. This verse proves this identification by the mention of *Urasa*, i.e. *Hazara* which can be reached from Kashmir only by crossing the *Krsna* (black) is the *Kisanganga* river which is on the route that is *mana.*
17. **Note.** *Urasa* given as a local name of the *gana* to *Panini*, iv.2. 82 is undoubtedly the ancient designation of the hill region which lies between the upper course of the *Vitasta* and the *Indus*. Its greatest district of *Hazara*. Lassen was the first to recognize in *Urasa* the territory of "Apara or Ovapara" which Ptolemy. VII I.45, places between the Bidaspes and Indus. Hiuen-Tsiang describes it as the 'Kingdom of *Wu-la-shi,'* situated to the North Western of Kashmir, and dependent on the latter (*Si-Yu-Ki,* 1. p. 147 and Life; p. 68). *Urasa* is probably meant also by the *Uraga* of the *Mahabharata* the *Puranas* and *Brhatsamhita*, along with those belong to the *Panjab* and *Simhapura* (Salt Range). The king of this region figures under the name of *Arsakes* in the account of Alexander's Panjab campaign. Kalhana's references to *Urasa* fully confirm the above identification and show that the close connection with *Kashmir* which existed in *Hiuen-Tsiang*' days, continued into later times. Under *Kalasa*, *Urasa* was occupied by a Kashmirian force which crossed the *Krsna* river i.e the *Krsnaganga* on the route. The daughter of *Abhaya* was married to *Bhoja*, the son of King *Harsa*. Payment of tribute by *Urasa* is mentioned in the reign of *Sussala*. Even *Tilakasimha* as lord of the Gate, levied tribute from the ruler of *Urasa*, who was subdued by the king's fierce lustre, after invading his land, and a victory of *Jayasimha* over *Dvitiya,* King of *Urasa*. *Dvitiya*, the lord of *Urasa*, he put to shame by defeating him, and through the king's power he took *Atyagrapura* strong in fighting men. The gloss of places *Bolyasaka* in *Dvaravati* near *Varahamula*. The term *dvaradhipa,* literally 'Lord of the Gate (or Gates)', along with its equivalents, *dvarapati, dvaresa, dvaradhisvara, dvaranayaka, dvaradhikarin,* is of most frequently occurance throughout the chronicle. It has hitherto be interpreted as denoting a chief

chamberlain or the administrator of a supposed province *Dvara* (*Dutt*). A careful examination of all the passages makes it, however, quite certain that it designated the high officer who held charge of the passes leading into Kashmir. It is very probably Kalhana explains here to one or several of the main passes which give access to the Valley of Kashmir. These entrances have always played an importnat part of 'Kashmir history', and have until quite modern times been specially guarded by watch-stations. The general use of the term *dvara* for these localities is proved by the passages quoted below, and by the employment in the *Rajatarangini* of the title *dvaradhipati, dvaresa,* or *dvaradhikarin*. The high officials thus designated were entrusted as 'Lords of the Marches' with the guardianship of these frontier passes. Of the latter, it displayed that they were all uniformly known by the designation *dvara* or 'gate'. That this was, indeed, the function of the officer variously named *dvaradhipa, dvarapati*, etc is made evident by a series of charateristic passages in the last two *Books. Salhana* put *Ujasuha, Lothana's* brother-in-law, who was fitted for assemblies of ascetics, into the office (of lord) of the Gate which required rude valour. It has been plainly told that the charge of the *dvara* required soldierly qualities and implied rough duties. *Ananta* had brought untimely demise of the number of Damaras, who losted his life in the warfare with the *Khasas* tribe, but few followers of this tribe rejected to retreat. It appears to us an officer holding the *dvaradhikara* who, like the *Dvaradhipa* of our passage, falls bravely in battle with the *Khasa*. That the latter held the territories immediately to the South and West of the Kashmir Valley, and were always troublesome neighbours. It appears that the name *Khasa* has been used since early times in Sanskrit literature for the designation of tribes settled in widely different parts of the Himalaya region. Term *Khasas* has been frequently mentioned in the Kashmir Chronicles. We find the rulers of *Rajapuri*, the modern *Rajouri*, described as 'Lords of the *Khasas* and their troops as *Khasas*. Proceeding from Rajouri to the East the valley of the upper Ans River, now called *Panjgabbar,* under the name of *Pancagahvara*, as a habitation of *Khasas*. Further to East lies *Banasala*, the modern *Banahal,* below the pass of the same name where the pretender *Bhikscara* sought refuge in the castle of 'the *Khasa*-lord', *Bhagika*. It shows that the whole of the valley leading from *Banahal* to the *Candrabhaga,* which is now called *'Bichlari,'* and which in the Chronicle bears the name of *Visaluta*, was inhabited by *Khasas*. Turning to the west of *Rajapuri,* we find a Khasa from the territory of *Parnotsa* or *Prunts* modern Punch, a person known as *Tunga,* who rose from the position of a cowherd to the Queen Didda's all powerful minister. The queen's own father, *Simharaja*, the ruler of *Lohara* or *Loharin*, is designated *Khasa*. It has been seen that his descendants, who after *Didda,* occupied the Kashmir throne, were looked upon as *Khasas*. Besides that, there were *Khasas* also in the *Vitasta* valley below Varahamula, is proved by the reference to *Viranaka* as 'a seat of *Khasas*'. Of this locality it has been shown that it was situated in the ancient *Dvaravati,* the present *Dvarbidi,* a portion of the *Vitasta* Valley between *Kathai* and Muzaffarabad. The position here indicated makes it highly probable that the *Khasas* are identical with the modern *Khakka* tribe, to which most of the petty hill-chiefs and gentry in the *Vitasta* valley below Kashmir belong. The name *Khakha* means *Pahari,* in Kashmiri singlarly known as *Khukh,* and in plural called *Khakhi* is the direct derivative of *Khasa.* In Sanskrit *S* being pronounced since early times in the Panjab and the neighbouring hill-tracts as *Kh* or *h.* The *Khakha* chiefs of the *Vitasta* valley as exercising judicial power over the commandant of a frontier fort, etc. Throughout the book, we see the successive 'Lord of the Gate' exercising military functions, particularly in connection with troubles in the border territories. From the expressions which Kalhana uses when recording the frequent transfers of the *Dvara* office, it is clear that the charge of the 'Gate' could be held ordinarly only by one person. Still more conclusive evidence is furnished by the fact that in all the numerous passages in which the detailed narrative of the last two books has occasion to refer to the successive *Dvarapatis,* we never find mention of more than one person holding this post at the same time. It is of interest to note this point as it indicates the difference between the 'Lord of the Gate' of the Hindu period and the *Margesas* or 'guardians of the routes' who figure so prominently in the narrative of the later Chroniclers. There *Margesas* (also called *margapa, adhvapa, adhvesa, margapesa*) are generally referred to in the plural, and in connection with particular routes across the mountains. There are clearly meant for the *Maliks* of Muhammadan times. These were feudal chiefs who held hereditory charge of specific passes, and were bound to furnish garrisons for the frontier posts on these passes in return for the revenue of certain lands assigned to them. Extensive as the power and privileges of the *Maliks* were down to the *Sikh* conquest, retained their semi-independent position until Sikh times, and along with their neighbours of the *Domba* clan, have ever proved troublesome neighbours for Kashmir. Of the marauding inroads which the *Khakha* made during the troubles of the Pathan rule, and later still, in *Shaika* Imam-ud-din's time, 1846, popular tradition in Kashmir has retained a vivid recollection. That the *Khasas* had already in earlier times deserved the character of expert plunders. In the Kashmir census report of 1891, p. 141, the *'Khakhe'* are entered with 4046 souls as a subdivision of the Muhammadan Hill-Rajputs. For some data regarding the modern history of the *Khakha,* (See lawrence Valley of Kashmir, p. 201). Thus, we find the valiant *Kandarpa* as 'Lord of the Gate' every engaged in expeditions against *Rajapuri* and other frontier territories. Of his successors it is especially noted that he was able to carry on his duties owing to his wealth, which permitted him to keep up a large armed force. Subsequently, when *Kandarpa,* had resumed once more the charge of the Gate, he successfully wards off an inroad of the pretender *Bhuvanaraja.* It is he, too, who endeavours to prevent the escape of the rebel prince, *Vijayamalla,* by closing the routes leading to the Darad territory. *Malla,* a member of the royal family, while holding temporarily the post of *Dvarapati,* under *Kalasa,* wages war on neighbouring chiefs and invades *Urasa.* Another lord of the Gate is represented it is clear that we must in them rather the successor of the old *drangadhipas* or commandants of frontier stations whom Kalhana mentions on particular routes of the 'Lords of the Gate' who held general charge of the approach to the valley. The official position of the *Dvarapati* must have been a very high one, as his post is repeatedly mentioned by Kalhana along with the chief state charges, such as the offices of the Prime Minister (*sarvadhikara*) the commander-in-chief (*Kampana*), chief justice (*Rajasthana*), the *padagra* post. It was superior post to that of a *Mandalesa or governor.*The post of the 'lord of the gate' is most frequently referred to under the name of *dvara, 'Dvara'* is here an abbreviation for *dvarakarya* or *dvaradhikara*. That the functions of the chief chamberlain, which the interpretation hitherto generally adopted has attributed to the *Dvarapat* were in reality discharged by another state official, will be seen from the account given of *Kalasa's* coronation. It has already been discussed that *Dvaravati* corresponds to the present *Dvarbidi*, the designation of that porition of the *Vitasta* valley which extends from Muzaffarabad to a short distance beyond the village of *Buliasa*. In the latter place, which is situated on the right bank of the Vitasta, 73° 5′ at the longtitude and 33° 11′ at the latitude and on the old route from Muzaffarabad to Kashmir, we can safely recognise Kalhana's *Bolyasaka* . The name *Peliasa*, under which the locality is shown on the map, is that in common use with *Pahari* population. The Kashmiris, however, settled in the valley below *Varahamula* at Kathai, Hattian, and other places, pronounce in variably the name as *Buliasa. Bulisasa* is phonetically the direct derivative of *Bolyasaka. Bulisasa* has given its name also to a well-populated valley which opens to the North of the village. Regarding the position of *Buliasa; Bolyasaka* on the old frontier of Kashmir territory in the *Vitasta* Valley. From the study we learn that it took the Kashmirian troops six days to reach the frontier of Kashmir territory at *Bolyasaka,* from the place where *Sankaravarman* was wounded. This locality has been identified with the present *Buliasa* on the right bank of the *Vitasta* about four miles below Kathai. From the latter place exaclty six daily marches are still counted to *Abbottabad* the modern administrative centre of the Hazara District. (*J.K.T.* p. 528). The route here followed (Via Muzaffarabad, Garhi Habibullah and *Mansahra*) has always been considered the easiest line of communication between Kashmir and the regions to the west. It may, therefore, safely be assumed to have been used also by the Kashmir army its return from the *Indus*. In view of this, and the close agreement of the distances, it seems probable that the encounter with the inhabitants of *Urasa* in which *Sankaravarman* was mostlly about *Abbottabad*. It is to be noted in this connection that *Mangali*, where popular tradition, locates the ancient capital of the country, lies on this route between *Abbottabad* and *Mansahra*. In the note, quoted reference has already been made to the high importance which was attached at all times to the guarding of these passes. The mountain-barriers which enclose Kashmir like great walls, leave but a small number of approaches practicable for a foriegn invasion. The history of Kashmir down to the present century shows clearly that it was on the defence of these approaches that the safety of the valley has always depended. We can hence easily understand why the protection of these passes, and the general command over the watch stations (*dranga* *dhakka*) established on them, should have been entrusted to a speical high officer, a kind of 'Lord of the Marches'.

18. **Note.** The name of *Bhiksacara* or *Bhikhra* 'beggar' which is here quoted from the list of Bihar names collected by Dr. Grierson, corresponds exactly to our *Bhiksacara.* The custom of giving opprobrious names to children born after the death of their elder predecessors, is widely spread throughout India. It takes its origin from the superstition that a disgusting name will save the child from evil influences which otherwise seem to threaten it. A full discussion of names of this kind will be found in Colonel Temple's *Proper Names of Panjabis.*
19. R.T. Vol.II Book VIII. pp. 2-3.
20. *Ibid.*
21. *Ibid.*
22. *Ibid.*
23. *Ibid.*
24. **Note.** By *Sanadroni* is meant here not the 'bath-tub' which was only brought to India by Europeans, but the place which is usually prepared in a native house for bathing purposes by separatng a cornor or part of a room from the rest by a low wall of plaster. Such a place is known in the lower hills and the Panjab by the name of *Sondri*, which is probably a derivative of *Snanadroni.* It is customary for Indian princes to hold a sort of small levee at their bath for selected courtiers.
25. R.T. Vol.II. Book VIII. p. 3.
26. *Ibid.*
27. **Note.** *Gaggacandra* is the same person as *Gagga* mentioned above, as the brother of the Damara *Janakacandra.* The full Sanskrit form of the name is *Gargacandra.* He helped only by his arm, killed and scattered the leaders of the league of conspirators. While *Gargacandra,* who was on *Salhana's* side, marched forth and took up a position at *Huskapura.* Few of his soldiers who survived with wounds, when the rest had been killed, were spared by *Gargacandra* from pity, after they had given up their arms, clothes and other (possessions). Most frequently, however, this personage is referred to by the abbreviated name *Garga*, who had arrogantly thought that *Garga* had been defeated after his younger brother's death, then heard of these events which were (to him) like annihilation. *Garga*, whom the cruel struggle made exceed the (proper) limits, ordered in his fury that the punishment due for high treason be executed upon the dead (*Radda*). The cheating king at *Garga* was *Bimba,* latter on he was put into the *Vitasta* river with a stone bound.
28. **Note.** By *Saddacandra* is possibly meant *Sadda,* the younger brother of *Gargacandra.* He was as good as others dead while in life, and died due to distressed curelty.
29. *R.T.* Vol.1I Book VIII. p. 3.
30. *Ibid.* p. 4.
31. *Ibid.*
32. **Note**. Emended *Laharam* for *Loharam.* It is evident from the above statement that *Janakacandra* and *Gargacandra* were Damaras of *Lohara* or *Lahara.*
33. *R.T.* Vol.II Book VIII. p. 4.

34. *Ibid.*
35. *Ibid.*
36. *Ibid.*
37. *Ibid.* p. 5.
38. **Note:** This statement compares with the term *Bahyali,* 'Outer court' of the palace, where an audience may be given by the monarch to people of lower position, outside the proper *asthana* or Darbar Hall during the time of *Durlabhavardhan,* when a *tanner* had to wish to see the ruler in the outer court, and the distinction of Diwan-i-Aam and Diwan-i-Khas at the Moghul court.
39. R.T. Vol.II. Book VIII. 5
40. *Ibid*
41. **Note.** Term *'Anuru'* (the thighless) is composed of two words *Anu+ru,* the charioteer of the sun, is compared to the king: The *Tritsu, Divodasa,* and *Kutsa* or *Purukutsa.* These two peoples, together with three others, the *Yadu,* the *TURVASU* and *ANU,* are frequently mentioned collectively in the *Rig-Veda* as "The five tribes' or Five Races". 'Ru' is the limbs (*anga*) of this tribe which is incomplete without *'Him'.*
42. R.T. Vol. II Book VIII. p. 5.
43. *Ibid.*
44. *Ibid.*
45. *Ibid.*
46. *Ibid.*
47. *Ibid.*
48. *Ibid.*
49. *Ibid.*
50. *Ibid. p. 6*
51. **Note.** From the statement we learn that the land revenue of the valley was collected in Hindu times, as it was until quite recently, for the most part in kind. The state sold its grain stores to the non-agricultural population of the city and towns at fixed rates, and thus, as in modern times, a preponderating influence over the grain prices. Under a provident administration the system afford the means of meeting famines arising from occasional bad harvests. It is evident that the system referred to is far more ancient in Kashmir than has been assumed by some writers at present.
52. *R.T.* Vol.II Book VIII. p. 6.
53. *Ibid.*
54. *Ibid.*
55. *Ibid.*
56. *Ibid.*
57. *Ibid.* p. 7.
58. *Ibid.*
59. Term *'Masjid'* is composed of two Arabic words *Mas+Jid, 'Mas'* means mind or *mana,* and *'jid'* means adamant originated *'adamas'* or invincible. Therefore, it shows that Muslims are also *Brahmana*, their minds are also wandering in the material life.
60. **Note**. It appears from the study that *Uchchala* was fond of horses, his favourite horse-trainers were also interested in generosity to plunder their

money which they collected from the same country as *Anantadeva* did during his reign. Now, history is going to 'repeat itself' as a dialogue between the *'present and the past'*. Let us look at the concept of *'laws'*. Throughout the eighteenth and nineteenth centuries, scientists assumed that 'laws of nature' i.e., 'Word' or *'Chamar'* or *'Sabda'*, *Newton's* laws of motion, *' the law of gravitation,' Boyle's* law 'the law of evolution', and so forth 'Word' or *'Nam'* or *'Kalma'* had been discovered and definitely established, and that the business of the scientist was to discover and establish more such laws by process of induction from observed facts. The word 'law' came down trailing clouds of glory from *Galileo* and *Newton*. Students of society, consciously or unconsciously desiring to assert the scientific status of their studies, adopted the same language and believed themselves to be following the same procedure. The political economists seem to have been first in the field with *Gresham's* law, and Adam *Smith's* laws of the market. *Burke* appealed to ' the laws of commerce, which are the *'laws of nature'*, and consequently the *'Laws of God' (Thoughts and Details on Scarcity* (1795) in *the works of Edmund Burka* (1846) vol. IV, *p. 270*. He deduced that it was not 'within the competence of the government, taken as government, or even of the rich, as rich, to supply the poor those necessaries which it has pleased the *Divine Providence* for a while to withhold from them. *Malthus* pro- pounded 'a law of population'; *Lassalle* an iron 'law of wages'; and *Marx* in the preface to *Das Capital* claimed to have discovered 'the economic law of motion of modern society'. *Buckle* in the concluding words of his *History of Civilization* expressed the conviction that the course of human affairs was 'permeated by one glorious principle of universal and undeviating regularity'. Today this terminology sounds as oldfashioned as it is presumptuous; but it sounds almost as old fashioned to the physical scientist as it does to the social scientist in the *Indian History*. In the year before *Bury* delivered his inaugural lecture, the French Mathematician *Henri Poincare* published a small volume called *La Science et L' hypothese* which started a revolution in scientific thinking. *Poincare's* main thesis was that the general propositions enunciated by scientists, where they were not mere definitions of disguised conventions about the use of language, where hypotheses designed to crystallize and organise further thinking, and were subject to verification, modification or reputation. All this has now become something of a commonplace. ***Newton's*** boast 'Hypotheses non fingo' rings hollow today; and though scientists, and even social scientists, still sometimes speak of law, so to speak, for old time's sake, they no longer believe in their existence in the sense in which scientists of the eighteenth and nineteenth century universally believed in them. It is recognised that scientists make discoveries and acquire fresh knowledge, not by establishing precise and comprehensive laws, but by enunciating hypotheses which open the way to fresh inquiry. A standard text-book on scientific method by two *American* philosophers describes the method of science as 'essentially circular'. *We obtain evidence for* principles *by appealing to empirical material, to what is alleged to be 'fact', and we select*, analyse, and interpret empirical material on the basis of principles. (M.R. Cohen and E. Nagel; *Introduction to Logic and Scientific method;* 1934, New York; p. 596). The word *'reciprocal'* would perhaps have been preferable to *'circular'* ; for the result is not to return to the same place, but to move forward to fresh discoveries through this process of interaction between principles and facts, between theory and practice. All thinking requires acceptance of certain presuppositions based on observations, which make scientific thinking possible but are subject to revision in the light of that thinking. These hypotheses may well be valid in some context or for some purposes, though they turn out to be valid in others. The test in all cases is the empirical one whether they are in fact effective in promoting fresh insights and adding to our knowledge. The methods of *Rutherford* were recently described by one of his most distinguished puplis and fellow-workers: He had a driving urge to know how nuclear phenomena worked, in the sense in which one could speak of knowing what went on in the Kitchen. We do not believe that he searched for an explanation in the classical manner of a theory using certain basic laws; as long as he knew what was happening he was contented. (Sir Charles Ellis; *In Trinity Review.* 1960, Cambridge, lent term; p. 14). This explanation is suitable for those historians, who deliberately or interntionally left this task as a basic laws of research and contented with the theory of mind or *Brahman.* The status of the hypotheses which has been used by the historian in the process of inquiry seems remarkable similar to that of the hypotheses used by the scientist. There is another example of *Max Weber*" famous diagnosis of a relation between the *Protestantism* and *Capitalism.* Today it is a law for the common people, though it might have been welcomed as such in an earlier period of the *Indian History.* It is a hypothesis which, though modified to some extent in the course of the inquiries which it inspired, has beyond doubt enlarge our understanding of both these movements. Or take a statement like that of Marx: 'The hand-mill gives us a society with a feudal lord; the stream mill gives us a society with an individual capitalist'. (Marx-Engels; *Gesamtausgabe,* i, vi, p. 179). This is not in modern terminology of a law, though Marx would probably have claimed it as such, but a fruitful hypothesis point the way to further inquiry and fresh understanding. Such hypothesis are indispensable tools of thought. The well-known German economist of the early nineteenth century, *Werner Sombart,* confessed to a 'troubled feeling which overtook those who had abandoned Marxism. *At that time (he wrote) we lose the comfortable formulas that have hitherto been our guides amid the complexities of existence of 'Word' or 'Nam' or 'Chamar', we feel like drowning in the ocean of facts until we find a new foothold or learn to swim.* (Werner Sombart; *The Qunitessence of Capitalism, English tr; 1915;* New York; p. 354). The controversy about periodization in history falls into this category. The division of history into period is not a fact, but a necessary hypothesis or tool of thought, valid in so far it is iluminating, and dependent for its validity on interpretation. Historians who differ on the question when the *Middle Ages* ended differ in their interpretation of certain events. The question is not a question of fact; but it is also not meaningless. The division of history into geographical sectors is equally not a fact, but a hypothesis: to speak of European history may be a mischievous in others. Most of the historians assume that Russia is part of Europe; some passionately denied it. The bias of the historian can be judged by the hypothesis which he adopted. There is one more example on the method of social science, since it comes from the great social scientist who was trained as a physical scientist. *Georges Sorel,* who practised as an engineer before he began in his forties to write about the problems of society, emphasised the need to isolate particular elements in a situation even at the risk of over-simplifying. One should proceed (he wrote) by feeling one's way; one should try out probable and partial hypothesis, and be satisfied with provisional approximations so as always to leave the door open to progressive correction. (Georges Sorel; *Materiaux D'une Theorie Du* Proletariat; London; 1919; p. 7). This is far cry from the nineteenth century, when scientists, and historians like Acton, looked forward to one day establishing, through the accumulation of well attested facts, a comprehensive body of knowledge which would settle all disputed issues once for all. Now a days both scientists and historians entertain the more modest hope of advancing progressively from one fragmentary hypothesis to another, isolating their facts through the medium of their interpretations and testing their interpretations by the facts; and ways in which they go about it do not seem to us essentially different. According to *Edward Hallett Carr* the pattern of history takes shape in the brain of the historian, and is fashioned not only by the events, he is describing but also by the world in which he is living, is supported by an overwhelming weight of experience; and although professional historians still sometimes put forward unguarded professions of objectivity in *'History'*, the 'conditioned' character of all historical writing has now become almost a commonplace. Creators of historical systems are not exempt from this rule. The idea of progress which inspired nineteenth-century A.D. systems and the idea of cyclical movement and decline which inspired more recent systems have been transparently derived not so much from a dispassionate analysis of the past as from the emotional impact of the current situation. Even in detail those systems reflect the particular bias of those who consturct them. *Hegel* found the culmination of the historical process in the Prussian State, Spencer in the free trade, free competition and free contract of *mid-Victorian* England. *Spengler* owed the immense popularity of his work to the occasion which it provided for his compatriots to treat the downfall of Germany in 1918 as an integral part of the predestined "decline of the west". It was the process of the *'Words'* or *'Nam'* to deepening pessimism about the future of *Western civilization* which marks successive volumes of *Professor Toynbee's 'Study of History'* reflects the increasing solicitude of the 1930's about the weakensses and failures of British policy. Articulate human groups share a natural human inclination to attach universal significance to their own experiences. (*The New Society*; London; Reprinted 1960; pp. 11-12. Hereafter written as N.S.). As we come to our own times history blends into remembered experience. Here we are close to the events, are watching struggles still unresolved, with their protagonists still alive and active. All this makes it especially difficult to comprehend what is happening, to analyse and judge the significance of the movements of science and society. Yet despite this the effort must be made, for while it may suit historians in general to avoid dealing with recent period until time allows disinterested appraisal, that is doubly impossible here. A book that sets out, as this one does to show the connexions between science and social forces can be useful only if it can show how those relations, as we find them here and now, have arisen out of their previous history. No gap can be allowed between present and past. But to omit the story of science in the twentieth would exclude the most important part of the whole argument, for it is in this twentieth century that science has come for the first time into its own. For more Scientific work has been done in the last sixty years than in the whole of previous history. And this is no mere quantiative growth; at the same time there has been greater advance in the knowledge of the fundamental nature of matter, animate and inanimate, than in any comparable period in the past. We may reasonably speak of a second *Scientific Revolution* in the twentieth century. Further, and this touches more closely the purposes of this book, for the first time in history science and scientists havebeen involved directly and overtly in the major economic, industrial and military developments of their time. The problem is no longer, as was the case in the earlier chapters of this book, to demonstrate how science has affected the course of history. The effects of science in the past were real enough, but they had to be sought to. The danger had been that science would be thought of as an appendage *'Word'* or *'Nam'* or *'Chamar'* is interesting, brilliant, but remote from the main stream of *'History'*. Now, half-way through the twentieth century, the danger is the opposite one, that of giving science too much credit for good or ill in the tremendous and disturbing changes, the wars and revolutions, that this century has already witnessed. It is no accident that the revolutions in science and society should occure together, but it would be too simple a view to make either one the consequence of the other. The interactions have been far more subtle and 'reciprocal', and their disentangling will be the main task of the remaining chapters of this book. What need to be sought out, at every major turn of events, are the social and economic forces that have helped to determine the general directions and speeds of scientific advance, and conversely, the points at which scientific discoveries have come to modify profoundly the course of economic and even political events. (J.D. Bernal; *Science in History*; Vol. III. England; third,edition 1965; pp. 704-05. Hereafter cited as S.H.) Since the time of *Karl Marx* a scientific truth as 'a statement which has been publicly accepted by the experts. Neither of these formulas is entirely satisfactory *'Word'* or *'Sabad'* for reasons which will appear when we come to discuss the question of objectivity. But it was striking to find a historian and a physicist independently formulating the same problem in almost exactly the same words. Analogies are, however, a notorious trap for the unwary; and we want to consider respectfully the arguments for believing that great as are the differences between the mathematical and the natural sciences, or between different sciences within these categories, a fundamental distinction can be drawn between these sciences and history, and that this distinction makes it misleading to call *the word 'History'* and perhaps also the other so called social sciences *'Word'* or *'Chamar'* by name of science. This view may be said to start with *Aristotle,* who declared the poetry was *'more philosophical'* and *'more serious'* than history, since poetry was concerned with general truth and history with particular. A host of later writers, down to *Collingwood* inclusive, made a similar distinction between science and history. This seems to rest on misunderstanding between the *'Chamar'* and *'Brahman'*. (R.G. Collingwood; *Historical Imagination;* London; 1935; p. 5). Those who are often accused of constructing, or believing 'in', such a scheme, we will quote by the way of summing-up a passage from one of *'His'* letters which puts the matter in its right perspective. Events strikingly similar, but occuring in a different historical milieu, lead to completely dissimilar results. By studing each of these evolutions separately and then comparing them, it is easy to find the key to the understanding of this phenomenon; but it is never possible to arrive at this understanding by using the passe-partout of some historical philosophical theory whose great virtue is to stand above the *'History.'* (Marx and Engels, *Works* (Russian ed.), xv, p. 378). The letter from which this passage is quoted appeared in the *Russian Journal Otechestvennye Zapiski* in 1877. *Professor* Popper exists to associate mark with what he calls *'the central mistake of historicism',* the belief that historical tendencies or trends 'can be immediately derived from universal laws alone'. (*The Poverty of Historicism,* New York; 1957; pp. 128-9). It has been rightly observed that *History* is concerned with the relation between the unique and general that is *'Nam'* or *'Word'*. As a historian, you can no more separate from these words or give precedence to one over the other, than you can separate the fact and interpretation. Some people, therefore, speak not of 'Cause' in history, but of 'explanation' or 'interpretation', or of 'the logic of the situation', or of 'the inner logic of events'. We reject the casual approach in history, but it is the functional approach towards the man. We see in the world that men were 'not governed uniquely, but by their fantasies', their behaviour followed certain laws or principles derived from 'the nature of things'. This is perhaps the place for a brief remark on the relation between history and sociology. Sociology at present faces two opposite dangers *'Chamar'* the danger of becoming ultra-theoretical and the danger of becoming ultra-empirical. The first is the danger of losing itself in abstract and meaningless generalizations about society in general. *'Society'* with a big *'S'* is as misleading a fallacy as *'History'* with a big *'H'*. This danger is brought nearer by those who assign to sociology the exclusive task of generalizing from the unique events recorded by *History*: it has even been suggested that sociology is distinguished from history by *'laws'*. This appears to the view of Professor Popper; (*The Open Society;* 2nd edition; 1952; Vol. II. New York; p. 322). The uniqueness of the social law in history is that 'Wherever the freedom of thought and of the communication of thought, is effectively protected by legal instituions and institutions essuring the publicity of discussion, there will be scientific progress. This was written in 1942 or 1943, and was evidently inspired by the belief that the western democracies, in virtue of their institutional arrangements, would remain in the van of scientific progress *'Chamar'* or *'Word'* a belief since dispelled, or severely qualified, by developments in the Soviet Union. Far from being a law, it was not even a valid generalization. The other danger is that which has been foreseen by *Karl Mannheim* almost a generation ago, and very much present today of a sociology 'split into a series of discrete technical problems of social readjustment. (*Ideology and Utopia;* Austriala, (English Tr; 1936); p. 228). No doubt, sociology is concerned with historical societies, every one of which is unique and moulded by specific historical antecedents and conditions. But to attempt to avoid generalization and interpretation by confining oneself to so-called 'technical' problems of enumeration and analysis is merely to become the unconscious apologist of a static society. Sociology, if it is to become a fruitful field of study, must, like history, concern itself with the relation between the unique and the generalbut it must also become dynamic *'Word'* or *'Spirit'* a study not of society at rest (for no such society exists) but of social change and development. For the rest, we would like to say that the more historical sociology be exists, and the more sociological history be exists. Therefore, it is better for both the subjects. Now the frontier between both of them is widely opened as a two-way of traffic. It is better to understand that some should be unhappy than that none should be happy, which would be the case in a general state of equality. (Boswell, *Life of Doctor Johnson;* New Zealand; Everyman edition II; 1776; p. 20). This has the qualification of *'purity'* or *'whiteness'* in the behaviour; (J. Burckhardt; *Judgements on History and Historians*; 1959; p. 85) sheds tears of light over the *'silenced moans'* of the victims of progress, 'who, as a rule, had wanted nothing else but *Parta tueri',* but is himself silent about the moans of the victims of the *ancient regime* who, as a rule had nothing to preserve. But it is in periods of radical change that the issue appears in its most dramatic form; and it is here that we find it easiest to study the attitude of the historian towards it. Let us take the story of the industrialization of *Great Britain* between the period of 1780-1870 A.D. Virtually every historical will treat the industrial revolution, probably without discussion, as a great and progressive achievement. He will also describe the driving of the peasantry off the land, the herding of workers in unhealthy factories and unsanitary dwellings, the exploitation of child labour. He will probably say that abuses occured in the working of the system, and that some employers were more ruthless than others, and will dwell with some unction on the gradual growth of a humanitarian conscience once the system has to be established. Study displayed that *'History'* is about the most cruel of all goddesses, and she leads her triumphal car over heaps of corpses, not only in war, but also in 'peaceful' economic development. And we men and women are unfortunately so stupid that we never pluck up courage for real progress unless urged to it by sufferings that seem almost out of proportion. (Letter of 24 February 1893 to *Danielson in Karl Marx and Friedrich Engels:* Correspondence 1846-1895 (1934); p. 510). Now we take up the example of 'determinism' as a historian, it appears the *'Word'* or *'Nam'* is uncontroversial in the history of man as it is a 'mysterious power of breaking laws of his own being as proof that no 'inevitable sequence' could exist in history (C. Kingsley; *The Limits of Exact Science as Applied to History;* U.S.A; 1860; p. 22). Therefore, 'determinism' is a problem not of history, but of all human behaviour. Professor Popper has rightly observed that 'everything is possible in human affairs', either meaningless or false. (K.R. Popper; *The Open Society;* 2nd edition; London; 1952, Vol.II; p. 197). Again, we look at the historian. Like the ordinary man, he believes that human actions have causes which are inprinciple ascertainable. It is the special function of the historian to investigate, these causes. This may be thought to give *'Him'* a special interest in the determined aspect of human behaviour; but he does not reject free will *'Word'* except on the untenable hypothesis that voluntary actions have no cause. Nor is he troubled by the question of inevitability. The first thing to be made clear from the study of the *'Word'* is that this question has nothing to do with the issue of 'determinism'. 'The Greeks', observed Gibbon' ' after their country had been reduced to a province, imputed the triumphus of *Rome* no to the merit, but to the fortune, of the republic'. (*Decline and Fall of the Roman Empire*, Chapter XXXVIII). It is interesting to note that the *Greeks*, after their conquest by the *Romans,* also indulged in the game of historical 'might-have-been *'Nam'* or *'Word'* the favourite consolation of the defeated: if Alexander the Great had not died young, they told themselves, ' he would have conquered the West and Rome would have become subject to Greek kings'. (K. Von Fritz, *The Theory of the Mixed Constitution in Antiquity;* New York; 1954; p. 395). The question when the decline of Roman civilization began *'Chamar'* quite apart from the more exciting question why *'He'* is still undecided by history. Two thousand years hence the final verdict on the nineteenth century may still be as uncertain as it is today the historian is like an observer watching a moving procession from an aeroplane; since there is no constant or ascertainable relation between the speed, height and direction of the aircraft and the movement of the procession, changing and unfamiliar perspectives are juxtaposed in rapid succession, as in a cubist picture, none of them wholly false, none wholly true. Any static view of history purporting to be recorded from a fixed point by a stationary observer is fallacious. Let us sum up, in the light of these reflections, what we mean by the historical approach and how we think it applicable to the problems which we have to face. History seeks to link the past with the future in a continuous line along wich the historian himself is constantly moving. It is clear that we should not expect to extract from history any absolute judgements, either on the past or on the future. Such judgements it is not in its nature to give. All human judgement, like all human action, is involved in the logical dilemma of determinism and free will. The human being is indissolubly bound, in both his actions and his judgements, by a chian of causation reaching far back into the past; yet he has a qualified power to break the chain at a given point *'Chamar'* the present *Brahman*' and so alter the future. In common-sense language; he can decide and judge for himself, but only upto a certain point; for the past limits and determines his decision and his judgement in innumerable ways. To admit that our judgements are wholly and irrvocably conditioned is to plead moral and intellectual bank ruptcy. But to recognize the conditioned element in them is the best way to put us on our guard against too readily yielding to intellectual fashions *'Word'* or *'Kalma'* of which the nineteenth century belief in progress and the twentieth cetury belief in decadence are excellent examples. (N.S. pp. 13-14) This backward-Looking view which makes us the helpless victims of the past is one of the gravest symptoms of our present crisis. The danger which confronts us was stated more than a hundred years ago by *Alexis de Tochquevilla* in the preface to his *Democracy in America*. The Christian nations of ourage seem to us to present a most alarming spectacle, the impluse which is bearing them along is so strong that it cannot be stopped, but it is not yet so rapid that it cannot be guided; their fate is in their hands; yet a little while and it may be so no longer. The first duty which is at this time imposed upon those who direct our affairs is to educate the democracy; to warm its faith, if that be possible; to purify its morals; to direct its energies, to substitute knowledge of business for its in experience, and an acquaintance with its true interests for its blind propensities; to adopt its government to time and place, and to modify it in compliance with the occurances and the actors of the age. A new science of politics is indispensable to a new world. This, however, is what we think of least; launched in the middle of a rapid stream, we obstinately fix our eyes on the ruins which may still be described upon the shore we have left, while the current sweeps us along, and drives us backward towards the gulf. (Ibid. p. 15). However, we resist the temptations of determinism and of scepticism, we must be cautious about yielding too readily of the brandishments of utopia Utopianism means a rejection of past. It denies the validity of history, substituting for it an indulgence in wich dreams about what might have happen if only George III had not lost the American colonies, if only the internal combustion engine for the atom bomb had not been invented, if only Kerensky had beaten the *Bolsheviks* in 1917 *'Word'* the sort of speculation belongs not to serious history, but to the competitions column of the weeklies. In its visions of the future it constructs imaginary commonwealth having no lineal or causal connexion with the past, and therefore unrealizable. The sane student of history must reject these wish-dreams, these speculations, these castles in the air, even at the risk of being branded as a determinist. If somebody who believes that monarchy in the United States, we shall tell him that he is wasting his time, since the history of the last 150 years is against him. But that doesnot make us a determinist. This function of the historian is not to reshape or reform the past, but to accept it and to analyse what he finds significant in it, to isolate and illuminate the fundamental changes at work in the society in which we live and the perhaps age-old processes which lie behind them; and this will entail a view (which, since it will be present even if it is unconscious, had much better be consciously recognized and deliberately avowed) of the processes by which the problems set to the present generation by these changes can be resolved. The historian undertakes a two-fold operation: to analyse the past in the light of the present and the future which is growing out of it, and to cast the beam of the past over the issues which dominate present and future. His aims and purposes will ultimately be derived from values which have their source outside history; for without these history itself must become meaningless *'Chamar'* a mere succession of action for the sake of action, and change for the sake of change. But the translation of these values into terms of policy is historically conditioned and subject to all the imperfections of the historical process and the application of policy to a particular historical situation is also closely involved in the understanding and acceptance of that situation. Well meaning reformers who profound utopian solutions of political problems commonly fail to recognize how far self-interest has intruded into the formulation of their ideal in terms of policy, and how complicated are the historical issues involved in its application. A historically-minded generation is one which looks back, not indeed for solutions which cannot be found in the past but for those critical insights which are necessary both to the understanding of its existing situation and to the realization of the values which it holds. (Ibid. pp. 17-18). Through the centuries that followed improved techniques of production led to the growth of cities, bringing the decay of the small self-sufficient unite and a new division of labour between town and country, the development of international trade and the beginnings of international banking and finance, and then, in the so-called mercantilist age, the consolidation of large potentially self-sufficient national markets. Through the same centuries new conceptions of the social relations and social obligations were growing up side by side with the old patterns and gradually driving them out *'Word'* first the new and revolutionary conception of the enterprising individual who enriches himself in competition with other individuals by providing services useful to the community, and then the equally new and revolutionary conception of national loyalities replacing, on the one hand, the old loyalities to the universal Church and Empire (Ibid. pp. 19-20). It is known to us that nineteenth-century economic society produced its own corresponding political order and political philosophy. In this society of free and equal individuals harmoniously competing against one another for the common economically *'Word'* or *'Chamar'* to control production or trade, prices or wages; and still less politically *'Chamar'* to guide and influence opinion. It held the ring to prevent foul play and to protect the rights of property against malefactors. Its functions were police functions. It was what *Lassalle,* the German socialist, contemptuously called the "night-watchman state". There is no more fascinating theme in contemporary history than to follow the stages through which '*Laissez-faire* "night-watchman state" of the nineteenth century has been transformed into the "Welfare state" of today *'Word'* at one and the same time its logical opposite and its logical corollary. The process was, of course, gradual and had begun long before the twentieth century or the First World War. While the *Industrial Revolution* was still in its infancy, *Robert Owen* has issued a warning against the danger of giving it its head and pleaded for state action to curb some of its consequences: *The general diffusion of manufacturers throughout a country ( he wrote in 1817) generates a new character in its inhabitants; and, as this character is formed on a principle quite unfavourable to individual or general happiness it will produce the most lamentable and peremanent evils unless its tendency be counter-acted by legislative interference and direction* (*Ibid.*. pp. 21-22). The notion of a New Society in which individuals start equal on equal terms in each generation *'Word'* the unqalified recognition of *La Carriere Ouverte aux* talents *'Chamar'* is soon tripped up by what seems to be a deep-seated human instinct. However, firmly we may in theory believe in an equal start for everyone in the race, we have no desire that our children should start equal with the children of the *Joneses 'Word'* assuming that our greater wealth or more highly placed connexious enable us to give them the initial advantage of better nutrition, better medical care, better education or better opportunities of every kind. (Ibid. p. 23). Let we quote from a recent biography by a well-known American scholar of perhaps the greatest of the American financiers and trust-builders- *The Great Pierpont Morgan*, by F.L. Allen: By instinct if not by reason, most business men hate competition. *'Word'* a man's competitor is the fellow who holds down his prices, cuts away his profits, tries to seize his markets, threatens him with bankruptcy, and jeopardizes the future of his family. *'Sabad'* it is hardly an accident that most of the Americans who at the beginning of the twentieth century were charged with being monopolists had got a good look in their youth at competition at its savage and unbridled worst and had decided to do something about it. (Ibid.p. 25). It was part of the normal procedure of punishing and expelling the inefficient, and operated as such in the nineteenth century with comparatively moderate results in economic dislocation and human suffering *'Nam'* results which were accepted as the proper and inevitable cost of a working economic system. But in the twentieth century both the practice and the theory of periodic economic crises were rejected as intolerable *'Word'* partly because humanitarian people refused any longer to believe that men who had so brilliantly mastered the secrets of material production were unable to devise some less wasteful and preposterous method of organising distribution, but mainly because the great orgnaised forces of capital and labour now both revolted more and more impatiently to the state to rescue than from its impact. If they for help came even more strongly from the side of capital than from that of labour, this was probably because the capitalists had closer affiliations to the ruling class and more direct and impressive means of access to its ear. It was thus the capitalists *'Chamar'* the industralists, farmers and financiers *'Word'* who, unwilling to see the capitalist theory of the elimination of the unfit through periodic crises applied foundations of an ordered national economy. They were fully justified in so doing. The structure of industry and finance in the twentieth century had been so firmly integrated and concentrated that its main sectors were no longer separable and concentrated that its main sectors were no longer separable either from one another or from the national economy as a whole. It was unthinkable that a great bank or a great railway, a major unit in the steel or chemical industries, should be would up for failing to meet its obligations (Ibid.

pp. 27-28). This fantastic nightmare is a sufficient answer to the plea that there was nothing wrong with the capitalist system, but only with the measures taken by governments *'Sabad'* or by capitalists themselves *'Word'* to interfere with its free operation. (*Ibid.* p. 32). Now, we have thus arrived at a paradoxical position. *Laissez-faire* individualist capitalism the word *'Israel'* means God's chosen people the regime of private enterprise in the true sense of the term spiritually, it does not refer to any particular nationality, but to the true seekers, those whom God has chosen to call back to himself and, has evolved by inherent process of development into monopoly capitalism (*L.O.S.J.* p. 27) Monopoly capitalism has provoked and made inevitable the intervention of the state as a more or less active directing force in the economic order. This is the system which in its fully developed form is known in English as "planning", in German as *"Planwirtschaft"*, in French as *"une economie dirigee"* and by Marxists as "State monopoly capitalism". But this system Bible you will find the expressions, "Sons of God", "the power to become sons of God," "those who are led by the spirit are sons of God," "the manifestation of the sons of God", we should be called sons of God," "now are we the sons of God". On the other hand, here we have the statement," the only begotten son of God." This could be a transposition of words and may be read, "only the begotten son of God," for this would coincide with all the other statements in the Bible which, whatever, it is, is not socialism *'the Celestial Music'* is confronted by an unexpected difficulty. (Ibid. p. 23). Hitler made it at a time when he was under heavy obligations to the big German industrialists and could scarcely have afforded to antagonoze them. It provides full employment and can therefore be made acceptable to the worker. The dilemma of this choice is, however, its transient and impermanent character. It is not our task to discuss current rearmament policy. Nothing that we have to suggest is intended to support the view that Britian has at the present time reached the physical or psychological limits of her capacity. But, taking a long-term view such limits obviously exist *'Holy Ghost'* or *Holy Spirit* for Britian as for other countries. Neither a war economy nor a rearmament economy provides a conceivable basis for a lasting social order. War itself would not solve the problem of man, but *'Word'* except for those whom it annihilated altogether. Whatever we left after war would have to take up again the planning of a social and economic order directed to some other purpose, and judged by some other criterion, than that of efficiency for war. Therefore, our interpretation of history and diagnosis of the present and future are sound with *'Sound Current'* and in these lectures we can claim to offer no more than interpretation and diagnosis and to show how they are interwined with one another. *My meat is to do the will of 'Him' that 'He' sent to me and to finish 'His' work.* As we have reached a point in history where the process of transition from the nineteenth-century *Laissez-faire* capitalist order offers us no alternative, short of annihilation in war, to a social and economic order which we can call the "Welfare state," the "social service state" or simply "Socialism". It has often been informed that war is a forcing house of socialism. The same is partly true even of rearment, since the diversion of scarce resources to purpose of defence clearly involves a new emphasis on equal distribution of what remains *'Word'* or *'Nam'* a policy of "fair shares for all". But the essence of socialism resides in the manner in which production is organised, in the purposes which inspire the public control and planning of the economy. You cannot in these days plan for inequality. Once you can no longer explain inequalities either as the salutary result of a natural economic process or as incidentals in an economic organisation primaxily designed to prepare for war, it must become a main purpose of economic policy to eliminate them. This is the political connexion between planning and socialism. In theory, they are separable; historically, they spring from different sources. But, once the historical evolution of the capitalism system has made a controlled and planned economy necessary, and once the temporary expedient of planning for war has become obsolute, to plan for socialism is the only available alternative. This dilemma also provides the key to another conflicted question *'Divine Being'* the relation between democracy and socialism. Both words are vague and susceptible of varities of interpretation. But they are widely accepted as the embodiment of the political and economic aspiration of the modern world. It has often been said by the historian that the liberty and equality of political democracy are hallow unless they are completed by economic liberty and equality. (N.S. pp. 37-38). But where the line is drawn between the rights of the individual and those of society *'Word'* or *'Sabad'*, to put it differently, what is the balance between the rights and the obligations of the individual in society *'Word'* or *'Rita'* is an empirical question which men have settled in very different ways at different periods of history. In the feudal period of the European history the role of the individual in society was determined by hereditary status combined with ownership of land and social relations were woven round a traditional framework of mutual obligation founded on hierarchy; and so solid and resistant was the structure that centuries of gradual change were required to undermine and destroy it. It was left the English revolution, following the trail blazed by the French Revolution and joining hands with the Industrial Revolution in Europe to strike the final below. Society founded on heirarchy *'Chamar'* though even then only in Western Europe *'Cooli'* was at last swept away. The New Society was to be in principle a society of free and equal individuals. Relations between them were henceforth to be determined not by status, but by contracts entered into by them of their own free will. No period before the nineteenth century would have questioned the right of society to compel men to work. In many societies certain classes of the population were exempted from "work" in the narrower sense; in some countries work in the sense was performed mainly by salves. But that the working classes, *'Barwala', 'Duma', 'Chamar' 'Nai', Chura, Megh, Candala, Jat, Gujar, Bakarwal, Dhobi, Chhimba, Lohar, Tarkhăn, Chamrang, Batwal Mallah, Gudaria, Cheera,* etc or "the poor" as they were customarily called in England united well on into the nineteenth century. They were under an obligation to work, and that this obligation, like any other social obligations, could and should if necessary be enforced by

'Law of Nature' was taken for granted. English legislation of the *Tudor* period, when the sanctions of the Mediavel order were breaking down, was explicit and severe: Persistent vegrancy was a capital offence. The Parish had the duty of providing relief for the indigent. But this was coupled with the duty of compelling the ablebodied among them to work for the Parish. So long as, the feudal organisation of society prevailed and the local community remained strong, the legal and moral compulsion to work had been offset by the legal and moral obligation of society to see that nobody starved in bad times. Poverty was not yet either a sin or a disgrace; the attitude towards the relief of the indigent was comparatively tolerant. But when the foundations of capitalism were laid and organised manufacture with hired labour became common, voices begn to be raised against this leniency. In 1704 Defoe published a Pamphlet entitled *Giving Alms no Charity and Employing the Poor a Grievance to the Nation.* He argued that if the poor were relieved they would remain idle, or alternatively that, if they were set to work in public institutions, the private manufacturer was equally deprived of his source of labour, the conclusion *Lord* expressed in modern terms *Divine* being that they should be thrown on the labour market and allowed to starve if they failed to find a place there. A few years later *Mandeville's Fable of the Bees* pointed the conclusion that the poor "have nothing to stir them up to be servicable but their wants, which it is prudence to relieve, but folly to cure", and that "to make society happy it is necessary that great numbers should be wretched as well as poor." The Industrial Revolution, beginning to gather momentum in Great Britain towards the end of the eighteenth century, completed the transformation. Its demand was nothing less than to drive a hitherto predominantly rural working class into urban workshops and factories. No social habit impelled men and woman towards this novel and unattractive form of employment to creat this habit the strongest complusions and incentives would be called for. The enclousers were providing the motive force to drive the workers off the land. But the force could no longer operate fast enough or powerfully enough if the brake were applied in the form of relief which enabled the unemployed or under-employed to remain where they were. In 1785 *William Townsend* in his *Dissertation on the Poor laws* put the case against the old system of Laws without squeamishness. *Hunger will tame the fiercest animals, it will teach decency and civility, obedience and subjection, to the most perverse. In general it is only hunger which can spur and goad them (the poor) on to labour; yet our laws have said they shall never hunger. The laws, it must be confessed, have likewise said they shall be compelled to work. But then legal constraint is attended with much trouble; violence and noise; creats ill will, and never can be productive of good and acceptable service; whereas hunger is not only peaceable, silent, unremitting pressure, but, as the most natural motive to industry and labour, it calls forth the most powerful exertions; and when satisfied by the free bonuty of another, lays lasting and sure foundations for good will and gratitude. The slave must be compelled to work, but the free man should be left to his own judgement and discretion; should be protected in the full enjoyment of his own, be it much or little, and punished when he invades his neighbour's property.* There might have seemed something ironical about the "judgement and discretion" left to the free worker to starve at will; but this is perhaps the first occasion in literature on which the dilemma of the choice between freedom from want and freedom from legal constraint was so cogontly and uncompromisingly put. Though *William Townsend* was a less original and distinguished writer than *Defoe* or *Mandeville* proved fruitful. The rationalization was worked out later, and fitted into the general philosophy of *Laissez-faire*. Society had no call to intervene in the working of the economic order, this contact cannot be made with the a Master of the past any more than we can contact God directly, for this is God's method or rather had a duty not to intervene in the political system precisely because those workings resulted (to use once more *Macaulay's* words quoted in the previous paragraph) in conferring on "industry and intelligence" the "natural reward" of prosperity, and on "Idleness and folly" the "natural punishment" of poverty. Just as the *entrepreneur* who was worsted in competition with his rivals was thereby proved to have been inferior to them in intelligence or application and thus deserved the msiery and dishnour of the bankruptcy court, so the worker who failed to maintain himself in rivalry with his fellow-workers was *ipso facto* convicted of laziness and folly and justly condemned to the penalties of poverty and squalor. If the possession of wealth was the reward of virture, remarked in one of his dialect poems, "the poor i' the loomp is bad". The inscrutable workings of providence could thus be vindicated. "To make society happy," as *Mandeville* had said, "it is necessary that great numbers should be wretched as well as poor," and this hypothesis was rendered tolerable by the assumption that they were poor because they were bad. Social stability rested on the unspoken belief that there would always be enough bad, and therefore poor, people to make the wheels go round. Perhaps today the authorities of countries whcih rely extensively on penal labour for public works sometimes similarliy congratulate themselves on the fortunate dispensation of providence which keeps up the supply of criminals. These developments were gradual and piecemeal. It appears that two bitter phrases which attained universal currency *"tanner"* "the dole" and "the means test" *"Chamar"* recall the controversies of the period. The widespread survival of this mood among the former ruling and privileged groups has a logical and extremely serious consequence. It encourages the survival of a similar mood among the workers. They also spend too much time looking back *'tanner'* not, indeed, eagerly, but anxiously *"Chamar"* towards the ruins; they also are preoccupied with the outlook of the *laissez-faire* world of the past. And this happens for two reasons. As in 1944 the *coalition Government* solemnly announced in a *White Papers* that they "accept as one of their primary aims and responsibilities the maintenance of a high and stable level of employment after the war". The *Labour Government* after 1945 took over this obligation and added fresh stones to the already impressive edifice of social services. Details of the structure have been sharply criticised by the opposition. But its main pillars *Chura, Chamar, Duma, Candala, Megh, Jat, Gujar, Bakarwal, Dhobi, Lohar,*

*Tarakhan, Nai, Chamrang, Batwal, Barwala, Cheera, etc.* full employment, the health services and the food subsidies we have all received explicit conservative endorsement. So far we have come on the road to the welfare state. We need not put a sentimental halo round the industrial workers. Some of *them are sons of God* though probably not more than in other sections of the community *but prodigal sons* are taking things a lot too easily. Some of them are making hay while the sun shines *'Chamar'* under the impression that it may not shine very long. But there is still a great deal to be lived down in the way of resentments from the past and fears for the future. Fear of unemployment, doubt wether we have yet really turned our back on the methods of the past. When we realize that *Reality* with ourselves, we become whole pure, and worthy of becoming one with the *Lord.* After such *Saints* mentioned above and *Mystics* leave the world, we deviated far from their real teachings and become entrangled in rites and rituals, and ceremonies, which lead us outwards. Thus we arrest the real teachings in small, narrow compartments and give them the forms of religious, nations, and countries. Then we begin to quarrel with one another. These are the most serious obstacles of all on the side of the workes in the way of the approach to the *'New Society'*. The sum of what has happened since the dawn of the present century has only destroyed one of the well-laid foundations of the *Industrial Revolution* but is bringing us back to once familiar and universally accepted doctrines: first, that society has an obligation to provide a decent standard of life for all its members; and second, that society has an obligation to provide useful or productive work within their capacity for them to perform. But the turn of the wheel has not yet reinstated the third doctrine which is necessary corollary of the other two *'Radha Soami'* that society has both an obligation and a right to see that they perform that work. This reinstatement has become essential. "You cannot have social security in this country", said Mr. Bevin in a speech in the *House of Commons* in 1943, "Without having some obligation." Yet it would be foolish to pretend that a return to conceptions of social obligation prevalent before the Industrial Revolution can take the form of a mere restoration of the *status quo ante.* A century of history cannot be simply wiped out. The social habits and labour incentives of the pre-industrial period cannot be resumed. But all that we have yet succeeded in doing is to destroy the philosophy, habits and incentives which for a century past have made the wheels of industry turn, without putting anything in their place. The task ahead is nothing less than the creation of a new philosophy which will furnish an incentive and a reinforcement for a new social habit of work. The first and most obvious incentive suggested is to increase the share of the worker in the proceeds of his work. Humane people who recognise that the "economic whip" of hunger and unemployment has become intolerable and unacceptable, but are yet reluctant to abandon the foundation of economic motive on which the *Laissez-faire* philosophy rests, take refuge in the idea of substituting the positive inducement of higher economic rewards for the negative deterrent of economic penalties. It is true enough that men who enjoy higher wages and therefore a higher standard of living are on the whole capable of more productive work than those of lower grades. It is also true that generous piecerates can stimulate production, at any rate for a time. But when we pass beyond the limited scope of these observations, the fallacy of believing in her wages as a main incentive to replace fear of want becomes quickly apparent. The consequences of this phenomenon lie not far beneath the surface. Fear of want is so fundamental, so animal, a force that it possesses a driving power different not merely in degree, but in its sheer elemental nature, from that of any more refined economic motive, and the promoters of the system of private enterprise were perfectly right in treating it as the only adequate incentive for which a place could be found in their philosophy of economic self-interest. The lure of higher wages has none of this Univeral driving-power. The man who finds his earning power enhanced by higher wages may prefer to take the benefit in the form not of increased income, but of increased leisure *'Word'* or *'Nam'* perhaps for himself, perhaps for his wife and children, who need no longer be sent out to work, so that rusing wages may even be reflected in falling productiion. While the desire to avide hunger is a universal human motive, the desire for a higher standard of living, once a conventional level of subsistence has been reached, is perhaps the exception rather than the rule. The stimulus to production obtainable from higher rewards is at best a wasting assest. The second group of remedies designed to revive the flagging labour incentive is directed not to the reumneration but to the status of the worker. The establishment of works councils with powers over matters of discipline as well as organisation, access by the workers representatives to production costs and balance-sheets, representatives of workers on the board, profit-sharing and co-partnership schemes, and many similar devices have been tried or advocated. The general verdict is that they are good as far as they go without going very far. Improved working conditions and greater opportunities of consultation between management and workers are always welcomed and ally discontent, but they have little positive result in creating fresh incentives or in making the worker feel that the success of the enterprise is a matter of personal concern to himself and has a moral claim of his most efficient service. A certain element of make-believe attending all such efforts is revealed in the slogan "industrial democracy" sometimes applied to them. Everyone, workers included knows that an industrial concern cannot be run by methods of democratic control; and the kind of democracy meant resembles at best that formerly adopted in crown colonies where the nominated representatives of the govemor. Outvoted the elected representatives of the people on any vital issue. The third source from which a new incentive for labour might be derived is the nationalization of industry, which represents the conceptions of industrial democracy on the national plane rather than on that of the particular factory or industry. This is a more real and more substantial proposition. The essence of so-called private enterprise even when it takes the form of large-scale monopoly or oligopoly, is that it is capable of making only an economic appeal to the worker. It practice and aim is profit-earning; its philosophy of work recognises material gain as the sole effective stimulus. Once, it departs from this premise, it becomes a public utility and had better be recognised and organised as such. It is true that, as has often been observed the attitude of workers in state or municipal undertaking or in public corporations has never been, and is not today, notably different from that of workers for private enterprises. But this is scarcely a relevant argument. The workers know quite well that the national economy, so far as major decisions of policy go, is a single entity; and in *Great Britain* it is not yet the nationalized sector which dominates industrial policy. We have no yet invited the worker to work in a society in which he is a full and equal partner and takes his full part in the runing of affairs, including the management of its industries and its economic policy. Our inclination is to believe that the nationalization of the major part of industry would be a necessary condition of the transition from purely economic incentives to incentives which include a sense of social obligation on the part of the worker; and we would add this to the reasons advanced in the previous lecture why, in the predicament at which we have arrived, we have to advance towards socialism as there defined *'Sabad'* or perish. But while this may be a condition precedent of the solution of our problem, it does not by itself provide a solution; and it is not our purpose to gloss over the basic difficulty of labour incentives under any kind of socialist order. It is common in discussions of this subject to speak of "work" as if it were just work, exactly as in discussions of international trade we speak of "imports" and "exports" as if the things we buy and sell were just imports and exports. Of course, work is not just work. Let us begin by admitting that few of us ever stop to reason or reflect about the incentives which make us work. The work we do has become a normal social habit, and it would be intolerable if every day or every week we paused on our way to the office or the factory to ask ourselves why we are doing it. Nevertheless, it is the incentives consciously or unconsciously recognised as valid which determine the social pattern; without them the pattern will gradually fade and disintegrate. What is happening around us at the present time is that the incentives of the old order have run down, that the habit of work is deteriorating and that the incentives of the *'New Society'* have not yet been created. It would be absurd to deny that man needs to work, that he derives from work of satisfaction which he can be get from nothing else, and that this satisfaction can be derived from any kind of work, however arduous, however tedious and however apparently distasteful in itself, provided it is felt to have a meaning and to serve a purpose. In deed, we suspect that the differences in satisfaction derived by different individuals from different kinds of work are due far more to temperamental differences between the individuals than to 'Objective' differences between the work done by them. But it is an illusion to suppose that human nature in itself provides a stimulus to work of a kind which will secure the performance of the tasks necessary to the existence of society. All that human nature does is to provide material which is capable of responding to external incentives of sufficient cogency and vigour. The incentives required are of two kinds *'Word'* positive and what 'I" or 'ego' will tremblingly and delicately call negative. As we have seen, increased rewards, increased inducements, are not enough. In two words, the donkey needs to see the stick as well as the carrot. We suppose, we have been more fortunate than most people in being able to choose congenial jobs. We have often worked because we wanted to and often because of something we wanted to get: but, if we are frank with ourself, we have also sometimes worked because, if we had stopped working, the consequences for us would have been in one way or another disagreeable. We suspect that, if we examine our hearts, that is true of everyone. Everyone has mixed motives; and, in that queer conglomeration of conscious, half-conscious and unconscious impulses which drive us to work, we believe that desire to avoid unpleasant consequences is always one element. The provision of positive incentives to work in the *'New Society'* will not be an easy task. But the most difficult task of all is to devise the ultimate and final sanction to replace the ultimate sanction of hunger *'Word'* the economic whip of the old dispensation. Moreover, in a society which rightly rejects the pretence of separating economics from politics and denies the autonomy of the economic order, that sanction can be found only in some conscious act of society. We can no longer ask the invisible hand to do our dirty work for us. We confess that we are less horror struck than some people at the prospect which seems to us unavoidable, of an *"Ultimate Power"* of what is called direction of labour resting in some arm of society; whether in an organ of state or of trade unions. We should indeed be horrified if we identified this prospect with a return to the conditions of the pre-capitalist era. The economic whip of *laissez-faire* indubitably represented an advance on the serf-like conditions of that period; in that relative sense, the claim of capitalism to have established for the first time a system of "free" labour deserves respect. But the direction of labour as exercised in Great Britain in the Second World War seems to us to represent as great an advance over the economic whip of the heyday of capitalist private enterprise as the economic whip represented over pre-capitalist serfdom. Much depends on the effectiveness of the positive incentives, much, too, on the solidarity and self-discipline of the community. After all, under the system of *Laissez-faire* capitalism the fear of hunger remained an ultimate sanction rather than a continuously operative force. It would have been intolerable if the worker had been normally driven to work by conscious fear of hunger; nor, except in the early and worst days of the Industrial Revolution, did that normally happen. Similarly in the society of the future the power of direction should be regarded not so much as an instrument of daily use but rather as an ultimate sanction held in reserve where voluntary methods fail. It is inconceivable that, in any period or in any conditions that can now be foreseen, any organ of state in Great Britain would be in a position, even if it had the will, to marshal and deploy the labour force our the whole economy by military disciple like an army in the field. This, like other nightmares of a totally planned economy, can be left to those who like to frighten themselves and others with scare crows. The attitude of the *'New Society'* to work is perhaps the most crucial issue which it had yet to face, since the fate of every society depends in the long run on the productivity of its workers. Whatever may be true of the political rights of man, the economic rights of man are meaningless and valueless without the acceptance of correlative economic obligations. A society which undertakes to ensure freedom from want to its members must be able to count on keeping up a level of organised production sufficient to meet their basic needs. Yet on no issue is the transition from the conceptions of the old society to those of the new marked by more hopeless confusion. The *laisez-faire* view of wages as the price of labour has long been tempered by the principle of a minimum wage adjusted to need, by family allowances and by social insurance; differences of remuneration originally designed to provide an incentive for the most intelligent and most industrious have been increasingly ironed out by the incidence of a highly progressive income tax; and the whole structure has not been overlaid by the structure of the welfare state in flat paradox with the original design of the edifice. And this fog of confusion about positive incentives is made thicker by almost total reluctance to face the necessity of some form of sanction for a direction of labour to take the place of the discarded *'Chamrang'* rightly and necessarily discorded *'tanner's* economic whip. On no subject is discussion more urgently needed *'Barwala'* means "aboriginal" and most of all among workers themselves; for this is not a question which can simply be left to politicians, intellectuals or even trade union leaders. It will be difficult to provoke that discussion untile more confidence has been gained that we have once for all cast aside our nostalgia for the economic whip, for the salutary dose of unemployment, for the ruins on the shore that lies behind; and it will be difficult to conduct it in isolation from such other issues as the nationalization and management of industry. Nevertheless, no subject is more vilal; for, as *Professor Hawtrey* has said, "what differentiates economic systems from one another is the character of the motives they involve to induce people to work". This decision will do more than any other to determine the fate, and mould the shape, of the *'New Society'*. Therefore, mass democracy call just as much as individualist democracy for an educated society as well as responsible and courageous leaders; for it is only thus that the gap between leaders and masses, which is the major threat to mass democracy, can be bridged the task is difficult but not hopeless; and just as *Great Britain* has done more than any other country during the last five years to mark out new lines of social and economic advance, so we believe that she has better opportunities than any other country to lay the foundation of an educated mass demoocray. The main outlines of the social revolution have been described in previous lectures. It forms the transition from the "night-watch man" to the *"social service"* or "welfare" state. *"Word"* or *"Nam"* the state of which we demand that it shall bring about a larger measure of equality than every before between its citizens i.e *Chamar, Barwalas, Doma, Candala, Megh, Batwal, Cheera, Lohar, Tarkhan,* etc. "fair shares for all"; that it should as far as possible ensure both freedom and equality of opportunity of all; that it should so plan and direct the national economy that the periodical crises inherent in *laissez-faire* systems should be avoided; the full employment may be secured for all who are able to work, and that the natural resources and national man-power may be applied to the production of those things that are most needed, rather than of those things that are most needed, rather than of those things which can be sold at the highest profit; and that it should so plan and direct our international trade that our scarce resources may be used to bring in those overseas supplies of which we are most in need, and on the most favourable terms. These are new and revolutionary functions for the state to perform, and the attempt to perform them will certainly bring with it many initial mistakes. The Revolution of 1917, have occured in backward Russia in the middle of the first World War, had to face the handicap, first of a primitive economy hopelessly shattered and dislocated by the impact of large-scale war, and secondly, of a politically primitive community unused to any form of government save an enlightened feudal autocracy. These conditions, which soon began to inspire horror and dismay even in circles that had at first greeted it with sympathy and enthusiasm. The attitude of Western Countries towards the *'Russian Revolution'* has been extraordinarily ambivalent. Sane judgement has always recogniged that there was something in the *'Russian Revolution'* to be learned as well as much to repeal. But the proportion in which the two reaction should be blended has always been controversial. In part, divisions of opinion about it have been divisions between *Right* and *Left*. But in part also the division has been chronological, opinion having varied from period to period to match the changing state of relations between the Western Countries and Soviet Russia. These two great forces which is transforming the face of twentieth-century politics and helping to mould the shape of the *'New Society'* the social revolution. The other is the colonial revolution. In the early years of the century, when the world was still dominated by the political presuppositions of *laissez-faire*, it expressed itself at first in political demands for the withdrawal of the capitulations in Egypt and Turky, for self-government in India, for the abolition of the unequal treaties of China. The underlying essence of the colonial revolution is today economic rather than political, and this gives the best hopes to the world of being able to weather it without disaster. The economic view of imperialism, promulgated by J.A. Hobbon, by Lenin and by a host of other writers, has now thoroughly penetrated the consciousness of the leaders of the so-called backward peoples; and they are turning against Europe the economic doctrines which they have learned from Europe, as they formerly did the political doctrines of Bright and J.S. Mill. The Colonial Revolution advancing side by side with social revolution and forming part of it, is the main reason why the world picture in the middle of the twentieth century. The nineteenth century world economy was a coherent and highly integrated structure *'Word'* artificial but efficient. The predominance of the industrial nations was unequivocally recognised; the development of the backward countries was carried out in a way, and at a place, which suited their interests and satisfied their requirements. International trade flowed on lines which contributed most to the prosperity and greatness of the Industrial countries. No question of a class came it was between two advanced industrial nations; and the colonical peoples were objects of the dispute, not motive factors in it. The vast change that has come over our international society today is that the former backward peoples are no longer passive objects of policy, but driving forces. They have taken the initiative and placed the former great *Industrial Powers* on the defensive. They have obtained recognition in principle of the doctrine of equal partnership. What has not yet been achieved is the translation of this doctrine into political, and the *Encyclopaedia of Religion and Ethics* states, "Mystical experience is as old as humanity, is not confined to any one racial stock, is undoubtedly one of the original grounds for personal religion and does not stand or fall with the truth of falsity of the metaphysically formulated doctrine of mysticism". It is still more important and the core of the teachings of *Hinduism, Judaism and Islam*, and the Sikh scriptures contain teachings of the *'Word'* or *'Nam'* in the Purest form Christ was nothing if he was not a true mystic into economic terms. The undeveloped countries are at once in possession of vast reserves of unused man-power. We do not yet know much the *'Word'* is the life of our souls; it is the life of the mind and the body, and its withdrawal means instant death. Of course, physicians give hundreds of different reasons for death but these are material actions. The real cause of death is always the withdrawal of the *'Name'* or *'Holy Spirit'* the essence of the soul, from the body at the appointed time at any rate not nearly enough law books give the meaning of 'Truth', nor do ordinary people understand it. *Truth,* in the mystic sense as used by *Kabir, Nanak, Ravi Dass* and other perfect saints, has nothing to do with speaking the truth or dealing with historic or other truths or with gauging political, social or economic conditions accurately about the conditions of the industrialization of backward territories in the twentieth century. Technical aid, and the planning and organization of their economies are perhaps quite necessary, and quite as likely to yield spectacular results, as the large-scale investment of foreign capital, particularly if this brings too many strings with it. Capital investment, technical aid, planned national econonmies, planned international trade this path of the *'Nam'* has been in existence ever since creation, and it is not the monopoly of any nation, race, caste, colour or religion. It is the bestower of all various, all goodness and greatness, all these elements are necessary if the colonial revolution is to be guided to a successful and peaceful consummation. It would be a rash man who would undertake to arrange these four elements in order of importance. But it is certain that an attempt to operate with only one or two of them will end in frustration. While the chief contemporary issues in international politis are intimately bound up with the social and colonial revolutions and cut across national boundaries, the most delicate question to control the tongue in spiritual progress and the one in which our diplomacy is most concerned with the material body we function in the material world. After death, when we move in the astral world we function with the astral body. If by the grace of the Lord and a true master we go to the causal world, we function with the causal world, we function with the causal body. And if we are fortunate enough to progress still further, we see ourselves as pure souls, part of the lord himself. This is journey of self-realization, is that of the relations between America and Europe. Of the many differences of outlook for which the broad Atlanic is main responsible, one is however, much they shrink from war, are none the less able to look beyond a potential third world war, to the prospect, however illusary, of peace regained, just as Europeans in the 1930's were still able to look beyond the potential second world war. Today Europeans know that little or nothing worth saving of Europe can survive a third war; they are not concerned, like many Americans, with the question how it is to be avoided. And the fate that awaits Europe in the event of another war gives Europeans a far greater moral right to make their voices heard in the international councils than could be claimed in virtue of their actual of potential contribution to the military strength of an allaince. In professer Toynbee's brilliant epigram, " No annihilation with representation." The function of this last lecture is to draw together some of the threads which we have been spinning over the past five weeks and draw out the rudimentary pattern of some conclusions. The hope with which we embarked on these lectures realizing who we really are a hope not perhpas easily realizable in our time and this ultimately leads to God-realization, or becoming one with the lord was to be able combine honesty and frankners with a measure of reasoned optimism for the future. It may be thought that we have passed too lightly over the possibility of catastrophe. Of that possibility we have throughout been intellectually conscious. But no society can live and function under the constant obsession of its own impending dissolution; the hypothesis of survival must be accepted, faith in the possibility of survival must exist, in order that society may be able to live and work for it. It may be thought that we have not dwelt with sufficient emphasis on the predicament in which we find ourselves. The gravity of the predicament we have no inclination to deny. What we wish to deny is that there is any predetermined pattern in history or pre-arranged destiny which condemns us to despair. As Lenin, who being a good Marxist, was certainly not blind to the determinist elements in history; once remarked: "There is no situation from which there is absolutely no way out." So much we would say with confidence of our present stiatuon. But this does not mean that every conceivable exit is open. The dielmma of froe will and determination is logically inescapable. We are both free and not free. Time is short, and if we waste to much of it trying all the wrong exits we may well perish in the conflagration. The enquiry on which we have engaged in these lectures rests on the belief that the study of history will held in the discovery which exits are available and which are not. The crisis has caught us kill, kill, kill and eat, eat, eat is the order of the day, and the most astounding part of it all is that we fail to see that we must pay for our actions to revert to our old metaphor stillness and silence are their watchwords in mid-stream. The fierce current which has borne us away from moorings on the shore behind us is threatening to carry us down into the gulf. We can avoid disaster only if we bend all our efforts to navigate our ship towards the unknown shore in front. If too many of our crew are too much absorbed in nostalgic contemplation of the ruins on the backward shore, the navigation of the help goes be default, and the prospect of our only means of escape is put in serious jeopardy. Let us repeat, however, the *Caveat* which we put forward in our lecture, that no historical judgements are absolute and that any historical interpretation depends in part on the values held by the historian, which will in turn reflect the values held by the age and society in which God lives. It is therefore incumbent on the historican, whether explicity or by implication, to make clear the values on which his interpretation rests, and thus we shall attempt to do. But first let us contest an obvious criticism. Does not the admission that the values held by the historian necessarily enter into the history that he writes deprive history of any objective character i.e. '*Nam*'. Can history in these conditions be more than a reflection of the whim of the historian? Now it is to use foolish and misleading to deny the subjective element in history. Any one who believes in the *Divine right* of kings, *Dr. B.R. Ambedkar* used to say that his *'Father'* sang those hymns with such depth of devotion that everyone who heard *'Him'* was moved to the core and the impression left on the minds of the children was remembered throughout their lives, a belief beyond the scope of argument caste-system, brahminism, ritualism, idol worship, pilgrimages and ascetism is bound to regard the last 150 years as a period of retrogression; and if he is a historian of that period, he will weave his facts into a pattern of decline. But this does not mean that history is purely subjective. Life rejects these logical dilemmas of choice between opposites. The question of whether man is free or determined, like the famous question about the hen and the egg, permits of two paradox answers, both equally valid. *'History'* is both subjective and objective. The historian takes his raw material, the dry bones of fact, and articulating them under the inspiration of his own sense of values, turns them into the framework of living history. No metaphor can be fully appropriate or expressive, since any metaphor must be taken from the field either of science or art, and history is, properly speaking, neither science nor art, but a process containing some elements of both. But, however, much we may insist on the subjective element in history, we do regard objectivity as something towards which the historian should strive, even if he cannot fully attain it. In what sense, then, do we believe that history can become more objective? It is sometimes said that, with the development of mass civilization, the values which the historian brings to study of history may tend to reflect less of personal idiosyncrasy and more of the conditons of his age and society, in other words, to become collective rather than individual values; but, in so far as this change is real at all, we are not sure that the view of history through collective eyes is necessarily more objective than the view through the eyes of an individual. Then it is sometimes said that the improved techniques at the disposal of the historian for establishing his facts *'True Worship of the Lord'* is notably the vast progress in statistical resources and methods of 'His' teachings will make history more objective. The historian has reason to congratulate himself on far richer resources of all kinds than were enjoyed by his predecessors. He can, and should, write better history; but, once again, we are not sure that this technical advance makes the function of interpretation any more independent of the values which the historian himself brings to it. Thirdly, we tempted by the view that the historian's own greater consciousness of the subjective element in his work will help to make him more aware both of his own limitations and of the character of his own achievements. "Those historians who have no theory", observes Professor Hancock, "fill the vacuum with their prejudices." The most suspect historian is the one who makes the loudest professions of impartiality. The most objective historian on this view is the one who is most careful to check his own subjective interpretations by the equally subjective interpretations of others. But in the long run we are not sure that we can wholly separate objectivity from belief in the truth of the values which we hold; and this makes it all the more incumbent are to be examine some of the pre-suppositions whih we have brought to the subject of these lectures and which have no doubt contributed to our interpretations and conclusions. The first relates to the role of reason in human affairs. In speaking of the flight from reason as an element in the transition from individualism to mass democracy, we referred to the influence of Marx and Freud. Both these thinkers were rationalists: they did not dethrone reason itself, but appealed from the over-simplified view of reason taken in the eighteenth and ninteenth centuries to a subtler and more sophisticated analysis. Other nineteenth-century thinkers went further in their assault on reason. Kierkegaard was perhaps the first who, by way of reaction against Hegel's exalation of a rational reality, depicted man as a lonely and helpless figure planted in the midst of an irritional external world; and the sudden and belated popularity of Kierke-gaard's doctrines a century after they were first formulated is a tribute to our preoccupation with this most profound of all the problems of our contemporary mass society. Dostoevsky carried the revolt against reason from the philosophical to the ethical and political plane by making the rational morality of the Utilitarians the central target of his attack. The Utilitarians believed that man could be made moral by appealing to his rational sense of his own interest. For Dostoevsky man was in revolt against the tyranny of reason and dominated by the impulse to sin against his own interest; rational conviction could provide no bulwark against evil. Such a belief, transferred to the political world, clearly made nonsense both of political freedom and of clearly made nonsense both of political freedom and of political democracy. "To begin with unlimited freedom is to end with unlimited depotism," declares one of the characters in Dostoevsky's novel *The Devils*. To deny the validity of reason is to reject any form of government based on the hypothesis of rational discussion followed by a counting of heads. Democracy in any shape or form has no meaning or validity for Dostoevsky. He provides the best possible negative proof that a belief in reason is a pre-requisite of belief in democracy. Both Kierkegaard and Dostoevsky, as well as many others who have followed in their wake, drew the same conclusion from their diagnosis of the fundamental irrationality of the external world and of human nature: the leap into religion. Kierkegaard, having dwelt on the helplessness of the individual, preached the mystical union of the individual soul with God, thus saving the autonomous individual but merging him in a divine infinity. Dostoevsky believed that freedom and salvation could be attained only by the individual who merged himself in the community of the Orthodox Church, the Catholic Church having already become an instrument of reason and therefore of tyranny; the Orthodox Church and the Russian autocracy based on it provided the only foundation for a stable and ordered society. A third great thinker, Nietzsche, travelled the same path as Dostoevsky to a different and more logical conclusion. Having exposed the hollowness of all reason, of all democracy, of all conventional morality, he equally rejects the leap into religion of Kierkegaard and Dostoevsky. Nietzsche follows the path till he reaches a complete and absolute follows the path till he reaches a complete and absolute nihilism never perhpas achieved before or since in human thinking. Human action is deprived not merely of any rational motive but of any super-rational motive. It becomes simply the expression of a biological urge to self-assertion; the will to power. Standing beyond good and evil, and recognizing no conscious ultimate purpose, Nietzsche's superman is the perfect animal. Nietzsche is at the opposite pole to those who subordinate means to ends and hold that the end sanctifies the means. He believes only in action as a good in itself without reference to ends. The political thinker who took most from Nietzsche was the syndicalist philosopher Sorel who preached the myth of the general strike as a value in itself, and declared "that the movement is everything, the goal nothing". Mussolini proclaimed himself a pupil of Sorel. But neither Fascism nor Nazism was in true Nietzschean tradition. The glorification of the state or the nation in which they indulged would have seemed to Nietzsche quite as vulgar and bogus as the bourgeois ideals of liberal democracy. Nietzsche is an important thinker because he alone carried the revolt against reason to its ultimate limit, and thus provided the proof of this world is full of darkness and illusion, we have come to give you the light of understanding, the light of truth. Have faith in light and follow our teachings, and you will not have to back in this world again and again. You will be liberate from this darkness. Once more a negative proof that man, when he cuts adrift from reason, denies his own nature and is lost. But when today we reassert our belief in reason, we can no longer accept much that was commonly accepted in the nineteenth century. We can no longer belive with Hegel in a metaphysical or divine reason in-herent in reality and in the process of history. We can no longer believe that all the highest impulses in human nature derive from reason. Least of all can we believe that the appeal to reason will always be the decisive force that determines political and social action. We have learned to penetrate deeply enough into the springs of human action to recognize that what appear on its surface as rational motives are often only rationalizations of our irrational impulses. But none of these disillusionments and discoveries enable us to dipense with reason as the organizing factor in our life and in our society. Just as the approach to a more objective history becomes possible only when we recognize and accept the subjective element which it inevitably contains, so the recognition and acceptance of the irrational element in human behaviour is the first step towards the fuller and more effective development of reason. The fatal barrier to the solution of any problem is to ignore or deny its existence. The gravest obstacle today to the building up of an effective mass democracy comes not from those who are aware of the irrational character of many of our contemporary democratic processes, but from those who are blind to it. To unmask the irrational by stripping from it is hypocritical fig-leaf of false reason is a salutary and necessary task. But this does not entail a panic flight from reason into the anti-rationalism of Kierkegaard and Dostoevsky or into the irrationalism of Nietzsche; on the contrary, it is an essential part of the movement towards understanding and overcoming the irrational. Reason is an imperfect instrument: it is good to recognise and study its imperfections. But we should do ill to throw overboard the compass of reason if we hope to advance towards democracy in our time. We cannot indeed share the radiant faith professed by the Utilitarians a century ago and by Mr. Bertard Russell today in the capacity of reason to transform human nature in a single generation through the process of education. Reason, like other good things, is sometimes discredited by the exaggerated claims of too enthusiastic Pundits. But in that interplay after the death of a saint people get involved in organising his teachings into a religion. or, as if we like, that struggle of *Kal*, the ruler of the three material worlds, not of saints but between the forces of good and evil which makes up human nature, reason is on the whole, to be found on the side of the angels; and we do not believe that we shall do ourselves anything but harm if we dethrone reason because reason has turned out to be less powerful or less self-sufficient than we thought, and take refuge in a cult of the irrational, even if it disguises itself as the super-rational. But the concept towards which the modern historian needs most of all to define his attitude is freedom. It is perhaps difficult today to realize the immense impact of the French revolution in the contemporary world. Let us recall the remark of Goethe, that most sober and balanced of men of genius, at Valmy: "Here and now begins a new epoch of world history, and you can say that you were there". Under the same inspiration Hegel described history as "nothing else than the progress of the consciousness of freedom". And a hundred years after the great event the cautious Acton was to write: "Never till then had men sought liberty knowing what they sought". There may be some hyperbole about this claim. But, though some anticipations can be found in primitive Christianity and some perhaps in the English Puritan Revolution, it is on the whole fair to attribute to the French revolution, it is on the whole fair to attribute to the French Revolution the conception of universal liberty as the goal of human endeavour. Hitherto freedom had meant freedom for some people to do certain things. Henceforth the demand was freedom in general, freedom as a matter of principle, freedom for all. The makers of the French Revolution did not know what this meant; indeed, we have been trying to find out ever since. It is now apparent that the consequence of the French Revolution was to change the conception of freedom in two ways. By universalizing freedom, it linked it with equality; if all were to be free, then all must be equal. Secondly, it gave freedom a material content;

for, once freedom was extended from the limited class which could take economic well-being for granted to the common man who was concerned first and foremost with his daily bread, freedom from the economic constraint of want was clearly just as important as freedom from the political constraint of kings and tyrants. The generation following the French revolution resisted both these conclusions. The third estate, but not the fourth, was the beneficiary of the liberty and equality conferred by the revolution. The new liberal doctrine which denied the competence of the state to intervene in the economic process created a new view of economic liberty and stultified the proposed extension of equality from politics to economics. But after the middle of the nineteenth century this attempt to limit the implications of the revolution broke down under the weight of the new industrial age and of the new mass civilization. In the twentieth century hardly anyone openly contests any longer the two propositions that freedom means freedom for all and therefore equality, and that freedom, if it means anything at all, must include freedom from want. Pious acceptance of these propositions does not, however, always carry with it willingness to accept their application in terms of policy; and it is here perhaps that we have to take a stand and define our values. If anyone maintains that it is desirable to achieve the greater freedom of the few at the cost of the lesser freedom of the many, or, in *Mandeville's* phrase, to make society happy by keeping many people wretched and poor, we can make one of two replies. In the first place, we can assert our views against him as an ultimate difference in values about which one does not argue: one believes in the freedom of the few as a proper aim and purpose or one does not. Secondly, we can reply that the course of history is, according to our interpretation, set against the realization of such a conception of freedom: we might say to the champion of freedom for the few, as we said in the first lecture to the hypothetical champion of monarchy in the United States, that the whole history of the last 150 years is ranged against us. But if we countered with the charge that we had arrived at the interpretation of history through the medium of our own values, we should have no completely conclusive answer. Perhaps we might say that our interpretation of history seems to us more objective than his, precisely because our values are truer, and therefore lead to less distortion, than the said historians. But this might imply that those values which are approved and realized by the course of history are truer than those which are rejected; and this in turn might involve in acceptance of a belief in progress in history in the palace of Ravan, who had innumerans, and countless grand daughters, in the palace today utterdarkness prevails a nor a is light there a point to which we shall return later. Having made clear my belief that freedom in our day as a goal of political action and political endeavour must mean freedom for all, let us come to its practical applications and embarrassments. Mill's famous formula recognized liberty for all and therefore comprised equality in liberty. But Mill's liberty was limited to the political and intellectual sphere; when he wrote his famous treatise at the end of the 1850's he had not advanced, even as far as he advanced later, towards the problems of mass civilization and of economic liberty and equality.

Even in the political sphere the proposition that our freedom is valid only in so far as it does not limit the freedom of others constitutes a far more serious qualification of absolute liberty than Mill himself realized. But, when we advance beyond the political sphere, the qualification becomes so far-reaching as to necessitate something almost like a re-definition of our whole conception of freedom; and it is at this point that some of those who appeared to accept the doctrine of freedom for all seem to fall by the wayside and revert to the doctrine of freedom for some. For, when we consider the paraphernalia of controls and rationing and taxation necessary to the organization of freedom from want for all, and the restrictions which these involve on the cherished liberties of some, it is not unnatural that some of these some feel that the new freedoms are not an extension of the old freedoms, but their negation. Enough volumes have been written on this theme in the last few years to fill a book-case. You can hardly pick up a newspaper today without finding an article or a letter that re-hashes the familiar argument. Nor can we escape from the dilemma. The price of liberty is the restriction of liberty. The price of some liberty for all is restriction of the greater liberty of some. While we shall not minimize the reality of this issue and the differences of values involved, more nonsense is talked on the subject of controls than on any other in current politics; and some of this nonsense we can dispose of forth-with. When a boy, one could travel up Whitehall in a horse-bus or a hansom cab or on a bicycle, and, having reached the north end, turn right without more ado into the stand and washed in clear, runing water a distance of 100 yards or so after two or three days of drying, the fibres are tried into bundles and sent to the mills to catch one's train at Charing Cross. Today one travels up Whitehall by motor-bus or car, and having reached the north end and stopped at the traffic lights, one makes a compulsory circuit of Trafalgar Square, stops at more traffic lights, and at last, having travelled well over a quarter of a mile, doubles back into Charing Cross Station in time to miss one's train. What a monstrous infringement of the liberty of the individual! Could one demand a clearer proof how far we have travelled on the road to serfdom? Yes, it was better when one could reach Charing Cross in two minutes by travelling 100 yards. Yes, it was better when one could walk into any grocer's shop and buy 5 Ib. of sugar for a shilling. The difference is that traffic controls never became an issue of party politics and are now forty years old, so that they have acquired a patina of uncontroversial antiquity which makes it almost sacrilegious to question them; there is no black market in dodging the traffic lights. The rules are simply accepted, for all their in-convenience to the individual, as a normal, decent amenity of civilized society in a city where the pressure of traffic outruns the comfortbale capacity of the streets. When demand outruns supply, and our sense of fairness requires to make an attempt to satisfy all demands in more or less equal proportions, then there is nothing for it but the queue after the queue at the grocer's shop or the queue at the traffic lights. These are the conditons of scarcity: they will be overcome when we can affrod to build enough parkways or fly-overs to carry our traffic and to put enough of the basic necessaries in the shops. For the present, however, in the crowded mass civilization in which we live, these conditions have become inescapable. To raise the banner of freedom for all is to accept as a normal, decent amenity of the New Society those controls which are necessary to effect the orderly equal distribution of scarce resources of the souls is *'Word'* whether the resources in question are food and clothing or space on the roads. This does not imply that all existing controls are either well conceived or well administered; it cannot be assumed without question that een our traffic regulations are the best in the world. But, in principle, scracity always makes controls necessary. In conditions of scarcity, control to assure equal distribution is not a negation of freedom, but a vital step on the road to freedom from the material world that freedom which can only come in full with full abundance. These problems of distribution are not, in our view, the major problems of freedom in the New Society. The economic condition of freedom is the creation of abundance through the right allocation of our human and material resources to the requirements of production; and here too there will have to be traffic·regulations and traffic lights which are restrictions on liberty but are none the less, rightly regarded, necessary milestones on the road to freedom. The political condition of freedom based on spiritually *'Word'* and economic and political conditions are not really separable 'Word' is the realization by the new mass democracy of the prinicple of government of all and by all and for all. These are high ideals, and politics is the art of the possible. Whole books are written nowadays on the study of nature though perhaps some of them were hardly necessary word to explain how foolish, and even how wicked, it is to hope to achieve the millennium on earth. It has become fashionable among some writers to dwell with almost sadistic pleasure on the fact of original sin. This is the truth, but certainly not the whole truth, and perhaps not even the most important and relevant part of the truth. Let us at any rate sometimes remind ourselves that mankind is also capable of great achievements and has great achievements to its credit. We may be utopian if we except to attain our goal. But we shall indubitably fail if we have no goal ahead by which to set our course, or if we shrink from the difficulties and hardships that are encountered on the way. The French revolution was, inspite of its national origin and title, a European event in an age when Europe still dominated the world. The revolution of today is still more certainly a world event, and its future does not turn on the destiny of a single country. In these lectures we have tried, looking both forward and backward, to chart the course of the revolution in the midst of which we are living. We see its workings everywhere today, sometimes in sharp and rugged outline, sometimes dimly and half hidden beneath an apparently unruffled surface, in Europe, in Asia (perhaps at this moment most of all in Asia), in Africa, in the Americas. We cannot escape it: we can only seek to understand it and to meet it. But we are, for natural reasons, more particularly concerned with the destinies of Great Britain and western Europe and with the implications of the world revolution for these countries. And here one is bound to note discouraging symptoms. Two world wars, of which the first had its main centre, and the second one of its main centres, in western Europe, have helped to create there a condition of material exhaustion and moral lassitude. Material difficulties in the present and graver apprehensions for the future have revealed themselves in those theories of historical decline, of judgement in history, or of a retreat into an ivory tower of pure knowledge, which are so widely current in Great Britain and western Europe at the present time. Two factors are at work here. The first is the same which accounted for the immense vogue of Spengler's Decline of the West in Germany after the first world war. The sense that Germany had lost her place among the great nations began to spread in the interval between the two world wars to the nations of western Europe, and after the second world war struck firm roots there. The shifting of the centre of gravity of the world to other continents translated itself into a belief in universal decay. In Great Britain, in particular, the temptation to identify the end of British supremacy with the impending end of civilization became increasingly hard to resist. The almost unchallenged British supremacy of the nineteenth century was the result of a fortunate opportunity seized with energy and enterprise *'Chamar'* the long start enjoyed by Britain in that complex series of developments known as the Industrial Revolution. It was an accident whose results could not last for ever. By the beginning of the twentieth century the British lead was being overtaken by Germany and by the United States. After the first world war the world economy and the world financial system, built as it was on the international division of labour between metropolitan industrial nations and dependent colonial peoples, crumbled in ruins: after the second world war Great Britain- looks like much of the rest of the world '*Word*' was the impoverished debtor of the United States. Whatever the situation of the rest of the world had been, and whatever the prospects of civilization in general, these straitened circumstances in Britain, and the sense of economic dependence succeeding economic supremacy, could hardly fail to encourage an inclination to look back to a golden age in the past and promote pessimistic estimates of future potentialities. The second factor in the spread of a pessimistic outlook was domestic. The vast majority of the ruling groups in Great Britain, in every branch of the national life, still belong, either by birth or by adoption, to the class which was the main beneficiary of British prosperity and power before 1914, and are therefore under the impression of a steep decline not only in British power and prosperity as a whole, but, within the country, in the power and prosperity of the class to which they belong. Before 1914 concessions by the British ruling class to other groups in the interests of social cohesion and social stability had been made out of a rising standard of living. They had been made at the cost of a curtailment of a natural increase, but not found except for a very small and highly privileged group left at the cost of an actual decline. In the last thirty years the situation has changed rapidly; and, with the decline in Britain's power and prosperity, the cost both of armaments and of social services has been met by progressively depressing the living standards of a large part of the ruling class. There is thus a dual reason for the pessimistic and fatalistic mood which has become visible in the

British approach to contemporary problems: the decline in British power and prosperity, and the decline in the power and prosperity of that group in British society which has a paramount share in determining policy and opinion. It is on any reckoning extraordinarily difficult for groups or individuals who have enjoyed prosperity under a certain dispensation, and learned to regard the beliefs on which that dispensation rested as eternally valid, to re-adapt themselves to a world in which that dispensation has passed away for ever and its beliefs are shown to be more than a reflexion and expression of the interests that upheld it. Once upon a time we had an uncle who beguiled his declining years by explaining to all who would listen that the world was going rapidly from bad to worse. But, being by nature a cheerful soul, he always ended his lament with the same aphorism: "Well, if we are all going down the drain, let us go down the drain with our top-hats on". This country today is full of old gentlemen 'Word' some of them not so old, and some of them in important places of the *heaven* who are far less worried by the prospect of going down the drain than by the prospect that the gale may blow off their top-hats. Respect for tradition is all right in its way, provided we do not smother ourselves with it. Nostalgia for the ruins on the shore that lies behind is a natural and venial human sentiment. But indulgence in it may easily become politically fatal. It is tempting to discover here what we will not call a law of history, but the explanation of a common historical phenomenon. Those powerful and decisive historical upheavals which we call revolutions, without confining the term to upheavals which are brought about or accompanied by violence, have frequently led to a displacement of power by violence, have frequently led to a displacement of power and leadership from one country to another, as if it was not possible for the same role to be played by the same country in successive and different periods of history; and, if this is true, we would suspect that the explanation lies in the difficulty which occurs in inducing any powerfully established ruling group to abandon the privileges which it enjoyed in the period of its supremacy and to adapt itself to the revolutionary process of transition from one period to the next. No inherent reason exists why we in this country should succumb to the same experience. It does indeed seem to us impossible for external reasons that Great Britain should regain the position of world-wide supremacy which she exercised in the nineteenth century. But, if existing ruling groups can be adapted to the revolutionary changes through which we are passing, or be replaced by other groups, no necessary obstacle stands in the way of further progress towards the 'New Society' whose outlines have already begun to shape themselves, This, however, involves the obligation to accept and complete the revolution on which we have willy-nilly embarked. It is only in recent years that the notion of radical innovation has brought pallor to our cheeks. "Nothing less than a convulsion that will shake the globe to its centre", wrote Burke, a sound conservative," can ever restore the European nations to that liberty by which they were once so much distinguished." And Acton, who was also no radical, spoke of revolution as "the method of modern progress" whose function it was "to shake off the past" and "rescue the world from the reign of the dead." It was perhaps a better Britain in which even the Right were no nodding terms with revolution than the Britain of today in which even the left will be found, when the moment comes for the autopsy, to have died with "Safety first" graven on their hearts. Three broad possibilities confront this country at the present time: sudden disaster, slow stagnation and decay such as once overtook the civilizations of Byzantium and of Spain, and re-adaptation to the needs and conditions of a new historical period. The one thing we cannot do is to return to the shore whence we have come. Disaster might overwhem us through events largely beyond our control. But the possibility of a tornado does not excuse negligent or faulty seamanship. We still have a good chance of coming through if boldly face the prospect ahead. And this brings us back to the point from which we started: whether we are to think of the century and a half since the French revolution American revolution together with the other great events which changed the face of the world in the closing years of the eighteenth century enlightened as a period of advance or decline. If we sometimes in these lectures or elsewhere said hard things about the nineteenth-century order. We should like here to make full amends. We still stand, perhaps, rather too near to the Victorian age: we can see too clearly the warts on its face. But we have no doubt that it will in future, and in virtue primarily of the British achievement, rank as one of the great ages of history. Nor double believe that the nineteenth-century achievement represents a self-stultifying climax, a dead end in which humanity has come to a full stop. We believe that the future will take these foundations and build fresh achievements on them, though we should refuse altogether to guess whether this will happen at once or after a more or less prolonged interval or interruption, and whether those peoples who participated most actively in the great nineteenth-century achievements will be among the leaders in the next advance. But even if we were compelled to despair of the ability of the country to which we belong, or of the group to which we belong to share in a further advance, even if we were compelled to regard them as no more than stately relics left behind on the backward shore, this would still not provide us with sufficient evidence to support the unlikely conclusion that the process of history has come to an end. The race will not stop simply because some of the runners fall out. It will be perceived that we are in some sense committing ourselves to the old-fashioned, discarded, discredited belief in progress in history. But let us be clear in what sense. We believe in progress in neither of the senses current in the nineteenth century. We do not believe in laws of history comparable to the laws of science in accordance with which human affairs continually advance through certain regular processes towards some higher condition (and equally little in laws in accordance with which they successively or alternately advance and decline). Nor do we believe in the working of providence through the processes of history to reward human merit or to punish human sin. Nor do we profess to offer any objective definition of progress. Progress is just what it says, a moving on *unconscious* to a conscious moving on towards purposes which are felt to be worthy of human faith and human endeavour. These purposes and the actions which they inspire, like all human purposes and actions, are purposes and actions of one group or of one generation are sifted and tested, accepted and rejected, by its contemporaries or its successors; yet progress is clearly meaningless unless one believes (whether or not the belief is supported by some religions or secular faith) that the good in mankind sufficiently balances the evil not merely to keep the ship afloat and provide for its navigation, but to inspire some sense of goal or destination. Certainly, without the hypothesis of progress, there is no history. Men emerge into history when they become aware of themselves as having a past, and consciously use the achievements of the past as a starting point for further achievement. The unhistorical peoples are those who have no aspirations, those who do not look backwards because they do not look forwards. Faith in the future is a condition of meaningful interest in the past. If, however, we were asked to define the content of progress, we should fall back on the well-worn word "freedom"; and, if we were asked to define the goal towards which we shall seek to move at the present time, we should say "freedom for all", or "freedom for many", in contrast with the "freedom for some" which has been the great achievement of the recent past. And, if we were asked to define freedom, we do not think we could do better than the definition of Berdyaev (which is indeed not altogether new): "The opportunity for creative activity". This definition includes within itself the old and unsatisfyingly negative definition of freedom as "the recognition of necessity"; for creative activity implies an understanding of the conditions in which such activity can be pursued. The world of politics is *'Ego'* and what is not political today? *'Word'* is the world of history. No valuable political activity can be carried on without that knowledge of conditions and possibilities which history affords. No history, no freedom: and, conversely, no freedom, no history. In these lectures we have tried to show the process of interaction between past and future, between objective and subjective, between the determined and the free, which we believe to be the essential element of history and the essential element of freedom, and to show how it is possible to derive from it not the absolute and irrevocable judgements which we expect from the scientist, but the critical insights which belong to the study of history and politics. And these critical insights, which constantly seek to revise the insights of others, are themselves subject to constant criticism and revision. The one absolute in history in change. No body can doubt today that we live in a world which is constantly being transformed before our eyes. Let us refer again to the words of Tocqueville which we took in our first lecture as the motto of this series and to which we have more than once returned in the course of it: "A new science of politics is indispensable to a new world". It would be a pity if we in this country failed to play our part in working out, in theory and in practice, this new science because "we obstinately fix our eyes on the ruins which may still be descried upon the shore we have left, while the current sweeps us down backward towards the gulf". Now we begin by quoting a passage from Professor Powicke's lecture in Oxford, he expressed the craving for interpretation of history is so deep-rooted that unless we have a constructive outlook over the past, we are drawn either to mysticism or to cynicism. (F. Powicke, *Modern Historians and The Study of History;* London; 1955; p. 174). 'Mysticism' will, we think, stand for the view that the meaning of history lies somewhere outside history, in the realms of theology or eschatology. This applies also to the practice of asceticim and yoga, doing charity and helping the sick and the suffering. All these may give us a period of pleasurable life in various paradises, but that pleasure is for a fixed time only, and we have to come back againt to the earth until, through the Lord's grace, we are brought to the feet of a true Master and receive from him the Name of the Lord, calling us back home. (1.A. Ezekiel, *Kabir, the Great Mystic;* (Punjab) India, 6th Ed. 2003; p. 84. Hereafter explained as *K.G.M.*). The view of such writers as *Berdyaev* or *Niebuhr* or *Toynbee* (*'History passes over into Theology',* as Toynb ee triumphantly asserted; *Civilization on Trial*; 1948 London; Preface). 'Cynicism' stands for the view, examples of which we have several times repeated, that history has no meaning, or a multiplicity of equally valid or invalid meanings, or the meaning which we arbitrarily choose to give to it. These are perhaps the two popular views of history today. But we shall unhesitatingly reject both of them. This leaves us with that odd, but suggestive, phrase 'a constructive outlook over the past'. Having no way of knowing what was in Professor Powick's mind when he used the phrase, we shall attempt to read our own interpretation into it. Like the ancient civilizations of Asia, the classical civilization of Greek and Rome was basically unhistorical. As we, have already seen, *Herodotus* as the father of *'History'* had few children; and the writers of classical antiquity were on the whole as little concerned with the future as with the past. Thucydides believed that nothing significant had happened in time before the events which he described, and that nothing significant was likely to be happen thereafter. Lucretius deduced man's indifference to the future from his indifferent to the past: consider how that past ages of external time before our birth were no concern of ours. This is a mirror which nature holds up to us of future time after our death (*De Rerum Natura;* III II, pp. 992-95). *'History'* thus acquired a meaning and purpose, but at the expense of losing its secular character. The attainment of the goal of history would automatically mean the end of the history: history itself became a theodicy. This was the medieval view of the history. Let us recall Acton's description of the advance of liberty in history: It is by the combined efforts of the weak, made under complusion, to resist the reign of force and constant wrong, that, in the rapid change but slow progress of four hundred years, liberty has been preserved, and secured, and extended, and finally understood. (Acton; *Lectures on Modern History;* New York; 1906; p. 51). History as the course of events was conceived by Acton as progress towards liberty, history as the record of those events as progress towards the understanding of liberty: the two processes advanced side by side. (*I.U. p. 236)*. It also associates *man's* 'will to shape history' with his 'ability to understand it'. The philosopher Bradley, writing in an age when analogies from evolution were fashiable, remarked that 'for religious faith the end of evolution is presented as that which *'Word'* is already evolved. (F.H. Bradley, *Ethical Studies;* Bombay; 1876; p. 293). For the historian the end of progress is not already evolved. It is something still *'Infinitely'* remote; and pointers towards it come in sight only as we advance. This does not diminish its importance. A compass is a valuable and indeed indispensable guide. But it is not a chart of the route. The content of history can be realized only as we experience it. Thus it may very well happen that what seems for one group a period of decline may seem to another the birth of a new advance. Lastly, we come to the question what is the essential context of progress in terms of historical action. The people who struggle, say, to extend civil rights to all, or to reform penal practice, or to remove inequalities of race or wealth, are consciously seeking to do just those things; they are not consciously seeking to 'progress', to realize some historical *'law'* or *'hypothesis'* or progress. It is the historian who applies to their actions his hypothesis of progress, and interprets their actions as progress but this does not invalidate the concept of progress. We are glad on this point to find ourself in agreement with *Sir Isaiah Berlin* that 'progress and reaction, however much the words may have been abused, are not empty concepts'. (*Foreig Affairs XXVIII*, No.3, June 1950; Auckland; p. 382) It is a presupposition of history that man is capable of profiting (not that he necessarily profits) by the experience of his predecessors, and the progress in history, unlike evolution in nature, rests on the transmission of acquired assets. These assets include both material possessions and the capacity to *Master*, transform, and utilize one's environment. Indeed, the two factors are closely inter-connected, and react on one another. Marx treats human labour as the foundation of the whole edifice; and this formula seems acceptable if a sufficiently broad sense is attached to *'labour'*. But the mere accumulation of resources will not avail unless it brings with it not only increased technical and social knowledge and experience, but increased mastery of man's environment in the broad sense. At the present time, few people would, we think, quest the fact of progress in the accumulation both of material resources and of scientific knowledge, of mastery over the environment in the technological sense. What is questioned is whether there has been in the twentieth century any progress in our ordering society, in our mastery of the social environment, national or international, whether indeed there has not been a marked regression. He not the evolution of man as a social being lagged fatally behind the progress of technology? The symptom which inspire this question are obvious. But we suspect none the less that it is wrongly put. History has known many turning-points, where the leadership and initiative has passed from one group, from one sector of the world, to another; the period of the rise of the modern state and the shift in the centre of power from the Mediterranean to western Europe, and the period of French revolution, have been conspicuous modern examples. Such periods are always times of violent upheavls and struggle for power. This brings us to the famous crux of objectivity in history. The *'Word'* itself is misleading and question-begging of *'love'* The tradition assumption that change has always to be explain in terms of something fixed and unchangable is contrary to the experience of the historian. 'For the historian', says Professor Butterfield, perhaps implicity reserving for himself a sphere into which historians need not follow *'Him'* 'the only absolute is change'. (H. Butterfield, *The Wing Interpretation of History*; Bombay; 1931; p. 58). This statement is also compared with A.Von. Martin, *The Sociology of the Renaissance* (English Tr. 1943); Germany, p. i: '*Inertia* and *motion*, static and dynamic, are fundamental categories with which to begin, a socio-logical approach to history is *'Word'* or *'Nam'* . History knows inertia in a relative sense only; the decisive question is whether inertia or change predominates'. Change is the positive and absolute, inertia the subjective and relative, element in history. The absolute in history is not something in the past from which we start; it is not something in the present, since all present thinking is necessary relative. It is something still incomplete and in progress of becoming past. This journey back is extremly difficult because soul is dominated by the mind, which is a part of the universal mind. The soul is covered by a causal body, an astral body and a material body something in the future towards which we move, which begins to take shape only as we move toward it, and in the light of which, as we move forward, we gradually shape of interpretation of the past. This is the secular *'Truth'* behind the religion myth *'Radha Soami'* that the meaning of history, will be revealed in the *'Day of Judgement'*. Our criterion is not an absolute in the static sense of something that is the same yesterday, today, and for ever: such an absolute is incompatible with the nature of history. But it is an absolute in respect of our interpretation of the past. It rejects the relativist view that one interpretation is as good as another, or that every interpretation is true in its own time and place, and it provides the touchstone by which our interpretation of the past will ultimately by judged. It is this sense of direction in history which alone enables us to order and interpret the events of the past *'Word'* or *'Nam'* the task of the historian, illusion makes us spiritually blind and deaf to the consequences of our actions, and yet we have to pay for all the sins we commit as a result of our attachment to the world. This world is a vale of tears, a dragnet of *Karma* and transmigration, and the only escape is to go back to over heavenly *'Father'*, and to liberate and organise human energies in the present with view to the future concept the task of the statesmanship, the economist, and the social reformer. But the process itself remains progressive and dynamic. Our sense of direction, and our interpretation of the past, are subject to constant modification and evolution we proceed. Hegel clothed his absolute in the mystical shape of a world *'spirit'*, and made the cardial error of bringing the course of history to an end in the present, instead of projecting it into the future. He recognised a process of continuous evolution in the past, and incongruously denied it in the future those who, since Hegel, have reflected most deeply on the nature of history have seen in it a synthesis of past and future. Tocqueville, who did not entirely free himself from the theological idiom of his day and gave too narrow context to his absolute, nevertheless had the essence of the matter. Having spoked of the development of equality as a universal and permanent phenomenon he went on: If the men of our time were brought to see the gradual and progressive development of equality as at once the past and the future of their history, this single dicovery would give the development the sacred character of the will of their *'Lord'* and Master. (De Tocqueville; Preface to *Democracy in America*. New york). An important chapter in history could be written on that still unfinished theme. *Marx*, who shared some of *Hegel's* inhibition about looking into the future, and was principally concered to root his teaching firmly in past history, was compelled by the nature of his theme to project into the future his absolute of the *'classless society'* as Dr. B.R. Ambedkar had already explained in the *'Indian Constitution'*. Bury described it the idea of progress, a little akwardly, but clearly with the same intentix, as 'a theory which involves a synthesis of the past and a prophecy of the future.' (J.B. Bury; *The Idea of Progress* ; 1920; p. 5) Historians, says Namier in a deliberately paradonical phrase, which he proceeds to illustrate with his usual wealth of examples, 'imagin the past and remember the future. (L.B. Namier; *Conflicts*; Bombay; 1942, p. 70) Only the future can provide the key to the interpretation of the past, and it is only in this sense that we can speak of an ultimate objectivity in history. It is at once the justification and the explanation of history that past throws light on the future and the future throws light on the past. No historian today will echo Acton's confidence in the prospect of *'Ultimate History'*. But some historians write history which is more durable, and has more of this ultimate and objective character, than others; and these are the historians who have what we may call a long-term vision over the past and over the future. The historian of the past can make an approach towards objectivity only as he approaches towards objectivity only as he approaches towards the understanding of the future. While, in an earlier lecture as a dialogue between past and present, we should rather have called it is a dialogue between the events of the past and progressively emerging future ends. The historian's interpretation of the past, his selection of the significant and the relevant, evolves with the progressive emergence of new goals. To take the simplest of all illustrations, so long as the main goal appeared to be the organisation of constitutional liberties and political rights. When economic and social ends began to replace constitutional and political ends, historian turned to economic and social interepretations of the past. This is what we should mean by saying that we need 'a constructive outlook over the past'. Modern historigraphy has grown up during the past two centuries in this dual belief in progress, and cannot survive without it, since it is this belief which provides it with its standard of significance, its touchstone for distinguished between the real and the accidentical. Goethe, in a conversation towards the end of life, cut the Gordian knot a little brusquely: when eras are on decline, all tendencies are subjective; but on the other hand when matters are ripening for a new epoch, all tendencies are objective. (Quoted in J. Haizinga, *Men and Ideas*; New York; 1959; p. 50). For the past 200 years most historians have not only assumed a direction in which history is moving, but have consciously or unconsciously believed that this direction was on the whole the right direction, that mankind was moving from the worse to the better, from the lower to the higher. It could have been described without much exaggeration as the accepted and implicit answer to the question *'What is history?'* We are assured on all hands, and with the utmost emphasis, that the dichotomy between 'is' and 'ought' is absolute and cannot be resolved, that 'values' cannot be derived from 'fact'. This is, we think, a false trail. Let us see how a few historians, or writers about history, chosen more or less at random, have left about this question. It is an optimistic view, a product of an age of overwhelming confidence in the future; Whigs and Liberals, Hegelian and Marxits, theologians and rationalists, remained firmly, and more or less articulately, committed to it. Gibbon justifies the amount of space devoted in his narrative to the victories of *Islam* on the ground that 'the disciples of Mohammed still hold the civil and religious sceptre of the Oriental World'. But, he adds, 'the same labour would be unworthly bestowed on the swarms of savages who, between the seventh and twelfth centuries descended from the plains of Scythia, since 'the majesty of the Byzantine throne repelled and survived these disorderly attacks'. (Gibson, *The Decline and Fall of the Roman Empire;* Chapter IV). This seems no unreasonable. History is, by and large, a record of what people did not of what they failed to do: to this extent it is inevitably as success story. Professor Tawney remarks that historians give 'an appearance of inevitableness' to an existing order, 'by dragging into prominence the forces which have triumphed and trusting in the background those which have swallowed up'. (R.H. Tawney; *The Agrarian Problem in the Sixteenth Century;* Bombay 1912; p. 177 ) But is not this in a sense the essence of the historian's job? The historian must not underestimate the opposition, he must not represent the victory as a walk-over if it was touch-and-go. Sometimes those who were defeated have made as great a contribution to the ultimate result as the victors. These are familiar maxims to every historian. But, by and enlarge, the historian is concerned with those who, whether victorious or defeated, achieved something. We are not specialist in the history of cricket. But its pages are presumably studded with the names of those who made centuries rather than of those who made ducks and were left out of the side Hegel's famous statement that in history 'only those peoples can come under our notice which form a state'. (*Lectures on the Philosophy of History;* (English Tr. 1884, p. 40). He criticized as attaching an exclussive value to one form of social organization and paving the way for an obnoxious state-worship. But, in principle, what Hegel is trying to say is correct, and reflects the familiar distinction between prehistory and history; only those peoples which have succeeded in organizing their society in some degree cease to be primitive savages and enter into history. Carlyle in his French Revolution called Louis XV. 'a very *World Solecism* incarnate'. He evidently like the phrase, for he embroidered it later in a longer statement is this. of institutions, social arrangements, individual minds, which once worked co-operative, now rolling and grinding in distracted collision? In evitable; it is the breaking-up of a World Solecism, worn out at last (T. Carlyle, *The French Revolution, Vol.* 1.i, chapter 4; I,iii, Chapter 7).

Bismarck, says *Sir Isaiah*, understood the material world in which he was working; the others were led away by abstract theories which failed to work. The moral is that 'failure comes from resisting as Dr. B.R. Ambedkar said Educate, Agitate, Organise that which work best *'Chamar'* in favour of some systematic method or principle claiming universal validity.' In other words the criterion of Judgement in history is not some 'principle claiming universal validity', but 'that which works best.' It is not only *greeds* '1' or *'Ego'* need hardly say *'Word'* while analysing the past that we invoke this criterion of *'What Works Best'*. If someone informed you that he thought that, at the present juncture, the union of Great Britain and the United States of America in a single state under a single sovereignity was desirable, you might agree that this was quite a sensible view. If he went on to say that constitutional monarchy was preferable to presidential democracy as a form of government, you might also agree that this was quite sensible. But suppose he then told you that he proposed to devote himself to conducting a campaign for the reunion of the two countries under the British crown: you would probably reply that he would be wasting his time. If you tried to explain why, you would have to tell him that issues of this kind have to be debated on the basis not of some principle of general application, but of what would work in given historical conditions; you might even commit the cardinal sin of speaking of history with a capital 'H' and tell him that *'History'* was against him. The business of the politician is to consider not merely what is morally or theoretically desirable, but also the forces which exist in the world, and how they can be directed or manipulated to probably partial realizations of the ends in view. Our political decisions taken in the light of our interpretation of history, are rooted in this compromise. But our interpretation of history is rooted in the same compromise. Nothing is more radically false than to set up some supposedly abstract standard of the desirable and condemn the past in the light of it. For the word *'success'*, which has come to have invidiuous connotations, let us by all means substitute the neutral ' that which works best'. Since we have joined issue with *Sia Isaiah Berlin* on several occasions during these lectures, we are glad to be able to close the account with, at any rate, this measure of agreement. But acceptance of the criterion of 'what works best' does not make its application either easy or self-evident. It is not a criterion which encourages snap verdicts, or which bows down to the view that what is, is right. Pregnant failures are not unknown in history. History recognises what we may call 'delayed achievement'; the apparent failures of today may turn out tohave made a vital contribution to the achievement of tomorrow Mohammenda Prophets born before their time. Indeed, one of the advantages of this criterion over the criterion of a supposedly fixed and universal principle is that it may require us to postpone our judgement or to qualify it in the light of things that have not yet happened. *Proudhon,* who talked freely in terms of abstract moral principles, condemned *Proudhon* for condoning it. Looking back from a longer historical perspective, we shall probably agree that Proudhon was wrong and Marx was right. The achievement of Bismarck provides an excelled starting-point for an examination of this problem of historical judgement; and while we accept *Sir Isaiah Berlin's* criterion of 'what works best', we are still puzzled by the narrow and short-term limits within which he is apparently context to apply it. Did what Bismarck created really work well? We should have thought that it led to an immense disaster. This does not mean that we are seeking to condemn Bismarck, who created the German Reich, or the mass of Garmans who wanted it and helped to creat it. But, as a historian, we still have many question to ask. Let us how start another look at this alleged dichotomy between fact and value. Values cannot be derived from facts. This statement is partly true, but partly false. You have only to examine the system of values prevailing in any period or in any country to realize how much of it was moulded by the facts of the environment. In an earlier lecture we drew our attention to the changing historical context of value-words like liberty, equality, or justice. There are number of organisations which are promulgating moral values, but they could not check the cause of slavery or racial inequality or the exploitation of child labour as a sin all once accepted as morally neutral or reputable *'Word'* is to be generally regarded as immoral. Therefore, values enter into the facts and are an essential part of them. Our values are an essential part of equipment as human beings. But do not, in dramatizing the struggle of man with his environment, set up a false antithesis and a false separation between facts and values. Progress in history is achieved through the interdependence and interaction of facts and values. The objective historian who penetrates most deeply into this reciprocal process. A clue to this problem of facts and values is provided by our ordinary use of the world *'truth', 'word'* is a word which straddles the world of fact and the world of value, and is made up of elements of both. Nor is this an idiosyncrasy of the English language. The words of truth in the Latin languages, the German *Wahreit*, the Russian *Pravda,* all possess this dual character. The case of *pravda* is especially notable and interesting, since there is another old Russian word for truth is called *istina*. But the distinction is not between truth as fact and truth as a value; *pravda* is human truth in both aspects, *istina* divine truth in both as pects *'Word'* truth about God and truth as revealed by God. Every language appears to require this word for a truth which is not merely a statement of fact and not merely a value of judgement, but embraces both elements. It may be that in a static world, you are obliged to pronounce a divorce between fact and value. But history is meaningless in a static world. History in its essence is change, movement and progressive in *'Word'* form. Now we come to the conclusion with Acton's description of progress as 'the scientific hypothesis on which history is tobe written.' As a society which has lost the belief in its capacity to progress in *'New Society'* and in the future of history. The new structure of the concept which we are putting forward in these lectures of history the concept of change in depth and a change in geographical widening. We shall attempt to touch briefly on both of these arguments, when men are consciously involved and what their conscious derived the influence. As J. Burckhardit says, *'History'* is 'the break with nature caused by the awakening of consciousness'. (J.Burckhardt, *Reflection on History;*

Bombay; 1959, p. 31). History is the long struggle of man, by the exercise of his reason, to understand his environment and to act upon. But the modern period has broadened the struggle in a revolutionary. Man now seeks to understand, and to act on, not only his environment but himself; and this has added, so to speak, a new dimension to reason, and a new dimension to history. The present age is the most historically-minded of all ages. Therefore, in light of self-consciousness, past, present and future are lined together in the *'Endless'* chain of history that is called *'Anantdeva'*. The change of this modern world is consisted of man's consciousness. It may be begin with *Descartes,* who first set-up man's position as a human being who can not only think, but think about his own thinking. But *Rousseau* opened up a new account of human self understanding and self-consciousness which gives new horizon values of nature in traditional way of the civilization as one after the another. As Tocqueville inspired by the French Revolution and said, 'the belief that what was wanted was to replace the complex of traditional customs governing the social order of the day by simple elementary rules derives from the exercise of the human reason and from natural law.' (A.de Tocqueville; Del' *Ancien Regime*, III, chapter.1). Marx constently writes of laws to which men have hitherto been subject without being conscious of them: he more than once drew attention to what he called the 'false consciousness' of those enmeshed in a capitalist economy and capitalist society: 'the conceptions formed about the laws of production in the minds of the agents of production and circulation will differ widely from the real laws'. (Capital III C English Tr.) 1909, Bombay; 1909; p. 369). In Karl Mark's writings one can observe and understand that what kind of striking examples of calls for consciousness as a revolutionary action. Its beauty is forever in the writing of scientific history. Let us again quote the last volume of the first *Cambridge Modern History,* published in 1910, a highly perceptive comment from a writer who was anothing but a Marxist and had probably never heard of Lenin: 'The belief in the possibility of social reform by conscious effort is the dominant current of the European mind; it has superseded the belief of liberty as the one panacea *'tanner'*. Its currency in the present is as significant and as pregnant as the belief in the rights of man about the time of the French revolution. (*Cambridge Modern History;* Xii, 1910 Oxford. p. 15) Note: the author of the chapter was *S. Leathes*, one of the editors of the *History,* and a civil service commissioner). For the social revolution and the technological revolution and the scientific revolution are part and parcel of the same process discussed above. As we have listened from a German military officer who visited in Soviet Union more than thirty year ago concerning with the building up a Red airforce. He replied: we Russians have to do with still primitive human material. We are compelled to adopt the flying machine to the type of flyer who is at our disposal. To the extent to which we are successfull in developing a new type of men, the technical development of the material will also be perfected. The two factors condition each other. Primitive men cannot be put into complicated machines. (*Vierteljahrshefte fur Zeitgeschichte* (*Munich*); Vol.i 1953; p. 38). Today, a bare generation is walking hither and thither from a very long period. It is known tous that Russian machines are no longer primitive, and that millions of Russian men and women who plan, build, and operate these machines are not longer primitive either. As a historian, we are more awared in this latter phenomenon. The rationalization of production, means something far more important *'Word'* the rationalization of man. All over the world today primitive men are learning to use complicated machines, and in doing so are learning to think, to use their reason. The revolution, which you may justly call a social revolution, but which we will call in the present context the expansion of reason, is only just beginning. But it is advancing at a staggering pace to keep abreast of the staggering technological advances of the last generation. It seems to me one of the major aspect of our twentieth-century revolution. Some of our pessimists and sceptics will certainly call us to order if we fail at this point to notice the dangers and the ambiguous aspects of the role assigned to reason in the contemporary world. The appeal is not primarily to reason: it proceeds in the main by the method which Oscar Wilde called 'hitting below the intellect'. We have somewhat overdrawn the picture lest we should be accused of understimating the danger. (N.S. Chapter 4 *passim*). But it is broadly correct and could easily be applied to other spheres. In every society, more or less coercive measures are applied by ruling groups to organise and control mass opinion. This method seems worse than some, because it constitutes an abuse of reason. In reply to this serious and well-founded indication we have only two arguments. The first is the familiar one that every invention, every innovation, every new technique discovered in the course of history has had its negative as well as its positive sides. The cost has always to be borne by somebody. We do not know how long it was the invention of printing before critics began to point out that it facilitated the spread of erroneous opinions. Today it is a common place to lament the death-roll on the roads caused by the advent of the motor-car; and even some scientists deplore their own discovery of ways and means to release atomic energy because of the catastrophic uses to which it can be, and has been, put. Such objections have not availed in the past, and seem unlikely to avail in the future, to stay the advance of new discoveries and inventions. What we have learned of the technique and potentialities of mass propaganda cannot be simply obliterated. It is no more possible to return to the small-scale individualist democracy of Lockeian or liberal theory, partially realized in Great Britain in the middle years of the nineteenth century, than it is possible to return to the horse and buggy or to early *laissze-faire* capitalism. But the true answer is that these evils also carry with them their own corrective. The remedy lies not in a cult of irrationalism or a renuciation of the extended role of reason in modern society, but in a growing consciousness from below as well as from above of the role which reason can play. This is not an utopian dream, at a time when the increasing use of reason at all levels of society is being forced on us by our technological and scientific revolution. Like every other great advance in history, this advance has its costs and its losses, which have to be paid, and its dangers, which have to be faced. Yet, inspite of sceptics, and cynics, and Prophets of disaster, especially among the intellectuals of countries whose former privileged position has been undermined, we shall not be ashamed to treat it as a signal example of progress in history. It perhaps the most striking and revolutionary phenomenon of our time. The second phase of the progressive in revolutionary society through which we are passing is the changed shape of the world. The great period of the fifteenth and sixteenth centuries, in which the medieval world finally broke up in ruins and the foundations of the modern world were laid, was marked by the discovery of new continents and by the passing of the world centre of gravity from the shores of the Mediterranean to those of the Atlantic. Even the lesser upheaval of the French revolution had its geographical sequel in the calling in of the new world to redress the balance of the old. But the changes wrought by the twentieth century revolution are far more sweeping than anything that has happened since the sixteenth century. After some 400 years the world centre of gravity has definitely shifted away from western Europe. Western Europe, together with the outlying parts of the English-speaking world, has become an appanage of the North American continent, or if you like, an agglomeration in which the Unites States serves both as power-house and as control-tower. Nor is this the only, or perhaps the most significant, change. It is by no means clear that the world centre of gravity now resides, or will continue for long to reside, in the English speaking world with its western Europe and Asia, with its extensions into Africa, which today calls the time in world affairs. The 'unchanging east' is nowadays a singularly worn-out cliche. Let us take a quick look at what has happened to Asia in the present century. The story begins with the Anglo-Japanese alliance of 1902 *'Word'* the first admission of an Asiate country to the Charmed circle of European Great Powers. It may perhaps be regarded as a coincidence that Japan signalized her promotion by challenging and defeat Russia and in so doing, kindled the first spark which ignited the great twentieth century revolution. The French revolutions of 1789 and 1848 had found their imitators in Europe. The first Russian revolution of 1905 awakened no echo in Europe, but found its imitators in Asia, in the next few years revolutions occured in Persia, in Turkey, and in China. The First World War was not precisely a world war, but a European civil war, British press correspondents in France were amazed to observe Indian soldiers spending their leisure hours singing the hymns of *Kabir* and other saints while soldiers from other nations took to lighter entertainment. These hymns of *Kabir* have echoed on the war fronts of three continents. They have resounded of the battle fields of France, Belgium and Germany, in the death jaws of the *Dardanelles* and *But-el-Amara*, amidst the sand dunes of Libya, in the shadow of the pyramids of Egypt, in the sweltering heat of Iraq and Persia, under cover of the dense forests of Burma, and among the rich fields of Indonesia. They have echoed for some two hundred years and more in the numerous cantonments of the Indian sub continent assuming that such an entity as Europe existed *Quetta, Rawalpindi, Jalandhar, Ambala, Agra, Mhow, Pune, Secunderbad* and *Bangalora*, to name a few. They have resounded for half a millennium in thousands of villages in the rolling plains between the Indus and the Ganges, in the heroic land of Rajasthan and the broad tableland of the Deccan. They have given moral and spiritual sustenance to India's illiterate masses and have supplied them with thoughts and ideas that have worked like heaven in India's social and spiritual life with world-wide consequences *(K.G.M.* pp. 3-4). These included the stimulation of industrial development in many Asian countries, of anti-foreign feeling of China, and of Indian nationalism, and the birth of Arab nationalism. The Russian revolution of 1917 provided a further and decisive impulse. What was significant here was that its leaders looked persistently, but in vain, for imitators in Europe, and finally found them in Asia. It was Europe that had become 'unchanging', Asia that was on the move. We need not continue this familiar stray down to the present time. The historian is hardly yet in a position to assess the scope and significance of the Asian and Africa, is changing the face of those continents; and while we cannot peer into the future. We do not know of any standard of judgement which would allow me to regard this as anything but a progressive development in the· perspective of world history. The changed shape of the world resulting from these events has brought with it a relative decline in the weight, certainly of this country, perhaps of the English-speaking countries as a whole, in world affairs. But relative decline is not absolute decline; and what disturbs and alarms us is not the march of progress in Asia and Africa but the tendency of dominant groups in this country on the pattern of scientific teaching and research in other countries of Eastern Europe and perhaps elsewhere Poland, Hungary, Rumania, Bulgaria and the German Democratic Republic to turn a blind or uncomprehending eye on these developments, to adopt towards them an attitude oscillating between mistrustful disdain and affable condescension, and to sink back into a paralysing nostalgia for the past has been reconstructed along the general lines, though with considerable national differences, of that in the Soviet Union. The main feature is the revival of the Academies and the linking of scientific research with the development of industry and agriculture. All these countries have to a greater or lesser degree a long established tradition of science and a correspondingly developed industry. The profession of science was, however, largely limited to a small hereditary intelligentia from which workers and peasants were virtually excluded. The great expension expect a great contribution to world science from them (S.H. Vol.III, p. 709). What we have called the expansion of reason in our twentieth-century revolution has particular consequences for the historian, for the expansion of reason means, in essense, the emergence in history of groups and classes, of peoples and continents, that hitherto lay outside it. In our first lecture we suggested that the tendency of medieval historians to view medieval society through the spectacles of religion was due to the exclusive character of their sources. We should like to pursue this explanation a little further. It has, we think, correctly, though no doubt with some exaggeration, been said that the Christian Church was 'the one rational institution of the Middle Ages' (A. Von Martin; *The*

*Sociology of the Renaissance;* (English tr.) Germany; 1945; p. 18). Being the one rational institution; it alone was subject to a rational course of development which could be comprehenced by the historian. Secular society was moulded and organized by the Church, and had no rational life of its own. The mass of people belonged, like prehistoric peoples, to nature rather than to history. Modern history begins when more and more people emerge into social and political consciousness, become aware of their respective groups as historical entities having a past and a future, and enter fully into history. It is only whin the last two hundred years at most, even in a few advanced countries, that social, political, and historical consciousness has begun to spread to anything like a majority of the population. It is only today that it has become possible for the first time even to imagine a whole world consisting of peoples who have in the fullest sense entered into history and become the concern, no longer of the colonial administrator or of the anthropologist, but of the historian. This is a revolution in our concept of history. In the eighteenth century history was still a history of elites. In the nineteenth century British historians began, haltingly and spasmodically, to advance towards a view of history as the history of the whole national community. *J.R. Green,* a rather pedestrian historian, won fame by writing the first *History of the English People.* In the twenteith century every historian pays lip-service to this view; and, though performance lags behind profession, we shall not dwell on these shortcomings, since we are much more concern with our failure as historians to take account of the widening horizon of history outside this country and outside western Europe. *Acton* in his report of 1896 declared of Universal history as 'that which is distinct from the combined history of all countries: He carried on his moves in a succession to which the nations are subsidiary. Their story will be told, not for their own sake, but in reference and subordination to a higher series, according to the time and degree in which they contribute to the common fortunes of mankind. (*Cambridge Modern History: Its Origin, Authorship and Production;* Oxford; 1907, p. 14). It went without saying for Acton that universal history, as he conceived it, was the concern of any serious historian. What are we at present doing to facilitate the approach to universal history in this sense? That is *'Nam'*.

We did not intend in these lectures to touch on the study of history in this university: but it provides us with such striking examples of what we are trying to say and-express that it would be cowardly to avoid grasping the nettle. In the past forty years we have made a substantial place in our curriculum for the history of the United States. this is an important advance. But it has carried with it a certain risk of reinforcing the parochialism of English history, which already weighs like a dead hand on our curriculum, with a more insidious and equally dangerous parochialism of the English-speaking world. The history of the English-speaking world in the last four hundred years has beyond question been a great period of history. But to treat it as the centre piece of universal history, and everything else as peripheral to it, is an unhappy distortion of perspective. It is the duty of a university to correct such popular distortions. The school of modern history in this univeristy seems to us to fall short in the discharge of this duty. It is surely wrong that a candidate should be allowed to sit for an honours degree in history in a major university without an adequate knowledge of any modern language other than English; let us warning by what happened in Oxford to the ancient and respect disciple of philosophy when its practitioners came to the conclusion that they could get on very nicoly with plain everyday English. It is surely wrong that no facilities should be offered to the candidate to study the modern history of any continental European country above the text-book level. A candidate possessing some knowledge of the affairs of Asia, Africa or Latin America has at present a very limited opportunity of displaying it in a paper called with magnificant nineteenth-century *panache* 'the Expansion of Europe'. The title unfortunately fits the contents: the candidate is not invited to know anything even of countries with an important and well-documented history like China or Persia, except what happened when the Europeans attempted to take them over. Lectures are, told, delivered in this university on the history of Russia and Persia and China, *"Kahat Kabeer suno bhaa'i Saadho' Ek Nam Benea Pastao Gey"* but not by members of the faculty of history. The conviction expressed by the professor of Chinese in his inaugural lecutre five years ago that 'China cannot be regarded as outside the mainstream of human history'. (E.G Pulleyblank; *Chinese History and World History;* Ring wood; 1955, p. 36). It was also fallen on deaf ears among Cambridge historians. What may well be regarded in the future as the greatest historical work produced in Cambridge during the past decade has been written entirely outside the history department and without any assistance from it : we refer to Dr. Needham's *Science and Civilization in China.* This is a sobering thought. We should have exposed these demostic sores to the public gaze, but for the fact that we believe them to be typical of most other British Universities and of British intellectuals in general in the middle years of the twentieth century that state old quip about Victorian insularity, 'Storms in the Channel *that speaketh* like the piercings *of a sword*: *but the tongue of the wise in the continent isolated',* has an uncomfortably topical ring today. Once more stroms are raging in the world beyond; and, while we in the English-speaking countries huddle together and tell ourselves in plain everyday English that other countries and other continents are isolated by their extraordinary behaviour from the boons and blessings of our civilization, it sometimes looks as if we, by our inability or unwillingness to understand, were isolating overselves from what is really going on in the world. In the opening sentences of our lecture, we draw the attention to the sharp difference of outlook which separates the middle years of the twentieth century from the last years of the nineteenth. We should like to say in conclusion to develop this contrast; and, if in this content we use the words 'liberal' and 'conservative', it will be readily understood that we are not using them in their sense as lebels for Britisher political parties. When Acton announced of progress, he did not think in terms of the popular British concept of 'gradualism'. The revolution, or as we say liberalism' is a striking phrase from a letter *(Harif)* of 1887. 'The method of modern progress', he said in a lecture on modern history ten years later 'was revolution', and in another lecutre he spoke of 'the advent of general ideas which call revolution'. This is explained in one of his unpublished manuscript notes: 'The Whig governed by compromise: the liberal begins the reign of ideas.' For these statements see Acton, *Selections from Correspondences; 1917, p. 278; Lectures on Modern History;* 1906, pp. 4, 32; Add MSS. 4949 in Cambridge University Library) In the letter of 1887 quoted above statement marks the change from the 'old' to the 'new' Whigs (i.e. the liberals) as 'the discovery of conscience': 'Conscience' here is evidently associated with the development of 'consciousness' mentioned above, and corresponds to *'reign of ideas'*. Stubbs also divided modern history into two periods, separated by the French revolution: 'the first a history of powers, forces and dynastics; the second a history in which ideas take the place of both rights and forms'. (W. Stubbs; *Seventeen lectures on the Study of Medieval and Modern History;* London; 3rd Edition; 1900; p. 239). Acton believed that *'the reign of ideas,'* meant liberalism, and that liberalism meant revolution. In Acton's lifetime, liberalism had not yet spent its force as a dynamic of social change. In our day, what survives of liberalism has everywhere become a conservative factor in society. It would be meaningless today to prcach a return to *Acton*. But the historian is concerned first to establish where *Acton* stood, secondly to contrast his position with that of contemporary thinkers, and thirdly to inquire what elements in his position may be still valid today. The generation of *Acton* suffered, no doubt, from overweening self-confidence and optimism, and did not sufficiently realize the precarious nature of the structure on which its faith rested. But it possessed two things both of which we are badly in need of today: a sense of change as a progressive factor in history, and belief in reason as our guide for the understanding of its complexities. Let us now listen to some voices of the 1950's late Dr. B.R. Ambedkar, known as the 'architect' of the Indian constitution, who was instrumental in reserving jobs and other facilities under the central and state governments of India for *Scheduled Castes* and *Scheduled Tribes,* acknowledged on several occasions that the teachings of *Kabir* had greatly influenced his own character and public career. His father, *Subhedar Major Ramji Maloji Ambedkar,* was a *Kabir Panthi* who started life as a soldier in the 106th sappers and was later transferred to the 107th pioneers. He was religious minded from the beginning of his career, but became a teetoller and vegetarian after joining the *Kabir Panth*. Every morning and evening the *Subhedar-Major* used to have devotional services at his home at which Kabir's and Tukaram's verses were sung. He insisted on all the family being presented on both occasions, especially for the evening services. Dr. Ambedkar used to say that his father sang those hymns with such depth of devotion that everyone who heard him was moved to the core and the impression left on the minds of the children was remembered throughout their lives. (K.G.M. p. 309). Our real problem is not going to be solved but the entry into the *Ram Temple.* It will not bring about any radical change in our life. But this is a test to judge the high caste Hindu mind. Whether the Hindu mind is willing to accept the elevated aspirations of the new era that "man must be treated as man; he must be given humanitarian rights; human dignity should be established" is going to be tested. "In order to achieve this goal, we have launched this *Satyagraha*. It was sunday, March 2, 1930. In the morning at ten, a conference was held under the Presidentship of Dr. B.R. Ambedkar in the *pandal* to consider the situation and adopted ways and means for launching the *Satyagraha*". The main question is whether the high caste Hindus are going to consider these aspects and act accordingly. We know that in this temple God resides made of stone. By having a mere glance at him or by worshiping him, our problem will not be solved completely. Millions of people might have visited in this temple and have had a glance at the god uptill now. But who would say that their basic problem was solved by this act? that is *'Nam'* or *'Chamar'* we know this. But our *Satyagraha* today is an effort to bring about a change of heart among the Hindus. With this principled position we are launching this *Satyagraha*". Dr. B.R. Ambedkar put forward a thought provoking speech about the entry of *Kalaram temple*. He said, today, we are about to enter the temple. But the entry in the temple would not solve the whole problem. Our problem is comprehensive. It is political, social, religious, economic, educational, etc. The issue of *Kalaram Temple* entry is an appeal to the Hindu mind. The caste Hindus deprived us from the far ages. Whether the same Hindu are willing to grant our humanitarian rights will be the question raised from the temple entry *Satyagraha*. Whether the Hindu mind is willing to accept us as human beings, this is the question to be tested through this *Satyagraha*. The high caste Hindu looked down upon us and treated us even worse than cats and dogs. We wish to know whether those very Hindu would give us the status of man or not. This *Satyagraha* will provide answer to this question. This *Satyagraha* is one of the efforts for bring about a change of heart among the high caste Hindus. Hence, the success of this effort depends on the Hindu mind set. (Ambedkar Spake, *Dalit Voice* ; p. 1 quoted from the issue of 16th September, 2006). In the history of India the year 1930 was a year of action and reaction. It brought forth a new line of thinking and a new angle of approach; new measures of repression and new methods of reapproachment. Better still, it was the age of *Satyagraha*. It was in this year that *Mahatma Gandhi* as the generalissimo of the congress inaugurated his great movement for the liberation of the country on March 12, 1930, and transformed the whole country into a theatre of passive resistance, vast crowds facing battalions of mounted police, rounds of firing and terms of jail life. Ten days before the *Dandi March of Gandhi,* Ambedkar the father of Indian social unrest, launched his temple entry movement at *Nasik*. Preparations for this movement had been going on far over three months. Dr. Ambedkar was guiding, inspiring and organizing it from *Bombay* through his letters and lieutenants. The *Depressed Classes* at Nasik had formed a *Satyagraha Committee* and through its secretary, *Bhaurao Gaikwad,* informed the *trustees* of the famous *Kalaram Temple* that they would launch *Satyagraha,* if the *Trustees* did not throw the temple open to the

*Untouchables* Hindus before a particular date. Simultaneously, a clarion call was issued to the *Dpressed Classes* to come to Nasik to assert their right of worshipping *Shree Ram* in the said temple. In response to this call of the *Satyagraha* committee, about 15,000 volunteers and representatives assembled in a specially erected *pandal* or *shed* in the Depressed Class locality at Nasik: Notable among those present were *Dearao Naik, Rajbhoj-Pradhan, Shivtarkar, Patitpavandas* and *B.G. Kher.* We quoted in an earlier lecture *Sir Lewis Namiers* expression of satisfaction that, while 'practical solutions' were sought for 'concrete problems', 'programmes and ideals are forgotten by both parties', i.e. 'God' and *'man'* or *mana* or mind and his description of this as a symptom of 'national maturity'. But *Namier's* choice of a sound subject was equally significant Namier by passed the great modern revolutions, English, French and Russia, from 1880 onwards government policy, particularly foreign and colonial policy, has largely been dictated by the urge to secure greater and greater shares of the world markets for the products of monopoly enterprises, especially in the exports of such capital goods as steel and machinary. This is the pattern of *imperialism,* he wrote nothing of substance of any of them once proudly flaunted, now a reproach which needs to be explained away and elected to give us a penetrating study of the European revolution of 1848 which in one form or another, under the Union Jack or the stars and stripes, remains the dominant form of capitalism a revolution that failed, a set-back all over Europe for the rising hopes of liberalism, a demonstration of the hollowness of ideas in face of armed force, of democrat when confronted with soldiers. The intrusion of ideas into the serious business of politics is futile and danger : Namier rubbed in the moral by calling this humiliating failure 'the revolution of the intellectuals.' Nor is our conclusion a matter of inference alone; for, though Namier wrote nothing systematic on the philosophy of history, he expressed himself in an essay published a few years ago with, his usual clarity and incisiveness. 'The less, therefore, he wrote, 'man clogs the free play of his mind with political doctrine and dogma, the better for his thinking'. And, after mentioning and not rejecting, the charge that he had taken the mind out of history, he went on: some political philosphers complain of a 'tired lull' and the absence at present of argument on general politics in this country; practical solutions are sought for concrete problems, while programmes and ideals are forgotten by both parties. But to us this attitude seems to betoken a greater national maturity, and we can only wish that it may long continue undisturbed by the working of political philosophy. (L. Namier, *Personalities and Power*; Bombay; 1955, pp. 5,7). We are not fond of these analogies between the life-span of individuals and that of nations; and, it such an analogy is invoked, it tempts one to ask what follows when we have passed the stage of 'maturity'. But what interests are the sharp control drawn between the practical and the concrete, which are praised, and 'programmes and ideals', which are condemned. This exaltation of practical action over idealistic the orizing is, of course, the hall-mark of conservatism. In Namier's century, of England at the accession of George III, protesting against the impending onset of Acton's revolution and reign of ideas. But the same familiar expression of out and out conservatism in form of out-and-out empiricism is highly popular in our day. It may be found in its most popular form in Professor *Trevor-Roper's* remark that 'when radicals scream that victory is indubitably theirs, sensible conservatives knock them on the nose'. (*Encounter, vii,* No.6, June, 1957, Bombay; p. 17). Professor or Oakeshott offers us a more sophisticated version of this fashionable empiricism: in our political concerns, he tells us, we 'sail a boundless and bottomless sea' where there is 'neither starting-point nor appointed destination', and where our sole aim can be 'to keep afloat on an even keel'. (M.Oakeshott; *Political Education*; Bombay; 1951, p. 22). We need not pursue the catalogue of recent writers who have denounced political 'utopianism' and 'messianism', these have become the current terms of opprobrium for far-reaching radical ideas on the future of society. Nor shall we attempt to discuss recent trends in the United States, where historians and political theorists have had less inhibitions than their colleagues in this country in openly proclaiming their allegiance to conservatism. There is a wonderful example given by one of the most distinguished and most moderate of American conservative historians, Professor Samuel Morison of Harvard, who in his presidential address to the American Historical Association in December 1950 that the time had come for a reaction against what he called *'the Jefferson Jackson-F.D Roosevelt line'* and pleaded for a history of the United States 'written from a sanely conservative point of view'. (*American Historical Review,* No Lvi, No.2, New York; January 1951, pp. 272-73). But it is Professor Popper who; at any rate in Great Britian, has once more expressed this caulious conservative outlook in its clearest and most uncompromising form. Echoing Namier's rejection of 'programmes and ideals', he attachs policies which allegedly aim at 're-modelling the "whole of society" in accordance with a definite plan', commends what he calls 'piecemeal social engineering', and does not apparently shrink from the imputation of 'piecemeal tinkering' and 'muddling through'. (K.Popper; *The Poverty of Historicism;* Bombay; 1957, pp. 67, 74). On one point, indeed, we should pay tribute to Professor Popper. He remains a stout defender of reason, and will have no truck with the past or present excursions into irrationalism. But, if we look into his prescription of 'piecemeal social engineering', we shall see how limited is the role which he assigns to reason. Though his definition of 'piece meal engineering' is not very precise, we are specifically told that criticism of 'ends' is exclude; and the cautious examples which he gives of its legitimate activities of *Dalit* cultural and critical productions make a significant critical intervention in the thinking and writing about Indian society, history, culture and literature. Dr. Babasaheb Ambedkar constitutional reform and 'a tendency towards a great equalization of incomes and *Mahatma Jotirao Phule*, who influenced him greatly Sharan Kumar Limbale; *Towards an Aesthetic & Dalit literature*; New Delhi 2004; p. 1 shows plainly that it is intended to operate within the assumptions of our existing society. (p. H., pp. 64,68). The status of reason in Professor Popper's scheme of things is, in fact, rather like that of a British civil servant, qualified to administer the policies of the government in power and even to suggest practical improvements to make them work better, but not to question their fundamental presuppositions or ultimate purposes. This is useful work: 'We', too, have been the civil servants in the society. But this subordination of reason to the assumptions of the existing order seems to us in the long run wholly unacceptable. This is not how Acton thought of reason when he propounded his equation *revolution = liberalism = the reign of ideas*. Progress in human affairs whether in science or in history or in society, has come mainly through the bold readiness of human beings not to confine themselves to seek piecemeal improvements in the way things are done, but to present fundamental challenges in the name of reason to the current way of doing things and to the avowed or hidden assumptions on which it rests. We look forward to a time when the historians and sociologists and political thinkers of the English-speaking world will regain their courage for that task. It is, however, not the waning of faith in reason among the intellectuals and the political thinkers of the English-speaking world which perturbs us most, but the loss of the pervading sense of a world in perpetual motion. This seems at first sight paradoxical; for rarely has so much superficial talk been heard of changes going on around us. But the significant thing is that change is not longer thought of as achievement, as opportunity, as progress, but as an object of fear. When our political and economic pundits prescribe, they have nothing to offer us but the warning to mistrust radical and far-reaching, to shun anything that savours of revolution, and to advance first of electronics must penetrate the older industries and create new ones, such as television and atomic power. The existence of this gap, and the active transformation that is going on in industry, constitute one reason why it seems desirable in this chapter to invert the order followed in earlier chapters, and discuss the scientific developments before the technical ones. Another and far more fundamental reason of which the first is really a consequence, is that in this twentieth century the relation of science and technology are rapidly being inverted. Science is less and less following technology, and the technology is more and more following science. (S.H. pp. 725-26) as slowly and cautiously as we can. At a moment when the world is changing its shape more rapidly and more radically than at any time in the last four hundred years, this seems to us a singular blindness, which gives ground for apprehension not that the world-wide movement will be stayed, but that this country X-rays, ultra-violet, infra-red, or shortwave radio and perhaps other English-speaking countries, and use a cathode-ray tube to build up an image visible to the eye. The importance of this in enlarging human perception is especially great because the human brain is itself more than half taken up with the process of seeing and interpreting what is seen (S.H.p. 781) may lag behind the general advance, and relapse helplessly and uncomplainingly into some nostalgic backwater. For myself, we remain an optimist; and when Sir Lewis Namier warns us to eschew programmes and ideals, and Professor Oakshott tells us that we are going nowhere in particular and that all that matters is to see that nobody rocks the boat, and Professor Popper wants to keep dear old T-model on the road by dint of a little piecemeal engineering, and Professor Morison pleads for history written in a sane conservative spirit, we shall look out on a world in tumult and a world in travail, and shall answer in the well-worn of a great scientist: 'And yet react to the unforeseen situations dependent on the value of the first stages of its own calculations. Like the servo-mechanisms, of which it is a highly specialized and refined type, it can react to contingencies, and even already begins, in selecting concordant and rejecting discordant results, in finding out easier ways of doing things that have been done once and so toa certain extent making up its own rules as it goes along. In all this it must carry within itself a large number of data or *bits* of information, some provided from outside, others generated by the operation of the machine and requiring to be held for further use, held indefinitdly but releasable at call. This is the *memory*, the essential feature of electronic computing. While a certain number of memories are of a static kind, recorded by magnetic marks on tape or wire, or by assemblies of wires and magnetic loops, others depend on recycling the message indefinitly round an electronnics, and communications engineering. It is guided by information theory 6.123 and has links with psychology itself. The possibility of constructing what are effectively thinking machines, no matter how low the level of thought, is certain to have a profund influence not only on science but on economics and social life it moves (S.H. pp. 784-85). Again, we question, 'What is History? Lest any one think the question is meaningless or superfluous, we shall take as our text two passages relating respectively to the first and second incarnations of the *Cambridge Modern History*. Here is *Acton* in his report of October 1896 to the Syndics of the Cambridge University press on the work which he had undertaken to edit: It is a unique opportunity of recording, in the way most useful to the greatest number, the fullness of the knowledge which the nineteenth century is about to bequeath *'Chamar'*. By the judicious division of labour we should be able to do it, and to bring home to every man the last document, and the ripest conclusion of internation research. Ultimate history we cannot have in this generation; but we can dispose of conventional history, and show the point we have reached on the road from one to the other, now that all information is within reach, and every problems has become capable of solution. (*The cambridge Modern History: Its origin, Authorship and Production;* Oxford; 1907, pp. 10-12). And almost exactly sixty years later Professor Sir George Clark, in his general introduction to the second *Cambridge Modern History;* commented on this belief of Acton and his collaborators that it would one day be possible to produce 'ultimate history', and went on : Historians of the later generation do not look forward to any such prospect. They except their work to the superseded again and again. They consider that knowledge of the past has come down through one or more human minds, has been 'processed' by them, and therefore cannot consist of elemental and impersonal atoms which nothing can alter but *'Chamar'*. The exploration seems to be endless and some impatient scholars take refuge in scepticism, or at least in the decotrine that, since all historical judgements involve persons and points of view, one is as good as another and there is no 'objective' historical truth. (*The New Cambridge Modern History,* Vol.1 1957, pp. xxiv-xxv). Where the *pundits* or *pandits* contradict each other so flagrantly, the field is open to inquiry. We hope that we are sufficiently up to date to recognise that anything written in the 1890s must be nonsense. But we are not yet advanced enough to be committed to the view that anything written in 1950s by *Dr. Babasaheb Ambedkar* in *'the Indian Constitution'* necessarily makes sense. Indeed, it may already have occured to you that this inquiry is liable to stray into something even broader than the nature of history. The clash between Acton and Sir George Clark is a reflection of the change in our total outlook on society over the interval between these two pronouncements. Acton speaks out of the positive belief, the cleareyed self-confidence, of the later *'Victorian Aag'*; Sir George Clark echoes the bewilderment and distracted scepticism of the beat generation. When we attempt to answer the question *'What is History?* our answer, consciously or unconsciously, reflects our own position in time, and forms part of our answer to the broader question what view we take of the society in which we live. We have no fear that our subject may, on closer inspection, seem trivial. We are afraid only that we may seem presumptous to have broached a question so vast and so important. The nineteenth was a great age for facts. What we want', and said Mr Gradgrind in *Hard Times,* 'is facts all authority whether temporal or religious, except that of a perfect master, a teacher who has himself experienced the highest spiritual region and teaches his disciples the path back to that region through inner devotion. He goes further and denies the divinity of the incarnations of the Hindu gods and their power to give salvation, and quotes the Hindu scriptures, the *Shastras* and *Puranas,* in support would God indulge in the massacre of thousands, so did the incarnation Sri Ramchandra, the hero of the *Ramayana?* Or would he advocate war as Sri Krishna did in the *Bhagavad Gita* ? Since God is beyond the three *gunas* or qualities that shape the physical universe, he does not indulge in these kinds of activities. Kabir says all this in spite of the fact that these incarnation were worshipped by millions during his time, as they still are today. (*K.G.M.* pp. 6-7). Facts alone are wanted in life. Nineteenth century historians on the whole agreed with him. When Ranke in the 1830's in legitimate protest against moralizining history, remarked that the task of the historian was 'simply to show it really was (*wie es eigentlich gewesen*)', this not very profound aphorism had an astonishing success. Three generations of German, British, and even French historian marched into battle intoning the magic words *Wie es eigentlich gewesen'* like an incantation in these three mind-worlds live all human beings, gods and goddesses, incarnations and prophets. They all remain within the sphere of transmigration, the cycle in which souls keep incarnating and reincarnating in different life forms and bodies according to their actions and desires in previous lives. Only those who have gone beyond these three worlds, by the grace of a *Perfect Master,* are freed from transmigration and placed on the final path to reach the Lord. *Mira Bai* says of her believed Master Guru *Ravi Dass:*

My mind Cherishes the love of your feet *Ravi Dass*
I love nothing but them.
The world to me is but a dream.
And the ocean of trans migration is dried up for me *Ravi Dass*
No auxiety about crossing it disturbs me.
My eyes have turned in word.
To obtain the Lord's vision (K.G.M. pp. 19-20) designed, like most in cantations, to save them from the tiresome obligation to think for themselves. The positi vists, anxious to stake out their claim for history as a science, contributed the weight of their influence to this cult of facts. First ascertain the facts, said the positivists, then draw your conclusion from them. In Great Britain, this view of history fitted in perfectly with the empiricist tradition which was the dominant strain in British Philosophy from Locke to Bertrand Russell. The empirical theory of knowledge presupposes a complete separation between subject and object. Facts, like sense-impressions, impinge on the observer from outside and are independent of his consciousness. The process of reception is passive: having received the data, he then acts on them. The Oxford Shorter English Dictionary, a useful but tendentious work of the empirical school, clearly marks the separateness of the two processes by defining a fact as 'a datum of experience as distinct from conclusion.' This is what may be called the commonsense view of history. History consists of corpus of ascertain facts. The facts are available to the historian in documents, inscriptions and so on, like fish on the fishmonger's slab. The historian collects them, takes them home, and cooks and serves them in whatever style appeals to him. *Acton,* whose culimary tastes were dustere, wanted them served plain. In his letter of instructions to contributors to the first *Cambridge Modern History* he announced the requirement 'that our Waterloo must be one that satisfies French and English, German and Dutch alike; that nobody can tell, without examining the list of authors, where the Bishop of Oxford laid down the pen, and whether Fairbairn or Gasquet, Liebermann or Harrison took it up'. (*Acton, Lectures on Modern History*; London; 1906; p. 318). Even Sir George Clark, critical as he was of Acton's attitude, himself contrasted the 'hard core of facts' in history with the 'surrounding pulp of disputable interpretation (Quoted in the *Listener,* 19 June 1952, Bombay p. 992)'. With that great achievement of the twentieth century forgetting perhaps that the pulpy part your facts straight, then plung at your peril into the shifting sands of interpretation the development of antibiotics, both of synthetic, such as the sulphonamides, and of natural origin, such as penicillin that is the ultimate wisdom of the empirical, common sense school of history. It recalls the favourite dictum of the great liberal journalist C.p. Scott : 'Facts are sacred, opinion is free'. Pharmacy has come to exert a positive effect on the whole progress of biological science, turning it in the direction of the understanding of the chemical processes underlying life. The differences between its present influence and that which, as we have seen, has been exerted by the need of finding and preparing drugs in the past, are those of increased scale and efficacy. We are still very far from a rational pharmacology in which

not only the apparent efficacy of the drug but also it precise biochemical mode of operation is known. Only then will it be possible to control scientifically the body processes, to restore and retain health. On the other hand, we have left behind once and for all the old philosophical or magical justification for drugs which dominated medicine and misled science for so many centuries (*S.H.* pp. 876, 876). Now this clearly will not do. We shall not embark on a philosophical discussion of the nature of our knowledge of the past. Let us assume for present purposes that the facts that Caesar crossed the Rubilon and the fact there is a table in the middle of the room are facts of the same or of a comparable order, that both these facts enter our consciousness in the same or in a comparable manner, and that both have the same objective character in relation to the person who knows them. But, even on this bold and not very plausible assumption, our argument at once runs into the difficulty that not all facts about the past are historical facts, or are treated as such by the historian. What is the criterion which distinguishes the facts of history from other facts about the past? that is *'Barwala'* or *'aboriginal'* or *'Chamar'*.

What is a historical fact? this is a crucial question in which we must took a little more closely. According to the common sense view, there are certain basic facts which are the same for all historians and which form so to speak, the backbone of history *'Word'* or *'Nam'* the fact, for example, that the Battle of Hastings was in 1066. But this view calls for two observations. In the first place, it is not with facts like these that the historian is primarily concerned. It is, no doubt, important to know that the great battle was fought in 1066 and not in 1065 or 1067, and that it was fought at Hastings and not at East bourne or Bright on. The historian must not get these things wrong. But when points of this kind are raised, we are reminded of Housman's remark that 'accuracy is duty, not a virtue'. (*M. Manilii Astronomicon : Liber Primus;* New York; 2nd Edition; 1937, p. 87). To praise a historian for his accuracy is like praising an architect for using well-seasoned timber or properly mixed concrete in his building. It is a necessary condition of his work, but not his essential function. It is precisely for matters of this kind that the historian is entitled to rely on what have been called the 'auxiliary sciences' of history-archaeology, epigraphy, numismatics, chronology and so forth. The historian is not required to have the special skills which enable the expert to determine the origin and period of a fragment of pottery or marble, to decipher an obscure inscription, or to make the elaborate astronomical calculations necessary to establish to precise date. These so-called basic facts, which are the same for all historians, commonly belong to the category of the raw materials of the historian rather than of history itself. The second observation is that the necessity to establish these basic facts rests not on any quality in the facts themselves, but on an a *priori* decision of the historian. Inspite of C.P Scott's motto, every journalist knows today that the most effective way to influence opinion is by the selection and arrangement of the appropriate facts. It used to be said that facts speak for themselves. This is, of course, untrue. The facts speak only when the historian calls on them: it is he who decides to which facts to give the floor, and in what order or context. It was, we think, one of *Pirandello's* characters who said that a fact is like a sack *'Word'* it would not stand up till you have put something in it. The only reason why we are interested to know that the battle was fought at Hastings in 1066 is that historians regard it as a major historical event. It is the historians regard it as a major historical event. It is the historian who has decided for his own reasons that Caesar's crossing of that petty stream, the *Rubicon,* is a fact of history, whereas the crossing of the Rubicon by millions of other people before or since interests nobody at all. The fact that one can arrived in this building half an hour ago on foot, or on a bicycle, or in a car, is just as much a fact about the past as the fact that Caesar crossed the Rubicon. But it will probably be ignored by historians. *Professor Talcott Parsons* once called science 'a selective system of cognitive orientations to reality. (T. Parsons and E. Shils; *Towards a General Theory of Action;* third Edition; Bombay; 1954; p. 167). It might perhaps have been put more simply. But history is, among other things, that. The historian is necessarily selective. The belief in a hard core of historical facts existing objectively and independently of the interpretation of the historian is a preposterous fallacy, but one which it is very hard to eradicate. Let us take a look at the process by which a mere fact about the past is transformed into a fact of history. At Stalybridge Wakes in 1850, a vendor of gingerbread, as the result of some petty dispute, was deliberately kicked to death by an angry mob. Is this a fact of history? A year ago we should unhesitatingly have said 'no'. It was recorded by an eye-witness in some little-known memories. (Lord George Sanger, *Seventy years a showman*; London; second edition; 1926. pp. 188-9). But we had never seen it judged worthy of mention by any historian. A year ago Dr. Kitson Clark cited it in his Ford lectures in Oxford. (Dr. Kitson Clark; *The Making of Victorian England,* 1962). Does this make it into a historical fact? Not, we think, yet. Its present status, we suggest, is that it has been proposed for membership of the select club of historical facts. It now awaits a seconder and sponsors. It may be that in the course of the next few years we shall see this fact appearing first in footnotes, then in the text, of articles and books about nineteenth century England, and that in twenty or thirty years time it may be a well-established historical fact. Alternatively, nobody may take it up, in which case it will relapse into the limbo of unhistorical facts about the past from which Dr. Kitson Clark has gallantly attempted to rescue it. What will decided which of these two things will happen? It will depend, we consider, on whether the thesis or interpretation in support of which Dr. Kitson Clark cited this incident is accepted by other historians as valid and significant. Its status as a historical fact will turn on a question of interpretation. This element of interpretation enters into every fact of history. We are allowed a personal reminiscence? When we studied ancient history in this university many year ago, we had as a special subject 'Greece in the period of the Persian Wars'. We collected fifteen or twenty volumes on our shelves and took it for granted that there, recorded in these volumes, we had all the facts relating to our subject. Let us assume interesting.

brilliant, but remote from the main stream of history. Now, half-way through the twentieth century, the danger is the opposite one, that of giving science to much credit for good or ill in the tremendous and disturbing changes, the wars and revolutions, that this century has already witnessed. It is no accident that the revolutions in science and society should occur together, but it would be too simple a view to make either one the consequence of the other. It was very nearly true that the interactions have been far more subtle and reciprocal, and their disentangling will be the main task of the remaining chapters of this book. What need to be sought out, a every major turn of events, are the social and economic forces that have helped to determine the general directions and speeds of scientific advance, and conversely, the points at which scientific discoveries have come to modify profoundly the course of economic and even political events. (S.H. pp. 703-04). And those volumes contained all the facts about it that were then known, or could be known. It never occurred to us to inquire by what accident or process of attrition that minute selection of facts, out of all the myriad facts that must once have been known to somebody, had survived to become the facts of history. We suspected that even today one of the fascinations of ancient and medieval history is that it gives us the illusion of having all the facts at our disposal within a manageable compass: the nagging distinction between the facts of history and other facts about the past vanished, because the few known facts are all facts of history. As Bury, who had worked in both periods, said, 'the records of ancient and medieval history are starred with lacunae'. (J.B. Bury, *Selected Essays*; Bombay; 1930; p. 52). History has been called an enormos jig-saw with a lot of missing parts. But the main trouble does not consist in the lacunae. Our picture of Greece in the fifth century B.C. is defective not primarily because so many of the bits have been accidentally lost, but because it is,by and large, the picture formed by a tiny group of people in the city of Athens. We know a lot about what fifth-century Greece looked like to an Athenian citizen; but hardly anything about what it looked like to a Spartan, a Corinthian, or a The ban-not to mention a Persian, or a slave or other non-citizen resident in Athens. Our picture has been preselected and predetermine for us, not so much by accident as by people who were conciously or unconciously facts which supported that view worth preserving. In the same way, when we read in a modern history of the middle ages that the people of the middle ages were deeply concerned with religion, we wonder how we know this, and whether it is true. What we know as the facts of medieval history have almost all been selected for us by generations of chroniclers who were professionally occupied in the theory and practice of religion, and who therefore thought it supremely important, and recorded everything relating to it, and not much else. The picture of the Russian peasant as devontly religious was destroyed by the revolution of 1917. The picture of medieval man as devoutly religious, whether true or not, is indestructible, because nearly all the known facts about him were preselected for us by people who believed it, and wanted others to believe it, and a mass of other facts, in which we might possibly have found evidence to the contrary, has been lost beyond recall. The dead hand of vanished generations of historians, scribes, and chroniclers has determined beyond the possibility of appeal, the pattern of the past. 'The history we read, writes Professor Barraclough, himself trained as a medievalist, 'though based on facts, is, strictly speaking, not factual at all, but a series of accepted judgements'. (G. Barraclough, *History in a Changing World;* London; 1955; p. 14). But now we turn to the direction of our study towards the modern historians. The ancient or medieval historian may be grateful for the vast winnowing process which, over the years, has put at his disposal a menageable corpus of historical facts. As Lytton Strachey said, in his mischievous way, 'ignorance is the first requisite of the historian, ignorance which simplifies and clarifies, which select and omits.' (Lytton Strachey, *Preface to Victorians*; London). When we tempted to someone in writing ancient and medieval history, we find consolation in the reflexion that they are so competent mainly because they are so ignorant of their subject. The modern historian enjoys none of the advantages of this built-in ignorance. He must cultivated this necessary ignorance for himself *'Word'* the more so the nearer he comes to his own times. He has the dual task of discovering the few significant facts and turning them into facts of history, and of discarding the insignifcant facts as unhistorical. But this is the very converse of the nineteenth century hereby that history consists of the compilation of a maximum number of irrefutable and objective facts. Anyone who succumbs to this hereby will either have to give up history as a bad job, and take to stamp-collecting or some other form of antiquarianism, or end in a madhouse. It is this hereby which during the past hundred years has had such devastating effects on the modern historian, producting in Germany, in Great Britain, and in the United States, a vast and growing mass of dry-as-dust factual histories, of minutely specialized monographs of would-be historians knowing more and more about less and less, sunk without trace in an ocean of facts. It was, we suspect, this hereby is a shinning 'Light' within every one of us, but we do not see that *'Light'* now. When we close our eyes we see only darkness within. Why do we not see that 'Light'? Because in the process of creation, the soul, in its descent, became embedded and extangled with the mind to such an extent that the mind prevents the 'Light' of the soul from shinning through. This is because, having come from the *'Father'* to the level of creation, the soul as forgotten the creator. And the mind, being attached to the creation and its sensual pleasures, has collected a lot of sins, or *Karmas* or actions, during many past lifetimes. This has clouded the mind to such an extent that it has become an impenetrable covering over the soul rather than the alleged conflict between liberal and Catholic loyalities a veil of darkness, which prevents us from enjoying or seeing the *'Light'*. The veil of darkness is composed of the sins we have committed in our past births. That is why Christ says, 'Repent ye: for the kingdom of heaven is at hand' and "the kingdom of God is with you". The *'Father'* is not to be seen outside. He is within every one of us, but before we can see *'Him'* within we have to repent, in order to remove that veil of darkness. Repent for what? Just after taking birth, a child has not done anything in this world to repent for, so why can he not see the *'Father'* within himself? Because he has done something in his past lives, so he has to repent for all the *Karmas* he has been carrying from birth to birth, (*L.O.S.J.* pp. 12-13), which frustrated Acton as a historian. In an early essay he said of his teacher Dollinger: 'He would not write with imperfect materials, and to him the materials were always imperfect' (Quoted in Gp. Gooch, *History and Historian in the Nineteenth Century;* London; p. 355) After sometimes Acton said of Dollinger that 'it was given him to form his philosophy of history on the largest induction every available to man'. (*History of Freedom and Other Essasy;* Londone; 1907; p. 435). Acton was surely here pronouncing an anticipatory verdict on himself, on that strange phenomenon occupant the Regius Chair of Modern History in this University has ever had *'Word'* but who wrote no history. And Acton wrote his own epitaph, in the introductory note to the first volume of the *Cambridge Mordern History* published just after his death in the *'Nam'*, when he lamented that the requirements pressing on the historian 'threaten to turn him from a man of letters into the compiler of an encyclopedia" (*Cambridge Modern History,* Vol.6 Xfore; 1902. p. 4). Something had gone wrong. What had gone wrong was the belief in this untiring and unending accumulation of hared facts as the foundation of history, the belief that facts, a belief at that so unquestioning that few historians then thought it necessary, *Dharamdas* became more and more restless, neglected his business and wondered about in search of the *Sadhu* until all his wealth was exhausted and the family was reduced to poverty. At last he became desperate and went to the bank of the Ganges to drown himself. Then the Sadhu appeared on the scene "why did you not reveal yourself to me earlier?" *Dharamdas* asked the *Sadhu* Because I am not a fly on a lump of sugar." replied the Sadhu. Dharamdas remembered his wife's remark, prostrated himself at the feet of the *Sadhu* and some still think it unnecessary today and became his devoted disciple. After becoming Kabir's disciple, Dharmdas underwent a transformation so fundamental that ultimately, it is said, he became one of his master's successors to ask themselves the question 'What is history? (*K.G.M.* pp. 26-27). The nineteenth century fetishism of facts was completed and justified by a fetishism of documents. The documents were the Ark of the Covenant in the temple of facts. The reverent historian approached them with bowed head and spoke of them in awed tones. If you find it in the documents, it is so. But what, when we get down to it, do these documents from the Orthodox view point, with his frank rejection of institutional religion and external observances, Kabir was a heretic. He denounced the whole appratus of Hindu and Muslim piety decrees, the treaties, the rent-rolls, the blue books, the official correspondence, the private letters and diaries the temple, the mosque, the priest, the scriptures tell us? No document can tell us more than what the author of the document thought as of the little consequence of God -realization. Repeatedly, he proclaimed that he was neither a Hindu nor a Muslim, but he is a *Schedule Caste.* (Ibid. p. 7), what he thought had happened, what he thought ought to happen or would happen, or perhaps only what he wanted others to think he thought, or even only what he wanted others to think he, or even only what he himself thought he thought. None of this means anything until the historian has got to work on it and deciphered it. The facts, whether found in document or not, have still tobe processed by the historian before he can make any use of them: the use he makes of them is, if we may put it that way, the processing process. Let we illustrate what we are trying to say an example which we happen to know well. When Gustav Stresemann, the Foreign Minister of Weimar Republic, died in 1929, he left behind him an enormous mass saints tell us that we have been wandering for untold ages. We have been born in the vegetable kingdom, in the animal kingdom, as birds of the air and as fish of the waters. We have been born as human beings as well, and have then gone to lower species again in the hierarchy of creation. We have stored in our minds all the past experiences 300 boxes full every thought that has passed through our minds, every act we have performed of papers, official, semi-official, and private, nearly all relating to the six years of his tenure of office as Foreign Minister this friends and relatives naturally thought that a monument should be raised to the memory of so great a man. His faithful secretary Bernhard got to work; and within three years there appeared three massive volumes of some 600 pages each, of selected documents from the 300 boxes, with the impressive title *Stresemanns Vermachtxis*. In the ordinary way of documents themselves would have mouldered away in some cellar or attic and disappeared for ever; or perhaps in a hundred years or so some curious scholar would have come upon them and set out to compare them with Bernhard's text. What happened was far more dramatic. In 1945 the documents fell into the hands of the British and American Governments, who photographed the lot and put the photostats at the disposal of scholars in the Public Record Office in London and in the National Archives in Washington, so that, if we have sufficient patience and curiosity, we can discover exactly what Bernhard did. What stresemann died, his western policy seemed to have been crowned with a series of brilliant successes and yet we know nothing of the consequences of our thoughts and actions (*Ibid.*. p. 106). Locarno, the admission of Germany to the League of Nations, the Pawes and Young plans and the American loans, the withdrawal of allied occupation armies from the Rhineland. This seemed the important and rewarding part of Stresemann's foreign policy; and it was not unnatural that it should have been over-represented in Bernhard's selection of documents. Stresemanns eastern policy, on the other hand, his relations with the Seviet Union, seemed to have led nowhere in particular; and since masses of documents about negotiations which yield only trivial results were not yet interesting and added nothing to Stresemann's reputation, the process of selection could be more rigorous. Stresemann in fact devoted a far more constant and anxious attention to relations with the Soviet Union, and they played a far larger part in his foreign policy as a whole surmise. But the Bernhard volumes compare favourably, we suspect, with many published collections of documents on which the ordinary historian implicity relies. This is not the end of our story. Shortly after the publication of Bernhard's volumes, Hitler came into power. Stresemann's name was consigned to oblivion in Germany, and the volumes disappeared from circulation: many, perhaps most, of the copies must have been destroyed Today *Stresemanns Vermachtni* is a rather rare book. But in the West Stresemann's reputation stood high. In 1935 and English publiser brought out an abbreviated translated of Bernhard's work, Kabir uses the most incisive of shock methods to arouse us from our stupor of ignorance and superstition. These methods reflect the tumult of his times, when people of all religious were subject to orthodoxy demanding outward observances and were susceptible to charlatans promising salvation through relics, rites and rituals. But though times have changed, humanity really has not a selection from Bernhard's selection; perhaps one-third of the original was omitted. Sutton, a well-known translator from the German, did his job competently and well. The English version, he explained in the preface, was slightly condensed, but only by the omission of a certain among of what, it was felt, was more empheral matter '*Word*' or '*Nam*' of little interest to English readers or students (Gustav Stresemann, *his diaries, Letters* and *Papers*, i. Bombay, 1935, Editor's Note). We still have the same propensity for rituals and lazy thinking, making Kabir's wit and biting humar equally relevant today (Ibid. p. 40). This again is natural enough. But the result is that Stresemann's eastern policy, already under-represented in Bernhard, recedes still further from view, and the Soviet Union appears in Sutton's volumes merely as an occasional and rather unwelcome intruder in Stresemann's predominantly western foreign. Yet it is safe to say that, for all except a few specialists Sutton and not Bernhard greed not be confined to wealth. In India, we are greedy for large families. We must have sons and grandsons, daughter and granddaughters, son-in-law and daughters-in-law, grandsons-in-law and granddaughters-in-law, uncles and aunts, nephews and nices. They are supposed to add to our glory. But what a glory Our palatial mansions are in continuous turmoil, peace and quite are impossible, and bickering and squabbles, quarrels and skirmishes, spite and jealosy are an accepted part of life. What opportunity can there be for peace and quite contemplation of the lord in such circumstances? Of course, the routine rituals of a big house are carried out and still less the documents themselves the priest gets his daily coin, the gods get a few flowers represents for the western world the authentic voice of Stresemann. Had the documents perished in 1945 in the bombing, and had the remaining Bernhard volumes disappeared, the authenticity and authority of Sutton Sultan would naver have been questioned. Many printed collections of documents, gratefully accepted by historians in default of the originals, rest on no securer basis than this all quite devoid of real devotion. (*K.GM* . p. 127). But we want to carry the story one step further. Let us forget about Bernhard and Sutton, and be thankful that we can, if we choose, consult the authentic papers of a leading participant in some important events of recent European history. What do the papers tell us? Among other things they contain records of some hundreds of Stresemann's conversations with the Soviet Ambassador in Berlin and of a score or so with Chicherin. These records have one feature in common. They depict Stresemann as having the lion's share of the conversations and real his arguments as invariably well put and cogent, while those of his partner are for the most part scanty, confused and unconvincing. This is a familiar characteristic of all records of diplomatic conversations. The documents do not tell us what happened, but only what Stresemann thought had happened, or what he wanted others to think, or perhaps what he wanted himself to think, had happened. It was not Sutton or Bernhard, but Stresemann himself, who started the process of selection. And, if we had, say, Chicherin's records of these same conversations, we should still learn from them only what Chicherin thought, and what really happened would still have to be reconstructed in the mind of the historian. Of course, facts and documents are essential to the historian. But do not make a fetish of them. They do not by themselves history; they provide in themselves no ready-made answer to this tiresome question 'What is history?' At this point we should like to say a few words on the question why nineteenth-century historians were generally indifferent to the philosophy of history. The term was invented by Voltaire, and has since been used in different senses; but we shall take it to mean, if we use it at all, our answer to the question, 'What is history? The nineteenth century was, for the intellectuals of Western Europe, a comfortable period exuding confidence and optimism. The facts were on the whole satisfactory; and the inclination to ask and answer awkward questions about them was correspondingsly weak. Ranke piously believed that divine providence would take care of the meaning of history, if he took care of the facts; and Burckhardt, with a more modern touch of cynicism, observed that 'we are not initiated into the purposes of the eternal wisdom? Professor Butterfield as late as 1931 noted with apparent satisfaction that 'historians have reflected little upon the nature of things, and even the nature of their own subject'. (H. Butterfield; *The Whig Interpretion of History;* Bombay; 1931; p. 67). But our predecessor in these lectures, Dr. A.L. Rowse, more justly critical, wrote of Sir Winston Churchills *World Crisis* the way of the world is vigorous activity and ceaseless talk his book about the First World War activity for getting honour and position, and talk to the same end. The mystic wants none of these and knows where they lead. *Saint James speaks very strongly concerning the troubles that can be caused by an unbridled tongue: 'For in many things we offend all. If any man offend not in word, the same is a perfect man, and able also to bridle the whole body. Behold, we put bits in the horses' mouthes, and they may obey us; and we turn about their whole body. Behold also the ships, which though they be so great, and are driven of fierce winds, yet are they turned about with a very small helm, whithersoever the governor listeth. Even so the tongue is a little member, and boasteth great things. Behold, how great a matter a little fire kindleth! And the tongue is a fire, a little fire kindleth! And the tongue is a fire, a world iniquity: so is the tongue among our members, that it defileth the whole body, and setteth on fire the course of nature; and it is set on fire of hell. For every kind of beasts, and of birds, and of serpents, and of things in the sea, is tamed, and hath been tamed of mankind: But the tongue can no man tame; it is unruly evil, fully of deadly poison.*

*Saints* instruct us not only to avoid indulging in slander and petty talk overselves, but also to avoid hearing the slander of others. We become party the slandes when we give ear to it, and contradicting slander leads only to worthless disputations. Saints therefore advise us to get away from such company. *Nivrittinata* says, "We should shut out mouth on hearing slander and mediate on God".

Sants even instruct us to avoid hearing our own praise or the praise of others. Why is this so? Hearing our own praise leads to feeding our own ago, which is harmful spiritually. When we see or hear anything praiseworthy, we must raise our hands in thanks to the Lord and sing his glory. All greatness is his. All praise belongs to the lord. Nivrittinath says on this subject:

*We should never hear our own praise,*
*And when anyone praises us*
*We should merge our consciousness*
*Inwards, in God*

Mysticism demands perfect stillness and invincible repose of the body, the mind and the soul. It involves no running about, no going to temples or pilgrimages, no heated discourse, no sharp-brained discussions. Kabir saw the spiritual worlds with his spiritual eyes and described them to the extent that they could be described in material language. But, most of what mystics experience cannot be described, so they are sometimes accused of being secretive. Saints would like the World to know everything, but they cannot tell everything for important reason his book about the First World War, the world is not prepared to know these things. Vijaydasa explains:

The devotees of God are like fire
covred with ashes;
If seen, they are uncouth
And difficult to approach.
They meditate on God within,
They remain in the company of seekers,
They remain in the Company of virtues;
Their talk and behaviour is uncommon.
They mix not with the deceitful.

Disciples are not allowed to reveal their spiritual experiences. This has led to confusing mysticism with mystery. But disciples are ordered to keep silent for two important reason: first, the revelation of inner spiritual experiences may pamper the desciples' vanity and thus prevent their further progress and second, the world does not believe in such revelatioins and only makes mockery of them. Christ warned his disciples against revealing inner secrets, saying: "Give not that which is holy unto the dogs, neither cast ye your pearls before swine, lest they trample them under their feet, and turn again and rend you", that, while it matched Trotsky's *History of the Russian Revolution* in personality, vividness, and vitality, it was inferior in one respect: It has 'no philosophy of history behind it.' (A.L Rowse, *The End of an Epoch; Mecico;* 1947; pp. 282-3). British historians refused to be drawn, not because they believed the history had no meaning, but because they believed that its meaning was implicit and self evident. The liberal nineteenth-century view of history had a close affinity with the economic dectrine of *laissez-faire 'Word'* also the product of a serene and self-confident outlook on the world. Let everyone get on with his particular job, and the hidden hand would take care of the universal hormony. The facts of history were themselves a demonstration of the supreme fact of a beneficent and apparantly *'Infiniti progress'* towards higher things. This was the age of innocence, and historians walked in the Garden of Eden, without a scrap of philosophy to cover them, naked and unashamed before the god of history. Since then, we have known Sin and experienced a Fall; and those historians who today pretend to dispense with a philosophy of history are merely trying, vainly and self-consciously, like memebrs of a nudist colony, to recreate the Garden of Eden in their garden suburb. Today the awkward question can no longer be evaded. During the fast fifty years a good deal of serious work has been done on the question 'What is history? It was from Germany, the country which was to do so much to upset the comfortable reign of nineteenth-century liberalism, that the first challenge came in 1880s and 1890s to the doctrine of the primacy and autonomy of facts in history. The philosophers who made the challenge are now little more than names: Dil they is the only of the them who has recently received some belated recognition in Great Britain. Before the turn of the century for any attention to be paid to heretics who attacked the cult of facts. But early in the new century, the torch passed to Italy, where Croce began to profound a philosophy of history which obviously owed much of German masters. All history is 'contemporary history', declared Croce: 'The content of this celebrated aphorism is as follows: 'The practical requirements which underline every historical judgement give to all history the character of "contemporary history", because, however remote in time events thus recounted may seem to be, the history in reality refers to present needs and present situations wherein those events vibrate". (B. Croce, *History as the Story of Liberty; English Tr; London; 1941; p. 19*). The contemporary history is consisted essentially in seeing the past through the eyes of the present and in the light of its problems, and that the main work of the historian is not to record, but to evaluate: for, if he does not evaluate, how can he know what is worth recording? In 1910 the American historian, Carl Becker, argued in deliberately provacative language that the facts of history do not exist for an historian till he creates them. (*Atlantic Monthly;* Atlantic; 1910, October, p. 528). These challenges were for the moment little noticed. It was only after 1920 the Croce began to have a considerable vogue in France and Great Britain. This was not perhaps because Croce was a subtler thinker or a better sylist than his German predecessors, but because, after the First World War, the facts seemed to smile on us less propitiously that the years before 1914, and we were therefore more accessible to a philosophy which sought to diminish their prestige. C roce was an important influence on the Oxford philosopher and historian Collingwood, the only Britisher thinker in the present century who has made a serious contribution to the philosophy of history. He did not live to write the systematic treatise he had planned, but his published and unpublished papers on the subject were collected after his death in a volume entitled *'The Idea of History'*; which appeared in 1945. The views of collingword can be summarized as follows. The philosophy of history is concerned neither with 'the past by itself' nor with, 'the historian's thought about it by itself', but with 'the two things in their mutual relations'. This dictum reflects the two current meanings of the word *history* '*Word' or 'Nam'* the inquiry conducted by the historian and the series of past events into which he inquires. 'The past which a historian studies is not a dead past, but a past which in some sense is still living in the present'. But a past act is dead, i.e. meaningless to the historian, unless he can understand the thought that lay behind it. Hence 'all history is the history of thought', and 'history is the re-enactment in the historians mind of the thought whose history he is studying' the reconstitution of the past in the historian's mind is dependent on empirical evidence. But it is not in itself an empirical process, and cannot consist in a mere recital of facts. On the contrary, the process of reconstitution governs the selection and interpretation of the facts: this, indeed, is what makes them historical facts. *'History'*, says Professor Oakeshott, who on this point stands near to Collingwood, 'is the historian's experience. It is "made" by nobody save the historian: to write history is the only way of making it.' (M. Oakeshott, *Experience and Its Modes;* London; 1933; p. 99). This searching critique, though it may call for some serious reservations, brings to light certain neglected truths, i.e., *'Chamar', Barwala, Megh, Tarkhan, Doma, Batwal, Jat, Candala, etc.*

In the first place, the facts of history never come to us pure', since they do not and cannot exist in a pure form: they are always refracted through the mind of the recorder. It follows that when we take up a work of history, our first concern should be not with the facts which it contains but with the historian who wrote it. Let us take as an example the great historian in whose honour and in whose name these lectures were founded. G.M. Trevelyan, as he tells us in his autobiography, was 'brought up at home on a some what exuberantly whig tradition'. (G.M. Trevelyan; *An Autobiography,* New York; 1949; p. 11). And he would not we hope, disclaim the title if we described him as the last and not the least of the great English liberal historians of the Whig tradition. It is not for nothing that he traces back his family tree, through the great Whig historian George Otto Trevelyan, to Macaulay, incomparably the greatest of the Whig historians. Trevelyan's finest and maturest work, *England under Queen Anne,* was written against that background, and will yield its full meaning and significance to the reader only when read against that background. The author, indeed, leaves the reader with no excuse for failing to do so. The historian starts with a provisional selection of facts, and a provisional interpretetion in the light of which that selection has been made men and women throughout the world today are searching, perhaps more earnestly than ever before for the basic truths of life and the ultimate meaning of human existence. Many are longing for certainty in a world where it often seems that the only certain thing is uncertainty. 'For change along is constant', as the poet says. In the Wester countries of today particularly, life seems to contain everything by others as well as by himself. As he works both the interpretation and the selection and ordering of facts undergo subtle and perhaps partly unconscious changes through the reciprocal action of one or the other. And this reciprocal action also involves reciprocity between present and past, since the historian is part of the present and the facts belong to the past. The historian is part of the present and the facts belong to the past. The historian and the facts of history are necessary to another. The historian without his facts is rootless and futile; the facts without their historian are dead and meaningless. Therefore, our first answer to the question 'What is history?' is that it is a continous process of interaction between the historian and his facts, an unending dialogue between the present and past except meaning. Inspite of his intellectual and scientific advancement, the modern man is still groping in the dark in so far as spiritual matters are concerned and does not know where to seek the light. Modern man has found that material progress, however, useful it may be, does nothing to satisfy his deeper aspirations. And largely as a result of scientific progress, man today is troubled and unhappy, and lives in fear rather than in hope as he looks towards the future Man's knowledge of the visible material world has increased to an almost unimaginable extent, but his knowledge of the invisible worlds of the spirit is less, perhaps, than in any previous period of history. Right-minded persons in all countries today are troubled by the crumbling of traditional values, the spiritual disorientation and the moral degradation seen in the present-day world, and are striving to find dependable spiritual values for themselves. For even in this twentieth-century materialistic and scientific world, men and women still feel that they have souls. But this feeling by itself is of little practical help. Those who are touched with spiritual longing still ponder the question: What shall we do to find souls. (Joseph Leeming; *Yoga And The Bible*; Punjab (India); Ninth Edition 2004; pp. 1-2. Hereafter cited as Y.B.) The question which comes first *Chamar* society or the individual *'World'* is like the question about the hen and the egg. Whether you treat it as a logical or as a historical question, you can make no statement about it, one way or the other, which does not have to be corrected by an opposite, and equally one-sided, statement. Society and the individual are inseparable; they are necessary and complementary to each other, not opposites. 'No man is an island, entire of itself', in Donn's famous words: 'every man is a piece of the continent, a part of the main'. (Donne; *Devotions Upon Emergent Occasions;* No. XVii). That is an aspect of the truth. On the other hand, take the dictum of J.S. Mill, the classical individualist: 'Men are not, when brought together, converted into another kind of substance'. (J.S. Mill; *A System of Logic*, vii.1). Of course not. But the fallacy is to suppose that they existed, or had any kind of substance, before being 'brought together'. As soon as we are born, the world gets to work on us and transforms us from merely biological into social units. Every human being at every stage of history or pre-history is born into a society and from his earliest years is moulded by that society. The language which he speaks is not an individual inheritance, but a social acquisition from the group in which he grows up. Both language and environment help to determine the character of his thought; his earliest ideas come to him from others. As has been well said, the individual apart from society would be both speechless and mindless. The lasting fascination of the Robinson Crusoe myth is due to its attempt to imagine an individual independent of society. The attempt breaks down. Robinson is not an abstract individual, but an English man from York, he carried his Bible with him and prays to his tribal God. The myth quickly bestows on him his Man Friday; and the building of a new society begins. The other relevant myth is that of Kirilov is Dostoyevsky's *Devils* who kills himself in order to demonstrate his perfect freedom. Suicide is the only perfectly free act open to individual man, every other act involves in one way or another his membership of society Durkheim, in his well-known study of suicide, coined the word *anomie* to denote the condition of the individual isolated from his society *'chamar'* a state especially conducive to emotional disturbance and suicide; but he also showed that suicide is by no means independent of social conditions. It is commonly said by anthropologists the primitive man is less individual and more completely moulded by his society than civilized man. This contains an element of Truth. Simpler societies are more uniform in the sense that they call for, and provide opportunities for, a far smaller diversity of individual skills and occuptions than the more complex and advanced societies. Increasing individualization in this sense is a necessary product of modern advanced society, and runs through all its activities from top to bottom. But it would be a serious error to set up an antithesis between this process of individualization and the growing strength and cohension of society. The development of society and the development of individual go hand in hand, and condition each other. Indeed what we mean by a complex or advance society is a society in which the inter-dependence of individuals on one another has assumed advanced and complex forms. It would be dangerous to assume that the power of a modern national community to mould the character and thought of its individual members, and to produce a certain degree of conformity and uniformity among them, is any less than that of a primitive tribal community. The old conception of national character based on biological differences has long been exploded; but differences of national character arising out of different national backgrounds of society and education are difficult to deny. That elusive entity (human nature' has varied so much from country to country and from century to century that it is difficult not to regard it as a historical phenomenon shaped by prevailing social conditions and conventions. There are many differences between, say, Americans, Russians and Indians. But some, and perhaps the most important, of these differences take the form of different attitudes to social relations between individuals, or in other words, to the way in which society should be constituted, so that the study of differences between American, Russian, and Indian society as a whole may well turn out to be the best way of studying differences between individual Americans, Russians and Indians. Civilized man, like primitive man, is moulded by society just as effectively as society is moulded by him. You can no more have the egg without the hen than you can have the hen without the egg. It would have been unnecessary to dwell on these very obvious truths but for the fact that they have been obscured for us by the remarkable and exceptional period of history from which the western world is only just emerging. The cult of individualism is one of the most pervasive of modern history myths. According to the familiar account in Burckhardt's *Civilization of the Renaissance in Italy,* the second part of which is subtitled 'The Development of the Individual, the cult of the individual began with the Renaissance, when man, who had hitherto been 'conscious of himself only as a member of a race, people, party, family, or corporation, at length 'became a spiritual individual and recognised him as much.' Later the cult was connected with the rise of capitalism and of Protestantism with the beginnings of the Industrial Revolution, and with the doctrines of *Laissez-faire*. The rights of man and the citizen proclaimed by the French revolution were the rights of the individual. Individualism was the basis of the great nineteenth-century philosophy of utilitarianism. Morley's essay *on compromise*, a characteristic document of Victorian liberlism, called individualism 'the religion of human happiness and well-being'. Rugged individualism' was the keynote of human progress. This may be a perfectly sound and vaild analysis of the ideology of a particular historical epoch. But what we want to make clear is that the increased individualization which accompanied the rise of the modern world was a normal process of advance civilization. A social revolution brought new social groups to position of power. It operated, as always, through individuals and by offering fresh opportunities of dividual development; and, since in the early stages of capitalism the units of production and distribution were largely in the hands of single individuals, the ideology of the new social order strongly emphasized the role of individual initiative in the social order. But the whole process was a social process representing a specific stage in historical development, and cannot be explained interms of a revolt of individuals against society or of an emancipation of individuals from social restraints. Many signs suggest that, even in the western world, which was the focus of this development and of this ideology, this period of history has reached its end. We need not insist here on the rise of what is called mass democracy, or on the gradually replacement of predominantly individual by predominantly collective forms of economic production and organization. But the ideology generated by this long and fruitful period is still dominant force in Western Europe and throughout the English-speaking countries. When we speak in abstract terms of the tension between liberty and equality, or between individual liberty and social justice, we are apt to forget that fights do not occur between abstract ideas. These are not struggles between individuals as such and society as such, but between groups of individuals in society, each group striving to promote social policies favourable to it and to frustrate social policies inimical to it. Individualism, in the sense no longer of a great social movement but of false opposition between individual and society, has become today the slogan of an interested group and because of it controversial character, a barrier to our understanding of what goes on in the world. We have nothing to say against the cult of the individual as a protest against the perversion which treats the individual as a means and society or the state as the end. But we shall arrive at no real understanding either of the past or of the present if we attempt to operate with the concept of an abstract individual standing society. And this brings us at last to the point of my long digression. The common sense view of history treats it as something written by individuals about individuals. This view was certainly taken and encouraged by nineteenth century liberal historians, and is not in substance incorrect. But it now seems over-simplified and inadequate, and we need to probe deeper. The knowledge of the historian is not his exclusive individual possession:men, probably, of many generations and of many different countries have participated in accumulating it. The men whose actions the historian studies were not isolated individuals acting in a vacuum: they acted in the context, under the impulse, of a past society. In our last lecture we described history in the present and the facts of the past. We now want to inquire into the relative weight of the individual and social elements on both sides of the equation. How far are historians single individuals, and how far products of their society and their period? How far are the facts of history facts about single individual and how far social facts? The historian, then, is an individual human. Like other individuals, he is also a social phenomenon, both the product and the concious or unconscious spokesman of the society to which he belongs; it is in this capacity that he approaches the facts of the historical past. We sometimes speak of the course of history as a 'moving procession'. The metaphor is fare enough, provided it does not tempt the historian to think of himself as an eagle surveying the scene from a lonely crag or as a V.I.p. at the saluting base. Nothing of the kind! The historian is just another dim figure trudging along in another part of the procession. And as the procession winds along, swerving now to the right and now to the left, and sometimes doubling back on itself, the relative positions of different parts of the procession are constantly changing, so that it may make perfectly good sense to say, for example, that we are nearer today to the middle ages than were our great-grandfathers a century ago, or that the age of Caesar is nearer to us than the age of Dante. New vistas, new angles of vision, constantly appear as the procession men and women throughout the world today are searching, perhaps more earnestly than ever before for the basic truths of life and the ultimate meaning of human existence many are longing for certainty in a world where it often seems that the only certain thing is uncertainty 'For change alone is constant', as the poet says. In the western countries of today particularly, life seems to contain everything and the historian with it except meaning. In spite of his intellectual and scientific advancement, the modern man is still groping in the dark in so far as spiritual matters are concerned, and does not know where to seek the light moves along. The historian is part of history. The point in the procession at which he finds himself determines his angle of vision over the past (*Y.B. p. 1*). This truism is not less true when the period treated by the historian is remote from his own time. When we studied ancient history, the classics on the subject were the 'supreme Father's love and power are boundless, and the purpose of his divine plan is to bring back to their original home those who have become ready to return as a result of their experience on earth. This return can be achieved only with the help and guidance of a living master. Accordingly, as part of the diuin plan, there have always been on earth one or more living masters, to whom mankind and probably still are the prodigal sons of God. Grote's *History of Greece* and Mommsen's *History of Rome* could turn for help (Ibid. p. 4). Grote, an enlightened radical banker writing in the 1840s, emboided the aspirations of the rising and politically progressive. British middle class in an idealized picture of Athenian democracy, in which pericles figured as a Benthamite reformer and Athens acquired an empire in a fit of absence of mind. It may not be fenciful to suggest that Grote's neglect of the problem of slavery in Athens reflected the failure of the group to which he belonged to face the problem of the new English factory working class. Mommsen was a German liberal, disillusioned by the muddles and humiliations of the German revolution on 1848-49. Writing in the 1850's every religion has two aspects the decade which saw the birth of the name and concept of *Realpolitik* the outer or exoteric, and the inner or esoteric. The history of religions shows us that in the beginning each one centred about a spiritualised *God-man* or *Master*, one who was in close and constant unity with God. To him was given the mission of preaching the doctrine, and the power of bringing his followers into touch with the inner reality, of teaching them how they could rise up, enter the kingdom of heaven, and commune with their creator. This esoteric form of the teachings continued as long as the Master or his spiritually advanced successors were on the earth to teach and guide spiritual seekers. But when the leadership passed into the hands of those who were less spiritually advanced, and lost the spiritual presence and power of God-man who was the original preception, the path lost the power of giving its followers directed and conscious contact with their creator. Thereafter, by degrees it became largely a matter of creeds, dogmas, prayers, rites and ceremonies. Entering the kingdom of heaven then became largely a hope that might be realised after death, rather than a definite and vital experience here and now, made possible by the spiritual power of the living master. But there always are living masters in the world, revealing the true spiritual way. There are such masters even today, pointing out, with their divine power, the inner or esoteric path to those interested. (Y.B. pp. 16-17). Mommsen was imbued with the sense of need for a strongman to clear up the mess left by the failure of the German people to realise its political aspirations; and we shall never appreciate his history at its true value unless we realize that his well-known idealization of Caesar is the product of this yearning for the strong man to save Germany from ruin, and that the lawyer-political Cicero, that ineffective chatterbox and slippery procrastinator, has walked straight out of the debates of the Paulikirche in Frankfurt in 1848. Indeed, we should not think it an outrageous paradox if someone were to say the Grote's *History of Greece* has quite as much to tell you today about the thought of the

English philosophical radicals in 1840s as about Athenian democracy in the fifth century B.C. or that anyone wishing to understand what 1848 did to the German liberals shold take Mommsen's *History of Rome* as one of his textbooks. Nor does this diminish their stature as great historical works. We have no patience with the fashion, set by Bury in his inaugural lecture, of pretending that Mommsen's greatness rests not on his *History of Rome* but on his corups of inscriptions and his work on Roman constitutional law: this is to reduce history to the level of compilation. Great history is written precisely when the historians vision of the past is illuminated by insists into the problems of the present. Surprise has often been expressed that Mommsen failed to continue his history beyond the fall of the republic. He lacked neither time, nor opportunity, nor knowledge. But, when Mommsen wrote his history, the strong man had not yet arisen in Germany. During his active career, the problem of what happened once the strong man had taken over was not yet actual. Nothing inspired Mommsen to project this problem back on to the Roman scene; and the history of the empire remained unwritten. It would be easy to multiply examples of this phenomenon among modern historians. In our last lecture we paid tribute to G.M. Trevelyan's *England Under Queen Anne* as a monument to the wing tradition in which he had been reared. Let us now consider the imposing and significant achievement of one whom most of us would regard as the greatest British historian to emerge on the academic scene the First World War: Sir Lewis Namier. Namier was a true conservative *'Word'* not a typical English conservative who when scratched turns out to be 75 percent (%) a liberal, but a conservative such as we have not seen among British historians for more than a hundred years. Between the middle of the last century and 1914 it was scarcely possible for a British historian to conceive of historical change except as change for the better. In the 1920s, we moved into a period in which change was beginning to be associated with fear for the future, and could be thought of as change for the worse a period of the rebirth of conservative thinking. Like Acton's liberalism, Namier's conservatism derived both strength and profudity from being rooted in a continental background. It is perhaps worth remarking that the only other considerable conservation British writer of the period between the wars, Mr. T.S. Elliot, also enjoyed the advantage of a non-British background; nobody brought up in Great Britain before 1914 could wholly escape the inhabiting influences of the liberal tradition. Unlike influences of the liberal tradition. Unlike Fisher or Toynbee, Namier had no roots in the nineteenth-century liberalism, and suffered from no nostalgic regrets for it. After the First World War and the abortive peace had revealed the bankruptcy of liberalism, the reaction could come only in one of two forms *'Word'* socialism or conservatisim. Namier appeared as the conservative historian. He worked in two chosen fields, and the choice of both was significant. In English history he went back to the last period in which the ruling class had been able to engage in the rational pursuit of position and power in an orderly and mainly static society. Somebody has accused Namier of taking mind out of history. The original criticism in an anonymous article in *the Times*

*Literary Supplement* of 28 August 1953 on 'The Namier view of History', ran as follows: Darwin was accused of taking mind out of the universe, and Sir Lewis has been the Darwin of political history *'Word'* in more senses than one'. Then Darwin made another scientific revolution; and social scientists taking their cue from biology, began to think of society as an organism. But the real importance of the Darwinian revolution was the Darwin, completing what lyell had already begun in geology, brought history into science. Science was concerned no longer with something static and timeless, as las as 1874, Bradley distinguished science from history as being concerned with the timeless and 'abiding'. (F.H. Bradley, *Collected Essays*, Bombay; 1935, i, p. 36). but with a process of change and development. Evolution in science confirmed and complemented progress in history. Nothing, however, occured to alter the inductive view of historical method which we described in our first lecture: first collect your facts, then interpret them. It was assumed without question that this was also the method of science. This was the view which Bury evidently had in mind when, in the closing words of his inaugural lecture witnessed a strong reaction against this view of history. Collingwood, when he wrote in the 1930s, was particularly anxious to drew a sharpline between the world of nature, which was the object of scientific inquiry, and the world of history; and during this period Bury's dictum was rarely quoted except in terms of derision. But what historians failed to notice at the time was that science itself had undergone a profound revolution, which makes it seems that Bury may have been more nearly right than we had supposed, though for the wrong reason. Why Lyell did for geology and Darwin for biology has now been done for astronomy, which has become a science of how the universe came to be what it is ; and modern physicists constantly tell us that what they investigate are not facts, but events. The historian has some excuse for feeling himself more at home in the world of science today than he could have done a hundred years ago. When we were very young, we were suitably impressed to learn that appearances not withstanding, the whole is not a fish. Nowadays these questions of classification move one less; and it does not worry us unduly when we were assured that history is not a science. This terminological question is an eccentricity of the English language. In every other European language, the equivalent word to 'science' includes history without hesitation. But in the English speaking world this question has a long past behind it, and this issues raised by it are a convenient introduction to the problems of method in history. At the end of the eighteenth century, when science had contributed so triumphantly both to man's knowledge of the world and to man's knowledge of his own physical attributes, it began to be asked whether science could not also further man's knowledge of society. The conception of the social sciences, and of history among them, gradually developed throughout the nineteenth century; and the method by which science studied the world of nature was applied to the study of human affairs. In the first part of this period the Newtonian tradition prevailed. Society, like the world of nature, was thought of as a mechanism; the title of a work by Herbert Spencer, *Social Statics*, published in 1851, is still remembered. Bertrand Russell reared in this tradition, later recalled the period when he hoped that in time there would be 'a mathematics of human behaviour as precise as the mathematics of machines. (B. Russel; *Portraits of Memory*; Bombay; 1958; p. 20). It is not perhpas a very fortunate pharse, but one can see the point which the critic was trying to make. Politics at the accession of George III were still immune from the fanaticism of ideas, and of that passinate belief in progress, which was to break on the world with the French revolution and usher in the century of triumphant liberalism. No ideas, no revolution, no liberalism: Namier chose to give us a brilliant portrait of an age still safe those who long to become *chelas,* or disciples of a true spiritual master, are the seekers. If they succeed in finding a genuine. Master their search will be at an end, for the Master will show them the way to the eternal light of God. The master, moreover, will be a living master, one who walks the earth today, followed and loved and worshipped by his disciples, as was Jesus some two thousand years ago. For a living master is needed to set the disciple's feet on the path. In the past the search for a genuine master was purposely made more difficult that it is today. Disciples were accepted only after the most severe tests. Now the masters have modified this policy. During recent years they have accepted practically all who have applied for initiation, unless their *Karmas* or actions though not to remain safe for long their deeds in earlier lives from all these dangers have been too evil. This is partly because there are many more seekers today whohave reached the point of being ready for the path (Y.B. p. 9) or let us take a distinguished example nearer home. In the iconoclastic 1930s, when the liberal part had just been snuffed out as an effective force in British politics, Professor Butterfield wrote a book called *The Whig Interpretation of History*, whiel enjoyed a great and deserved success. It was remarkable book in many ways the fact that the spiritual work of the Masters is an exact science is quite difficult for some in the west to grasp, accustomed as they are to thinking of religion and spirituality as matters of faith and belief of alone. But the readers for whom this book is intended will find that the Master's science contains the inner essence and truth of every extent world religion. And it gives its followers not only hope for the future, but positive certainity and present realization. This is possible because the masters are not mere preachers, but may accurately be described as super-scientists are totally unaware, and they use laws to hasten the spiritual development of their disciples. (Y.B.p. 13). Not least becasue, though it denounced the Whig interpretation over some 130 pages, it did not (so far as we can discover without the help of an index) name a single Whig except Fox, who was not historian, or a single historian save Acton, who was no Whig H. Butterfield, *The Whig Interpretation of History* (New York; 1931; on p. 67) the author confesses to 'a healthy sort of distrust' of disembodied reasoning'. But anything that the book lacked in detail and precision it made up for in sparkling invective. The reader was left in no doubt that the whig interpretation was a bad thing; and one of the charges brought against it was that it 'studies the past with reference to the present'. On this point Professor Butterfield was categorical and severe: The study of the past with one eye, so to speak, upon the present is the source of all sins and sophistries in history, of the *'Word'*. It is the essence of what we mean by the word 'unhistorical' (H. Butterfield; *Interpretation of History The Whig;* New York; 1931, pp. 11, 31-32). Twelve years elapsed. The fashion for iconoclasm went out. Professor Butterfield's country was engaged in a war often said to be fought in defence of the constitutional liberties embodied in the Whig tradition, under a great leader who constantly invoked the past 'with one eye, so to speak, upon the present'. In a small book called *The Englishman and His History* published in 1944, Professor Butterfield not only decided that the Whig interpretation of history was the 'English' interpretation, but spoke enthusiastically of 'the Englishman's alliance with his history and of the 'marriage between the present and the past'. (H. Butterfield, *The Englishman and His History,* New York; 1944; p. 2, 4-5). To draw attention to these severals of outlook is not an unfriendly criticism. It is not our purpose to refute the proto-Butterfield with the deutero-Butterfield sober. We are fully aware that, if anyone took the trouble to peruse some of the things wrote before, during and after the war, he would have no difficulty at all in convincing us of contraditions and inconsistencies at least as glaring as any we have detected in others. Indeed we are not sure that we should envy any historian who could honestly claim to have lived through the earth shaking events of the past fifty years without some radical modifications of his outlook. Our purpose is merely to show how closely the work of the historian mirrors of the society in which he works. It is not merely the events that are in flux. The historian himself is in flux. When we take up a historical work, it is not enough to look for the author's name on the title page: look also for the date of publication or writing to understand the work of the Masters and the ultimate purpose and goal of human life, it is necessary to have at least an outline knowledge of the structure of the great universe of universe of universes, of which the physical universe is but the lowest, darkest, and smallest part. This information, as taught by the great Saint and masters of the east, is given briefly here. (Y.B. p. 19). It is something even more revealing the philosopher is right in telling us that we cannot step into the same river twice, it is perhaps equally true, and for the same reason, that two books cannot be written by the same historian. And, if we move for a moment from the individual historian to what maybe called broad trends in historical writing, the extent to which the historian is the product of his society becomes all the more apparent. In the nineteenth century, British historian with scarcely an exception regarding the course of history as a demonstration of the principle of progress; they expressed the ideology of a society in a condition of remarkably rapid progress. History was full of meaning for British historian's as long as it seemed go be going our way; now that it has taken a wrong turning, belief in the meaning of history has become a heresy. After the First World War, Toynbee made a desperate attempt to replace a line ear view of history by a cyclical theory in every instance, the esoteric teaching is not a man-made one, but a God-made one. For in each instance the founders of religions and the genuine. Masters have taught, not their own doctrine, but the doctrine or system of him who sent them to this world. And this is the age-old natural and perfect system designed by the Creator for the express purpose of liberating man from the bondage of the body and mind and enabling him to enter and enjoy the kingdom of heaven here and now as well as in the future. It is only the living masters who can show us how to do this here and now, however, while all religion point to the hope of it after death the characteristic ideology of a society in decline. Marcus Aurelius in the twilight of the Roman Empire consoled himself by reflecting 'how all things that are now happening have happened in the past and will happen in the future' (To *Himself*, X, p. 25); as is well known, Toynbee too the idea from spengler's *Decline of the West.* Since Toynbee's failure, British historians have for the most part have content to throw in their hands and declare that there is no general pattern of history at all. A banal remark by Fisher to that effect in *Preface* dated, 4 December 1934, to *A History of Europe,* has achieved almost as wide a popularity as Ranke's aphorism in the last century. If anyone tells me that the British historians of the last thirty years experienced this change of heart as the result of profound individual reflexion and of the burning of midnight oil in their separate garrets, we shall not think it necessary to contest the fact. But we shall continue to regard all this individual thinking and oil-burning as a social phenomenon, the product and expression of a fundamental change in the character and outlook of our society since 1914. There is no more significant pointer to the character of a society than the kind of history its writers or fails to write. Geyl, the Dutch historian, in his fascinating monograph translated into English under the title *Nepolean For and Against,* shows how the successive judgements of Franch nineteenth-century historians on Napolean reflected the changing and conflicting patterns of French political life and thought throughout the country. The thought of historians, as of other human beings, is moulded by the environment of the time and place. Acton, who fully recognised this truth shought for an escape from it in history itself. History (he wrote) must be our deliverer not only from the undue influence of other times, but from the undue influence of our own, from tyranny of environt and the pressure of the air we breathe. (Acton, *Lecturers on Modern History*; 1906; p. 33). This may sound to optimistic an assessment of the role of history. But we shall venture to believe that the historian who is most conscious of his own situation is also more capable of transcending it, and more capable of appreciating the essential nature of the differences between his own society and outlook and those of other periods and other countries, than the historian who loudly protests that he is an individual and not a social phenomenon. Man's capacity to rise above this social and historical situation seems to be conditioned by the sensitivity with which he recognises the extent of his involvement in it. In our first lecture we said: Before you study the history study the historian. Now we would add: Before our study the historian study his historical and social environment. The historian, being an individual, is also a product of history and of society; and it is in this twofold light that the student of history must learn to regard him. Let us now leave the historian and consider the other side of our equation *'Radha Soami'* disciples the facts of history and there are many of them in the light of the same problem. Is the object of the historian's inquiry the behaviour of individuals or the action of social forces? Here we are moving on to well-ground When Sir Isaiah Berlin published few years ago a sparkling and popular essay extitled *Historical Inevitability* who have advanced some distance on the path and having many times gone with the master into the higher, heavenly worlds, have expressed how these spiritual journeys reveal the masters dual nature. The following description of this experience is adapted from the book *With a Great Master in India*: Looking at the master as a mere man, such disciples say, one can form no conception of his true greatness. But when one travels with him on the path that passes upward through the heavenly regions, then say it is no uncommon sight to witness hundreds of thousands of souls, all radiant in their own light, but all the following him and worshipping him in loving adoration disciples who have made these journeys add that the throngs that attend the master in the heavenly realms run even into millions of souls. And the higher up one goes with him, the greater he is seen to be. He is literally and truly the *'King of Kings'* in all the regions of light and pure spirituality. But returning to earth again, he says never a word about these frequent journeys, and appears among his disciples simply as a loving, patient father ministering to his little children. It is from dwelling so continually in the higher worlds that the masters have the highest spiritual knowledge and are able to transmit it. They teach what they have learn, not on hearsay or from book learning, but through first hand personal experience. As Jesus said: '*Verily, Verily, I say unto thee, we speak that we do know, and testify that we have seen.' (John 3:11) (Y.B. p. 61).* What we shall call the Bad King John of history at first glance there may seem to be no connection between the two quotations given above. Both statements, however, refer to the same great truth the view that what matters in history is the character and behaviour of individuals the *'Word'* of God, which in essence is the might y outpouring stream of boundless love, life and power emanating without ceasing from the *'Supreme Creator'* of the universe. The *'Word'* of God is, and always has been the most important factors in the teaching of masters has a long pedigree of the teachings of Jesus as well as of the masters of today. It is mentioned under different names in the scriptures of all the great world religions mentioned, though its meaning has been known to but few of the followers of these religions. The Hindu scriptures call it *Anahat Shabd,* or the *Unstruck Music,* and also *AkashBani, the Celestial voice.* Mohammedans call it *Kalma or Word* and *Kalam-i-Ilahi* or *'Voice of God'*. Zoroaster speaks of it as *Sraosha,* meaning 'the sound from the sky. The early Greek philosophers who had learned the spiritual secrets of *'India'*, refer to it as the *'Logos'*, while some called it the music of the spheres. Socrates speaks of it as an *'Inner Sound'* that transported him to realms of transcendent and divine beauty. The masters of today call it *'Nam'* meaning *'Name'* or *'Word'* (of God); and also *Shabd* (Pronounced *Shubud),* which means Sound, or more particularly, spiritual sound. In the English language the *'Word'* is called the sound current or the *'Audible Life Stream'*. These names are given to it- because the *'Word'*, which is God in dynamic action, can be heard by human beings whose inner ear has been opened by a Perfect Master the ability to hear the 'Sound current is given by the master to each disciple at the time of initiation. The light of the current of the *'Word'* can also be seen by a master's disciples. For the primal manifestations of the Supreme Father to human beings appear in the form of *'Inner Light and Sound'*, both of which are inherent in and emanate from the 'Sound current'. The fact that the *'Word'* is audible is one of the most vital of all facts to the disciple. For when he hears the sacred and sublime music of the *'Sound current'*, he hears God himself. The Audible life stream 'unspoken language', and His 'unwritten Word'. The term *'Sound Current'* is new to most western readers, and because of this fact, its identity with familiar terms used in the Bible must be made abundantly clear. The *'Sound Current'* is the *'Holy Spirit'* or *'Holy Ghost'* are used, they refer to the *'Sound Current'* or the *'Word'*. In this book also, the terms are used inter changeably (*Ibid.* pp. 33-34). The desire to postulate individual genius as the creative force in history is characteristic of the primitive stages of historical consciousness. The ancient Greeks liked to label the achievements of the past with the names of eponymous heroes supposedly responsible for them, to attribute their epics to a bad called Homer, and their laws and institutions to a lycurgus or a Solon. The same inclination reappears at the Renaissance, when Plutarch, the biographer-moralist, was much more popular and influential a figure in the classical revial than the historians of antiquity. In this country, in particular, we all learned this theory, so to speak, at our mother's knee; and today we should probably recognise that there is something childish, or at any rate childlike, about it. It had some plausibility in days when society was simpler, and public affairs appeared to be run by a handful of known individuals. It clearly does not fit the more complex society of our times; and the birth in the nineteenth century of the new science of sociology was a response to this growing complexity. Yet the old tradition dies hard. At the beginning of this century, 'history is the biography of great men' was still a reputable dictum. Only ten years ago a distinguished American historian accused his colleagues, perhaps not too seriously, of the 'mass murder of historical characters' by treating them as 'puppets of social and economic forcies. (*American Historical Review, Lvi,* No.1 (January 1951), p. 279). Addicts of this theory tend nowadays to be shy about it; but, after some searching, we found an excellent contemporary statement of it in the introduction to one of Miss Wedgwood's books. *The behaviour of men as individual (she writes) is more interesting to us than their behaviour as groups or classes. History can be written with this bias as well as another; it is neither more, nor less, misleading 'Word'. This book 'Nam' is an attempt to understand how these men felt and why, in their own estimation, they acted as they did (C.V. Wedgood; The King's Peace;* Bombay; 1955; p. 17). This statement is precise; and since Miss Wedgwood is a popular writer, many people, we are sure, think as she does. Dr. Rowse tells us, for instance the Elizabethan system broke down because James we were incapable of understanding it, and that the English revolution of the seventeenth century was an 'accidental' event due to the stupidity of the two first stuart kings. (A.L Rowse, *The England of Elizabeth;* Bombay, 1950, pp. 261-62, 382). It is fair to point ouf that in an earlier essay Mr. Rowse condemned 'historians who think that the Bourbons failed to re-established the monarchy in France after 1870 just because of Henry V's attachment to a little white flag'. (*The End of an Epoch;* 1949, p. 275). It is believed perhaps reserves such personal explanation for English history. Even Sir James Neale, a more austere historian than Dr. Rowse, sometimes seems more eager to express his admiration for Queen Elizabeth than to explain that the Tudor monarchy stood for; and *Sir Isaiah Berlin*, in the essay which we have just quoted, is terribly worried by the prospect that historians may fail to denounce Genghis Khan and Hitler as bad men. (I. Berlin; *Historical Inevitability;* New York; 1954; p. 42). The Bad King John and Good Queen Bess theory is especially rife when we come to more recent times. It is easier to call communism 'the brain child of Karl Marx' (we pluck this flower from a recent stockbrokers circular) than to analyse its origin and character, to attribute the Bolsehvik Revolution to the stupidity of Nicholas II or to German gold than to study its profound social causes, and to see in the two world wars of this century the result of the individual wickedness of Wilhelm II and Hitler rather than of some deep-seated breakdown in the system international relations. Miss Wedgwood's statement, then, combines two propositions. The first is that the behaviour of men as individual is distinct from their behaviour as members of groups or classes, and that the historian may legitimately choose to dwell on the one rather than on the other. The second is that the study of the behaviour of men as individuals consists of the study of the conscious motives of their actions. After what we have already said, we not labour the first point. It is not that the view of man as an individual is more or less misleading than the view of him as a member of the group; it is the attempt to draw a distinction between the two which is misleading. The individual is by definition a member of a society, or probably of more than one society how long ago the descent of the soul took place, history does not record, for the life span of the historical civilizations known to us is very brief, a matter of some five or six thousand years; But the master, whose knowledge of human history on this earth extends over a far longer period, say that many individuals who are now on earth have been coming here in different forms for many millions of years. We came down through the higher-worlds and finally came into this world. But once here, we became absorbed in the fascinating panorama of the show and lost all recollection of our Father. The masters sometimes compare us with a child who goes to a fair holding onto his father's hand, but lets go of the father's hand and wanders happily on looking at the many attractions of the fair, even hoping that his father will not find him to take him home call it group; class, tribe, nation, or what you will. (Y.B. p. 75-6). Early biologist were contented to classify species of birds, beasts, and fishes in cages, aquariums, and showcases, and did not seek to study the living creature in relation to its environment. Perhaps the social science today have not fully emerged from that primitive stage.

Some people distinguish between psychology as the science of the individual and sociology as the science of society, and the name 'psychologisim' has been given to the view that all social problems are reducible to the analysis of individual human behaviour. But the psychologist who failed to study the social environment of the individual would not get very far. Modern psychologist have none the less been convicted of this error: 'Psychologists as a group have not treated the individual as a unit in a functioning social system, but rather as the concrete human being sho was then conceived as proceeding to form social systems. They have thus not adequately taken account of the peculiar sense in which their categories are abstract'. (Professor Talcott Parsons in the Introduction to Max Weber, *The Theory of Social and Economic Organization;* New York; 1947. p. 27). It is tempting to make a distinction between biography; which treats man as an individual, and history, which treats man as part of a whole, and to suggest that good biography makes bad history. 'Nothing causes more error and unfairness in man's view of history', Acton once wrote, 'than the interest which is inspired by individual characters'. (*Home and Foreign Review,* January 1863; p. 219). But this distinction too, is unreal. Nor do we want to take shelter behind the victorian proverb placed by G.M. Young on the title-page of his book *Victorian England* : 'Servants talk about peopled, gentlefolk discuss things'. This idea was elaborated by Herbert Spencer in his most solemn style in *The Study of Sociology*, Chapter 2: 'If you want roughly to estimate anyone's mental calibre, you cannot do it better than by observing the ratio of generalities to personalities in his talk to obtain knowledge of God we must necessarily go to one who knows God's science and is himself proficient in it. It is only the person who has a conscious experience or realization of God who can impart God-knowledge. Within the Master there is the one great power of God, and through him human beings can reach that power. Inwardly, the master is at one with the universal spirit, and is entrusted with the missionof bringing individuals into direct contact with God. (Y.B. p. 61). How far simple truths about individuals are replaced by truths abstracted from numerous experiences of men and things. And, when you have thus measured many, you find but a scattered few likely to take anything more than a biographical view of human affairs. Some biographies are serious contributions to history: in our own field, Isaac Deutscher's biographies of Stalin and Trotsky are outstanding examples. Others belong to literature, like the historical nove. 'To Lytton Strachey', writes Professor Trevor-Roper, historical problems were always, and only, problems of individual behaviour and individual eccentricity *'Nam'* or *'Word'*. Historical problems, the problems of politics and society, he never sought to answer, or even to ask'. (H.R. TrevorRoper; *Historical Essays;* London; 1957; p. 281) Nobody is obliged to write or read history; and excellent books can be written about the past which are not history. But we think we are entitled by convention complete surrender to the will of the most is the ultimate test of real discipleship. One who does not so surrender himself is not a disciple but a rebel, not a soldier but a mutineer. Kabir calls upon his disciples to surrender themselves to the master as a *pativrata,* a chaste and faithful wife, surrenders herself to her husband. The word *Pativrata* must be explained, as it has no exact equivaent in the English language. It refers to much more than physical chastity as we propose to do in these lectures it connotes complete physical, intellectual, moral, and spiritual surrender to one's husband. Of course, the husband is also bound by similar lofty duties towards his wife and children to reserve the word 'history' for the process of inquiry into the past of man in society, (*K.G.M.* pp. 157-58). The second point i.e that history is concerned to inquire why individuals in their own estimation, acted as they did, seems at first sight extremely odd; and we suspect that Miss Wedgwood like other sensible people does not practise what she preacher. If she does, she must write some very queer history. Everyone knows today that human beings do not always, or perhaps even habitually, act from motives of which they are fully conscious or which they are willing to avow; and to exclude insight unconscious or unavowed motives is surely a way of going about one's work with one eye wilfully shut. This is, however, what, according to some people, historians ought to do. The point is this. So long as you are contented to say that the badness of King John consisted in his greed or stupidity or ambitioin to play the tyrant, you are speaking in terms of individual qualities which are comprehensible even at the level of nursery history. But, once you begin to say that King John was the unconscious tool of vested interests opposed to the rise of power of the feudal barons, you not only introduce a more complicated and sophisticate view of King John's badness, but you appear to suggest that historical events are determined not by the conscious actions of individuals, but by some extraneous and all-powerful forces guide the unconscious will. This is, of course, nonsense. So far as we are concerned, we have no belief in *'Divine Providence,' 'World Spirit'* Manifest Destiny'. *History* with a capital H, or any other of the abstractions which have sometimes been supposed to guide the course of events; and we should endorse without qualification the comment of Marx: History does nothing, it possesses no immense wealth, fights no battles. It is rather *man*, real living *man* who does everything, who possesses and fights. (Marx-Engls; *Gesamtausgabe,* i, iii, p. 625). The two remarks which we have to make on this question have nothing to do with any abstract view of history, and are based on purely empirical observation. The first is that history is to a considerable extent a matter of numbers. Carlyle was responsible for the unfortunate assertion that 'history is the biography of greatmen'. But listen to him at his most eloquent and in his greatest historical work: *Hunger and nakedness and nightmare oppression lying heavy on twenty-five million hearts: this, not the wounded varities or contradicted philosophies of philosophical advocates, rich shopkeepers, rural noblesse, was the prime mover in the French Revolution; as the like will be in all such revolutions, in all countries (Carlyle); History of the French Revolution;* III, chapter 1.) Or, as Lenin said: 'Politics begin where the masses are; not where there are thousands, but where there are millions, that is where serious politics begin'. (Lenin; *Selected Works;* vii, p. 295). Carlyle's and Lenin's millions were millions of individuals:

there was nothing impersonal about them. Discussions of this question sometimes confuse anonymity with impersonality. People do not cease to be people, or individuals to individuals because we do not know their names. Mr. Eliot's 'vast, impersonal forces' were the individuals whom Clarendon, a bolder and franker conservative, calls 'dirty people of no name'. (Clarendon, *A Brief View & Survey of the Dangerous & Pernicious Errors to Church & State in Mr. Hobbes's Book entitled Leviathan; London; 1676; p. 320*). These nameless millions were individuals acting more or less unconscioulsy, together, and constituting a social force. The historian will not in ordinary circumstances need to take cognizance of a single discontented peasant or discontented village. But millions of discontented peasants in thousands of villages are a factor which no historian will ignore. The reasons which deter Jones from getting married do not interest the historian unless the same reasons also deter thousands of other individual of Jones's generation, and bring about a substantial fall in a marriage-rate: in that event, they may well be historically significant. Nor need we be perturbed by the platitude that movements are started by minorities. All effective movements have few leaders and a multitude of followers; but this does not mean that the multitude is not essential totheir success. Numbers count in history. Our second observation is even better attested writers of many different schools of thought have concurred in remarking that the actions of individuals human beings often have results which were not intended or desired by the actors or indeed by any other individual. The Christian believes that the individuals, acting consciously for his own often selfish ends is the unconscious agent of God's purpose. Mandeville's 'private vices-public benefits' was an early and deliberately paradoxical expression of this discovery. Adam Smith's hidden hand and Hegel's 'cunning of reason', which sets individuals to work for it and to serve its purposes though the individuals believe themselves to be fulfilling their own personal desires, are too familiar to require quotation. 'In the social production of their means of production' wrote Mark in the preface to his *Critique of Political Economy*, 'human beings enter into definite and necessary relations which are independent of their will'. 'Man lives consciously for himself', wrote Tolstoy in *War and Peace,* echoing Adam Smith, 'but is an unconscious instrument in the attainment of the historic universal aims of humanity'. (L. Tolstoy; *War and Peace; IX, Chapter* 1. Oxford). And here, to round off this anthology; which is already long enought, is Professor Butterfiled: 'There is something in the nature of historical events which twists the course of history in a direction that no man ever intended? (H. Butterfield; *The Englishman and His History;* Bombay 1944; p. 103). Since 1914, after a hundred years of only minor local wars, we have had two major world wars. It would not be a plausible explanation of this phenomenon to maintain that more individuals wanted war, or fewer wanted peace, in the first half of the twentieth century than in the last three quarters of the nineteenth. It is difficult to believe that any individual willed or desired the great economic depression of the 1930s. Yet it was indubitably brought about by the actions of individuals, each consciously pursuing some totally different aim. Nor does the diagnosis of a discrepancy between the intentions of the individual and the results of his action always have to wait for the retrospective historian. 'He does not mean to go to war', wrote Lodge of Woodrow Wilson in March 1917',' but we think he will be carried away the events'. (Quoted in B.W. Tuchman, *The Zimmerman Telegram;* New York; 1958; p. 180). It defies all the evidence, to suggest that history can be written on the basis of 'explanation in terms of human intentions'. (The phrase is quoted from 1. Berlin, *Historical Inevitability;* Bombay 1954; p. 7). It appears that the writing of history in these terms displays to be commended or of accounts of their motives given by the actors themselves, of why 'in their own estimation, they acted as they did'. The facts of history are indeed facts about individuals, but not about actions of individuals performed in isolation, and not about the motives, real or imaginary, from which individuals suppose themselves to have acted. They are facts about the relations of individuals to one another in society and about the social forces which produce from the actions of individuals results often at variance with, and sometimes opposite to, the results which they themselves intended. One of the serious errors of Collingwood's view of history which we discussed in our last lecture was to assume that the thought behind the act, which the historian was called on to investigate, was the thought of the individual actor. This is a false assumption. What the historian is called on to investigate is what lies behind the act; and to this the conscious thought or motive of the individual actor may be quite irrelevant. Here we should say something about the role of the rebel or dissident in history. To set up the popular picture of the individual in revolt against society is to reintroduce the false anti-thesis between society and the individual. No is fully homogeneous. Every society is an arena of social conflicts, and those individuals who range themselves against existing authority are no less products and reflexions of the society than those who uphold it. Richard II and Catherine the great represented powerful social forces in the England of the fourteenth century and in the Russia of the eighteenth century: but so also did Wat Toyler and Pugachev, the leader of the great serf rebellion. Monarchs and rebels alike were the product of the specific conditions of their age and country. To describe Wat Toyler and Pugachev as individuals in revolt against society is a misleading simplification. If they had been merely that, the historian would never have heard of them. They owe their role in the history to the mass of their followers, and are significant as social phenomena, or not at all. Or let us take an outstanding rebel and individualist at a more sophisticated level. Few people have reacted more violently and more radically against the society of their day and country than Nietzsche. Yet Nietzsche was a direct product of European, specifically of German, society whoever studies and practises this science with the help and guidance of a properly qualified teacher, will receive increasing confirmation of the existence of God and the truth of his own divinity through his own first-hand experience. The science of the Masters is thus an empirical science, based on verification through personal experience. It methods are exact and its results uniform. In all ages of the world, among all races and in all countries, all who follow its methods achieve exactly the same results. The fact that the spiritual work of the masters is an exact science is quite difficult for some in the west to grasp, accustomed as they are to thinking of religion and spirituality as a matter of faith and belief alone. But the readers for whom this book is intended will find that the Master's science contains the inner essence and truth of every extent world religion. And, it gives its followers not only hope for the future, but positive certainty and present realization. This is possible because the masters are not mere preachers, but may accurately be described as super-scientists. They have knowledge of laws of which the material scientists are totally unaware and they use these laws to hasten the spiritual development of their disciples or *Sikhs*. (*Y.B. p. 13*). A phenomenon which could not have occurred in China or Peru. A generation after Nietzsche's death it became clearer than it had been to his contemporaries how strong were the European, and specifically German, social forces of which this individual had been the expression; and Nietzsche became a more significant figure for prosperity than for his own generation. The role of the rebel in history has some analogies with that of the great man. The great-man theory of history to the mass of mankind, the gateway to this vast universe of higher worlds is locked and impenetrable, for they wish to hear nothing of it. But for those who are ready for the path, the gate is automatically opened. For the Master holds the key which is the *'Word'* a particular example of the Good Queen Bess School the link between man and his Creator has gone out of fashion in recent years, though it still occasionally rears its ungainly head. And he offers it to all who qualify. But rightly using the key, the mortal man can unlock the gate and enter the path that leads ever upward, through all the universe of higher, finer worlds, to the regions of immortality. Then, indeed, does he experience the greatest good fortune that can come to any man. (Ibid. p. 142). The editor of a series of popular history text-books, started after the second world war, invited his authors 'to open up a significant historical theme by way of a biography of a great man', and Mr. A.J.P. Taylor told us in one of his minor essays that the history of modern Europe can be written in terms of three titans: Napoleon, Bismarck, and Lenin'. (A.J.P. Taylor, *From Napoleon to Stalin;* Bombay; 1950; p. 74). It appears though in his more serious writings he has undertaken no such rash project. What is the role of the great man in history? The great man is an individual, and, being an outstanding individual, is also a social phenomenon of outstanding importance. 'It is an obvious truth', observed Gibbon, ' that the times must be suited to extraordinary characters, and that the genius of Cromwell or Retz might now expire in obscurity.' (Gibbon; *Decline and Fall of the Roman Empire;* Chapter; IXX) Marx, in *The Eighteenth Brumaire of Louis Bonaparte* diagnosed the converse phenomenon: 'the class war in France created circumstances and relations which enabled a gross mediocrity to strut about in a hero's garb'. Had Bismarck been born in the eighteenth century the progress of the physics, after the group of discoveries just referred to, was halted by the First World War, which brought to an abrupt end the first heroic period of modern physics. The war drew some scientists, but by no means the majority, into war service;

but even where it did not, it effectively held up, except in neutral countries, the purely scientific research of the non-mobilized experimental scientists. The theoretical scientists for the most part, however, went on working, and it is in that period that one of the greatest advances in the history of human thought took place an absurd hypothesis, since he would not then have been Bismarck the completion by Einstein in 1915 of the *general theory of relativity.* Now relativity belongs in essence which more to the science of the nineteenth than to that of the twentieth century. The keynote of twentieth-century science was discontinuity and atomism; relativity, on the other hand, is still a continuum and field theory; but the fields of relativity are far more generalized than the electro-magentic fields of Maxwell. They are the new fields of space and time. The special theory of relativity which Einstein put forward in 1905 had shown that, as only relative motion could be observed, space and time were to a certain extent interchangeable, depending on the movement of an observer. Ten years later Einstein was able to bring the hitherto arbitrary and occult force of gravitation into the generalized picture of space and time, but to do this he had to break away not only from the mechanics of Newton, but from the still more firmly based geometry of Euclid. Relativity, for all its popular vogue, is still a theory very difficult to grasp. Its importance in science however, depends on two closely linked relationships: the equivalence of mass and energy, and the special limiting character of the velocity of light. The first of these, expressed in the formula $E=mc^2$, where E stands for energy, m for mass, and C for velocity of light, was to provide the theoretical expression of the enormous energies locked in the atom. These were afterwards shown to be the sources of all the concentrated energy in the universe an absurd hypothesis, since he would not then have been Bismark the energy of the sun and the stars, those first nuclear-energy piles. The sun warms us, in fact, by getting lighter, burning up its hydrogen into helium, a form of fire which the successors of prometheus, undeterred by the fate, are bring down from heaven in the form of the hydrogen bomb. The limiting character of the velocity of light is an equally significant fact. By showing that all velocities are relative Einstein was also able to explain that, inspite of continuous acceleration, no particle could travel faster than the critical velocity of light, for as it approached that velocity its energy and its mass increased simultaneously so that it became harder and harder to make it go faster. (*S.H.* pp. 742-43). He would not have united Germany and might not have been a great man at all. But one need not, we think, as Tolstoy does, decry great men as no more than 'labels giving names to events'. Sometimes of course the cult of the great man may have sinister implications. Nietzsche's superman is a repellent figure. It is not necessary for us to recall the case of Hitler, or the grim consequences of the 'cult of personality' in the Soviet Union. But it is not our purpose to deflate the greatness of great men: nor do we want to subscribe to the thesis that 'great men are almost always bad man'. The view which we would hope to discourage is the view which places great men outside history and sees them as imposing themselves on history in virtue of their greatness, as 'jack-in-the-boxes who emerge real continuity of history'. (V.G Childe; *History; Bombay*; 1947. p. 43). Even today we do not know that we can better Hegel's classic description: The great man of the age is the one who can put into words the will of his age, tell his age what its will is, and accomplished it. What he does is the heart and essence of his age; he actualizes his age. (Hegel; *Philosophy of Right;* English Tr. Bombay 1942; p. 295). Dr. Leavis means something like this when he says that great writers are 'significant in terms of the human awareness they promote' (F.R. Leavis; *The Great Tradition;* New York; 1948; p. 2). The great man is always representative either of existing forces or of forces which he helps to create by way of challenge to exist authority. But the higher degree of creativity may perhaps be assigned to those great men who, like Cromwell or Lenin, helped to mould the forces which carried them to greatness, rather than to those who, like Napoleon or Bismark, rode to greatness on the back of already existing forces. Nor should we forget those men who stood so far inadvance of their own time that their greatness was recognised only by succeeding generations. What seems to us essential is to recognise in the great man an outstanding individual who is at once a product and an agent of the historical process, at once the representative and the creator of social forces which change the shape of the world and the thoughts of men. History, then, in both senses of the word good thoughts and actions means good *Karma,* which reveals itself in the form of happiness or good fortune of various kinds meaning both the inquiry conducted by the historian and the facts of the past into which he inquires material, mental, or spiritual is a social process, in which individuals are engaged as social beings; and the imaginary antithesis between society and the individual is no more than a red herring drawn across our path to confuse our thinking in the same or in future lives. Bad thoughts and actions imply bad *Karma*, which must be paid for by experiencing equivalent unhappiness, pain or suffering (Y.B. pp. 105-106). The reciprocal process of interaction between the historian and his facts, what we have called the dialogue between present and past, is a dialogue not between abstract and isolated individuals, but between the society of today and the society of yesterday. History, in Burckhardt's words, is 'the record of what one age finds worthy of note in another (J. Burckhardt; *Judgements on History and on Historian*; Bombay; 1959; p. 158). The past is intelligible to us only in the light of the present to enable man to understand the society of the past, and to increase his mastery over the society of the present, is the dual function of history.

61. *R.T.* Vol.II. p. 7
62. *Ibid.*
63. **Note**. The *Smrticandrika* (1.pp. 198-99) quotes 26 verses on the worship of *Narayana* the last of which is the well-known verse *'dhyeyah sada savitrmandala 'Nam' madhyavarti, etc* and the same work (on *sraddha* p. 354) quotes a verse of Narada in which *Sunday* and *Sankranti* are mentioned that they used to assembled for *Satsang*. (*H.D.* Vol.1. p. 470)
64. R.T. Vol.II. p. 7
65. **Note.** It shows the *Nandiksetra*, the complex of sacred and profane

buildings which had gathered around the ancient temple of Siva Bhutesvara at *Buthiser* is meant here. "As the twon of *Bhutesa,* which had been destroyed by a conflagration, has quickly recovered its (former) splendour by the power of your order, thus O king *Uchchla*, may you restore to happiness and comfort this, your own city, which has been destroyed by the five fires of Kayasthas, (royal) relatives, (obnoxious) regulations (*'Word' Klpti*), ministers and solemn fasts (*prayopavesa*)*!"*. When Stein examined these ruins in August, 1891, we came across unmistatable signs of later restoration, executed with interior materials, especially in the first or western group of the temples. These repairs may well be attributed to *Uchchala* on the strength of our passage, no subsequent reference to a restoration of this kind being found in the *Rajatarangini* or the later Chronicles.

66. *R.T.* Vol.II. p. 7
67. **Note.** Vishnu-*Cakradhara* had an ancient shrine on the alluvial plateau or *Udar,* which lies on the left bank of the Vitasta, one mile below the town of Vijabror. The plateau bears to this day the name of *Tsakadar Udar*. Kalhana mentions frequent the temple and hill of *Cakradhara;* which also served in times of trouble as a fortified position. The *Nilamata,* 1170, mentions *Cakradhara* in the first place among the forms of Vishnu and gives a fragmentary account of the legend connected with this place of worship for the latter also *Haracar.* For a suggestion as to the exact position of the temple accounts for the great scarcity of stone remains now found on the northern extremity of the latter, which is detached from the rest of the plateau by a dip in the ground, Stein have found on a visit paid to the site in September, 1895, traces of a quadrangular enclosure, about forty yards square, marked by hollows in the ground. Could these hollows be the last indications of the wooden walls which enclosed the shrine?
68. **Note.** *Yogesa* is found as a name of Vishnu in the *Nilamata*, 1138. No temple dedicated to the god under this name is referred to elsewhere. But possibly the shrine named in our passage is identical with that of Vishnu *Yogasayin*, mentioned near the confluence of the *Vitasta* and *Sindhu*, there stands the temple of *Hrsikesa Yogasayin*.
69. **Note.** Regarding the worship of Agni *Svayambhu*, 'the self-created Fire,' at *Suyam*, or in the language of the villagers *Suyam,* is the name of a spot, situated half a mile to the South West of the village Nichahom, at the elevation of 74° 10′ longitude and 34° 22′ latitude in the Machipur Pargana, where Volcanic phenomena are observed in a shallow hollow formed between banks of clay and sand. In certain years vapours issue here from fissures of the ground, then sufficiently to boil the *Sraddha* offerings, which the pilgrims place there. When Stein visited the site in September, 1892, the phenomenon was said not to have taken place for the last fifteen years. But the soil of the hollow appeared even then bright red, like burned clay, and was furrowed by narrow fissures. Pt.Govind Kaul attended a pilgrimage to *Svayambhu* in the year 1876, when the symptoms were noticeable for about ten months. Vignc, *Travels, II.* p. 280, mentions occurrences of the phenonmenon at the beginning of the present century. For earlier reference, see *Ain-i-Akbari;* vol.II p. 365 also

compares with Lawrence, Kashmir *Valley;* pp. 42-43. The *Svayambhumahatmya* relates at length the legend how Siva (*Svayambhu*) at the request of the gods who were hard pressed by the *Asuras*, took there the incarnation of *Kalagnirudra.*

70. **Note.** The name of *Parihasapura* is preserved in that of the Pargana *Paraspor* which, as indicated on the Survey may, comprises the well-defined little tract lying between the marshes on the left bank of the *Vitasta* immediately to the South West of Shadipur. The identity of the names *Parihasapura* and *Paraspor* is evident on phonetic grounds, and was known to the authors of the Persian chronicles (Haidar Malik, Muhammad, 'Azim, Birabal Katsera). It cannot be doubted that we have to look among the ruins here described for the five great buildings which *Lalitaditya* erected at *Parihasapura.* They are named in the chronicle known as *Parihasakesava, Muktakesave, Mahavaraha, Govardhanadhara* and *Rajavihara.* The first four were temples dedicated to the worship of Visnu. The last as its name shows, was a Buddhist convent. Subsequently, in the account of the war between king *Harsa* and the pretender *Uchchala,* we read of the latter taking up a position at *Parihasapura*, which is rightly enough described as difficult of access owing to the steep slopes of the plateau and the water around. For the night *Uchchala* took his quarters in one of the quadrangles (*Catuhsala*). When the royal troops had stormed *Parihasapura,* the *Rajavihara* was burned down, as *Uchchala* was erroneously believed to have taken refuge in it. The silver image of Vishnu *Parihasakesava,* was subsequently carried away and broken up by King *Harsa.* A new statue of the god was put up by *Uchchala* after his conquest of the throne. The final destruction of the temples of *Parihasapura* is attributed by the Muhammadan chroniclers and *Abul-i-Fazl* to Sikandar Butshikast (1389-1413 A.D.). The latter author records a curious story about a Sanskrit inscription discovered on that occasion. Where the name *Parihasapura* is found in the later Sanskrit Chronicles it must be understood as referring to the district, the modern *Paraspor.* However, this may be, it is of interest to find that the *Paraspor* ruins, about which no tradition whatever can be traced at present, were yet, at a comparatively so recent time, generally attributed to Lalitaditya's buildings.
71. *R.T.* Vol.II. p. 7.
72. **Note.** After defeating the King of *Kanyakubja* in battle, that king of surpassing valour carried of his throne, the ensign of royal power.
73. **Note.** Regarding *Jayamati's* antecedents a dancing girl of the family of the female dancer *Kanasravati,* had adopted a girl of unknown origin called *Jayamati.*
74. *R.T.* Vol.II. p. 8.
75. *Ibid.*
76. *Ibid.*
77. **Note.** The verse here quoted is found in *Manusmrti* that Queen *Srilekha,* daughter of the illustrious *Yasomangala*, as her husband was of feeble power indulged in licentious conduct with somewhat. The variations are evidently due to Kalhana having quoted from memory. For the meaningless *daynascatah* we have to read, in accordance with the

original text, '*dayinahsathah,* as already suggested by Durgaparsad.

78. R.T. Vol. II. p. 8
79. *Ibid.*
80. *Ibid. Note.* The words in the first half -verse may alsobe taken as referring to a Vetala whom a magician (*sphurata*) binds by spells (*guna*), and subjects to his will, but who ultimately devours his master, as related in many an edifying story of the *Kathasaritsagara,* etc.
81. *Ibid.*
82. *Ibid.*
83. *Ibid.* p. 9.
84. **Note.** It appears that there are *samyavada*, perhaps *samyavadi* has to be corrected. Connected with *Sihrasa Rai* ruler of Sind dynasty of *Sudra* family Known by Durgaprsada.
85. R.T. Vol.II. p. 9.
86. **Note.** This musical party is still known to strolling players in Kashmir by beating pots is an accomplishments.
87. R.T Vol.II p. 9.
88. **Note.** *Bhurja* is the inner bark of the Himalayan birch (*Baetula Bhojpatr*), which has been used in Kashmir and in the adjoining hill regions as the general writing material (*bhurajapattra*) up to the 17th century A.D. Regarding its preparation for writing purposes, etc, compare this *report* with Prof. Buhler; pp. 29-30. Birch-bark is still largely used by village shopekeepers, *Patvaris* and others in Kashmir for keeping brief notes and accounts. The custom of writing with a white chalky paint on small blackboards of wood or slate has been duly noted by (Alberuni; *India*; vol. i, p. 182). It prevails to this day in Kashmir, as all over Northern India, among school-children and shopkeepers.
89. *R.T.* Vol.II. p. 9.
90. *Ibid.*
91. *Ibid.*
92. Term *Stavarajas* means 'Chief hymn', is the designation of panegyrical texts in praise of particular deifies such as are found in the *Mahabharata, Puranas* and other collections like *Bhismastavaraja, Mahapurusastavaraja* in the *Mahabharata,* the *Ganesastavaraja* in the *Bhavisyapurana*, etc.
93. **Note.** Term *Durgottarinividya*, 'the knowledge which helps across dangers' is perhaps the name of a tantric text, or probably another designation of the well known *Durgamahatmya* or *Devimahatmya.*
94. *R.T Vol.II* p. 10.
95. *Ibid.*
96. *Ibid.*
97. *Ibid.*
98. *Ibid.*
99. *Ibid.* p. 11.
100. **Note.** The anecdote which related with the Hindu law regarding deposits. The detailed references contained in the Smritis and other legal texts as to the means by which the peculation of deposits may be prevented, and as to the legal procedure in such suits, show how frequent cases similar to that related in our text must have been at all times. The law books

clearly indicate two different kinds of deposits, open or closed contrined in the *Manusmriti*, VIII, p. 185. King's decision based on VIII; pp. 150-156 as an evidence furnished by the new coins as to the merchant having treated the deposit as an open one. Having used the amount deposited for trade, purposes, the merchant is bound to pay interest for it just as if he had taken the money on loan. In the same way, the depositor is obliged to pay interest on the advances he had drawn from the merchant. Stratagems like the one employed by *Uchchala*, are recommended to the judge already by the Smritis in suits of this kind where direct proofs are not available.

101. **Note.** Learned *Bhatta Udbhata* as an *Alamkarika* or writer on poetics. His *alamkarasastra,* a short treatise, has been discovered by Prof. Buhler mention on Report; p. 65. The first question which presents itself, concerns the value of the term *Dinnara,* which we find almost invariably used or implied in Kalhana's monetary statements. This word, undoubtedly derived from the *denarius* of the West, is well known to Sanskrit lexicography as the designation of a gold-coin, usually spelt *dinara.* In this case term *dinara* or *dinnara* had to be taken in the general sense of 'coin' or 'money', was made quite evident by the passage, the fact underlying this poetically extravagant statement is that *Harsa* is the only later Kashmir king of whom authentic gold and silver pieces have hitherto been found. Here we have clearly the word *dinnara* in the sense of *mudra,* 'coin' distinctly given to it by the *Unadikosa.* As regards the second class of the passages we have important evidence from the Kalhana's *Rajatarangini* expresses '*dinnaranam dasasatim'* (ten hundred *dinnaras*). He again states that *dinnarah* means the same as *dyar* in Kashmir. The latter word is commonly used to this day in the sense as 'money', in particular, 'coined money' or 'cash'.
102. **Note.** It is come to our notice instead of the word *attamatra* we use word *antamatra* which gives no sense to word *attamatra* had been conjectured in the proposed study of the term *arthamatra* 'Sum of money' which compared in the alphabet *S.V.* means to win the victory of *Sant. rth* and *tt* are very easily confused in Sarada writing. The sums thus advanced to the depositor are referred as *dravinena 'word' attena*, 'money taken up'. Therefore Durgapr. hasdattamatra, evidently a correction.
103. *R.T.* Vol.II. p. II.
104. **Note.** It is important to note that the expression of term *trimsadvisma* must be understood as 'twenty or thirty' and not as 'fifty' because we are informed that the deposit was handed to the merchant under King *Kalasa*. Even taking as the extreme time limits *Kalasa's* nominal coronation in *Lokakala* 4139, and the year of *Uchchala's* death, *Lokakala* 4187, the interval is less than fifty years. Between the accession of *Kalasa* and *Uchchala* about thirty-eight years intervened and between the dates of their death twenty-two years.
105. *R.T.* Vol.II p. 11.
106. *Ibid.*
107. *Ibid.*
108. *Ibid.*
109. *Ibid.*

110. *Ibid.*
111. *Ibid.*
112. *Ibid.*
113. **Note.** The gourd (*Lagenaxia* vulgaris used in Sericulture), is generally used in Kashmir and the Panjab as a vesicatory. For this purpose a small opening is made at one end of the fruit and the latter filled with smoke over a fire. The gourd is then applied to the suffering part of the body. Where it causes blisters. The moisture which the fire draws out of the gourd is compared to the sweat-drops (or tears) which appear on the sanctimonious merchant when he attends daily to his sacrificial fire. Any one who has visited a bazaar in Northen India will find it easy to recall to his memory figures which might have sat for the humorous, if not very complimentary, portrait drawn hereby the author.
114. *R.T.* Vol.II. p. 12.
115. **Note.** The interpretationof the first half-line (*Yad adau sreyasa iti nyastam asreyase padam*) is very doubtful. In translating as above, we assume that *sreyase* and *asreyase* were mercantile terms, corresponding to our 'profit' and 'loss', or credit and debit. The merchant would thus say that the depositors account had turned, owing to the several advances, from a credit account into a debit one.
116. *R.T.* Vol.II. p. 12.
117. *Ibid.*
118. *Ibid.* p. 13.
119. *Ibid.*
120. *Ibid. Note. Sraddhapaksa* or 'Sraddha-fortnight' is the designation of the dark half of the month *Asvina,* when special sacrifices to the Manes are described. For the latter, offerings of the articles mentioned in the text are obligatory. Compare regarding the *Sraddhapaksa,* which is still religiously observed in Kashmir and popularly known as *Kambaripach* (in Sanskrit *Kamaripaksa*), *Nilamata Purana*; p. 748. A reference to special bathing in connection with these sacrifices occurs in the *Vijaesvaramah* compared with *Padmapur*, where the *Sraddhapaksa* is understood under the term *aparapaksa*.
121. **Note.** Certain mendicants established at Srinagar, but recruited from the Panjab and known as *Sutrasahi*, still practise exactions by threatning to remove their testicles, in case they are refused alms.
122. **Note.** The *dhupa* is an incense prepared prepared from the roots of the *dupa* plant (Jurinea macrocephala), which grows on the Kashmir mountains and is largely exported to India.
123. **Note.** Term *Sanda,* not found in our dictionaries, is certainly the Sanskrit name of the plant known in Kashmir as *hand.* The latter is found growing wild all over the Valley, and is valued as a vegetable and for its medical properties. According to Dr. Elmslie's *Kashmiri Vocabulary;* p. 130, the botanical name of the *hand* is Cichorium intybus.
124. **Note.** The expression *bhattapada* rendered above by 'Guru', has already occured in this text, as an honorific designation of Tantric teachers.
125. R.T. Vol. II. p. 13
126. **Note** We understand this and the preceding verses to mean that the merchant makes out a bill not only for the cost of the articles supplied

by us from time to time, but also for the interest due on these advances. The total of these sums, according to the reckoning exceeds the amount of the original deposit. The latter is treated by the merchant as if it were a closed one, i.e not bearing interest. Hence it is he who claims to be paid up by his customer, compare the verses following.

127. **Note.** The word *Ujjamadhana* composed of two words *Ujjama+dhana, Ujjama* we take as the Sanskrit original or representative of the Kashmir *'Uzum', 'debt'*. The word is found in the *Lokapr* i., in the expressions *dinnarojjamacirika* 'acknowledgement of a debt in cash', *dhanyojjamcirika,* 'acknowledgement of a debt in rice', *bhandojjamacirika*, 'acknowledgement of a debt on pawn, and also in a bond formulary•given, *ib.* Ksemendra, *Samayam, Viii* p. 96, uses in the same sense the term *Ujjamapattrika* also compared with *ujjamatandula* 'rice advanced on interest', *ib*, ii.78. Term *Ujjama* means '*unique* living *manas'* in single form like God or *'Nam'*
128. *R.T.* Vol. II. p. 14.
129. **Note.** In the Kashmiri proverb *mudarsrakh* is known 'a knife with honey' and still it is called as *Ksuram Ksaudropaliptam.* It is often used of an arrangement which seems fair on the first book and is yet unjust.
130. *R.T.* Vol. II p. 14.
131. *Ibid.*
132. **Note.** Word *tanka* means here, as well as simply 'coin-type' or 'die', and does not, as assumed as by Cunningham. It has been designate a coin of 'fine gold', compared as the victory of Sant, S.V. *tankapati,* 'mint-master', *tankasala*, ' mint'.
133. *R.T.* Vol. II. p. 14.
134. *Ibid.*
135. **Note.** In Sarada writing the short mark for 'T' is liable to be misread for: (*Visarga*) at the end of the words; if followed by a *Danda* as per their deposit.
136. **Note.** At the request of the councillor, the King granted to the claimant the house of merchant, together with his properity, and exiled the defendant from the land. Therefore, for the punishment inflicted by *Yasaskara* in a similar case.
137. *R.T.* Vol.II. p. 15.
138. *Ibid.*
139. *Ibid.*
140. *Ibid.*
141. *Ibid.*
142. *Note.* The fifth head of Brahman has been burn off by the fire of *Uchchala* or Siva's eye.
143. *R.T.* Vol.II. p. 15.
144. *Ibid.*
145. *Ibid.*
146. *Ibid. p. 16. Note.* In every month on the day of solemn reception, these emblems of regal dignity were brought from his house to be used in the royal assambly. It compares with the expression *masarghadina.*
147. *Ibid.*
148. *Ibid.*

149. *Ibid.*
150. *Ibid.*
151. *Ibid.*
152. Note. It has already been indicated above in the passage that *Visalata* must be identified with the valleys drained by the *Bichlari* river, a tributary of the Chenab. This hill district, situated immediately to the South of the *Divasar* and *Shahabad* Parganas, is now called generally Banahal, after the pass of that name to which it forms the approach. The name *Visalata* is probably preserved in that of the river *Bichlari*. *Visalata* is mentioned as the route by which the pretender *Bhiksacara* intends to invade *Devasarasa,* i.e. *Divasar*. The reference to the crossing of the mountains, show clearly that the king's troops, when dislodged from *Devasarasa* (Divasar) by *Prthvihara,* flee to the South towards the mountains bordering Kashmir. The mention of the *Vitasta* as the end point of the pursuit seems therefore, strange on the first look. Stein also believes that Kalhana, wishes in reality to refer to the locality. Where the source of the *Vitasta* is traditionally placed. This is the *Naga* at *Vithavutur,* the *Vitastatra* of the *Rajatarangini,* close to *Vernag* in the Shahabad Paragana. Immediately above *Vithavutur* begins the ascent to the Banahal pass, by which *Janakasimha* and other ministers escaped to *Visalata*. It is possible that the *Vitastantam* of the text is a corruption for *Vitastatram,* in which case we should have a reference to the actual village of *Vithavutur.* We read of some Kashmiri nobles who, after being pursued to *Vitastatra* (below the *Banahal* pass), take refuge with the *Khasas* in *Visalata* after crossing the mountain range. The King (*Uchchala*), who was very far-sighted, apprehended an enterprise coming from the house of *Dengapala* by the way of *Visalata*. *Dengapala,* a *Khasa* chief, who according to *Thakkura* resident on the banks of the *Chandrabhaga,* gave him his daughter *Bappika* (in marriage) and took him to himself. It is spoken to him as threatening to advance against Kashmir from *Visalata*. *Mallakostha* wished to bring back *Bhiksacara* and sent his own troops to him to *Visalata*. Thus, then *Lavanya Jayyaka* brought back to the King *Janaka (Simha), Srivaka* and the rest from *Visalata*. He proceeded at the commencement of the winter to *Visalata,* planning *Sujji* should arrive after bathing in the *Ganga*. Others have declared that his above described acts were obtained predominance when the city (of *Nara*) had been burned through the wrath of the Naga.
153. *R.T.* Vol.II. p. 16.
154. *Ibid.*
155. *Ibid.*
156. *Note*. As soon as he listened the news of his opponents death, he was marching upon the city lusting for the throne, he was as King addressed by *Tilaka,* the son of *Kaka*. It seems that *Kaka* was the father of *Tilaka* '*Kakavamsya*', who with his relatives is so frequently mentioned in the succeeding narrative. *Tilaka, Sobhaka* and others, who held high posts under *Uchchala* and his successors belongs to it mentioned in the below passage. It makes clear from the study that *Kaka* was not a physicians but he was in the form God or *'Nam'*. For education or *Vaidya*, a later hand in 'single' form has been corrected *'Vaisya'* which would turn the

families here mentioned into *Vaisyas.*

157. *R.T.* Vol. II. 16.
158. *Ibid.*
159. **Note.** *Gaggacandra* is the same person as *Gagga*, mentioned above as the brother of the Damara *Janakacandra.* The full Sanskrit form of the name is *Gargacandra,* already mentioned above. Most frequently, however, this personage is referred to by the abbreviated name *Garge* in the passage.
160. *R.T.* Vol. II. p. 17.
161. **Note.** *Tilaka* and *Janaka* are often referred to in the subsequent narrative by their full names *Tilakasimha* and *Janakasimha.*
162. *R.T.* Vol. II. p. 17.
163. *Ibid.*
164. *Ibid.*
165. *Ibid.*
166. *Ibid.*
167. *Ibid.*
168. *Ibid.*
169. *Ibid.*
170. **Note.** The best-cultivated and brodest part of the Valley of *Loharin* lies about eight miles above the *Mandi,* at the elevation of 74-23′ logitude and 33°-48′ latitutde. The cluster of large villages situated here (distinguished after the tribal names of their inhabitants as *Tantrivand, Gegivand*, and *Doivand*) are jointly known by the name of *Loharin,* and may be regarded as the centre of the district. Through *Loharin* proper and then through a side-valley descending from the mountains on the North leads the path to the Tosamaidan pass, which since earlier times to the present day has formed one of the most-frequented and the best routes from the Western Panjab to Kashmir. The importance of this route and the easy communication thereby established, explains the close political relations of *Lohara* with Kashmir as well as the prevalance of a Kashmiri population in the present Loharin. In examining the main passages of the *Rajatarangini* bearing on Lohara with a view to providing its identity with the modern *Loharin*, it will be most convenient to follow the order of Kalhana's narrative. *Vigraharaja's* expedition took place soon after the death of *Samgramaraja* which fell at the commencement of the month *Asadha* (June-July). At that season the shortest route for the invader lay over the Tosamaidan pass. This notwithstanding its weight (circ. 13,500 feet above the sea level), is open for traffic of all kinds from May till November. The practical possibility of covering the distance within the above time was tested by us in 1892, on the tour referred to. Leaving Loharin on the morning of the 19th August, with baggage-animals and load-carrying *'coolies', or 'Chamars'* we reached without difficulty, on the evening of the following day, the edge of the Tosamaidan plateau above the village of Drang. From there half a day's march across the level valley would suffice to bring one to Srinagar. *Vigraharaja's* son and successor *Ksitiraja,* whom we find also mentioned as ruler of *Lohara* in *Bilhana's Vikramankadevacarita,* resigned his throne in favour of *Utkarsa,* the grandsonof King *Ananta* and younger

brother of *Harsa*. When *Utkarsa,* on *Kalasa's* death (A.D. 1089), was called to rule over Kashmir, he united with his new kingdom the territory of *Lohara*. This henceforth became the mountain fastness and place of safety for the Kashmir rulers in the troubled times of the succeeding reigns. In the time of *Harsa* we hear of an expedition sent against *Rajapuri*, the modern Rajauri, which takes the route *via* Lohara, i.e. over the '*Tosamaidan Pass*. when, subsequently, the pretender *Uchchala*, the descendent of a side branch of the house of Lohara, made his first irruption into *Kashmir* from *Rajahri*, he held his small band of followers through the territory of the Governor of Lohara. He defeated the latter's forces at *Parnotsa* or Poonch, surprised the commandant of the *Dvara*, and safely reached the rebel camp in *Kramarajya,* the western portion of the valley. Kalhana's special reference to the consternation caused by the sudden appearance of the pretender is significant. It clearly connected with the fact that *Uchchala's* invasion took place at the beginning of the month *Vaisakha*, i.e. April. At that time the Tosamaiden pass, according to the information collected by us at *Loharin,* can be crossed only on foot and with some difficulty. Fuller details regarding the topography of Lohara are to be found in the narrative of the events which took place there during the rule of *Jayȧsimha*, i.e. in Kalhana's own time. It has been shown that this invasion of *Sussala* was made in all probability by the Tosamaidan route. *Varahavarta* might therefore be placed at or near the present village of *Varahagam*, situated in the Biru Pargana about three miles to the East of *Drang*. (The place is marked on the map as *Waragam).*

171. *R.T.* Vol.II. p. 18.
172. *Ibid.*
173. **Note.** The text reveals the scarcely attack of the king on *'Sussala'*
174. *R.T.* Vol.II. p. 18.
175. *Ibid.*
176. *Ibid.*
177. *Ibid.*
178. **Note.** *Selyapura* is the modern town known as *Silipor,* situated on the route from the Tosamaidan to Srinagar. It is a large village in the Dunts Pargana, at the elevation of $74^0$ - 45' longitude and $34^0$ -1' at latitude. This identification is supported mentioned above where from we see *Selyapura* is connected with *Sussala's* march from Lohara to Srinagar. *Silipor* lies on the direct route connecting the Tosamaiden pass, and thus Lohara (*Loharin*), with its capital.
179. *R.T* vol. II; p. 18.
180. *Ibid.*
181. *Ibid.*
182. *Ibid.*
183. *Ibid. Note* See the reference of the term *Kalinjara* in elsewhere in this book.
184. *Ibid.*
185. **Note.** The text of this verse permits of difference interpretations. It seems to us that it contains certain reference as a authority of *Kalha,* who will protected *Sussala's* dominion i.e, *'Nam'* or *'Word'*. Therefore, it appears

from the study that the marriage of *Sussala* with *'Kalha's* grand daughter in the preceding verses would be meaningless.

186. *R.T.* Vol.II. p. 19 *Note.* This route mostly followed by *Sussala* to defeat the *Daradistani.*
187. *Ibid.*
188. *Ibid.*
189. *Ibid. Note.* See the reference of the *Darsanapala* in elsewhere.
190. *Ibid.*
191. *Ibid.*
192. *Ibid.*
193. *Ibid.*
194. *Ibid.*
195. *Ibid.*
196. *Ibid.*
197. *Ibid.*
198. *Ibid.*
199. *Ibid.*
200. *Ibid.*
201. *Ibid.*
202. *Ibid.*
203. *Ibid.* p. 20.
204. **Note.** It appears from the study that *Asamati* had brought away from *Naravarman,* and who had come provided by the former with gold for the journey. When *Asamati* had died, and the gold given for the expedition had been exhausted, his father-in-law too became in time slack in his attentions. It is still customary in Kashmir Brahman families to call the eldest woman of the household by the honorific name of *Didd* (Didda), given in recollection of the great queen. The 'Sahi princesses' are *Harsa's* queen.
205. *R.T.* Vol.II. p. 20.
206. **Note.** The *Naravarman* has already mentioned in elsewhere in the genealogical lists of the later *Paramara* rulers of *Malava.*
207. *R.T.* Vol.II. p. 20.
208. *Ibid.*
209. *Ibid.*
210. *Ibid.*
211. *Ibid.*
212. *Ibid.*
213. *Ibid.*
214. *Ibid.*
215. **Note.** It was the autumn, he enjoyed inworship of Siva, plunging into the lotus which rise of *Agastya*, the star of canopus, in the month of *Bhadrapada,* is supposed to mark the end of the raining season which renders the streams impure and turbid.
216. *R.T.* Vol.1 p. 21.
217. **Note.** *Jayasimha's* actual accession in *Lokakala*, 4203 (A.D.1128), he was treacherously murdered on the new moon day of *Phalguna* in the year (of the *Laukika* era four thousand two hundred and) three, after having passed fifty-five years in life, not his *Abhiseka* in 4199. His father

had him crowned as King on the first day of *Asadha,* and then indicated to him all the main principles of government, saying with a faltering voice: " May you support that burden under which your father and uncles have tried out, not being able to carry it upon you, O my brave (son), devolves this load". Our passage permits us to fix the date of *Jayasimha's* birth which had not been specified, at *Lokakala*, 4181, (A.D. 1105-06). A reference at present, in the twenty-fourth year of the *Laukika* (era), on thousand and seventy years of the Saka era have passed. Regarding the *Laukika* or *Saptarsi* era, which has remained in current use among the Brahman population of Kashmir to the present day, it compared the remarks of Prof. Buhler, *Report;* pp. 59 sq. He was the first to bring the initial date of this era, viz; *Caitra sudi* I of *Kalisamvat* 25 (expired) or the year 3076-75 B.C., to the notice of European scholars and to account for the equation given in our verse.

The following calculation shows that the year in which Kalhana wrote his introduction, was *Laukikasamvat* 4224:-

Distance between *Kali* 25 (initial date of *Laukika* era) and the initial date of the Saka era = 3154

Distance between *Sakasamvat* 1 and Kalhana's time = 1070

Total of *Saptarsi* years ..........................................= 4224

The omission of the centuries in giving *Laukika* dates is an ancient custom, as shown by the dates recorded in this era in inscriptions and *M.S.S.* For a full discussion of the facts connected with the *Laukika* cycle and its use in the hill regions neighbouring on Kashmir; Sec Cunninghan; (*Indian Eras*; pp. 6-17)

218. *R.T.* Vol. II. p. 21.
219. *Ibid.*
220. **Note.** Kalhana wants to express the name *Jayasimha,* as that of *Buddha Sarvarthasiddha,* has both an etymological and conventional meaning, equally applicable to the King. Such words are designated as *Yogaruda.*
221. *R.T.* Vol.II. p. 21.
222. **Note.** The reddish colour of the feet of the son is an indication of auspicious sign of the *'Nam'* or *'Word'* ; compared with *Brhatsamhita, ixviii* ; . pp. 87, 97
223. *R.T* Vol.II. p. 21.
224 *Ibid.*
225. *Ibid.*
226. *Note.* After this event no reference will be made subsequently about the *Mallamatha.*
227. *R.T.* Vol.II. p. 21.
228. *Ibid.*
229. **Note.** *Uchchala* left the palace and proceeded to the *Navamatha,* thinking that this place round which the *Vitasta* formed (as it were) a most, was inaccessible to the enemy. On the fifteenth day of the bright half of *Asvina* in the year (of the *Laukika* era four thousand two hundred and) even (A.D 1135) the king placed him under guards in the *Navamatha.* It seems from the Kalhana's words that *Jayamati* intended it to be called after her husband, as it has been given in the above mentioned example.
230. **Note.** The *Sullavihara* was completed by *Jayasimha,* his uncle and three temples of his father (*Sussala*) had already built but they remained

unfinished till date. Now he started to build on the bank of the *Vitasta* three high temples under his own name and the names of his mother-in-law and wife. This virtuous lady burned herself in her house together with her nurse *Candri,* who felt unable to funeral libations of her whom she had brought up as a child with her own milk.

231. *R.T* Vol.II. p. 22.
232. *Ibid.*
233. **Note.** We can safely identified that *Varhatacakra* site lies to the south of this hamlet of *Tsakavadar* (marked *'sheikhwadda'* on the map) in Bombay the modern name is the exact phonetic derivative of a form *Cakra-Varhata,* in which the two words of the compound name have been transposed. Kalhana's *tsaka,* means 'wheel', is the representative of Sanskrit *Cakra.* For *Vadar* less then *Varhata,* it should be noted that in rustic form *Kalhana's* 'r' at the end or in the middle of the words is almost invariably pronounced as *'d'*, and that final *'t'* is regularly changed into *'r'*, compared with *Kasthavata* greater than (7) *Kastavar, ghotaka* greater *than (7) gura,* 'horse' etc. Alternative forms of village names in which the words composing them can be transposed, are not unknown in Kashmir. Thus, e.g. a village of the *Phak* Pargana is known both as *Dara-Sadapor* and *Sadapor-Dara*, and another in the Vular pargana, both as *Kai-Chach koth* and *Chachkoth-kai.*
234. **Note** The localities connected with this adventure of *Uchchala* can be fixed without difficulty also compared with *Nilamata, Purna* ; 1040. As the piligrimage of king *Uchchala* is mentioned above in the statement. The past of this range covered the fire hills leads the route from the northern parts of *Kramaraja* towards *Svayambhu.* Near the village of *Dachaldor* it enters the valley contracts above the village of *Rajpor* into a narrow wooded gorge. This for a distance of about one mile would offer excellent opportunities for a sudden attack, such as that described in the text. The path runs along the bottom of the gorge and follows the tortuous course of the stream between steep cliffs. A visit stein paid to this neighbourhood in September, 1892, showed us that this path could easily be blocked by a small number. Higher up near *Svayambhu* itself the country is comparatively opened and formed by a series of grassy spurs with broad shallow valleys between them.
235. *R.T.* Vol.II. p. 22.
236. **Note.** The name *Kambalesvara* can be recognised without difficulty in the present *Krambhar*; the name of a village situated at the foot of a low hill range in the Machipor pargana, about at the elevation of 74°-15′ longitude and 34°-26' latitude (marked *Krombhur* on map). For the phonetic relation between Kalhana's (-har less than (<) Sanskrit-e) *svara.* This remarks compared with *Triphar* less than (<) *Tripuresvara* and other Kalhana's local names derived from Sanskrit names ending in *-isvara.*
237. *R.T.* Vol.II. p. 22.
238. *Ibid.*
239. *Ibid.*
240. *Ibid.*
241. *Ibid.*
242. **Note.** *Chudda* and his brothers, as descendants of *Kamadeva, Yasaskare's* grandfather, could claim relationship with a former dynasty.

243. **Note.** *Radda*, *Chudda* and *Vyadda* were the sons of a common soldier of the name of *Sadda*. They were also made ministers by that King *Uchchala*. As it is known to us that in the village of *Pisacakapura,* a householder, *Viradeva* by name, had a son called *Kamadeva,* the grandfather of *Yasaskara*. This son being distinguished by good qualities, such as the pious performance of ablutions etc, and having acquired a knowledge of *Aksaras,* became a boys teacher in the house of *Meruvardhana*, and in course of time treasurer (*ganjadhikarin*).
244. *R.T* Vol.II. p. 23.
245. *Ibid.*
246. *Ibid.*
247. *Ibid.*
248. **Note.** The *Lavata* of our passage is evidently the same person who is referred a load-carrier (bharik) by origin drew by his favour a pay of two thousand *Dinnaras*.
249. *R.T.* Vol.II. p. 23.
250. *Ibid.*
251. **Note.** From the study we learn formerly people of this country had, with the single exception of the king, worn their hair loose, had carried no head-dress and no ear-ornaments, where they are going to bareheaded as the former habit of Kashmirians.
252. *R.T.* Vol.II. p. 23.
253. *Ibid.*
254. *Ibid.*. 23-24.
255. **Note.** This reference to the *rajasthana* is curious. Neither of *Chudda* nor of any of his brothers has it been previously stated that they held the high post of *Rajasthaniya*, which is last mentioned above as filled by *Bhogasena*. It is therefore probable that the word has not to be taken here in the technical meaning *Alamkara* in *Jayasimha's* reign, but in the wider sense indicated by the translation. Thanks to the king's lustre, the enemy was defeated also by *Sajjaka,* who, being a soldier of rustic origin, (had become) superintendent of the *S'eda* office (*rajasthana*)*;* where an account office (*seda*) is designated as a *'Rajasthana'*.
256. *R.T.* Vol.I. p. 24.
257. *Ibid.*
257. *Ibid.*
258. *Ibid.*
259. *Ibid.*
260. *Ibid.*
261. *Ibid.*
262. *Ibid.*
263. **Note.** The exact character of the post of *pravesabhagika* is uncertain. He was *Barwala* or aboriginal always in moving process. It might have been a subordinate official of the treasury who received the actual tax-payments (*pravesa*), corresponding to the modern *Khazanchi* (*Petivol in Kashmir*).
264. *R.T.* Vol.II. p. 24.
265. *Ibid.*
266. *Ibid.*

267. *Ibid.* pp. 24-25.
268. *Ibid.* p. 25.
269. *Ibid.*
270. *Ibid.*
271. *Ibid.*
272. **Note.** *Vartula* means *'Nam'* is the war of love or 'Lord of the Universe' and Raja *Shajapala,* the 'Lord of *Vartula'*, as well as the *Yuvarajas* of the chiefs of *Trigarta* and *Vallapura,* (called) *Balha* and *Anandaraja*, five in all, met in some place, and after making a compact for the journey visited *Kuruksetra. Kuruksetra,* the traditional scene of the battle of the *Kurus* and *Pandavas,* is the plain stretching south of *Thanesvar* towards Panipat. Owing to its very numerous *Tirthas,* it has remained a favourite goal for pilgrimages to the present day. Though the point is not clearly mentioned in the text, it seems probable that the five hill chiefs had proceeded to *Kuruksetra* on a joint tour of pilgrimage. The compact to which Kalhana refers, may either have been intended to guarantee mutually the safety of their respective territories during their absence, or to insure greater security for the chiefs on the journey. *Kuruksetra* had then been for about a century in Muhammadan hands. For another reference to the *Kuruksetra*, prince (*Raj Kumar*) has to decided to attack with solar eclipse, met there the *Cavanya* and abandoned from necessity his former enemity (against him). The only other mention of it we can trace is in *Vikram.* XViii. 38, where, 'a lord of *Bhartula'* is mentioned among the hill chiefs defeated by king *Anantadeva.* As *Ba* and *ch* are easily confused in *Sarada* writing (which also *Bilhana* used) it is scarcely doubtful that both names refer to the same tract. Can *Vartula* be the hill-district of *Batal* shown on the map as situated on the North bank of the Chenab and to the South West of Banahal or *Visalata*? movement of the stream with the 'Almighty Power' i.e. *'Nam'*.
273. **Note.** Smt. Amrita Devi, she is known as *Mata Kalasi* or *'Pure thought'*.
274. *Note.* After the death of *Sahajapala*, his son *Sangramapala* had been placed on the throne of *Rajapuri.*
275. *R.T.* Vol.II. p. 25
276. *Ibid.*
277. *Ibid.* 115.
278. *Ibid..* p. 25.
279. *Ibid.*
280. *Ibid.*
281. *Ibid.*
282. *Ibid. p. 26.*
283. *Ibid.*
284. *Ibid.*
285. *Ibid.*
286. *Ibid.*
287. *Ibid.*
288. *Ibid.*
289. *Ibid.*
290. *Ibid.*
291. *Ibid.*

292. *Ibid.*
293. *Ibid.*
294. *Ibid.*
295. *Ibid.*
296. *Ibid.*
297. *Ibid. p. 27.*
298. *Ibid.*
299. *Ibid.*
300. **Note.** *Katar* is a large double-edged dagger fitted with a peculiar hilt. It was much used once in Northern India, for representation see e.g Egerton, *Handbook* of *India Arms*, p. 102, Fig. 340.
301. *R.T.* Vol. II. 27.
302. *Ibid.*
303. *Ibid.*
304. *Ibid.*
305. *Ibid.*
306. *Ibid.*
307. *Ibid.*
308. *Ibid.*
309. *Ibid.*
310. *Ibid.*
311. *Ibid.*
312. *Ibid.*
313. *Ibid.* p. 28
314. *Ibid.*
315. *Ibid.*
316. *Ibid.*
317. *Ibid.*
318. *Ibid.*
319. *Ibid.*
320. *Ibid.*
321. *Ibid.*
322. *Ibid.*
323. **Note.** *Ravana's* defeat by Hanumat's monkeys is alluded to. 'The *Kuru* Lord' is *Duryodhana*, who was kicked on the head by *Bhima* at the end of their combat.
324. R.T. Vol.II. p. 28.
325. *Ibid.*
326. *Ibid.*
327. *Ibid.*
328. *Ibid.*
329. **Note.** It has been already discussed in elsewhere in the text that *Mahasarit* is the present *Mar* stream which flows from the Dal Lake, and with its branch called *Tsunth Kul* ('the apple tree canal) reaches the *Vitasta* opposite to the *Sher Gadi* palace and a little below the first bridge. Between the *Mahasarit* and the *Vitasta* lies the great island of *Mayasum* (*Makrikasvamin*). At the western end of this island, and a short distance above the first bridge, the river bank was used as a burning ground for Hindus until some forty years ago. Close to it the Christian cemetery of

the Shaikh Bagh has been established. It has been rightly expressed by the Kalhana after wandering from the three places known as Poonch to Jammu, than Jammu to Kargil and from Kargil to Jammu. He reached a stream which skisted the burning ground and was bordered by trees looking terrible in the light of numerous funeral pyres.

330. *R.T.* Vol.II. p. 29.
331. *Ibid.*
332. *Ibid.*
333. *Ibid.* p. 30.
334. *Ibid.* p. 29.
335. **Note.** The royal force is feeling panic to disappear the Ekangas from the scene, because they are the enemies of the 'History' and for them the main 'Gate' has been closed by the *Simhadvara,* literally means 'the loins' gate'.
336. *R.T.* Vol.II. p. 29.
337. *Ibid.*
338. *Note.* Nothing is known of the *Diddasvamin* temple and of *Diddapura.* The *Matha* here referred to is undoubtedly the *Diddamatha.* Now it is known as *Didamar* at present in Srinagar, situated between the sixth and seventh bridges on the right bank of river. This identification is well known to Pandits, and is borne out by numerous passages of the later chronicles which refer to that part of the city under the name of *Diddamatha.*
339. *R.T.* Vol. II, p. 30.
340. **Note.** Events are here alluded when *'History'* has to change to which much have been related with *Sakaksa* the three *Aksaras* missing in 'A' at the commencement of 'New Era'. A younger brother of *Garga,* called *Sadda,* without any noticed he will kill him, wounded by the sword and then he will flee from his own country.
341. *R.T.* Vol. II p. 30.
342. *Ibid.*
343. *Ibid.*
344. *Ibid.*
345. **Note.** At the moment when *'Deepit Raj'* seized by an abdominal disease, he had *Varnata,* the son of his paternal grand-uncle *Ramadeva,* consecrated as a King by the ministers, *Ekangas* and feudal chiefs and entrusted him (to their care). For A° *bhajad* read with L° *bhajan* for a short time became the successor of *Yasakara.*
346. *R.T.* Vol.II p. 30.
347. *Ibid.*
348. *Ibid.*
349. **Note.** Perhaps we-ought to correct *phullito* for a *Phalito,* 'which bore blossoms at night.'
350. *R.T. Vol.II.* p. 31
351. *Ibid.*
352. *Ibid.*
353. *Ibid.*
354. *Ibid.*
355. *Ibid.*

356. *Ibid.*
357. *Ibid.*
358. *Ibid.*
359. **Note.** It was customary in case the heir to the throne was a young child, to place him in the arms of an elder relative, and to perform the *Abhiseka* ceremony for both jointly. This was to assure the safety of the heir during his infancy, and his subsequent accession to the actual power. Compare, for example, with the story of Bhoja's *Abhiseka* along with his uncle Munja, as told at the commencement of the *Bhojaprabandha*. The person in whose arms *Gargachandra* washed in particular to have Uchchala's infant son consecrated is *Sihasramangala*. He exiled in anger *Sihasranmangala*, whom *Garga*, as the guardian of *Uchchala*'s son, had wished to elevate to the throne.
360. *R.T.* Vol.II. p. 31.
361. *Ibid.*
362. *Ibid.*
363. *Ibid.*
364. *Ibid.*
365. **Note.** *Vigraharaja's* expedition took place soon after the death of *Samgramaraja* which fell at the commencement of the month *Asadha* (June-July). At that season the shortest route for the invader lay over the Tosamaidan Pass. He (*Vigraharaja*) had already in Didda appeared as a pretender. After the death of *Samgramaraja* (A.D. 1028), he made a second unsuccessful attempt to seize the Kashmir throne. It has been shown with the help of 85, marched from Lohara for Srinagar, burned on the way the Kashmirian frontier station (*dvara*), and appeared after two and half days hard marching before the capital. There he was defeated and slain. This news was reached within no times.
366. *R.T.* Vol. II, p. 32.
367. *Ibid.*
368. *Ibid.*
369. *Ibid.*
370. *Ibid.*
371. *Ibid.*
372. *Ibid.*
373. *Ibid.*
374. *Ibid.*
375. *Ibid.* pp. 32-33.
376. *Ibid.* p. 33.
377. *Ibid.*
378. **Note.** *Sussala* must have proceeded by one of the routes which lead from the *Sadrun* Valley of the Vitasta below *Varahamula*. It is exactly by one of these routes (over the Hajji Pir or *Pajjla* Passes), that Prunts is most conveniently approached from Kashmir. In the above mentioned reference, we read that *Sussala*, after reaching *Kasthavata*, is stopped by an opposing force assembled at *Huskapura*. In like manner we find in our own narrative that *Phalguna*, when stopped on the way to *Parnotsa*, returns from *Kasthavata* to *Varahaksetra*, i.e. *Varahamula*. *Sussala*, some months later, succeeded in wresting Kashmir from his half-

brother *Salhana*. He subsequently used the stronghold of Lohara for the custody of his dangerous relatives and as the hoarding-place of his treasures, accumulated by an oppressive rule. When threatened by the rebel forces of the pretender *Bhikscara* he sent his son and family, in the summer of A.D. 1120, to Lohara for safety, and followed them himself in the month of Margasirsa of that year *via Hu*[illegible]*pura*. In the following spring, the pretender *Bhiksacara* despatched a force *via Rajapuri* in order to attach *Sussala* in his mountain fastness. These troops, advancing from the south, were met by *Sussala* at *Parnotsa,* and there utterly routed. During the remainder of Sussala's reign we hear of *Lohara* only once more, when *Jayasimha* is brought back to Kashmir after three years residence at *Lohara*, and met by his father by at *Varahamula*. Fuller details regarding the topography of Lohara are to be found in the narrative of the events which took place there during the rule of *Jayasimha*, i.e in Kalhana's own time of the princes whom *Sussala* on his accession to the Kashmir throne had confined at *Lohara, Lothana* with five of his relatives, was in A.D. 1130 still in captivity there.

379. *R.T.* Vol. II. p. 33.
380. *Ibid.*
381. *Ibid.*
382. **Note.** *Bilvavana,* otherwise unknown, was probably a locality in the Valley of the Vitasta, below *Varahamula*, where *Khasas* are settled to the present day.
383. *R.T.* vol. II. p. 33.
384. *Ibid.*
385. *Ibid.*
386. *Ibid.*
387. *Ibid.*
388. *Ibid.*
389. *Ibid.*
390. *Ibid.*
391. *Ibid.* p. 34
392. *Ibid.*
393. *Note.* Kalhana refers here clearly to one of the rope bridges, or *Jhulas*, which until a few years ago formed the only communication across the *Vitasta* in the Valley below *Varahamula*. These ropes bridges are suspension bridges of the simplest construction, and generally formed of three cables made of twisted twigs. Owing to the swaying of these cables to and fro in the wind, and to the steep gradients on either side, the passage of a *Jhula* of any great span is nervous work for those unused to it. Occasionally when there is a high wind, the crossing of such a *Jhula* is dangerous even for those accustomed to the work from childhood. These bridges are quite impassable for four footed beasts, unless carried on a man's back. As the latter operation assume that *Sussala's* horse in reality swam across the river. In cases where the condition of the river bed and the current permits of this expedient, ponies are generally aided in swimming by a rope bridge. Those who have had the doubtful pleasure of crossing some of the *Jhulas* in the hills neighbouring on Kashmir,

will readily pardom Kalhana for having slightly enaggerated the difficulties of such a crossing. Compare regarding *Jhulas*; (J.K.T. *p. 122).*

394. *R.T.* Vol. II. p. 34.
395. *Ibid.*
396. *Ibid.*
397. *Ibid.*
398. *Ibid.*
399. **Note.** *Viranaka* has been identified with the present *Viran* in the *Vitasta* Valley opposite to *Buliasa Bolyasaka*. A son of *Sukhraja's* sister, whom he had made 'Lord of the Gate' (*dvaradhipa*), met his death through negligence at a place called *Viranaka*. Of the latter place, we know for certain that it lay on the very border of Kashmir territory. And the circumstances under which *Viranaka* is mentioned both in our passage and make it clear that it too must have been in the immediate vicinity of the Kashmir frontier towards the *Khasas*. The gloss $A^2$, places *Bolyasaka* 'in *Dvaravati* near *Varahamula'*. *Dvaravati* corresponds to the present *Dvarabidi,* the designation of that portion of the *Vitasta* valley which extends from above *Muzaffarabad* to a short distance beyond the village of *Buliasa*. In the latter place, which is situated on the right bank of the *Vitasta*, $73^0$-51' logitude, and $34^0$-11' latitutde, and on the old route from Muzaffarabad to Kashmir, we can safely recognise Kalhana's *Bolyasaka*. The name *Peliasa*, under which the locality is shown on the map, is that in common use with the *Pahari* population. The Kashmiris, however, settled in the valley below *Varahamula* at *Kathai, Hattian*, and other places pronounce invaribly the name as *Buliasa*. Of this stein was able to convince ourselves by inquiries made at different occasions and in different occasions and in different localities. *Buliasa* is phonetically the direct derivative of *Bolyasaka*. *Buliasa* has given its name also to a well-populated valley which opens to the North of the village. Regarding the position of *Buliasa; Bolyasaka* on the old frontier of Kashmir territory in the *Vitasta* valley. From the position of *Viramaka*, as ascertained in the preceding note, we may safely conclude that the same route was followed also on the outset of the expedition. Among the territories on the *Indus* which can be reached by this route, some, like *Cilas*, and *Sazin,* lie almost due North, others to the North western of Kashmir. Hence Kalhana's expression *Uttarapatha* is sufficiently accurate.
400. *R.T.* Vol.II. p. 34.
401. *Note.* Correct with Durgaparsad *mirbhayo dandayat Khasas.*
402. *R.T.* Vol. II p. 35
403. *Ibid.*
404. **Note.** *It is clear* from the study that the bridge near the 'Gate' of *Varahamula* is meant here. Regarding this watch-station, which was the best known of all the 'Gates' of Kashmir. It is very probable that Kalhana refers here to one or several of the main Kalhana refers here to one or several of the main passes which give access to the valley of Kashmir. These entrances have always played an important part in *Kashmir* history, and have until quite modern times been specially guarded by watach-stations. The general use of the term *dvara* for those localities is proved by the *passage,* quoted below, and by the employment in the

*Rajatarangini* of the title *dvaradhipati, dvaresa, or dvaradhikarin.* The high officials thus designated were entrusted as 'Lords of the Marches' with the guardianship of these frontier passes frequently occurrence throughout the Chronicle. It has been noted as the 'Western gate' by *Hiuen-Tsiang* and *Ou-Kong*; see our *Notes on Ou-K'ong*; p. 23. Alberuni too, *India*; vol.1. p. 207, tells us of "the watch-station *Dvar* on both sides of the river *Jailam*". The position of the watch-station on the right river bank is marked in all probability by the old ruined gateway still known as *Drang*, which was guarded until some twenty years ago, compared Craft and Treback; *Travels in the Himalayan Provinces of Hindustan and the Punjab; in Ladakh and Kashmir;* (from 1819 to 1825); New Delhi; Reprint 1986.vol.II p. 280. Hereafter referred as T.H.p. H.).

405. *R.T.* Vol. II. p. 35
406. *Ibid.*
407. *Ibid.*
408. *Ibid.*
409. *Ibid.*
410. *Ibid.*
411. *Ibid.*
412. *Ibid.*
413. **Note.** The name of *Salhana's* brother is given here A and L as *Lasthana*, which is probably a legitimate Sanskrit variant for the *Lothana,* a Prakrit form. Also see the comparative statement of *Garga* and *Gargacandra* for *Gagga* and *Gaggacandra.*
414. *R.T.* Vol. II. p. 35.
415. *Ibid.*
416. *Note. Bimba* and *Nilasva* must be the name of territorial division of Kashmir proper which, however, cannot be identified now. It has already mentioned in elsewhere in this text.
417. *R.T.* Vol. II. p. 36.
418. *Note.* The locality meant by *Halaha* is unknown. The only other reference to it is contained that he threw himself into a hill fort called *Ratnavarsa* and having been deprived of his horses and deserted by his followers, was invested from a distance by the king, if our emedation there of *Halaha* for *Phalaha* is justified.
419. **Note.** The distinction between *bahya* ('outer') and *abhyantara* (inner') among the royal servants is repeatedly mentioned below. From the use made of the expression *bahyabhrtya,* the king, on the other hand, being afraid of him, excluded *Rilhana* from (private) councils, familiar conversations, and other confidential occasions as if he had been one of the outer court (*bahya*). It would appear that by *Abhyantara* are meant the officials who, owing to high position and direct connection with the court, could claim admittance into the royal excluded. For a similar distinction observed at the Moghul court (*Diwan-i-Am, Diwan-i-Khas*), *see* Bernier *Travels in India*; p. 265. The term *bahyali* appears to be the general designation of the outer portion of the palace, where an audience may be given by the monarch to the people of lower position, outside the proper *asthana* or Darbar Hall.
420. *R.T* Vol.II. p. 36.

421. *Ibid.*
422. *Ibid.*
423. *Ibid.*
424. *Ibid.*
425. *Ibid.*
426. *Ibid.*
427. *Ibid.*
428. **Note.** *Lothika* was the daughter of *Samgramraja* for securing his assistance, she was married to the superintendant of the *Diddamatha, Preman* by name, who possessed wealth, courage and other (good qualities). She constructed the *Lothikamatha,* and founded another Math a under the name of her mother *Tilottama. Hariraja* was also thrown himself into the *Lothikamatha*, there troops were sent by the *Srilekha* where, he killed and his followers set fire (to the place) with courage and bold step.
429. R.T. Vol.II. p. 36.
430. *Ibid.*
431. **Note.** The position of the sacred site of *Tripuresvara* (or *Tripuresa*) can be fixed with great probability near the modern village of *Triphar.* The latter lies at the evaluation of 74°- 50′ longitude and 34°-9′ latitude in the valley opening to the East from the North East corner of the Dal, and at a distance of about three miles from the latter. Apart from the name *Triphar,* which evidently stands in the same relation to *Tripuresvara* as *Kother* < (greater than) *Kapatesvara, Jyether* < (greater than) *Jyesthesvara, Amburher* < (greater than) *Amaresvara, Krambhar* < (greater than) *Kambalesvara*. This identification is supported by the following evidence. The IV *Adhyaya* of the *Sarvavatara or Jyesthesvara,* as worshipped '*sthane Tripuresvarasamjnaka'*. This locality, which according to the legend related in that text, took its name from the demon *Tripurai* destroyed there by siva, is described as situated close to Mount *Mahadeva*, and on the bank of the *Mahasarit* river. The former is certainly the peak still known by that name (*Mahadeo* of the maps) which rises immediately to the east of *Tripura*, and is to the present day the object of a pilgrimage.
432. *R.T.* Vol.II. p. 37.
433. *Ibid.*
434. *Ibid.*
435. *Ibid.*
436. *Ibid.*
437. *Ibid.*
438. *Ibid.*
439. **Note.** It makes clear from the study that one must have come down from the theory of *anumartum* and *Vasantim,* as rain entered into the dry earth and give it new life.
440. *R.T.* Vol. II p. 37.
441. *Ibid.*
442. *Ibid.*
443. *Ibid.*
444. *Ibid.*

445. *Ibid.*
446. **Note.** Term *Salha* is an abbreviation of *Salhana* who is fighting for the celestial victory.
447. *R.T.* Vol. II p. 37.
448. *Ibid. p. 38. Note.* To obtain the beauty of *Varahamulena*, one must have to go at the low level otherwise one has to go for the destruction whcih is the way of the Brahman.
449. *R.T* Vol. II. p. 38.
450. *Ibid.*
451. *Ibid.*
452. *Ibid.*
453. *Ibid.*
454. *Ibid.*
455. *Ibid.*
456. **Note.** *Gunalekha* is mentioned as King *Jayasimha's* wife. She was (then) five years old, and consulted about this with his (*Parmandi's*) maternal uncle, the son of *Garga* (*Pancacandra*).
457. *R.T.* Vol. II; p. 38.
458. *Ibid.*
459. **Note.** Here we see a kind of portcullis has been mentioned by Kalhana and proved as undesirous for the enemies of *'Nam'*.
460. *R.T.* Vol. II. p. 38.
461. *Ibid.*
462. *Ibid.*
463. *Ibid.*
464. **Note.** It appears from the study that *Sanjapala* was explained in the house of the laws on the matter of his simplicity. But they will have to bear the brunt of the expliotation who they were, they were the mean fellow and could not recognise him that he is a *Sant* kind of man, even his wife *'Pusapa Lata'*, she was with them. *Sant* do not bother for that because they are the load carrier of the human beings. It is their insult not the *Sant. Sant* always lives in Heaven, but he watches the every activity of the living being from the very core of the heart. Let them do, balance sheet has been prepared for them, the account will be settled at the right time, i.e., on the day of judgement.
465. *R.T.* Vol. II. p. 39.
466. *Ibid.*
467. **Note.** The position of *Patamgagrama* is equivalent to the *'Word'* or *'Nam'*. He is 'Supreme Power" when we go for the study of the said term.
468. *R.T.* Vol. II p. 39.
469. *Ibid.*
470. *Ibid.*
471. *Ibid.*
472. *Ibid.*
473. *Ibid.*